ANCIENT AND MODERN PERSPECTIVES ON THE BIBLE AND CULTURE

Essays in Honor of Hans Dieter Betz

Hans Dieter Betz

ANCIENT AND MODERN PERSPECTIVES ON THE BIBLE AND CULTURE
Essays in Honor of Hans Dieter Betz

Edited by

Adela Yarbro Collins

Scholars Press
Atlanta, Georgia

ANCIENT AND MODERN PERSPECTIVES ON THE BIBLE AND CULTURE

Essays in Honor of Hans Dieter Betz

Edited by
Adela Yarbro Collins

Library of Congress Cataloging in Publication Data

Ancient and modern perspectives on the Bible and culture : essays in honor of Hans Dieter Betz / edited by Adela Yarbro Collins.

p. cm.— (Scholars Press homage series ; no. 22)

Essays based on a symposium presented at the University of Chicago, Oct. 8–10, 1996

Includes bibliographical references and index.

ISBN 0-7885-0521-1 (cloth : alk. paper)

1. Bible—Socio-rhetorical criticism—Congresses. 2. Religion and culture—Mediterranean Region—History—Congresses. 3. Christianity and culture—History—20th century—Congresses. 4. Religion and philosophy—Mediterranean Region—History—Congresses. 5. Philosophy, Ancient—Congresses. I. Betz, Hans Dieter. II. Collins, Adela Yarbro. III. Series.

BS521.9.A53 1999

220.6'7—dc21 98-47964
CIP

Printed in the United States of America
on acid-free paper

Table of Contents

Contributors

Elizabeth Asmis is Professor of Classics at the University of Chicago.

David E. Aune is Professor of New Testament at Loyola University Chicago.

James Barr is Professor Emeritus at Vanderbilt and Oxford Universities.

Walter Burkert is Professor Emeritus of Classics at the University of Zürich.

Hubert Cancik is Professor of Classics at the University of Tübingen.

Hildegard Cancik-Lindemaier is a scholar of Classics living in Tübingen.

Adela Yarbro Collins is Professor of New Testament at the University of Chicago Divinity School.

John J. Collins is Professor of Hebrew Bible at the University of Chicago Divinity School.

Detlev Dormeyer is Professor of Biblical Studies at the University of Dortmund.

Arthur Droge is Professor of Early Christianity at the University of California at San Diego.

Ithamar Gruenwald is Professor of Jewish Thought and Mysticism in the Department of Jewish Philosophy at Tel Aviv University.

David Hellholm is Professor of New Testament at the University of Oslo.

Roy Kotansky is a scholar of New Testament and Classics living in Santa Monica, California.

Edgar Krentz is Professor of New Testament at the Lutheran School of Theology in Chicago.

Margaret M. Mitchell is Professor of New Testament at the University of Chicago Divinity School.

James M. Robinson is Professor of New Testament at the Claremont Graduate School.

Jonathan Z. Smith is Professor of Religion and the Humanities at the University of Chicago.

Kathleen O'Brien Wicker is Professor of Religion and Humanities at Scripps College and The Claremont Graduate School.

ABBREVIATIONS

AAWM	Abhandlungen der Akademie der Wissenschaften in Mainz
AB	Anchor Bible
ABD	D. N. Freedman (ed.), *Anchor Bible Dictionary*
Aesch.	Aeschylus
Ag.	*Agamemnon*
Eum.	*Eumenides*
AJP	*American Journal of Philology*
ANRW	*Aufstieg und Niedergang der römischen Welt*
APA	American Philological Association
APF	*Archiv für Papyrusforschung und verwandte Gebiete*
Apoll. Rhod.	Apollonius Rhodius
Argon.	*Argonautica*
Apollod.	Apollodorus
Apollon.	Apollonius
Hist. Mir.	*Historia Mirabiles*
Apul.	Apuleius
Met.	*Metamorphoses*
Aristoph.	Aristophanes
Ach.	*Acharnenses*
Av.	*Aves*
Ra.	*Ranae*
Aristot.	Aristotle
An.	*De Anima*
Eth. Eud.	*Ethica Eudemia*
Eth. Nic.	*Ethica Nicomachea*
Hist. An.	*Historia Animalium*
Metaph.	*Metaphysica*
Part. An.	*De Partibus Animalium*
Rhet.	*Rhetorica*
Arrian	
Anab.	*Anabasis*
ARW	*Archiv für Religionswissenschaft*
ASMS	American Society of Missiology Series

Athen.	Athenaeus
Deipn.	*Deipnosophistae*
BAGD	W. Bauer, W. F. Arndt, F. W. Gingrich, and F. W. Danker, *Greek-English Lexicon of the New Testament*
BAR	British Archaeological Reports
BBB	Bonner biblische Beiträge
BETL	Bibliotheca ephemeridum theologicarum lovaniensium
BIBAL	Berkeley Institute of Biblical Archaeology and Literature
Boeth.	Boethius
Cons.	*De Consolatione*
BTB	*Biblical Theology Bulletin*
BTH	Beiträge zur historischen Theologie
BThSt	Biblisch-Theologische Studien
BZNW	Beihefte zur *ZNW*
CAD	The Assyrian Dictionary of the Oriental Institute of the University of Chicago
CAH	*Cambridge Ancient History*
CB.NT	Coniectanea biblica. New Testament Series
CBQ	*Catholic Biblical Quarterly*
Cic.	Cicero
Att.	*Ad Atticum*
Fam.	*Ad Familiares*
Fin.	*De Finibus Bonorum et Malorum*
Nat. Deor.	*De Natura Deorum*
Phil.	*Orationes Philippicae*
Tusc.	*Tusculanae Disputationes*
CQ	*Classical Quarterly*
CRINT	Compendia Rerum Iudaicarum ad Novum Testamentum
Demetr.	Demetrius
Eloc.	*De Elocutione*
Did.	*Didache*
Dio C.	Dio Cassius
Dio Chrys.	Dio Chrysostom
Or.	*Orationes*
Diod. S.	Diodorus Siculus

Diog. Laer.	Diogenes Laertius
DJD	Discoveries in the Judaean Desert
DK	H. Diels and W. Kranz, *Die Fragmente der Vorsokratiker*
EHPR	Etudes d'histoire et de philosophie religieuses
EKKNT	Evangelisch-katolischer Kommentar zum Neuen Testament
Epic.	Epicurus
Men.	*Ad Menoeceum*
Epictet.	Epictetus
Diss.	*Dissertationes*
Epiph.	Epiphanius
Haer.	*Haereses*
EPRO	Études préliminaires aux religions orientales dans l'Empire romain
ErFor	Erträge der Forschung
ETL	*Ephemerides theologicae lovanienses*
Eur.	Euripides
Ba.	*Bacchae*
Herc. Fur.	*Hercules Furens*
Eus.	Eusebius
Hist. eccl.	*Historia Ecclesiastica*
EWNT	H. Balz and G. Schneider (eds.), *Exegetisches Wörterbuch zum Neuen Testament*
FRLANT	Forschungen zur Religion und Literatur des Alten und Neuen Testaments
FTS	Frankfurter Theologische Studien
GRBM	Greek, Roman, and Byzantine Monographs
GRBS	*Greek, Roman, and Byzantine Studies*
HALAT	W. Baumgartner, ed., *Hebräisches und aramäisches Lexikon zum Alten Testament*
Herm.	*Hermas*
Sim.	*Similitude(s)*
Vis.	*Vision(s)*
Hes.	Hesiod
Theog.	*Theogonia*
HNT	Handbuch zum Neuen Testament
HNTC	Harper's NT Commentaries

Hom.	Homer
Il.	*Iliad*
Od.	*Odyssey*
Horace	
Sat.	*Satirae*
HTKNT	Herder's theologischer Kommentar zum Neuen Testament
HTR	*Harvard Theological Review*
Iambl.	Iamblichus
Protr.	*Protrepticus*
ICC	International Critical Commentary
IOS	*Israel Oriental Studies*
JBL	*Journal of Biblical Literature*
JBTh	*Jahrbuch für biblische Theologie*
JIES	*Journal of Indo-European Studies*
Jos. Asen.	*Joseph and Aseneth*
Joseph.	Josephus
Ant.	*Antiquitates*
Ap.	*Contra Apionem*
Bell.	*Bellum Judaicum*
Vit.	*Vita*
JR	*Journal of Religion*
JSNT	*Journal for the Study of the New Testament*
JSNTSup	Journal for the Study of the New Testament—Supplement Series
JSPSup	Journal for the Study of the Pseudigrapha—Supplement Series
JTS	*Journal of Theological Studies*
Just.	Justin Martyr
Dial.	*Dialogus cum Tryphone Judaeo*
KNT	Kommentar zum Neuen Testament
KP	*Der Kleine Pauly*
LCL	Loeb Classical Library
Livy	
Epit.	*Epitomae*
LSJ	Liddell-Scott-Jones, *Greek-English Lexicon*
Luc.	Lucian
Hermot.	*Hermotimus*

Nigr.	*Nigrinus*
Vit. Auct.	*Vitarum Auctio*
Bis acc.	*Bis Accusatus*
M. Ant.	Marcus Aurelius Antoninus
Max. Tyr.	Maximus of Tyre
M-W	R. Merkelbach and M. L. West, *Fragmenta Hesiodea*
n. s.	new series
NASB	New American Standard Bible
NEB	New English Bible
NovT	*Novum Testamentum*
NovTSup	Novum Testamentum, Supplements
NT	New Testament
NTD	Das Neue Testament Deutsch
NTOA	Novum Testamentum et Orbis Antiquus
NTS	*New Testament Studies*
NZSTh	*Neue Zeitschrift für systematische Theologie und Religionsphilosophie*
OBO	Orbis biblicus et orientalis
OCD	*Oxford Classical Dictionary*
Orig.	Origen
Comm. in. Ioh.	*Commentarii in Johannem*
OTP	James H. Charlesworth, ed., *The Old Testament Pseudepigrapha*
Pall.	Palladius
Hist. Laus.	*Historia Lausiaca*
Paterculus	
Hist. Rom.	*Historiae Romanae*
Paul. Diac.	Paulus Diaconus
Paus.	Pausanias
PhAnt	Philosophia antiqua
Philostr.	Philostratus
Vit. Ap.	*Vita Apollonii*
Pind.	Pindar
Isthm.	*Isthmian Odes*
Nem.	*Nemean Odes*
Olymp.	*Olympian Odes*
Plat.	Plato
Alc.	*Alcibiades*

Ap.	*Apologia*
Charm.	*Charmides*
Crat.	*Cratylus*
Gorg.	*Gorgias*
Leg.	*Leges*
Phaed.	*Phaedo*
Phaedr.	*Phaedrus*
Resp.	*Respublica*
Symp.	*Symposium*
Theaet.	*Theaetetus*
Plin.	Pliny the Elder
Hist. Nat.	*Naturalis Historia*
Plin.	Pliny the Younger
Ep.	*Epistulae*
Plot.	Plotinus
Enn.	*Enneads*
Plut.	Plutarch
Comm. Not.	*De Communibus Notitiis*
Sert.	*Sertorius*
Stoic. Rep.	*De Stoicorum Repugnantiis*
Porphyr.	Porphyry
Vit. Plot.	*Vita Plotini*
Ps.	Pseudo
Pss. Sol.	*Psalms of Solomon*
RAC	*Reallexikon für Antike und Christentum*
RB	*Revue biblique*
RGRW	Religions in the Graeco-Roman World
RhM	*Rheinisches Museum für Philologie*
RHPR	*Revue d'histoire et de philosophie religieuses*
RivB	*Rivista Biblica*
RSF	*Rivista di studi fenici*
RSV	Revised Standard Version
RTL	*Revue théologique de Louvain*
RVV	Religionsgeschichtliche Versuche und Vorarbeiten
SBLSBS	Society of Biblical Literature Sources for Biblical Study
SBLSS	Society of Biblical Literature Semeia Studies
SCHNT	Studia ad corpus hellenisticum novi testamenti

SEÅ	*Svensk Exegetisk Årsbok*
Sen.	Seneca
Ben.	*De Beneficiis*
Ep.	*Epistulae Morales*
SHAW	Sitzungsberichte der Heidelberger Akademie der Wissenschaften
Sib. Or.	*Sibylline Oracles*
SM	Sermon on the Mount
SNTS	Society of New Testament Studies
SNTU	*Studien zum Neuen Testament und seiner Umwelt*
SP	Sermon on the Plain
SQAW	Schriften und Quellen der Alten Welt
ST	*Studia Theologica*
Stob.	Johannes Stobaeus
Ecl.	*Ecloge*
SUNT	Studien zur Umwelt des Neuen Testaments
SVF	H. F. A. von Arnim, *Stoicorum Veterum Fragmenta*
T. Naph	*Testament of Naphtali*
TAPA	*Transactions of the American Philological Association*
TDNT	G. Kittel and G. Friedrich (eds.), *Theological Dictionary of the New Testament*
Tg. Jon.	*Targum (Ps.-) Jonathan*
Tg. Onq.	*Targum Onqelos*
THAT	E. Jenni and C. Westermann (eds.), *Theologisches Handwörterbuch zum Alten Testament*
Theocr.	Theocritus
THKNT	Theologischer Handkommentar zum Neuen Testament
TU	Texte und Untersuchungen
TWAT	G. J. Botterweck and H. Ringgren (eds.), *Theologisches Wörterbuch zum Alten Testament*
TWNT	G. Kittel and G. Friedrich (eds.), *Theologisches Wörterbuch zum Neuen Testament*
UNT	Untersuchungen zum Neuen Testament
UTB	Uni-Taschenbücher
WBC	Word Biblical Commentary
WMANT	Wissenschaftliche Monographien zum Alten und Neuen Testament

WUNT	Wissenschaftliche Untersuchungen zum Neuen Testament
Xenoph.	Xenophon
Mem.	*Memorabilia Socratis*
ZDPV	*Zeitschrift des deutschen Palästina-Vereins*
ZGL	*Zeitschrift für germanistische Linguistik*
ZKG	*Zeitschrift für Kirchengeschichte*
ZNW	*Zeitschrift für die neutestamentliche Wissenschaft*
ZPE	*Zeitschrift für Papyrologie und Epigraphik*
ZTK	*Zeitschrift für Theologie und Kirche*

Introduction

Each of the contributions to this volume demonstrates dramatically the fruitfulness of reading a text in more than one cultural context. The essays in Part One deal with the ancient Mediterranean world. These show the profound interrelationship of philosophy and religion and one religion with another in antiquity. James Barr argues that the discipline of natural theology was born in the interaction of Jewish tradition with Greek philosophical thought. His respondent, John J. Collins, explores the tension in natural theology between the truth and ethics of reason and those of revelation. Hubert Cancik, in a way that corrects and supplements the work of Arthur D. Nock, argues that the phenomenon of "conversion" in Greek tradition has its home in philosophical circles, much more so than in religious ones. His respondent, Edgar Krentz, shows how Cancik's study illuminates early Christian texts and raises the question whether there was a literary genre "conversion account" in antiquity. Walter Burkert and Elizabeth Asmis explore archaic, classical and Hellenistic Greek language and images for the inner self and its parts, which are at times in conflict with each other and at times in harmony. These analyses create an invaluable context for understanding the apostle Paul's remarks about the inner self, its conflicts and transformations. They also raise significant questions about what it means to be an embodied self. Burkert pays special attention to the texts that regard the inner self as superior to the body and the body as a limitation of the self. Asmis emphasizes texts that speak about the body as a home, as a framework in which the self can live. Hildegard Cancik-Lindemaier discusses the philosophical and literary nature of the letters of Seneca and their rhetorical function. As a collection they provide a kind of autobiographical narrative of the moral progress of Seneca, presented not so much as a model to be imitated, but as the report of a fellow traveler from which his named addressee, and no doubt an anticipated wider audience, may learn. This essay is a fascinating case study which invites comparison and contrast with Paul and his letters. Margaret Mitchell provides a telling comparison of the collection of Seneca's letters with the so-called Pastoral Epistles of the New Testament, the letters to Timothy and Titus. By means of a painstaking analysis of the literary history of the Gospel of Matthew, James M. Robinson contributes to the reconstruction of the cultural transformations of the early Christian movement, especially from predominantly Jewish Christian forms to Gentile Christian types. In my response, I challenge the idea that literary history is a mirror of cultural and religious history. In his study of the stilling of the storm and the healing of the demoniac in Mark 4:35–5:43, Roy Kotansky illuminates the text's mythic features and its affinity with the legends and cult of Heracles in relation to ancient Gadeira, near the Pillars of Herakles, the strait of Gibraltar. In his response, David Aune defends the association of these narratives with ancient Galilee and points out the political implications of their symbolic characteristics.

The essays in Part Two show how themes from ancient Jewish and Christian movements are enculturated or interpreted today. Ithamar Gruenwald argues that the apocalyptic mentality is very much alive today in Israel and that its embodiment in that context sheds light on apocalyptic phenomena in antiquity. In particular, he suggests that the widespread association of apocalypticism with sects is dubious. It makes more sense to see apocalyptic movements as attempts to reform or persuade the whole society in which they occur. He also implies that apocalypticism is inherently violent. In his response, Jonathan Z. Smith provides some helpful cross-cultural reflections on the phenomenon. He challenges the idea that apocalypticism is inherently violent and calls for further study of the question why some apocalyptic groups become violent and others do not. David Hellholm, in interpreting the beatitudes, shows how the twentieth century discipline of text-linguistics can uncover the profound ambiguity of the beatitudes attributed to Jesus, when they are read in isolation. It can then assist in determining the meaning of these beatitudes in the context of the life of Jesus and in the various literary contexts in which they were transmitted thereafter. Detlev Dormeyer draws a striking analogy between the Gospel of Matthew, with its beatitudes and talk about the mysteries of the kingdom, and the ancient mystery religions, which also acclaimed the initiates blessed. Kathleen O'Brien Wicker provides fascinating case studies of conversion to forms of Christian faith that are adapted to indigenous African cultures. These case studies illuminate the cultural factors in the conversion of the apostle Paul. In his response, Arthur Droge challenges the notion that "conversion" is a cross-cultural category and highlights its specifically Christian and western characteristics.

As a collection, the essays in this volume illustrate the pluralism of methods in biblical studies and classics. Some of the authors employ tried and true methods to achieve fresh insights. James Barr discerns the beginnings of systematic thought in the traditionally non-systematic biblical genres. Walter Burkert reconstructs the history of an idea by selecting and reading closely a large number of texts from different points in the history of Greek literature. James M. Robinson employs literary methods to discern stages in the composition of texts. Roy Kotansky adapts the approach of the history of religions school. Hubert Cancik and Hildegard Cancik-Lindemaier rely on traditional methods, but innovate in their use of "narrative philology." Ithamar Gruenwald and Kathleen O'Brien Wicker take a comparative approach related to cultural studies with sociological and anthropological sensitivities. David Hellholm transforms the traditional methods of form and redaction criticism and the reconstruction of tradition-history by approaching the questions addressed by such methods from a text-linguistic point of view. The result is an exhibition in which works never before seen together illuminate one another in surprising and fascinating ways.

The essays and responses published in this volume derive from a conference celebrating the scholarship and teaching of Hans Dieter Betz that took place at the University of Chicago, October 8–10, 1996. It was sponsored by the Dean and Faculty of the University of Chicago Divinity School and by the Department of New Testament and Early Christian Literature in the Division of the Humanities of the University of Chicago. I would like first of all to thank Dieter Betz for being the kind of scholar and teacher who could inspire such a symposium. He revealed over lunch with a few friends one day that, as a young man, he had wanted to become an artist. This revelation made sense to his interlocutors because it correlated with his extraordinary creativity as a scholar.

When most New Testament scholars were interpreting their texts almost exclusively in relation to the Hebrew Bible and post-biblical Jewish texts, Dieter insisted on and demonstrated the relevance of Greek and Roman models and traditions. He did not neglect the

Jewish context of early Christianity, however, as his collaboration with Ithamar Gruenwald, for example, shows. When historically oriented rhetorical criticism was virtually unheard of among scholars of early Christianity, he pioneered a rhetorical approach to the Sermon on the Mount and to Paul's letter to the Galatians. His voice in the wilderness at first met with great resistance. It is a tribute to his leadership and powers of persuasion that these approaches are widely accepted and practiced today.

To the degree that such a thing is possible in the twentieth century, Dieter approximates the Renaissance ideal of the polymath. Equally at home in Greek and Roman religion and philosophy as in the texts of early Christianity, he has a wide network of colleagues here at the University of Chicago and throughout the United States, Europe, Israel and South Africa. He has educated a significant number of students from a variety of backgrounds who are emerging as leaders in the field of New Testament studies.

Thanks are also due to W. Clark Gilpin, Dean of the University of Chicago Divinity School, for his generous support of the conference, both intellectually and financially. Tim Child, Sandra Peppers and Linda Aldridge of the Divinity School did much to see that the conference went smoothly. Many colleagues collaborated with the editor of this volume in conceiving the idea for the conference and planning it, especially Ithamar Gruenwald, David Hellholm, John J. Collins, Elizabeth Gebhard, Elizabeth Asmis, and Chris Faraone. Matthew Jackson-McCabe, Jeffrey Asher and Eric Sorensen contributed enormously to the preparation of the manuscript for publication.

Finally, all the contributors to the volume are to be thanked heartily for creating a stimulating symposium and for offering the fruits of their scholarly labors in honor of Dieter Betz to the community of scholar-teachers and students and to other interested members of the public.

Adela Yarbro Collins
University of Chicago
April, 1998

Greek Culture and the Question of Natural Theology

James Barr

The subject of natural theology is an ancient one and historically of great importance. But in the biblical studies of the twentieth century it has been severely neglected; indeed, much that has been written about the Bible leaves the impression that its ultimate aim has been to depict the Bible as a purely revelational document and one from which every trace of natural theology is absent.[1] If in fact we find that the Bible itself gives clear evidence of depending on natural theology, or implying it, then a great deal of fresh thinking has to be done. Here today we have several people who have done work in this direction: certainly Professor John J. Collins, certainly also Professor Betz, whom I remember consulting about the matter, and also myself. Given this strong measure of agreement, I do not propose to spend time arguing that there *is* natural theology in the Bible, or at least something like it, or something that implies it. This I take to be already proven. What I want to do is to go on to the next step: given that something akin to natural theology is well founded in the Bible, I want to ask: can we find out something more about how it got there, how it worked, perhaps whether there are different tendencies within it, and whether we can see some sort of development between different aspects of its impact. But I want to begin with the contribution of Professor Betz.

Betz presented highly important evidence in this respect, some of which was published as far back as 1985. I refer to the Excursus entitled "Paul's Agrarian Theology," contained in his commentary on

---

[1] I leave aside the question of the various meanings which the phrase "natural theology" has had in the history of ideas. For my purpose, as the term is mostly used today, it means any theology based on what human beings, simply as human beings, may know, as distinct from revelational theology, built upon special interventions or communications of the divine. On the origin of the idea, in St. Augustine's discussion of Varro, see W. Jaeger, *The Theology of the Early Greek Philosophers* (Oxford: Clarendon, 1947) 2–4. As I myself have used the term, it can be expressed as "anterior knowledge," i.e., knowledge of God, of humanity, or of the world that is available and accessible to humans and is thus "anterior" to any special revelation.

2 Corinthians 8 and 9.[2] Now I am not sure that he there says anything about the position of traditional theologians, or that he even uses the term "natural theology" itself. He starts from an actual, fairly limited, group of texts and expounds them in such a way as to show their literary coherence and thereby their original separate unity. But in so doing he produces exegetical thoughts which cannot fail to be relevant for the general question of natural theology.

He is talking about passages of Paul like the following: "he who sows sparingly, sparingly will he also reap, and he who sows bountifully, bountifully will he also reap" (2 Cor 9:6) and "the one who provides 'seed for the sower and bread for consumption' will provide and [indeed] increase your seed and multiply the fruits of your righteousness" (2 Cor 9:10). Commenting on these and other similar expressions, Betz provided the important Excursus I have mentioned, and here are some salient remarks from within it:

> Paul's argument in vv. 6–14 is founded throughout upon presuppositions which belong to the realm of ancient agriculture. . . . Ancient agriculture never confined itself to purely practical matters, but embraced the entire science of household economy, in which religion played a role that can hardly be overestimated. To this agrarian religion there also belonged a particular kind of "theology" which made use of reflections on such proverbial wisdom and of religious practices and the concepts connected with them. This complex of secondary reflection also played a role in ancient philosophy, and therefore was capable of being integrated into the philosophical systems of various schools. This agrarian theology is certainly pre-Christian and also pre-Jewish—in fact, it is simply the common possession of all of antiquity. But, as Paul's use of these ideas demonstrates, they could also be easily integrated with Christian thought.[3]

And here Betz goes on to quote the Greek material, starting of course with the most obviously "agrarian" of all writings, Hesiod's *Works and Days*. And so, to quote again:

> The religious-spiritual dimension of agriculture was familiar to everyone in the ancient world. Thus when Paul contrasted sowing "sparingly" with reaping "bountifully," he made reference to the presuppositions of an agrarian theology known to all. It was possible for him to pass back and forth between the material and spiritual aspects of the concept without expressly calling the

---

[2] H. D. Betz, *2 Corinthians 8 and 9: A Commentary on Two Administrative Letters of the Apostle Paul* (Hermeneia; Philadelphia: Fortress, 1985) 98–100.

[3] *Ibid.*, 98.

> transition to his readers' attention. Precisely what seems confusing to modern man was a self-evident fact of life for the ancients.[4]

This passage on "Agrarian Theology" is far from the only one in Betz's commentary that is relevant to our theme. Compare again his section on pp. 111–115, where we hear at one point that "Paul's language and thought seem very close to that of Greek religion" and "The ideas that Paul expressed here correspond to an extraordinary degree to those found in Greek religion."[5] As I have argued elsewhere, any sort of transreligiosity brings us close to natural theology. On p. 111 we read that "these ideas must be very old, and must have constituted part of the generally accepted wisdom tradition in antiquity," a point illustrated from a Mesopotamian wisdom poem.

Now, as I say, all these facts and interpretations are highly relevant to the general question of natural theology, but Professor Betz refrains—at least in that book—from discussing the latter as a general question, preferring close textual commentary. In my own work I went the other way, seeking to approach the whole theological question and the reasons why natural theology has been so much in disfavour, but refraining from trying to gather all the detailed textual evidence that might easily be found. But the resurvey of the detailed textual evidence is the next step to be taken, and this is where Betz stands strikingly ahead of us all.

Now let me explain just why this matter of "Agrarian Theology" might be so important for the general question of natural theology. In the tradition of natural theology, certainly Christian but also Jewish, natural theology has meant in effect the taking of a tradition of Greek philosophy as a system of presuppositions upon which revealed theology might rest. Thus Platonism, Aristotelianism, and Stoicism are all familiar classic examples of philosophies which have been taken as acceptable intellectual bases for theology: the same could not be said, however, of some other Greek philosophical traditions, for example the Epicurean, which tended to be condemned by the Jewish-Christian tradition, and the Sceptical. Now the importance of this is that those who have opposed natural theology have commonly done so for just this reason: that is, because they understood it to mean the

---

4 *Ibid.*

5 *Ibid.*, 112, 115.

importation of a Greek philosophical system in its entirety. For exactly this reason, the modern denial of natural theology within Christianity was commonly associated with a strong hostility to Greek thought. Nowhere was this hostility more clearly stated, in an influential writing, than by Emil Brunner in his *The Divine-Human Encounter*:

> The decisive word-form in the language of the Bible is not the substantive, as in Greek, but the verb, the word of action. The thought of the Bible is not substantival, neuter and abstract, but verbal, historical and personal.[6]

And again:

> The New Testament differs from the Old in a manner which is seductive and dangerous for our generation. The New Testament is written in Greek. It makes use of Greek concepts to express the message of salvation in Christ. . . . The Greeks are our scientific tutors. Owing to the unprecedented esteem and practical significance which science enjoys today, the Greeks are more than ever the tutors of our time. Even the thinking of the ordinary man, who knows nothing of the Greeks, is infused with Greek thought from the school, the newspaper and daily associations.
>
> Now it is a strange paradox of reality that the Gospel is presented to us in the language and concepts of the people whose thought constitutes today the greatest opposition to the content of the Gospel. To mention only one example, the Greek conception of spirit, and therefore of the true and the good, is a kind which equates spirit with the abstract and represents the physically concrete as its opposite, as that which ought not to be. . . . The identification of the spiritual with the abstract is one of the most fateful facts of our intellectual history. . . . for us the Greek conceptual world of the New Testament is above all a hindrance because it presents the temptation to Hellenize the content of the New Testament. . . . In the Old Testament we come upon a world completely unaffected by the whole Hellenic spirit. . . . That which is peculiarly biblical, veiled in the New Testament under Greek form, appears to us in Old Testament form unveiled—yes, perhaps even enhanced, in a certain sense exaggerated. But this is what we need especially today; and this is why for us the Old Testament is necessary in a special way for understanding the New.[7]

---

[6] E. Brunner, *The Divine-Human Encounter* (London: SCM, 1944) 32; German original, *Wahrheit als Begegnung* (Berlin: Furche-Verlag, 1938); for the impact of this book, cf. B. S. Childs, *Biblical Theology in Crisis* (Philadelphia: Westminster, 1970) 17, 45; G. E. Wright, *God Who Acts* (London: SCM, 1952) 90.

[7] Brunner in his article "The Significance of the Old Testament for our Faith," *The Old Testament and Christian Faith* (ed. B. W. Anderson; New York: Harper and Row, 1963) 247–49; German original, "Die Bedeutung des Alten Testaments für unsern Glauben," *Zwischen den Zeiten* 8 (1930) 30–48. Cf. J. Barr, *Old and New In Interpretation: A Study of the Two Testaments* (London: SCM, 1966; 2nd ed. 1982) 45.

As in all these things, there are many apparent contradictions. For example, Brunner was not against natural theology in the way Karl Barth was, and indeed it was his proposal to search for a new natural theology for his time that led to the violent strife between the two of them. Nevertheless it was Brunner who provided, more even than Barth, the conceptuality in which the opposition to natural theology was to be expressed and understood, at least for a generation or two. Curiously, Brunner in his opposition to Barth never really valorized the one weapon that might have been fatal to the Barthian cause, namely the evidence that the Bible itself contained, affirmed or at least implied natural theology. It is as if he thought that the Bible itself took the Barthian position, but there were reasons in the modern situation why natural theology should be pursued. Anyway, for many people working in the theology of the forties and fifties it was Brunner who provided the standard conceptuality of attitudes about Greek thought and natural theology.

This leads me to the thought that Betz's "Agrarian Theology" brings to my mind. As he rightly points out, the agrarian theology "played a role in ancient philosophy." But his agrarian theology is not a simple takeover of any such philosophy: rather, it is more like a pre-philosophy, which then also supplies certain ingredients within later philosophies. It goes back to Hesiod; in part it may go back to Mesopotamian times. Now what I am going to suggest is that this may be true not only of agrarian theology but also of much of the Bible's own natural theology, and especially so in its earlier stages, and particularly in the Hebrew Bible itself. In other words, I am asking if we may distinguish different kinds of natural theology, and whether there may be some kind of development visible, in which we may see on the one hand old kinds of pre-philosophical wisdom and on the other obvious dependence on Greek philosophic terms and categories. And is there a stage at which the interaction between these different types makes some substantial difference to the total biblical tradition? I will suggest that there may indeed be such a stage.

First however we have to discuss one very general and profound question, namely how far *theology* is a correct term for the material we find in the Bible. For there are very different ideas of what *theology* is and where and when it started. One fashionable idea is that theology is a late phenomenon. Seen this way, it belongs to the scholastic and dogmatic trends, visible especially in Christianity: its peak periods lie in the Fathers of the fourth century or so, in the Middle Ages, in the Reformation, in modern dogmatic theology. Before this time, there was not any real theology. Seen this way, the Bible did not contain theology, or only very little. Jewish opinion, though not universally, tends to depict theology as a Christian operation, something Jews do not like and do not operate. According to this view, most ancient religion got along very well without theology. This opinion has been very popular over the last century or so. The history of religions has often followed this path; sometimes it has been marked by an animus against theology, against any theology of any kind and at any time.

But the opposite tendency also exists. The idea of "biblical theology" may, in one of its definitions, suggest that the Bible is full of theology or at least implies it. The term *theology* is sometimes used of very ancient phenomena: in studies of ancient Egypt, for instance, "the Memphite theology" has been a customary phrase. As is familiar, or should be, the Greek word *theologia* is first found in Plato (*Resp.* 379a). In this sense, Werner Jaeger wrote, "theology is a specific creation of the Greek mind. . . . Theology is a mental attitude which is characteristically Greek."[8] Plato and Aristotle may not be so very early, in comparison with Ancient Egypt, but they are amply earlier than the beginnings of Christianity. And, as we have seen, Dieter Betz sees an "agrarian theology" that reaches back into ancient times. I suspect that some trends in the history of religions are becoming more willing than in the past to accept "theology" as a respectable term. A good example can be seen in the work of Rainer Albertz.[9] Albertz is emphatically against the idea of biblical theology or Old Testament theology and thinks that any attempt at such a discipline should be abandoned and replaced by the history of religion. But this does not mean that he himself abandons the term "theology." On the contrary, he finds "theology" within the Hebrew Bible and in great profundity, especially in a movement like the Deuteronomic reforms. In other words, the

---

[8] W. Jaeger, *The Theology of the Early Greek Philosophers* (Oxford: Clarendon, 1947) 4.

[9] Rainer Albertz, *A History of Israelite Religion in the Old Testament Period* (2 vols.; London: SCM, 1994).

history of religions has to include theology as a constituent of religion, where theology in fact exists.

Paradoxically, however, modern theologians, as distinct from biblical scholars, are themselves if anything becoming more dubious about the use of "theology" within the Bible. Ebeling is one of the major theologians to express this tendency. He has become cautious about saying that anything in the Bible is actually "theology." Thus in a famous and widely-read article he asserted:

> A further thing that has become problematical is the application of the concept "theology" to the actual content of the Bible. . . . [From a certain angle] there would be real sense in speaking of theology even in the New Testament, above all in Paul and the author of the Fourth Gospel. On the other hand it would be questionable to describe, say, the preaching of the individual Old Testament prophets as theology. But it is certainly capable of theological explication. From this the conclusion follows that although the Bible for the most part does not contain theology in the strict sense, yet it does press for theological explication.[10]

The important thing about this is that it does not come from the more sceptical, anti-theological wing of study, but from a major theologian himself. Likewise in a more recent time Dietrich Ritschl, in a chapter entitled "The Fiction of a Biblical Theology," wrote:

> The question is whether the Bible contains theology in the sense that contemporary theology could get its content directly from it or find a model for its work in the way in which the Bible presents things. Certainly parts of the biblical writings were "theology" in a particular way for the believers of their time. But that does not mean that the theological content could be transferred directly to later times or situations. Strictly speaking, most parts of the Bible cannot be transferred. The wisdom literature in the Old Testament and in the New may be an important exception.
>
> Theology in the sense of theorizing with a view to regulative statements exists in the biblical writings only in an approximative sense.[11] Only with qualifications and under certain conditions can we talk of "the theology of Deutero-Isaiah," of Lucan or Johannine "theology;" it is easier to speak of Pauline theology because in Paul there are detailed declarations, arguments and definitions that we can follow. And yet even in comparison with the christologies, doctrines of the Trinity, doctrines of the church, of grace, of man

---

[10] G. Ebeling, "The Meaning of 'Biblical Theology,'" *Word and Faith* (London: SCM, 1963) 79–97, here 93–94; originally published in *JTS* 6 (1955) 210–225.

[11] I here translate this sentence in a different way from that of the English translation of Ritschl's book.

and so on, the letters of Paul are theology only in the inauthentic sense of the word.[12]

Now we cannot hope to settle this question altogether within a single paper like this present one. Perhaps it suggests that there are several *kinds* or levels of theology, one of which is very "primitive," in the sense that it goes back a very long time, another much more "adult," in the sense that it emerges in a comparatively late stage. The older natural theology expresses itself in folk wisdom, proverb, story and ritual. It may belong to several quite different religions or religious currents. The more adult expresses itself in argument. It is linked with religious conflict. The two may overlap, in that the later type can be found as far back as in ancient Egypt and the earlier type is still to be found in Paul. In the Hebrew Bible I would think that Proverbs contains a mixture of that older "gnomic" wisdom, along with developed rhetorical and doxological passages. Qohelet is more concerned with observation, deduction and argument: maybe not religious conflict, but certainly religious crisis. The Wisdom of Solomon is more definitely argumentative and polemic: it much more obviously takes up Greek categories and Greek arguments, but then its argument is substantially against the Greeks with their polytheism and supposed idolatry and in favour of the Jewish tradition. Different types are thus mixed up—as we see in Paul, who follows older wisdom in his "agrarian theology," but follows the Wisdom of Solomon in the argument of Romans 1–2.

We have thus to offer some sort of preliminary statement of what is "theology," as distinct from other sorts of religious assertion or expression, as distinct, let us say, from much of the material of the Bible. This may doubtless be questioned and contradicted, but here is what I propose. To qualify as theology something has to be discriminatory, that is, it has to make a distinction as against some other possibility; it has to be argumentative, that is, it has to give grounds—not necessarily rational grounds, but grounds of some kind—for its position; it has to be abstracted—I do not say "abstract," but abstracted—in the sense

---

[12] D. Ritschl, *The Logic of Theology* (London: SCM, 1986) 68; Ritschl may well have altered his view of these matters more recently—see his article, "Wahre, 'reine' oder 'neue' biblsiche Theologie? Einige Anfragen zur neueren Diskussion um 'biblische Theologie,'" *JBTh* 1 (1986) 135–150—but the view as stated by him in his *The Logic of Theology* remains a good basis for discussion.

that it is not a mere repetition or rewording of a religious utterance, but is meant to have validity of its own; it has to have some claim to universality, and thus not be limited to one set of circumstances only. Thus much of the biblical material can be classed as "story:" story is not itself theology (this is intended in contrast with much that claims to be "narrative theology"), but is the raw material for theology (Dietrich Ritschl). Thus the teaching of Jesus in the Synoptic Gospels is not theology, and few Christians have ever been happy with the idea that Jesus was a theologian. But these Gospels are certainly material that invites and requires theological explanation. They may also *imply* theology; but if so they do not make it explicit.

Now this is linked once again with the question of Greek thought. In the same article Ebeling went on to argue: "It could be shown that theology arises from the meeting of the biblical testimony to revelation with Greek thinking, and that these two elements are constitutive for the nature of theology."[13] Something similar was said by the Old Testament scholar Rudolf Smend.[14] Thus two points are tied together: firstly, whether the Bible contains theology; secondly, whether theology as such is tied up with contact with Greek thought.

Perhaps before we go any farther we might look at some objections which have been levelled against Ebeling's arguments by Hans Hübner. In his stimulating *Biblische Theologie des Neuen Testaments,* he has taken up and discussed just these points made by Ebeling.[15] Can one not perceive, he asks, a *theological* conception underlying the narrative representations of the Gospels?[16] These conceptions clearly show theologically reflective and argumentative features, and to such a degree that one can speak of the respective theologies of the

---

13 Ebeling, *Word and Faith,* 93–94.

14 R. Smend, asking the question whether the phenomenon theology really exists in the Old Testament, writes: "One will not be able to force the New Testament scholar or, most completely, the dogmatician, whose texts—*overwhelmingly trained on Greek thought* [my italics]—have so much higher a degree of reflection, to answer this question in the affirmative." See his "Theologie im AT," *Die Mitte des Alten Testaments* (Munich: Kaiser, 1986) 104–117, here 116; originally published in *Verifikationen: Festschrift für Gerhard Ebeling zum 70. Geburtstag* (ed. E. Jüngel et al.; Tübingen: Mohr, 1982) 11–26.

15 H. Hübner, *Biblische Theologie des Neuen Testaments* (3 vols.; Göttingen: Vandenhoeck & Ruprecht, 1990–95) 1. 24–26.

16 *Ibid.*, 26.

individual Synoptic evangelists. "Naturally the theology of the New Testament authors is not academic theology in the modern sense, but the spiritual achievement of these men is theologically reflective argumentation."[17] So, he concludes, "The New Testament is thus a highly theological book."[18]

It seems to me, however, that Hübner is wrong in this and that Ebeling was right. *Of course* the Synoptic Gospels are "theological:" that is not to be doubted. So is the New Testament as a whole. They imply theology and, as Ebeling and Brunner said, they invite theological explication. But that a text is "theological" is not the same as saying that it is theology. The contents of most parts of the Synoptic Gospels are not theology. Theology may well be implicit in them, but a text is theology only when theology is made explicit in it. One way of expressing the task of biblical theology, or of theological exegesis, is to say that it seeks to make explicit the implicit theology of the texts. But this is needed precisely because the the texts themselves for the most part are not theology. If they were theology, in the proper sense, there would be no need for a discipline such as biblical theology.

Hübner has reacted also against the second remark of Ebeling just quoted, and again, in my opinion, wrongly. Quoting the same passage from Ebeling as I have done, he says that "for Ebeling two elements are constitutive for theology, namely (a) the biblical testimony to revelation and (b) Greek thought. Where these two constituents are to be found in the New Testament, there could one speak of theology, thus for example with Paul or the author of John."[19] But Hübner here takes Ebeling as if the latter thought of contact with Greek thought as a *condition* for the presence of theology. I understand Ebeling as meaning it as a mere matter of fact: where we do find theology in the proper sense, there it is in fact in connection with Greek thought (and so also Smend as quoted above). This seems correct. Whether contact with Greek thought is a *necessary* condition or not, factually it is, in the biblical tradition and its marginal congeners, mostly in contact with Greek thought that we find something like explicit theology.

---

[17] *Ibid.*, 26.

[18] *Ibid.*, 28.

[19] *Ibid.*, 25.

This then outlines our first question: given that there is doubt whether "theology," or even "approximations to theology," exist within the Bible, can we do anything further to define them? I would say that, on the basis of these considerations, the Bible contains *some* material that is really "theology," but only some. But if there are only occasional pieces of theology in the Bible, where did they come from? How did *any* theology get into the Bible?

From this it is an easy move on to our second question: is there a connection between theology, on the one hand, and Greek thought, on the other? In this we come at once upon another conflict of modern discussion. For the Biblical Theology Movement, using the terms of Childs, not only was sure that the Bible was thoroughly theological and (probably) implied that much of its contents were theology, but it also insisted that, if the intellectual foundation of that theology came from anywhere, it came from the Hebrew Bible. The Hebrew Bible was the source and pattern upon which the theology of the New Testament and of Christianity in general was based. Biblical theology, with its basis in Hebrew thought, was seen as special and characteristic precisely in its *difference*, its *contrast*, from the world of Greek thought. No one doubts that this was a central and characteristic emphasis of the Biblical Theology Movement.

But, as we have seen, exactly here, these older certainties have been questioned by more recent arguments: Greek thought is constitutive of theology, not in the sense that it is absolutely necessary, but at least in the sense that much or most of what is real theology, within the biblical and later traditions, factually exists in contact with Greek thought.

This brings us back to one particular book which I mentioned briefly earlier, namely the Wisdom of Solomon. I have elsewhere stressed the importance of this work for the concepts used by Paul in his arguments in the opening chapters of Romans. Natural theology, in the sense in which the term is most commonly used, is central to the Wisdom of Solomon and is followed by Paul in Romans. And in a certain sense the Wisdom of Solomon, at least in this part of it, is not only a work of natural theology, but more a work that is strictly theology, in the modern sense of the term, than is anything in the Hebrew Bible. In a sense, therefore, natural theology is not only present at this stage, but natural theology forms the prime stage of theology itself. Therefore, far from it being the case that natural theology is a late-comer and intruder which threatened to spoil the continuity of revelational theology, it may be natural theology that provided a substantial contribution to the appearance and centrality of theology within the Jewish-Christian tradition at all.

It is striking that this decisive intellectual step was taken in a book widely considered to be "apocryphal." The Wisdom of Solomon lay outside the Jewish canon, at least the later canon as it now exists.[20] Whether the book is counted as "canonical" for religion or not, I would call it a "biblical book;" and its historic place in the rise of "theology" to importance cannot be disregarded.

The Wisdom of Solomon, however, though it certainly included natural theology, and though it certainly relied on Greek concepts and categories in large measure, can still not be regarded very easily as a work of Greek philosophy. Only to a very limited extent can the natural theology of the Bible be described as a taking over of Greek philosophy or of any particular Greek philosophy. There may indeed be a substantial use of terms and modes of thought which are adapted from Greek philosophy: but in terms of actual content, of actual convictions the acceptance of which is being demanded, the opposite is often the case. Jewish natural theology, as found for instance in the Wisdom of Solomon, while using Greek thought forms is to a large extent in combat with Hellenism. Similarly, later in Christianity, Fathers like the Cappadocians who greatly developed the tradition of natural theology did so as part of their *controversy* with the Greeks.[21]

To give one salient example of this, the idea of *creation*. Much natural theology has been *creation theology*: it has reasoned, in a partly or wholly philosophical manner, from the fact of creation. Creation manifested essentials of the nature of God, it also proved certain

---

[20] John Barton writes: "A few books now reckoned deutero-canonical, apocryphal, or even pseudepigraphical may have enjoyed a status they subsequently lost in Judaism. The Wisdom of Solomon and 1 Enoch may be examples of the latter category." See his "The Significance of a Fixed Canon in the Hebrew Bible," *Hebrew Bible/Old Testament. The History of its Interpretation.* Vol. 1, *From the Beginnings to the Middle Ages* (ed. M. Sæbø; Göttingen: Vandenhoeck & Ruprecht, 1996) 71.

[21] On this see now the imposing work of J. Pelikan, *Christianity and Classical Culture. The Metamorphosis of Natural Theology in the Christian Encounter with Hellenism* (New Haven: Yale University Press, 1993).

things about humanity. But creation was a subject on which Greek philosophy was decidedly weak. Becoming, coming to be and passing away, the origination of things, the original principle of being—on all these it had spoken. But creation by a massive act of one God, bringing all things into existence in a clear temporal sequence chronologically linked with all subsequent history—this comes from the Hebrew Bible, and especially from the completed Pentateuch. Natural theology might seek to express this in categories taken from Greek philosophy, but the essential content in this case at least came from the Bible.

On the other hand one cannot insist that this is always so. When it comes to be recognized, as it surely will, that natural theology has a significant place within the Bible, many will seek to comfort themselves with the thought that, even if the source is natural theology, that content is transformed and used to convey only new revelational material. Betz, however, says that this is not so. Certainly it was sometimes so: Paul's use of these ideas [of agrarian theology] shows that they "could easily be integrated with Christian thought."[22] But, he goes on,

> Yet it is remarkable that he did so little to make these ideas Christian. In the entire section [2 Cor.] 9:6–14, which presents a unified train of thought, there is nothing which could be designated as specifically Christian. The concept "the gospel of Christ" constitutes the only exception, but this concept plays no role in the argument itself. Thus we must reckon with the fact that the entire complex derives essentially from pre-Pauline, Hellenistic-Jewish theology. If this is granted, then we may conclude that even at a later time Paul could still have recourse to complexes of thought which actually belonged to his pre-Christian period.[23]

If this is right, then natural theology was not merely a vehicle to be transformed and used for a revelatory Christian message: it could be used by Paul just as it was, as effective natural theology.

Here we can bring in another very useful point made by Betz: he points out that, when Paul quotes an authoritative sentiment, it may be uncertain whether he is quoting the Old Testament in Greek or a Greek proverb which happens to be similar to a biblical passage.[24] This is very significant. Much attention has been given in recent work to the

---

22 Betz, *2 Corinthians 8 and 9*, 98.

23 *Ibid.*, 99.

24 Cf. *ibid.*, 102–4, 113, with reference to Prov 11:24, Isa 55:10.

New Testament's scriptural quotations; see for instance the substantial volume edited by D. A. Carson and H. G. M. Williamson, *It is Written: Scripture Quoting Scripture.*[25] It has been suggested that the true basis for a New Testament theology would be found in the quotations, an idea thought of by C. H. Dodd and adopted with greater emphasis by Hübner. But any such procedure runs the risk of exaggerating the importance of the quotations, for one would have to write a companion volume listing all the arguments in the New Testament which do not include a scriptural quotation, or where, as in the cases Betz mentions, it is impossible to be sure whether the passage is a quotation or a Greek proverb that happens to be similar.

Remember how much of Paul's exposition of the resurrection in 1 Corinthians 15 depends upon a sort of philosophical argument and how little upon scriptural quotation, and similarly in the Areopagus speech of Acts 17 how little depends on the biblical quotations and how much greater the input from the Greek poet quoted. The balance between scriptural quotation and other kinds of expression or argumentation has to be carefully observed. Otherwise one is in danger of imputing to the New Testament writers a sort of biblicism which may misrepresent them.

A word here must be added about monotheism: we already mentioned the polytheism of the Greeks as an aspect against which Jewish natural theology was often directed. I want to stress this. A modern canonical critic like Brevard Childs despises the importance of this concept. The term "monotheism," he tells us, is "theologically inert and fails largely to register the basic features of God's self-revelation to Israel.[26] That is only an expression of his own theology of today. In the first century, I would think it likely that monotheism was far more important than all the salvation history stressed by von Rad and others or the kerygma and canonicity which are so much

---

[25] D. A. Carson and H. G. M. Williamson, eds., *It is Written: Scripture quoting Scripture* (New York: Cambridge University Press, 1988).

[26] B. S. Childs, *Biblical Theology of the Old and New Testaments: Theological Reflection on the Christian Bible* (Minneapolis: Fortress, 1983) 355; cf. 360.

emphasized in Childs' own work.[27] And monotheism was central as a focus for the natural theology of the time.

I return in conclusion to one of the points made at the beginning. It is a mistake to regard natural theology, as it is manifested within the biblical tradition, as being basically the acceptance of some one Greek philosophy as the foundation for Jewish or Christian theology. Rather, as Dieter Betz's thinking suggests to us, natural theology came from a source much older, much more diffuse, more practical and less rationally controlled, a source that fed also into Greek philosophy as it fed into biblical religion. This means that the recognition today of natural theology as an important aspect within the Bible may be, and I think should be, seen as something quite different from the adoption of some given philosophy, Greek or modern, as the authoritative basis upon which modern theology should be founded. And if this is right, for the recognition of it we owe much to our friend and colleague Hans Dieter Betz.

---

[27] For a profound and detailed analysis see Yehoshua Amir, "Die jüdische Eingottglaube als Stein des Anstoßes der hellenistisch-römischen Welt," *JBTh* 2 (1987) 58–75.

The Tension Between Revelation and Natural Theology

John J. Collins

No scholar has done more than James Barr to try to bring clarity and rationality to the recalcitrant subject of biblical theology and to break down the facile polarities of the so-called Biblical Theology Movement, such as the contrast between Greek and Hebrew thought. He is surely right to locate the origins of theology, as that discipline flourished historically in the western world, in the fusion of Greek and Hebrew thought that took place above all in Alexandria around the turn of the era. I have no quarrel with his account of the historical development. I would like to take the discussion a little further, however, by asking about the coherence of the theology produced by this fusion. Barr has correctly noted that this theology worked in categories and terms of Greek culture and used its methods of argument, but that its main affirmations did not come out of the Greek tradition. My question is whether this attempt to combine Greek categories with Hebraic content did not result in incompatibility, and whether as a result there are not serious fissures in the foundations of the edifice of western theology. I will focus my question on the Wisdom of Solomon, which provides the clearest example of natural theology in the canonical and deutero-canonical literature.[1]

Central to the theology of the Wisdom of Solomon is the figure of Wisdom or Sophia, which is identified in the opening chapter as "a holy spirit" (*pneuma*) which is benevolent (*philanthropon*) and identical with the spirit of the Lord that fills the whole earth. The idea of a cosmic *pneuma* or spirit was an important element in Stoic philosophy, probably first developed by Chrysippus. The *pneuma* was the soul of the universe, a fiery substance which permeated and vivified all reality,

[1] For a fuller discussion see John J. Collins, *Jewish Wisdom in the Hellenistic Age* (Old Testament Library; Louisville: WestminsterJohnKnox, 1997) 178–232; "Natural Theology and Biblical Tradition: The Case of Hellenistic Judaism," *CBQ* 60 (1998) 1–15.

identical with the Logos, or rational principle of the universe. The Stoic overtones of Wisdom are especially evident in Chapter 7, where wisdom is said to have a fine physical quality, subtle, agile, lucid and more mobile than any motion, and to pervade all things by reason of its pureness. The Stoic Logos is an immanent deity, identical either with the world itself or with the active force within it. The Wisdom of Solomon, like the entire Jewish tradition, insisted on a transcendent creator God, who "created the world out of formless matter" (11:17) (not, it should be noted, out of nothing). The relation of Wisdom to this creator God is addressed in Wis 7:25–26: she is "an exhalation from the power of God, a pure effluence from the glory of the Almighty . . . an effulgence of everlasting light." This language is reminiscent of the Platonic tradition rather than Stoicism, insofar as it implies a God beyond this world. Plato used the analogy of light and the sun to explain the relationship between the good as present in the world and the Idea of the Good. The net effect, however, is that Wisdom takes the Stoic concept of the Pneuma or Logos and subordinates it to a transcendent God, who is affirmed as its source.

Some of the most distinguished commentators on the Wisdom of Solomon, such as Paul Heinisch[2] and Chrysostom Larcher,[3] have concluded that the author of Wisdom did not really understand his philosophical sources, and that he combined them in an incoherent manner. David Winston, however, has argued effectively for the philosophical coherence of Wisdom.[4] The philosophical background of the book should not be sought in classical Platonism or Stoicism, but in the Middle Platonism that flourished around the turn of the era, which absorbed ideas from the Peripatetics and the Stoics.[5] Especially important for Middle Platonism was Plato's dialogue, the *Timaeus*. In that dialogue (§ 28) Plato asks:

> was the world . . . always in existence and without beginning? or created, and had it a beginning? Created, I reply, being visible and tangible and having a

---

[2] P. Heinisch, *Die griechische Philosophie im Buche der Weisheit* (Münster: Aschendorff, 1908) 155.

[3] C. Larcher, *Études sur le Livre de la Sagesse* (Paris: Gabalda, 1969) 235–36.

[4] D. Winston, *The Wisdom of Solomon* (Anchor Bible 43; New York: Doubleday, 1979) 33.

[5] On Middle Platonism, see J. Dillon, *The Middle Platonists: A Study of Platonism, 80 B.C. to A.D. 220* (London: Duckworth, 1979).

> body, and therefore sensible; and all sensible things are apprehended by opinion and sense and are in a process of creation, and created. Now that which is created must as we affirm of necessity be created by a cause. But the father and maker of all this universe is past finding out. . . .

Plato also refers to "the father and maker" as Craftsman or Demiurge, and then proceeds to call him "God." He also endows the world with a soul, so that it is deathless and self-sufficient, and it too can be called a god. We find, then, in Plato's *Timaeus* the seeds of a philosophical theology which could affirm an immanent deity, or world-soul, in the manner of the Stoics, but also a transcendent creator deity beyond this world. Such a philosophy was quite congenial to the philosophically minded Jews of Alexandria. It was exploited for theological purposes by Philo of Alexandria, who has a fair claim to be considered the first systematic theologian of the western tradition. The Wisdom of Solomon, too, must be seen in the context of the fusion of Platonism and Stoicism around the turn of the era. Seen in this context, it should not be judged incoherent. Its combination of immanent Pneuma and transcendent creator was at least compatible with a significant philosophical current of its day.

Because of the mediating role of the Logos or Pneuma, human beings can hope to arrive at a knowledge of God. Hence the famous passage in Wisdom of Solomon 13, where the author deliberates about the culpability of those who fail to arrive at a knowledge of God: "Vain by nature were all who were ignorant of God and were unable to know the Existent One from the good things that are seen, or to recognize the Craftsman through attention to his works. . . For from the greatness and beauty of created things is their author correspondingly (*analogōs*) perceived." Despite the immanence of God in Stoic theology, the manner of argumentation there too is rather similar to what we find in the Wisdom of Solomon: "We alone of living things know the risings and settings and the courses of the stars . . . and contemplating the heavenly bodies the mind arrives at a knowledge of the gods" (Cicero, *De Natura Deorum* 2.253). The Wisdom of Solomon assumes that Gentiles can be held responsible for failing to arrive at a knowledge of the true God. The author provides only minimal arguments, but he could claim adequate support for such a position among the philosophers of his day. In this case, philosophical reasoning could be employed plausibly to support the faith inherited from his religious tradition.

The belief in a creator God, then, does not seem to me to pose insurmountable problems within the context of Hellenistic philosophy. A more severe problem arises in connection with the issues of universalism and particularism. According to Wisdom of Solomon 1, Wisdom is a benevolent spirit (*philanthrōpon*). God, we are told, loves all things that exist and hates none of the things that He has made, for His imperishable spirit is in all things (11:24–12:1). The notion of philanthropia was also a Stoic concept, grounded in the affinity between the divine and the human that is established by the Logos. The world, we are told, is "the common dwelling-place of gods and men, or the city that belongs to both."[6] The Republic of Zeno is said to have been aimed at this one point, "that our household arrangements should not be based on cities or parishes, each one marked out by its own legal system, but we should regard all men as our fellow-citizens, and there should be one way of life and order, like that of a herd grazing together and nurtured by a common law."[7] Zeno did not think that all human beings shared this fellowship, but declared the good alone to be true citizens.[8] For the Stoics, however, there could be no assumption that the distinction between good and bad coincided with ethnic divisions.

For anyone nourished on the Hebrew Bible or Septuagint, however, such an assumption was not easily discarded. The second half of the Wisdom of Solomon is a homily based on the Exodus, which seems to identify the righteous with the people of Israel. Israel is never mentioned by name. Instead it is called "a holy people and blameless race" (10:15), but also "your people," "your children," and the like, even "God's son." Ethnic continuity is undeniably a factor. Wis 18:6 refers to the Israelites of the Exodus as "our ancestors." Conversely, the enemies of the Jews were "an accursed race from the beginning" and their wickedness was inbred (12:10–11). Even though we are told at the end of chapter 11 that God loves all things that exist "for they are yours," this is followed at the beginning of chapter 12 by a

---

[6] Cicero, *De natura deorum,* 2.147 § 154.

[7] Plutarch, *Moralia: On the Fortune or the Virtue of Alexander* 1.6 (329A-B).

[8] Diogenes Laertius, *Lives and Opinions of Eminent Philosophers,* 7.1 § 33.

statement that God hated those who lived long ago in the holy land, because of their abominable practices. Wisdom goes on to show how both the Egyptians at the Exodus and later the Canaanites deserved to be punished. Consequently, some modern critics speak of "undisguised particularism"[9] and see the book as an attack on Gentile religiosity.[10] These assessments exaggerate the polemical character of the book, and do not do justice to its avowed universalism, but there is an undeniable tension here between the biblical notion of a chosen people and the Stoic ideal of philanthropia. Undoubtedly this tension was exacerbated by the experience of the Jewish community in Alexandria in the time of Caligula and the succeeding decades, when it was increasingly beset by a rising tide of Greco-Egyptian hostility. Within a century the once-flourishing Jewish community of Alexandria would be wiped out. Inevitably, this unfortunate history led to a negative perception of the Gentiles. But it must be admitted that the problem was circular to a degree. The Jewish claim to be a chosen people was far older than the Hellenistic-Roman era. One of the factors that exacerbated Gentile hostility to the Jews was the perception that they were anti-social and misanthropic, because they held back from full participation in the life of the city.

The problem posed by ethnic particularism in the Wisdom of Solomon is not necessarily endemic to all biblically based theology, but it is illustrative of a deep rooted problem. Natural theology, by its own resources, may take many forms, but it is unlikely to lead to the affirmation of all biblical claims or of all Christian dogma or Jewish law. Some distinctive biblical claims, such as creation, can be defended on philosophical grounds. Attempts to rationalize other biblical postulates, such as the laws of Leviticus, or the election of Israel, quickly become forced and artificial. The same might be said of attempts by Christian apologists to defend the unique truth of Christianity or the divinity of Christ. Consequently, natural theology in the Christian tradition has always operated under a reservation. Reason can never dispense with faith. Similarly, in the Alexandrian Judaism of Philo or the Wisdom of Solomon, Greek philosophy can be

---

[9] J. Reider, *The Book of Wisdom* (New York: Harper, 1957) 41.

[10] J. Barclay, *Jews in the Mediterranean Diaspora, from Alexander to Trajan (323 BCE—117CE)* (Edinburgh: T. & T. Clark, 1996) 181–91.

embraced to a great degree, but in the end it is subordinated and placed in the service of biblical revelation. Even Philo, whose engagement with Greek philosophy was deeper and broader than that of any of his contemporaries, used it essentially for apologetic purposes. In his *Life of Moses* he still professes the hope that "each nation would abandon its peculiar ways, and, throwing overboard its ancestral customs, turn to honouring our laws alone" (*Vit. Mos.* 2.44).

The situation of the Jews in Alexandria was complicated by political and social issues, but it also illustrates an historical problem that was inherited by Christianity. At the root of this problem is the discrepancy between two sources of theological authority, the one relying on revelation, the other on philosophical reasoning. I submit that two thousand years of western theology show that these twain never fully meet, although they may converge on many issues. St. Paul can make use of natural theology when he is arguing against homosexuality in Romans, but he can still dismiss the wisdom of the Greeks as mere folly when it conflicts with his faith. Therein lies the problem of natural theology in the biblical tradition, and indeed of any theology that accepts the Bible, in either Testament, as inspired, foundational revelation. By this conclusion I by no means mean to disparage the elements of natural theology that we find in the Bible and to which James Barr and Dieter Betz have drawn attention. Quite the contrary. But we must also recognize that within the biblical world, of either Testament, there remains an uneasy tension between Athens and Jerusalem.

Lucian on Conversion: Remarks on Lucian's Dialogue *Nigrinos*

Hubert Cancik

§1 Lucian and Conversion: Defining the Topic

§1.1 On the Current State of Research

Forty years ago, when Hans Dieter Betz wrote his dissertation in Mainz on *Lucian of Samosata and the New Testament*, the term "popular philosophy" was something many a theologian in West Germany could not "think any good of at all,"[1] and Lucian was regarded as one of the worst. In an essay of 1921 Otto Weinreich, speaking for many scholars, summed up the prejudice as follows:[2]

> Lucian . . . had the fickle instincts of a journalist, was capable of any metamorphosis, always swimming with the tide; someone who changed himself from Syrian to Hellene, who abandoned sculpture because rhetoric offered better profits, who slid from rhetoric to philosophy, presented himself as a Platonist, then turned into a half-Cynic, landing finally in shallow Epicureanism and nihilistic scepticism, once he had the security of a halfway decent position, cracking jokes about anything and everything, presumably to his own and his audiences' great delectation.

Rootless and therefore infinitely adaptable, an atheist and nihilist, a Syrian and a journalist: these key words evoked then, in the early days

---

[1] So, looking back, H. D. Betz, *Der Apostel Paulus und die sokratische Tradition* (Tübingen: Mohr [Siebeck] 1972) 2. (The dissertation was received in the winter of 1958/59 by the Theological Faculty of the Johannes-Gutenberg-Universität, Mainz, and published in 1961.) I would like to thank Christine Baatz, Tübingen, for translating my essay into English.

[2] O. Weinreich, "Alexander der Lügenprophet und seine Stellung in der Religiosität des 2. Jahrhunderts n. Chr.," *Neue Jahrbücher für das klassische Altertum* 24 (1921) 129–151, here p. 130. In contrast cf., e.g., the reasons which Max Oberbreyer put forth in favour of Lucian as a school author, following Fr. Aug. Wolf (1791), Mathiä, Fritzsche, Eyssel, Schöne, Jacobitz, J. Sommerbrodt (1860); he concludes: "Es ist kein genügender Grund vorhanden, der . . . Moral (sc. of Lucian) den Stempel der Frivolität aufzudrücken oder die Lauterkeit seiner Gesinnung zu verdächtigen" (*Lucian's Ausgewählte Schriften übersetzt von C.M. Wieland* [Leipzig: P. Reclam, 1877] 7).

of the Weimar Republic, the clearly delineated stereotype of an enemy: the sensationalist, the homeless intellectual, "the Jewish press."[3]

Half a century's research has altered fundamentally our knowledge of what is called Greek and Roman popular philosophy, as well as the categories for its historical classification and philosophical evaluation. This can be learned by looking at the volume *Hellenismus und Urchristentum*, the series Studia ad Corpus Hellenisticum Novi Testamenti[4] or the research report on Lucian presented by Diskin Clay in 1992.[5] Starting from this research, I would like to draw attention now to the theme of conversion, which Lucian treats so frequently and significantly, but which as far as I can see has not been examined in the scholarly literature.[6]

As a base text I have chosen, for biographical and panegyrical reasons, the dialogue *Nigrinos*.[7] My aim is twofold and pertains to both the history of ideas and the history of literature: (a) the phenomenon of recruitment and conversion to a philosophical school (αἵρεσις) and (b) the form of the autobiographical conversion story, which itself turns into a "missionary sermon."

§1.2 Conversion in Religion and Philosophy

§1.2.1 Ancient philosophy is a style of thought, a way of life, a school (αἵρεσις, βίος, σχολή). In the extreme case it lays claim to one's

---

[3] For evidence from the circle of Richard and Cosima Wagner, see Fr. Nietzsche, "Sokrates und die Tragödie" (Basel, 1870): "Dieser [scil. moderne] Sokratismus ist die jüdische Presse." (G. Colli and M. Montinari, eds., *Friedrich Nietzsche. Sämtliche Werke. Kritische Studienausgabe* [München: Deutscher Taschenbuch Verlag, 1980] 14.101).

[4] The series is edited by H. D. Betz, G. Delling, W. C. van Unnik and G. Mussies. Up to now the following authors have been dealt with: Apollonius of Tyana; Dio Chrysostom; Plutarch's theological writings; Plutarch's ethical writings.

[5] D. Clay, "Lucian of Samosata: Four Philosophical Lives," *ANRW* 2.36.5 (1992) 3406–50. (The four are Nigrinus, Demonax, Peregrinus, Alexander Pseudomantis).

[6] In H. D. Betz, *Lukian von Samosata und das Neue Testament: Religionsgeschichtliche und paränetische Parallelen. Ein Beitrag zum Corpus Hellenisticum Novi Testamenti* (Berlin: Akademie-Verlag, 1961), "conversion" is not treated as a topic in paraenetic literature or religious history.

[7] H. D. Betz commenced his disquisition upon Lucian with the *Nigrinos*.

whole life and rewards it with one moment on the summit of Stoic wisdom.[8]

Ancient philosophy is research, free research, not commissioned or ordered by a temple, a religion, or the state, but a field of intellectual activity in its own right. It is a small or perhaps even a large component of the general education of the individual. It is received in most cases as a part of rhetoric or literature. The role of a philosopher is demanding; a philosophical school is a strenuous institution, its aim nothing short of complete truth, μόνη—"the only truth" is to be sought for.[9] Therefore, turning to philosophy or to one of its schools is a decision that can change the whole outer and inner life of a person considerably. It is specific to Greek and Roman culture that such decisions about personal ways of life, perfection, and supreme happiness are reflected on less in the framework of religion than in philosophy.

§1.2.2 For the three authors which I would like to present you, Lucian and, for the sake of providing a contrast, Epictetus and Apuleius, the constitution of the "inner man" had been defined long ago. In ethics, the theory of the soul, anthropology and the theory of knowledge, the large systems—Platonism, Stoicism, Epicureanism—had defined the central terms: "Soul and mind, conscience and affect, freedom, will, decision." Alongside these are images and expressions that give nuance to these terms, illustrate them and render them comprehensible to the non-specialist: *persona* (mask, role, "person"), the interior space of the human being (ὁ ἐντὸς ἄνθρωπος),[10] the I, the self, the oneness (*unum*) of the human being.[11]

Myth, art and science have either anticipated or translated these insights. Tragedy reveals the madness of the heroes—Heracles, Orestes, Athamas, Pentheus—as the fractured unity of the person,

---

[8] Luc. *Hermot.* 6.

[9] Luc. *Hermot.* 27; 45–46.

[10] a) Plat. *Resp.* 9.588c–589b; cf. the later development of the image in Plotinus (*Enn.* 5.1.10: εἴσω ἄνθρωπος) and Prophyry (in Stob. *Ecl.* 3.581.17; 582.21); b) Stoa: Seneca, *Ep.* 7.12; 23.3–5; 25.6; 80.10; 119.11: *beatus introrsum*; Seneca, *De providentia* 6.5; M. Ant. 7.59: ἔνδον βλέπε.

[11] Sen. *Ep.* 121.22: *Magnam rem puta unum hominem agere. Praeter sapientem autem nemo unum agit, ceteri multiformes sumus.*

schizophrenia.[12] Comedy shows Amphitruo's messenger who, confronted with his double, asks himself:[13] "Where have I perished? Where have I been changed? Where have I lost my form?" *ubi ego perii? ubi immutatus sum? ubi ego formam perdidi?*

§1.2.3 For the popular philosophers and philosophizing men of letters that are to be discussed here, the conceptualization of gradual and sudden change and the question of the unchangeable in the succession of changing phenomena were likewise developed in detail in those philosophical systems. The different forms of movement, of Being and Becoming and the identity of structure and substance in all their sudden changes and unexpected turns had been examined in ontology and physics.

The analogous thesis, that man had to preserve his Self during all successive stages of life, is the basis of Stoic anthropology and ethics.[14] This principle could be more sharply defined in the doctrine of the transmigration of souls—and of course it could easily be parodied as well. Pythagoras taught that you were once someone other than you are now and that after some time you will turn into yet another.[15] Here, too, myth anticipated and received: all metamorphoses experiment with transformation and identity. Is Daphne a laurel tree? Does the narcissus know that previously it was a human being? Which is more amazing, the metamorphosis of a woman into a sadly crying sea-bird (Halcyone) or the metamorphosis from the state of infancy to old age?[16]

In ethics this is the question concerning the original core of a person and the unity of the human being:[17] Only as "one" is a human being "perfect" and "wise." How do I become wise? Two alternatives will be discussed here, the Stoic and the Cynic: through a break with

[12] Cf. the satire on madness by Horace *Sat.* 2.3, esp. vv. 132–141.

[13] Plautus *Amphitruo* 455–57.

[14] See M. Forschner, *Die stoische Ethik. Über den Zusammenhang von Natur-, Sprach- und Moralphilosophie im altstoischen System* (2d ed.; Darmstadt: Wissenschaftliche Buchgesellschaft, 1995) 142–44.

[15] Luc. *Vit. Auct.* 5–6.

[16] (Pseud.?) Luc. *Halcyon or On Transformations* (LCL, vol. 8).

[17] Seneca *Ep.* 121.22.

society and the conversion to philosophy or through learning, through gradual self-transformation.

The ideas of the inner man and his capacity for change were developed in Greek and Roman culture outside their religions. A "structural change from religions of conciliation to religions of salvation"—if this can be proven at all—thus cannot be postulated in these cultures as the driving force for this development. This is connected with the fact that Greek and Roman religions, with few exceptions, do not recruit and convert. These religions spread by other means: through merchants, soldiers and colonists. Geographical expansion, it is true, took place in accordance with rites prescribed for departure, victory or the founding of cities. But there was no military campaign undertaken, no group of colonists sent on their way with the aim of spreading Greek or Roman religion. Accordingly, Greek and Roman religions either absorbed foreign cult practices (*sacra peregrina* became *sacra recepta*) or at least did not prevent their private practice.

These general principles need to be supplemented by mention of some exceptions and special cases. The suppression of the Bacchanalia in Italy (186 BCE) is, according to the offical version, the suppression of criminal and anti-Roman machinations. The Bacchus religion as such was not prohibited nor was the worship of other divinities enforced.[18]

Only a few examples of individual religious conversion have come to my attention. Horace says—though it is uncertain how seriously this is meant—that a flash of lightning from the blue had forced him "backwards" (*retrorsum*) from Epicurean philosophy; that from that time on he ceased to be the "sparing worshipper of the gods" that he had been before.[19] The most important exceptions to this general picture are the *Constitutio Antoniniana* (212 CE) on "universal civil rights in the Roman empire" and the story of the conversion and salvation of Lucius in Apuleius, which will be discussed in the last part of this essay.

---

[18] H. Cancik-Lindemaier, "Der Diskurs Religion im Senatsbeschluß über die Bacchanalia von 186 v. Chr. und bei Livius (B. XXXIX)," *Geschichte—Tradition—Reflexion. Festschrift für Martin Hengel zum 70. Geburtstag* (ed. H. Cancik, H. Lichtenberger, P. Schäfer; 3 vols.; Tübingen: Mohr [Siebeck] 1996), vol. 2: *Griechische und römische Religion* (ed. H. Cancik) 77–96.

[19] Horace *Carmina* 1.34.1: *Parcus deorum cultor.*

§2 Lucian's Dialogues on Conversion.

§2.1 Nigrinos: "Transposing, Re-educating, Re-composing"

§2.1.1 In his long life (ca. 120—after 180 CE), Lucian of Syrian Samosata witnessed many transformations, reported and reflected upon them. Of Syrian ancestry, a barbarian and poor, by trade a stonemason, he became a Hellene and wealthy. He was a lawyer and orator, who transformed himself into a philosophizing essayist. Around 155 CE in Rome he met a philosopher of the Socratic-Platonic school by the name of Nigrinos. According to Lucian, Nigrinos' "Encomium of Philosophy"[20] and a lecture on the cities of Athens and Rome converted him to a new philosophical, truly happy life.[21]

The two cities, he says, had been described as symbolic places: Rome as the theatre of Tyche and Nigrinos, the observer (ἐπίσκοπος); the Athenians as the custodians of culture (παιδεία) which gradually transforms even rich luxury seekers from abroad: these are re-educated and transposed to a pure conduct of life; (chap.12): ἠρέμα τε μεθαρμόττουσι καὶ παραπαιδαγωγοῦσι καὶ πρὸς τὸ καθαρὸν τῆς διαίτης μεθιστᾶσιν.

Lucian describes in the form of a Platonic dialogue both the lecture and its effect on him. Two friends converse about the lecture of an absent third party. Under the title "The Philosophy of Nigrinos" he sends this text and an accompanying letter to Nigrinos in Rome.

Just what is genuine and what fictitious autobiography in this text must remain an open question. What is clear is that Lucian's "Nigrinos" is the longest, oldest text to survive from antiquity whose thematic frame is the autobiographical account of a conversion to philosophy.

§2.1.2. The conversion that Lucian experienced occurred "suddenly" and led to a full transformation (μεταβάλλεσθαι). He has found true happiness, has been "thrice blessed" and that "in a very short time:"[22]

---

[20] Luc. *Nigr.* 4. Quotations are from the English translation by A. M. Harmon (*Lucian* [LCL; Cambridge, MA: Harvard University Press, 1992] vol.1).

[21] *Nigr.* introductory letter; 1; 3–4.

[22] *Nigr.* ch.1; cf. ibid., ἄφνω μεταβέβλησαι; on liberation through philosophy cf. 19f. - A sudden conversion may also be induced by a religious experience.

"once a slave, I am now free, once poor, now rich indeed, once witless and befogged, now saner."

Thus in the first chapter of his *Nigrinos*, Lucian fundamentally expounds the theme of his narrative frame. He aims at the psychology of the sudden change, analyses the altered state of the inner man, and reflects upon the question how this experience and the situation that brought it about can be faithfully transmitted.

Conversion is described in the first place as a healing process. Lucian searched for a doctor for an eye disease; he found a philosopher, who then brought him from a darkling life into the light:[23] "and I looked up . . . in a great light. In consequence, I actually forgot my eye and its ailment." "Healing" and "enlightenment" are the experiences and the imagery used to describe the process of conversion and to reflect upon it.

The encounter with the philosopher arouses strong emotions and is described in luxuriant, sometimes excessively figurative language. As the sirens sing, as the nightingales sing, as ambrosia delights and lotus—so overpowering is the ring of Nigrinos' words:[24] ". . . at the moment I could not imagine what had come over me. I cried and laughed, I felt pain and joy. It was as if I was drunk, possessed, crazed." Transformation, ecstasy through love, wine and inebriation are the experiences, words and images with which Lucian describes the pathos[25] of his conversion and through which he tries to interpret it, combining it with the common erotic and dionysiac physiognomics and psychology.

The intensity of the experience and the importance of the teachings he receives urge the newly converted to communicate them. The friend, to whom Lucian explains everything, is to be won over as a "witness" (μάρτυς). The convert likes to repeat what he has learned:

Plutarch tells the myth of a certain Aridaios who, in a state of apparent death, had a vision of the eschatological punishment of the souls; when he awoke a μεταβολή to a virtuous (not to a religious) life had taken place, the change being emphasized by a new name—Thespesios—given to him during his vision: Plut. *De sera numinis vindicta* 563 D.

[23] *Nigr.* 4.

[24] A paraphrase of chaps. 3–5 follows.

[25] *Nigr.* 4; 5; with *figura etymologica* and heightened by the myth of the Phaeacians in chap. 35: τὸ τῶν Φαιάκων πάθος ἐπεπονθεῖν.

"It is sweet to me to remember." Even when he does not have any listeners, he repeats the teachings to himself, two or three times a day:[26] He reflects on them, turns them over in his mind; he visualizes, as lovers do, the absent speaker by repeating his words and even by seeming to talk with him. Thus the teacher remains present at all actions of the converted (παρ-εἶναι), and in the end he even makes an appearance in the dialogue: Lucian starts off with a report on the teachings of Nigrinos, but then, suddenly, Nigrinos himself speaks in the first person (chap. 17). The convert turns into the teacher.

This transition from a pupil into a teacher, from one who has just been converted to a "messenger" (ἄγγελος), brings a number of problems with it. Is the message authentic? Is the messenger legitimate and competent? Lucian recognized this problem as well, a problem that all expanding spiritual movements share.[27] He makes a clear distinction between the teacher and the messenger. The latter is no more than an actor in the theatre: He speaks the text which another has written or spoken. But he knows that he cannot pass on the oral teachings he has received in the same order, nor in the way Nigrinos himself could. He does not attempt to imitate the person of Nigrinos. Instead, Lucian wants to speak to his friend as a friend "without a mask."

In the Platonic dialogues similar considerations have come down to us as regards the authenticity of the conversations ascribed to Socrates. According to the frame narrative in the Theaitetos,[28] Eukleides takes "notes" immediately after the encounter with Socrates (ὑπομνήματα) and later, when he has peace and quiet enough to recall everything, he writes down the conversations in a more detailed form; he questions Socrates again about what he has forgotten and then corrects what he has already written. Thus "the whole logos" has been written down in a small book (βιβλίον) that can be read aloud now.

The early Christian authors gave similar consideration to the transmission of Christ's words. They emphasize the difference between

---

[26] The following is based on chaps. 6–7.

[27] The following is based on chaps. 8–11.

[28] Plat. *Theaet.* 143.

their teacher and the disciples to explain why the words of Jesus appear in a different form and order in the gospels.[29]

§2.1.3 Topological aspects

(a) The paradigm of "ecstatic confessions" was not created by Lucian. It is possible to make out this kind of confession in the New Comedy, perhaps even in Menander himself. Lucian made extensive use of the writers of comedy.[30] It may even be the case that he found the paradigm for his representation of the awakening to philosophy already in comedy. The most important witness to the paradigm is the monologue in Papyrus Didot b (mid-second century BCE).[31] The opening reads:

> Well, here is solitude; whatever I say, there's nobody here to listen. Gentlemen, believe me: I have been dead the whole of my life so far. There seemed no difference between the beautiful, the good, the holy and the evil,—such was the cloud of darkness that used to hang about my wits, I fancy. It hid all this from me, made it invisible. Now that I have come here, I have come to life again for the future, like a man who lies down in Asclepius' temple and is saved; I walk and talk and think. I never discovered the sun before—so big so fine . . . .

The speaker, probably a young man from the countryside, experiences Athens as a place of light, of salubrity, of new life. Since the text suffers increasingly large gaps from this point on, it remains unclear whether the speaker has turned to a particular "philosophy,"[32] or whether the

---

[29] Cf. Papias, in Eus. *Hist. eccl.* 3.19.15, on the arrangement of words and deeds of Jesus in the gospel of Mark.

[30] Cf. Scholion to the *Dialogi Meretricii*: "You should know that all these hetairas have their origin in comedies, actually from all comic poets, but particularly from Menandros who has prepared all the topics for Lucian." Cf. J. Ledergerber, *Lukian und die altattische Komödie* (Einsiedeln: Benziger, 1905).

[31] R. Kassel and C. Austin, *Poetae Comici Graeci* (Berlin and New York: de Gruyter, 1995), vol. 8: "Adespota," no. 1001; cf. K. Gaiser, "Ein Lob Athens in der Komödie (Menander, Fragmentum Didotianum b)," *Gymnasium* 75 (1968) 193–219 (without referring to Lucian). The fragment is attributed to Menander by Herzog, Zuntz and Gaiser; references in Kassel and Austin, *Poetae Comici Graeci*, ibid. Philemon (*Philosophi*), Alexis, Theogenes and Poseidippos have also been proposed as authors. English translation by D. L. Page, *Select Papyri*, Vol. 3, *Literary Papyri. Poetry*" (LCL; London: Heinemann, 1950) 227.

[32] A *subscriptio* (?) after line 15 says: ἀρίστων φιλόσοφος μαθήματα; the meaning is not clear, see Kassel and Austin, *Poetae Comici Graeci*, ad. loc.

beautiful, sophisticated city awakened him: theatre and acropolis are explicitly mentioned (v. 15).

The imagery of the comedian is identical with Lucian's: disease/healing, death/resuscitation (ἀνα-βεβίωκα), light/darkness. This imagery, plus the conventional topoi in the encomium on Athens and the type of speech of the effusive confession, connect Lucian's *Nigrinos* directly or via a prosaic intermediate source to Hellenistic comedy.

(b) The conclusion of *Nigrinos* is formed by the following three elements:

(1) the parable of the good bowman (chaps. 36–37), a long impressive allegory of the right λόγος προτρεπτικός, that is, a recruitment speech for philosophy or a missionary sermon;

(2) the evocation of the mythical bowmen who brought "light" and "healing:" Teucros and Telephos (chaps. 37–38);[33]

(3) a comparison from the Cynics: the teachings of Nigrinos shall spread like rabies.

The allegory, as is known, runs like this:

> The soul of a well-endowed man resembles a very tender target. Many bowmen, their quivers full of words of all sorts and kinds, shoot at it during life, but not with success in every case. Some draw to the head and let fly harder than they should: though they hit the target, their arrows do not stick in it, but owing to their momentum go through and continue their flight leaving only a gaping wound in the soul. Others, again, do the opposite; themselves too weak, their bows too slack, the arrows do not even carry to the target as a rule, but often fall spent at half the distance; and if ever they do carry, they . . . do not make a deep wound . . . . But a good bowman like Nigrinus first of all scans the target closely . . . he dips his arrow . . . in a sweet gently working drug, and then shoots with skill. The arrow driven by just the right amount of force, penetrates to the point of passing through, and then sticks fast and gives off a quantity of the drug, which naturally spreads and completely pervades the soul. That is why people laugh and cry as they listen, as I did (chaps. 36–37).

The images of the bowman, target (σκοπός) and chase, are old and well-related philosophical imagery.[34] Their rearrangement in Lucian

---

[33] a) Teucros: Hom. *Il.* 8.282 (Agamemnon to Teucros): "Shoot so that you may become a light for the Greeks." b) Euripides, Telephos frg. 724 (A. Nauck, *Tragicorum Graecorum Fragmenta* [2d ed.; Leipzig: Teubner, 1889] = C. Austin, *Nova Fragmenta Euripidea* [Berlin: de Gruyter, 1968] frg. 132): "The one who has hurt, will heal."

as a comprehensive allegory give his dialogue a magnificent conclusion.[35] In this way Lucian takes up again the reflections he had made in the first part (chaps. 8–11) on the authenticity and communicability of a direct, immediate experience, of "Urgeschichte" (a foundation story), so to speak. The parable of the good bowman now brings in figurative form a didactics and psychology of the philosophical recruitment speech.[36]

§2.2 *Polemo mutatus* and Dionysius ὁ μεταθέμενος (Lucian, *Bis accusatus*)

1. In his essay *The Double Indictment* Lucian reports on seven legal cases argued in Athens, among them[37] (a) Intemperance vs. the Academy, because of the kidnapping of Polemo; and (b) Stoa vs. Pleasure, because Pleasure had coaxed away her lover Dionysius. The court procedures in which the allegorical figures take part is the frame within which Lucian attempts to examine (a) the conversion from vice to Platonic philosophy and (b) the conversion from one school of philosophy to a rival one.

Intemperance will have it represented that the Academy had "torn" Polemo "away" from her, had stolen him out of her hands, had

---

[34] Roswitha Alpers-Gölz, *Der Begriff "Skopos" in der Stoa und seine Vorgeschichte* (Hildesheim and New York: Olms, 1976); K.-H. Rolke, *Die bildhaften Vergleiche in den Fragmenten der Stoiker von Zenon bis Panaitios* (Hildesheim and New York: Olms, 1975). Cf. the simile in Panaitios, frg. 109 (M. van Straaten, *Panaetii Rhodii Fragmenta* [3d ed.; Leiden: Brill, 1962]); Chrysippos, *SVF* 3 frg. 280.

[35] T. W. Rein, *Sprichwörter und sprichwörtliche Redensarten bei Lucian* (Tübingen: Mohr [Siebeck], 1894); O. Schmidt, *Metapher und Gleichnis in den Schriften Lucians* (Winterthus: Geschwister Ziegler, 1897); J. Bompaire, *Lucien ècrivain* (Paris: de Boccard, 1958) 424–26: Les métaphores et comparaisons; K. Berger, "Hellenistische Gattungen im NT," *ANRW* 2.25.2 (1984) 1110–1124 (§ 9): similes; 1240: man-hunting (cf. Mark 1:17; Luke 5:11).

[36] Cf. A. Bonhoeffer, "Ein heidnisches Pendant zum neutestamentlichen Gleichnis vom Sämann," *ARW* 11 (1908) 571–72. Bonhoeffer finds in Lucian "a classical expression of the deepest really religious emotion" and compares the conversion of Shaul, the repentance of Peter and the adulteress, as well as the Letter to the Hebrews 4:12. A principal contrast to the New Testament is, according to Bonhoeffer, that salvation is limited to men of good nature (εὐφυεῖς). He overlooks, however, the universalism of Greek ethics and education, particularly in Stoicism and Cynism. Cf. H. D. Betz, "Jesus and the Cynics: Survey and Analysis of a Hypothesis," *JR* 74 (1994) 453–457.

[37] Lucian, *Bis acc.* 13.

enslaved him and "re-educated" him (μετα-διδάσκειν), changing him completely. A flourishing man had turned into a shrunken, bent body; he had "unlearned" (ἀπο-μαθεῖν) the joyful songs. The conversion was triggered by a speech of Academia: Polemo heard her while the doors were standing open, just as she spoke to the members (ἕταιροι) about virtue and temperance. Though he had originally intended to disturb the speech, he was overcome by it. He sobered himself, laid down his garlands, told the flutist to be silent, and woke up "as it were, from profound sleep" (chap. 17).

This topos of "awakening" is a further element from the classical imagery for conversion and salvation to appear with healing and enlightenment. It is the speech of the Academy that converts Polemo, together with the community (συνουσία) of Academics.

The Academy defends herself against the accusation of kidnapping:[38] "Taking this man . . . when he was in a ridiculous plight . . . I converted him (ἐπι-στρέφειν) and sobered him, and made him from a slave into a well-behaved, temperate man . . . ." The Academy wins her suit by a great majority; Polemo is snatched away from Intemperance and becomes a member of a new community.

2. The second law suit, Stoa vs. Pleasure (defended by Epicurus) is structured as a counterpoint: this time Pleasure wins unanimously. She has "drawn to her" (περι-σπᾶν, προσ-άγεσθαι) the former Stoic Dionysius, and "forced" him to "abandon" the Stoa (ἀπ-έχεσθαι). The conversion from one school to another is described as a "flight" and a "liberation," two more classical concepts redolent of everyday experience applied to the radical change of the inner man.[39] Dionysius escaped from Stoa like someone who cuts through his chains, like a shipwrecked person who swims to safe harbour, like a supplicant who finds refuge at the Altar of Mercy.

3. There is a historical kernel in both of these cases. They lead into the first half of the third century BCE. Dionysius is the paradigm of an apostate: ὁ μεταθέμενος is his epithet.[40] Polemo is the paradigm for a

---

[38] Up to chap. 17. In the LXX and the NT ἐπι-στρέφειν—"turn about, turn round"—is frequently used for Hebr. שׁוּב, "to convert."

[39] *Bis acc.* chap. 21. The "defection" is stylized with topics of the conversion story. The conflict between two women over a lover is a comedy motif.

[40] Cf. Diog. Laer. 7.166; Cic. *Tusc.* 2.25.60.

man who suddenly and unexpectedly changes for the better. Horace makes reference to him as "the changed Polemo" (*mutatus Polemo*) in that satire in which the poet is almost overcome by a fanatic converted to Stoicism.[41] These historic patterns for philosophical conversion show that conversion narratives, like these transmitted by Lucian, have a long, rich, pre-Christian tradition.

The twin court cases that form the conclusion of this series and have given the text its title also lend an autobiographical turn to this essay.[42] Rhetoric accuses the Syrian, that is, Lucian, of having broken his marriage to her. The latter, for his part, accuses her of infidelity; he confesses to having an enduring affair with Dialogus, the son of Philosophy, and publicly dismisses Rhetoric. The Syrian wins his case by a large majority. In this trial, the key terms "marriage" and "love" bring to bear another large reservoir of experiences and feelings, images and words, that point to cultural, ethical and philosophical involvement and commitment.[43] Thus the arsenal of motifs, "marriage" and "adultery," "love" and "infidelity" (γάμος, μοιχεία, ἔρως), added at the end of the dialogue, may be seen as a climax to the series of images we have already mentioned, such as "healing," "enlightenment," "flight" and "liberation." With their help Lucian develops the discourse of his essay *The Double Indictment* on inner change and conversion.

§2.3 From Protreptikos to Apotreptikos (Lucian, *Hermotimos*)

1. Lucian gives the theme of change a paradoxical twist in his dialogue *Hermotimos, or Concerning the Sects* (that is, on the affiliation with philosophical schools: Ἑρμότιμος ἢ περὶ αἱρέσεων).

For many years Hermotimos has been on his way to the summit of Stoic philosophy. There on high are Wholeness and Happiness. His friend Lykinos, his interlocutor, seems to be considering joining the Stoic school. He asks Hermotimos therefore what had given him the

---

[41] Horace *Sat.* 2.3.254, according to R. Helm (*Lukian und Menipp* [Leipzig and Berlin: Teubner, 1906] 283–85) from Stoic-Cynic tradition (see Epictet. *Diss.* 3.1.14; 4.1.30 and Diog. Laer. 4.16). Cf. Diog. Laer. 2.77 and Horace *Sat.* 2.3.100–2: the anecdote about Aristippus; Diogenes refers to the tradition of "people around Bion."

[42] Lucian *Bis acc.* 25–34.

[43] Here, too, the comedy is an important source for Lucian.

first impulse to philosophy and for what reason he had chosen particularly to join the Stoa:[44] "In whom did you believe then?" τῶι ποτε πιστεύσας; How did Hermotimos know that the Stoa was "the only true" philosophy (μόνη ἀληθής), that she alone was the one, direct and rightful way for everyone?[45]

In this dialogue Lucian made abundant use of this world of images—way (ὁδός)[46] and disorientation,[47] crossroad and ascent, turning aside and turning back[48]—in order to illustrate more vividly the subject of orientation and change of direction.

2. The conversation soon comes to an impasse: it cannot be established beforehand and without doubt, which philosophy is the rightful one. Nor can one test it by experience, for the two friends calculate that it would take more than two hundred years to try out each one of the schools. Yet only this way could the one rightful philosophy be determined (chap. 48). This loss of direction provokes a sudden change (chap. 86). Since Hermotimos cannot demonstrate to his friend the turning to philosophy, Lykinos starts, as it were, a "*logos apotreptikos.*" The philosophers in their schools are simply afraid of "turning back" (chap. 75). They never leave the school, but press as many as possible to enter it (προτρέπουσιν), so that their own false decision would not become evident. Only a few brave men admit to having deceived themselves and move others away (ἀποτρέπουσιν) from making similar errors. Only those who shed light upon the deception of school philosophy are the true philosophers. Hermotimos, who has been on the road toward the summit of Stoic wisdom for twenty years, is struck dumb. He is near to tears and bemoans the waste and the lost time.

Here the protreptic topoi for describing a turning towards Philosophy are inverted.[49] It is Lykinos who demands the sobering up

---

[44] Luc. *Hermot.* 15: this question is asked twice.

[45] Luc. *Hermot.* 15; cf. 32–34; 52; 27: μίαν εἶναι τὴν ἀληθῆ ὁδόν; 46.

[46] Luc. *Hermot.* 1–8 passim; 30; 52: "there are many paths to philosophy and each one claims that it leads to virtue;" 63.

[47] ἀνέξοδα—"blind alleys" (chap. 15); ἀπορία (chaps. 27; 70).

[48] ἀναστρέφειν (chap. 75; chap. 28); μεταχωρεῖν (chap. 84). Lucian applies the well known crossroad parable also to his own life; Luc. *Somnium.*

[49] Cf. *Nigr.* 3–4 and 38; 5.

of Philosophy, the enlightenment of Philosophy, a re-education, a turning away from Philosophy (μετα-μαθεῖν, μετα-χωρεῖν).

The speech of dissuasion succeeds. A symbolic action makes the inner turning visible, externalizes it, as Hermotimos lays aside the rough mantle, the garb of the philosophers. He will cut his long thick beard and put on a purple gown, so that all will see that he no longer takes part in philosophical sophistry.

Lykinos is the saviour—from the turbulent waters, from shipwreck, from darkness. Hermotimos will celebrate a feast of salvation (*sotēria*), because he has been saved from the school-philosophy by superhuman intervention. Yet the dialogue does not end on an edifying note. The newly converted non-philosopher displays the overreaction of the converted: "If I should happen upon a philosopher along the way, I would shun him and give him a wide berth as with rabid dogs."

§2.4 Lucian and the Philosophical and Historiographical Tradition

1. The three examples that I have presented, *Nigrinos*, *The Double Indictment*, *Hermotimos*, do not simply narrate three cases of conversion. Rather, Lucian constructs, not without personal engagement,[50] three different types: the ecstatic exuberance of a young man in the *Nigrinos*, the legal debate between the schools over affiliation and the wooing of members from other schools in *The Double Indictment*; and the arduous, but finally radical withdrawal of an experienced professional philosopher in *Hermotimos*. Lucian is concerned with the role of the "philosopher," and he works on a phenomenology of the different schools.[51] He experiments with the linguistic fields of reference and imagery that regard turning back, breaking off, salvation and new beginnings: the way and the ascent; light and darkness; love, marriage and infidelity; disease and healing; sleep and awakening; and

---

[50] The *Nigrinos* is stylized as a confession addressed to the teacher; it is Lucian, the Syrian, who is *bis accusatus*; Hermotimos' interlocutor is called "Lykinos" (i.e. Lucian).

[51] In this respect these and other texts of Lucian's are contributions to a (theoretical) conception of the shape of the philosopher as such; cf. O. Gigon, "Antike Erzählungen über die Berufung zur Philosophie," *Museum Helveticum* 3 (1946) 21; H. Cancik and H. Cancik-Lindemaier, "Senecas Konstruktion des Weisen. Zur Sakralisierung der Rolle des Weisen im 1. Jh. n. Chr.," *Weisheit. Archäologie der literarischen Kommunikation* (ed. A. Assmann; München: Fink 1991) 205–22.

enslavement and liberation. Lucian reflects on the conditions under which the choice for one school must be taken. This choice cannot be justified rationally: this is the lesson Hermotimos learns. The choice of one's school is not only a matter of choosing the right system of thought. For the ancients it means the choice of a way of life, a form, a "model" of dress and beardstyle. Whoever dares make this leap requires "belief" (πιστεύειν), trust in a man whom he can "follow" (παρακολουθεῖν) for personal and decidedly non-philosophical reasons.[52] Consultation of an oracle can further the decision-making process. Socrates and Aristotle are well attested examples of how Apollo's oracle calls philosophers to their vocation.[53] Thus philosophy and religion, rationality and irrationality are tied together in these conversion narratives.

2. The wealth of Lucian's texts on the theme of conversion, their linguistic richness, the variety of motifs and the high level of reflection demonstrate that Lucian continues an old and important tradition. The vocation to philosophy, as Olof Gigon has shown, is one of the most typical situations created by the classical bios of a philosopher:[54] "The way to philosophy" is one of those "borderline experiences" (Gigon's term), "where the possession or the lack of a philosophical attitude is most clearly dramatized and manifested." Thus Lucian's examples and sources—Polemo and Dionysius, Menippus and Bion[55] as well as the New Comedy—lead back to the anecdotal and historiographical tradition and to the confessions and the legends of the school-followers of the late classical and early Hellenistic period: Socrates and Xenophon, to whom Socrates said "Follow me and learn;"[56] Diogenes and Zeno, who visited the oracle together: Diogenes received the reply that "he should mint the coins anew;" Zeno rather that "he should couple with the dead." Both made the right decision, the one to revalue all values and the other to study the

---

[52] "Belief:" *Hermot.* 7: "I believe what my teacher says;" chaps.15; 17–18; 27; 29; 30; 47; 72; 73; 74 (repeatedly); 75.

[53] a) Aristot. *On Philosophy* frgs. 1–3 (R. Walzer, *Aristotelis Dialogorum Fragmenta* [Florence: G. C. Sansoni, 1934]); b) Aristot. *Letter to Philip of Madedonia*, frgs. 652–653; cf. Gigon, "Erzählungen," 18; c) cf. *Hermot.* 16.

[54] Gigon, "Erzählungen," 2. Lucian is not dealt with by Gigon.

[55] Luc. *Bis acc.* 16–18; 19–21; cf. Helm, *Lukian und Menipp*, passim.

[56] Diog. Laer. 2.48.

writings of the philosophers.[57] The richness of this tradition is discernible to us almost exclusively in fragmentary form or in later compilations. Lucian, however, stands out as a well-preserved and original representative of this tradition.[58]

§3 Lucian's Concept of Conversion Compared with Epictetus and Apuleius

§3.1. Epictetus and the Conversion to Cynicism

Epictetus (ca. 50–125/130 CE) came from Phrygian Hierapolis, was a slave in Rome and a Stoic philosopher. In the third book of his lectures, which were edited by his student Arrian (cos. 130 CE), there appears the diatribe *On Cynicism*.[59] In it, Epictetus does not develop Cynicism as a philosophical system, but rather describes the situation of a man who wants to become a Cynic and the role he would then have to assume.

Do nothing "without God," is the first admonition (2), and "Think the matter over more carefully, know yourself, ask the Deity, do not attempt the task without God" (53; 9). For the Cynic life is not an improved continuation of the solid middle-class existence that the candidate had known up until then (9–12). Rather, "First, in all that pertains to yourself directly you must change completely from your present practices . . ." (13). A "sudden change" (μεταβολή) of the governing principle (*hegemonikon*) is the precondition for assuming the role of a Cynic in public, as well as the proof that he who has assumed it has done so truly and rightfully.[60] The profession of the Cynic constitutes a break with his earlier life and a breaking away from his social environment.[61] He leaves wife and child, house and possessions,

---

[57] Diog. Laer. 6.20; 7.2.

[58] In this respect the following texts are particularly promising: *Kataplus*, *Vitarum auctio* and *Somnium* (including the allegory "Lucian at the crossroad"). M. Goodman did not use these texts (*Mission and Conversion: Proselytizing in the Religious History of the Roman Empire* [Oxford: Clarendon, 1994]); his theses concerning conversion in Greek philosophy are therefore to be modified.

[59] Epictet. (-Arrianus), *Diss.* 3.22. Quotations from the translation by W. A. Oldfather, *Epictetus. The Discourses as Reported by Arrian, the Manual, and Fragments* (2 vols.; LCL; Cambridge, MA: Harvard University Press; vol. 1, 1925; vol. 2, 1928).

[60] The wording follows *Diss.* 3.21.3.

[61] *Diss.* 3.22.45–47 (irony!); 67–69; cf. 3.21.8.

he lives outside the polis and its amenities, without servants or a fixed abode. The series of negations is long: ἄπολις, ἄοικος, ἀκτήμων, ἄδουλος; οὐ γυνή, οὐ παιδία. The decision to "leave" (3.21.8) so much should not be taken lightly. "But in such an order of things as the present" the Cynic ought to be "without disctraction" (3.22.69). When "the God" sends you on your way (46), you have to be free of all obligations: those towards the mother-in-law, the relatives of your wife, your wife, your child (70–72). Only in this way can the Cynic be messenger, servant, spy, herald of the gods, overseer, physician of humanity, and witness. Even the series of positive aspects to the Cynic's role is impressive; the Greek words demonstrate the closeness to early Christian ideas: ἀπόστολος (cf. 46), διάκονος, κατάσκοπος, ἄγγελος, κῆρυξ (69); ἐπίσκοπος (72; 77), ἰατρός (73), μάρτυς (88)—or anglicized: "apostle, deacon, angel, bishop, martyr."[62]

The difference from the concept of inner change as developed by Seneca is apparent: in Seneca gradual "transfiguration," unobtrusive "progress" of the inner man; in Epictetus the break with all things of importance for men of the ancient world: *polis*, *familia*, children. But this break should not occur impulsively and emotionally, when you are high on the beautiful words of a philosophical guru. Therefore at the end of this discourse, Epictetus repeats his admonishment: "Such is the nature of the matter about which you are deliberating. Wherefore . . . . put off your decision and look first at your endowment" (107).

§3.2 From Ass to Pastophoros

§3.2.1 Apuleius, *Metamorphoses* XI

Apuleius, a Platonic philosopher, orator and lawyer from Madauros in Numidia, composed his romance *The Metamorphoses*[63] around 160–170 CE, probably in Carthage. The protagonist is Lucius, a young

---

[62] Epictetus' sources concerning the role of the Cynic might possibly be inferred from a comparison with Lucian; Helm suggests: Menippos, *Diogenes for Sale* (*Lukian und Menipp*, 247). Cf. Epictet. *Diss.* 4.1 ("On Freedom").

[63] Apuleius, *Apologia* 24. The date of the *Metamorphoses* is uncertain. W. Haupt suggests a rather late date: 170–175 CE (epilogue to *Apuleius, Der goldene Esel* [2d ed.; Frankfurt/Main: Suhrkamp, 1981], 333). Occasionally a Greek model of Apuleius is ascribed to Lucian or to an imitator of Lucian; cf. J. G. Griffiths, *Apuleius of Madauros. The Isis-Book (Metamorphoses, Book XI) edited with an Introduction, Translation and Commentary* (Leiden: Brill, 1975) 1.

man from Corinth, who is allured by curiosity and sensuality to Thessaly, the land of the witches. There he finds sensual love and magic, more than is good for him. In one magical experiment he is mistakenly turned by his lover into an ass. Execution of the counter-spell is prevented by the attack of a band of robbers, who drive away the ass. Lucius the ass tries to get away again and again. Each attempt fails miserably. Instead of attaining freedom, he falls ever deeper into the world of the robbers, into slavery and moral ruin. Though he knows of the magical agent that can save him—he must eat roses—he never succeeds in making use of it. Either the security is too tight for him to be able to nibble at the blooming roses in a garden, or it is not the right time of year.[64] At the end of his long odyssey, the ass must lie with a woman, a mixer of poisons, in a public spectacle. She, however, is condemned to the arena to be killed by wild animals, so that her sexual partner also finds himself in danger of his life.

The *peripeteia* takes place when his fall has reached the lowest point and the danger is at its greatest.[65] It is already spring again; the roses are beginning to bloom (10.29.2) and this is his best hope. The ass flees for fear and shame,[66] but even this flight would have failed had it not been that the queen of the heavens "suddenly" appeared from the sea, the full moon of springtime with her otherworldly radiance. The deity speaks: "Behold, Lucius, . . . I have come, I, the mother of the universe, mistress of all the elements . . . my real name (is) Isis. . . . Now stop your tears . . . . Now by my providence your day of salvation is dawning—*iam tibi providentia mea inlucescit dies salutaris*" (11.5).

There follow the exorcism of Lucius, the initiation into the mysteries of Isis and Osiris, and finally the ascent into the priesthood of the greatest Temple of Isis in Rome, the *Iseum Campense* in the Campo Marzio.[67] The *reformatio* is a miracle,[68] but this time in the

---

[64] Roses: 2.16; 10.29: spring; 11.6.

[65] Cf. *Met.* 9.13: *ad ultimam salutis metam detrusus.* This idea is widespread. It is based on the experience that in cases of emergency people may discover forces unknown to them before. Cf. Seneca *Naturales Quaestiones* 3 prol. 8: *ad imum delatus es nunc locus est resurgendi.*

[66] *Met.* 10.34.1: *non de pudore iam, sed de salute ipsa sollicitus.* For *salus*—"life" and "salvation"— cf. *Met.* 3.29; 11.1.3; 11.5.4 et al.

[67] Nock does not ask either the literary question concerning the relationship between *Met.* I-X and *Met.* XI or the theological question as to how the

context of true religion rather than black magic. The odyssey of the ass and the conversion narrative in the end join together in a typical miracle story. The crowd is astonished and praises the deity. News of the event spreads and the miracle recruits new believers.[69]

§3.2.2 Conversion, Salvation, and Confession

a) In Apuleius the Isis-religion is presented as a religion of salvation. It teaches that man cannot escape from his wretched fortune by his own strength. Neither through education (cf. *Met.* 1.1–2) nor through magic can he attain to the truth and knowledge of salvation. Neither by cunning nor by effort does the ass succeed—not even in seizing the desperately needed roses. Despite all attempts to save himself he continues to fall deeper and deeper. Only a deity can save him. Only she can "reform" (*reformare*) the ass and lead Lucius through the mysteries in a symbolical death to "rebirth:" then he is *renatus*.[70]

The relation postulated by religion between inescapable guilt and undeserved salvation forms the thematic context of the two parts of the *Metamorphoses* (I-X/XI). Their narrative interweaving takes the form of the *peripeteia* at the end of the tenth book.[71]

b) There are frequent contrasts between the ass's world of misfortune and Isis' world of salvation: here there is impatient curiosity, there, stepwise instruction through the mystagoge; instead of magic (esp. 3.15) in the room of the beloved Photis, the mysterium in the community of Isis; the slavish subjugation to physical lust (*serviles voluptates*: 11.15) is transformed into freedom and pure, child-like love, and the bond with the great mother-goddess; from the lover's lesser

---

"transformation" of the ass into a man is conceived of and what kind of guilt is taken away by what kind of divine action (*Conversion: The Old and New in Religion from Alexander the Great to Augustine of Hippo* [London, Oxford and New York: Oxford University Press, 1972] 138–155).

[68] *Met.* 11.13.4. This "reformation" is anticipated in the ass story in 3.19.2; 3.21; 3.23; 3.25 et al.

[69] Conversion leads to mission; cf. the conversion-stories in Lucian.

[70] *Met.* 11.14.1; 11.16; cf. 11.21.6–7; cf. Paul, Romans 13.

[71] The questions concerning the literary unity of the *Metamorphoses*, their either comic (also in book 11) or serious-satirical (also in books 1–10) character throughout, the reference to mystery-cults (in the Psyche-narrative exclusively?) continue to be disputed; see the history of research in Griffiths, *Isis-Book*.

light of magic (Photis), from the darkness of his wanderings, Lucius reaches the light; from death into light, from stormy seas into the peace of the harbour—and whatever other images may be employed to describe unexpected salvation.

c) Apuleius' romance contains autobiographical elements, but the degree of their fictitiousness is a matter of debate. In any case the romance is also a confession, at the end of which the first-person narrator Lucius, who had just been an ass, reveals himself as the "Man from Madauros" (11.27). Thus the theological teachings of the romance—inescapable guilt and undeserved salvation, "reformation" and "rebirth"—turn into a personal testimony. At the end there is the call into the priesthood of Isis. After repeated rites of ordination, the former ass becomes Pastophoros—yes! one of the elders of the college on the Iseum Campense. Only thus does he come to belong completely to the saving mother.[72] Proudly—thus reads the last sentence of the romance—he wears his full tonsure as a priest of Isis. The man who had sung in a prose hymn the longest and most beautiful praise of his beloved's hair (*Met.* 2.8–9) leaves the narrative completely bald-headed. This and many other external signs reveal the dramatic reversal that the life of Lucius has undergone: from ass to Pastophorus.

The Isis-religion, in which the theme of this radical change of the inner and outer man is developed, is a religion of salvation and as such part of the Greek religion in Corinth and of the Roman religion in the city of Rome.

§4. Results

§4.1 According to the method of narrative philology (*enarratio auctorum*), I have presented three authors of the imperial period that seem to be useful for the study of the history of conversion in the ancient world: Lucian, Epictetus and Apuleius. The genre of conversion narrative is well attested in Greek and Roman literature. The most important elements of the genre are the imagery-rich narrative of the conversion experience, if need be with fictional self-description; instruction by a teacher; recruiting for a new school; topoi of salvation and miracle stories.

---

[72] Cf. 11.6.4: *cuius beneficio redieris ad homines, ei totum debere quod vives.*

§4.2 The worlds of experience and imagery by which the change of the inner man are rendered comprehensible involve darkness and enlightenment; sleep and awakening; healing; images of peregrination: the ascent to the summit of wisdom, orientation, turning back; slavery and liberation; love, marriage, and (un)faithfulness. The respective discourses lead into physiognomics, medicine, *hodogetike*, law and erotology.

Examples of these conversion narratives are to be found from the Hellenistic period on. They are widely disseminated in the various genres of popular literature (Menippean satire, diatribes of the Cynics and Stoics, New Comedy, and Romance) and were also transmitted in the so-called lower classes of society.

§4.3 In the classical work on *Conversion*, the above-mentioned authors are not presented at all or are incompletely presented.[73] The longest classical narrative of a conversion that has come down to us, at least to my knowledge, namely, Lucian's *Nigrinos*, is not treated at all. The literary and theological question concerning the relation between the two parts of Apuleius' *Metamorphoses* is not discussed.

§4.4 Lucian, Nigrinos

§4.4.1 In Lucian's oeuvre, "conversion, vocation and choice of modes of life" are frequently treated as important topics. In the *Nigrinos* conversion to philosophy is the central theme of the frame narrative;

---

[73] Cf. Nock, *Conversion*, 138–155 on Apuleius book 11: the story of Amor and Psyche is not taken into consideration; it is not recognized that the greatness of salvation is measured by the depth of guilt. Nor does Nock realize (chap. 11) the meaning of Seneca's *Epistles* as a process of *profectus* and "conversion." Nancy Shumate, in her study on *Crisis and Conversion in Apuleius' Metamorphoses* (Ann Arbor: University of Michigan Press, 1996), interprets the romance correctly, to my mind, "specifically as a narrative of conversion" (p. 1). The pattern of this "genre" guarantees the unity of the romance. My interpretation of Apuleius focuses on religious conversion; cf. H. Cancik and H. Cancik-Lindemaier, "*patria—peregrina—universa.* Versuch eine Typologie der universalistischen Tendenzen in der Geschichte der römischen Religion," *Tradition und Translation. Zum Problem der Übersetzbarkeit religiöser Phänomene. Festschrift für Carsten Colpe zum 65. Geburtstag* (ed. C. Elsas et al; Berlin and New York: de Gruyter, 1994), 64–74, §4: "Exklusive Universalisierung: *numen unicum* (Apuleius)." Shumate emphasizes the epistemological process: "Questions of epistomology lie at the heart of the Metamorphoses" (p.43). I am grateful to Hans Dieter Betz for having brought this important and well documented book to my attention.

and in so far as the juxtaposition of Athens to Rome implies the choice of the right life, the middle section of the *Nigrinos* is also to be brought into strict relation with this theme of conversion. The theme is not only developed by narrative means, but also in the author's reflection on whether the further transmission of the learning is authentic or not; on how the relation of teacher to student becomes that of student to student; and on how the recruiting can hit its mark.

§4.4.2 Two hundred years after *Nigrinos* the biographer Eunapius (380/390 CE) wrote:[74] "Lucian of Samosata is a man who tries seriously to provoke laughter; he recorded the life of Demonax, a philosopher of his times; in that book and in very few others was he completely serious" (δι' ὅλου σπουδάσας). In my opinion the *Nigrinos* belongs to these few serious writings. The lucid outlook, the serene and graceful narrating, the choice of dignified material and the confident, accomplished exposition make of this dialogue a "truly Greek" work.

---

[74] Eunapius, *Vitae sophistarum* (introduction); cf. H. Cancik, "Bios und Logos. Formengeschichtliche Untersuchungen zu Lukians 'Demonax,'" *Markus-Philologie* (ed. H. Cancik; Tübingen: Mohr [Siebeck], 1984), 115–130.

Conversion in Early Christianity

Edgar Krentz

I am privileged to respond to Hubert Cancik today—and that for two reasons: (1) To honor Hans Dieter Betz as a major scholar in the fields of New Testament and the Early Roman empire. I value his friendship highly. He is a stimulating colleague, a gracious participant in the scholarly life of the community of New Testament teachers in the Association of Chicago Theological Schools, one whose literary productivity constantly amazes this lesser colleague.

(2) I am delighted to respond to Professor Cancik's paper, which renews, even if somewhat tenuously, ties of affection for the Eberhard-Karls Universität of Tübingen in Germany, where I spent a delightful year in 1963–64 and participated in Hildebrecht Hommel's Hauptseminar, Antikes im Neuen Testament. Professor Cancik stands in a long series of Tübingen classicists who have enriched New Testament research.

Professor Cancik, directing our attention to Lucian's *Nigrinus*, *Bis Accusatus*, and *Hermotimus*, extends the research with which Professor Betz entered the scholarly world.[1] His paper opens up new facets of Lucian's thought, especially from the *Nigrinus*, to illuminate an aspect of ancient religion and philosophy, the formal character of ancient conversion narratives. In my brief remarks I hope to underscore some things Professor Cancik said, to suggest something of their significance for one or two New Testament texts, and to raise a few questions for discussion.

Professor Cancik discusses the "conceptual and literary history" of the conversion narrative. He identifies three types of philosophic conversion: (1) the ecstatic movement over to a new way of life of a young man in *Nigrinos*; (2) the juristic controversy among philosophical schools for adherents in *Bis Accusatus*; and (3) apostasy, the radical debarkation of an old philosopher from his school in *Hermotimus*, that

---

[1] Hans-Dieter Betz, *Lukian von Samosata und das Neue Testament. Religionsgeschichtliche und paränetische Parallelen, ein Beitrag zum Corpus Hellenisticum Novi Testamenti.* (TU 76; Berlin: Akademie-Verlag, 1961).

is, conversion away from philosophical commitment. Professor Cancik contrasts these to two other conversion accounts: Epictetus' description of conversion to Cynicism and Apuleius' account of Lucius' conversion and initiation as a follower of Isis.

Thus there are differing forms of conversion: the philosophic through hearing a teacher/speaker; the call to leave everything behind and follow one's true inner being and conversion to religious devotion via the irruption of a deity to free one from guilt. But they exhibit a common literary form: a presentation of the conversion experience rife with pictorial elements, at times with a fictive personal witness; the speech of a teacher; recruitment for the new direction in life; topoi of salvation and miraculous story. The accounts make use of various popular literary genres, even when used in the so-called lower levels of society.

As Professor Cancik notes, modern scholars do not discuss the literary form of conversion narratives. Arthur Darby Nock's standard monograph contains no literary or formal analysis of the many texts he studies,[2] nor does the study by Beverly Roberts Gaventa.[3] Alan Segal[4] has the most extensive discussion of conversion in recent literature, but he too does not discuss literary form. In his survey of the philosophical lives in Lucian, Diskin Clay comes closest as he looks at "Philosophical Paragons."[5] Neither C. P. Jones (*Culture and Society in Lucian*[6]) nor Christopher Robinson (*Lucian*[7]) discusses philosophical conversion. The term does not appear in the index of Jones' useful

---

[2] Arthur Darby Nock, *Conversion: The Old and the New in Religion from Alexander the Great to Augustine of Hippo* (London: Oxford University Press, 1961 = 1933).

[3] Beverly Roberts Gaventa, *From Darkness to Light: Aspects of Conversion in the New Testament* (Philadelphia: Fortress, 1986).

[4] Alan F. Segal, *Paul the Convert: The Apostolate and Apostasy of Saul the Pharisee* (New Haven: Yale University Press, 1990) 72–149. In his recent book, *Paul and the Gentiles: Remapping the Apostle's Convictional World* (Minneapolis: Fortress, 1997), Terrence L. Donaldson devotes some time to Paul's conversion, but does not deal with the form of conversion narratives (pp. 13–18).

[5] Diskin Clay, "Lucian of Samosata: Four Philosophical Lives (Nigrinus, Demonax, Peregrinus, Alexander Pseudomantis)," *ANRW* 2.36.5, 3406–3450.

[6] C. P. Jones, *Culture and Society in Lucian* (Cambridge and London: Harvard University Press, 1986).

[7] Christopher Robinson, *Lucian and His Influence in Europe* (Chapel Hill: University of North Carolina Press, 1979).

monograph; his discussion of the *Nigrinus*[8] focuses on the philosopher and his anti-Rome speech, while almost totally disregarding the narrator, whose role he sums up in one sentence: "His visit to the famous Platonist Nigrinus corrects his spiritual vision when he learns not to admire wealth, reputation, and the like." We owe Professor Cancik thanks for the new questions he has put to Lucian's texts and the resulting identification of a pattern in conversion narratives. Moreover, his typology of conversion stories will enrich research in many areas—especially New Testament studies, where the Apuleius material has tended to dominate discussion.[9]

Professor Cancik does not apply this typology to texts from the New Testament or other early Christian texts in his paper. Indeed the only reference to the New Testament he gives points to parallels between language in Epictetus and the New Testament. Since Professor Betz has concerned himself with the relationship of the New Testament to Graeco-Roman culture—and specifically with Lucian—I turn to the question, "Does the New Testament reflect the conversion narratives Prof. Cancik identifies in his paper?" *Partim*, I answer. First of all we should note that there are very few conversion narratives *per se* in the New Testament. Are we to interpret the change in Cleopas and his companion (his wife?) as a conversion story (Luke 24:13–32)? Are the call narratives in the gospels conversion stories, especially that of Peter in Luke 5:1–11? What of the Gerasene demoniac's going out to preach (Mark 5:1–20, especially vv. 19–20)? Or the Samaritan woman of John 4:28–30? They are certainly not all of the same type.

The majority of the clear conversion narratives are found in the book of Acts: Pentecost (Acts 2:37–42), Simon Magus in Samaria (Acts 8:4–13), the eunuch of Ethiopia (Acts 8:27–39), Saul (Acts 9:1–18; 22:3–21; 26:9–20), Cornelius (Acts 10:24–48), Sergius Paulus (Acts 13:4–12), Lydia (Acts 16:13–15), the jailer of Philippi (Acts 16:25–34), Athenians (Acts 17:16–34), Corinthian gentiles (Acts 18:7–10), and the

---

[8] Jones, 84–87.

[9] I think here especially of Martin Dibelius' use of this material in the interpretation of Colossians: "Die Isisweihe bei Apuleius und verwandte Initiations-Riten," *Botshaft und Geschichte* (ed. Günther Bornkamm; Tübingen: Mohr [Siebeck], 1956 [=1917]) 2.30–79; English translation, "The Isis Initiation in Apuleius and Related Initiatory Rites," *Conflict at Colossae* (rev. ed.; ed. Fred O. Francis and Wayne A. Meeks; SBLSBS 4; Missoula: Scholars Press, 1975) 61–121.

Ephesian magicians (Acts 19:13–20). Some, but not all, of these narratives credit conversion to Christian proclamation, the equivalent of the philosophical speech. Others reflect different patterns: confrontation with a heavenly being or the desire to get a benefit (Simon Magus). We will return to some of these narratives.

Professor Cancik's analysis illuminates some texts in the New Testament very well. I shall deal here only with one, 1 Thessalonians, the oldest text in the New Testament. Paul does not narrate a conversion, as do the texts Professor Cancik discusses, but he clearly refers back to the Thessalonians' conversion (1 Thess 1:9–10): "for they themselves announce concerning us what sort of an entrance we had with you, and how you turned to God from statues, to serve a God who is alive and authentic, and to await his son from the heavens, whom he raised from the dead, Jesus, the one rescuing us from the wrath that is on the way."[10] This change from the worship of traditional Greek gods (called here images, statues, εἴδωλα) is clearly conversion. But of what type?

In 1 Thess 2:2–8 Paul presents himself as a traveling speaker in language that is similar to Dio Chrysostom's description of the true philosopher: "We *grew bold of speech* in our God *to speak to you the good news about God* in a great *struggle*. For our *exhortation* did not arise from deceit or from impurity or treacherously, but just as we have been tested and approved by God to be entrusted with the good news, that is how we are speaking, *not as one pleasing people*, but [pleasing] God who puts our hearts to the test. For we were *never in a flattering speech*, just as you know, or *on a pretext of making a profit*, God be our witness, *or seeking a reputation from people, neither from you or from others*, although we were able to use pressure as apostles of Christ. But we were gentle among you, as if a wet nurse were fondling her very own children; thus longing for you we decided to share with you not only *the good news about God* but our very own lives, because you became dear to us."[11] I

---

[10] All translations are my own. αὐτοὶ γὰρ περὶ ἡμῶν ἀπαγγέλλουσιν ὁποίαν εἴσοδον ἔσχομεν πρὸς ὑμᾶς, καὶ πῶς ἐπεστρέψατε πρὸς τὸν θεὸν ἀπὸ τῶν εἰδώλων δουλεύειν θεῷ ζῶντι καὶ ἀληθινῷ (10) καὶ ἀναμένειν τὸν υἱὸν αὐτοῦ ἐκ τῶν οὐρανῶν, ὃν ἤγειρεν ἐκ [τῶν] νεκρῶν, Ἰησοῦν τὸν ῥυόμενον ἡμᾶς ἐκ τῆς ὀργῆς τῆς ἐρχομένης.

[11] ἐπαρρησιασάμεθα ἐν τῷ θεῷ ἡμῶν λαλῆσαι πρὸς ὑμᾶς τὸ εὐαγγέλιον τοῦ θεοῦ ἐν πολλῷ ἀγῶνι. 3 ἡ γὰρ παράκλησις ἡμῶν οὐκ ἐκ πλάνης οὐδὲ ἐξ

cite this long passage because the underscored terminology is close to that of Dio Chrysostom in *Or.* 32.1–24, where he contrasts true and false philosophers.[12] Paul's use of this terminology suggests that he appeared to the Thessalonians like a wandering philosophical teacher.

Now, given Professor Cancik's analysis, this letter's language is congruent with Paul's description of their conversion. Paul stresses their radical shift from commitment to images to worship of a God who is alive and authentic (1:9–10). He calls this a λόγος τοῦ θεοῦ and εὐαγγέλιον τοῦ θεοῦ. He points out their experiences and feelings as they heard his words (1:5–6), which resulted in their becoming repeaters of the word (1:8). Paul praises them for imitating him—and the Lord. He accounts for his absence from them, that is, he is not present (παρεῖναι, 2:17–20). His letter is an extended exhortation, παράκλησις, which calls them to a life that conforms to their convictions. They are sons of light and of day (5:5), not of night and darkness. Like Nigrinos, Paul's own way of life corresponded to his logos. I repeat, 1 Thessalonians is not a conversion story, but it reflects the language of conversion evidenced in the *Nigrinos*. This linguistic context may account for the almost complete lack of the use of the Old Testament in the letter: no citations, no references to OT figures or cult, no use of the exodus, etc.

The story of Thecla in the *Acta Pauli* is a conversion story in which she becomes a Christian as a result of hearing a sermon by Paul (though the sermon *per se* is not given).[13] Her life changes. In spite of

---

ἀκαθαρσίας οὐδὲ ἐν δόλῳ, 4 ἀλλὰ καθὼς δεδοκιμάσμεθα ὑπὸ τοῦ θεοῦ πιστευθῆναι τὸ εὐαγγέλιον, οὕτως λαλοῦμεν, οὐχ ὡς ἀνθρώποις ἀρέσκοντες ἀλλὰ θεῷ τῷ δοκιμάζοντι τὰς καρδίας ἡμῶν. 5 οὔτε γάρ ποτε ἐν λόγῳ κολακείας ἐγενήθημεν, καθὼς οἴδατε, οὔτε ἐν προφάσει πλεονεξίας, θεὸς μάρτυς, 6 οὔτε ζητοῦντες ἐξ ἀνθρώπων δόξαν οὔτε ἀφ᾽ ὑμῶν οὔτε ἀπ᾽ ἄλλων, 7 δυνάμενοι ἐν βάρει εἶναι ὡς Χριστοῦ ἀπόστολοι. ἀλλὰ ἐγενήθημεν νήπιοι ἐν μέσῳ ὑμῶν, ὡς ἐὰν τροφὸς θάλπῃ τὰ ἑαυτῆς τέκνα, 8 οὕτως ὁμειρόμενοι ὑμῶν εὐδοκοῦμεν μεταδοῦναι ὑμῖν οὐ μόνον τὸ εὐαγγέλιον τοῦ θεοῦ ἀλλὰ καὶ τὰς ἑαυτῶν ψυχάς, διότι ἀγαπητοὶ ἡμῖν ἐγενήθητε.

[12] See Abraham Malherbe, "'Gentle as a Nurse:' The Cynic Background to 1 Thessalonians 2," *NovT* 12 (1970) 203–17, reprint in idem, *Paul and the Popular Philosophers* (Minneapolis: Fortress Press, 1989) 35–48. See also his *Paul and the Thessalonians: The Philosophic Tradition of Pastoral Care* (Philadelphia: Fortress Press, 1987), passim.

[13] See the Acta Pauli in *Acta Apostolorum Apocrypha* (ed. R. A. Lipsius and M. Bonnet; Leipzig: in aedibus Hermanni Mendelssohn, 1891; repr. Darmstadt:

the pressure from her parents, she refuses to marry Thamyris, the young man selected for her by her father. Brought before Castellius, the Roman governor, she remains steadfast, even when condemned to be immolated. Saved miraculously, freed by the governor, she eventually dresses as a male, follows Paul to Myra, and becomes a teacher of the word of God in Seleucia. Hers is a conversion caused by teaching.

Professor Cancik did not refer to the *Poimandres* (Corpus Hermenticum 1), which also supports his analysis. It comes close to the type of revelation discourse leading to conversion that occurs in Apuleius, *Metamorphoses* 11. The details cannot be presented here. But there is a revelation, a logos, from outside, accompanied by the metaphors of light, birth, radical change (divinization), a new life style, the telling of the story to another, and the praise of the revealer.

Problematic Conversions: Variant Conversion Stories

Other conversion stories do not fit the pattern observed. What does one make of the Lystra narrative in Acts 14:8–18, where a lame man becomes an adherent, appealing for aid before Paul speaks to him, and where Paul's oration prevents the inhabitants from worshipping Barnabas and him? Or the Athenian Areopagus address in Acts 17:16–33? Might one understand these two narratives as anti-philosophical addresses which do not convert philosophical auditors. I think that is at least an interesting question to pose.[14]

Recently Krister Stendahl questioned whether we should call Paul's Damascus experience a conversion at all, since Paul after Damascus still worshipped the same God, the God of Abraham, Isaac, and Jacob, whom he worshipped before he met the resurrected Jesus.[15] Stendahl suggests that we speak of a call narrative, not a conversion. The question is, did not such call narratives seem very similar to the

---

Wissenschaftliche Buchgesellschaft, 1959) 1. 235–72; English translation in *New Testament Apocrypha* (ed. Wilhelm Schneemelcher; Eng. tr. ed. R. McL. Wilson; Rev. ed.; Cambridge: James Clarke; Louisville: Westminster/John Knox, 1991) 2.239–46

[14] I am aware that the "standard" view is that these are models of how to present the good news to non-Jewish audiences.

[15] Krister Stendahl, "Paul Among Jews and Gentiles," *Paul Among Jews and Gentiles and Other Essays* (Philadelphia: Fortress Press, 1976) 7–23.

conversion of the Cynic philosopher in Epictetus? In short, can we make this genre more precise as we define it over against the call narrative tradition of the Old Testament?

Other forms of conversion are dissimilar to that which Professor Cancik details. There is, for example, conversion that results from a young man studying with teachers of differing philosophical schools· Justin Martyr was first a Stoic, then Peripatetic, Pythagorean, and Platonist before becoming a Christian "Philosopher."[16] Josephus presents his early life as a movement through the three sects (Pharisees, Sadducees and Essenes) to following one Bannus in the wilderness before deciding intellectually for Pharisaism.[17] Here conversion is the result of study and intellectual satisfaction leading to a reasoned decision.

There is also the stock story of the young man who comes to philosophy as the result of growing independence and the development of rationality. Maximus Tyrius described the myth in which Prodicus brings the young Heracles to two roads, those of Pleasure and Virtue, presented as two women, one chastely dressed, one arrayed like a courtesan.[18] Heracles abandons Pleasure to follow Virtue.

Non-philosophical conversions are surprisingly different. Ramsey MacMullen, for examplc, argues that conversion to Christianity via "intellectual pilgrimage" was restricted to the upper classes, for example, to Justin Martyr, Tatian, Menippus in Lucian, and Plotinus in the post New Testament period. The demonstration that the God of Christianity was more powerful than the gods of traditional Greek religion, of the many mystery cults, of city cults, or ruler worship led

---

[16] Just. *Dial.* 2.3–6. L. W. Barnard, *Justin Martyr: His Life and Thought* (Cambridge: Cambridge University Press, 1971) 6–12; Robert M. Grant, *Greek Apologists of the Second Century* (Philadelphia: Westminster, 1988) 50–51. M. B. Trapp in Maximus of Tyre, *The Philosophical Orations*, tr. with Introduction and Notes by M. B. Trapp (Oxford: Clarendon Press, 1997) notes the philosophical pilgrimage of Galen (5.41–2 Kühn). In that light he argues that the quest of Hermotimus after twenty years is a parody of this model.

[17] Joseph. *Vit* 2.

[18] Max. Tyr. 14.1 (Trapp, 125–26). Trapp calls attention to the conversion of Polemo (Diog. Laer. 4.16) as an example.

more often to conversion.[19] The lower classes were converted by miracle, as is reflected in the Acts of John, the Acts of Peter, and by the stories that circulated about Gregory Thaumaturgus or, at a later date, Porphyry of Gaza.[20]

Some NT conversion stories support MacMullen's proposal. The Lukan call of Peter would be one such. I also think of those narratives in Acts about Simon Magus, Sergius Paulus, the jailer at Philippi, and the Ephesian magicians. The Philippian jailer is a striking example. After the earthquake, discovering Paul and the other prisoners still in the jail—though set free from their chains—he burst out "What must I do to be saved?" Paul's answer first announces the name of Jesus to him. He seems to be overcome by the power of Paul's tutelary deity, who controls natural phenomena for the benefit of Paul (shades of Dionysos in Euripides' *Bacchae*). One finds the same reaction to miraculous deeds in other Acts narratives.

That raises questions worth discussing. (1) Is there a difference between philosophical conversion (à la Lucian and others) and what, for want of a better term, I would call religious experiential conversion (MacMullen's type)? Might each not awaken reactions that use similar language, for example, is Lucius' conversion in Apuleius' *Metamaorphoses* 11 really a narrative of the same order as the *Nigrinus*? Or does he experience a miracle that later must be followed by instruction and initiation? (The same would be true of Paul's conversion.) I am struck by Professor Burkert's words in *Ancient Mystery Religions*. In the chapter titled "Personal Needs" he writes about the relation of votive religion to mystery cults. Personal initiation was largely parallel to votive religion in motivation and function, he argues. It is a new form in a similar quest for salvation, that is, initiation is a response to a benefit conferred. The parallelism

> . . . is not even absent from the famous text of Apuleius on the Isis initiation of Lucius—the only extant account of a mystery initiation in a first-person style.

---

[19] Ramsay MacMullen, *Christianizing the Roman Empire (A. D. 100–400)* (New Haven and London: Yale University Press, 1984) 22 (of Jesus), 25–42. He concentrates on post NT materials of the second century and following.

[20] See Marcus Diaconus, *Vita Porphyrii* (ed. Societatis Philologae Bonnensis Sodales; Leipzig: B. G. Teubner, 1895) 19 (rain miracle), 34, etc.

> This has been called a conversion in the full sense.[21] Yet in spite of the religious rhetoric, the picture is not dominated by spiritual preoccupations [might we also add philosophical or ideational?]; it remains realistic and is fused with normal psychology in an interesting way. The so-called conversion to Isis does not result in withdrawal from the world and worldly interests; on the contrary, the runaway student who had been roaming wildly through the Greco-Roman world now finally becomes integrated into respectable society. He starts his career as a lawyer in Rome and proves to be quite successful. This is felt to be a result of the favor of Isis and Osiris: they are givers of riches, *ploutodotai,* quite deservedly in this case because the repeated initiations had literally cost a fortune and deprived the man from Madaura of all his father's inheritance.[22]

(2) That suggests another problem. How should one define "conversion"? The question is more than idle, since definition often determines findings. Lewis R. Rambo, in his recent encyclopedia article on conversion,[23] defines conversion as follows: "Conversion will be viewed as a dynamic, multifaceted process of change. For some, that change will be abrupt and radical; for others, it will be gradual and not inclusive of a person's total life" (p. 73). Just how radical, abrupt or total a change must there be? Arthur Darby Nock seems to limit the use of the term "conversion" to a change that involves "body and soul," to use MacMullen's phrase. Conversion demands renunciation, a new start, commitment to a new theology, a new life in a new people. Therefore, for Nock "the only context in which we find it in ancient paganism is that of philosophy, which held a clear concept of two types of life, a higher and a lower, and which exhorted men to turn from the one to the other."[24] MacMullen rejects this limitation on historical grounds, since many who converted to Christianity did not have this total commitment demanded by Nock. The problem of definition is more than word-play.

---

[21] Nock, 155, explicitly draws a parallel to "a man received into the Catholic church." Burkert comments: "I see no special justification for the Pauline formula 'living in the world, but not as of the world' being applied to Lucius." Burkert, note 23, p. 140.

[22] Walter Burkert, *Ancient Mystery Cults* (Cambridge and London: Harvard University Press, 1987) 17.

[23] Lewis R. Rambo, "Conversion," *The Encyclopedia of Religion,* ed. Mircea Eliade (New York: Macmillan; London: Collier Macmillan, 1987) 4. 73–78.

[24] Nock, 14.

The motto of the University of Chicago is *Crescat scientia, vita excolatur.* I have high respect for Professor Cancik's presentation. He has made a strong case for a type of conversion that results from argumentation or proclamation. His typology stimulates one to further examination of significant texts both in the New Testament and the world in which its nascent history unrolled. He has, at least for this hearer, increased the knowledge that informs the study of the New Testament; he has certainly shown how life was fundamentally changed by conversion in the first century. The Chicago motto has here been carried out.

Towards Plato and Paul: The "Inner" Human Being

Walter Burkert

The Discovery of the Mind is the title of a famous and important book by Bruno Snell. "The Disovery of the Body" would be a title more in accordance with the tendencies of the present day.[1] It is not only the case that general interest in theory and practice, from psychoanalysis through health care to recreational activities, is mainly concerned with the individual body today; it is especially the breathtaking progress made by science in understanding the functions of the living organism, including the brain, neuronal transmitters, moods, and consciousness, that makes us rethink the traditional hierarchy of mind and body.

The common concept still today is that there is "mind" or "soul" "within" the body, "within" the living person. There is the traditional and remarkable formula of an "inner" human being, characterized by "soul" or "heart," and distinct from the corporeal woman or man whom I see standing or sitting before my eyes, clad with skin and normally with clothes. The formula is anchored in the Christian tradition, as it is used several times by St. Paul and becomes ubiquitous in later Christian literature, but its origin is in fact in Plato, some 400 years before Paul; no doubt it shows the indebtedness of Paul to Hellenistic philosophy, even if the intermediates seem to be lost to us.[2]

---

[1] Bruno Snell, *The Discovery of the Mind* (Oxford: Blackwell, 1953); originally published as *Die Entdeckung des Geistes* (Hamburg: Claaszen & Goverts, 1946; 4th ed. reprinted Göttingen: Vandenhoeck & Ruprecht, 1975). For contrast see G. Rappe, *Archaische Leiberfahrung: Der Leib in der frühgriechischen Philosophie und in außereuropäischen Kulturen* (Berlin: Akademie Verlag, 1995); in general, cf. J. Assmann, ed., *Die Erfindung des inneren Menschen* (Gütersloh: Gütersloher Verlag, 1993).

[2] See T. K. Heckel, *Der Innere Mensch: Die paulinische Verarbeitung eines platonischen Motivs* (Tübingen: Mohr [Siebeck], 1993); K. Berger, "Innen und Außen in der Welt des Neuen Testaments," *Die Erfindung des inneren Menschen,* 161–167; Markschies, "Die Platonische Metapher vom 'Inneren Menschen'. Eine Brücke zwischen Antiker Philosophie und Altchristlicher Theologie," *ZKG* 105 (1994) 1–17; Markschies, "Innerer Mensch," *RAC* 18 (1997) 266–312. In fact there

It is the prehistory of both Plato's and Paul's concepts which is to be explored here.

It was Bruno Snell who showed that the concepts of body and mind as evidenced in language are not just "natural" nor ubiquitous, but different as to cultural groups and historical epochs. Homer, Snell insisted, has neither a clear and simple word for "soul" nor for "body;" the "discoveries" of these concepts, the changes in wording and imagination are to be documented step by step; Snell undertook to do this within Greek literature.[3] Still following the impulse of Bruno Snell, we should be conscious of the fact that we cannot posit Homer as an absolute beginning—there are about 2000 years of documented literary and mental history before Homer— and that we are not so sure about "progress" in mental history. There may be changing ideological postulates rather than "discoveries," regarding the relation of mind and body, the construct of an "inner" sphere of mind, *psyche*, or personality, in opposition to outward reality.

The "inner" dimension usually gets the positive accent even today, not only in many variants of esotericism or sects, but also in important trends of modern consciousness. Tales of Hermann Hesse, whose books became bestsellers in the United States some 30 years ago, bear the comprehensive title *Route to the Interior, Weg nach Innen*.[4] Most

---

is no attestation of the term ἐντὸς/εἴσω ἄνθρωπος between Plato and Paul, even if Philo comes close to it; the term becomes common with post-Pauline Gnostics and with the later *patres*, with evident recourse to Plato; see below notes 53 and 56. Markschies holds that Paul coined the term afresh by himself, without knowing about Plato. This seems hardly credible, even if Paul no doubt makes quite an original use of it.

[3] The problem raised by Snell, whether Homer has a concept of the "person" including responsible "decision," has started a long controversy; suffice it to refer to C. Voigt, *Überlegung und Entscheidung. Studien zur Selbstauffassung des Menschen bei Homer* (Ph.D. diss., Hamburg, 1932; repr. Meisenheim: A. Hain, 1972); K. Lanig, *Der handelnde Mensch in der Ilias* (Ph.D. diss., Erlangen, 1953); A. Lesky, *Göttliche und menschliche Motivation im homerischen Epos* (SHAW 4; Heidelberg: Carl Winter Universitätsverlag, 1961); H. Lloyd-Jones, *The Justice of Zeus* (Berkeley: University of California Press, 1971); A. Schmitt, *Selbständigkeit und Abhängigkeit menschlichen Handelns bei Homer* (AAWM 5; Mainz: Akademie der Wissenschaften und der Literatur, 1990).

[4] Hermann Hesse, *Weg nach Innen* (Berlin: S. Fischer, 1931; Frankfurt am Main: Suhkamp, 1947; [West Germany]: Deutsche Buch-Gemeinschaft, 1973). A famous poem by Rainer Maria Rilke, "Es winkt zu Fühlung fast aus allen Dingen . . .," created the German word *Weltinnenraum*.

people today will think of India's spiritual tradition in such a context, as did Hermann Hesse. But it is in fact the tradition of Platonism and Neoplatonism which has been effective in our tradition all the time. "To follow the way to the interior" is a maxim of Plotinus. Plotinus also wrote: "Everything is within."[5] No Eastern guru could outdo this.

Still one should probably not forget the warning—voiced above all by the angry young people of 1968—that the relegation to the "interior," *Innerlichkeit*, can be used by ruling classes as a deceptive strategy to deprive the inferiors of their share in "outward" resources. In this respect, even the Bible is not above suspicion: if St. Peter, in his first letter, recommends "the hidden human being of the heart, in the imperishable sphere of the gentle and quiet spirit, that is of high value in the sight of god,"[6] this makes a fine text for general sermons; but as, in its context, this is a recommendation especially for women, warning them against "outward" adornments, husbands will be quick to appreciate that "inner riches" do not cost them money. Yet there are much more horrible consquences of an extreme and exclusive valuation of the "inner" dimension. Plotinus, for whom "everything is within," was so prudish that he would never visit a public bath, and he died from this neglect of his body, as Porphyry attests.[7] A Christian ascetic is reported to declare about his body: "It is killing me—I am killing it."[8] There are saints starving to death in non-Christian religions, too. Such victories of the "inner person" are lethal.

To begin in quite a general perspective: "In" is a preposition which belongs to the Indoeuropean heritage of our languages, which means that already some 5000 or 6000 years ago the contrast between "exterior" and "interior" was consciously expressed. We may go much farther back with the obvious statement that it was biology that invented the "interior" sphere: One decisive step in evolution was the formation of a "cell," separated from what is outside by the cellular

---

[5] Plot. *Enn.* 1.6.8.4, συνεπέσθω εἰς τὸ εἴσω; 3.8.6.40 πάντα εἴσω. A Gnostic text declares: "what is inside of you is what is outside of you . . . ;" Nag Hammadi Codex VI, Tractate 2, p. 20, lines 18–20 (*The Nag Hammadi Library in English* [ed. J. M. Robinson; 3d ed.; Leiden: Brill, 1988] 302–3).

[6] 1 Pet 3:4: ὁ κρυπτὸς τῆς καρδίας ἄνθρωπος ...

[7] Porphyr. *Vit. Plot.* 2.

[8] Pall. *Hist. Laus.* 2.1.

membrane, which still must be permeable in certain ways. All higher forms of life are dependent on this invention. It was repeated in the progress of evolution with the construction of a skin enclosing the whole body of a multicellular being, separating the interior from the environment, guaranteeing protection which must not become isolation. In a special way, finally, the central organ of higher animals, the brain, has become an "interior," as it is encapsulated in a solid shell, protected from the outside and yet designed for communication through input and output, with openings for the spinal chord, the eyes and the ears.

More flexible, yet based on these foundations, is the actual experience of the human being. Each finds himself constructed as an individuum, within one's own skin, with proper genetical code, proper immune system, proper nervous system and brain, and yet always communicating with others and dependent on them. Since language intervenes as the decisive medium of intelligence, the facts of "in" and "out" are being transformed into a dialectic of what is closed and hidden or else disclosed and plain. The management of reality presupposes the discovery that there is a consistency in things beyond immediate sensation, that things we cannot see, hear, smell or grasp at the moment still exist, even if concealed. It is an important question of developmental psychology to ascertain when exactly a baby comes to understand this fact. If things can be concealed, you can manage to do so yourself, you can hide yourself. But since intelligent beings are curious, what seems to be hidden has a very special attraction. To hide, to search, to find out what may be "in" the black box has become a favourite game of intelligence.[9] So much about anthropological fundaments of "in" and "out."

In consequence, we should not wonder that the question about an "inner" dimension of the human being does come up less in self-reflection than in searching for the "real" ideas and intentions of a partner. We understand each other both through words and through body language. Yet if there is concealment, the situation becomes

---

[9] See Walter Burkert, "Der geheime Reiz des Verborgenen: Antike Mysterienkulte," *Secrecy and Concealment. Studies in the History of Mediterranean and Near Eastern Religions* (ed. H. G. Kippenberg and G. S. Stroumsa; Leiden: Brill, 1995) 79–100.

ambivalent. Each child will learn soon that it is not advisable to show or to speak out everything one is feeling, that one should, for example, smile to fulfill social expectations; in immediate consequence, this must raise suspicions: what really is behind, beneath, inside such a smile? The "inner person" is discovered as a problem: what is happening "in" the partner, in his head—or is it "in his heart"?

To speak of the "heart" in such a context is still so common that we hardly realize that we are using a strange metaphor. In fact we are confronted with a short circuit that happens in most archaic languages and civilizations: The hidden sources of behavior, the feelings and thoughts of a partner are assigned to the organs which really are to be found inside of the skin, which could be extracted and brought to light, even if this would be a circumstantial and violent operation. Both quite common and uncommon, even grotesque, opinions may be voiced in the process.

A certain knowledge of human anatomy can be assumed even for the earliest periods; this is propagated in language, not without disfigurations and misunderstandings. In the Indoeuropean tradition of our own languages, we find words for heart, lungs, liver, and kidneys as well as for eyes, ears or feet, which takes us at least 5000 years back. Of course there was no scientific anatomy, but still what may be called accidential anatomy, cuts and woundings, also, in addition, sometimes strange funerary rituals. Egyptian embalming presupposed the removal of the bowels; the heart was replaced by a scarabaeus.[10] The embalmer thus had very detailed knowledge about the "interior" of a human being. Moreover the similarity of all mammals, as regards "interiors," was well known from butchery in hunt and sacrifice; the organs have the same names in humans and animals, be it heart, liver, or kidneys. The special use of the liver in mantic procedures spread from Assytria to Greece, Etruria, and Rome.[11] That the pulse of the heart—you feel it beating—is driving the blood through the arteries has always been known; one can even

---

[10] H. Bonnet, *Reallexikon der ägyptischen Religionsgeschichte* (Berlin: de Gruyter, 1952) 297–98, *s.v.* "Herzskarabäus;" 481–87, *s.v.* "Mumifizierung." See also J. Assmann, "Zur Geschichte der Herzens im Alten Ägypten," *Die Erfindung des inneren Menschen*, 81–113.

[11] See Walter Burkert, *The Orientalizing Revolution* (Cambridge, MA: Harvard University Press, 1992) 46–53.

cut out the throbbing heart, as was done in certain sacrifical rites, and see the consequences.[12] Everybody also knows that we can eat heart, lungs, liver, and kidneys, we are familiar with their taste; and whoever bites the gall bladder will not fortget its distasteful bitterness.

These realistic "interiors" of the human being are set in direct correspondence to feeling and thinking. Some forms of experience are available or even unavoidable for everyone, the beatings of the heart, the reactions of stomach and bowels; in interpretation and linguistic fixation there may be special developments nonetheless. This is even true of the heart. To give some details: Akkadian, the main language of cuneiform script, has a general word for the "interior" of man, *kabittu*, rarely specified in an anatomical way—it seems to be the liver, but there is another unambiguous word for "liver" (*amutu*)—but constantly applied in describing emotions: joy and wrath, relaxation and alarm. The *kabittu* desires and gets to rest; it rejoices, becomes light and radiant, or fiery in wrath.[13] Even more often the word *libbu*, "heart," is used for "inner" emotions, joy, fear, and desire; it is also quite normal to say that this happens "in the heart" (*ina libbi*), which means doubling the "interior" dimension, heart in the breast and joy in the heart. Hebrew is not basically different—the Hebrew word לב or לבב exactly corresponds to *libbu*. We may still have in our ears the pronouncement that God "looks at the heart." "Man sees what is for the eyes, but the Lord looks for the heart." "This people . . . honour me with their lips, while their hearts are far from me."[14] We also know, what has become proverbial, that the Lord examines "heart and reins"—sacrificial practice has become psychology.[15] Characteristics of the "heart" are courage, joy, pain, compassion, desire, but also intelligence, plans, and will, in short, all "interior" motions; in biblical language, "thinking" and "speaking" is performed "in the heart;" even Mary at the birth of Christ "keeps the

---

[12] See Walter Burkert, *Homo Necans* (Berkeley: University of California Press, 1983) 6.

[13] W. von Soden, *Akkadisches Handwörterbuch* (Wiesbaden: Harrassowitz, 1965–1981) 416; *CAD*, *s.v.*

[14] 1 Sam 16:7; Isa 29:13; cf. *HALAT*, 488–491. Cf. Rappe, *Archaische Leiberfahrung*, 287–311. See also Assmann, "Zur Geschichte der Herzens im Alten Ägypten."

[15] Ps 7:10; Jer 11:20; 17:10; 20:12; cf. *TWNT*, *s.v.* καρδία.

words and moves them in her heart."[16] We may wonder at the expression of a "circumcised heart," as the outward sign of religious classification becomes interiorized. "Uncircumcised with respect to hearts and ears," Stephen scolds the Jewish public in Acts; his words "cut like a saw through their hearts" and make them "grind their teeth;" then they start throwing stones: here there is movement from "interior" motion through "exterior" reaction to aggressive action.[17]

If we have a look at the early Greek, that is, Homer's usage, we meet with the "heart" again, κῆρ, καρδίη. Love and joy, anger and sorrow occur "around the heart," περὶ κῆρι, or "at the heart," κηρόθι.[18] The heart's special power is in fighting: "to make war and to fight incessantly with the heart," καρδίηι ἄλληκτον πολεμιζέμεν ἠδὲ μάχεσθαι, is a Homeric formula (*Il.* 2.452; 11.12; 14.152). The same idea is expressed by the adjective θρασυκάρδιος, "bold of heart." In the *Odyssey* the functions of the "heart" are richer and more complex than in the *Iliad*; even pain "dives into the heart" and "grows in the heart" (*Od.* 18.348; 20.286), the heart "undulates" in thinking (17.489). Notorious is the scene when Odysseus the beggar watches the maiden servants going to bed with the suitors: his heart "barks within himself," ἔνδον ὑλάκτει (20.13), whereupon the noble sufferer speaks the winged words: "endure this, oh my heart; even worse didst thou endure . . ." (20.18). This is an "inner" dialogue of conscious will and primitive macho-emotion, which makes the "heart" give sounds like an animal.[19] For Archilochus, the brave man should be "full of heart," leaving no room for cowardice.[20] What we hardly find in archaic Greece is any relation of the heart to love, or to god; *sursum corda* would hardly have been understood by then—it came from Hebrew to Christian liturgy.

---

[16] Luke 2:19.

[17] Acts 7:51.

[18] See Bruno Snell, ed., *Lexikon des frühgriechischen Epos* (Göttingen: Vandenhoeck und Ruprecht, 1955-), *s.v.*; cf. Rappe, *Archaische Leiberfahrung*, 35–95.

[19] On speaking organs in Homer and Pindar, see H. Pelliccia, *Mind, Body, and Speech in Homer and Pindar* (Göttingen: Vandenhoeck & Ruprecht, 1995) esp. 220–21 on *Od.* 20.1–3.

[20] Archilochus frg. 114,4 (M. L. West, ed., *Iambi et Elegi Graeci* I [2d. ed.; 2 vols.; Oxford: Oxford University Press, 1989]).

The other important "inner" organ is the "liver" together with "bile." The word for bile, χολή, is linguistically tied to current words for anger and wrath, χόλος, κεχολῶσθαι.[21] It may be true that humans vomit bile in cases of extreme agitation; it happens much more often in literature. Dominant is the association of the bile's taste with anger. "You have not got bile on your liver," Archilochus scolds a fellow without character (234); "this city without gall, oppressed by a demon," Alcaeus chides his fellow-citizens.[22] To feel wrath is part of a man's virtue, and it has its proper place "within" the body.

Strange and much-discussed within Homeric psychology is the role of the diaphragm, the φρένες: These are made the proper organ of "thinking" which we think should be done rather within the head. There is no doubt about the anatomical place of φρένες in Homer's text; the φρένες, "dark round around," are enclosing the liver (*Od.* 9.301); they are black, being filled with energy at an attack of fury (*Il.*1.103). But normally it is thinking, reflection, that goes on within the φρένες, according to the formulaic diction of the epic.[23] The verb φρονέω with its many uses and derivations means mental activities and dispositions; φρόνησις comes to denote intelligence in general; φρενῖτις is a disease of thinking, which is submerged in "frenetic" applause. I think the basic experience which gave its meaning to φρένες is the harmony of the body as it becomes apparent in breathing. The diaphragm is active in regulating the breath; breathing and spiritual experience go together, as any Yogi may teach. Good breathing means good thinking, and a disturbance of breath indicates a disturbance of thought: this was expressed originally by εὔφρων and ἄφρων. Mental activity is found to be bound to the corporeal state.

Another psychosomatic expression has come about in Hellenistic Greek and spread through the usage of the New Testament: compassion as motion in the bowels. An old word for the inner parts is σπλάγχνα, used especially in the context of butchery in hunt and sacrifice. But from the New Testament onwards σπλαγχνίζεσθαι means "to have compassion." There is a Hebrew word in the

---

[21] J. Irmscher, *Götterzorn bei Homer* (Leipzig: O. Harrassowitz, 1950) 8–10.

[22] Archilochus frg. 234 (West, *Iambi et Elegi Graeci*); Alcaeus frg. 348 (E. Voigt, ed., *Sappho et Alcaeus*, [Amsterdam: Athenaeum 1971]).

[23] See Snell, *The Discovery of the Mind.*

background, רחם/רחמים, which means "to love" and "to have compassion;" the older layers of the Septuagint use the old Greek verbs ἐλεεῖν and οἰκτίρειν for translation. רחם also means uterus; some kind of etymology seems to have influenced the creation of the new word.[24] At any rate the verb σπλαγχνίζεσθαι is an example of how psychosomatic expressions for "inner" emotions may rise afresh even in a period when intellectuals have long agreed on a clean separation of "outward" and "inward" processes in anthropology. Εὔσπλαγχνος ("compassionate") is still current in modern Greek.

Back to Homer: φρένες is often associated with θυμός, a general word for psychic energy; besides, there is another word for energy, μένος, quite an old Indoeuropean formation; there is also νόος for the mind's perception. Θυμός and μένος have their place within the breast; the dead have lost both: θυμός leaves the limbs in the process of dying; the dead are called ἀμενηνὰ κάρηνα in the Homeric formula. What is characteristic is the multiplicity of synonyms in the sphere of the "psyche," without explicit declaration about their mutual relations. There is no comprehensive word for "soul" or "psyche"—it was Bruno Snell who insisted on this fact. But this can be shown to be just normal in many archaic languages and civilizations.[25] Of course the word ψυχή does occur in Homer, but mainly in the formulaic description how it leaves the human being at death and goes to the house of Hades, to continue a shadowy existence, without μένος, nay without φρένες.

In spite of this whole psychosomatic conglomerate, the separation of "outward" and "inward" behavior can be fully described even at the level of Homeric language, especially in the situation of concealment and deception. Achilles, in the Iliad, has the famous saying: "Hateful for me like the doors of Hades is the person who conceals one thing in his φρένες and says something else" (*Il.* 9.312). This very feat, on the other hand, is a specialty of Odysseus. When, in the *Odyssey*, the beggar is seated in front of his wife, who is weeping bitterly for her husband (19.210–212), "in his θυμός he felt compassion for his moaning wife, but his eyes stood fast like horn or iron in the eyelids: by cunning he

---

[24] See *TWNT, s.v.*

[25] See J. Bremmer, *The Early Greek Concept of the Soul* (Princeton: Princeton University Press, 1983).

concealed his tears." Something is happening "within" Odysseus, but this is not allowed to come out; what he is hiding is called by the word for outward reality, "tears," not "compassion" (though the poet could have said: ἔλεον δ' ὅ γε κεῦθε δόλοισιν instead of δόλωι δ' ὅ γε δάκρυα κεῦθεν). When the suitors have been slain, Odysseus does not allow Eurykleia to burst into a jubilant cry: "Within the θυμός, woman, you may rejoice, but restain yourself and do not give a piercing shriek: it is impious (οὐχ ὅσιον) to rejoice over slain men" (*Od.* 22.411–12). Ritual piety applies to outward behavior only; in the hidden regions, "within the θυμός," there is no constraint, one may rejoice "heartily."

There is a certain development in psychological expressions from the *Iliad* to the *Odyssey*. The next generations of poets, the so-called lyric poets, proceed on these lines, retaining still the unclear conglomerate of designations and the psychosomatic integration of feelings. Think of the famous ode of Sappho, translated by Catullus, which describes the shock of erotic experience: the heart in the breast is made to flutter, the tongue is broken, a fine fire runs underneath the skin, eyes and ears are failing, sweat is pouring down, there is trembling and pallor, next to death[26] —these are all "outward," corporeal events marking what is happening "inside," "beneath the skin;" there is no need for a word such as *psyche.*

Two passages more, from early tragedy, from Aeschylus' *Oresteia*: at the beginning of the *Eumenides*, we are at Delphi; Orestes has taken sanctuary at the altar of Apollo, and through the power of the god the pursuing Erinyes have fallen asleep around the altar. Enter the spectre (εἴδωλον) of Klytaimestra, who speaks to the sleeping demonesses: "Look in your heart at my wounds. For sleeping consciousness (εὕδουσα γὰρ φρήν) is illuminated with (special) eyes . . . ."[27] There is an "inner" view in dreaming, with eyes closed, which can perceive appearances, such as persons who have long been dead. We must translate φρήν by "consciousness" here, rather than by "diaphragm;" but to designate the "interior" the poet just uses καρδία, "heart," not "soul," and the "illumination" is due to special "eyes," not to mental power. Clairvoyance occurs by "heart."

---

[26] Sappho frg. 31 (Voigt, *Sappho et Alcaeus*); Catullus 51.

[27] Aesch. *Eum.* 103–5.

Another passage from the same trilogy: when Agamemnon, back from Troy, has entered his palace where the murder is being prepared, the uncanny feelings of the chorus concentrate in a remarkable song (1025–1033): "Were it not that one fate ordained by the gods does restrain another fate from winning the advantage, my heart, outrunning my tongue, would pour this out. But as it is, it roars in the dark, pained to the core (θυμαλγής) and without hope ever to unravel anything to timely purpose, out of my mind which is glowing under ashes:"

εἰ δὲ μὴ τεταγμένα
μοῖρα μοῖραν ἐκ θεῶν
εἶργε μὴ πλέον φέρειν,
προφθάσασα καρδία
γλῶσσαν ἂν τάδ' ἐξέχει.
νῦν δ' ὑπὸ σκότωι βρέμει
θυμαλγής τε καὶ οὐδὲν ἐπελπομέ–
 να ποτὲ καίριον ἐκτολυπεύσειν
ζωπυρουμένας φρενός.[28]

Feelings we can fully understand and share are expressed in a language which is as impressive as it is strange. Consciousness is "glowing under ashes," as if to be set ablaze; movements of the heart are felt to rise from normal beatings to a permanent roar of alarm, as if the heart would jump up, overrunning the checkpoint of the "tongue" and pour out its boiling contents, all the distress which has been assembling "in the heart;" yet it remains stable in spite of the uproar, falling back to hopelessness, unable to "develop" a timely solution, while the glowing fire remains alive. There is, after all, an order of fate sanctioned by the gods, boundaries established in the whole of the *kosmos*, which makes even the "inner" organs of the human being keep to their boundaries. It is magnificent how the poet succeeds in transmitting emotion, just because there is no separation of corporeal organs and activities of the "soul."

---

[28] Aesch. *Ag.* 1025–1033; E. Fraenkel hardly does justice to the passage (*Aeschylus. Agamemnon* [3 vols.; Oxford: Clarendon, 1950] 2. 463–466); see K. Reinhard, *Aischylos als Regisseur und Theologe* (Bern: A. Francke, 1949) 22–25; 162.

The situation is found to change radically just after Aeschylus. In consequence, as it appears, of a surprising interaction of religious lore and rational activities. There suddenly appears the doctrine of transmigration; Pythagoras is named as the first preacher of this dogma; but there is no first hand evidence preserved about this guru.[29] It is plausible that the idea of transmigration should have been borrowed from India—both India and Samos, Pythagoras' homeland, had just become parts of the Achaemenid empire, and Indians and Ionians were bound to meet when delivering their tributes at the New Year Festival at Persepolis. But there is not even documentary evidence for India at this period.

The idea of transmigration has remained popular to the present day; it is said to be accepted by a sizeable portion of modern Westerners. In Greek literature we first meet with a derogatory poem of Xenophanes, about 500 B.C.: Pythagoras, meeting a man who is beating his dog, says "Stop, do not hit him, for verily this is the *psyche* of a friend, whom I recognized, hearing his voice."[30] This text does not say that a man's soul is "in" the dog, but that Pythagoras hears the cries of the soul—and not of the dog's vocal cords. The word *psyche* marks identity, but its essence and whereabouts remain unclear. More precise is the word which soon appears in the context, ἔμψυχον, to characterize the "living being:" ἔμψυχον clearly says "there is a *psyche* within," ἐν—ψυχή; a parallel, possibly older expression is ἔνθεος, the word for "enthusiasm," which equally says: "there is a god within," ἐν—θεός.

We need not dwell on the characteristics of reincarnation, including the personal identity through many lives, the justice of retribution in the sequence of lives, an eventual judgment of the dead and intermediate sojourns in the beyond. We have diverging descriptions by Pindar, Empedocles and Herodotus in the fifth century; in the fourth century, we get the great myths of Plato. What matters in our context is that the individual essence of a person now

---

[29] See H. S. Long, "A Study of the Doctrine of Metempsychosis in Greece from Pythagoras to Plato" (Diss., Princeton University: 1948); K. von Fritz, "ΕΣΤΡΙΣ ΕΚΑΤΕΡΩΘΙ in Pindar's second Olympian and Pythagoras' Theory of Metempsychosis," *Phronesis* 2 (1957) 85–89; Walter Burkert, *Lore and Science in Ancient Pythagoreanism* (Cambridge, MA: Harvard University Press, 1972).

[30] Xenophanes DK B 7.

concentrates in one concept and designation, ψυχή, the "soul," which is taken to be independent from the "body," σῶμα, and may be contrasted with it, even if each living being must have a ψυχή "within" the body.

Empedocles, figuring as a prophet in his poem *Katharmoi*, even changes the perspective: The question is no longer what is "in" a living body, but how the transcendent *ego*, which may also be called *daimon*, chased from one incarnation to another, is provided with the respective body from time to time: This is a kind of garment presented by some superior power, which "clothes" the individual with the "unknown garment of flesh."[31] The body as a garment of the undying soul—this idea was to have a great progeny in Gnosticism; the parallel expression that the body is a "hut" or "dwelling-place" for the soul appears in the Pythagorean tradition and, strangely enough, in Democritus;[32] both the "hut" and the "clothing" imagery are taken up by St. Paul in 2 Corinthians.[33]

This does not mean that corporeal reality should vanish from view: the question how the soul can get into the body is asked in an absolutely realistic mood. The simplest answer is that souls are in the air, "borne with the winds" (Aristot. *an.* 407b 22), and thus one soul "slips into" the body with the first breath of a new-born being. Even more drastic is the affirmation that the soul is a snake, which slips out of sight at death; somehow then it must re-enter a mother's uterus during or before pregnancy. It was generally believed that the snakes possess the secret of immortality, since they can shed their "old age" by sloughing their skin. In Hesiod's *Catalogues*, in a fragmentary and unclear context, the sloughing of the snake is described in these words: "Only a *psyche* is left"—which evidently will build up a new body with the new skin.[34]

---

31 Empedocles DK B 126; see G. Zuntz, *Persephone: Three Essays on Religion and Thought in Magna Graecia* (Oxford: Clarendon, 1971) 256; 405–6.

32 Democritus DK B 37; 57; 187; 223; 270; 288; frequent in Ps.-Pythagorean writings, see the index in H. Thesleff, ed., *The Pythagorean Texts of the Hellenistic Period* (Abo: Akademie, 1965). Democritus knew about Pythagoras; there was a book *Pythagores* among his writings (DK A 33 I.1). According to Plato, the Orphics called the body a prison or preservation-place for the soul (*Crat.* 400c, *Phaed.* 62b).

33 2 Cor 5:1–4.

34 Hes. M-W frg. 204, 139.

Even before and without explicit doctrines of reincarnation, various ideas about the soul dwelling in a body, both realistic and uncanny, make their appearance in folklore. For Homer already, the *psyche* "flies out" at death—from where exactly, remains to be debated. There are characteristic tales how from the mouth of a sleeping person a mouse, a weasel, or some other small animal is seen to escape, which leaves the human as if dead for some time, until the animal is observed to come back; woe if anything is changed with regard to the sleeper: the soul will not find its way back, and the sleeper will remain dead. The model tale is in Paulus Diaconus, featuring a certain king Guntram; the Grimm brothers already collected many variants. A Greek version names Hermotimos of Klazomenai, whose ψυχή would go wandering while he was lying dead, until "the soul would enter again, after a certain time, as into a sheath (ἔλυτρον) and wake up the body." The story was known to Aristotle.[35]

Thus for a long time and in many places, the beliefs about a "soul" encapsulated "in" the body were firmly and realistically held; the use of Greek language, since the fourth century, conforms, as does normal philosophy, even if there remained to be discussed where exactly the soul could be found, in the heart, in the blood, in the arteries, in the brain, or dispersed through the whole of the body, and which should be its proper essence: breath, *pneuma*, fire, or some special element such as *aither*. Fantasy could dwell on the materialistic aspects: in Greek comedy it was said that Daedalus, artist of the miraculous, had poured mercury into hollow statues and thus made them alive: they had to be fettered to remain in their respective sanctuaries.[36] There is also the myth about the robot who was the guardian of Crete, Talos the giant, running around the island without pause: He was filled within with melted metal; Medea killed him by pulling out the plug.[37]

---

[35] See Bremmer, *The Early Greek Concept of the Soul*, 14–53. Guntram: Paul. Diac. 3.34; Hermotimos: Apollon. *hist. mir.* 3; cf. Aristot. *Metaph.* 984b19; Burkert, *Lore and Science in Ancient Pythagoreanism*, 152; J. Grimm and W. Grimm, *Deutsche Sagen* (repr. ed; Darmstadt: Wissenschaftliche Buchgesellschaft, 1977) nos. 248–250; 461; ii, *Deutsche Mythologie* (3 vols.; 4th ed. repr. Graz: Akademische Druck, 1953) 2. 906.

[36] Philippus comicus frg. 1 (R. Kassel and C. Austin, *Poetae Comici Graeci* [Berlin and New York: de Gruyter, 1983]) = Aristot. *an.* 406b15; cf. K. Meuli, *Gesammelte Schriften* (Basel: Schwabe, 1975) 1038–39.

[37] Apollodorus, *Bibliotheca* 1.9.26.

This is parody. This does not exclude that one may feel one's own soul within the body, as in the famous love epigram: "Kissing Agathon, I had my soul on my lips; poor thing, it came up as if it would pass over."[38] We may also assume that in the circle of a guru such as Pythagoras psychic experience was trained in a certain way, comparable to Yoga; Empedocles said about Pythagoras: "For whenever he reached out with all his diaphragm (πραπίδες), he easily saw each of all the things that are, in ten and even twenty generations of men." "Interior" organs are "reaching out" to grasp. Empedocles tells his pupil Pausanias, regarding the elements of knowledge: "If you stem them under your stout diaphragm (πραπίδες) and contemplate them with good will in pure exercises (μελέται), these will assuredly all be with you throughout your life, and you will gain many other things from them, for of themselves they will cause each to grow in its own way . . . ."[39] This is psychic exercise, uniting body and mind in an unbroken continuity.

Yet it was not only speculation and training à la Pythagoras that made the pair of "soul and body" current usage: more pervasive was the contribution of those whom we used to call sophists. Plato has done his best to denigrate them, but even his dialogues clearly show what their aim was and their merit to which we are all indebted: they invented and propagated higher education. They proposed to "make men better" for the competition of life through teaching. Competitive "virtue," *arete*, was the recognized goal in Greek morality; victory in one of the great athletic games was one of the obvious illustrations. Sportsmen no doubt are "made better" by training, *askesis*; by analogy, the sophists were offering new forms of "training." But what is the object of such "training"? Not muscles and sinews, as with a sportsman, but something else: the *psyche*. This is the programmatic text of an

---

[38] Diog. Laer. 3.32 = *Anthologia Palatina* 5.78; on the attribution to Plato, see W. Ludwig, "Plato's Love Epigrams," *GRBS* 4 (1963) 59–82; German text in G. Pfohl, ed., *Das Epigramm: Zur Geschichte einer inschriftlichen und literarischen Gattung* (Darmstadt: Wissenschaftliche Buchgesellschaft 1969) 56–84.

[39] Empedocles DK B 129; B 110; cf. Burkert, *Lore and Science in Ancient Pythagoreanism*, 137–38; P. Kingsley, *Ancient Philosophy, Mystery, and Magic. Empedocles and Pythagorean Tradition* (Oxford: Clarendon, 1995); on DK B 110, see esp. Rappe, *Archaische Leiberfahrung*, 179–186.

epigram in honour of Gorgias, set up at Olympia: "None of mortals ever found a more beautiful technique than Gorgias for training the soul for the contests of virtue."[40] "Training the soul for the contests of virtue," ἀσκῆσαι ψυχήν, this can be taken as a key word for the sophists' enterprise.

The principle is adopted and modfied by Socrates: in the midst of diverging and controversial testimonies about Socrates, this one formula is attested most firmly, by Plato, Xenophon, and others: The essential task for humans is "to care for the soul," ψυχῆς ἐπιμελεῖσθαι.[41] Plato has Socrates explain this in a compelling way in his *Apology*. "Caring for one's soul" in the Socratic sense, in order that it should be "as good as possible," this is more important than all the other goals for which people are normally striving, enjoyment, riches, power—these will forthwith be called "external goods" in philosophical ethics. This makes the "contests" recede to the background, as each is caring for his own soul; one may as well say "caring for oneself," ἑαυτοῦ ἐπιμελεῖσθαι. The "self" thus becomes separated from the body; it can even enter into opposition to the body: caring for the soul may lead to corporeal death, as Socrates shows in an exemplary way. This means unprecedented "freedom" of the soul: evil can do no harm to what is "good" (*Apol.* 30c).

With Socrates, we have entered the realm of Plato, whose dialogues bring Socrates to life. Plato created what philosophy has meant ever since. From this huge field, we are just taking up one aspect here. From Socrates who professed to know nothing, Plato makes the momentous step to the postulate of absolute knowledge, which, however, cannot refer to anything within our changing and unstable world. The existence of absolute knowlede is proved by the *a priori* character of mathematics: there is "being," "holding forever the same

---

[40] Gorgias DK 82 A 8 = Inschriften von Olympia no. 293 = P. A. Hansen, *Carmina Epigraphica Graeca Saeculi IV A. Chr. N.* (Berlin: de Gruyter, 1989) no. 830. Cf. A. Henrichs, "Zwei Fragmente über die Erziehung," *ZPE* 1 (1967) 45–46: τὸ μὲν σῶμα γυμνασίοις ἀσκεῖν, τὴν δὲ ψυχὴν λόγοις.

[41] Plat. *Ap.* 29d, 30a; (Plat.) *Alc.* I 128b–130e; Xenoph. *Mem.* 1.2.4, 19; used as a catchword in polemics against the Socratics by Isokrates 13.8. See W. K. C. Guthrie, *A History of Greek Philosophy*, vol. 3, *The Fifth-Century Enlightenment* (Cambridge: Cambridge University Press, 1969) 3. 467–473.

relation," available not to sensation but to thinking; yet the subject of thinking is "soul," ψυχή. Thus absolute knowledge is found to carry the soul, the subject of thought and cognition, out of the boundaries of its imperfect and perishable body and makes it plausible that soul itself should be close to absolute being, ungenerated and imperishable, immortal. "Immortality" was reserved to the gods in the traditional, "Homeric" view; it is made a property of the human soul in Plato's philosophy. "Immortality of the soul" has become the credo of Platonism and, for a long period, of Christianity too.

Plato sees the soul in opposition to the body, and he is inclined to accept the doctrine of transmigration, not as a dogma, but as a "probable myth." At any rate "soul" enjoys priority over against the body; most importantly, it is the soul that moves the body—an important proof for the soul's immortality is derived from reflecting on the "principle of motion."[42] For a human being, everything depends upon the status of the soul, which should be "beautiful" and "good." This gives enhanced relevance to the Socratic principle of "caring for the soul."

"Soul," for Plato, is not only separable from the body, but immaterial, incorporeal in the full sense; thus it is not only inaccessible to the senses, but also not confined to any place, neither "within" nor "without" the body. And yet descriptions in common language can hardly do without topography; the metaphors of "within" and "without," even if left behind in theory, prove to be indispensable in the practice of speaking or writing about the "soul." It is here that Plato opens up the dimension of the "inner" personality.

In *Charmides*, Plato introduces Charmides as a youth of oustanding beauty to the gymnasium. "What a beautiful face," Chairephon says; the answer is: "Well, if he will consent to undress, you will not even see his face, so beautiful is he in his totality." This is a homoerotic remark about nudity at the verge of indecency. Of course we are curious about what is underneath the clothes. But Socrates immediately goes further, "Let us undress him first as to his other properties," he says, "and have

---

[42] Plat. *Phaedr.* 245c-e; cf. *Leg.* 894b–896d. On the problems of the soul's immortality within Plato's philosophy, see T. A. Szlezák, "Unsterblichkeit und Trichotomie der Seele im zehnten Buch der Politeia," *Phronesis* 21 (1976) 31–58.

a look at his soul, before contemplating his body."[43] As the body is hiding in the clothes, the soul seems to be hiding in the body; it is the soul which is more interesting, says Socrates; he is about to lay it bare in philosophical discourse.

At the end of *Gorgias,* the judgment of the dead is described in the form of myth. This judgment will definitely decide which humans are either good or bad, against the fascinating thesis of Kallikles that the great personality, by transcending and destroying the ridiculous morality of the weaker ones, is really admirable, "beautiful," and "good." But normal human beings, Socrates holds, are unfit to become judges in this context, "because they have their eyes, ears, and their whole body hanging as a cover before their soul." The soul is encapsulated in an envelope which hinders clear sight; even the eyes are obstacles rather than instruments for seeing. Hence "it is necessary to judge people in the state of nakedness, that is, death; and the judge must be naked too, contemplating with his soul the soul of each person."[44] What a *gymnasion* of the dead! The body itself is the decisive wrapping, the garment of the soul as Empedocles had it. Cognition and judgment concern what has been inside, the "pure" soul.

In the *Symposion,* the "interiors" are presented in another memorable image, Socrates himself setting the example. Socrates, Alkibiades explains, is similar to a wooden Silenus as it can be found in a carpenter's shop, with a bald head, a flat nose, ridiculous of appearance and anything but beautiful; yet if such a Silenus is opened, it is found to contain statues of gods within. We must admit we do not know from other sources about wooden boxes of this kind, but the simile is unmistakeable.[45] Once more Plato makes the corporeal appearance the "outside" in opposition to what is "within;" and the "interior" alone is valuable, even divine. It is the "soul" of Socrates which has the unique effect on others, teaching and effecting the "good." Plato thus has created the concept of "inner values"—a formula often misused and ridiculed since.

---

[43] Plat. *Charm.* 154de.

[44] Plat. *Gorg.* 523d. Cf. E. R. Dodds, *Plato. Gorgias* (Oxford: Clarendon, 1957) 372–78.

[45] Plat. *Symp.* 215ab. One may compare the Aesopian fable about gold contained in a statue of Hermes; see Babrius 119 (B. E. Perry, *Aesopica,* vol. 1, *Greek and Latin Texts* [Urbana, IL: University of Illinois Press, 1952] 432, no. 285).

Of course, an inverse relation between inside and outside is equally possible. The corporeal beauty of Alkibiades or Charmides does not guarantee the quality of the "inner person." In the *Alkibiades* of Aeschines, Alkibiades, perfectly endowed with all the outward values, is made to burst into tears, as Socrates is pointing out his inner deficit.[46] More drastic is the language of Jesus when he calls the lawyers and Pharisees hypocrites: "like tombs," he says, "covered with whitewash: they look good from outside, but inside they are full of dead men's bones and all kinds of filth."[47]

The formula "the inner human being" finally comes to the surface in Plato's *Politeia*. In this dialogue Plato is asking the basic question of morality: What does it help a person to be moral? Will not the immoral be better off in all circumstances? Plato's answer is that the soul of each one is in need of a well-ordered interior system, of "inner" justice. This is more important than any outward success or catastrophe. This point is clarified by constructing the system of society, the state, with its functions of nourishment, defence, and rulership—Plato is bold enough to assign rulership to philosophy. If the classes fulfill their necessary functions, the state is well-ordered and "just." The same is true for what happens "within" a single person (435e): there are three functions of the soul, three parts, desire, courage, and the thinking mind. These parts may well be in conflict with each other; desirable is their harmonious collaboration, which is "justice," not as an "outward" but as an "inner activity."[48] This makes a soul qualify as "good" in all respects.

The parallel established between state and soul opens up quite a new level of metaphorical language to illustrate the "inner" dimensions, leaving far behind the old popular anatomy of "heart" and "bile." There were highly developed forms of political discourse in Greek, with descriptions of stable systems and analysis of violent social struggle; the pattern of three possible constitutions had long been developed, monarchy or tyranny, oligarchy, and democracy, and traumatic experience of revolutions and counter-revolutions was not

---

[46] Aischines frgs. 46, 51, 52 (G. Giannantoni, *Socratis et Socraticorum Reliquiae* [4 vols.; Naples: Bibliopolis, 1990] 2. 606, 609).

[47] Matt 28:27, ἔσωθεν—ἔξωθεν; cf. Acts 23:3.

[48] Plat. *Polit.* 443c: ἐκτὸς πρᾶξις—ἡ ἐντός.

lacking in the host of Greek city-states. This would provide narrative models to describe all kinds of dramatic events and conflicts, of breakdown and dominance within the soul. *Psyche* becomes a battlefield in Platonic language, with Platonizing presuppositions: "If somebody thinks he is suffering wrong, doesn't *thymos* boil in him and rage and take sides with what he considers just, and through hunger and cold and all such sufferings, enduring this, he strives for victory, and he does not desist from his noble goals until he either achieves the end or has to die; or, like a dog by his shepherd, he is called back by reason, which is present with him, and becomes mild and tractable again." This is the "inner" conflict of rage and reason, recalling the "barking heart" of Odysseus—the Homeric verse is explicitly quoted—and yet surpassing it by far in dramatic language.[49]

Later on, in the eighth book, psychology turns into politics: Plato states that to each form of constitution a certain type of man corresponds, the oligarchic, the tyrannic, and the democratic personality. Each of them is defective as against the ideal type. But just as constitutions change in a certain sequence, there is a parallel process of depravity in humans. With special delight in poignant satire, Plato presents democracy and the democratic personality, the excess of freedom—critics of contemporary society often cannot refrain from quoting from these passages. The oligarchic personality turns democratic, Plato says, if a youth, brought up in parsimony and without proper education, comes to taste the full varieties of pleasure; this is reinforced "from without" by problematic friends, while he is still waging "battle with himself within himself;"[50] in the process, the multitude of pleasures may increase, so that some quasi-democratic majority comes into existence "within this man;" and "finally this majority conquers the acropolis of the soul of this youth, because they found out that this acropolis was not occupied by learning, by beautiful activities, by true doctrines, which are the best guardians and protectors in the thoughts of men. . . . False and preposterous doctrines and opinions have rushed up instead of these, and have occupied the place; they close the doors of the royal wall within this man, they do not let pass any auxiliary force. . . . Shame is called silliness by them,

---

49 Plat. *Resp.* 440cd, 441b.

50 Plat. *Resp.* 560a: μάχη ἐν αὐτῶι πρὸς αὐτόν.

and ignominiously thrown out into exile, moderation is called cowardice, is bespattered with mud and driven out. . ." (560b-d). The conquest of the acropolis is followed by the exile of the opponents; then the image changes from civil war to mystery initiation: "They make void of all this the soul of the person who is possessed by them and initiated with great rituals, and they purify it, and afterwards they introduce, brilliant and with a great chorus, hybris, anarchy, prodigality, and shamelessness, crowned with wreaths and praised by them in eulogy. . ." (560d-e).[51] The dramatic change of personality is presented in the image of a perverse exorcism: purification first, to create the "void," which can be filled subsequently by new powers, hailed by the jubilant chorus of the initiates.

I am reminded by this passage of a strange saying of Jesus:[52] "When the unclean spirit goes out of the man, it passes through desert places seeking rest, and does not find it. Then it says, 'I shall go back to the house from whence I came;' and arriving, it finds the house in a state of holiday, cleaned and adorned; then it goes and takes with itself seven other spirits that are worse than itself, and they come in and take up their dwelling there; and the final state of this man becomes worse than the first." This is the same imagery, the same topology, one might say, of psychic catastrophe: make the house void and clean, as if in preparation for a festival, to receive new and noble hosts. Yet instead of divine powers evil ones are found to enter. The context is different, of course; Jesus is describing the failure of therapy, the failure of exorcism—which, as a healer, he may have experienced—whereas Plato has a more general event of psychic depravation. What is common is the imagery of an enclosed "inner" space, a "house" where the dramatic conflicts are going on.

Plato goes on to describe further reversals within the soul, especially the change from the democratic to the tyrannic personality. We need not rehearse this in detail; let us quote the final summary (588d): "Imagine one figure," Socrates says, "of a multiple, many-headed beast, bearing round about the heads of both tame and of wild animals, which can change itself and make grow from itself all that. . . . Imagine

---

[51] Plat. *Resp.* 560de; cf. Walter Burkert, *Ancient Mystery Cults* (Cambridge, MA: Harvard University Press, 1987) 97.

[52] Matt 12:43–45, shorter in Luke 11:24–26.

one other figure: a lion, and finally, a man. . . . Now combine these three figures into one, so that somehow they should grow together. . . . Now construct round about them from without the figure of one being, a human being, so that for him who cannot see the inside, but only the outward wrappings, it should appear to be just one animal, the human animal." This is the human being as constructed before, with the tripartite soul: the mutiple desires, the lion's courage, and the very property of humanity, the thinking mind. It is all important, Plato says, not to feed the multiple animal too much, nor even the lion, but the human part: "It is useful to do and to say everything from which this part of the human, the inner human being, will be strongest (ὅθεν τοῦ ἀνθρώπου ὁ ἐντὸς ἄνθρωπος ἔσται ἐγκρατέστατος); and for that many-headed creature he will care like a farmer, feeding and fondling the tame parts, but not allowing the wild parts to grow, making his ally the lion's nature."[53] This is a new chapter of mythology transferred to the "inside," while the "exterior" is being constructed by secondary acts. The "inner human being" is the verily human part of humans; Plato is adamant that this is the rational part, and that it should dominate the other constituents—in contrast to what moderns would claim to be the "inner" and "authentic" feelings undermining the pale façade of "rationality." Plato seems to be forgetting that it is in fact the multi-headed creature which feeds the human partner, which cares for the very basis of individual life in all its complexity; there is no use for a dead lion. Well, Plato does acknowledge that it is the evils of the body that make us die, not the evils of the soul, which allow certain people to go on living quite happily. The soul is immortal, Plato insists; thus it is all the worse to create immortal evil.

Hellenistic philosophy has followed Plato in speaking of the "inner" dimensions which are relevant for a person's freedom and responsibility. Many impressive formulations recur in post-Hellenistic authors such as Seneca, Epictetus and Marcus Aurelius. Seneca, for example, states that there is no outward defence which will ward off every attack of fortune. Hence protection must be built up "inside:" *nullus* . . .

---

[53] Plat. *Resp.* 589a. This very passage, in a Coptic redaction, is contained in the Nag Hammadi Library, Codex VI, tractate 5 (Robinson, *Nag Hammadi Libary*, 318–20).

inexpugnabilis murus est. intus instruamur.[54] The "soul inside" may may be raised to even higher rank as "spirit" or "god" dwelling "inside" the human person, so that the self is turned into a "temple" of the sacred.[55] Paul and others, especially Gnostics, were following the lead of popular philosophy in adopting these formulas, including the "inner human being," ὁ ἔσω ἄνθρωπος.[56]

Still, as said already in the introduction, we can hardly acquiesce in the triumph of progress, having arrived at the discovery of the "inner" dimensions of the "soul," the "inner human being" with all its complexity and almost unlimited opportunities. "Ouside" reality does not cease to make itself felt, and deplorable or even horrifying consequences of a total victory of the "inner self" are not lacking.

Aristotle, for one, did not follow Plato in the constructs of an "inner world." There is a characteristic passage from the lost *Protreptikos*, which still tries to recommend higher values as against the beautiful body, such as that of Alcibiades: "If one were sharp-eyed as Lynkeus, who could see through walls and trees—who would ever feel the sight (of a human) was bearable, if he could see of what horrible things a human is composed?"[57] Aristotle, the doctor's son, knows about anatomy; contemplating the "inside" of the human animal, he finds nothing but strange and disconcerting organs: we are back to heart and liver, gall-bladder, bowels and diaphragm. We cannot get rid of reality, even if Aristotle too proposes to understand this by recourse to the higher principles of Nature.

Let us close with a sentence of Plato, which is aiming at an ideal synthesis of "inside" and "outside." This is the final prayer to Pan and the Nymphs that Socrates pronounces at the Ilissos river: "Give me that

---

[54] Sen. *Ep.* 74.19. The "good" and happiness are "within" the person, *introrsum*: *Ep.* 119.11; cf. 7.12; 23.5; not *extrinsecus*: *Ep.* 9.15. Epictet. *Diss.* 2.5.5: the "good" is ἔσω ἐν τοῖς ἐμοῖς; cf. 3.15.13; conscience is a "seer (*mantis*) within," 2.7.3. M. Ant. 7.59: ἔνδον ἡ πηγὴ τοῦ ἀγαθοῦ.

[55] Epictet. *Diss.* 2.8.11–13: "you are carrying a god in yourself." For Plotinus it is a "common idea" (κοινὴ ἔννοια) that everybody has a "god" in himself (τὸν ἐν ἑκάστωι θεόν): *Enn.* 6.5.1.

[56] Paul, Rom 7:22; 2 Cor 4:16; Eph 3:16. See notes 2, 6 and 53. The image of the "temple:" Paul 1 Cor 3:16; 6:19; 2 Cor 6:16; cf. *Barn.* 16:8, 10; *TWNT* 4.890–91.

[57] V. Rose, ed., *Aristotelis. Fragmenta* (3d. ed; Leipzig: Teubner, 1886) Fr. 59 = W. D. Ross, ed. *Aristotelis. Fragmenta Selecta* (Oxford: Clarendon, 1955) *Protrepticus* Fr. 10a (Iambl. *Protr.* 47.5; Boeth. *Cons.* 3.8).

I become beautiful in the inner dimension; and what I have outside, be tied in friendship to what is inside."[58] Let us hope for friendship and harmony in what is tied together to keep the human person alive.

Modern science, following Aristotle, is on its triumphant way to the disclosure of the tiniest details of corporeal reality, especially the functions of nerves and brain, the basis of feelings and moods, perceptions and thoughts. This means that the deconstruction of Platonic dualism is continuing. There does not seem to be any "interior" hiding place left for "higher" entities within the human animal. This leaves philosophy, which means the "knowledge of things divine and human," according to the Stoic definition, with a momentous challenge: how to preserve the full dimensions of humanity.

---

[58] Plat. *Phaedr.* 279bc; cf. K. Gaiser, "Das Gold der Weisheit. Zum Gebet des Philosophen am Schluß des *Phaidros*," *RhM* 132 (1989) 105–40.

Inner and Outer Selves in Harmony

Elizabeth Asmis

Walter Burkert has treated us to a fascinating study, enriched with a marvelous array of examples. The way he has put together the examples illuminates each one of them. The topic appears more interesting than ever. Instead of simply tracing a linear development, Burkert shows us a series of explorations, each of which is intriguing in its own right. The inner person appears multi-faceted, a worthy subject for further exploration. Burkert regrets the possible loss of the inner self to the outer body; and he leaves us with the challenge of rediscovering the self.

I would like to take up this challenge by adding a few more examples. In response to Burkert's powerful defence of the inner self, I feel compelled to offer a little help to the body. I don't disagree with any part of Burkert's analysis. I would just like to shift the balance a little, and perhaps even help out the inner self in this process.

First, I can't resist trying out an answer to a question that Burkert has provocatively inserted in his paper. Burkert uses the little word "strangely" in reference to Democritus' metaphor of the hut. He says: "the . . . expression that the body is a 'hut' or 'dwelling-place' for the soul appears in the Pythagorean tradtion and, strangely enough, in Democritus." I suspect Burkert has an answer that he'd like us to puzzle out for ourselves. So here goes. What is so strange about Democritus' comparison of the body to a hut? Burkert suggests a parallel with the metaphor of the garment; I wonder what else the metaphor of the hut captures. Democritus' term is σκῆνος, which is related to σκηνή, "tent," and has the basic meaning of "hut" or "tent." What is good about a hut or tent is that it serves as a shelter. It is a protective environment that allows activity to go on within. A garment, too, protects, but it is primarily a cover, and it can be used to deceive. A hut is simply functional: it does not pose. Its task is to provide a safe space for the occupant. It makes few demands, as Democritus points out; its value, he says, lies in its strength.

Democritus stands out among Greek philosophers for his innovative and vivid use of metaphors. He has the inanimate atoms groping, for example, toward each other and turning in rhythmic patterns (DK 68 A 38); the atoms crowd one another like a throng in the marketplace (DK 68 A 93a). In another use of the term σκῆνος, he compares the womb to a hut, providing shelter for the embryo (DK 68 A 152); if the shelter is dissolved, the embryo aborts.

What special sense, then, did he pick out by the comparing the body to a "hut"? Democritus believed that the soul, like everything else, is atoms. The soul-atoms are especially fine, fiery atoms, interspersed with the atoms of the body in such a way as to infuse it with life. Aristotle made fun of this idea, as Burkert reminds us, by saying that this is like pouring mercury into the body (*an.* 406b15–22). Aristotle here resorts to the commonplace metaphor of the body as a vessel. Democritus' hut, though, carries a more specialized sense. We live, Democritus explains, by drawing in breath from the environment; the incoming atoms replenish the atoms that continually leave the body. Death comes when the body can no longer hold the atoms inside; they rush out, bombarded by atoms from outside (Aristot. *De respiratione* 471b). The body no longer resists the pressure from outside and lets the inner breath escape.

If we put together the theory and the metaphor, the image that comes to mind is that of a strong, cold wind battering the hut and breaking down its protective barrier, so that the inner warmth escapes. We might go further and say that the hut gives each individual a personal space in the universe: it provides a shelter for each person to shape his own life. Each occupant warms a fire within the hut, so to speak, warding off the blows from outside. However inert in itself, the body is a framework that makes possible individual life.

Indebted to Democritus, Epicurus also proposed an atomist theory of the soul. In place of Democritus' metaphor of the hut, he uses the more prosaic term "sheltered." The soul, he says, is "sheltered" by the rest of the atomic compound (*Men.* 64–65). The verb is στεγάζειν, which can often be translated simply as "enclose," but whose primary meaning is to "provide a roof." In typical fashion Epicurus has diluted Democritus' metaphor, but the basic idea is the same: the body provides a protective cover that allows the soul to exercise its function.

Democrtius' view of the body as a hut makes a striking contrast with another metaphor: the comparison of the body to a tomb. Here is an enclosure of a very different sort. The Greek saying has a powerful ring: σῶμα σῆμα; "the body is a tomb." The view is attributed to the Pythgorean Philolaus (Clement of Alexandria, DK 44 B 22). Socrates in Plato's *Gorgias* (493a2) says that he heard it from some wise man. The saying is also mentioned in Plato's *Cratylus* (400c1–2) as an explanation of the word σῶμα. With just a little change of vowel, Socrates suggests, the term σῶμα, "body," is the same as σῆμα, "tomb." Another explanation, which is attributed to the Orphics, is that the word is derived from the verb σῴζειν (*Crat.* 400c4–9). Paradoxically, the body is thought to save the soul by serving as a prison that punishes the soul for its sins. In the *Phaedo*, Plato stresses the life-destroying force of this prison: bound within the body, the soul is corrupted by it. What humans must do to save the life of the soul is to practice the death of the body.

As a tomb, the body provides the opposite kind of housing from the hut: whereas the hut shelters life, the tomb encloses death. It is tempting to speculate that Democritus knew the well known saying σῶμα σῆμα and responded to it by proclaiming: σῶμα σκῆνος, "the body is a hut:" the body does not destroy life, it shelters it.

In the *Phaedo*, Plato presents a stark dichotomy between soul and body: the soul is the inner self, corrupted by the body and yearning to escape from it. In the *Republic* and elsewhere, he offers a more complicated view of the relationship between body and soul. Dividing the soul into three parts, he offers a gradation of interaction between the soul and the body. The intellect is now separated off as the innermost soul. At the very interface with the body is the desiring soul; it is necessarily corrupted by the body. In the middle is the spirited part, which can join forces with either the desiderative or the intellectual part of the soul. Plato compares the desiderative part to a many-headed monster, the spirit to a lion, and the intellect to a human being; all is wrapped up in the guise of a single human figure. The intellect is the real self; and it may escape corruption by dominating the desiderative part. Plato now gives the human being the opportunity to save the soul in this life by exerting power over the body. The body is still a corrupting force, but it is at a remove from the innermost self. In the best case, as Alcibiades depicts Socrates in the *Symposium*, the intellectual part exists as a kind of divinity within us.

In the *Republic* and elsewhere, Plato doesn't view the body simply as a hindrance: it offers some help to the intellect, but it does this in the context of having messed up the intellect. In the *Timaeus*, Plato shows us how thoroughly perturbed the soul becomes when encased in the body. But he also extends it some powerful help. A human being can reintroduce order into the soul by attuning it to the motions of the soul that extends through the universe as a whole. The inner being overcomes the body by joining forces with the outer world.

Let us return for a moment to the Epicurean soul. Here, too, we have an innermost soul, the intellect. While the soul as a whole is spread throughout the body, the intellect is concentrated within the heart as a particularly fine network of atoms. The body provides a protective barrier that allows the soul and intellect to stay together and ward off a hostile environment. Chaos reigns outside the person: there is increasing order and power as we move to the innermost mind. Anticipating Seneca's exhortation to build our defences inside the walls, Lucretius describes the innermost mind as the guardian within who protects the barriers of life (*On the Nature of Things* 3.396–97; cf. 3.324)

In opposition to both the atomists and Plato, the Stoics offered a different image of the soul. I will conclude with this metaphor; and it is perhaps the most strange. The Stoics compared the soul to an octopus (Aetius, *SVF* 2.827). The octopus has one head and seven tentacles (not eight, as we define it; the Greek word for "octopus" is simply πολύπους, "many-foot"). The head stands for the command center, the mind. The Stoics are not known for their sense of poetry or their humor. But to fully appreciate this image, we must visualize the octopus head, together with the sac-like trunk, as forming a big tubular shape in the middle, surmounted by two prominent eyes. The eyes are sharp-sighted. The seven long, sinuous tentacles stand for the seven functions of the soul: the five senses, speech, and reproduction. Each of these functions has its own bodily organ. As Aristotle also knew, one of the tentacles does indeed serve for reproduction (*Hist. An.* 524a9). Just like the octopus head, the Stoic intellect has its own functions, but it also reaches out through the body to exercise other functions. The soul is a unity allowing the mind to receive information from the body and pass back commands from itself. The mind is not besieged by the body; it smoothly controls it.

The Stoics' many-footed octopus offers an imaginative response to Plato's composite beast. Our desires are not so many animal heads, threatening to lurch out of control; they are just feet, responding to directions from a command center. Aristotle compares the feet of an octopus to hands. Indeed, the octopus' limbs may be viewed as so many groping instruments, just as Empedocles viewed the senses of the body (DK 31 B 2 and 3). There is no wild lion; the closest counterpart is the jet of black ink that the octopus emits to get away from its enemies. In the Stoic metaphor, the inner self is smoothly integrated with the body. The octopus head is perhaps unappealing as a representation of the inner self. But there is a payoff: mind and body are seen to work together. And not only that: they are smoothly integrated with the entire environment. The body is not interposed between mind and the universe as an obstruction. There is an unbroken continuity between innermost self and outermost environment. The mind, together with the body, is in harmony with the deity that suffuses the entire world.

This bit of "aquatic" theology (if you allow me) seems to fit our own ecological age. It certainly did not commend itself to the later Stoics, who preferred Plato's image of the god within us. Epictetus and Marcus Aurelius, in particular, thought of the body as something vile, a shell to be discarded, a mixture of mud and blood and gore. But here I would like to remind you of a story told by Aristotle (*Part. An.* 645a17–21). In defence of the study of blood, flesh, bones, and the lower animals in general, he quotes the words of Heraclitus to some friends who were hesitating as they entered the lowly hut in which he was warming himself by the stove: "Here too are gods."

Seneca's Collection of Epistles: A Medium of Philosophical Communication

Hildegard Cancik-Lindemaier

Introduction

It is not the least among Hans Dieter Betz's achievements that he has drawn the attention of theologians—and not of theologians alone—to the "high-level philosophical reflection" of "Greek and Roman philosophers" in the Hellenistic and Roman periods. He pleads for a re-evaluation of Plutarch against the judgement of philologists who spoke favourably of his "warm, kind, and human personality," but disregarded the writings of the 'epigone' and did not appreciate the task "of interpreting Greek philosophical and ethical traditions to the educated society" of the Romans.[1]

I propose to inquire more closely about the Roman element in philosophical thinking and practising, that is, to consider not only Romans writing in Greek, like Mestrius Plutarchus, but also Latin-speaking Romans. This inquiry, it seems to me, necessitates a revision of the term 'popular philosophy' and a focus on the theoretical differences persisting in that apparent *koinon* of philosophers,[2] taking "seriously" both Plutarch's polemic distance from Stoicism and Seneca's paradoxical synthesis of Stoic and Epicurean ideas.

In this essay I approach the interpretation of Seneca's epistles in three steps: considering first, briefly, the notion of moral progress within the Stoic system, second Seneca as an independant Stoic philosopher, and finally the epistles as a medium for expressing and communicating moral progress.

§1 A Philosophy of moral progress

---

[1] H. D. Betz, ed., *Plutarch's Ethical Writings and Early Christian Literature* (SCHNT 4; Leiden: Brill, 1978) 4–5, referring esp. to Konrat Ziegler and Eduard Zeller, and p. 6. I am grateful to Julia Mentan (of Seattle and Tübingen) for having revised my English version.

[2] "Elements drawn mainly from the Platonic, Peripatetic and Stoic schools had become amalgamated to a conglomerate of ideas which Plutarch shared" (Betz, *Plutarch's Ethical Writings*, 6, referring generally to D. Babut).

§1.1 The Concept of Nature: φύσις—*natura*

a) In Stoic anthropology time is an important factor. The individual passes through different phases, until the logos has reached full growth. In Stoic ethics the concept of progress—προκοπή—corresponds to this physical or biological evolution. Being a natural event, προκοπή was held to be an ἀδιάφορον,[3] that is, morally neither good nor bad and thus, of course, subject to change in time, whereas there is no alteration in the concept of good or virtue itself, neither by time nor by quantity. Consequently, time is of decisive importance in Seneca's philosophy—philosophy to be taken *au pied de la lettre* as striving for wisdom, not the status of being wise.

Nature, as the Stoics conceived it, is the organizing principle in a system of relations and functions; this organizing principle is itself dynamic; it has inscribed time-indexes. This is true for the nature of humans, the animal kingdom and finally the all-embracing system of the world (κόσμος).[4] The Stoics, then, did not consider the notion of "nature" and the determinations derived from it, such as "natural, given by nature, according to nature" (κατὰ φύσιν, φυσικός), as if it meant a complete set of fixed aptitudes with inherent objectives.

b) Expressions such as "by nature, natural, in a natural way" are meant to incorporate the phenomena into the comprehensive system which sustains and explains their existence (materialism, monism). Thus they are described as facts which can be verified by observation,[5] but they are not bound to an automatism which has been fixed once and for all. The whole is a flexible structure in which many factors in different phases cooperate with one another.

c) The category of κατὰ φύσιν is relative. It has different meanings according to the status of a being: for an animal κατὰ φύσιν is κατὰ

---

[3] More precisely, it is a προηγμένον: *SVF* III frg. 127 (Diog. Laer. 7. 106); III frg. 136 (Stob. *Ecl.* 2.80.22); III frg. 135 (Diog. Laer. 7.107): προηγμένα δι' αὐτά (in opposition to δι' ἕτερα).

[4] See J. M. Rist, "Three Stoic Views of Time," *Stoic Philosophy* (Cambridge: Cambridge University Press, 1980) 273–288; a more doxographical survey: J. Blänsdorf, *Das Paradoxon der Zeit* (Heidelberger Texte. Didaktische Reihe 13; Freiburg and Würzburg: Ploetz, 1983) 9–18.

[5] An example taken from Sen. *Ep.* 121.19: chickens do not flee from geese, but from hawks; this is a strategy of self-preservation, which is prior to any experience of threat.

τὴν ὁρμήν, according to the drive; for beings endowed with reason, however, it means τὸ κατὰ λόγον ζῆν ὀρθῶς—to live according to the λόγος in the right way.[6]

d) This proportion is valid also for the lifetime of an individual. The logos of a child is not yet fully developed; the category of what is, for a child, κατὰ φύσιν corresponds to that of an animal.[7] This is why a child can aspire to what—according to his or her nature—is advantageous and avoid what is harmful. With regard to ethics, however, these actions are intermediates—μέσα—since reason, which makes an action a moral one, is not yet fully developed.[8] The more the individual evolves in age and education, the more his or her understanding, will, decision, and activity become pronounced. "By nature" does not mean "automatically;" there is no hidden biologism in ethics.

§1.2 *prima conciliatio*—οἰκείωσις

a) The condition which makes possible a life "according to nature" is given by nature. The Stoic doctrine of οἰκείωσις—*prima conciliatio*—"being and becoming akin to oneself," means that every living being, from the very moment of his or her birth onward, is concerned about conserving him or herself and that he or she is aware of it.[9] As John Rist[10] has pointed out, this theory is the logically necessary basis for the distinction between those "indifferent things," ἀδιάφορα—*indifferentia,* which are to be preferred (προηγμένα) and those which are to be rejected (ἀποπροηγμένα).

---

6 Diog. Laer. 7.86: τὸ κατὰ λόγον ζῆν ὀρθῶς γίνεσθαι (τοῖς λογικοῖς) κατὰ φύσιν.

7 Sen. *Ep.* 124.9.

8 *SVF* III frg. 183 (Cic. *Fin.* 3.6.22): *non inest in primis naturae conciliationibus honesta actio.*

9 For a short survey, see P. Steinmetz, "Die Stoa," *Grundriss der Geschichte der Philosophie. Begründet von F. Ueberweg. Völlig neu bearbeitete Ausgabe. Die Philosophie der Antike* (vol. 4.2; ed. H. Flashar; Basel: Schwabe, 1994) 613–15 and 545 on Zeno. Cf. in particular Sen. *Ep.* 121.14 and *SVF* III frgs. 178–183; further *SVF* II frg. 724 (Plut. *Stoic. Rep.* 1038b): ἡ γὰρ οἰκείωσις αἴσθησις ἔοικε τοῦ οἰκείου καὶ ἀντίληψις εἶναι.

10 Rist, *Stoic Philosophy*, 68–74, with discussion of different views proposed and rejection of Dirlmeier's thesis of peripatetic origin.

b) The principle of οἰκείωσις—*prima conciliatio*—operates in every phase of the individual's evolution. Every new level preserves the preceding ones.[11] The constitution of the self has to be accomplished anew on every level, first of all in the elementary sense of biology. As soon as the logos is fully developed, that is, at the end of childhood, about the fourteenth year, the mental and ethical evolution commences.[12]

§1.3 Virtue—the Sage—Proceeding towards Virtue (ἀρετή—ὁ σοφός—προκοπή)

a) The ethics of the Stoics is said to be "rigid," above all because they do not admit any differences of quantity or grades within virtue. One cannot be more or less virtuous; virtue is not defined, with Aristotle, as the middle between two extremes, nor the culmination of a continuum. There is a neat distinction which does not admit any compromise: either one is virtuous, or one is not;[13] and if one is virtuous, one possesses all virtues at once: there is but *one* virtue.

b) Possession of virtue, and that means total absence of evil, is that which characterizes the Stoic sage (ὁ σοφός), and him alone. This concept evoked mockery and derision in ancient times which has continued to the present day. Attributes like ἀπάθεια, ἀταραξία, and αὐτάρκεια have constantly been misunderstood, or at least interpreted *in malam partem*. Nietzsche, for example, who should have known better—being an expert on Diogenes Laertius—did not shy away from writing "der stoische Hornochs"—the Stoic blockhead.[14] In

---

[11] *SVF* III frgs. 186–188 (Cicero, *Fin.* 3).

[12] *SVF* I frg. 149 (= II frg. 835); II frgs. 83; 764. For a comprehensive discussion, see Maximilian Forschner, *Die stoische Ethik. Über den Zusammenhang von Natur-, Sprach- und Moralphilosophie im altstoischen System* (2d ed.; Darmstadt: Wissenschaftliche Buchgesellschaft, 1995) 144–159.

[13] See, e.g., Seneca, *Ep.* 66.7: *Ceterum multae eius* [sc. of an *animus* which has become identical with *virtus*] *species sunt, quae pro vitae varietate et actionibus explicantur: nec minor fit aut maior ipsa. Decrescere enim summum bonum non potest nec virtuti ire retro licet: sed in alias atque alias qualitates convertitur ad rerum quas actura est, habitum figurata.* For a historical analysis of these dogmata, see H. J. Kraemer, *Platonismus und die hellenistische Philosophie* (Berlin and New York: de Gruyter, 1971) 227–29. Sen. (*Ep.* 66) gives an elaborate discussion of the equality of all goods; in this letter, a series of dogmatic considerations beginning with *Ep.* 65 is continued.

[14] Posthumous papers of the winter of 1887–88: *Friedrich Nietzsche. Sämtliche Werke. Kritische Studienausgabe* (ed. G. Colli and M. Montinari; München: Deutscher

a word, the construct called ὁ σοφός is probably the most famous of the so called "Stoic paradoxes".[15]

It is not possible here and would be beyond my competence to delineate the systematic premises of this construction; let me only emphasize two points. First: the Stoics insisted on the reality and materiality of virtue. That is why they insist on the reality of the σοφός, albeit a "hidden" reality.[16] Second: the Stoics did not give way to the dualistic temptation. They insisted on the principal goodness of nature, also of human nature. Hence the particular hostility in the controversy between orthodox ecclesiastical writers and the so called Pelagians, especially between Augustine and Julian of Eclanum.[17]

§1.4 Time—Progress—Evolution in Stoic anthropology

a) Given the premise that there can only be a sudden and unmediated change from vice to virtue, an evolution seems to be excluded.[18] There is, indeed, no evolution within virtuousness itself; there is, however, progress (προκόπτειν) on the way that leads towards virtuousness.[19] Virtuousness is a state of mind (διάθεσις)[20] in

---

Taschenbuch Verlag, 1980) 13. 125; Stoicism as "a work of Semites," ibid., 114. Nietzsche, to be sure, had once known better: see the letter to his friend Carl v. Gersdorff, February, 20th, 1867, speaking about his disquisitions on Diogenes Laertius: "Wenn ich Dir eine Lektüre empfehlen darf, die Dich zugleich an das Alterthum fesselt und an Schopenhauer erinnert, so nimm einmal die epistulae morales des Seneca vor" (*Friedrich Nietzsche. Sämtliche Briefe. Kritische Studienausgabe* [ed. G. Colli and M. Montinari; München: Deutscher Taschenbuch Verlag, 1986] 2. 201).

15 The fragments put together in *SVF* III, chap. IX, *de sapiente et insipiente*, can also be read as a history of prejudice, polemics and arrogance, let alone many a modern book on Stoic philosophy.

16 There is a small tradition claiming that the sage himself is not aware of the sudden μεταβολή that separates him completely from evil: *SVF* III frgs. 540 (Stobaios) and 541 (Philo). Plutarch is the most explicit on this point (see below §1.5), but, given his polemical intentions, caution is needed.

17 John Rist thinks that in fact Julian "has passed up the opportunity to develop a searching critique of Augustine's fundamental claims about the soul and the body," that he failed "as a philosopher" (*Augustine: Ancient thought baptized* [Cambridge: Cambridge University Press, 1994] 327).

18 This is the way the adversaries of the Stoics usually argue; see, e. g., the section on Plutarch below, §1.5.

19 This is Zeno's concept (esp. *SVF* I frg. 234); see Steinmetz, "Die Stoa," 545; on Sen. *Ep.* 66 (*paria bona*), cf. O. Luschnat, "Das Problem des ethischen Fortschritts in der alten Stoa," *Philologus* 102 (1958) 193.

which ethical actions will always be performed successfully and with perfect ease. It is possible to approach this state of the mind by a long training (ἄσκησις, *meditatio*).[21] Whoever succeeds in attaining this state is wise. This state itself (εὐδαιμονία), finally attained, as we know, by a sudden change (μεταβολή), does not admit modifications either of quantity or of time.[22]

Simplikios (first half of the sixth century CE), when commenting on Aristotle's categories, observed a close relationship between the Stoics' natural predisposition (προϋπάρχειν) for a progress towards virtue and what the Peripatetics call "natural virtue" (φυσικὴ ἀρετή).[23] As Aristotle points out,[24] a distinction is to be made between the "natural virtue" which is present from the very moment the individual is born and virtue in the strict sense (κυρία ἀρετή).[25] Since these "natural virtues" are not yet guided by reason (νοῦς), they may possibly become harmful (βλαβεραί),[26] which is evidently an analogy to the Stoic definition of progress existing in the field of ἀδιάφορα and being itself an ἀδιάφορον.

Here we grasp the traces of a broad discussion among the different philosophical schools. And we can see that—beyond systematic differentiations and oppositions—there was a consensus in ancient philosophy that humans were endowed by nature with the faculty of ethical development and improvement. Philosophers did not conceive of nature as essentially weak or corrupted, although there were—as in Orphism—religious conceptions of a primordial guilt. The discussions

---

[20] Definitions: *SVF* II frg. 393; III frgs. 104 and 105.

[21] Aetius gives Chrysippus' definition of philosophy as different from wisdom: *SVF* II frg. 35; *SVF* III frg. 278 (Chrysippus according to Stobaios): . . . ἀρεταὶ . . . δυνάμεις ἐκ τῆς ἀσκήσεως περιγιγνόμεναι.

[22] All individuals who have reached this state are equal, although they do not lose their peculiarities; they are equal as regards virtue: *Ep.* 79.8–9.

[23] *SVF* III frg. 217.

[24] E. g., Aristot. *Eth. Nic.* 6.13. 1144 b.

[25] Like the Stoics, Aristotle thinks that there is an equivalence between children and animals: ὑπάρχειν φύσει πως—εὐθὺς ἐκ γενετῆς—καὶ γὰρ παισὶ καὶ θηρίοις αἱ φυσικαὶ ὑπάρχουσιν ἕξεις. Cf. the concept of οἰκεῖόν τι πρὸς τὴν ἀλήθειαν in Aristot. *Eth. Eud.* 1.6 (1216b 31) and *Rhet.* A1 1 (355a 15–17). Cf. also for the same function the terms συγγενικόν or σύμφυτον in Epicurus' letter to Menoikeus (Diog. Laer. 10.129), although these are attributes of ἡδονή.

[26] *Eth Nic.* 6.13 (1144b 9).

among the schools attest to an elaborate level of debate and a strong effort towards precise concepts and a consistent terminology, in spite of the ambiguities of the "natural" language.[27]

§1.5 Plutarch on the Stoic notion of Progress

Among the works Plutarch dedicated to his prominent Roman friend, Q. Sosius Senecio, there is a tractate entitled "How a man may become aware of his progress in virtue"—πῶς ἄν τις αἴσθοιτο ἑαυτοῦ προκόπτοντος ἐπ' ἀρετῆι.[28] Plutarch, it is known, filled many pages with what he called the Stoics' inconsistencies. According to him, there cannot be progress if there is not a gradual abatement of vice and that means, degrees of evil, which the Stoics, of course, did not admit.[29]

Plutarch scholars often agree with him that there is something against common sense in Stoicism. André Philippon even excuses Plutarch for not distinguishing between progress "towards" virtue and progress "in" virtue, since only Stoics would claim that there was a difference.[30] William C. Grese argues that Plutarch was focusing on the ancient Stoa, whereas contemporary Stoics would largely have agreed with him.[31] Plutarch, however, when arguing against the Stoics, did not concede that there were "modern" Stoics, to whom his criticism did

[27] I can only refer to the broad branch of Stoic logic. Cf. particularly the texts von Arnim has put together under the heading περὶ σημαινόντων ἢ περὶ φωνῆς, e.g., *SVF* II frg. 151 (p. 25, lines 21–23) = Varro, *De Lingua Latina* IX 1. Concerning the principle of anomaly: . . . *Chrysippus de inaequabilitate cum scribit sermonis, propositum habet ostendere similes res dissimilibus verbis et dissimiles similibus esse vocabulis notatas, id quod est verum,* frg. 152 (p. 45, line 29) = Gellius, XI 12: *Chrysippus ait, omne verbum ambiguum natura esse, quoniam ex eodem duo an plura accipi possunt.*

[28] Cited here: "Progress;" neither the Latin nor the modern versions render the Greek title correctly.

[29] Plut. *Progress* 2.75 F (*SVF* III frg. 535); unawareness: Plut. *Comm. Not.* 19. 1063 A and *Progress* 1. 75 C (*SVF* III frg. 539).

[30] *Plutarque, Oeuvres Morales. tome 1, 2e partie* (ed. A. Philippon et al.; Paris: Les Belles Lettres 1989): "Comment on peut s'apercevoir qu'on progresse dans la vertu," texte établi et traduit par André Philippon, 143–211; see introduction, 149.

[31] W. C. Grese, "De Profectibus in virtute," *Plutarch's Ethical Writings and Early Christian Literature,* 11–31; here 11, nn. 4 and 13. Grese refers to A. Bonhoeffer, *Die Ethik des Stoikers Epiktet* (Stuttgart: Enke 1894) and refuses to consider the relationship between Plutarch and Stoicism, since he is concerned with Plutarch's relationship to the New Testament. Grese erroneously attributes the term προκόπτων to the new Stoics (p. 13).

not apply. Grese does not realize the contemporary character of Plutarch's polemics and misses the philosophical problem as such and also its significance for the New Testament, which is his focus. Thus, for instance, the opposition, in Paul, between sudden transformation effected by baptism or by grace and gradual change is reduced to a juxtaposition of a more Plutarchian or a more Stoic impact.[32]

Evidently, it is the very notion of moral progress and a specific theory about its conditions, that is, evolutionary processes, which interested Plutarch. He compiled comparisons from craftsmanship and medicine in order to prove the importance of gradual improvement in any field of experience whatsoever and famous examples—such as Miltiades and Themistocles[33]—in order to demonstrate that without consciousness of improvement there would not be moral acts at all. Plutarch, to be sure, must have expected this to be of interest also for his addressee Sosius Senecio, a Roman politician who had been a consul three times and was held to be a close confidant of the emperor Trajan.[34] It is hardly credible that this gentleman would have paid attention to a merely scholarly discussion about doctrines which nobody professed any longer. There was a contemporary discussion about evolutionary concepts, and there was rivalry among different philosophical school traditions. Whether Plutarch did not grasp the Stoics' conception of προκοπή as an "intermediate," or was not willing to, his arguments against "the so called progress" (ἡ λεγομένη προκοπή) of the Stoics appear to be blurred by polemics.[35]

§2 Moral Progress in Seneca

§2.1 Seneca—a Stoic Philosopher

§2.1.1 Seneca, the Statesman, the Philosopher and the Poet

Lucius Annaeus Seneca was born about 4 BCE. His family, the *Annaei*, belonged to the Spanish nobility, but they mostly lived in Rome, respectively in imperial service in Egypt or Greece. Lucius

---

[32] Grese, ibid., 11–12.

[33] *Progress* 14.84 B-C. This famous anecdote was used by Kierkegaard; see H. Cancik(-Lindemaier), *Untersuchungen zu Senecas epistulae morales* (Spudasmata 18; Hildesheim: Olms) 106.

[34] Cf. C. P. Jones, *Plutarch and Rome* (Oxford: Clarendon, 1971) 54–57. Sosius Senecio was also a friend of Pliny (*Ep.* 1.13; 4.4).

[35] *SVF* III frg. 535 (= *Progress* 2).

Annaeus Seneca the younger, the philosopher and poet, had two brothers: the elder one, L. Annaeus Novatus through adoption became L. Iunius Gallio Annaeus Novatus. He was *proconsul* of the province Achaia in 51/52; an inscription of his, as is well known, gives us one of the few certain dates for the biography of Paul. The younger brother, L. Annaeus Mela, was the father of the poet M. Annaeus Lucanus, who wrote the epic about the civil war between Caesar and Pompey. We also know of outstanding female members of this family, above all Helvia, Seneca's mother; he dedicated one of his *Consolationes* to her.

Seneca commenced his first career as a brillant orator; he escaped a death sentence under Caligula and was exiled by Claudius from 41 to 48. Called back by Agrippina, he started his second career; as the tutor of young Nero, Seneca won influence and wealth. For about seven years he was one of the mightiest men in Rome. After withdrawing from the court, he applied himself to his literary work, writing, among others, the *Epistulae morales ad Lucilium.* In 65 he was given an order to kill himself;[36] no male member of the Annaean family survived this year.

The enormous prose oeuvre which Seneca has left is usually classified as writings in popular philosophy. The discussion about whether and to what end the philosopher could have written the ten tragedies attributed to him appears to be settled; most scholars agree about the authenticity of at least eight of them—all on classical themes of Greek mythology.

A statesman who declares himself to be a philosopher and is writing poetry—poetry written by a statesman, who is also a philosopher—philosophical works composed by a poet, who is also a statesman: these different perspectives shed light on the complexity of Seneca's personality and work. Focussing on the statesman's presumably last philosophical work, the *Epistulae morales ad Lucilium,* we are to remember that we are dealing also with a poet's work. It is the work of a philosopher, who had once started as an adherent to the Pythagoreans and the Roman Sextii and finally applied himself to Stoicism. Nevertheless, he quotes Epicurus continuously and refers to Plato and

[36] Tacitus *Annals* 15.60–64.

Aristotle, claiming that he is free to receive whatever is good from whosoever has found it.[37]

§2.1.2 *profectus*

"It is a mistake on our part," says Seneca, "to make the same demands upon the sage and upon one who is still progressing."[38] The argument evokes Chrysippus' classical distinction between wisdom and philosophy.[39] Like Chrysippus, Seneca defends the Stoic sage against those who perceive him as a mere fiction, something which is neither natural nor human.[40] He affirms that the sage is a real possibility, and he invests in him all attributes of perfection.[41] In all these topics, Seneca agrees with the ancient Stoic tradition. Time and again he refers to its sophisticated terminological distinctions and theories about changing significance of words according to theoretical and pragmatic contexts, such as: "The sage does not suffer injustice (*iniuria*); nevertheless the person who has attacked him will be condemned, since he has done him injustice (*iniuria*)."[42]

On the other hand, what really matters is less the delineation of the ideal than the way to reach it. Seneca does not hesitate to exalt the figure of the sage in formulas of religious language,[43] but the very emphasis and emotional depth of this imagery reveals his preoccupation with those who are not wise and their progress towards virtue and wisdom. This is the field where he develops psychological analysis and reflections about the conditions of ethically relevant acts: "a great part of progress is the desire to progress. Of this I am aware: I

---

37 For Seneca's originality, see Cancik(-Lindemaier), *Untersuchungen*, 80–88.

38 *Ep.* 71.30: *hoc loco nostrum vitium est qui idem a sapiente exigimus et a proficiente.* The English translations are by Richard M. Gummere, if not indicated otherwise; *proficiens* ("one who is still progressing") is my translation. For the topic of *sapiens/proficiens* in the composition of books 8–9, see Cancik(-Lindemaier), *Untersuchungen*, 149.

39 *SVF* II frg. 35.

40 Cf. *SVF* III frg. 545 (Plut. *Stoic. Rep.* 17).

41 Cf., e.g., the catalogue in Diog. Laer. 7.117–131.

42 Sen. *Ben.* 2.35 (*SVF* III frg. 580).

43 This tendency is found also in Epictetus. Cf. H. Cancik and H. Cancik-Lindemaier, "Senecas Konstruktion des Weisen. Zur Sakralisierung der Rolle des Weisen im 1. Jh. n. Chr.," *Weisheit. Archäologie der literarischen Kommunikation* (ed. A. Assmann; München: Fink, 1991) 205–22.

will and I will with my all my heart." (*magna pars est profectus velle proficere. Huius rei mihi conscius sum: volo et tota mente volo*; *Ep.* 71.36). There is a new stress on the experience of willing and of failing.

§2.2 Time—Progress—Will

In the first book of his epistles, which is an exposition of the whole work, Seneca has gathered the relevant topics. The most general end is to become onself (*suum fieri*). The path goes from things "outside" and "alien" (*extra nos*) which do not pertain to us, towards the inside, where the real good is to be found. This process will occupy a lifetime; saving time therefore is the first imperative.[44] "Everything," says Seneca, "is alien, time alone is ours," and is yet the most futile of all things; it is given by nature; it can be taken away by whomsoever, and we'll never get it back (*Ep.* 1.3). Humanity lacks time: "one has been cast upon a point of time."[45] Time, as an essential element of human existence, is present in the whole work in a great variety of aspects: reflections on present, past and future,[46] on memory, history and cosmology[47] and the ever-recurring experience of urgency.

The experience of an essential lack of time provokes a perception of progress *e negativo*, and so does failure: "and indeed this very fact is proof that my spirit is altered into something better, that I can see its own faults, of which I was previously ignorant."[48] There is clearly awareness of progress—Seneca uses among others the terms *emendari, transferri, mutari, transfigurari*—but it is clearly conceived of as a progress within the status of not being good.

The second condition necessary for progress is volition: *quid tibi opus est ut bonus sis? velle* (*Ep.* 80.4); *volo et tota mente volo*; will is a great

---

[44] *Ep.* 1; cf. *Ep.* 88.39: *tempori parce.*

[45] *Ep.* 77.12; cf. *Ep.* 49.3: *punctum est quod vivimus et adhuc puncto minus*; *Ep.* 48.12; *Ep.* 49.2: *infinita est velocitas temporis . . . .*

[46] *Ep.* 120.18, referring to *Ep.* 77.11: *non eris nec fuisti.* But cf. *Ep.* 79.17: *Paucis natus est, qui populum aetatis suae cogitat. Multa annorum milia, multa populorum supervenient; ad illa respice.*

[47] *Ep.* 101.5: *volvitur tempus rata quidem lege sed per obscurum*; *Ep.* 79.2.

[48] Cf., e.g., *Ep.* 6.1: *et hoc ipsum argumentum est in melius translati animi, quod vitia sua, quae adhuc ignorabat, videt.* Cf. also *Ep.* 118.2: *sua satius est mala quam aliena tractare, se excutere . . . .*

part of progress, at the end it will itself be transformed into a habit:[49] *perseverandeum est . . . donec bona mens sit quod bona voluntas est* (we must persist . . . until it shall be the perfect state of mind that is good will).

Seneca's concept of will deserves closer examination; there might be more than "voluntarist emphases," *pace* John Rist,[50] and it is, in my opinion, not a requirement to find something like "a faculty called the will." I would prefer to extend the inquiry into Seneca's psychological insights to the mechanisms of will and desire and to include, for instance, statements like this:[51] *non quia difficilia sunt non audemus, sed quia non audemus, difficilia sunt* ("we do not lack confidence, because things are difficult, but things are difficult, because we lack confidence"). It is doubtlessly correct and necessary to take the arguments of Stoic philosophers, Seneca included, as what they were intended to be, namely philosophical questions and answers, and to confront them with philosophical questions of ours. The specifics of the philosophical topics found in Seneca, however, cannot be grasped, when isolated, as if they were "fragments." They actually are embedded in a philosophical project, that is, moral progress in practice, and realized in a particular literary form, that is, written epistles. This is the framework of a philosophical interpretation as well.[52]

---

[49] *Ep.* 16.1. Cf. *Ep.* 95.57–58: *Actio recta non erit nisi recta fuerit voluntas. Rursus voluntas non erit recta nisi habitus animi rectus fuerit: ab hoc est enim voluntas . . . . si vis eadem semper velle, vera oportet velis.* Here *recta voluntas* is probably identical with διάνοια, but I doubt that the accumulation of forms of *velle* at the end is but a rhetorical highlight. For distinctions between willingly (*voluntarium*) and unwillingly (*non voluntarium*), cf. Sen. *De ira* 2.1–4 (a psychology of anger); cf. *Ep.* 66.16: *omne honestum voluntarium est.*

[50] Rist claims that there is no decisive difference between Seneca's and Chrysippus' concepts of knowing and willing and rejects Pohlenz' idea of a specifically Roman mentality in Seneca's *voluntas*, but finally admits "voluntarist emphases" (*Stoic Philosophy*, chap. 12, "Knowing and Willing," 219–32, esp. 226–31); idem, "Seneca and Stoic Orthodoxy," *ANRW* 2.36.3 (1989) 1993–2012, esp. 1999–2003 (on *Ep.* 113).

[51] *Ep.* 104.26. Gummere's translation slightly altered.

[52] As a whole, the contribution of John Rist cannot be overestimated; the review by W. Görler in *Philosophische Rundschau* 19 [1972/73] 289–300, in my opinion, has missed the point. But the discussion on *Ep.* 71.36 (*Stoic Philosophy*, 226), reducing the argument to something self-evident ("only an imbecile would deny it") does not account for the specific emphasis that results from the context and is an integral part of the philosophical argument.

Up until now the approach seems to be barred by the generalizing assumption that "modern" concepts—especially of will—were introduced into antiquity only by Christian theologians. Let me quote, as one voice out of many, Albrecht Dihle:[53] "St. Augustine was . . . the inventor of our modern notion of will" . . . "for the needs of his specific theology." . . . "he was greatly helped and tacitly guided by the Latin vocabulary of his time." I would propose an inquiry into "the needs" of Seneca's philosophy and a renunciation of a metaphysical hypostasis of Latin vocabulary.[54]

§2.3 A Goal beyond the Human: κατόρθωμα—*rectum, recte factum*[55]

We may call Seneca's conception of progress an anthropology of being "on the way." Plutarch's charge that there is no progress possible in Stoic ethics is certainly not valid. Seneca has unfolded in his collection of letters an outstanding documentation of moral progress and yet never deviated from the dogmata of ancient Stoicism. He has consciously integrated teaching into this process—at various points with varying rigour and emphasis; there is hardly a branch of Stoic philosophy that is not taken account of, or, at least, touched upon. And he explains why theory is indispensible in certain phases of progress; appropriately, he does this in the latter part of his corpus of epistles.[56]

Seneca, of course, has made a choice; he does not reproduce the system, he presupposes it. The epistles cannot be understood without

---

[53] A. Dihle, *The Theory of Will in Classical Antiquity* (Berkeley, Los Angeles, London: University of California Press, 1982) 144; in Seneca Dihle finds but "a vague voluntarism" (135); Augustine's introspection is called "psychology;" Seneca's is not. It is hard to see how the tradition of Latin vocabulary should have had such different results. Seneca was given a profounder analysis by A. J. Voelke, *L'idée de volonté dans le stoicisme* (Paris: Presses Universitaires de France, 1973); cf. esp. 191–200: comparing Augustine, Voelke distinguishes the theological dogma and the philosophical argument.

[54] Cf. J. Rist's critical remarks on Pohlenz regarding the Roman character of *voluntas* in Seneca (*Stoic philosophy*, 226–27).

[55] *SVF* III frgs. 13–15 (Cicero, *Fin.*).

[56] See *Ep.* 95 and its correspondent, *Ep.* 94, on *decreta* and *praecepta*; cf. *Untersuchungen*, 42–45.

this system.[57] They are evidence for Stoic ethics at work, not for the system.

How then does it work? Let us look at what is, with regard to the system, the end of this process: the only achievement that deserves this name, the ethically right action—*recte factum*, κατόρθωμα—is left to the sage alone. Ethically speaking all other people are performing but *peccata*—ἁμαρτήματα;[58] even when performing appropriate acts, (μέσα) καθήκοντα—*officia*, which are according to nature (κατὰ φύσιν), they do not escape from the realm of immoral acts.

How are we to understand this fact? Are we to assume that the Stoics were considerably inconsistent when displacing the goal of their ethics beyond human capacities, although they held that philosophy had to foster both the individual and the society of humankind? Or were they, for systematic reasons—such as theodicy for instance—bound to construe the ideal as an inviolable one? And did they thus, paradoxically perhaps, gain ground to meet—in practice—the more serious challenges, which occur in the sphere of intermediates (ἀδιάφορα) and demand appropriate acts (καθήκοντα), according to intricate circumstances and sometimes even against all appearances (καθήκοντα ἄνευ περιστάσεως— καθήκοντα περιστατικά)? And finally, supposing that their ethical project was principally insufficient, would it be inappropriate to state that the aporias still persist? It is nearly impossible to avoid key words, such as "casuistry" or "freedom of conscience" or "Gesinnungsethik"—let alone the theological loci of salvation and sin. "Grateful, then," says Seneca, "is also he, who only wants to be, and has no witness to this will but himself."[59]

§3 Expression and Communication of Moral Progress: the Epistles as a Medium

---

[57] The problem is that (a) this system has come down to us only in fragments distorted by misunderstanding and polemical interests and scattered in a way that we often cannot even measure the distances which separate them; (b) we do not know how Seneca learned this system nor in what form he had it in hand. How many volumes of the old Stoics had he actually read?

[58] For a quick summary, see the clear picture in Steinmetz, "Die Stoa," 546; 544–46; Zeno's doctrine: 615–16.

[59] Sen. *Ben.* 4.21 (*SVF* III frg. 509); cf. frg. 508 (my translation); cf. *Ep.* 110.20: . . . *id ages ut sis felix, non ut videaris, et ut tibi videaris, non aliis*; *Ep.* 113.32: ... *saepe iustus esse debebis cum infamia, et tunc, si sapis, mala opinio bene parta delectet.*

§3.1 The Literary Form of the Epistles

Seneca's *Epistulae morales*, as they have come down to us, are a series of 124 letters, all written by Seneca and addressed to his friend Lucilius. They do not constitute a correspondence, since there are no answering letters, nor are they half of a correspondence. They are a literary work, which includes the addressee's response as an integrated part of the composition. Thus, these letters are fictional, insofar as they were neither sent nor received, nor gathered by the addressee or someone else. The subdivison into books—we have twenty, but there is evidence that there were at least twenty-two[60]—belongs to a composition following philosophical needs and literary categories. The entire topic of letter-writing is present and used to create the literary framework of the genre;[61] at the same time it is transformed into a medium of this particular philosophical project, namely, a communication among friends about moral progress, or should we say a moral autobiography in dialogue?

There are many models and parallels for every single element in Seneca's work in Greek and Roman literature. There are Epicurus' letters to his pupils, which combine philosophical doctrines with personal admonitions, given by a teacher who is also a friend.[62] There are Plato's letters—authentic or not—whose collection Franz Dornseiff has interpreted as "an epistolary novel about Plato in Sicily" composed soon after his death.[63] There is—almost contemporary with Seneca—a series of seventeen epistles,[64] written presumably in the first half of the first century CE and attributed to Chion of Heraclea, a pupil of Plato's, who killed Klearchos the Tyrant of Heraclea (Pontos) in 352 BCE. The subject matter is the philosophical legitimization of tyrannicide,

[60] Gellius, 12.2.3, quotes from a twenty-second book of the *epistulae morales ad Lucilium.*

[61] For a survey see Cancik(-Lindemaier), *Untersuchungen*, 46–68.

[62] Special edition: P. von der Mühll, *Epicuri Epistulae tres et ratae sententiae* (Stuttgart: Teubner, 1975; originally published 1922).

[63] Franz Dornseiff, *Echtheitsfragen antik-griechischer Literatur* (Berlin: de Gruyter 1939) 31.

[64] Fifteen epistles are addressed to Chion's father Matris, one to the tyrant Klearchos, the seventeenth to Plato; see I. Düring, *Chion of Heraclea* (Göteborg: Wettergren & Kerbers, 1951).

founded upon a Platonizing[65] philosophy about freedom and the affinity between man and god. "All letters are," as the editor I. Düring observes, "integrated parts of a carefully prepared composition;" he calls them "the only example of a novel in letters."[66] All these examples—fictional or real—have one factor in common, that is the intimacy, intensity, and authority of personal commitment. I need not point out how Paul used these qualities of the epistolary genre for teaching, educating, exhorting, consoling his communities and presenting himself as the witness to his faith.

The primary function of letters, to establish communication between writers and recipients, favours psychological considerations and insight. This may be one reason why in the Augustan period Roman poets chose this medium, which is the most poetic and even lyric of prose genres. Ovid sent verse letters from his place of exile to Rome and made Greek heroines write letters to their beloved, almost infinitely varying the topics of the genre. He thus produced what, according to Greek rhetoric, a letter was to be: an image of one's soul.[67] Horace, who was the first to give the letter the rank of high poetry, collected and deliberately arranged a selection of his epistles and thus created the book of epistles as a literary entity.

In ancient literature, then, the epistolary genre proved to be a suitable literary medium for the representation of interior processes. Seneca the poet, whose tragedies exhibit a particular sensibility for the psychological mechanisms of error, anxiety, passion, and crime—

[65] Düring, *Chion*, 21–22.

[66] Düring, *Chion*, 14, 7, 18, 23, with remarks on the history of the epistolary genre.

[67] Demetr. *Eloc.* § 227 (3rd century BCE). Cf. in general: Klaus Thraede, *Grundzüge griechisch-römischer Brieftopik* (Zetemata 48; München: Beck, 1970). W. G. Müller gives a history of the topos from antiquity to Samuel Richardson ("Der Brief als Spiegel der Seele. Zur Geschichte eines Topos der Epistolartheorie von der Antike bis zu Samuel Richardson," *Antike und Abendland* 26 [1980] 138–57). In the novels in letter form—*Pamela* and *Clarissa* by Richardson (first half of the eighteenth century)—it appears to have reached its goal: the fiction of the highest authenticity; it is noteworthy that the letter form is used to reveal the inner character of women, but Müller does not refer to Ovid's heroines. The modernity of Seneca's letters is emphasized when compared to this genre of eighteenth century English literature.

providing eventually a comment upon his century—was certainly aware of this.[68]

Finally, Seneca the statesman knew Cicero's letters and discreetly compared them with his own. Having quoted the words that Cicero wrote to his friend Atticus, "Even if you have nothing to say, write whatever enters your head,"[69] Seneca continues, ". . . there will always be something for me to write about, even omitting all the kinds of news with which Cicero fills his correspondence;" then he adds a list of politicial and financial issues, like those that recur in Cicero's letters.[70] Thus rejecting what preoccupies Cicero, Seneca indirectly gives a definition of what his epistles are intended to do: "But it is preferable to deal with one's own ills rather than with another's—to sift oneself and see for how many (vain) things one is a candidate, and cast a vote for none of them" (*Ep.* 118.2). A truly Stoic stance and, given the time and the situation when the epistles were written (after 62), a pertinent witness to himself. "This, my dear Lucilius," Seneca continues, "is a noble thing, this brings peace and freedom—to canvass for nothing, and to pass by all the elections of Fortune."

§3.2 The presence of Addressee and Writer

In addition, an every-day letter, as is evident by its introductory formula, provides a stage for the meeting of writer and receiver. The every-day letter compensates for the deficiency that the receiver is not present. In the epistle this compensation is made a virtue, that is to say, a literary and philosophical device for staging a process of communication. Hence, autobiographical witness and representation of the addressee are constituent parts of the genre.

Thus, for instance, Seneca's remarks on Lucilius' epistolary style are intended to represent the friend's mind (*Ep.* 59.5–6). "I thank you for writing to me so often for you are revealing your real self to me in the only way you can. I never receive a letter from you without being in your company forthwith. If the pictures of our absent friends are

---

[68] On Seneca's "psychology," see, e.g., J. Rist, "Seneca and Stoic Orthodoxy," 2011–12; for an evaluation of the psychological achievements in Seneca's tragedies, see ibid., 1197.

[69] Cic. *Att.* 1.12.4.

[70] *Ep.* 118.1–2, quoting Cic. *Att.* 1.12.4 and 1.12.1; cf. Sen., *Ep.* 9 7.4–6: quotations from Cic. *Att.* 1.16.5.

pleasing to us, though they only refresh the memory and lighten our longing by a solace that is unreal and unsubstantial, how much more pleasant is a letter, which brings us real traces, real evidences of an absent friend! For that which is sweetest when we meet face to face is afforded by the impress of a friend's hand upon his letter—recognition." (. . . *amici manus epistulae impressa praestat agnoscere*; *Ep.* 40.1).

Letters are *amicorum colloquia absentium* as Cicero puts it;[71] Seneca, in his epistles, continually returns to this topic, sketching thus a theory of the genre with regard to subject matter, style, atmosphere and efficiency.[72] In epistle 55 he pushes it to a paradox: "I would therefore have you share your studies with me, your meals and your walks. We would be living within too narrow limits if anything were barred to our thoughts. I see you, my dear Lucilius, and at this very moment I hear you; I am with you to such an extent that I hesitate whether I should not begin to write you notes instead of letters. Farewell."[73] These words, at the same time, ingeniously allude to an essential claim of Stoic ethics, namely to free oneself from the limits imposed by time, space and all types of circumstances—in a word, by chance. Seneca's project even extends beyond the boundaries of individual life to posterity; referring to Epicurus whose letters, just as Epicurus had promised, had made Idomeneus more renowned than his own deeds, Seneca promises fame to Lucilius (*Ep.* 21.3–5).

Plato's dialogues present Socrates and his followers directly at work—hence their beautiful liveliness which makes one forget the structures underlying all of these spontaneous pros and cons. Thus we hardly can imagine a literary form more appropriate to Socrates than the dialogue—when handled by a poet like Plato.

Epicurus wrote letters to his pupils and friends Herodotus, Pythokles, and Menoikeus, while his garden was still flourishing.[74]

---

[71] Cic. *Phil.* 2.4.7; *Att.* 12.39.2; cf. Cancik(-Lindemaier), *Untersuchungen*, 51–52.

[72] Cf., e.g., *Ep.* 38.1; 40.1; 67.2; 75.1.

[73] *Ep.* 55.11; cf. *Ep.* 34.1; 35.3; 38.1.

[74] H. S. Long, ed., *Diogenes Laertius. Vitae philosophorum* (2 vols.; Oxford: Clarendon, 1964). Book 10.35–83 (to Herodotus); 84–117 (to Pythokles); 122–135 (to Menoikeus). The letter to Herodotus is perhaps a draft or a copy of a draft, including marginal notes without final corrections with regard to style etc. Nevertheless, it is clear from Epicurus' own words that the letter—representing an "epitome" of his physical teachings (Diog. Laer. 10.35)—is intended to be

These letters are "real," insofar as there may have been accidentally a practical necessity for writing; they were, at the same time, literary, insofar as carefully composed, reproducing Epicurean doctrine and lifestyle, and most certainly meant to be read not only by their formal addressees. Since the master himself is speaking, the epistle is the appropriate literary form; it is a philosophically suitable medium, since colloquia among friends in the garden are an essential in Epicurus' philosophy. In each of the letters at least two of them are—though absent—present. Their literary character was, finally, sealed by the fact that they were collected and published.

When Seneca was writing his letters, there was no longer an Academy, a Lykeion, a Garden, a Stoa. Athens was little more than a utopia of philosophers. Cicero already had described his visit in the manner of a "voyage sentimental" or a pilgrimage: *quacumque enim ingredimur, in aliqua historia vestigium ponimus.*[75] There was Rome, the city, the metropolis of an empire, there was the imperial court and all those circumstances that threatened life and almost prohibited philosophy. Seneca's friend Lucilius was a Roman magistrate who had to be abroad as a procurator in Sicily. Thus Seneca had to write their friendship, if not their lives. His choice of genre is intelligible.

§3.3 The Autobiographical Element—Progress in Dialogue

3.3.1 Striving for progress towards virtue means learning through practice and implies carefully observing and scrutinizing oneself. Since this does not happen as an autobiographical monologue, but as communication among friends,[76] the result is mutual education. Thus teaching turns into learning, and learning means sharing the other's quest. "I am not so shameless to undertake to cure my fellow men

---

published. Cf. J. M. Rist, *Epicurus: An Introduction* (Cambridge: Cambridge University Press, 1972).

[75] Cic. *Fin.* 5.2.5; cf. *Fam.* 13.1; Epicurus' *vestigia,* i.e., his house, remain at Athens. There is no longer a *contubernium;* new ways of communicating have to be found, covering large distances in space and time.

[76] Seneca uses the verb *communicare* exclusively in the epistles; with the exception of two passages, *Ep.* 27.1 and 109.9, all occurrences are in the first book: *Ep.* 3.1; 5.7; 6.2; 7.10; 10.1. This may be significant, for this is the introductory book in which the fundamental concepts of the entire work are to be emphasized; e.g., *Ep.* 3, 6 and 9 are concerned in detail with friendship; see Cancik(-Lindemaier), *Untersuchungen,* 61–66.

when I am ill myself. I am, however, discussing with you the troubles which concern us both, and sharing the remedy with you, just as if we were lying in the same hospital. Listen to me, therefore, as you would if I were talking to myself. I am admitting you to my inmost thoughts, and am having it out with myself, merely making use of you as a pretext."[77] The letter offers the atmosphere of intimacy which is to protect the most personal communications.

The message transmitted is not knowledge but seeking. ". . . read (my works) as if I were still seeking, and were not aware of, the truth, and were seeking it obstinately, too." Seneca does not conceive of himself as a teacher nor as simply a follower. His is a particular concept of originality and creativity—which is usually called eclecticism: "For I have sold myself to no man; I bear the name of no master; I give much credit to the judgment of great men; but I claim something also for my own. For these men, too, have left to us, not positive discoveries, but problems whose solution is still to be sought."[78]

Seneca's self-representations cover a broad scale of experiences and of narrative types. No happening in every-day life is too banal to be taken as a starting point of meditation and to be related, in order to show what cannot be taught. The testimony that Seneca gives of himself may, as in *Ep.* 108, structure the whole of a letter.

3.3.2 In *Ep.* 108, then, Seneca records his journey to philosophy, how in his youth he attended the lectures of Attalus, the Stoic, and those of Sotion the Pythagorean, and how he attempted to practice what he was taught; how, following Sotion and Sextius, he abstained from meat and how he came to abandon this practice: during the first years of Tiberius' reign, foreign cults had been introduced in Rome which practised abstinence from certain kinds of meat;[79] whoever did so was suspected of superstition. Seneca changed his lifestyle at the request of his father, "who did not fear persecution but hated philosophy" (*Ep.* 108.22). This ironic remark stresses the remem-

---

[77] *Ep.* 27.2; *Ep.* 67.2: *itaque et de hoc quod quaeris quasi conloquar tecum; quale sit una scrutabimur.*

[78] *Ep.* 45.4. Cf. below on *Ep.* 108.38: appropriating what has been taught.

[79] Seneca alludes to the year 19 CE; cf. Tacitus *Annals* 2.85.

brance of terror in the past rather than concealing it. The past, no doubt, is meant to shed light on the present.

There are good reasons to read the whole passage under the heading, given by Seneca himself, quoting Attalus in the beginning of epistle 108: *"idem," inquit, "et docenti et discenti debet esse propositum: ut ille prodesse velit, hic proficere"* (108.3) ("The same purpose should possess both master and scholar—an ambition in the one case to promote, and in the other to progress"). It is this that Seneca apparently is illustrating, when he records his first steps. There is, however, a rupture in the middle of the text (§ 23). Seneca cuts off the demonstration of a teacher being taught, focusing on the shortcomings of teaching and of scholarly approaches in general. The second half of *Ep.* 108 deals with the moralist interpretation of poetry—here as often it is Vergil's—in contrast to what grammarians and philologists do. (Here I will not go into details; it would be all too disappointing for my guild.)

The letter concludes with a plea for making words become deeds (§ 35). All that has been taught belongs to others, unless one has made it one's own: *faciant quae dixerint* (§ 38). A deep perspective on the Stoic system is opened, evoking the physical concept of οἰκείωσις, the dialectics between what is "alien" and what pertains to us, and summing up the whole in the most important imperative of a philosopher's life: *congruentia vitae et doctrinae.*

Seneca developed all this within the framework constructed by the first and the last sentences of this letter. In the very end Seneca promises to respond, in a following letter, to what Lucilius had demanded, and what had properly been the starting point for *Ep.* 108. At the beginning (§ 1), Seneca recalled that Lucilius had required books "embracing the whole department of moral philosophy" and offered advice as to how to digest all this knowledge; the advice, realized as the communication of Seneca's personal experience, eventually occupies the whole of a long letter. The topic of letter-writing provides the means of integrating this message into a carefully balanced composition.[80]

---

[80] Actually, *Ep.* 108 is strongly linked to the following, much shorter, letter, which deals with the Stoic topic of "whether a wise man can help a wise man" (*an*

3.3.3 The corpus of epistles is a narrative performance of moral progress. To conclude, it may be sufficient to repeat some key ideas: Seneca has projected a pedagogic movement, based upon Stoic morals and presupposing the whole system of Stoic philosophy; the needs of the educational progress produce the rhythm of the composition, such as, variation between more doctrinal parts in descriptive language and paraenetic parts in prescriptive language immediately aiming at practice. This process is, for philosophical reasons, conceived of as mutual, to be realized in the continuous communication of friends. The letter is the literary form which appropriately grants the intimacy required for representing a face-to-face communication. The corpus of epistles enables the writer to construct the reciprocity of representation and self-representation: thus progress in dialogue is staged. Seneca has alluded to the interior dialectic of this relationship in a saying borrowed from Hecato:[81] "If you would be loved, love" (*si vis amari, ama*).

---

sapiens sapienti prosit) and which again is concluded (*Ep.* 109.17–18) with a reference to the introduction of *Ep.* 108.1.

[81] Seneca *Ep.* 9.6. Cf. the broad discussion about the "golden rule" and Matt 7:12 in: H. D. Betz, *The Sermon on the Mount: A Commentary on the Sermon on the Mount, including the Sermon on the Plain (Matthew 5:3–7:27 and Luke 6:20–49)* (Hermeneia; Minneapolis: Fortress, 1995) 508–19.

Reading to Virtue

Margaret M. Mitchell

It is my pleasure to respond to Dr. Cancik-Lindemaier's rich and stimulating paper on Seneca's *Epistulae morales* as a part of this conference in honor of my teacher and friend, Hans Dieter Betz. Among the many things I have learned from Dieter, the one which stands foremost for me today, on the occasion of this conference, is the enjoyment of collegiality with others in the common enterprise of the scholarship which so fascinates us. Dieter is the quintessential conversation partner: attentive, insightful, informed, expansive, creative, inexhaustible. I have learned from him the inestimable importance of the scholarly virtue of cooperation. In the good words of Seneca: *Nullius boni sine socio iucunda possessio est.*[1]

The essential thesis of Dr. Cancik-Lindemaier's paper, "Seneca's Collection of Epistles, a Medium of Philosophical Communication," is that this collection of one hundred and twenty-four epistles must be understood as "a philosophical project, that is, moral progress in practice, and realized in a particular literary form" (p. 99). Dr. Cancik-Lindemaier suggestively terms Seneca's letter collection "a communication among friends about moral progress, or should we say a moral autobiography in dialogue?" (p. 102). In my response I would like to comment first on this specific argument about Seneca's epistolary corpus, and then, in the interdisciplinary spirit of this conference, as of Hans Dieter Betz's scholarship, also suggest some implications of Dr. Cancik-Lindemaier's arguments for the study of the New Testament.

Most interesting for me is Dr. Cancik-Lindemaier's thesis that "the corpus of epistles is a narrative performance of moral progress" (p. 109). The initial question this raises is "moral progress for whom?" For Seneca? For Lucilius? For the reader whom Seneca expects to take up

---

[1] "No good thing is pleasant to possess, without friends to share it" (*Ep.* 6.4, text and trans. Richard M. Gummere, *Seneca ad Lucilium epistulae Morales* [LCL; Cambridge, MA and London: Harvard University Press, 1953], as throughout this response).

this correspondence later, as he explains, for example, in *Ep.* 8: "I am working for later generations, writing down some ideas that may be of assistance to them."[2] It seems clear that Dr. Cancik-Lindemaier is arguing that the moral progress which receives narrative performance in the letter corpus is *both* that of the epistolary author, Seneca, and that of his historical recipient Lucilius, in which all other readers are likewise invited to participate. The communal nature of the ethical education Cancik-Lindemaier envisions in the epistolary narrative demands that the progress of all parties be part of the "narrative" which is in the process of performance, indeed of creation, as the work unfolds. Thus, if I understand correctly, the literary form of the letter collection is the medium by which one can "read into virtue" by both gazing there upon the image of the soul of Seneca in progress, and composing, through following his example and specific precepts, one's own self-portrait in the fleshly deeds and choices of one's life. Thus the "autobiography" which is "performed" here is simultaneously that of Seneca and that of the reader; hence the curious but apt oxymoron, "a moral autobiography in dialogue" (p. 102).[3]

If one agrees with this thesis, the issue of the relationship between the individual letter and the whole corpus in the "narration of moral progress" becomes quite acute. Though in her book and in this paper, Dr. Cancik-Lindemaier is well appreciative of the hermeneutical signficance for each individual letter of the context formed by the total *Briefcorpus*, as also by its division into books,[4] I would be most interested to hear more about how she views the structure of this letter collection in relation to the "narrative" which she views it as creating.[5]

---

[2] *Posterorum negotium ago; illis aliqua, quae possint prodesse, conscribo.* See also 8.6 on "commun[ing] in such terms with myself and with future generations" [*si haec mecum, si haec cum posteris loquor. . .*].

[3] Yet, nonetheless, the reader's moral autobiography is only fostered, but not scripted, in the narrative which the letter collection as it stands creates (thus the distinction Dr. Cancik-Lindemaier makes between the autobiographical witness of the author and the representation of the addressee ["Seneca's Collection of Epistles," 104]).

[4] Hildegard Cancik, *Untersuchungen zu Senecas Epistulae morales* (Spudasmata 18; Hildesheim: Olms, 1967) 138–140.

[5] This question intersects, of course, with two recent lines of scholarship, on the literary structure of Seneca's *Epistulae morales* and on ancient psychagogical techniques. See, for instance, Cancik, *Untersuchungen*, 139–51; Gregor Maurach,

For example, a too simplistic model would hold that a letter collection creates a "moving picture" of the soul of its author, Seneca, since one by one the static snapshots of his soul which are conveyed by the individual letters are placed before the eye of the reader. Then, like a child's deck of cards which, when shuffled, shows a dog jumping over a fence or a girl dancing, the epistolary collection can create the element of time necessary both for the cultivation of virtue (according to Seneca's pedagogy) and for the creation of "narrative." The picture will move correctly, however, only if the cards are in the right order. But this model, though theoretically sensible, does not account for the complexly diachronic nature of the portraits of Seneca's soul and his progress which are found *within individual letters,* as Seneca uses flashbacks, future visions, cross references to previous letters, and other dramatic techniques to display the intricacies of the progress toward virtue within a single epistle. So what we have are one hundred and twenty-four individual moving portraits within a macro-genre of moving portrait. But what are the ordering principles in forming that macro-genre, and how do they affect the act of reading this text, reading toward virtue?[6] Are individual epistles (such as *Ep.* 108, which Dr. Cancik-Lindemaier analyzed in her paper) microcosms of the whole, both structurally and in terms of psychagogic technique? Does the complete work display a careful architecture which corresponds to the moral curriculum toward virtue,[7] or is its plan more discursive, less

Der Bau von Senecas Epistulae morales (Heidelberg: Winter, 1970); Erwin Hachmann, *Die Führung des Lesers in Senecas* Epistulae morales (Orbis Antiquus 34; Münster: Aschendorff, 1995); Clarence E. Glad, *Paul and Philodemus: Adaptability in Epicurean and Early Christian Psychagogy* (NovTSup 81; Leiden: Brill, 1995), esp. 53–181.

[6] Another interesting feature of the "narrative performance" would be its renewed and different effect on the one re-reading the text as compared with the person who reads it for the first time. How would it work as a "review curriculum," in contrast to an initial tutorial in moral progress?

[7] A further question is how this architectonic masterpiece might have been experienced (or not) in the history of reception of this work. Would anyone have read the whole work, *seriatim,* to gain this effect? This is an important question that one should ask also in relation to recent intricate literary-critical studies of New Testament Gospels, for instance, since we have no evidence in early church history of the Gospels being consumed as narrative wholes (see Harry Y. Gamble, *Books and Readers in the Early Church* [New Haven: Yale University Press, 1995] 216: though *lectio continua* was practiced from early on, it meant *seriatim,* reading a text

carefully set out, therefore less (strictly speaking) "narratological"? Surely it is a long, repetitious and rather serpentine experience reading through Seneca's letters, isn't it? How essential is the order and composition of the letter collection to the "narrative performance of moral progress" which it is designed to engender?[8] Must the reader complete a *lectio continua* of the whole circuit of one hundred twenty-four epistles, or could one receive the benefit of this correspondence-course in virtue without experiencing the full extent of the corpus, in its present order? What if one took Seneca's own advice, in *Ep.* 2, and focused on only a few selected portions rather than reading widely in this epistolary library?[9] Further, can one analyze the composition of the whole letter-collection without attending to its ending, which we do not have (for Dr. Cancik-Lindemaier alludes to at least two more books of epistles which are not extant)?[10] Or is the open-endedness itself part of the narrative effect? Such questions might frame on-going

---

week to week, not in one sitting). For one study which examines the "orality" of the Gospel according to Mark, with further bibliography, see Christopher Bryan, *A Preface to Mark: Notes on the Gospel and its Literary and Cultural Settings* (New York/Oxford: Oxford University Press, 1993).

8 What is the history of this arrangement? How much of it, and the division of the epistles into books, was the work of Seneca?

9 See also *Ep.* 6, where Seneca tells Lucilius that he has marked out selected passages in the philosophical works he is sending him so that he doesn't have to wade through the whole writings to find them. But we find the exact opposite advice in *Ep.* 33.5: "For this reason, give over hoping that you can skim, by means of epitomes, the wisdom of distinguished men. Look into their wisdom as a whole; study it as a whole [*tota tibi inspicienda sunt, tota tractanda*]. They are working out a plan and weaving together, line upon line, a masterpiece, from which nothing can be taken away without injury to the whole [*ex quo nihil subduci sine ruina potest*]!" Or, on the contrary, should we reject any idea of wholesale digestion of the total work, a text-corpus which itself recommends that one take in only one thought per day (*Ep.* 2.4–5; 4.5)? Note also that the early epistles conclude with "the thought for the day" [*hodiernum*].

10 The remark above assumes that the missing books which Dr. Cancik-Lindemaier mentions ("Seneca's Collection of Epistles," p. 102) would have continued after *Ep.* 124. At any rate, that epistle does not have any formal concluding character to it, though in theme it is fitting enough. It is interesting that none of the compositional analyses of this letter collection which I have looked at (Cancik, *Untersuchungen*, 140–151; Maurach, *Der Bau von Senecas* Epistulae morales; Hachmann, *Die Führung des Lesers)* treats any epistle beyond number 88. What does that imply about the composition of the literary whole?

conversation on Dr. Cancik-Lindemaier's suggestive thesis on Seneca's *Epistulae morales* as "a narrative performance of moral progress."

I should now like to turn to the comparative part of my response, and it won't surprise you that within the New Testament it is Paul who comes to my mind immediately in this context. In fact, this comparison suggested itself to readers from very early on in the church, as we know from the fourth-century fictional correspondence between the two, in which Seneca, using an epistolary commonplace apt in the context of this afternoon's lecture, says to Paul: "do you not wish me to rejoice that I am so close to you that I may be thought your second self?"[11]

The collection of Paul's letters does not appear to have been arranged with a psychagogical intent such as Dr. Cancik-Lindemaier has identified for Seneca.[12] There were several early versions of the collection of Paul's letters, which apparently focused more on the *number* of the letters (or churches addressed—the "letters to seven churches collection") than the *order* of the letters as conveying special meaning.[13] The compositional principle which is retained in the finally published shape of the corpus is neither pedagogical nor literary, but economical and practical: the letters to churches are arranged in descending length, from Romans to 2 Thessalonians, followed by the letters to individuals, similarly laid out from longest (1 Timothy) to shortest (Philemon).[14] Thus the collection of Paul's letters is essentially a reference collection, a fact also likely responsible for the well-known early Christian preference for the codex over the

---

11 *Non ergo vis laeter, si ita sim tibi proximus ut alter similis tui deputer?* (text Laura Bocciolini Palagi, *Il carteggio apocrifo di Seneca e San Paolo* [Accademia toscana di scienze e lettere "La Colombaria," "Studi" 46; Florence: Leo S. Olschki, 1978]; trans. Cornelia Römer in Hennecke-Schneemelcher, *New Testament Apocrypha*, ed. R. McL. Wilson [2 vols.; Louisville: Westminster/John Knox, 1992] 2.51 [*Ep.* 12]).

12 This may be impossible in a letter collection which contains letters to different addressees (this question might repay further investigation—perhaps the Socratic epistles could be usefully drawn in here).

13 See Harry Y. Gamble, "The Pauline Corpus and the Early Christian Book," *Paul and the Legacies of Paul*, (ed. W. S. Babcock; Dallas: Southern Methodist University Press, 1990) 265–80; idem, *Books and Readers in the Early Church*, 49–66.

14 David Trobisch, *Die Entstehung der Paulusbriefsammlung: Studien zu den Anfängen christlicher Publizistik* (NTOA 10; Göttingen: Vandenhoeck & Ruprecht, 1989) 56–61, 108–113.

scroll.[15] The corpus Paulinum is not an epistolary narrative or a letter collection arranged intentionally to create a narrative effect upon the reader when read *seriatim*.[16] Individual letters, however, may provide us with more like comparative material.

Within the epistles attributed to Paul, I would argue that it is the Pastoral Epistles,[17] 1 Timothy in particular, which resonate with the philosophical project and use of literary form which Dr. Cancik-Lindemaier has identified in Seneca's *Epistulae morales*. I will briefly describe the considerable similarities and at least one major difference between the two works,[18] as only a preliminary and suggestive glance at what New Testament scholars might learn from her work on Seneca.

Seneca's epistles and 1 Timothy share very similar epistolary dynamics. Like Seneca's epistles directed to Lucilius, 1 Timothy is a letter addressed to a single individual which clearly has a wider readership in mind. Both Seneca and the pseudonymous author who assumes the identity of the apostle Paul create in their epistolary self-representations *personae* which are wiser, more mature[19] than their recipients, who from their superiority will act as guides for the moral improvement of their correspondent. One might draw an interesting comparison in this regard with Seneca's fascinating three-fold identity

---

[15] This is the persuasive thesis of Gamble, "The Pauline Corpus," 275–78, and idem, *Books and Readers in the Early Church*, 62–66.

[16] Could this lack be part of the impetus for the composition of Acts (and later, the *Acta Pauli*)? Of course, the debates about the date of Acts, and about whether or not that author knew a collection (or which collection) of Paul's letters, go on. But certainly Acts provides a narrative framework for the ministry of Paul which is not to be found in the reading of the corpus of letters *seriatim*.

[17] Within the corpus of authentic Pauline letters, Romans perhaps has some similarities to what Dr. Cancik-Lindemaier describes as the goal of progress in virtue, if David Aune and others are right that Romans is a λόγος προτρεπτικός (David E. Aune, "Romans as a Logos Protreptikos in the Context of Ancient Religious and Philosophical Propaganda," *Paulus und das antike Judentum*, [ed. Martin Hengel and Ulrich Heckel; Tübingen: J.C.B. Mohr/Paul Siebeck, 1992] 91–124). Because Seneca's letters are important for Aune's thesis about Romans, this topic would require a full-scale discussion of its own.

[18] I shall concentrate my comparison on the first two books of the *Epistulae morales*, though not exclusively.

[19] Paul refers to Timothy's "youth" in 1 Tim 4:12; Seneca refers to the right path, "which I have found late in life" (*quod sero cognovi*) (*Ep*. 8.3; 26.1; cf. *Ep*. 35.3–4).

as philosopher, statesman and poet, for the author of the Pastorals is perhaps equal parts theologian, head of church polity and quoter of poetic fragments. In both sets of writings the author also engages a recipient whose persona is created solely through the dramatic representation in the letter itself (that is, neither collection is a correspondence with letters from both parties). Both letters, as expected, contain epistolary *topoi* of travel plans, desire to see the addressee, concerns about health and complaints about distance. In both sets of letters, the epistolary author inserts tidbits of personal information about contact with the recipient, but these serve only as jumping off places for moral exhortations of a more universal character. In such long sections of the letters, the actual named recipient (Timothy or Lucilius) can be lost from view entirely in the general exhortations to the virtuous or faithful life, but then he reappears always by the end of the letter, via a vocative address,[20] to receive some last minute specific and individualized instructions.

The express purpose of the two writings is also quite similar. The function of epistolary tutelage toward προκοπή in virtue, which Dr. Cancik-Lindemaier has identified in the epistles of Seneca, is matched in the summary exhortation of 1 Tim 4:15: ταῦτα μελέτα, ἐν τούτοις ἴσθι, ἵνα σου ἡ προκοπὴ φανερὰ ᾖ πᾶσιν ("practice these things, be in them, so that your progress might be manifest to all"). Both "Paul" and Seneca have as their purpose in writing the progress of their pupil, though in 1 Timothy it is progress in εὐσέβεια (or πίστις), whereas for Seneca it is progress in *virtus* (or *sapientia*). Both authors use their own progress as an example for imitation. Seneca, for instance, writes of his present progress each day,[21] while the pseudepigraphic Paul invokes his amazing progress from misguided persecutor to chosen, faithful missionary in 1 Tim 1:12–16, explicitly saying that Christ chose him to be an ὑποτύπωσις of those who will

---

[20] These are of course everywhere in the *Epistulae morales.* Compare, for example, *Lucili* in *Ep.* 13.16; 15.2, etc., *mi Lucili* in 13.8; 18.15, *Lucili carissime* in 23.6, and τέκνον Τιμόθεε in 1 Tim 1:18, and ὦ Τιμόθεε in 6:20 (cf. ἄνθρωπε θεοῦ in 6:11).

[21] *Ep.* 6.3: "you cannot conceive what distinct progress I notice that each day brings to me" [*concipere animo non potes, quantum momenti adferre mihi singulos dies videam*]. Cf. *Ep.* 6.7: "What progress, you ask, have I made? I have begun to be a friend to myself" [*Quaeris, inquit, quid profecerim? Amicus esse mihi coepi*].

later believe.[22] Both Seneca and "Paul" issue paraenetic calls for their recipients to devote themselves steadfastly to what is singularly important: in Seneca's case, to contemplative study of philosophy (for example, *Ep.* 14.11; 15.1–2), in "Paul's," to prayer (1 Tim 2:1–8). Both authors have confidence that progress can be achieved through "holding fast" to the precepts which they hand over in the epistles. Using characteristic paraenetic vocabulary, Seneca urges Lucilius to "hold fast, then, to this sound and wholesome rule of life" (*Ep.* 8.5 (*forma vitae*); cf. 16:6), and "Paul" urges Timothy to "flee"[23] vices, to "pursue" righteousness, piety, faith, love, endurance and meekness, to adhere to the "healthy teaching" (1:10; 6:3), and to "guard the deposit" (6:20). The author of 1 Timothy explicitly names the goal of such "instruction:" τὸ δὲ τέλος τῆς παραγγελίας ἐστὶν ἀγάπη ἐκ καθαρᾶς καρδίας καὶ συνειδήσεως ἀγαθῆς καὶ πίστεως ἀνυποκρίτου (1:5: "the goal of the instruction is love from a pure heart and a good conscience and unhypocritical faith"). Seneca, as is well known, is likewise concerned for the cultivation of a "good conscience" (*bona conscientia*).[24] The route to the progress each assists his pupil toward is in both cases to be found in "exercise" (*exercitatio*, γυμνασία), and both contrast exercise of body and mind, not surprisingly favoring that of the mind or soul over thc physical.[25] Both envision their students becoming in turn the teachers of others.[26]

---

[22] This contrast illumines the fact that, while Seneca uses his present self as an on-going example, Paul as an example refers exclusively to his past, with a sense of its closure, which is a clear indication of the pseudepigraphical character of 1 Timothy.

[23] Cf. Seneca *Ep.* 14.11: *ad philosophiam ergo confugiendum est.*

[24] E.g., *Ep.* 12.9; 23.7; 44.5; 97.12; also 1 Tim 1:19; 3:9 (cf. 4:2).

[25] Seneca recommends some simple physical exercises, such as running, weightlifting, jumping, and then says: "but whatever you do, come back soon from body to mind (*cito redi a corpore ad animum*). The mind must be exercised both day and night (*Illum noctibus ac diebus exerce*) . . . and this form of excercise (*exercitatio*) need not be hampered by cold or hot weather, or even by old age" (*Ep.* 15.3–6). Compare 1 Tim 4:7–8: "Exercise yourself toward piety. For bodily exercise is profitable a little bit, but piety is profitable in all things since it holds the promise of life now and in the future" (Γύμναζε δὲ σεαυτὸν πρὸς εὐσέβειαν· ἡ γὰρ σωματικὴ γυμνασία πρὸς ὀλίγον ἐστὶν ὠφέλιμος, ἡ δὲ εὐσέβεια πρὸς πάντα ὠφέλιμός ἐστιν ἐπαγγελίαν ἔχουσα ζωῆς τῆς νῦν καὶ τῆς μελλούσης) (cf. also 6:12).

[26] 1Tim 4:11; 6:2; *Ep.* 7.8–9; 33.9.

Even the specific content of some of the exhortations is very similar. Most predominant in Seneca's epistles, as one expects for a Stoic, is disparagement of worldly possessions, and pleas for indifference to material goods. Using the appropriate Stoic technical term, "Paul" urges that the life of piety be lived in αὐτάρκεια, "self-sufficiency" (6:6). Both Seneca and "Paul" emphasize that the key to virtue in this realm is in learning to be satisfied with what you have,[27] and both authors draw upon the commonplace that a person is born with nothing and will take nothing into the afterlife (1 Tim 6:7; *Ep.* 20.13; 102.24–25). Both urge their recipients away from the customary vices of jealousy, strife, and contention.[28] Both authors also villify those whom they regard as opponents of their way of life, sometimes by name,[29] and urge their recipient to avoid such persons and their dangerous, foolish speech.[30] Seneca and "Paul" agree in their favoring of "conservative" lifestyles, their advocation of "modesty" in comportment, and their disdain for ostentation and "novelty."[31]

Dr. Cancik-Lindemaier's argument, that Seneca's epistles depend upon a system of Stoic doctrines but do not present it wholesale, also corresponds with what we find in 1 Timothy. Here the "system" behind

---

[27] 1 Tim 6:8: ἔχοντες δὲ διατροφὰς καὶ σκεπάσματα, τούτοις ἀρκεσθησόμεθα ("having food and clothing we shall be content with these"); *Ep.* 20.8: *ut contentus sis temet ipso et ex te nascentibus bonis* ("to make you content with your own self and with the goods that spring from yourself"). Cf. *Ep.* 9.13 (*Se contentus est sapiens*), 18.5–7 (on testing oneself monthly by periods of being content only with meager diet and rough clothing), and throughout the corpus.

[28] E.g., 1 Tim 6:4; 6:11; *Ep.* 14.9–10.

[29] See, e.g., 1 Tim 1:20, and *Ep.* 5.1, and *Ep.* 29 (on Marcellinus).

[30] 1 Tim 1:3–7; 4:7; 6:3–5, 20–21; cf. *Ep.* 20.2; 29.7; 32.2; 48.12.

[31] See, for example, "Paul"'s call for σωφροσύνη in dress in 1 Tim 2:9, and Seneca's *Ep.* 5, against Cynic attire, which would be right at home in the Pastorals: "Philosophy calls for plain living, but not for penance; and we may perfectly well be plain and neat at the same time (*Frugalitatem exigit philosophia, non poenam, potest autem esse non incompta frugalitas*)." On disdaining "novelty," see 14.14: *Non conturbabit sapiens publicos mores nec populum in se vitae novitate convertet* ("the wise man will not upset the customs of the people, nor will he invite the attention of the populace by any novel ways of living"). See also the subsequent paragraph on *temperantia*: "although, as a matter of fact, good health results from such moderation." Seneca and "Paul" both argue against extreme asceticism and for a moderate path between it and luxury (1 Tim 4:1–10; *Ep.* 5.4–5). Compare also "Paul"'s call for *decorum* in conduct in 2:2: ἵνα ἤρεμον καὶ ἡσύχιον βίον διάγωμεν ἐν πάσῃ εὐσεβείᾳ καὶ σεμνότητι.

the letter is the gospel, that narrative of God's saving actions in Jesus Christ, which is referred to via shorthand abbreviations (such as τὸ εὐαγγέλιον τῆς δόξης τοῦ μακαρίου θεοῦ (1:11), and τὸ τῆς εὐσεβείας μυστήριον; 3:16).[32] Both make abundant use of quotations from authorities to punctuate their reference to this underlying system of commitments or beliefs, in Seneca's case to a variety of philosophers (in the first thirty epistles especially to Epicurus), in "Paul's" to early Christian credal or hymnic texts. Each has a formulaic way of introducing these quotations, Seneca by saying he will "give his daily gift" (*Ep.* 14.17) to Lucilius with his quote of the day,[33] and "Paul" with a characteristic expression, πιστὸς ὁ λόγος, found three times in 1 Timothy.[34] It is possible that a similar paradox of paraenesis is found in the two works also, as Seneca the Stoic urges progress toward virtue, and the Pauline author progress "in the faith," neither of which, ideally, can be achieved without a momentous conversion,[35] though the complexity of this topic, and the epistemological bases upon which it depends, would require more discussion than is possible here.[36]

Responsible comparative literary and philosophical studies of course require engagement with differences as well as similarities. Though the two epistolary works bear similarities in form, content,

---

[32] See also 1:15 (Χριστὸς Ἰησοῦς ἦλθεν εἰς τὸν κόσμον ἁμαρτωλοὺς σῶσαι); 2:4–6; 3:16; 4:10; 6:13–16. I have discussed this phenomenon in Pauline theology generally in Margaret M. Mitchell, "Rhetorical Shorthand in Pauline Argumentation: The Functions of 'The Gospel' in the Corinthian Correspondence," *Gospel in Paul* (ed. A. Jervis and P. Richardson; JSNTSup 108; Sheffield: Sheffield Academic Press, 1994) 64–90.

[33] *Cotidiana stips.* Or, often, "pay his customary contribution" (*diurna mercedula*; e.g., *Ep.* 6.7).

[34] 1:15; 3:1; 4:9; cf. 2 Tim 2:11; Tit 3:8. Quotations are also introduced in other ways (e.g., 2:5–6; 3:16; 6:15–16).

[35] See Cancik-Lindemaier, "Seneca's Collection of Epistles," 91–101, on the Stoic paradox. In 1 Timothy this becomes acute in exegesis of 2:15 and 4:16, and in the "admittedly peculiar treatment of faith (πίστις) in the Pastorals (J. N. D. Kelly, *The Pastoral Epistles* [HNTC; San Francisco: Harper & Row, 1960] 20).

[36] It appears that for Seneca, the source of knowledge of virtue is in nature (as Cancik-Lindemaier, "Seneca's Collection of Epistles," 89–91, argues, as explicated, e.g., in *Ep.* 13.15; 49.12), and in 1 Timothy, in tradition faithfully appropriated (3:15; 6:20); but this point requires a much fuller discussion than I can give it here.

and compositional techniques, a major difference is that Seneca's Stoic preoccupation with death is unmatched in 1 Timothy.[37] On the other hand, 1 Timothy contains a large quantity of group or institutional instructions—about bishops, deacons, widows and others in the church—which are not paralleled in Seneca's correspondence with Lucilius, which is entirely individual in scope (though it does deal with questions of the delineation between different philosophical schools). The author of 1 Timothy assumes a role of authority, therefore, above and beyond Timothy's piety, and extends that authority into unchallengeable legislation for a wider church social order. Timothy serves mainly as the shapeless conduit for his instructions. This is where the real versus the fictional quality of these two sets of correspondence is significant.[38] The author of the Pastorals used the pseudepigraphic correspondence to instruct a later generation, after the deaths of both Paul and Timothy.[39] Therefore, the "moral autobiography" which is given fictional expression in the epistolary framework in this case is the host for a conversation about the health and future of an entire organization of early Christian communities.[40] Moral autobiography has been transformed into

---

[37] There are no instructions about attitudes toward death or dying. Eternal life is mentioned in four places in the letter (1:16; 4:8; 6:12, 19); however, its meaning is not developed, but is assumed from the underlying gospel narrative. Neither, interestingly, is it used in a strong paraenetic vein. There is one interesting correspondence, however: in 5:6 the self-indulgent widow is described as ζῶσα τέθνηκεν ("though alive, she has died"), which is a commonplace drawn upon also by Seneca (see, e.g., *Ep.* 82.3–4: *otium sine litteris mors est et hominis vivi sepultura*).

[38] This is perhaps where the pseudepigraphon meets the "letter essay," as in the places where Seneca inverts the Ciceronian *sententia* which describes the letter as a conversation with absent friends by instead naming his letter as a conversation with himself, with the addressee perchance listening in (*Ep.* 26.7; 27.1; cf. *Ep.* 3.3, on this as linked with the friendship *topos*).

[39] Although both Seneca and Lucilius are alive and in contact at the time of the letters' composition, which is not the case with the pseudepigraphical 1 Timothy, still the dynamics are not entirely different, as Dr. Cancik-Lindemaier has stressed the extent to which also Seneca's letters are "fictive" in that the friendship with Lucilius is in a sense created via the letters ("Seneca's Collection of Epistles," 106: "Thus Seneca had to write their friendship, if not their lives"), and in that the letters were not sent to their putative recipient.

[40] Another minor difference, which points in the same direction, has to do with the treatments of slavery in the two works. While Seneca discusses slavery as a

moralizing polity, psychagogy into ecclesiagogy. Not surprisingly, also gone here is the *mutuality* in moral autobiography (contrast, for example, Seneca *Ep.* 23.1), for Paul is dead, and beyond προκοπή, now enshrined as a frozen example from the past.

In conclusion, Dr. Cancik-Lindemaier's provocative thesis about Seneca's epistles provides both many stimulating ideas about the role of epistles and implied narrative in moral development, and a most useful lens for understanding the peculiarity of the Pastorals among Paul's letters. In the latter case the letter has become a directive issued by the apostle to his church of later generations, about how it should order its life, instead of a conversation between friends about the moral life (the form which it mimics), a move which was to prove decisive for the history of reception of this text, especially as it was gathered into the sub-collection of the Pastorals and then into the corpus Paulinum, which became its primary interpretive context.

---

philosophical topic and engages the *topos* of true slavery and true freedom in relation to wisdom (e.g., *Ep.* 22), the author of 1 Timothy treats the issue on a strictly practical level (6:1–2), concerning the obedience of slaves to their masters, believing or unbelieving, betraying no philosophical interest (though Seneca himself can get into such particulars also, as in *Ep.* 47).

The Matthean Trajectory from Q to Mark[1]

James M. Robinson

Now that we have worked out a critical text of Q, with the sequence of Q[2] as well as its wording on much firmer ground than it has ever been before, we can extend redaction criticism beyond Matthew and

---

[1] I earlier used the term "Proto-Matthew" to highlight the difference between Matthew 3–11 and Matthew 12–28, with which the present paper is concerned. In an essay "The *Incipit* of the Sayings Gospel Q" (*Hommage à Étienne Trocmé. Revue d'Histoire et de Philosophie Religieuses* 75 [1995] 9–33, p. 33) I wrote: "The idiom τὸ εὐαγγέλιον τῆς βασιλείας may not have been first created by the final Matthean redaction, but may reflect a Q-like expansion of Q 3–7 into Matt 3–11 with some help from Mark, a kind of Proto-Matthew, which preceded the final Matthean redaction that included the later chapters which more slavishly follow Mark." Frans Neirynck responded with visible concern ("Q: From Source to Gospel," *ETL* 71 [1995] 421–430, here 426 n. 30): "It is amazing to read that 'the idiom τὸ εὐαγγέλιον τῆς βασιλείας . . . may reflect a Q-like expansion of Q 3–7 into Matt 3–11 . . .' (*The* Incipit, p. 33). Are we then in synoptic criticism to start again from the very beginning?" What Neirynck has in mind is evident from his paper, "The First Synoptic Pericope: The Appearance of John the Baptist in Q?" (*ETL* 72 [1996] 41–74), where he begins with his own teacher L. Cerfaux, who postulated a Papias-inspired Aramaic Matthew ("M") that was translated into Greek ("Mg") and then used by Matthew and Luke (hence the "minor agreements"), as well as by Mark, a kind of "Urevangelium" which Cerfaux' close colleague L. Vaganay designated Proto-Matthew. But ("The First Synoptic Pericope," 42): "Vaganay's theory of Proto-Matthew as the Synoptic source behind Mk 1,1–6 is now generally abandoned." As well it should be! In fact my agreement with Neirynck here is evident from my critique of the attempts by D.R. Catchpole and J. Lambrecht, both in 1992, to revive a similar position (see pp. 15–19 of my essay, "The *Incipit* of the sayings Gospel Q," and pp. 44–46 of Neirynck's "The First Synoptic Pericope"), and my criticism of the appeal to Papias in my essay, pp. 26–28. The future of synoptic criticism does in fact lie in moving forward upon the basis of the progress that has been made, not in returning to rightly discarded alternatives. What I have in view is not such a harmonistic "Urevangelium," but rather an installment in the composition of Matthew that has already begun to make use, even though minimally, of the Gospel of Mark. But I see that "Proto-Matthew" is a term much too encumbered by its previous usage for one to make use of it even in a quite different sense.

[2] See my essay on "The Sequence of Q: The Lament over Jerusalem," *Von Jesus zum Christus—Christologische Studien für Paul Hoffmann,* (ed. Ulrich Busse and Rudolf Hoppe; Berlin and New York: de Gruyter, 1998).

Luke's use of Mark, to their use of Q. The present paper seeks to initiate this second phase of redaction criticism.[3]

1. The Working Hypothesis

It was Q^{Matt}, the copy of Q that had been used and expanded in the life of the Matthean community, that the Evangelist Matthew used in composing canonical Matthew, which, according to the conventional wisdom as early as Rudolf Bultmann, consisted in working Q^{Matt} into the framework of the Gospel of Mark. But this standard definition of Matthean redaction leaves out a crucial ingredient: Matthew began this redactional procedure by imbedding Mark into his Q, not Q into Mark. The hold of Q on Matthew did not give way easily, but held on tenaciously through chapter 11, only then surrendering to the hegemony of Mark.

What goes on in Matthew 3–11 should not simply be included in the designation Q^{Matt}, for by Q^{Matt} one has in mind the glossing of Q by the Matthean community before the Evangelist Matthew set about merging Q with Mark to produce canonical Matthew. It is the intrusion of Mark into the Q-Matthew trajectory already in Matthew 3–11 that suggests one should not speak of a late draft of Q^{Matt}, but rather of a first installment of Matthew, now involving (to a limited extent) Mark and so deserving already the designation Matthew.

Striking insights in recent scholarship have led to the point of departure of this paper. Hans Dieter Betz, for two decades or more,[4] argued forcefully, but initially rather unconvincingly (to judge by early reviews[5]), that the Sermon on the Mount was not composed by the

[3] Two of my doctoral students, Linden Youngquist and Kathryn J. Silberling, have provided seminar papers, and the latter has completed a doctoral dissertation, "Orality and Intertextuality in Matthew: A Case for Literary Stratigraphy in the Gospel of Matthew" (Claremont Graduate University, 1997) working out some of these issues.

[4] Hans Dieter Betz, "Eine judenchristliche Kult-Didache in Matthäus 6,1–18," *Jesus Christus in Historie und Theologie: Neutestamentliche Festschrift für Hans Conzelmann zum 60. Geburtstag* (ed. Georg Strecker; Tübingen: Mohr [Siebeck], 1975) 445–457. It and subsequent essays on the Sermon on the Mount were published in Betz's *Essays on the Sermon on the Mount* (Philadelphia: Fortress, 1985), culminating in his Hermeneia commentary, *The Sermon on the Mount* (Minneapolis: Fortress, 1995).

[5] G. N. Stanton, *JTS* 37 (1986) 621–623; Charles E. Carlston, "Betz on the Sermon on the Mount — A Critique," *CBQ* 50 (1988) 47–57.

Evangelist, but was written a generation or more earlier, around 50 CE, as an epitome of Jesus' teaching for use in the Jewish Christian Mission authorized by the Jerusalem Council, with the Sermon on the Plain found in Luke being composed at about the same time as the epitome for the Gentile Christian Mission. In this way Betz was able to use the Sermon on the Mount as documentation for the other side of the Pauline debate analyzed in his Galatians commentary. Indeed Betz made a point of highlighting subtle anti-Pauline polemics he found imbedded in the Sermon on the Mount.

In any case, the Sermon on the Mount is not just the first of the five Matthean discourses. It is Betz who deserves credit for having called our attention to the unavoidable fact that the Sermon on the Mount is something special, not only as the classic statement of Jesus' teaching, but also in the way it came to be. But he did not succeed in explaining just how it did come to be.

If Betz has posed acutely the question of the origin of the Sermon on the Mount, it is Ulrich Luz who, in his exhaustive four-volume commentary on Matthew, has focussed attention on the origin of the Gospel of Matthew. In the introduction to his commentary, Luz made comments that seem to stand in some tension with each other:[6]

> . . . the Gospel of Matthew comes from a community which was founded by the wandering messengers and prophets of the Son of man of the Sayings Source and remains in close contact with them. The traditions of Q thus reflect, for the community, experiences from its own history. They are "its own" traditions.

If thus Matthew is the ultimate outcome of the Q community, it is difficult to explain Luz' other comment:[7]

> Matthew, who has taken over the narrative structure of the Gospel of Mark, is literarily a new concept of the Gospel of Mark and not a new conception of Q.

How is it that the Q community, now become the Matthean community, could give up its own Q priorities so readily, to become just a new concept of Mark? Was there no Q loyalty left? Is there not at least a last gasp of Q in Matthew's sense of values?

Luz did not pose this question. Yet it is to his credit that he clearly detected a crucial seam in Matthew between chapters 11 and 12. For this is precisely where Matthew shifts from his loyalty to Q and goes

---

[6] Ulrich Luz, *Matthew 1–7: A Commentary* (Minneapolis: Augsburg, 1989) 83.

[7] Ulrich Luz, *Matthew 1–7*, 75.

over to subservience to Mark. Yet, oddly enough, Luz did not find this, to me rather obvious, explanation for the seam he detected:[8]

> Beginning with ch. 12, the Gospel of Matthew follows closely the structure of Mark. Leaving aside the discourses, only few texts are inserted. But in chs. 3–11 non-Markan texts predominate. The sequence of Mark 1:1–2:22 seems to be presupposed in Matthew 3–11, but it determines the structure only minimally. It seems as if the evangelist Matthew [from chapter 12 on] relaxed in his redactional activity. The discrepancy between Matthew 1–1[1] and 1[2]–28 must be explained.

There is indeed a sudden shift between Matthew 11 and Matthew 12 in the way Matthew uses Mark. If Matthew 12–28 is striking in its almost complete subservience to Markan order, a quite different situation calls out for an explanation in Matthew 3–11.

There is, in addition to the shift between Matthew 11 and Matthew 12, an additional problem calling for explanation: Matthew 3–11 (actually only Matthew 8–10) had continued taking material from Mark in Markan sequence (with only Mark 2:1–22 and 4:35–5:17 in reversed order), getting as far down as Mark 13:13 par. Matt 10:21–22. So the further problem is that Matthew 12–28 returns to Mark 2:23, to move a second time through Mark, for example, reaches a second time Mark 13:13 at Matt 24:9c,13, finally to complete Mark at Matt 28:1–8. Put conversely, Matthew 3–11 went considerably beyond the point in Mark (2:22/23) where Matthew 12–28 began to take over the bulk of Mark in unaltered Markan sequence (Mark 2:23–16:8 par. Matt 12:1–28:8). It is this continuing Markan material in Matthew 8–10, derived from Mark 4:35/2:1–13:13, that is, from the part of Mark that will be reworked more fully in Matthew 12–28, that hence also calls for explanation. Why the repetitive scanning of Mark, once with more redactional energy, once more "relaxed," going with the flow? A solution is needed that will both make sense of Matthew going through the Markan material twice and of him working with such sharply diverging techniques.

The solution lies in recognizing that Matthew 3–11 is not primarily oriented to editing Mark, but rather to editing Q, or, to be more precise, editing the first major segment of Q, found in Q 3–7 = Matthew 3–11. For in these chapters Q, and following him Matthew, is

[8] Ulrich Luz, *Matthew 1–7*, 37. See also p. 42, and Luz, *Die Jesusgeschichte des Matthäus* (Neukirchen-Vluyn: Neukirchner Verlag, 1993) 19.

energetically perfecting the main (pre-)christological argument of Q, to the effect that Jesus is the Coming One predicted by John, a message intended only for Israel. For Matthew, this is a monument to and justification for the Q community, for having held out in Jesus' own lifestyle for so long, before in fact yielding to the unremitting pressure of the Gentile Christian community and its Gospel Mark. Mark is hence only a subordinate factor in Matthew 3–11, just as Q is only a subordinate factor in Matthew 12–28.

2. *The Archaizing, Archival Tendency in the Gospels*

Before going into more detail about the first major segment of Q that Matthew recognized as such and sought to perfect in chapters 3–11, it may be helpful to disgress a moment, to draw attention to a neglected aspect in the scholarship in our century regarding the Synoptic Gospels, but an aspect which is presupposed in speaking of Matthew 3–11 as a monument to and justification for the Q community, for having held out in Jesus' own lifestyle for so long.

Whereas the Nineteenth Century sought to read the Gospels as direct reports about Jesus around 30 CE, the Twentieth Century has read them first of all as reports about the Evangelists' times, with form criticism emphasizing the communities that transmitted the traditions and redaction criticism emphasizing the creative theologizing of the Evangelists themselves. While all this remains true, such an emphasis has perhaps unduly obscured another dimension, an archaizing, archival interest in portraying how it was back then for apologetic reasons, in the case of Luke to justify the successful Gentile church for promptly departing from Jesus' ways, in the case of Matthew to justify the failing Jewish church for clinging so long to Jesus' ways.

One has detected this archaizing, archival interest perhaps most clearly in the case of Luke. His two-volume policy took some pressure off of him to present in his Gospel an up-to-date form of Christianity, since that transparency of Jesus' biography to Luke's present time could be spelled out in fuller detail and in more direct language in the Acts of the Apostles. Luke also had a periodizing theology that permitted him to favor different procedures for different periods.

Thus, just as Luke can in Acts portray a sort of primitive "Communism" at the beginnings of the Jerusalem church without feeling obligated to portray the subsequent Gentile Diaspora church in such terms, even more can he portray the Mission of the Twelve and even the Mission of the Seventy-Two in his Gospel in a way quite different from his presentation of the Pauline Mission in Acts. To some extent, this is simply conforming to the facts of a changing mission practice, as Paul's concession of his diverging practice in 1 Corinthians 9 already makes clear. But, to some extent, Luke does discuss the problem in terms of his periodizing theology and presents a justification for telling how it was back then in distinction from how it is now.

Hans Conzelmann first drew attention to the overarching Lukan redaction in the Gospel:[9] After failing at the Temptation, the devil in Luke 4:13 left Jesus "for a time," and then, only after the idealized public ministry, re-emerged to enter Judas in Luke 22:3 and to tempt Peter in Luke 22:31. The period of Satan's absence, corresponding to what we call the public ministry of Jesus, is what Conzelmann defined as "the center of time," a paradise-like unrepeatable idyllic period of time. But what Conzelmann did not notice is that this center of time in Luke's presentation corresponds very closely to the limits of Q in Luke, from Luke 3:2 through Luke 22:30, since the idyllic center of time ends in the very next verse, Luke 22:31. For it is immediately after quoting the conclusion of Q in Luke 22:28, 30 that Luke presents Satan re-emerging to tempt Peter to betray Jesus. Then Luke moves in verses 35–38 to revoke quite explicitly the Mission Instructions of Q 10:4, urging the disciples instead to sell a tunic to buy a sword, so as to prepare the reader for the Markan sword used by a disciple in Gethsemane, reported next in verses 49–51. Here in effect Luke has closed down the epoch of Q, wonderful though it may have seemed, and "gets real." With Q safely behind him, Luke can proceed to follow Mark through the Passion Narrative.

This periodizing did not require Luke to omit the outdated and formally abrogated Mission Instructions; rather it permitted him to preserve them in their archaic form, still separated into Markan and Q versions, and not updated to conform to current practice. Matthew, however, clinging longer to the older procedures, had to make the

---

[9] Hans Conzelmann, *The Theology of St. Luke* (New York: Harper and Brothers, 1960). The title of the German original had brought to expression the central thesis about the public ministry as the center of time: *Die Mitte der Zeit* (Tübingen: Mohr [Siebeck], 1954).

adjustments called for by the passage of time, justifying, by appealing to Jesus' instructions, the exclusively Jewish Mission as it had been carried out to the exclusion of Gentiles and Samaritans up until quite recently (Matt 10,5b–6,23).

Much the same is true of the two versions of the Q-Sermon, Luke leaving it largely as it had been in Q^{Luke}, since he replaces it, as the Inaugural Sermon, with a much better Sermon, from his point of view, in the synagogue of Nazara (Luke 4:16–30), where Jesus explicitly argues that he fulfills Isaiah 61 (only implicitly used in one beatitude by Q and in others as well by Matthew), after having read it aloud. But Matthew retained the Sermon as it had lived and grown in the Matthean community for a generation, though, as Betz insists, it was still not worthy of Antioch's new designation "Christian." Yet Matthew still cherished it. Whereas Matthew's Great Commission of necessity discontinues explicitly the Mission limited to Israel, at least the Sermon on the Mount is quietly vindicated: ". . . teaching them to observe all that I have commanded you" (Matt 28:20).

If Luke spread Q throughout the whole public ministry of Jesus, since after all he had a second volume in which to move from the Jewish Christianity of Q to the Gentile church, Matthew had to compress most Q material, especially its older parts, into Matthew 3–11, so as to leave the space of Matthew 12–28 to work his way faithfully through Mark to evolve into the Gentile Mission he proclaims only at the very end (Matt 28:18–20). In Matthew 3–11, Matthew is presenting an idealized version of the traditional Q kind of Christianity, so as to have it on the record, an archaic archive vindicating the first major period of the Matthean community's own way of being Christian. Matthew's point is: though we will have to do it Mark's way, one can never say we were unfaithful in having done it so long in Q's—and Jesus'—way.

Thus both Luke and Matthew implement archaic apologetic interests in somewhat different ways, Luke with more relaxation describing how things were done back in the unreal (un-Satanic, unarmed) unique period of Jesus, where such was still viable, but Matthew justifying his community for having retained those practices up until recently, when the olden ways collapsed like a house of cards and had to give way to the success story of Gentile Christianity.

The present essay is oriented to this archaizing, apologetic interest of Matthew, the last stand of Jewish Christianity in Matthew 3–11, before Matthew simply copies out Mark in Matthew 12–28, only toning down unobtrusively here and there what seemed to him and his constituency to be Markan excesses. But Matthew also had to work his way out of the Q community's limitation to Israel. Hence, he has Jesus first give the Syrophoenician (now Canaanite) woman the standard Jewish-Christian reply (see Matt 10:6): "I was sent only to the lost sheep of the house of Israel" (Matt 15:24). But then, following through on Mark 7:24–30, he updates his position: "O woman, great is your faith! Be it done to you as you desire" (Matt 15:28). Matthew finally leaves far behind his Judaism, with blood on its hands for killing Jesus (Matt 27:25) and lies on its lips for accusing the disciples of stealing the corpse (Matt 27:62–66; 28:11–15), as Matthew's church marches forth with the Great Commission making disciples of all nations, no doubt much to the distress of the holdouts for Jewish Christianity, and with at least mixed feelings on the part of the Evangelist himself.

What is striking is the quantity of clusters from precisely the oldest layers of Q that are moved forward from later in "our" Q, to be crammed into Matthew 3–11, within the overarching outline of Q 3–7, which was the first major segment of Q. That is to say, the basic fact about Matthew 5–7, the Sermon on the Mount, as enlarged far beyond its original proportions by the interpolation especially of the oldest Q traditions, while retaining the overarching Q outline of the Sermon, is what is also true of the first major section of Matthew into which the Sermon was imbedded, as Q 3–7 was enlarged to become Matthew 3–11. What Betz drew attention to in Matthew 5–7 is part of a larger phenomenon in the Gospel of Matthew, to which Luz drew attention, namely the sharp divergence of Matthew 3–11 from Matthew 12–28. Hence, Matthew 3–11 calls for an overarching solution not limited to Matthew 5–7.

Luz quite rightly comments that "the combination of these two sources [Mark and Q] reflects a piece of the history of the Matthean community."[10] But he has not actually worked out the implications for the Matthean community's history. Rather than the Markan text simply dominating the Q-Matthean community, its Evangelist first took

---

[10] Ulrich Luz, *Matthew 1–7*, 82.

over what was needed from Mark within Q's own framework, using Q 3–7 as the basic outline of Matthew 3–11, and only from then on yielded to the overpowering Markan framework. Of course this is first of all an observation about the Matthean text, not the Matthean community, but it may well reflect an important transition in the Q-Matthean community that should not be overlooked. In view of the inroads of the Gentile Christian success story, culminating in the Great Commission, Matthew 3–11 seems to reflect the Q community perfecting its last will and testament, before moving via Mark into the mainstream of Christianity, to be canonized and thus rescued for posterity, for ourselves.

3. The Q Redaction's Organization of Q 3–7

We should first look at the organization of the first major section of Q, so as to be able to trace it more clearly in Matthew's redaction. Q used to be thought of only as a random, non-tendentious collection of sayings of Jesus, but the thesis of Dieter Lührmann[11] has by now gained rather universal acceptance, to the effect that Q reflects a quite distinct redactional activity. Lührmann's focus in analyzing the Q redaction was on its use of the Deuteronomistic view of history, God's devastating judgment on "this generation" of Israel for rejecting Jesus and the Q people. But the redactional work is evident not only in this theological *Tendenz*, evident primarily in later parts of Q (Q 11:49–51, followed directly by Q 13:34–35, as in Matt 23:34–39), which is most of what Lührmann saw, but also shows up clearly at the compositional level, especially in the first major section of Q: Q 3–7, before being transformed into Matthew 3–11.

Here one has first John's preaching about a Coming One and Jesus' receiving the Spirit at his Baptism (Q 3), then the Sermon (Q 6), the Healing of the Centurion's Boy (Q 7:1–10), the delegation of John's disciples to ask if Jesus is that Coming One (Q 7:18–23), and finally the coordination of John and Jesus with Wisdom's children (Q 7:24–35). (Lührmann, perhaps rightly, considered the Temptations of Jesus in Q 4 to be a later interpolation, as has, in fact, been rather frequently suggested.)

---

[11] Dieter Lührmann, *Die Redaktion der Logienquelle* (WMANT 33; Neukirchen-Vluyn: Neukirchner Verlag, 1969).

In Q 3, John's initial preaching had its center, from Q's point of view, in John's prediction of a Coming One who would carry out judgment on Israel. Even though this prediction may well have originally had God in view, yet for Q it already had Jesus in view. But this claim cannot be made explicit in Q 3, where it would seem simply preposterous, not to say blasphemous. The reader must be prepared for this early kind of incipient christological claim of Q by experiencing first the evidence. And the image of Judge would have to be modulated to approximate the Jesus tradition. Furthermore, for someone to be the Coming One would mean, in a Jewish context, to have been prophesied in the Old Testament. Hence Q, from its very beginning in Q 3 on, is looking for Jesus traditions that could document the prophecies from Isaiah summarized in Q 7:22 being fulfilled by Jesus:

> Go and tell John what you hear and see: The *blind see* and the lame walk, lepers are made clean and the deaf hear, and the dead are raised, and *the poor are evangelized.*

This learned saying[12] is a gleaning from throughout Isaiah, but is based primarily on Isa 61:1 LXX:

> The *Spirit* of the Lord is *upon me,* because he has anointed me, he has sent me to *evangelize the poor,* to heal the broken of heart, to proclaim liberty to the captives, *the recovery of sight to the blind,* . . . .

The *Spirit* had indeed descended *upon* Jesus at his baptism in Q 3:22,[13] the *evangelization of the poor* has taken place, as exemplified by the

[12] This list of healings from Isaiah may not be original to Q, for it is remarkably similar to the Qumran fragment 4Q521. In any case, it is surprising to find it in Q, since Q is not a collection of healings or miracle stories, such as the Semeia Source, but rather a collection of sayings, to which only the concluding item in the list, "the poor are evangelized," would seem to fit. Hence its focus on healings is all the more remarkable for Q. At the 1996 annual meeting of SNTS at Strasbourg, Hans Kvalbein presented a paper, "Die Wunder der Endzeit: Beobachtungen zu 4Q521," in which he argued that the healings are intended spiritually. But in Q, Matthew and Luke they seem to be taken more literally, though here too Jesus' healings are of course accorded spiritual significance.

[13] The rationale for all this taking place in the case of Jesus is his empowerment with the Spirit. It is largely for this reason that Jesus' baptism, though reduced in Luke to a genitive absolute, and put after John's imprisonment to accomodate Luke's periodizing schematism, should nonetheless be ascribed to Q (where the minor agreement of Q using the Isa 61:1 LXX preposition ἐπ' rather than Mark's εἰς for "upon" is a tell-tale sign).

Sermon in Q 6:20–49, beginning "Blessed are *the poor*, for yours is the kingdom of God," and the healings are exemplified by the Healing of the Centurion's Boy that follows immediately in Q 7:1–10.

Thus the two sections of Q handling the relation of John and Jesus (Q 3 and Q 7) form an *inclusio*, one with John predicting a Coming One, the other with confirmation to John that Jesus is that Coming One, the two separated by, or connected by, the material thought necessary to prove the argument that the Coming One is in fact Jesus: the Spirit coming upon Jesus, the Sermon for the Poor and the Healing of the Centurion's Boy. Thus Q 3–7 is a very well organized section of Q redaction. It is in fact Q's basic and decisive argument that Jesus is the fulfillment of biblical prophecy, that is, the Coming One, and hence the one whose sayings, when followed in practice, will save in the day of judgment. This is the core of Q's positive "theology."

Now Matthew apparently still understood all that, standing as he did in the Q heritage, and recognized its decisive importance. And so, before turning away from Q to a rather rote copying out of Mark in Matthew 12–28, he first presented in Matthew 3–11 an enlarged, improved, even more convincing argument that Jesus is, as Q had claimed all along, the Coming One. The Sermon on the Mount is part of this. It may well not have an adequate christology, if judged by the Markan standards of Matt 12–28, but it has a convincing (pre-) christology, if judged by Q's standards. (The ἔχρισέν με of Isa 61:1 is a christological point of departure not picked up explicitly either by Q or by Matthew.)

To make the Q Sermon weightier and more effective, Matthew could simply interpolate into the Sermon important clusters of archaic sayings that were available to him in Q, and in his other sources. But to produce healing narratives comparable to the list of Q 7:22, he could not build primarily on Q, which had only two healings, but had to turn to Mark, not primarily out of loyalty to Mark, but rather out of loyalty to Q, to bolster its decisive claim. Similarly the Mission Instructions of Q 10 were advanced into Matthew 10, that is, were put prior to Q 7 = Matthew 11. Here the Mission Instructions occur in greatly enlarged form, again in part using Mark, by imbedding in Q's Mission Instructions also Mark's Mission Instructions (putting Mark 6:8–11 into the Mission Instructions as Matt 10:9–11, 14), and by historicizing Mark's apocalypse (putting Mark 13:9, 11–13 into the Mission

Instructions as Matt 10:17–22). This then is followed by Matthew 11, an augmented version of Q 7 that then becomes the climax of the first main section of Q. All of this, put together, produces an even more impressive conclusion of the Q-oriented first part of Matthew.

This is the basic solution to Luz's conundrum cited above: "The discrepancy between Matthew 1–11 and 12–28 must be explained." For Matthew 3–11 is the last stand of Q, Matthew 12–28 the first victory of Mark.

4. Matthew 5–7: Archaic Clusters from Q Built into the Sermon on the Mount

The sections within Matt 3–11 do become more intelligible when seen from the perspective of the Q trajectory, as the work of the leader of a Q-Matthean community that did not give up its heritage easily. The Sermon on the Mount is a central part of this overarching tendency.

Günther Bornkamm, in his Presidential Address at SNTS in 1977,[14] posed acutely the redactional problem of the Sermon on the Mount: the first half of the Sermon is highly structured in a clearly recognizable way—beatitudes (Matt 5:3–12) are followed by hermeneutics (Matt 5:17–20), then antitheses (Matt 5:21–48) and then the cult didache (Matt 6:1–6, 16–18). The final section too, with the Golden Rule shifted to Matt 7:12, to conclude the body of the Sermon, followed by a conclusion, seemed intelligible enough. But this careful composition puts in sharp contrast the intervening last half of the body of the Sermon, Matt 6:19–7:11, where no rhyme or reason has been found to explain the seemingly random sequence of disparate materials.[15] Here one has 26 (or, if one adds the Lord's Prayer that seems a foreign body within the cult didache: 35) disorganized verses,

---

[14] Günther Bornkamm, "Der Aufbau der Bergpredigt," *NTS* 24 (1978) 419–32.

[15] A profound reason need not in every case be required. Matthew seems to have moved Q 12:33 about Treasure in Heaven, which in Q seems to have followed the Ravens and Lilies (Q 12:22–31 par. Matt 6:25–34), to a position prior to it (Matt 6:19–21), on the basis of a catchword connection, ἀφανίζω, used in quite different meanings in Matt 6:16 and 6:19–20. The baffling intrusion of Matt 7:6 about giving what is holy to dogs and throwing pearls before swine may at least in part be due to the catchwords βάλλω in Matt 7:5 and δίδωμι in Matt 7:7.

or, in terms of the subdivisions of Aland's *Synopsis*, seven or eight random pericopes ranging in size from one to ten verses.

Bornkamm made a valiant effort to solve this problem by arguing that this disorganized second half of the body of the Sermon on the Mount was organized around the Lord's Prayer found in Matt 6:9–13, with each petition of the Prayer corresponding to a section in the last half of the body of the Sermon. But a number of these correlations, as Bornkamm proposed them, are at best forced, at worst fanciful, when for example "Lead us not into temptation" finds its explication in not giving dogs what is holy or pearls to swine. It is almost as if the petition in the Prayer for which no clear saying can be found hence fits the saying for which no clear meaning can be found. From the failure of such topical justifications as that of Bornkamm, Betz drew the inevitable conclusion that one cannot make sense of the structure of the last half of the body of the Sermon in terms of some topical organization. The last word would seem to be Krister Stendahl's "resignation:"[16] "VI 19–VII 29 offers material which has been brought into the Sermon on the Mount by Matthew in such a manner that we find no clue as to its arrangement."

If one can hence concede that there is no clear topical structure to explain what we have in the last half of the Sermon, one is inclined to seek an explanation elsewhere. If, namely, instead of a nice outline, one seeks a meaningful compositional procedure, the seemingly jumbled section might make much more sense.

The standard treatment of the order of Q was provided by Vincent Taylor in two essays published in 1953 and 1959, where his argument in favor of Lukan order was based on a compositional procedure ascribed to Matthew.[17] He argued that the Lukan order is, as the English tradition had long maintained, the Q order, since Matthew

---

[16] Krister Stendahl, "Matthew," *Peake's Commentary on the Bible* (ed. M. Black and H. H. Rowley; Middlesex: Nelson, 1962), 779, cited in Bornkamm, "Der Aufbau der Bergpredigt," 425, and in Dale C. Allison, Jr., "The Structure of the Sermon on the Mount," *JBL* 106 (1987) 434.

[17] Vincent Taylor, "The Order of Q," *JTS*, n. s. 4 (1953) 27–31, reprinted in his *New Testament Essays* (Grand Rapids, MI: Eerdmans, 1972) 90–94; "The Original Order of Q," *New Testament Essays: Studies in Memory of T. W. Manson, 1893–1958* (ed. A. J. B. Higgins; Manchester: Manchester University Press, 1959) 246–269, reprinted in Taylor's *New Testament Essays*, 95–118.

really supports the Lukan order, once one has detected with Taylor's help Matthew's method: for each of his five discourses, Matthew scanned Q for sayings relevant to the theme of that discourse, plucking them out as he came to them in the Q order, and thus built his five discourses around different topics. When one then sees that each discourse individually follows Lukan order, it is apparent that the Lukan order is the Q order.

For the past generation one has tended to accept Taylor's insight, since it provides evidence for what one had already assumed. Yet it fails just when one needs it most, in the Sermon on the Mount: the Sermon on the Mount (Matthew 5–7) should, according to Taylor, begin, let us say as Matthew 5, with the first relevant material from the beginning of Q, namely the Sermon from Q 6. Then, let us say as Matthew 6, would come the relevant material from the first half of the remaining Q text, say Q 7–11, and finally, as Matthew 7, material from the last half of the remaining Q text, in Q 12–22. But that is precisely not what one finds in the Sermon on the Mount. Rather, the contents of the Sermon in Q 6 are expanded, accordion-like, to function as an outline for Matthew 5 and 7, but to skip Matthew 6 completely. Hence the Sermon on the Mount, in its use of the Q Sermon, is already one major exception to Taylor's "rule," in that it retains throughout the organizational structure of the Q Sermon, stretched out to become a kind of framework.

But even if one were to grant Taylor this one major exception to his theory, the bulk of the Sermon on the Mount, which is from elsewhere, calls for an explanation in its own right: the 48 verses of Matthew 5 become more than twice as large as the seventeen verses of the corresponding first half of the Q Sermon (6:20–36); Matthew 6 is not from the Q Sermon at all, but does contain 34 verses, much from elsewhere in Q; and Matthew 7, with its 27 verses, is more than twice the size of the corresponding thirteen verses in the last half of the Q Sermon (6:37–49).

One need only survey the sequence of the Q material brought into the Sermon on the Mount from elsewhere in Q, in terms of its Q = Lukan order, to see the patent improbability of Taylor's theory: Q 16:17; Q 12:57–59; Q 16:18; Q 11:2–4; Q 12:33–34; Q 11:34–36; Q 16:13; Q 12:22–31; Q 11:9–13; Q 13:23–24, 25–27. We are asked to assume that Matthew collected this material by reading Q in Lukan =

Q order! In a very few cases, of which Taylor makes much, one can make a selection from among this Q material that produces a sequence of a few items where the Matthean order fits the Q = Lukan order. But it is mathematically inevitable that somewhere Matthew would have the Q = Lukan order, given the length of the list, unless one were to assume Matthew consistently copied out Q from back to front.

Furthermore, to make sense of Taylor's theory, one would need to assume that Matthew went through Q with the given topic of a discourse in mind, to glean out what fits that theme to put into that discourse. Taylor's theory requires him to conjecture that Matthew went through Q several times in composing the Sermon on the Mount (since the sequence of the Q material in the Sermon on the Mount does not present a single correspondence to Lukan = Q order). But it remains completely unexplained why Matthew would choose sayings when going through Q for this purpose a second or third or fourth time that he would not have chosen already when going through Q on a previous occasion, if indeed he went through Q repeatedly collecting material on the same theme for the same discourse. And what was the theme that would explain the interpolations into the Q Sermon? When one moves beyond the appealing schematism to the specific texts, Taylor's theory simply fails to make sense of what often seems a disparate hodge-podge of sayings brought into the Q Sermon from elsewhere to enlarge it into the Sermon on the Mount.

This divergence of the reality of the Sermon on the Mount from Taylor's theory might however tend to indicate that the author of the Sermon on the Mount was the same Q-Matthean author who composed in a somewhat similarly non-sequential way, from later Markan (and Q) texts, the two chapters of Healings in Matthew 8–9 (see below). Also the Mission Discourse in Matthew 10 has in one regard a similar non-Taylor-like outlining structure to that of the Q Sermon in Matthew 5–7, when the conclusion of the Q Mission Discourse, Q 10:16, is deferred to the conclusion of the Matthean Mission Discourse, at Matt 10:40, just as the conclusion of the Q Sermon is used as the conclusion of the Sermon on the Mount. Such a rectification of Taylor's thesis would not basically undercut Betz's argument for a distinct author of the Sermon on the Mount, if one were to recast it in terms of a distinctive editorial policy for all of Matthew 3–11.

Even if one were to concede to Betz that there must have been some other author than canonical Matthew for the Sermon on the Mount, this would not in itself explain the chaotic Q sequence in the second half of the Sermon. Hence one may suggest, as an alternative explanation, a sequence of layering procedures, whose cogency would in each case have to stand on its own merits.

Not all of the layers could be as early as around 50 CE. For a last layer involved borrowings from Mark: the amputation of the offending eye and hand in Matt 5:29–30 probably comes from Mark 9:43–47, and the exhortation to forgive appended to the Lord's Prayer at Matt 6:14(–15) probably comes from Mark 11:25(–26). But, such concessions of peripheral Markan intrusion would not basically put in question Betz's early dating for the Sermon on the Mount, since the bulk of the composition could in any case be much older than Mark.

Yet another set of interpolations into the Sermon on the Mount may also be relatively late, for they come after the redaction has closed the body of the Sermon by shifting the Golden Rule from the middle (Q 6:31, in Matthean terms just after Matt 5:42) to near the end (Matt 7:12, before the conclusion began at Q 6:41). For a pre-Matthean redaction had rightly recognized that the body of the Q Sermon ended with the Speck and the Log in one's eye (Q 6:41–42 par. Matt 7:3–5). The Q Sermon's original conclusion or Peroration that followed consisted then in the exhortation actually to do what Jesus said: it is by one's fruits that one is known (Q 6:43–45 par. Matt 7:15–20), rather than by just saying "Lord, Lord" (Q 6:46 par. Matt 7:21–23); one is not only to hear but also to do Jesus' sayings, so as to build one's house on rock, not sand (Q 6:47–49 par. Matt 7:24–27). But into that original Peroration of the Q Sermon, consisting of only seven verses (Q 6:43–49), have been interpolated so much material that the conclusion has become more than twice as long as it originally was, now stretching to fifteen verses (Matt 7:13–27). This is more than half of chapter 7, but not much of it is related to the Peroration's purpose, to exhort one to do what Jesus has said. This bloating of the conclusion out of all proportion would hence seem to be later than the shift of the Golden Rule to mark the real end of the body of the

Sermon, since the Golden Rule now stands in a rather arbitrary position in the middle of Matthew 7.

Here, in this extended conclusion, is where one finds a Q cluster (Q 13:24–29) put redactionally partly into the Sermon on the Mount and partly into the following Healings: The sayings on the Two Ways and on the Evildoers (Matt 7:13–14,22–23) were brought forward from Q 13:23–24,25–27, to become an obviously late intrusion that disturbs the well thought-out concluding Peroration to the Q Sermon, and goes well beyond its appropriate dimensions. Then it is the remaining third of this same pericope (Q 13:28–29) that is also interpolated redactionally, to follow in Q order upon the other two parts of this pericope. But this third part of the Q 13 text is imbedded not in the Sermon on the Mount at all, but in what follows immediately after the Sermon in Q, the Healing of the Centurion's Boy (Matt 8:11–12). That is to say, Q 13:23–29 was interpolated not into the Sermon on the Mount, when it existed in isolation, but when it was already followed by the ongoing Matthean text. It was moved into Q^{Matt}, or into Matthew 3–11, not just into an isolated Sermon on the Mount.

One could, however, postulate with Betz an early draft of the Q Sermon in which it was subjected to an early enlargement, making use of small collections of sayings later to be incorporated into the Q redaction. For Taylor did not demonstrate that Q materials were already in the sequence of the Q redaction (the Lukan sequence) when they were introduced into the Sermon on the Mount. To the extent that these could be dated as early as mid-century, the initial layering within the Sermon on the Mount could be dated that early, and thus Betz' thesis could be, in the main, validated, even if the later layering in the Sermon on the Mount mentioned above would remain minor exceptions to Betz's thesis. The basic ingredients of such a reconstruction are as follows:

In the original Q Sermon (Q 6:20–49), the admonition to love one's enemies, with which the first half of the body of the Sermon culminates, includes the exhortation to pray for those who persecute you (Q 6:28). This exhortation to prayer could have been the occasion for the interpolation of the early Q pericope on Prayer, consisting of the Lord's Prayer (Q 11:2b–4) and its Interpretation: Ask, Seek, Knock (Q 11:9–10), illustrated by the human father's treatment of his son (Q 11:11–13). In the triad of Ask, Seek, Knock, it is clearly *Ask* that dominates the illustrations about *asking* for bread and fish and receiving them, rather than stones and snakes (Q 11:11–12). Indeed, the verb *ask* occurs five times in the five verses of this Interpretation. Now the Matthean introduction to the Lord's Prayer recognizes this focus on "*asking*," in that it concludes: "for your Father knows what you need before you *ask* him." Thus Matthew seems to have been aware that the Interpretation belonged to the Prayer, as in Q, where the Interpretation followed immediately on the Prayer. But in the Sermon on the Mount they are widely separated, forming the beginning and end of this disorganized second half of the body of the Sermon on the Mount (Matt 6:7–15; 7:7–11), which in turn calls for explanation:

The second of the three synonyms for prayer, "ask, *seek*, knock," recurs in the conclusion (Q 12:30–31) of another early Q pericope, about the Ravens and Lilies: "the Gentiles *seek*" food and clothing, but you are to "*seek* his kingdom, and these things shall be yours as well." Hence the pericope on the Ravens and Lilies could well have also been attracted into the context of the Prayer and its Interpretation. In fact it does crop up between them in the Sermon on the Mount (Q 12:22–31 par. Matt 6:25–33), no doubt as another kind of illustrative interpretation of the Prayer, now exemplified by the Ravens and Lilies (much as Luke 11:5–8 is a Lukan interpolation into the same position between the Prayer and its Q Interpretation, namely, an illustration of a friend seeking and receiving bread).

In support of the view that the Sermon on the Mount did associate the Ravens and Lilies with the Prayer and its Interpretation, one need only point out the redactional allusions to the conclusion of the Ravens and Lilies found in the Matthean context of the Lord's Prayer. For Q's conclusion of the Ravens and Lilies, "your heavenly Father knows that you *need* them all" (Q 12:30b par. Matt 6:32b), is echoed in the introduction to the Prayer in the Sermon on the Mount (Matt 6:8): "for your Father knows what you *need* before you ask him." And this conclusion of the Ravens and Lilies is immediately preceded in Q by an ethnic slur about Gentiles: "For the *Gentiles* seek all these things" (Q 12:32a par. Matt 6:32a). This has apparently triggered the Matthean redactional interpolation, in precisely the same position as in the Ravens and Lilies, that is to say, just before the reassurance that God knows our *needs*, of the ethnic slur about Gentiles: "Do not heap up empty phrases as the *Gentiles* do" (Matt 6:7). Thus the Ravens and

Lilies, as an illustrative Interpretation of the Lord's Prayer, is attached in the Sermon on the Mount to the Lord's Prayer by a kind of *inclusio*, the Matthean Prayer beginning with the ethnic slur (Matt 6:7), and the reassurance that God knows our every need (Matt 6:8), and the Ravens and Lilies concluding with the repetition of the same two striking traits (Matt 6:32a,b). The compiler of this part of the Sermon on the Mount sensed that they belong together.

But the close affinity, in the Sermon on the Mount, of the Lord's Prayer and the Ravens and Lilies is not limited to this shared framing *inclusio*. For the substance of the two pericopes is quite close. In the original Lord's Prayer of Q, the petition "Thy *kingdom* come" was followed directly by its practical concretization: "Give us this day our daily *bread*." This association of the kingdom with the daily provision of food is repeated at the conclusion of the pericope on Ravens and Lilies, to the effect that one should not have anxiety about *food* and clothing but instead seek the *kingdom*, and then such other things will also be supplied. It is by praying for the *kingdom* that one's *bread* is provided, just as it is in seeking only the *kingdom* that one obtains other things as well, such as *food* and clothing. Whoever did the layering in the composition of the second half of the body of the Sermon on the Mount must have been especially aware of this close substantive association of the Lord's Prayer with the illustrative Interpretation of the Ravens and Lilies.[18]

This redactor of the Sermon on the Mount interpolated into the Lord's Prayer his own (or his community's) interpretation of "*Thy kingdom* come:" "*Thy will* be done on earth as it is in heaven." Then he interpolated the same interpretation into the pericope on the Ravens and Lilies: "Seek first[19] *the kingdom of God* and *his righteousness*, and all these things shall be yours as well." Thus the clear recognition of the

[18] David R. Catchpole states that the Prayer and its Interpretation are "the only complex of Q material which could genuinely and without strain provide the argumentative basis upon which the ravens/lilies tradition builds" (*The Quest for Q* [Edinburgh: T. and T. Clark, 1993] 227).

[19] Bornkamm sees here an additional redactional allusion to the Lord's Prayer, "durch Hinzufügung von [427] πρῶτον, wodurch der Spruch deutlich an den Vorrang der ersten drei, insbesondere der 2. und 3. Bitte anklingt" ("Der Aufbau der Bergpredigt," 426–427). Bornkamm senses that the Matthean redaction recalls that in the Prayer the petitions for the kingdom and for God's will precede the petition for bread. This ingenious insight may be overdrawn.

original substantive interrelatedness of the Lord's Prayer and the Ravens and Lilies, and the compiler's own ethical interpretation of both, make clear why he would interpolate the Ravens and Lilies into the middle of his discussion of prayer, between the Lord's Prayer and its original Interpretation: Ask, Seek, Knock. Thus the Ravens and Lilies in effect replaces Ask, Seek, Knock as the first Interpretation of the Prayer in the Sermon on the Mount, whereupon Ask, Seek, Knock is relegated to third position, which, after other interpolations, becomes the very end of the body of the Sermon on the Mount (Matt 7:7–11). Like the Golden Rule (Matt 7:12), it comes to function as part of the body of the Matthean Sermon's concluding summary: the Golden Rule summarizes the central section of the Q Sermon in Matthew 5 about Focal Instances of Ideal Conduct and Love of Enemies, whereas Ask, Seek, Knock comes to summarize the added Q material about Prayer[20] moved by a compiler into the Sermon in Matthew 6.

These extensive interpolations of early collections, such as the Lord's Prayer and both its Interpretations, into the Q-Matthean Sermon, is in a sense a belated justification of Günther Bornkamm's sensitivity for the centrality of the Lord's Prayer in the second half of the Sermon on the Mount, without his strained and artificial association of each pericope in the second half of the Sermon with some petition of the Prayer. These interpolations of the Lord's Prayer and its Interpretations into the Sermon on the Mount even fit Vincent Taylor's observation that Matthew brought forward from later in Q items that fitted a topic under discussion, in this case Prayer, without the woodenness of trying to argue that Matthew brought them forward always in Q order (which obviously would not apply in the present case).

Betz's claim that (an early draft of) the Sermon on the Mount is old enough to provide documentation for Paul's debate with Jerusalem could now gain in probability, without the burdens either of the disassociation of the Sermon on the Mount from the Q trajectory or an

---

[20] Bornkamm recognizes this concluding role of the placement at Matt 7:7–11, once the intervening interpretation of the Lord's Prayer that Bornkamm was seeking to demonstrate had been completed in Matt 7:6 ("Der Aufbau der Bergpredigt," 430).

improbably early dating of the final Q redaction. One would, indeed, have to concede that not all of the Sermon on the Mount is of one piece, the result of a single composition. Yet that concession need not really upset Betz' basic position. An early layer, which has just been discussed in more detail, could indeed have been as early as 50 CE, if one agrees with Lührmann that an original "collecting" stage preceded the final "redacting" stage of Q. The work of the redactor did not consist only of collecting isolated sayings, but involved collecting already composed clusters, such as the Q Sermon, the Lord's Prayer, its original Interpretation Ask, Seek, Knock, and the Illustration about Ravens and Lilies. It is striking that the Sermon on the Mount gives preference to precisely such collections as have on other grounds been classified as early.

There could have been then a subsequent layer or subsequent layers, in which various other Q sayings were interpolated into the Sermon, as well as non-Q material, such as antitheses (Matt 5:21–39,43) and the cult didache (Matt 6:1–6,16–18), and various stray sayings such as giving what is holy to dogs and pearls to swine (Matt 7:6). Most important, there would have been the superimposition of an organizational structure on the Sermon, signaled by the subordination of everything to the Law and the Prophets, both in the hermeneutics (Matt 5:17–20) and in the Golden Rule, once it was removed from the middle of the Q Sermon and put as the conclusion to the body of the Sermon, as the quintessence of the Law and the Prophets (Matt 7:12).

This major structural redaction of the Q Sermon into what one could already call the Sermon on the Mount could also have taken place relatively early, at the Q^{Matt} stage, in any case before Mark became involved (from which, however, the "Mount" is derived, Mark 3:13a). For the Markan intrusion about amputating an eye or hand (Matt 5:29–30) seems appended to the antithesis On Adultery (Matt 5:27–28). And the intrusion about forgiving if one wants to be forgiven (Matt 6:14–15) seems appended to the Lord's Prayer (Matt 6:9–13). Thus the additions from Mark seem added to what were already secondary additions, and thus to take on a tertiary character.

Finally, there would seem to have been interpolations at the end of the process, when the original Peroration of the Q Sermon about actually doing what Jesus said was expanded with further Q material that also continued beyond the Sermon into Matthew 8.

5. *Matthew 8–9: Q 7:22's List of Healings Narrated with Mark's Help*

It is a striking and significant fact that Matthew 8–9 provides an instance of each of the kinds of healing listed in Q 7:22, the summary Jesus gave John's disciples to prove that he is the Coming One. When listed in Q's order, they are as follows:

"the blind receive their sight,"	Matt 9:27–31, from Mark 10:46–52
"the lame walk,"	Matt 9:1–8, from Mark 2:1–12
"lepers are cleansed,"	Matt 8:1–4, from Mark 1:40–45
"and the deaf hear,"	Matt 9:32–34, from Q 11:14
"the dead are raised up,"	Matt 9:18–26, from Mark 5:22–43
"the poor are evangelized"	Matt 5–7, from Q 6:20–49

Q itself had made a somewhat inadequate attempt to provide something for John's disciples, or at least the Q readers, to see (or hear or read), in that the Healing of the Centurion's Boy precedes immediately the arrival of John's disciples in Q. But a single undiagnosed healing hardly provides adequate documentation for a list of five specific maladies to motivate loyal Baptists to move from John to Jesus. Even Luke recognized this weakness, and so interpolated a verse immediately prior to Q 7:22 (Luke 7:21), to the effect that, when John's delegation arrived, Jesus was in the midst of a series of healings, concluding with the one with which Q immediately begins its list, the healing of the blind. The last in the list of healings, the raising of the dead, may also be responsible for Luke's interpolation of the story of the raising from the dead of the son of the widow at Nain (Luke 7:11–17), just prior to John sending his emissaries to Jesus (Luke 7:18–23). But only Matthew takes the apologetic need literally enough to compose two whole chapters telling in detail each healing story on the list.

Attention was drawn to these two chapters by Luz's rather shocking analysis.[21] He lays out, to his own consternation,[22] the bald facts that

---

[21] Ulrich Luz, "Die Wundergeschichten von Mt 8–9," *Tradition and Interpretation in the New Testament: Essays in Honor of E. Earle Ellis for his 60th Birthday*, (ed. Gerald F. Hawthorne and Otto Betz; Grand Rapids, MI: Eerdmans; Tübingen: Mohr [Siebeck], 1987) 149–165.

[22] See Luz's effort to cope with his resultant conclusion that Matthew invented unhistorical healing stories, which might seem to question Matthew's integrity:

Matthew, usually quite conservative regarding the tradition, here not only shifted healings out of their Markan order in a rather capricious way, clearly not interested in presenting them in their historical or even their Markan sequence, but even took a single healing such as that of Blind Bartimaeus, changed it into the healing of two anonymous blind persons, and then told the story twice, once at Jericho where it belongs, and once here at Matt 9:27–31, where Matthew desperately needed it, so desperately as to resort to this disturbing procedure. Why is he so desperate? Because the list of Healings in Q 7:22 puts in first place "the blind see," and no blind persons are healed in Q. So Matthew has to turn to Mark to get a Healing of a Blind Person. Matthew then does much the same with Q's Dumb Demoniac, a story is moved forward from its Q position (Q 11:14–15) to be used in Matt 9:32–34. Then, when it is repeated in its rightful Q position (Matt 12:22–24), the poor demoniac becomes blind as well as dumb, perhaps so that one will not notice it is a healing story that had already been used. What could have motivated the conservative Matthew to such drastic measures? His need to prove Q's case that Jesus is the Coming One!

We have seen that Q 7:22 is a kind of table of contents of the first major part of Q, in which the Q Sermon (Q 6:20–49) and Q's Healing of the Centurion's Boy (Q 7:1–10) are combined to prove to John's emissaries (or at least to the reader of Q) that Jesus is after all the Coming One. For Q 7:22 not only contains a list of healings inadequately represented in Q by the healing of the Centurion's Boy, but Q 7:22 concludes, following Isa 61:1, with the evangelization of the *poor*, which is a flash-back to the *incipit* of the Sermon, "Blessed are the *poor*, for yours is the kingdom of God." Now it is precisely these two Q sections, expanded in Matthew as the Sermon on the Mount (Matthew 5–7) and the Healings (Matthew 8–9), that cry out for some explanation in the work of Betz and Luz. But they are precisely those that an Evangelist with Q in mind would want most to strengthen. Hence to expand dramatically the Q Sermon into the Sermon on the Mount is quite analogous to escalating Q's Healing of the Centurion's Boy into a complete narration of all the healings of Q 7:22 in Matthew

---

"Fiktivität und Traditionstreue im Matthäusevangelium im Lichte griechischer Literatur," *ZNW* 84 (1993) 153–177.

8–9. Thus Matthew 5–7 and Matthew 8–9 belong together as a single phenomenon calling for a single explanation. Rather than the Sermon on the Mount being an isolated problem, as Betz presents it, it is part of a much larger Matthean problem, the vindication of Q.

6. Matthew 10 and 11: Q 10 Placed before Q 7

Matthew 10 is the greatly expanded Mission Instructions of both Mark and Q. Its credentials for inclusion in the section of Matthew oriented to Q become obvious when one notes the way in which the drastic rearrangement of Markan passages, shown to be characteristic of Matthew 8–9, continues in Matthew 10. The Markan material in Matthew 10 occurs in the following order: Mark 6:7; 3:14, 16–19a; 6:8–11; 13:9–13; 9:41. The pedantic following of Mark's order that characterizes Matthew 12–28 has obviously not yet begun. We still have to do with Matthew defending Q, not Matthew following Mark. Likewise, Matthew 11 is clearly on the Q side of the dividing line, since it consists almost exclusively of Q material. Mark takes over only with chapter 12.

The *inclusio* about John and Jesus that characterizes the first major section of Q (Q 3–7) has been expanded by Matthew to include very much material brought, as we have seen, from Q (and Mark) into Matthew 5–7 and from Mark (and Q) into Matthew 8–9. But perhaps even more striking in the expansion of Q 3–7 is the fact that this *inclusio* has been stretched one last time by pulling the Q Mission Instructions of Q 10 back into Matthew 10, a position prior to Q 7 = Matthew 11, that is to say, prior to the completion of the John-Jesus *inclusio* in Q 7, which hence is deferred until Matt 11:2–19. This explains why the Q 3–7 unit became a Matthew 3–11 unit. We hence need to look first at this shift of the Q Mission Instructions forward to become Matthew 10, prior to Q's delayed discussion of John and Jesus in Matthew 11.

Eduard Schweizer has provided a partial explanation for this inversion of sequence as follows:[23]

> Matthew does not place this reply to the Baptist [Matthew 11] directly after the miracles [of Matthew 8–9]: he first inserts chapter 10 because he wants to make

[23] Eduard Schweizer, *The Good News according to Matthew* (Atlanta: John Knox Press, 1975) 69–70.

> the point that the same authority to perform miracles is also given to the community . . . . Jesus' response to the disciples of the Baptist is thus also the response of the community to adherents of the Baptist in the [70] period of the evangelist.

That is to say, Matthew's message to the Baptists is that they have access to Jesus' healing power through the Q-Matthean community.

The Mission Instructions in Matthew 10 do contain a much more detailed listing of the disciples' healing powers than did Q, which had called only for healing the sick (Q 10:9), or than did Mark (6:7, 13), which had specified only exorcism. For the long list in the case of Jesus (Q 7:22 par. Matt 11:4) is matched by an almost equally long list in the case of the disciples (Matt 10:8): "Heal the sick, raise the dead, cleanse lepers, cast out demons."

But Matthew has much more at stake in the Mission Instructions than just offering healing power to the Baptists. His interest is primarily to validate the particularistic Q Mission, before having to abandon it. This is the ultimate reason that the Q^{Matt} Mission must be included in Matthew.

Betz had already noted in passing a similarity of the Mission Instructions of Matthew 10 to his early pre-Matthean Sermon on the Mount. For the primitive christology suggested by the role of Jesus as advocate rather than Judge at the Last Judgment in the Sermon on the Mount (Matt 7:21–23) crops up again in a similar Q text (Q 12:8–9) used in Matt 10:32–33, which leads Betz to comment:[24]

> The version in Matthew 10 cited here is found in a source which Matthew has taken up into his Gospel, the great Mission Discourse of Matt. 10:1–42, a work that resembles the pre-Matthean SM [Sermon on the Mount] in many respects.
>
> [62]In analogy to the SM, the question must also be raised with respect to the mission instruction whether it represents a Matthean or a pre-Matthean composition.

Indeed, the most flagrant instances of Matthean texts standing in such stark contradiction to Matthean theology that they must be pre-Matthean occur not in the Sermon, as Betz emphasizes, but rather in the Mission Discourse of Matthew 10. After all, it begins (Matt 10:5b–6):

> Go into no road of the Gentiles, and do not enter a town of the Samaritans, but go rather to the lost sheep of the house of Israel.

---

[24] Betz, *Essays on the Sermon on the Mount*, 142 and n. 62.

And it then ends (Matt 10:23):

> You will not have gone through all the towns of Israel, before the son of man comes.

This seems as flat a contradiction of the Great Commission as one could wish—or not wish! Clearly Betz's argument for an early dating of the Sermon on the Mount, since its theology is Jewish Christian rather than Matthean, applies in spades to this Mission Discourse! Hence a viable explanation of a pre-Matthean Sermon on the Mount should also explain the Mission Discourse of Matthew 10.

It is not surprising that a dissertation by a pupil of Betz, Eung Chun Park, investigates precisely the pre-history of Matthew 10.[25] He does establish the presence here of early tradition, but, in distinction from Betz's thesis, does not postulate a written source for Matthew 10 other than Q. Even Betz himself has had to temper somewhat the analogy:[26]

> The instruction to the missionary apostles in chapter 10 has some similarity with the SM, but closer examination reveals that it is quite different.

Yet what is indispensable for Betz in his appeal to Matthew 10 is affirmed succinctly by Park:

> Mt 10:5b–6 and 23, which were probably transmitted through Q^{Mt}, reflect an early Palestinian Jewish-Christian tradition, which belongs to a similar stage of the history of mission reflected by Acts 15 and Gal 2.

That is to say, Matthew 10 does after all supplement the Sermon on the Mount in documenting the situation reflected in Galatians, which was Betz's point of departure.

The difficulty in Betz's appeal to Matthew 10 lies, however, in the fact that Matthew 10 involves not only material from Q^{Matt}, but also a section from Mark. For a central section of the Markan apocalypse, Mark 13:9–13, has been moved forward into Matt 10:17–22. It is significant that here (at 10:18) Matthew omits the Markan reference (13:10) that "the gospel must first be preached to all nations," since Matthew's Q community had opposed the Gentile Mission. Later Matthew tucks it back in, at the end of the apocalyptic future (Matt

---

[25] Eung Chun Park, *The Mission Discourse in Matthew's Interpretation* (WUNT 2.81; Tübingen: Mohr [Siebeck], 1995).

[26] Hans Dieter Betz, "The Sermon on the Mount in Matthew's Interpretation," *The Future of Early Christianity: Essays in Honor of Helmut Koester* (ed. Birger A. Pearson; Minneapolis: Fortress, 1991) 258–275, here 263.

24:14). The particularism of the Q-oriented Matthew is at work not only in inserting Matt 10:5b–6, 23, but also in editing the Gentile Mission of Mark 13:10 out from Matt 10:18, in contrast to Matthew's final position in editing it back in at Matt 24:14. Hence one cannot simply ascribe the limitation to Israel of the Matthean Mission to Q^{Matt}, for it still prevails at the time when Mark is, at least to a limited extent, being built into Matthew.

A vestige of Mark's Gentile Mission does survive in Matt 10:18, when in the situation of persecution one is said to bear testimony to Jews *and Gentiles,* which may indeed reflect some awareness that elsewhere, along side the Matthean Jewish Mission, there is a Gentile Mission which is also persecuted. Betz appeals to this as documentation for a pre-Matthean source knowing about both of the Missions taking place side by side, such as is found in Galatians:[27]

> This division of the mission also corresponds to Paul's account about the separation of the mission in Gal 2:1–10. It may be that already the source of Q^{Matt} reflected this division, so that here also the evangelist was able to draw on an earlier source to make it fit his scheme.

But Betz's explicit appeal here to the deletion of the Gentile Mission at Matt 10:18 and its replacement by a vestige perhaps alluding to persecution during somebody else's Gentile Mission[28] does not really support his attempt to use Matthew 10 as an analogy to his early

---

[27] Betz, "The Sermon on the Mount in Matthew's Interpretation," 273.

[28] Betz, "The Sermon on the Mount in Matthew's Interpretation," 273 and n. 40:

> Matthew was certainly aware that there was a mission to the Gentiles and to the Samaritans, but that mission had to wait until after the resurrection of Jesus, when the then-reconstituted body of the eleven was charged with carrying out that mission too (28:16–20). [[40]See Matt 10:17–18 . . . . This prediction, contrary to Mark 13:9–10 but in agreement with Luke 21:12–13, does *not* refer to the mission and proclamation of the gospel to the Gentiles, but to the apostles' testimony of their persecution; καὶ τοῖς ἔθνεσιν explains that these governors and kings were Gentiles who, therefore, became early witnesses even before the mission to the Gentiles began. . . .] Matthew, therefore, knew that at first the Christian mission was to the Jews, preaching the same message as John the Baptist and Jesus (10:7; cf. 3:2; 4:17). This division of the mission also corresponds to Paul's account about the separation of the mission in Gal 2:1–10. It may be that already the source of Q^{Matt} reflected this division, so that here also the evangelist was able to draw on an earlier source to make it fit his scheme.

Sermon on the Mount. When he appeals to the "source of Q^{Matt}" to explain the explicit rejection of a mission to Gentiles and Samaritans in Matt 10:5b–6,23, these particularistic texts could indeed derive from Q^{Matt} in analogy to the Sermon on the Mount at 50 CE. But Matthew's redaction of Mark in Matthew 10 to reduce the Gentile Mission to a faint echo cannot support the dating of the Mission Discourse to 50 CE, any more than do the redactional interpolations of Markan material into the Sermon on the Mount permit such an early dating for the Sermon. For Mark was after all written around 70 CE.

To whatever extent one may appeal to Matthew 10 as an analogy to the Sermon on the Mount, the valid point would be that both include not only abstract concepts that are older than Matthew, but do indeed incorporate older clusters of material, in some kind of layering process that may have begun as early as Paul's Galatians, but continued as late as the beginning of Markan interpolations into Q^{Matt}. The flat contradiction between the Mission Instructions in Matthew 10 and the Great Commission in Matthew 28 proves that no-longer-valid traditions do get interpolated into Matthew, but that a completely independent authorship of the Sermon on the Mount around 50 CE is clearly no more indicated than is a completely independent authorship of the Mission Discourse. In both, the layering extends 20 years beyond 50 CE, into the time of Mark.

The Q community's own Mission, limited to Israel, seems for all practical purposes to have failed. The extensive instructions as to how to handle a town that rejects the disciples (Q 10:10–12), followed by the Woes on the Galilean towns (Q 10:13–15), seem to presuppose at most a very minimal success. Sophia's Saying (Q 11:49–51) and the Lament over Jerusalem (Q 13:34–35) involve Deuteronomistic incriminations againt Israel for the failure of the mission, and suggest God's abandonment of the temple to destruction. To underline this, Matthew advances from the Markan Apocalypse (13:9–13) a section into Matt 10:17–25 that Aland's *Synopsis* quite aptly entitles "The Fate of the Disciples."

7. The Baptist Connection

The Q community's unmediated access to God's acquittal, in bypassing the temple and the Jewish leadership to build on one's own "righteousness," would not have set well with the main stream of

Judaism. Such a Q community, not able to go into any Gentile road or Samaritan village, and hence quite literally, even geographically, limited to Israel, but yet not succeeding with main-line Judaism, may have found its only hope in the Baptists (a term not attested in Q), who also were self-righteous Jews who shared the Q community's bypassing of the temple establishment. Already in Q there was not only the delegation sent from John to Jesus (Q 7:18–23), but, in the continuation of that discussion, Jesus addressing the crowd as those that went out to the wilderness to see John (Q 7:24–26), suggesting some kind of shared constituency. It hence makes sense for the rather desperate Mission Instructions of Matthew 10 to be followed by a focus on Baptists in Matthew 11.

Matthew 11, John sending disciples to Jesus, is a passage derived from Q 7:18–35, which is the *inclusio* about John and Jesus with which Q 3–7 ends. But first one should note that when Matthew reintroduces John at the opening of Q 7:18 (Matt 11:2), he does so with the redactional comment that "John had heard from prison about the *deeds* of the Christ," and concludes the Q section about John redactionally (Matt 11:19), "wisdom is justified by her *deeds.*" Here Matthew would seem, with his focus on Jesus' *deeds,* to be exploiting all the redactional efforts he had undertaken to pull together the full list of Healings in Matthew 8–9, whose purpose is now clearly shown to be to point out how the Healings had already impressed John and would vindicate Sophia.

John's emissaries are not reported in Q to have responded on hearing Jesus' demonstration that he was the Coming One. But surely they cannot fail to be impressed by Matthew's much more rigorous presentation! Indeed, the target of Matthew's efforts would seem to have been the disciples of John.

This focus on the "*deeds* of the *Christ*" to convince Baptists is strikingly parallel to John 10:24, where the demand is made that if Jesus be the *Christ* he should tell them plainly, whereupon Jesus points to his *deeds* (John 10:25, 32, 33, 37, 38). For this is followed directly by a Baptist context with its focus on Jesus' signs (John 10:40–42):

> He went away again across the Jordan to the place where John at first baptized, and there he remained. And many came to him; and they said, "John did no sign, but everything that John said about this man was true." And many believed in him there.

It also recalls the situation that Luke reports in Acts 19:1–7, where Baptists receive the Holy Spirit through Christian baptism. The unusual (for Q) focus on Jesus' healings in Q 7:22, to convince Baptists that he is the Coming One, may be more intelligible in this context.

The Q community may ultimately have succeeded in effecting a conversion of, perhaps more nearly a merger with, the Baptists, indirectly documented in the Gospel of Matthew. This success may have forestalled the inevitable for a time, even if ultimately the inevitable did happen: the very painful choice between extinction or the absorption of the Q community, or at least its left wing, into the Gentile church. Those in the middle would have struggled on as "Jewish Christianity," later documented as Ebionite and/or Nazarene "heretics." Some may have become, or remained, Baptists. The right wing was perhaps absorbed back into emergent "normative Judaism."

The Mission of the Twelve in Mark (6:7–13) is followed by the lengthy narration of the death of John, as if to fill up for the reader the lapse of time involved in that Mission. After the death of John, Mark (6:30) concludes: "The apostles returned to Jesus, and told him all that they had done and taught." This then is followed by Jesus' invitation (Mark 6:31): "Come away by yourselves to a lonely place, and rest a while," which Luke takes to imply a retreat across the frontier to Bethsaida (Luke 9:10).

But Matthew recasts completely this whole section of the Mission of the Twelve (Mark 6:7–13), the Death of John (Mark 6:17–29), and the Return of the Twelve (Mark 6:30–31). The Death of John is deferred until Matt 14:3–12, though an echo may occur more nearly at its Markan position after the Mission of the Twelve in Matthew 10, namely, at Matt 11:2, where Matthew inserts redactionally that John was in prison when he heard about Jesus' deeds and sent his disciples to inquire. But Matthew omits completely Mark's report of the Return of the Twelve, which nonetheless seems to have intrigued him. For he does use the Markan language of the Return of the Twelve in two significant places, both of which have more to do with the disciples of John than with those of Jesus!

Q had never reported the outcome of the efforts of Jesus to convince John's disciples that he was indeed the Coming One. But Matthew had made a much more concerted effort to strengthen that argument in such a way that it would be simply irresistible. And then Matthew appended to the visit of the emissaries the Q Thanksgiving that reaches its peak in the claim that no one knows the Father except the Son. Thus the logic of Q 3–7, as Matthew has built it up, is focussed so as to exclude a mere allegiance to John (or to anyone else), which is then followed by an explicit and final invitation to come to Jesus (no doubt rather than to anyone else), which concludes the whole presentation of Matthew 3–11. (Matthew had already used the same chain of command leading to God via Jesus, based on Q 10:16, at the conclusion to the Mission Discourse in Matt 10:40–42.)

It is precisely here that Matthew makes use of a significant part of Mark's bypassed language from the Return of the Twelve. Mark 6:30: "Come . . . and rest a while" (δεῦτε ... καὶ ἀναπαύσασθε ὀλίγον) becomes in Matt 11:28–29: "Come to me, . . . and I will give you rest, . . . and you will find rest for your souls" (δεῦτε πρός με ... κἀγὼ ἀναπαύσω ὑμᾶς ... καὶ εὑρήσετε ἀνάπαυσιν ταῖς ψυχαῖς ὑμῶν). If this invitation, here elevated into familiar sapiential language, has for Matthew any specific audience other than the reader, it would refer to the preceding context, when Jesus was talking to the "crowds" that had gone "out into the wilderness to see" John (Q 7:24 par. Matt 11:7). This audience was, then, rather literally, a crowd of John's followers, who had heard and seen the demonstration that Jesus is the Coming One, and now are invited to become Jesus' followers.

Nor does Matthew 11, any more than Q 7, report on the outcome of Jesus' demonstration to the disciples of John and to the crowd of his followers that he is the Coming One. Yet when Matthew gets around to narrating the Markan story of John's death (Matt 14:3–12), it contains the rest of the Markan language from the Return of the Twelve that Matthew had omitted (Mark 6:30): "The apostles returned to Jesus, and *told* him all that they had done and taught." Matthew adds this motif at the conclusion of the story of the death and burial of John (Matt 14:12): "and they [John's disciples] went and *told* Jesus." In both cases, ἀπήγγειλαν is used. But this is not the only striking overlap. Mark 6:31 continues to the effect that Jesus told his returning disciples: "Come away by yourselves to a lonely place (κατ' ἰδίαν εἰς ἔρημον τόπον), and rest a while." But in Matt 14:13a, on hearing of John's death, Jesus "withdrew from there in a boat to a lonely place apart (εἰς ἔρημον τόπον κατ' ἰδίαν)."

Matthew has thus taken the Markan language of the return of Jesus' disciples (Mark 6:30–31) and used it, part in the embellished conclusion of Matthew 3–11 (Matt 11:28–30), and part at the arrival of John's disciples to Jesus after John's death (Matt 14:12b–13a). It is almost as if, according to Matthew, Jesus sent out his own disciples on their Mission, but those who reported back to him were not his own, but rather John's disciples, no doubt now after John's death thought of as having become Jesus' disciples. The fact that Matthew, in reporting on John's disciples at his death, has in mind the same Markan text of Jesus' own disciples reporting after their Mission which he used in Jesus' invitation at Matt 11:28–29, strengthens the probability that the conclusion of Matthew 3–11 also had in view John's disciples.

There is thus in Matthew 14 at least a hint at a success story with the Baptists, which, if true, might explain the way in which Matthew throughout puts sayings of John and Jesus on each other's tongues, and presents John as being on the Christian side of the divide (Matt 11:12–15), as well as perhaps helping to explain the heightened Baptist apocalypticism of the Gospel of Matthew. Matthew tells his community's founding story as the story of John as well as of Jesus.

The Thanksgiving of Q 10:21–22 par. Matt 11:25–27 and the Great Commission of Matt 28:28–30 have frequently been compared, in that they share a remarkable ascription of supreme authority to Jesus. The Thanksgiving at the conclusion of Matthew 3–11 begins: "All things have been delivered to me by my Father" (Matt 11:27a par. Q 10:22a); the conclusion of the Gospel of Matthew begins: "All authority in heaven and on earth has been given to me" (Matt 28:18).

From Q's dramatic ascription of exclusive authority to the Son, Matthew 3–11 moves directly to its final Altar Call (Matt 11:28–30):

> Come to me, all who labor and are heavy laden, and I will give you rest. Take my yoke upon you, and learn from me, for I am gentle and lowly in heart, and you will find rest for your souls. For my yoke is easy and my burden is light.

The Great Commission begins (Matt 28:19): "Go therefore and make disciples of all nations." The Altar Call and the Great Commission thus each provide the basis for a Mission. In the one case it is based on Q's christology, the evidence provided to John's emissaries that Jesus is the Coming One, in the other case it is based on Mark's christology, the kerygma of Christ's death and resurrection. Matthew 3–11 has a resounding, even if only temporary, conclusion in Q terms, quite comparable to the resounding final conclusion of the Gospel of Matthew in Markan terms. Matthew 3–11 thus presents the final stage in Q's trajectory, its enlargement into a first installment of Matthew, before almost exclusively Markan influence takes over to produce our canonical Matthew.

Literary History and Cultural History

Adela Yarbro Collins

In his recent book, *The Real Jesus*, Luke Timothy Johnson argues that there are cultural wars going on in the United States today within the churches and the universities and between the church and the academy.[1] He suggests that one manifestation of these wars is that scholars and theologians have been disabled from direct and responsible engagement with the scriptures in their religious dimension. The reason for this disability, he claims, is the hegemony of the historical critical method.[2] One of the faults that he finds with the historical critical method is its tendency to dissect literary compositions. Often associated with this dissection is the indemonstrable hypothesis that the various sources and redactional layers discovered in this way represent discrete stages of historical development.[3]

Now Johnson and other scholars who are inclined to a literary or theological approach to the Gospels are certainly right in emphasizing the importance of the Gospels as unified works with literary and religious purposes and effects. It is also true that the meaning of a particular passage which can be discovered most reliably is the meaning that it has as part of the work in which it occurs. But what is the most appropriate way to discover that meaning? It is a small step from ignoring the question of the pre-history of a text to assuming that it had no pre-history. Such an assumption leads to a distorted reading of the Gospels as texts which arose at a single point in time in a particular author's attempt to address the concerns of a single community. Or worse, it removes the text from any historical context at all, so that it can be filled with whatever content suits the reader.

I would like to defend, therefore, the position that James M. Robinson and Hans Dieter Betz have taken, namely, that it is both

---

[1] Luke Timothy Johnson, *The Real Jesus* (San Francisco: HarperSanFrancisco, 1996) 57–80.

[2] Ibid., 169.

[3] Ibid., 100–1.

necessary and worthwhile to attempt to trace the pre-history of the Sermon on the Mount and other passages in the Gospels. Professor Betz's argument that the Sermon on the Mount is an early epitome of the teaching of Jesus addressed to Jewish Christians is attractive and illuminating, however controversial, and Professor Robinson's challenge to Betz's reconstruction of the pre-history of this text has yielded new insights.

Robinson has succeeded in explaining the logic of the author's compositional and redactional activity in chapters 3–11 of Matthew. These chapters reflect intense editorial work, having as its goal the preservation and vindication of the Q tradition. Another point of equal importance and more general significance is Robinson's emphasis on "the archaizing, archival tendency in the Gospels" as a corrective to the overemphasis on the actualizing, theologizing and preaching tendency of these works.[4]

But the presentation that we have just heard also raises some unsettling methodological questions. Are authors masters of their sources or do sources control their authors? Did ancient authors experience "the anxiety of influence"? Is literary dependence in an ancient context a sign of submissiveness or subservience? To what extent should the Gospels (and their sources) be seen as community products or as the products of individual authors? Is the assumption justified that, because a different mode of composition is used in Matthew 3–11, these chapters were composed earlier than chapters 12–28? (In an earlier and longer version of Robinson's essay, I noticed the movement from "first phase of Matthean redaction" to "first stage of Matthew.") Was the identity of a particular ancient Christian community defined by a single document? Is it historically plausible to speak of "the Q community" or even "the Matthean community"? Does the Gospel of Matthew present in chapters 3–11 "an idealized version of the traditional Q kind of Christianity" in the intention of the author or an idealized version of the teaching and activity of Jesus?

I would like now to respond to a few particular points in Robinson's paper, using a "yes, but" kind of format. He argued that, in Matthew 3–11, the author was not primarily editing Mark. Rather he was editing Q with the help of Mark. Yes, but the explanation is not necessarily

[4] Robinson, "The Matthean Trajectory from Q to Mark," 126–30.

that he was still under the spell of Q. The compositional logic of the first part of Mark, chapters 1:1–8:26, is notoriously difficult to discern. Further, this portion of Mark emphasizes Jesus' role as teacher, but gives relatively little of his actual teaching. Thus an equally plausible explanation is that the author of Matthew improved on the structure and content of the first part of Mark with the help of Q.

Matthew follows Mark from Mark 1:1 to 1:20. He departs from Mark in a significant way at Mark 1:21. The reason seems to be, not that he is still loyal to Q, but that he found Mark 1:21–28 problematic. Vv. 21–22 speak of Jesus teaching in the synagogue in Capernaum and the audience marveling at his teaching. But vv. 23–26, instead of giving a sample of his teaching, relate an exorcism performed by Jesus in the synagogue instead. Then vv. 27–28 return to the theme of the impressiveness of Jesus' teaching. Mark presents a mysterious connection of mighty deeds with teaching, in which the mighty deeds validate the teaching and the teaching interprets the miracles. Matthew, however, preferred a more straightforward and edifying presentation of the teaching of Jesus as preserved in the version of Q available to him. He therefore omitted Mark 1:21–28 and inserted the Sermon on the Mount in its place. That this was his intention is shown by the transitional statement following the Sermon on the Mount (7:28–29), which takes up Mark 1:22.

Robinson has argued that the portion of Q preserved in chapters 3–7 of Luke contains an *inclusio* involving the relationship between Jesus and John and that it is a highly organized argument that Jesus is the coming one. Yes, that portion of Q seems to have had a certain logical organization, but it is probably too much to say that it is "very well organized" and that it is "Q's basic and decisive argument that Jesus is the fulfillment of biblical prophecy, hence the Coming One." The likelihood that only one miracle story was included in this section of Q and the observation that this story does not support the list of the mighty deeds of Jesus suggest rather that the scene in which John sends messengers to Jesus simply makes a claim about the significance of Jesus rather than concluding a self-conscious argument about his identity and role.

Yes, Matthew created an argument that Jesus was the coming one, but this is not a matter of loyalty to Q versus loyalty to Mark. Mark also has John predict one coming after him who will baptize with holy spirit. Rather than preferring Q or Mark over the other, he combines them in chapters 3–11.

Robinson has made many interesting observations about the composition of the Sermon on the Mount, but the argument that the "layering" he has discovered represents a process that occurred in stages over time is not entirely convincing.

One of the most provocative parts of the essay is its explanation of the fact that the author of Matthew moved the mission discourse forward from its place in Q following the scene in which John sent messengers to Jesus to a position preceding it. Robinson follows Eduard Schweizer in arguing that the mission instructions were moved forward because they portray Jesus giving healing power to the disciples. Since the messengers in the narrative represent "Baptists" that Matthew wanted to persuade to follow Jesus, the availability of this healing power is an enticement to accept the self-legitimation offered by Jesus in the encounter with the followers of John. Robinson goes further than Schweizer to argue that the placement of the mission discourse also has the purpose of validating the particularistic mission of the Q community. They were right, at least for a limited time, in confining their mission to "the lost sheep of Israel."[5] Although this argument is somewhat speculative, it is helpful and stimulating because it presses the question why this passage was moved forward and expanded.

An alternative solution begins with the tension between John's preaching about a coming one (Q3) and Jesus' response to John's query (Q7). John speaks of someone who is stonger than he, who will baptize, not only with holy spirit, but also with fire, who will winnow the wheat from the chaff and burn the chaff with unquenchable fire. As Robinson points out, this is a Coming One who is to carry out judgment upon Israel. Jesus' response in Q7, however, describes one who was indeed prophesied by scripture, but hardly a judge: he heals the blind, the lame, the deaf, and lepers; he raises the dead; and he announces good news to the poor. This tension may explain why Matthew moved the mission speech to a position prior to the query of John. It is in this speech that Jesus is portrayed in close association with judgment upon Israel. The disciples will indeed, especially in

---

[5] Ibid., 146.

Matthew's version, heal the sick and proclaim good news as Jesus has done. But the cities that do not welcome the disciples will meet a heavier penalty on the day of judgment than Sodom. The speech also contains Jesus' oracles of judgment against the cities that have refused to repent. Thus, by the time the disciples of John come to ask Jesus if he is the coming one, he has not only proclaimed good news to the poor in the Sermon on the Mount and performed all the miracles mentioned in Jesus' response; he has also pronounced judgment. The author of Matthew has thus created a narrative in which Jesus fulfills both the prediction of John in chapter 3 and the scripture cited by Jesus himself in chapter 11.

Finally, I would like to comment on the relation of the mission discourse to the great commission at the end of the Gospel of Matthew. Robinson has argued that the great commission, presented as given immediately after the resurrection of Jesus, justifies the preservation of archaic practices until shortly before the Gospel of Matthew was written. I find it difficult to follow him in this jump from a literary phenomenon to a historical claim. The tension between the particularism of the mission discourse in Matthew 10 and the universalism of the great commission seems rather to result from the archaizing, archival tendency that Robinson has called to our attention. The author of Matthew attempted to correct Mark's picture in which Jesus himself, before his death and resurrection, inaugurated the mission to the Gentiles.

I would like to conclude by thanking Professor Robinson for honoring Professor Betz and challenging all of us by grappling with the crucial though intractable issues involved in the reconstruction of literary and social history.

Jesus and Heracles in Cádiz (τὰ Γάδειρα): Death, Myth, and Monsters at the "Straits of Gibraltar" (Mark 4:35–5:43)

Roy D. Kotansky

When Jesus arrives in the land of the *Gadarēnoi* (Mark 5:1), an extraordinary chain of events unfolds. As he gets out of the boat, a demon-possessed man, whom no one could tame, recognizes Jesus from afar as the son of God and rushes down upon him, adjuring him not to cast him out of the land. The man with unclean spirit, we soon discover, is possessed of an entire phalanx of demons and would shatter any chains placed upon him. Night and day he cries out from the rock-hewn tombs among the mountains where he made his dwelling.[1] In place of outright banishment, the "legion" of demons are permitted, we are told, to inhabit a herd of two thousand swine grazing by the mountainside; the drove then promptly rushes off a cliff and drowns in the sea.

This remarkable account is but a single story in a group of several fabulous miracles gathered into one of two distinct collections, or "catenae," compiled sometime before the completion of Mark's Gospel.[2] In this study, I shall examine the nature of the first of these two catenae, with special reference to the "otherworldly" setting of Jesus' arrival into this land of the *Gadarēnoi*. Beneath the surface of a more "historical" casing, a "mythological" reading of the catena will aim at representing Jesus battling netherworld forces in a fabulous

[1] Mark 5:5 also describes the man "lacerating," or "breaking himself in pieces," upon the rocks; although the phrase κατακόπτων ἑαυτὸν λίθοις is ambiguous, it should not be construed as a maniacal act of "cutting himself with stones" (cf. 5:15), for the λίθοι are not the sharp hand-held stones with which the demoniac strikes himself, but the large monumental blocks (cf. BAGD, *s.v.*) of the cliff-tombs upon which the man is either clambering, or against which he is casting himself like waves against rocks.

[2] Catena I: Mark 4:35–5:43; 6:34–44; 53 [?]; Catena II: Mark 6:45–52; 7:24b–30; 32–8:10; see P. Achtemeier, "Toward the Isolation of Pre-Markan Miracle Catenae," *JBL* 89 (1970) 281–84; idem, "The Origin and Function of the Pre-Marcan Miracle Catenae," *JBL* 91 (1972) 198–211.

Land of the Dead. In order to reach this "No Man's Land," Jesus must first pass through to the other side of the sea, a sea whose primordial ferocity he also tames; but in the context of the miracle catena, it is not, we shall argue, the Sea of Galilee that Jesus transgresses, but the vast threshold of the mythic Ocean. By bringing together a series of literary and folkloric motifs, we suggest that Jesus sails to the ends of the earth as a superhuman hero encountering the Abyss and other monstrous forces allied with the powers of Death. To the mind's eye of the catena-writer, this voyage will serve as a kind of nautical *descensus ad infernos* that presents its hero as a figure already resurrected and empowered, a hero now living *in illo tempore*, or the Great Time.[3] Our study will depend on a broad reading of the text of Mark vis-à-vis specific myths relative to stories about the Straits of Gibraltar and the western Mediterranean, especially the cults and myths of Heracles Melqart at Cádiz, an eminent Tyrian city sitting at the farthest extremes of the known world. We shall also attempt to situate this interpretation within the early *Sitz im Leben* of the Hellenistic Church.

I. The Miracle Catena

The first Markan catena is comprised of a pastiche of folkloric narratives informed of both Greek and Near Eastern myth, with allusions to biblical Hebrew poetry and prophetic writings.[4] Its present

---

[3] I borrow terminology from Mircea Eliade, *Myths, Dreams, and Mysteries. The Encounter between Contemporary Faiths and Archaic Realities* (San Francisco: Harper & Row, 1960; repr. 1975) 23–38. The "Great Time" is that truth which exists apart from the instances of historic reality ("Profane Time"), and is the primordial cycle wherein the truth of all myth can and must be reenacted over and over again. In this study, "myth," then, does not represent an untrue mode of expression, but on the contrary, is the only real one pertinent to the understanding of the religious history of the miracle catenae.

[4] Achtemeier ("Origin and Function") looks for a broadly defined Mosaic typology from Exodus in the catenae; J. Duncan M. Derrett ("Contributions to the Study of the Gerasene Demoniac," *JSNT* 3 [1979] 2–17, esp. 9–10) and R. Schneck (*Isaiah in the Gospel of Mark, I-VIII* [BIBAL Dissertation Series 1; Vallejo: BIBAL, 1994] 133–58) isolate allusions to Isaiah; cf. further, J. F. Craghan, "The Gerasene Demoniac," *CBQ* 30 (1968) 522–36, esp. 529; Adela Yarbro Collins, "Rulers, Divine Men, and Walking on the Water (Mark 6:45–52)," *Religious Propaganda and Missionary Competition in the New Testament World: Essays Honoring Dieter Georgi* (ed. L. Bormann, K. del Tredici, & A. Standhartinger; Leiden: Brill, 1994) 207–27, esp. 213–14. With the notable exception of Jonah (below), I do not believe the catenae

form shows the artful insertions of fragments of an earlier pre-Markan travelogue; the insinuation of additional non-synoptic glosses; and general editorial reworkings. As a concatenation of divergent pre-Markan sources, the loose confederation of stories was forged to make a more cohesive unity from its sometimes unrelated parts; it will naturally look most like Mark in those places where kinship with Markan vocabulary can be established.[5] Nevertheless, its independent pre-Markan existence in some form or other is unmistakable.

The stories of the catena when contrasted with the assortment of other miracle traditions in the synoptics defy easy categorization, and, were it not for the fact that they are indeed preserved in canonical gospels, they would have been judged as apocryphal. The main themes of the catenae, in general, deal with nature miracles and healings tinged with a more fantastical coloring; they are far grander than the usual synagogal exorcisms and healings found elsewhere in Mark—narratives that are otherwise soundly anchored historically and geographically to specific cities, villages, synagogues, and controversies with Jewish leaders.[6] The miracles of the catenae—particularly the first—on the other hand, seem to describe unusual and remarkable events, unlike anything else encountered in the gospel tradition—the calming of an enormous tempest; the healing of a wild man possessed of two thousand demons; the saving of a woman menstruating for twelve years; the recalling of a little girl's soul back from the very dead; and the supernatural feeding of five thousand men on a grassy plain.

---

are intentionally patterned after biblical Hebrew midrash, but rather draw from an older depository of traditional Greek and Near Eastern myths that have also informed the writing of ancient Hebrew biblical texts.

[5] In a study to be addressed elsewhere, I take the catenae to be compositions independently formed just before the final redaction of canonical Mark; they seem to be centos made up of other, even older written compositions for which traces can be found in Markan contexts apart from the catenae themselves. These centos also include unique pre-Markan material that is genuinely *sui generis* and may have come from a common milieu.

[6] The miracles apart from the catenae belong to a more mundane sort: the alleviating of fever, the expelling of an annoying demon, or the restoration of a "withered" hand. Note the healings typical of the Markan "summaries" in 1:34; 6:5; 6:56. The miracles of the catenae group, on the other hand, which take over some stories from even older collections, are in part determined by more established literary expectations of what a Graeco-Semitic hero or *thaumaturge* might be expected to do.

II. The Sea-Context

Another feature of both miracle catenae is the close affiliation of their stories with the sea (ἡ θάλασσα): the calming of the storm (4:35–41) and the walking on water (6:45–52), of the second catena, occur at sea; the first catena's herd of pigs are cast back into the sea (5:13), just as the stories of the raised daughter, the hemorrhaging woman, and the prodigious feeding can all be placed within the context of the sea (5:21; cf. 6:45; 8:1–9).[7] Likewise, the second catena's Syrophoenician woman (7:24–30) is placed on the coast at Tyre; and the healing of the deaf-mute (7:32–37) occurs by the sea.[8]

With the exception of the story placed near Tyre, most readers will assume that the unqualified use of θάλασσα in the above contexts refers to the Sea of Galilee; but this is by no means certain. The second catena's naming of a "Greek woman of Syrophoenician birth"[9] in the coastal regions about Tyre, should give us reason to pause; it suggests the possibility that in the catenae—if not in all of Mark's gospel—there was at least some ambiguity about the use of the word, "the sea." Mark uses the full phrase "Sea of Galilee" only twice in all of his gospel; and although it is true that θάλασσα is the only term found in Mark to describe such a sea-lake, he makes clear the affiliation by supplying τῆς Γαλιλαίας.[10] Otherwise Mark employs the simple ἡ θάλασσα as a

---

[7] The feeding of the four thousand concludes immediately with an embarkation to the mysterious regions of Dalmanutha (8:10), on which see further below.

[8] Here, specifically the Sea of Galilee, according to 7:31: Καὶ πάλιν ἐξελθὼν ἐκ τῶν ὁρίων Τύρου ἦλθεν διὰ Σιδῶνος εἰς τὴν θάλασσαν τῆς Γαλιλαίας ἀνὰ μέσον τῶν ὁρίων Δεκαπόλεως. This is an editorial verse not usually considered part of the catenae (R. A. Guelich, *Mark 1–8:26* [Word Biblical Commentary 34A; Dallas: Word Books, 1989] 390; see discussion below).

[9] Mark 7:26: ἡ δὲ γυνὴ ἦν Ἑλληνίς, Συροφοινίκισσα τῷ γένει. The dual ethnicity of the woman—she is both a Hellenic woman and a Tyro-Phoenician (vs. a Libyo-Phoenician)—makes her a perfect candidate for the sort of fusing of "Helleno-Semitic" culture that the writer of the catenae wishes to foster. This combination of Greek and Semitic (= Punic/Phoenician) values lies at the heart of the mythology that went into the make-up of the pre-Markan catenae.

[10] The Call of Simon and Andrew in 1:16: Καὶ παράγων παρὰ τὴν θάλασσαν τῆς Γαλιλαίας εἶδεν Σίμωνα καὶ Ἀνδρέαν, κτλ.; and the catena "seam" at 7:31 (text given above)—a famous crux interpretum. The case of 2:13, another call-story that falls in between 1:16 and our next reference at 3:7, is unique in 1) retaining the ambiguous παρὰ τὴν θάλασσαν; 2) showing affinities with 3:7 in

kind of generic term for a large body of water.[11] We must permit the context to determine whether this will refer to the Sea of Galilee, or not; sometimes θάλασσα will seem rather to point to the Mediterranean seacoast—as the context of the Tyrian woman, above, suggests—and not to the Sea of Galilee. Will this not allow, then, for the possibility of a coastal localization for the rest of the catenae stories positioned near a θάλασσα?

It would not be prudent to read one Markan seaside context into another, for references to θάλασσα seem to refer to divergent bodies of water in the various pre-synoptic sources. It seems that there was some vacillation and confusion between a coastal and a lakeside venue in the Markan uses of θάλασσα and that the miracle catenae refer exclusively to marine settings. Apart from the editorial remark of Mark 7:31, "Galilee" is not part of the mind-set of the catenae narratives at all; neither is Capernaum nor Nazareth, its principal Synoptic cities.[12] If Galilee forms no part of the catenae geographies, references to a generic "sea" in them will not describe the Sea of Galilee, but the greater littoral of the adjoining seacoast.

III. The Retreat to the Seacoast

The first allusion to the sea in the first Markan catena occurs in a scheduled crossing of it in 4:35 ("Let us cross over to the other side"), without the word "sea" being named at all. Nevertheless, to determine what body of water it intends, we must go back to Mark 3:7, a fundamentally important θάλασσα-antecedent that describes a unique

---

making it a *teaching* summary; and 3) turning it into a call-story at 2:14, by use of the phrase καὶ παράγων εἶδεν Λευίν, κτλ.

[11] In two "seaside" sayings of Jesus apart from the pre-Markan catenae—the one about the offender being cast into the sea with a millstone around his neck (9:42), the other about a mountain being cast into the sea (11:23)—we do not know what "sea" is intended. In the first, Jesus is at Capernaum; but in the second, he is at Bethany, where the Dead Sea would be more proximate. In both, however, θάλασσα may have in mind the Mediterranean Sea and stem from traditions of Jesus having taught in a setting located along the Syro-Phoenician coast (cf. the proximity of the "salt-saying" in 9:50).

[12] "Galilee" occurs in Mark 1:9, 14, 16, 28, 39; 3:7; 6:21; 7:31; 9:30; 14:28; 15:41; 16:7 (cf. 14:70)—with a huge gap in the catenae sections; similarly, Capernaum (1:21; 2:1; 9:33) is not named in these sections either. For the catenae's cities, see note 17 below.

withdrawal to a seaside locale.[13] What is remarkable about the section contained in these verses (3:7–12) is its largely non-Markan character, a fact that should warn us not to "prooftext" it by assessing its context from unrelated verses.[14] A quick glance soon shows that θάλασσα in 3:7, too, is careful not to make any mention of the Sea of Galilee at all. This is hardly accidental, and a closer look will suggest that the writer had in mind the Mediterrean seacoast. Thus, the non-Galilean interpretation of the sea-stories would seem to carry over, as well, into sections not traditionally assigned to the first miracle catena. There are compelling reasons, however, to see these verses as a kind of editorial *incipit* composed by a later writer to introduce the whole of the miracle catena itself.[15]

Be that as it may, Jesus and his disciples are said to "withdraw" πρὸς τὴν θάλασσαν, with no mention of Galilee and its Lake Tiberias. A retreat to the "sea" could easily have meant a withdrawal then to the Mediterranean coast, only about twenty miles from Nazareth itself, and closer still to other Galilean cities not known to the synoptic record,

---

[13] The text begins: Καὶ ὁ Ἰησοῦς μετὰ τῶν μαθητῶν αὐτοῦ ἀνεχώρησεν πρὸς τὴν θάλασσαν· καὶ πολὺ πλῆθος ἀπὸ τῆς Γαλιλαίας, κτλ., "And Jesus, with his disciples, withdrew to the sea. And a mighty multitude from Galilee (began to follow)" etc. In between Mark 3:7 and 4:35, there also falls 4:1: Καὶ πάλιν ἤρξατο διδάσκειν παρὰ τὴν θάλασσαν ("And again he began to teach by the sea"), which ushers in the long Parable of the Sower (it is perhaps part of a larger version of the pre-Markan catena, as some have argued). But even here we find no mention whatsoever of the Sea of Galilee. The πάλιν, pointing back in the Markan narrative to the earlier "sea" referent at 3:7, will nevertheless provide our starting point.

[14] Vv. 7–9 of the section 3:7–12 have a number of "non-Markan" terms; note ἀνεχώρησεν, πλῆθος, πλοιάριον, προσκαρτερῇ, Ἰδουμαία, ἐπιπίπτειν etc. The vocabulary has its greatest affinities with John and Acts, although ἀναχωρεῖν is a favorite of Matthew's. The main reason for distancing vv. 10–12 from vv. 7–9, even though both sections may bave been brought together as a pre-Markan unit, is taken up in note 23, below.

[15] See previous note. Much discussion centers on whether Mark 3:7–12 is pre-Markan or a product of Markan redaction. I concur with Guelich (*Mark*, 142–44), who follows R. Pesch (*Das Markusevangelium* [HTKNT 2.1–2; 3rd ed. Freiburg: Herder, 1980] 198) in identifying this as a pre-Markan introduction to the cycle of miracles in Mark 4:35–5:43; 6:32–52; 6:53–56. Leander Keck recognizes a traditional core in vv. 7, 9–10, but still sees the summary related to the pre-Markan "divine man" miracle cycle ("Mk 3,7–12 and Mark's Christology," *JBL* 84 [1965] 341–58). I am undecided about what portion, if not all, of the catena material that Mark 3:7–12 introduces.

cities like Sepphoris, or Johannine Cana. All other Galilean cities of the Markan narrative—Capernaum and Bethsaida—are planted right along the shores of the Galilean lake, so (if indeed 3:7 intended *this* "sea") a mention of Jesus and his disciples now *withdrawing* to the very venue of the public ministry in which they were currently engaged would be so unusual as to be absurd: Jesus has just previously been mentioned as having healed a man with a withered hand at the Capernaum synagogue;[16] he is already in Galilee. In other words, he cannot now be said to *withdraw* to a place where he is already located.

The verb ἀναχωρεῖν in 3:7 represents a sizable retreat—the term is originally military, referring to the recession of large armies; the motion implied will thus entail some geographical distance. But to where does Jesus retire? Given the prospect that Jesus cannot "withdraw" to a place where he is already conducting his affairs, the only likely interpretation is that he pulls back to the nearby seacoast. The nondescript θάλασσα here, by virtue of the fact that it is *not* called a "Sea of Galilee" (as in 1:16), further favors the Mediterranean venue and militates against the Galilean.

The text that follows in Mark is especially telling in suggesting that such a sea is the coastal littoral: a great mass (πολὺ πλῆθος) begins to follow (ἠκολούθησεν) Jesus, a crowd coming, according to the geographic sequence, foremost from Galilee, Judaea, and Jerusalem; and then from Idumaea, the other side of the Jordan, and the area about Tyre and Sidon. The mention of Galilee first in the list is not to imply that more westerly folks, at some remove from the Sea of Galilee, began to gather along the shores of Lake Tiberias, but rather that lakeside folks began to move en masse due west towards the nearby coast. To Mark, whose Galilee contains only lakeside inhabitants to begin with, there is no populace away from the lakeshore to speak of, in any respect.[17] It would have been otiose to

---

16 Mark 3:1: Καὶ εἰσῆλθεν πάλιν εἰς τὴν συναγωγήν—with "again" and "*the* synagogue" harking back to the Capernaum synagogue of Mark 1:21; 2:1.

17 Mark's Gospel in general knows only of Καφαρναούμ (1:21; 2:1; 9:33), Βηθσαϊδάν (6:45; 8:22 [var.]), and Γεννησαρέτ (6:53). Other "lakeside" names of villages are problematic—the Γαδαρά/Γερασά/Γεργεσά of our study here, and the "Dalmanoutha" crux at 8:10 (see below). Ναζαρέθ, the only extra-lakeside Galilean town named in Mark (1:9), is less important to Mark than the titular Ναζαρηνός (1:24; 14:67; 16:6). Knowledge of Μαγδαλά (known as such only from

mention a great mass now *withdrawing* to the Sea of Galilee if the principal towns and villages of it were on its very shores.[18] Mark 3:7's great withdrawal to the sea, in point of fact, probably refers to the Mediterranean shore, specifically to the Syro-Phoenician coast around Mt. Carmel—that is, at the sinus known today as the Bay of Haifa, just north-by-northeast of Cape Carmel. A Mount Carmel context will then explain the ascent to "the mountain" (καὶ ἀναβαίνει εἰς τὸ ὄρος) that immediately follows in Mark 3:13.[19] If Mark's intention were to describe a gathering from the outer regions to Jesus within Galilee (and its lake-shores), a naming of Galilee itself would hardly have been necessary. Instead, what we find is a great crowd coming from Galilee as but one of a number of regions; all are following Jesus in a north-to-

Matt. 15:39), is only implied from the adjective Μαγδαληνή used of Mary in Mark 15:40, 47; 16:1, 9, although this belongs to an entirely "non-Galilean" source and context! Τιβεριάς (cf. John 6:1, 23; 21:1) on the western shore of the sea of Galilee is never mentioned in Mark, nor the other synoptics.

18 Even if villages and towns of Galilee *away from* the shores of its lake are known from the other gospels (e.g., Chorazin, Cana, Tiberias, and Nain), they are nonexistent to Mark. The only "extra-lakeside" village named in all of Mark is Nazareth, but this is mentioned only once (1:9); see previous note. The existence of extra-lakeside villages and cities from other literary and archaeological records has no place in the study of Mark. Why no gospel-writers name the metropolis of Sepphoris remains a mystery.

19 Less explicable is the crossing to Bethsaida in 6:45 in the Walking on Water episode (of the second miracle catena), where Jesus goes atop a mountain to pray, but ends up espying the disciples from its lofty vantage-point as they strain at the oars. There are no "Sea of Galilee" mountains to fit this description, either "kitty-corner" from Bethsaida, or elsewhere. Again, a solution would be to recognize πρὸς Βηθσαϊδάν as an early gloss on εἰς τὸ πέραν inserted to contextualize the story. Mark never otherwise adds a town of destiny with τὸ πέραν and has no real interest in Bethsaida (the only other occurrence at 8:22 carries the preferred (!) textual variant of Βηθανίαν in D; see further note 27 below). Further, the parallel to Mark 6:45 in Matt 14:22 says *nothing* of Bethsaida, mentioning only εἰς τὸ πέραν—a very important fact—especially since not a single ancient manuscript has attempted to harmonize Matt 14:22 with its Markan equivalent at 6:45 (Βηθσαϊδάν)! On the other hand, if Jesus were envisioned as looking down from the heights of Mt. Carmel as the disciples struggled to sail from Cape Carmel straight across the bay to Ptolemaic Acco, we would have the proper geographic setting. In the synoptics, Bethsaida is elsewhere only mentioned in the famous Q-logion, except for the peculiar occurrence at Luke 9:11. The placing of the town Bethsaida here in Mark is entirely incongruous. The possibility of a retreat to Caesarea Maritima on the coast just south of Mt. Carmel is discussed further below.

northwesterly route to the coast, with the exception of the Tyro-Sidonians who come down from the coast. Galilee is named first for its prominence and natural pairing with Judaea, and for the fact that it is still the closest district to the actual area of retreat, lying just east of the seacoast of Carmel-Acco.[20]

The sequence and breadth of the geographical groups said to follow Jesus thus represent a slow and steady migration of followers northward and westward from as far south as Idumaea and as far east as Peraea (and the Decapolis).[21] Included would have been populations from around Galilee, with which the geographical catalogue in 3:7–8 begins. But the idea that an early synoptic record was meant to imply that Jesus set up camp and ministered from the shoreline of the Syro-Phoenician coast will surely cast new light on much of the Markan story, not the least of which will be our understanding of the first miracle catena.

IV. Crossing the Sea

Once Jesus has relocated to the sea in Mark 3:7, it is a simple step to place him "again" (πάλιν) on the shore to teach the crowd in 4:1, the venue of the long parabolic section (4:3–34) including the Sower and its interpretation. Jesus is thus brought one noticeable step closer to actual embarkation in the portrayal of his teaching the crowd offshore from the boat. The teacher has his professorial chair (καθῆσθαι) in the ocean (ἐν τῇ θαλάσσῃ), but the crowd stays on the earth (ἐπὶ τῆς γῆς). The motif of a launching (εἰς πλοῖον ἐμβάντα) and of instruction on the sea not only foreshadows the memorable sailing that is to begin in 4:35, it places a necessary distance between Jesus as master of the watery abyss and the crowd that must remain on shore. The contrast between "in" the sea versus "upon" the land creates a

---

[20] The list ends emphatically with the naming of the regions περὶ Τύρον καὶ Σιδῶνα and encloses the whole with the phrase with which it began—πλῆθος πολύ—though in reverse order (chiasmus). On the importance of these two cities for the catena's *Sitz im Leben*, we will have more to say later.

[21] Peraea (Περαία) = τὸ πέραν τοῦ Ἰορδάνου in Mark 3:8 is the historic designation of the "land on the other side." The Decapolis, of course, is not specifically named, and its use in Mark is a crux interpretum.

thematic high/low antithesis that places Jesus down in the depths of Ocean but the masses elevated up on dry land.[22]

The long teaching section of chapter four also enables our author to provide a badly needed intermission to the fast pace of miracles and controversies of the preceding chapters; but the *incipit* he gives it forms a doublet with 3:9 and makes incongruous the sequence of events in 4:36, where the disciples take Jesus on board their prepared vessel.[23]

With the seaside context fixed along the shores of the Mediterranean rather than by the lake of Galilee, the reader is prepared for a large sea-crossing—or a series of them—not a mere jaunt across a lake. With Jesus and the crowd thus already gathered along the shores of the Mediterranean Sea, our writer prepares us for the hero's embarkation to the more mythic worlds of the Beyond where, as master of the unknown, he will tame the powers of Death and the

---

[22] A similar juxtaposition is encountered again in Jesus' emerging out of the sea in Mark 5:1 and meeting a demon coming down from the mountains—a demon, albeit, who ironically addressed Jesus as Son of God Most High! This kind of "coincidence of opposites" is characteristic of the kinds of events that take place in a "No-Man's Land" (on which I recommend W. Brashear, "Zauberformular" [Exkurse: Übergänge, Grenzen, Niemandsland]," *APF* 36 [1990] 61–74; and addenda: *APF* 48 [1992] 27–32). This will be examined in greater detail elsewhere.

[23] Mark 4:1 reads much like a variant on the peculiar Markan "gloss" of 3:9, where the preparation of a boat by the disciples enables a similar distance between Jesus and the pressing crowd. The difficulty there, of course, and proof indeed that the verse is an interpolation, is the fact that the following vv. 10–11 do not portray Jesus *teaching* from the offshore boat, but rather *healing* those who were physically touching him, something impossible if he were in a boat. Of the Greek texts of either version—that of 3:9 or 4:1—only 3:9 will go with the embarkation of 4:36, which has the disciples then take Jesus on board the "prepared" ship: καὶ εἶπεν τοῖς μαθηταῖς αὐτοῦ ἵνα *πλοιάριον* προσκατερῇ αὐτῷ διὰ τὸν ὄχλον ἵνα μὴ θλίβωσιν αὐτόν (3:9) . . . + καὶ ἀφέντες τὸν ὄχλον παραλαμβάνουσιν αὐτὸν ὡς ἦν ἐν τῷ πλοίῳ, καὶ ἄλλα *πλοιάρια* [! Byz. Fam. + L U 124 2 τ] ἦν μετ' αὐτοῦ (4:36). Of course, it is the separation of these two narratives by Mark and the inclusion of the verbal proclamation that creates the difficult incongruity of 4:36. With Mark 3:8–9 + 4:36 there is no conflict in the flow of the narrative: Jesus requests a ship to be made ready and heals the shoreline crowds as they press him. The arrival of evening, then, in 4:35, ends a long day of shoreline healing, not one of shoreline teaching. Jesus is then taken on board "as he was"—completely exhausted from his healing-service and presumably asleep (cf. 5:38). There may have been a series of verses lost between the sequence of 3:9–12 + 4:35, but the joining of these two narratives offers one explanation for the odd ὡς ἦν-clause. Cf. note 45, below.

Abyss. With the "ship-in-waiting" of 3:9 (along with the other seaworthy vessels named in 4:36), Jesus initiates his voyage with the proclamative words of 4:35: "Let us pass through to the other side" (διέλθωμεν εἰς τὸ πέραν). He is then received on board. What follows next—the strangely ocean-like ferocity of the tempest (4:37); the sense of distance implied in Jesus' deep sleep (4:38); the calm (4:39); the arrival in another land (5:1); and the telling of the series of fabulous stories that constitute the first catena—will all contribute to the notion that Jesus is undertaking a mythic sea-voyage into the Land of the Dead.

A. *The "Other Side."* The motif of a voyage to the "Other Side" is central to the sea-portrayals of the miracle catenae, particularly the first: the nominal form τὸ πέραν and its verbal counterpart διαπερᾶν are almost entirely restricted to these two collections.[24] That the catena episodes indeed intended large-scale sea-crossings, if only in a metaphorical sense, is again proved by a close reading of the verses with this noun and verb and from a study of the cognates outside the gospels.

As noted above, θάλασσα in Mark is ambiguous; it can refer to the Sea of Galilee or to the Mediterranean. When it comes to the actual crossings of such seas, the geographical context proves even more tenuous, and the assumption of a Galilean sea passage in the catenae becomes more and more difficult to sustain. In Mark 4:35, 5:1, and 5:21, where a crossing (τὸ πέραν) is first mentioned (with or without the actual word ἡ θάλασσα), nothing is ever said of a "Sea of Galilee" as such. Instead we find only the imprecise naming of an ocean-crossing. The original context of the catena sea-episodes, in either maintaining this sea-ambiguity, or never intending it at all, has for the reader automatically enlarged the θάλασσα to include the vast limen of the ocean: I believe that the composer of the catena actually meant to promote Jesus with his band as westward sailors, voyaging across the Mediterranean Sea, like a biblical Jonah towards a kind of mythic Tarshish.[25]

---

[24] Mark 4:35; 5:1, 21; 6:35, 45; 8:13. The only exceptions are the two references to the "other side" of the Jordan River in Mark 1:8; 10:1.

[25] Although I disfavor reading a Moses typology (note 4, above) into the Markan sea-crossing story—note, for example, that Moses parts the sea and walks

Accordingly, all the sea-crossings of both miracle catenae, at least in the mythic imagination, are to be construed as true sea-voyages; their destinations, when recorded, will not tally well with known geographies of the circum-Galilean region: does Jesus land at Gerasa, Gadara, Gergesa in 5:1—or does he land somewhere else? Where does Jesus make landfall when he "again" comes to the other side (πάλιν εἰς τὸ πέραν) in Mark 5:21?[26] Do the disciples in 6:45 attempt to sail towards Bethsaida or just to "the Beyond" (τὸ πέραν), as the Gospel of Matthew has it?[27] Where in Mark 8:10 are the regions of Dalmanou(n)tha, or Mount Dalmounai, a place name that has been

---

on dry land, while Jesus sails the sea and stills it—I am not opposed to seeing the influence of a specific Jonah typology (cf. Guelich, *Mark*, 266; J. Duncan M. Derrett, *The Making of Mark. The Scriptural Basis of the Earliest Gospel* [Warwickshire: P. Drinkwater, 1985] 97–98; Pesch, *Markusevangelium*, 278). Although there will be differences here too, Jonah (like Jesus) sleeps in the ship during a violent sea-storm (LXX Jonah 1:5: Ιωνας δὲ κατέβη εἰς τὴν κοίλην τοῦ πλοίου καὶ ἐκάθευδεν, κτλ.) and is indignantly roused by the captain. The storm abates once Jonah is willfully cast overboard, where he prays in the fish's belly for three days. This last motif, different of course from Jesus' own stilling of the storm, is echoed elsewhere in the Gospel tradition: Jonah's being in the belly of the fish symbolizes Jesus' own resurrection (Matt 12:40 Q). The added parallelism that our study will offer is that Jesus, like Jonah, sails to Tarshish, the region traditionally associated with Tartessos and Cádiz in Iberia, according to popular thinking. The equation of Tarshish with Tartessos and Gadir is discussed in M. E. Aubet, *The Phoenicians and the West: Politics, Colonies, and Trade* (Cambridge: Cambridge University Press, 1993) 176–79.

[26] Guelich rightly argues for the pre-Markan character of the verse (*Mark*, 295). But here I support rather those whom he criticizes (e. g., Schmidt), for they see the crossing "again" as a trip to the eastern side of the lake (to go εἰς τὸ πέραν is always to sail across the lake from west to east of the lake; πάλιν in Mark is usually "again/once more," not "back"). But in the new, broader context of the argument that we are promoting, this "seam" is intended to represent another trans-oceanic voyage in "magical" time. But the verse serves no other purpose than to situate the catena's next story also within the context of a mythic "sea-crossing" and to thereby emphasize the story's netherworld elements in the extremes of the world (cf. ἐσχάτως, v. 23). Mark 5:21 simply couples the preceding story with the Jairus account, whose καὶ ἔρχεται *incipit* shows that it originally belongs to an independent "land-based" source, not a "nautical" one (see next note).

[27] Also, the lake crossing in 8:13, presumably to Bethsaida in 8:22, has a telling variant in Bethany! It, too, uses a Markan travel-narrative formula usually used of Judean *land* excursions: Καὶ ἔρχονται εἰς ʽΒηθσαϊδάν [Βηθανίαν D pc it]. The landing at Gennesar/Gennesareth (Γεννησάρ/ Γεννισαρέτ/Γεν(ν)ησαρέθ/-τ = γῆν Ναζαρήθ?) in Mark 6:53 is considered an editorial gloss or perhaps a fragment of a lost portion of Catena I.

profoundly altered in many manuscripts to refer to districts or mountains of Magdala, Magada, Mageda, or Melegada?[28]

This state of affairs argues for "extra-biblical" towns and cities as the original destinies of the pre-Markan miracle catenae. There appears to have been an apparent attempt by later editors—or even by Mark himself—to harmonize the fabulous lands of the miracle catenae with the known geography of Palestine in order to ensure that they accorded with lakeside crossings. Regardless of the editorial ameliorations, the target cities of both catenae remain gravely troubled in their textual transmissions. It is as if in their final forms the actual sea-crossings, and the stories attached to them, preserved texts with fairly dependable readings, but that the extra-Palestinian identification of their destinies proved embarrassing and were consequently tampered with, resulting in the bewildering array of manuscript variants that we now possess. It seems, too, as in Mark 8:10, that entire narratives may have disappeared. It is our contention that the stories preserved in Mark 5:1–20 in particular, and those of the catenae in general, were cut from a more colorful "geographical" fabric than those used for the more "historical" portions of Mark's gospel. The geographical lands of these portions of the Markan narrative appear to be undergoing a kind of "mythologization," as their stories begin to be transformed into novellas. Such "novella"-type narratives allowed Jesus to sail to lands more distant, unknown, and mythological than those "authorized" by the more traditional ecumenical sources. These *Märchen* were consequently reshaped at a

---

[28] Viz. τὰ μέρη Δαλμανουνθά (Δαλμανουθά) / Μαγδαλά / Μαγεδά versus τὰ ὅρια / ὄρη Δαλμανουθά / Μελεγαδά / Μαγαδά versus τὸ ὄρος Δαλμουναί / Μαγεδά. In other words, the destinations of the second catena, if known, are even more confused than those of the first. This is precisely the state of affairs found in the apocryphal *Acts of Andrew and Matthias* (*AAMt*), where the Land of the Cannibals, called Myrmidonia, is preserved with numerous textual variants (Mermidona, Myrmidonia, Mirmidona, Mirmidonia, Myrmidona, Mirmydona, Myrmidon, Myrmidonensis, Mermedonia, Marmedonia, Marmadonia, Medea, Margundia, and Mirdone, Μυρμήνη, Μυρμήνις, Μύρνη, Μυρμήκη, Σμυρμήνη, and Σμύρνα). Note Dennis R. MacDonald, *The Acts of Andrew and the Acts of Andrew and Matthias in the City of the Cannibals* (SBL Texts and Translations 33; Christian Apocrypha Number 1; Atlanta: Scholars Press, 1990) 7–15, esp. 10–11, who rightly observes that "Myrmidonia belongs not on the map of the Roman empire but on the map of the imagination. The significance of Myrmidonia is not geographical but mythological."

later stage by scribal authorities in order to bring their geographies into line with the more conservative expectations of where Jesus lived and taught.

V. Death, Underworld, and Afterlife

Jesus' agenda of sailing to distant lands will accord well with the language and vocabulary of the catenae. Since the destiny of the nominal phrase τὸ πέραν signifies "the other side"—"what lies beyond" a body of water—it is cognate with πέρας, "limit, end; boundary" (pl., πέρατα); it should thus come as no surprise that the word is regularly used to refer to the limits of the known world.[29] To sail westward to the edges of the earth is to come to the streams of Ocean, where, too, the famous Elysian Plain was to be found.[30] In the oldest Greek concepts of the world, the entire earth, a flat disk, was surrounded by a vast river called Ὠκεανός (Ocean), a deity once known, with his wife Tethys, as the begetter of all gods.[31] When Helios sets in the west as the sun in his golden cup, he is believed to sail around the outer river of Ocean (or even under it, as in *Od.* 10.191) only to rise again in the east at daybreak. Stesichorus tells us that once he has "passed over Ocean" (ὄφρα δι' Ὠκεανοῖο περάσας), Helios arrives in the "depths of holy, dark night."[32] More importantly, when

---

[29] Its epic form πεῖραρ (πείρατα), thought from some contexts to refer originally to rope-ends, came also to mean one's doom, as in *Il.* 6.143; see, in general, Ann L. T. Bergren, *The Etymology and Usage of ΠΕΙΡΑΡ in Early Greek Poetry* (American Classical Studies 2; New York: APA, 1975). In the terminal land of the Phaeacians (see below), Odysseus metaphorically reaches the limits of his trials, πεῖραρ ὀϊζύος (*Od.* 5.289).

[30] In Homer, *Il.* 14.200, 301, the πείρατα γαίης—the limits of the earth—is where Okeanos lay (G. S. Kirk, J. E. Raven & M. Schofield, *The Presocratic Philosophers* [2nd ed.; Cambridge: Cambridge University Press, 1983] 13, no. 8). *Od.* 4.563, too, describes the Elysian Plain by these same πείρατα γαίης; and the famous asphodel meadows were situated "past the streams of Ocean" (*Od.* 24.13; cf. 11.539; G. K. Gresseth, "The Homeric Sirens," *TAPA* 101 [1970] 203–18, esp. 209). On the kindred "Isles of the Blessed" being there, too, see further below.

[31] Kirk et al., *Presocratics,* 10–15.

[32] D. Page, *Poetae Melici Graeci* (Oxford: Clarendon, 1967) 100, frag. 8, 1–4; Kirk & Raven (*Presocratics* [1st ed., 1957] 14–15, no. 8). This important fragment is omitted for economy in the second edition of Kirk et al., *Presocratics.* For Egyptian parallels, note H. Wagenvoort, "The Journey of the Souls of the Dead to the Isles of the Blessed," *Mnemosyne* 24 (1971) 113–61, esp. 118–19.

Odysseus sails to the streams of Ocean, in the twenty-fourth book of the *Odyssey*, he somehow arrives mystically in the land of the dead: "Past the streams of Ocean they went and the White Rock; past the gates of Helios and the realm of dreams. And quickly they arrived in the asphodel meadows. There dwell the souls, the phantoms of those who have ceased toil."[33] The underworld is regularly represented as lying in the mythological west.

In the catena's expedition Jesus, too, sails westwardly to the limits of the world and thereby crosses mystically into an underworld environment. His voyage in Mark 4:35 begins ominously at nightfall, ὀψίας γενομένης—a particularly unpropitious time for sailing. The phrasing not only recalls the night-time sinking of Helios into the depths of Ocean, it signals the first of several metaphorical interpretations of deeper importance: the time around sundown will prove symbolic of an expedition into the twilight world of the dead. Further, a series of allegorical clues within Mark 4:35–5:43 are subtly planted to re-situate the hero's environment from the mundane to the supramundane world; the "subtext" of the narrative subsumes recurrent themes of "rites of passage" and of transition under the larger umbrella of entrance into the macrocosm of the *Jenseits*. These allegorical clues we can note only in passing, as they deserve further study elsewhere: the "crossing through" (διέρχεσθαι) to the Other Side in itself signifies the journey of death (4:35); to dismiss the crowd (ἀφέντες τὸν ὄχλον) is to depart the known world (4:36); the receiving of Jesus "as he was" (ὡς ἦν) is to render him inert, as if he were already dead and laid in a tomb (4:36); his sleeping on the pillow is to represent his "sleep of death" (4:38),[34] just as the deceased girl in the narrative to follow will be referred to as "sleeping" (5:39). Furthermore, Jesus' being "raised" in 4:38 is to symbolize his

[33] Homer *Od.* 24.11–14: πὰρ δ' ἴσαν Ὠκεανοῦ τε ῥοὰς καὶ Λευκάδα πέτρην, / ἠδὲ παρ' Ἠελίοιο πύλας καὶ δῆμον ὀνείρων / ἤϊσαν· αἶψα δ' ἵκοντο κατ' ἀσφοδελὸν λειμῶνα, / ἔνθα τε ναίουσι ψυχαί, εἴδωλα καμόντων. This, the famous "second Nekyia" of Homer, is discussed in J. Russo, M. Fernandez-Galiano, & A. Heubeck, *A Commentary on Homer's Odyssey, Volume III. Books XVII-XXIV* (Oxford: Clarendon Press, 1992), 356–58; 360–62; cf. *Od.* 11.539.

[34] Noted, for example, in J. Bligh, "The Gerasene Demoniac and the Resurrection of Christ," *CBQ* 31 (1969) 383–90, esp. 385.

resurrection from the dead;[35] and the disciples' query, "Do you not care that we are perishing (ἀπολλύμεθα)?" will bring to a climax the motif of death and dying (4:38). Even the whole context of the sea can betoken the mythical "waters of death."[36]

After Jesus does make landfall, in that unfamiliar land that will form the centerpiece of our study, the theme of death continues: the demoniac who meets Jesus is a man who comes "out of the tombs" (5:2), has his dwelling "among the tombs" (5:3), and cries out night and day "among the tombs and mountains" (5:5). His proclaiming Jesus the "son of the highest God" (υἱὲ τοῦ θεοῦ τοῦ ὑψίστου, 5:7) is not only to mark Jesus as a Hellenistic θεῖος ἀνήρ, it is to emphasize the demoniac's own netherly status,[37] just as his request not to be tortured (μή με βασανίσῃς) borrows a metaphor of the torments of hell (5:7).[38] The eventual rushing of the demon-possessed pigs into the sea is to return them to their proper home in the Abyss (5:13).[39]

---

[35] Bligh, "Gerasene," 387, who anticipates Achtemeier's classic identification of the catenae by seeing the Marcan text of the "Gerasene" demoniac as the work of a "precanonical evangelist . . . who saw that the Galilean ministry was full of anticipations or prefigurements of the post-resurrection period." But the "resurrections" in the catenae are not so much "prefigurements" as resurrection stories in their own right. To the writer of the catenae, there is no Easter-event in the traditional Markan sense, for the raising of Jesus is, like the raisings of the vegetal gods with whom he is compared, a ritual that is continually reenacted in the life of the catena community: "they raise him" (ἐγείρουσιν αὐτόν, 4:35) may well refer to an annual rite of resurrection like the ἔγερσις of Melqart mentioned by Menander of Ephesus (2nd cent. BCE) *apud* Josephus, *Ant* 8.5.3 (= *Ap.* 1.116); see further note 169, below.

[36] Collins, "Rulers," 209 (with ref. to Dibelius).

[37] On the "divine man" typology, note the masterful study of H. D. Betz, "Gottmensch II (Griechisch-römische Antike und Christentum)," *RAC* 12 (1983) 234–311, with add. refs. Bligh ("Gerasene," 387) astutely compares the demoniac's recognition of Jesus as a rejoinder to the disciples' query of 4:41: "Who is this then that even the wind and the sea obey him?" It is another case of the unexpected description of events in "No Man's Land."

[38] This notion of infernal torment, also implied in Mark 5:29, 34, is made explicit in Luke's (16:23) description of Lazarus' "being in torment"(ὑπάρχων ἐν βασάνοις) in Hades (cf. E. P. Gould, *A Critical and Exegetical Commentary on the Gospel According to St. Mark* [ICC; Edinburgh: T & T Clark, 1896] 89).

[39] R. Kotansky, "Greek Exorcistic Amulets," *Ancient Magic & Ritual Power* (ed. Marvin Meyer & Paul Mirecki; RGRW 129; Leiden: Brill, 1995) 243–77, esp. 265–72. For Bligh, "the destruction of the herd of swine prefigures the overthrow of the powers of evil by the resurrection and glorification of Jesus" ("Gerasene,"

Similar thanatological themes will also run through each of the catena stories in sequence: the ruler's little daughter hangs precariously between life and death in the limen of the *eschatia*—the very edges of time and space; she has it, literally, in a lastly way (ἐσχατῶς ἔχει, 5:23). She is simultaneously "at her end" and "outside known geography," as she undertakes a voyage *in extremis.* Like the woman "in flux" with whom she is closely linked, the little girl needs not only to be healed but to be eschatologically saved (σωθῇ, 5:23; σωθήσομαι, 5:28).[40] Like Jesus, the daughter sleeps the sleep of death but is raised (ἔγειρε/ἀνέστη ... καὶ περιεπάτει, 5:42). There are, further, subterranean themes to be identified in the hemorrhaging woman that will point to her role as a kind of archetypal Lady of the Abyss.[41] With the final feeding of the five thousand (6:34–44), the theme of death and its conquest turns to one of Afterlife and symposiastic bliss.[42]

A. *The Mystic Calm.* A number of ocean calms in the epic tradition also seem to act as a folkloric literary device that signals the passing of the hero from the known to the unknown world of the *Jenseits.* These mystic "hushes" of the sea provide additional comparative evidence that prove particularly instructive for the understanding of the Markan narrative.

---

388). In the demons' plea not to be sent away, Luke 8:31 uses εἰς τὴν ἄβυσσον in lieu of Mark's ἔξω τῆς χώρας (5:10).

[40] "Salvation" is here eschatological, and healing is a form of salvation. There is also the motif of funerary lament (5:38), coupled with the fact that the names in the story contain theological "puns:" Jairus = "He (sc. God) raises (from the dead)"—C. E. B. Cranfield, *The Gospel According to Saint Mark* (Cambridge: Cambridge University Press, 1966) 183, misunderstands the pronominal referent(s)—and Talitha (= טַלְיְתָא, "young girl") also means "funerary pall," "shroud"(טַלִּית).

[41] A study to be taken up elsewhere. She plays the female counterpart (γυνή / ἐν ῥύσει αἵματος, 5:25) to the male demoniac (ἄνθρωπος ἐν πνεύματι ἀκαθάρτῳ) who form a kind of netherworld pair that are symbolically joined as the mother and father of the *korasion* (5:40–41).

[42] Collins rightly hints, for example, at the function of the feeding of the four thousand in Mark 8:1–10 as "a symbolic representation or a foreshadowing of the messianic banquet" ("Rulers," 225). That the feeding includes ideas about a concept of the "Isles of Blessed" is considered further below.

Jesus' calming of wind and sea serve as a precursor to his arrival in the "mystic" land of the *Gadarēnoi*. After his being roused from sleep, resurrection-like, Jesus' rebuking of the sea-wind produces an abatement of the elements which cedes to an eerie calm (γαλήνη μεγάλη), a calm matched in substance only by the ferocity of the storm that had just preceded (λαῖλαψ μεγάλη). In Homer, a similar "great storm" (μεγάλη λαῖλαψ) describes the tempest that Odysseus faces before he is borne back to Scylla and Charybdis, and eventually to Calypso.[43] Elsewhere, the motif of a calm affords a typical prelude to the heroic wayfarer's arrival into the land of myth. A similar γαλήνη, for example, precedes Odysseus' being cast ashore at Scheria (*Od.* 5.452), in the land of Phaeacians, who "for the poet ... live beyond the limits of the known world;" they, like the little daughter, are the ἔσχατοι dwelling far off in the distant sea.[44] Morever, when Alcinous, king of the Phaeacians, wishes to send Odysseus safely back home, he will do so by inducing in him a deep sleep, as he is wafted over the γαλήνη of the sea (*Od.* 7.319), presumably with a sort of magical suspension of real time in order to shorten the trip (*Od.* 7.325–26). When the feat is actually accomplished in *Od.* 13.75–77, Odysseus—like Jesus—is made to lie ritually in the ship's prow (πρύμνα) and to sleep a sleep as sound as death.[45] A similar

---

43 *Od.* 12.407–8: αἶψα γὰρ ἦλθε / κεκληγὼς Ζέφυρος *μεγάλῃ* σὺν *λαίλαπι* θύων. This is combined with a wind (ἀνέμοιο θύελλα, line 409) and wave (κῦμα, line 420) that destroys Odysseus' remaining ship (see below). Once the wind ceases (ἐπαύσατο λαίλαπι θύων, line 426), Odysseus must face alone the danger of the whirlpool and his continued adventures (cf. *Od.* 12.447–453 = *Od.* 7.253–256, the isle of Calypso).

44 A. Heubeck, S. West, & J. B. Hainsworth, *A Commentary on Homer's Odyssey, 1: Introduction and Books I-VIII* (Oxford: Clarendon Press, 1990) 294, with reference to ἑκὰς ἀνδρῶν ἀλφηστάων ("far from men of toil") at *Od.* 6.8; and to the Phaeacians as ἔσχατοι at *Od.* 6.205; further, Heubeck, et al., *Commentary*, 306, on the latter term as "outside, sc. the known world." For γαλήνη used at *Od.* 5.391, see below. On the rôle of the Phaeacians in the *Odyssey* in general, note C. Segal, *Singers, Heroes, and Gods in the* Odyssey (Ithaca and London: Cornell University Press, 1994) 15–25; 37–64.

45 He is first laid, almost ritual-like (cf. E. Cook, "Ferrymen of Elysium and the Homeric Phaeacians," *JIES* 20 [1992] 239–67, esp. 245), upon a blanket and a linen sheet in the stern (πρύμνης, *Od.* 13.75) where he sleeps a sleep "most likened to death" (θανάτῳ ἄγχιστα ἐοικώς, *Od.* 13.80). Then, upon arrival, Odysseus is lifted, with the wrappings, while he is still asleep (δεδμημένον ὕπνῳ, *Od.* 13.117–119). The imagery may help explain the odd καὶ παραλαμβάνουσιν

compression of travel-time seems to occur also in Mark's narrative of Jesus.

The land of the man-eating Laestrygonians in the tenth book of the *Odyssey* is reached by a harbor where breaks "no wave great or small," but there is a "bright calm all about" (*Od.* 10.94, λευκὴ δ' ἦν ἀμφὶ γαλήνη). We also find a paranormal intersection of night and day and a prodigious juxtaposition of opposing cliffs and headlands[46]—cliffs that will prove vital to the geography of our Markan tale, as we shall see. But such a folkloric motif of an ocean calm often presages impending doom: the enclosed harbor becomes for Odysseus and his men a death-trap, as the giant Laestrygonians hurl huge rocks upon the hero's fleet, spear them like sitting ducks, and carry them off to be eaten. All but one of the twelve vessels is destroyed, the one that carries Odysseus and his comrades to the isle of Circe, where the enchantress soon turns the hero's comrades into swine, of all creatures.[47]

αὐτὸν ὡς ἦν in Mark 4:36: Jesus is taken on board, mummiform, exhausted and in a death-like slumber. On the role of boats in Egyptian and Near-Eastern funerary ritual and myth in this connection, note too Cook, "Ferrymen," 254–55, 260.

[46] *Od.* 10.86: ἐγγὺς γὰρ νυκτός τε καὶ ἤματός εἰσι κέλευθοι ("For the passings of night and day are near"), a crux, apparently referring to a region of perpetual light; cf. lit. and discussion in A. Heubeck & A. Hoekstra, *A Commentary on Homer's Odyssey, 2: Books IX-XIII* (Oxford: Clarendon Press, 1990) 48 ("The lines convey a sense of the topographical strangeness of the legendary country"). For the cliffs, cf. *Od.* 10.87–88. On the Laestrygonians in general, see Heubeck & Hoekstra, *Commentary*, 47–48. The day-and-night expression reminds one of the far-western description of the transition between night and day at Gadeira (see below), which Philostratus, *Vit. Ap.* 5.3, describes as a sudden, paranormal burst of light.

[47] However important the Homeric parallel is, we can only pause here briefly to remark upon the folkloric motif of changing men into pigs (on which see Heubeck & Hoekstra, *Commentary*, 50–52), since the discussion of the Markan swine, below, is to assume a slightly different tack. With drugs and a magic staff, Circe transforms Odysseus' men into animals: "they had the head, voice, hair, and form of pigs, but their minds remained as before" (οἱ δὲ συῶν μὲν ἔχον κεφαλὰς φωνήν τε τρίχας τε / καὶ δέμας, αὐτὰρ νοῦς ἦν ἔμπεδος, ὡς τὸ πάρος περ, *Od.* 10.239–40). A similar transition from human to porcine state is reflected in the host of Markan demons that leave the man and enter into (i.e., "turn into") a herd of pigs. Although the metamorphosis is entirely "numinous" rather than "material," there is a transformation, nevertheless; an army of disembodied men (= legion) in effect turns into an army of corporeal swine.

The most famous of Odysseus' excursions into a "No-Man's Land" is that of the venture to the isle of the Sirens, followed by his encounter with Skylla, Charybdis, and the cattle of Helios Hyperion; it too is prefaced by the motif of a great calm:

τόφρα δὲ καρπαλίμως ἐξίκετο νηῦς εὐεργὴς
νῆσον Σειρήνοιιν· ἔπειγε γὰρ οὖρος ἀπήμων.
αὐτίκ' ἔπειτ' ἄνεμος μὲν ἐπαύσατο ἠδὲ *γαλήνη*
ἔπλετο νηνεμίη, κοίμησε δὲ κύματα δαίμων (*Od.* 12.166–169)

Meanwhile the well-built ship speedily came to the isle of the two Sirens, for a fair and gentle wind bore her on. Then presently the wind ceased and there was a windless calm, and a god lulled the waves to sleep.[48]

With this eerie lull,[49] which an unnamed *daimon* brings about, our hero's ears are stopped with wax and his hand and foot bound so that he can experience with relative immunity the alluring song of the Sirens, a song that announces a knowledge not only of Odysseus and his plight, but even of "all things that come to pass upon the fruitful earth" (trans. Murray). The Sirens are prescient because they are souls of the dead.[50] Their capacity for knowledge will match that of the Markan demoniac, possessed by a spirit of the dead, who will recognize Jesus by name and rank, a privilege not shared by Jesus, who must inquire about the demon's name and nature.

Straightaway after the Sirens, Odysseus and his comrades, less than successfully, navigate the gauntlet of the bubbling whirlpool of Charybdis and the sheer terror of Skylla (*Od.* 12.201–259). But when Odysseus and his remaining crew escape and beach their vessel, they improperly devour the kine of Helios. Accordingly, upon departure,

---

[48] Translation by A. T. Murray, *The Odyssey: Homer* (2 vols.; LCL; Cambridge, MA: Harvard, 1960–75) 1. 445.

[49] For other examples, see *Od.* 5.391, with the same expression preceding the aforementioned arrival in the land of the Phaeacians. Heubeck & Hoekstra (*Commentary*, 127) following Gresseth ("Sirens," 210) rightly note that the calm is intended as "a warning to Odysseus of imminent danger." For another such γαλήνη in a nether context, see the discussion below on the Argonauts' landing in Libya.

[50] For the Sirens representing souls of the deceased who sing their song in the Afterlife, note Heubeck & Hoekstra, *Commentary*, 118–19 (with lit.); Gresseth, "Sirens," 203–4. Sirens also have the ability to calm the sea-wind in the Hesiodic *Catalogue* (frag. 28 M-W): ἐντεῦθεν Ἡσίοδος καὶ τοὺς ἀνέμους θέλγειν αὐτὰς ἔφη (Schol. on Hom. *Od.* 12.168), just as Jesus calms the wind in Mark 4:39.

the heroic mariners are destroyed by a terrible tempest that pulls the ship back to Charybdis and sucks it down again; this time Odysseus alone survives by clinging to a life-saving fig-tree (*Od.* 12.432–436); but the venture is costly; the force of his original fleet has been pared down from a single vessel to a single man.

Each of the foregoing marine "sea-calms" in the epic tradition not only warns our adventurous hero of lurking danger, they collectively signal for the reader a bizarre entrance into a magic narrative where normal geographies are disposed of and where powerful archetypal dangers confront the hero. So too Jesus' journey to the Beyond represents a kind of magic voyage preceded by the mystic calm that marks the "No-Man's Land" separating the realms of the Known and Unknown. Like Odysseus with his fleet of vessels, Jesus embarks to magic realms with a little armada of sea-worthy vessels (4:37). But in the unfolding of the episode of 5:1–20, Jesus alone arrives in the *Peran* in a single boat, and alone encounters the demoniac. The disciples are strangely absent and reappear only in 5:31, in the story of the woman who touches Jesus' garment.[51] Like Odysseus before Circe, our hero must face his challenges in the unknown land entirely on his own.

As we shall see, journeys to the mystic lands in the epic tradition bring the hero and his crew face-to-face with the divine in many forms; nymphs, spirits, and sorceresses; unnamed δαίμονες, ungainly monsters, and unknown races of divine people populate the lands of epic heroes. There is always a peculiar mixing of historic names and peoples with supernatural beings and events. Even though the Gadarene tale will plant Jesus in a land bound by quasi-historic perimeters, it will remain the realm of wonder, just as Odysseus' ventures mingle inextricably the known aspects of the land of the Phaeacians and Laestrygonians with their unknown and mysterious geographical mien.[52] Mystic lands, especially those at the limits of the

[51] Although placed in the environment of the sea, as noted above, the combined story of Jairus' Daughter and Hemorrhaging Woman is, "genetically" speaking, a "landlocked" story: even if Jesus "crosses" to the other side in the story (διαπεράσανος . . . εἰς τὸ πέραν, 5:21), the narrative's introductory καὶ ἔρχεται (5:22) aligns it with other narratives in Mark that use the formula; all of these narratives appear to belong to "non-marine" contexts.

[52] The problems are discussed in Heubeck, et al., *Commentary*, 289–90, 294, who soften too much, though, the well-argued view that the Phaeacians act as

explored world, remain historically elusive; their names are familiar, but the terrain is not. The famed limits of the world's edge found at the Straits of Gibraltar, although fixed to an historical landmark, remained closely linked to the figure of Heracles whose pillars were thought to rest somewhere near the closest points of the two juxtaposed continents of Africa and Europe.

B. *The Pillars of Heracles.* Odysseus' navigation through the narrow straits between Skylla and Charybdis (or the Clashing Rocks),[53] although set in a mythological seascape, has occasioned speculation as to its precise location. Where in the ancient Mediterranean would such a whirlpool have existed? The classical locus is usually the straits of Messina between Italy and Sicily; however, motif for motif, those who have championed the Straits of Gibraltar have a better case for positioning Odysseus and his comrades at the edges of the world.[54] Hennig had argued for a giant octopus found beyond the Straits of Gibraltar as the model for the bizarre serpentine creature, Σκύλλα, described first in *Od.* 12.85–100. Strabo, too, in describing the ocean beyond the Pillars, names the various huge whale-like monsters that inhabit the sea.[55] It seems that witches, sea-monsters, and other dangerous forces were thought in ancient times to dwell near the edges of the known world, whether north, east, south, or west.

The far western threshold of the known world was marked in post-epic literature by the Pillars of Heracles. Certain death awaited those

---

netherworld ferrymen of the dead (most recently Cook, "Ferrymen"). So, too, the land of the Laestrygonians contains "realistic elements" (Heubeck & Hoekstra, *Commentary*, 47).

[53] The famous Symplegades or Planctae (*Od.* 12.61; 23.327; cf. Apoll. Rhod. *Argon.* 2.596, 645; 4.860, 924, 932, 939, etc.) were also equated with Skylla and Charybdis. The Hemeroskopeion, described below, was also the locale of a similar 'Wandering Rock' (*Planesia*); cf. Strabo 3.4.6.

[54] The issues are summarized conveniently in Heubeck & Hoekstra, *Commentary*, 121–22.

[55] Strabo 3.2.7. The identity of the various "whales" he describes is uncertain: ὄρυξ ("narwhal"?), φάλαινα ("whale"), φυστήρ ("whale"); γόγγροι ("conger-eels"—"of bestial size"—ἀποθηροῦνται); etc.; see the outstanding study of J. S. Romm, *The Edges of the Earth in Ancient Thought: Geography, Exploration, and Fiction* (Princeton: Princeton University Press, 1992) 190–91. Tacitus (2.24.4) describes in the north "powerful whirlwinds, unheard-of birds, sea-monsters, and ambiguous creatures partway between human and animal;" cf. Romm, *Edges of the Earth*, 146.

who sailed past them. Pindar, writing in the fifth century BCE, gives a perfect summary of ancient conceptions of the limits and dangers of this far-western region:

> εἰ δ' ἐὼν καλὸς ἔρδων τ' ἐοικότα μορφᾷ
> ἀνορέαις ὑπερτάταις ἐπέβα παῖς Ἀριστοφάνεος· οὐκέτι πρόσω
> ἀβάταν ἅλα κιόνων ὕπερ Ἡρακλέος *περᾶν* εὐμαρές,
> ἥρως θεὸς ἃς ἔθηκε ναυτιλίας *ἐσχατάς*
> μάρτυρας κλυτάς· *δάμασε* δὲ θῆρας ἐν πελάγεσιν
> ὑπερόχους, ἰδίᾳ τ' ἐξερεύνασε τεναγέων
> ῥοάς, ὁπᾷ πόμπιμον κατέβαινε *νόστου* τέλος,
> καὶ γᾶν φράδασε, κτλ.

> But, if the son of Aristophanes, being fair to look upon, and doing deeds that befit the fairness of his form, embarked on the highest achievements of manly prowess, no further is it easy for him to sail across the trackless sea *beyond* the Pillars of Heracles, which that hero and god set up as far-famed witness of the *furthest* limit of voyaging. He *quelled* the monstrous beasts amid the seas, and tracked to the very end of the streams of the shallows, there where he reached the limit that sped him home again, and he made known the limits of the land.[56]

The motifs in Pindar's account mirror the very themes in Mark's mythic voyage to the "Other Side:" Jesus, too, having sailed *beyond* the sea (τὸ πέραν), now comes to the *limits* of known reality, tames (δαμάσαι) the untamable daimon, and will of course—eventually—return home. Only heroes and divine figures could sail to the ends of the earth and return safely, at least in the context of myth. Although it was a literary and mythic commonplace that the crossing of the Straits of Gibraltar meant death or the coming into a kind of eerie netherworld, more historical accounts like those of the great Phoenician seafarer Hanno, or Himilco, have survived and tell in a marvelous way some of the unusual and fabulous wonders they saw in lands lying beyond known reality. It is to the genuine knowledge of

---

[56] *Nem.* 3.19–26. Translation adapted from J. E. Sandys, *The Odes of Pindar: Including the Principal Fragments* (rev. ed; LCL; Cambridge, MA: Harvard University Press, 1961) 337. Similar thoughts about the world's edge are reflected, too, in the 3rd *Olympian Ode*, in describing Theron of Akragas' superlative accomplishments in this, his "life-achievement" award: ". . . sorrow doth Theron by his deeds of prowess come unto the utmost verge, by his own true merit reaching even as far as the Pillars of Heracles. All beyond that limit cannot be approached, either by the wise or by the unwise; else may I be deemed a fool" (*Olymp.* 3.44; LCL, p. 39). In a word, to go further than the straits is a kind of hybris (cf. *Isthm.* 4.11–13).

such strange peoples and creatures living beyond the Pillars that we can often attribute the shaping of the seafaring tales of the epic and gospel traditions. Even though an eventual opening up of the unexplored regions may have served to "demystify" places like the far west, even well into Hellenistic and Roman times, myths about the edges of the world with its monsters prevailed in the popular imagination. The sea with its vastness remained an enigmatic and unfathomable realm of myth, monster, and mystery.

VI. The "Gadarene" Account

To return to our comparison of the mystic "calm" of the epic tradition with Mark: following the magical ocean calm—a calming, we may add, that Jesus himself causes, not some δαίμων—the unnamed voyagers of the pre-Markan narrative come "to the land of the *Gadarēnoi*" (καὶ ἦλθον . . . εἰς τὴν χώραν τῶν Γαδαρήνων). The particular phrase, "they came into the land of x," carries with it the ring of a far and distant place. We have already met up with it in the epic narratives describing the lands of the Laestrygonians and the Phaeacians, and, in the apocryphal acts, the land of the cannibal Myrmidons. The notion of an entrance into a faraway country signifies that the wayfarers have disembarked onto the mysterious shores of fable and not into the familiar territory of history. The expression calls to mind distant and unfamiliar places not belonging to the known geographies of the hero's frame of reference—for Odysseus, his island home of Ithaca; for Jesus, his Galilean homeland. No such geographic outlier as that embodied by the expression "in the land of the *Gadarēnoi*" occurs anywhere else in all of Mark's gospel, a fact that suggests we are dealing with an independent, non-Galilean source.[57] The sort of narratives that address someone else's land in such distant terms, especially when that land lies literally "beyond the sea," are also

[57] Note also the "mythic" use of a similar phrase in the *The Acts of Andrew and Matthias* (= *AAMt*), § 5 (MacDonald, *Acts of Andrew*, 80, n. 31): ἐν τῇ χώρᾳ τῶν ἀνθρωποφάγων, the Greek variant on Latin ms. *civitatis Mermedonie*. Further, the use of the genitive plural to describe the people of that land also adds to the geographic mystique, and distance, of the inhabitants. No such gentilic plural, especially with χώρα, is found anywhere else in Mark. The case of Mark 14:32, καὶ ἔρχονται εἰς χωρίον (οὗ τὸ ὄνομα Γεθσημανί), is curious in itself, but somewhat different.

characteristic of the so-called "circumnavigations" (περίπλοι) and of the whole category of adventure stories introduced thus far, from the ancient novel to the more epic tale of the argonautical sort.

In the epic tradition, sailing to mythic topographies often brings the hero into contact with a world of the dead, as noted above with the famous "second Nekyia" in *Odyssey* 24. In a similar vein, Apollonius Rhodius' *Argonautica,* whose heroic tale has in its entirety been called an elaborate journey to the underworld, tells of the Argonauts' arrival in the "land of Myriandynoi" (Μαριανδυνῶν . . . γαῖαν, 2.723; γῆν Μαριανδυνῶν, 2.748), a land marked by a peculiar underworld topography: there, there is an Acherousian headland lined with abysmally steep cliffs (κρημνοῖσιν . . . ἠλιβάτοισιν, 2.729; cf. 2.750), a cave of Hades covered by woods and rocks (2.735–36) that issues forth an "icy-cold breath" (ἀϋτμὴ πηγυλίς, 2.736–37), and the nether river Acheron itself (2.743).[58] The land is—as we shall see with Mark—both known and mysterious; both historic and mythic. It refers simultaneously to the geographic land of the southern coast of the Black Sea and mythologically to the realm of the Underworld from whose very entrance Heracles retrieves Kerberos, the hound of Hades.[59]

More towards the west, the Argonauts (*Argon.* 4.1232–34) later in their adventure come to another "land situated at the end, the limbo, of the world," as Kyriakou puts it;[60] there they encounter death in a different kind of mythic underworld, that of the land of Libya.[61] This

---

[58] The netherworld typology and its relationship to the *Odyssey* is most recently discussed in P. Kyriakou, "ΚΑΤΑΒΑΣΙΣ and the Underworld in the *Argonautica* of Apollonius Rhodius," *Philologus* 139 (1995), 256–64, esp. 256, who gives the pertinent literature. On Apollonius Rhodius, note also Romm, *Edges of the Earth,* 194–96. Steep cliffs, too, characterize the arrival of the Argonauts at their final destination at the Caucasian mountains of Cholcis, where Prometheus' liver is being devoured by the eagle (2.1247–1259). There at the Phasis river, they reach the farthest boundaries of the ocean (ἔσχατα πείρατα πόντου, 2.1261), although this time it is the eastern sea.

[59] K. Ziegler, "Mariandynoi," *KP* 3 (1979), 1024–25.

[60] Kyriakou, "Underworld," 259.

[61] Libya here and in most ancient sources is North Africa up to the Straits. The Argonauts arrive in Libya following a sea-storm, after having passed "the land of the Curetes" (4.1229) and "the land of Pelops" (4.1231). On the chthonian aspect of Libya, see Kyriakou, "Underworld," 259, n. 22 (with additional refs.).

strange country is marked by a vast empty mist (4.1246) and by the kind of "dead calm" (εὐκήλῳ . . . γαλήνῃ, 4.1249) that we have discussed above, a calm prescient of unwelcome events to come. The adventurers nervously query, "What land is this (τίς χθὼν εὔχεται ἥδε)? Whither has the tempest hurled us?"[62] There, defeated by the desolation of the land, the Argonauts are consigned to lie down "like lifeless spectres" (οἷον δ' ἀψύχοισιν ἐοικότες εἰδώλοισιν, 4.1280) to wait for death; they are, however, soon rescued by the intervention of a peculiar class of divine goddesses of the land (4.1321–1323), the Libyan Tutelary Daughters (Λιβύης τιμήοροι ἠδὲ θύγατρες, 4.1358), one of those unknown races of divine people mentioned above.

The epic voyage to a mythic land brings the hero into close contact with the world of the supernatural, that of Afterlife and the Beyond, in a word, a land not associated with normal existence; it is thus at once a magic land of blissful immortality and the domain of the less fortunate dead.[63] This theme is repeated over and over again in the telling of the various fairytale adventures of Odysseus and is one that will have bearing on our Markan story as well. In order to identify more specifically the land of Jesus' arrival we must focus upon the text of Mark 5:1 itself.

A. *The textual problem.* What actual place was this land of the *Gadarēnoi* that Jesus and his band finally obtain? The synoptic versions of the "legion"-story are plagued by a well-known textual conundrum. In each of the accounts, the name of the city describing the inhabitants of the land to which Jesus comes widely differs. Each synoptic parallel has a constellation of manuscripts associated with one of each of three principal gentilic groups, named from their respective townships: *Gadarēnoi, Gerasēnoi, Gergesēnoi, Gergustēnoi,* and even

---

[62] Translation from R. C. Seaton, *Apollonius Rhodius. The Argonautica* (LCL; Cambridge, MA: Harvard University Press, 1961) 379.

[63] Note, in general, C. Sourvinou-Inwood, *'Reading' Greek Death: To the End of the Classical Period* (Oxford: Clarendon, 1995) 17–92, esp. 71: "This fairyland [of the Phaeacians] is essentially non-human, at times super-human at others sub-human;" and esp. 37: "it is a common belief of seafaring people that the dead travel beyond the seas to a remote Land of the Dead."

Gazarēnoi.[64] Textual critics have favored the reading Γερασηνῶν for Mark and Luke, but Γαδαρηνῶν for Matthew, a fact that in itself betrays the inherent danger in slavishly counting manuscripts in weighing one reading against another: if Matthew used Mark, as most scholars maintain, the two evangelists' original readings would have to be identical, not different.[65]

But not only are the variant readings in gross divergence with one another, the identity of the cities, whatever the original readings, poses difficulties of their own. Both Gadara and Gerasa are well removed from any shore whatsoever, let alone one with cliffs; the latter city, in fact, on which the so-called "preferred" Markan reading is based, is as far removed from the Sea of Galilee as the Sea of Galilee itself is from the Mediterranean; Gadara hardly fares better, for it is also too far from the shore, and the only cliff-like formations in the area at all are those on the western side of the Sea of Galilee, the wrong side of the lake.[66] The only ancient site near the eastern shore of the Sea of Galilee was Hippos, an important metropolis altogether unmentioned

---

[64] See B. Metzger, *A Textual Commentary on the Greek New Testament* (London and New York: UBS, 1971) 23. The names are in the genitive plural, following the phrase "land of:" Mark 5:1 reads 1) Γαδαρηνῶν A C K̦ f^{13} syr^{p,h}; 2) Γερασηνῶν (ℵ* B D it vg cop^{sa}); 3) Γεργεσηνῶν (L ^{c}ℵ Δ Θ f^{1} syr^{s,hmg} cop^{bo}); 4) Γεργυστηνῶν (W syr^{hmg}). Matt. 8:28 gives for 1) (ℵ*) B C C^{txt} (Δ) Θ syr^{sph}; 2) it vg cop^{sa} syr^{hmg2}; 3) ℵ^{c} C^{mg} K L W ^{fl} f^{13} cop^{bo}. Luke 8:26 has 1) A K W Δ^{gr} Ψ f^{13} syr^{csph}; 2) p^{75} B D it vg cop^{sa}; 3) ℵ L X Θ f^{1} cop^{bo}. Γεργυστηνῶν in W (032)—the famous Codex Freerianus (with its unique "Freer Logion" at Mark 14:16), which B. Metzger typifies as "curiously variegated" (*The Text of the New Testament. Its Transmission, Corruption, and Restoration* [3rd ed. New York and Oxford, 1992] 57)—is supported by a marginal reading of the Harklean Syriac text, itself a slavish revision of the Greek. Greek γέργυρα (Dor.) / γόργυρα means "underground chamber" or "dungeon"(LSJ), so that "the land of the Γεργυστηνοί" could conceivably be a land of "troglodytes," about whom we have more to say below. Matt 8:28 adds the unique reading Γαζαρηνῶν (ℵ* = "land of the Gazarenes"), which corresponds to Judaean Gezer, far from any sea or lake.

[65] Given the priority of Mark, there is an internal inconsistency in electing Γαδαρηνῶν for Matt 8:28, but Γερασηνῶν for Mark 5:1; if Matthew used Mark as his source, then Γαδαρηνῶν cannot be the preferred Matthean reading without Γαδαρηνῶν also being the preferred Markan reading. Since Γερασηνῶν is relatively weakly attested in Matthew, and Γαδαρηνῶν comparatively stronger in Mark 5:1, Γαδαρηνῶν must be given preferential weight for Mark too.

[66] Viz. just north and south of Tiberias; see the superb aerial photographs in R. Cleave, "Satellite Revelations. New Views of the Holy Land," *National Geographic* 187/6 (1995) 88–105, esp. 89 (overleaf).

in the Bible, and nowhere near cliffs.[67] Had the pre-Markan catena narrative intended historical lake-crossings, Hippos would surely have been mentioned once, as a target city.

Our third reading, that of Gergesa, is the only reasonable possibility, topographically, but the least likely textually, historically, and archaeologically. McRay aptly summarizes the whole issue as follows:

> Gerasa, modern Jerash, can hardly be the location of the miracle story because it is 37 miles SE of the Sea of Galilee—too much of a run for the pigs. Gadara, which is to be identified with modern Umm Qeis, is also too far away, 5 miles SE of the sea. This leaves Gergesa, modern El Koursi, on the E bank of the sea as the only reasonable possibility, *if any credence is to be given to the geographical statements of the gospels* (italics mine).[68]

But the reading "of the Gergesenes" bristles with particular difficulties of its own, not the least of which is the insurmountable problem of identifying the city at all. There is absolutely no evidence that a Gergesa even existed. Josephus' silence suggests that it did not.[69] The attempted identification of Gergesa with El Koursi represents a counsel of despair aimed at reconciling the biblical text with an historical geography. Modern maps, like that found in the inside cover of the 26th edition of Nestle-Aland (1992), places a "Gergesa" conveniently resting on the eastern shore of the sea, but with a question mark. The recent contemporary map produced by the Survey of Israel project, with no confessional axe to grind, recognizes no Gergesa near the Sea of Galilee, nor anywhere, for that matter.[70] Thus,

---

[67] C. Burchard, "Hippos," *KP* 2 (1979) 1177–78; Y. Aharoni, *The Land of the Bible: An Historical Geography. Revised and Enlarged Edition* (2nd ed.; Philadelphia: Westminster Press, 1979) 381, n. 45.

[68] J. McRay, "Gerasenes," *ABD* 2 (1992) 991.

[69] Josephus is unaware of Gergesa and is at pains to state that no trace of the ancient OT Gergesites has survived (*Ant.* 1.6.2). Besides, the biblical Girgashites cannot be identified with a later, New Testament, land of Gergesenes, since the Canaanite tribe was located on the West side of the Jordan (cf. D. W. Baker, "Girgashite," *ABD* 2 [1992] 1028). The *ABD* also carries no entry on Gergesenes, as it does on Gerasenes and Gadarenes, respectively.

[70] Y. Tsafrir & L. Di Segni, eds. *Survey of Israel: Iudaea Palestina. Eretz Israel during the Hellenistic, Roman and Byzantine Periods* (Jerusalem: Israel Academy of Sciences and Humanities, 1993). The evidence for Gergesa's existence seems to come entirely from Origen. The town is apparently an etymological fiction (= "dwelling of those that have driven away;" cf. Metzger, *Textual Commentary*, 24 and n. 1) that

the clearly "orthodox" way out of the biblical conundrum—to adopt the "Gergesene" reading—embarrassingly falters; it creates a worse mess than the problem it attempts to solve.[71]

Textual science should alert us to the fact that something has gone badly awry in Mark 5:1 at an embryonic stage of transmission, long before any "early text" was established and certainly long before the development of any "text families;" for what we have here is not one good variant replacing another good one, nor a better reading replacing a poorer one, but rather a situation where no textual version is satisfactory. Whatever the original reading was, it was subject to replacement.

In concert with the themes of a fantastic sea-voyage argued thus far, an identification of the place name in 5:1 is to be resolved, I believe, in seeing it not as a reference to Gadara or Gergesa, at all, but to a place far removed from *terra Palaestina.* The location most likely to satisfy our travelers' destination may not have been, in fact, the "Gadara" just east of the Sea of Galilee, but rather a similar-sounding habitat far in the distant west: the magnificent fortress of Gadeira, modern Cádiz, the renowned island-city of the Phoenicians, lying just beyond the famous Pillars of Heracles at the opposite end of the Mediterranean.

Phonetic reasons, too, might support such a thesis, for "Gadeira" and "Gadara" share the same root in their underlying Semitic: *Geder* means "fence," "walled enclosure," or even a "pen" (for herds).[72] It is

---

was propagated by Origen to salvage the Markan narrative. But for modern scholars to endeavour to locate, even with a query, a "Gergesa" on a map betrays an attempt to circumvent scientific reasoning merely to maintain the integrity of a confessional position.

[71] R. H. Gundry adopts the Gergesene reading, although "hesitantly" (*Mark. A Commentary on His Apology for the Cross* [Grand Rapids: Eerdmans, 1993] 256). Cranfield's reasoning on the problem is highly specious (*Saint Mark*, 176).

[72] Phoenician *gdr* means "fence," "wall," or "walled enclosure" (cf. J. Hoftijzer & K. Jongeling, *Dictionary of the North-West Semitic Inscriptions*, pt. 1 [Leiden: Brill, 1995] 215, *s.v.*). Late Hebrew גֶּדֶר *geder* (*ha-geder* = "fence," "partition," or "pen") is also the spelling of Peraean Gadara, just as the cognate גָּדֵיר (late Aramaic גְּדֵירָה = "fence") is the Mishnaic Hebrew for Gadira / Cádiz (M. Jastrow, *A Dictionary of the Targumim* [Brooklyn: Shalom, 1967 repr.] 212, 215, *svv.*). We do not know, of course, what the original Phoenician vocalization would have been. See also the next note. A number of Hebrew cognates of *gdr* also refer to various biblical cities in Canaan and Judah: Beth-gader, Gederah, Gederoth, Gederathaim, Gedar etc.; see C. S. Ehrlich, "Geder," "Gederah" etc. in *ABD* 2 (1992) 925.

this virtual identity of the basic Semitic names for the cities that may have created confusion between the Phoenician and Galilean spellings in the eventual Greek transcription.[73]

An identification of the "land of the *Gadarēnoi*" in the distant horizon of the west will thus confirm our suspicions that the pre-Markan story is modelled on an Argonautical or Odyssean-like venture, for certain details of the pre-Markan story in 5:1–20, as we shall see, can be explained better within the context of a Phoenician Gadeiran topography than a Galilean one. In addition to the motif of arriving in a Land of Death that the "Gadeirite" setting seems to present, maritime Gadeira will also provide the necessary "local color" to the Legion-story that is embarrassingly absent with a "Sea of Galilee" topography: all along ancient Gadeira and the coasts of Spain one encounters steep cliffs abutting the shore's edge; there are herds of livestock in abundance (including pigs), as well as the necessary rocks and tombs. More importantly, however, other religious and mythological details seem to place Mark 5:1–17 squarely within a Gadeiran context. The Helleno-Semitic cult of Tyrian Heracles-Melqart, centered in the famous Herakleion of Cádiz, flourished up through New Testament times; it was a cult that, most strikingly, held swine to be taboo. Further, not only are motifs of a Herculean "strong man"-type to be extrapolated from the Markan verses, a particular Hercules-myth attached to Gadeira seems to lie at the very core of the account.[74] These and other parallels will suggest a surprising association between the Markan "Gadarēnoi"-episode and the Heracles "Gadeira" myth.

---

[73] In Greek the distinction is Γάδειρα vs. Γάδαρα (cf. Γαδαρεύς vs. Γαδειρεύς); however, by the time the story came into the NT canon, it may have already been "relocated" in Galilee; therefore, τῶν Γαδαρηνῶν need not presuppose an original text with τῶν Γαδειραίων, τῶν Γαδαρίτων or τῶν Γαδιτανῶν—a "Latinized" form common in Strabo (cf. 3.2.1), but not listed in LSJ, nor Supplements. Even τῶν *Γαδειρηνῶν, which is closest to Γαδαρηνῶν though not attested, is a possibility; cf. "Spanish" Γαδειραῖος, Γαδειρίτης and Γαδειρικός, ή, όν, without corresponding "Galilean" equivalents in Greek. The absence of corresponding forms may simply be an accident.

[74] Namely, the tenth labor of Heracles, the myth of the cattle of Geryon, discussed further below.

B. *Gadeira in Roman Times.* Gadir (modern Cádiz) was a Phoenician colony founded by Tyrian settlers ca. 1104–1103 BCE, according to traditional reckoning, at the divine behest of an oracle of Melqart;[75] reasons of a more economic sort, however, lay behind the settlement of the region: the exploitation of the abundant silver of the famous mines about the Quadalquivir basin.[76]

Phoenician Gadir,[77] known in Greek sources as Gadeira (τὰ Γάδειρα) and in Latin as *Gādes*, was situated on the western side of the cape at Tartessus—a region with which the city was often confused—just 97 kilometers northwest of the Straits of Gibraltar. Today, modern Cádiz rests at the end of a long peninsular finger attached to the mainland near San Fernando, formed from centuries of alluvial silting that has created an enclosed bay. In antiquity, this slender peninsula was detached from the mainland so that Gadeira was comprised of three long, closely adjoining islands lined with cliffs, particularly in the south.[78] The resulting archipelago, described by

---

[75] Strabo 3.5.5; Diod. S. 5.20.1–4; 25.10.1; on the foundation date, note Velleius Paterculus *Hist. Rom.* 1.2.3; Mela Pomponius 3.6.46 with discussion in Aubet, *Phoenicians,* 168–72; 221–23. Velleius Paterculus' foundation date of eighty years after the Trojan War (1104 or 1103 BCE) is generally disbelieved in favor of a more likely date around 800 BCE.

[76] Note Aubet, *Phoenicians,* 236–41; Strabo 3.2.8–9, on the authority of Poseidonius, remarks at length on the abundance of metals in the area, a fact that will also contribute much to the popular notion of the West as a kind of paradise of "prodigal fortune" (§ 9). But in this description he also aligns the wealth (*ploutos*) of the region with the proverbial "wealth" of the underworld: to the inhabitants it is not Hades, but Pluton (Wealth) who dwells below.

[77] Phoen. *gdr* = "(walled) enclosure" (see above). The etymology of the word also matches a play on words found in the Markan narrative, whereby *gdr* = *ʿdr* ("enclosure," "pen," "herd," or "flock"), a reference to the "herd" of pigs in the story (see further note 102 below).

[78] Today the cliffs at modern Cádiz are largely absent, as the width of the island/peninsula has shrunken considerably (see A. García y Bellido, "Hércules Gaditanus," *Archivo Español de Arqueologia* 36 [1963] 70–152, esp. 76). But cliffs are still present at the Isla de Santi Petri, at the opposite end of the peninsula; cf. too, the photographs of Quintero (P. Quintero [de Atauri], *Necrópolis Ante-Romana de Cádiz: Descripción de las excavaciones efectuadas, acompañada de un estudio de D. Antonio Vives sobre las monedas antiquas Gades* [Madrid: Hauser y Menet, 1915] 44; idem, *Cádiz. Primeros Pobladores: Hallazgos Arqueológicos* [Cádiz: Manuel Alvarez, 1917] plate). The 1564 plate reproduced in Miguel Martinez del Cerro, *Un Paseo por Cadiz. Ensayo historia intinerario artistico* (Cadiz: Editorial Escelicer, S.A. del Cerro, 1966) 15, shows the extent of the cliffs in the 16th century. It is important to note,

Pliny in the first century CE, included Kotinoussa, the long slender strip with the famous Herakleion at the southern tip, and the crowning island of Erytheia, where the walled city of Gadeira itself was located.[79]

Gadeira endured for centuries as a Phoenician city and became in the empire second only to Rome itself in size and commercial importance. Its greatest cultural and commercial zenith was achieved in the period from the first century BCE to the mid-first century CE, at which time it enjoyed close ties with Rome and Italy, even though it continued to hold on to its distinctively Punic character in language, culture, and religion.[80]

As the greatest of maritime cities in all of the Mediterranean, Gadeira exported to Ostia metals, textiles, fruits and vegetables, as well as honey, wine, bees-wax, and its own brand of pickled fish, for which its factories had become famous.[81] The imperial trade with Spain was

---

however, that the cliffy terrain of the whole region has created a kind of "mythology of cliffs," as discussed throughout this paper; the required terrain is largely one of mythic imagination and need not be physically identified; cf. note 94, below, and ref. at note 112.

[79] Pliny *Hist. Nat.* 4.22. Reconstructions of the archipelago vary; see the excellent maps in Aubet, *Phoenicians,* 224–25, with discussion. The original fortress in Gadir of Phoenician origin was enlarged in Roman times by Balbus of Gades so that the Nea Gadeira formed a twin city ("Didyme") with the older citadel (Strabo 3.5.3; Aubet, *Phoenicians,* 226). On a tiny island just north of Gadeira there was a temple of Astarte (Venus Maritima) with an oracle (Avienus, *Ora Maritima,* 85, 267–270; Aubet, *Phoenicians,* 226). Further, Kotinoussa also had a second temple dedicated to Baal Hammon (Saturn). This so-called *Kronion* (τὸ Κρόνιον, Strabo 3.5.3) lay opposite the *Herakleion,* on the other tip of the island near the city (Aubet, *Phoenicians,* 229–30).

[80] Cf. J. B. Tsirkin, "The Labours, Death and Resurrection of Melqart as Depicted on the Gates of the Gades Herakleion," *RSF* 9 (1981) 21–27; idem, "The Phoenician Civilization in Roman Spain," *Gerion* 3 (1985) 246–70, esp. 252, 259. Phoenician was still spoken in the region in the first century BCE/first century CE period (and later), as witnessed by their coin legends; Tsirkin, "Phoenician Civilization," 248, 249, 251, 256–57, 266 (citing A. Vives, *La moneda hispánica* [4 vols.; Madrid, 1924] 1 .16–17, 51–54, 60–62; 3.8–9, 14, 16–20, 27–32; 4 .12–14); cf. Aubet, *Phoenicians,* 217.

[81] Unrivalled for its commercial shipping, Gadeira had "huge pickled-fish factories"(Ταριχεῖαι μεγάλαι, Strabo 3.1.8). Aubet remarks further on Gadeira's famous shipyards and opulence (*Phoenicians,* 220). In addition to enormous mineral wealth, the Tartessian mainland (Turdetania) in general supplied the empire with a rich harvest of wheat, oil, and wine (Strabo 3.2.6). E. Albertini

primarily an export business that had its main market with Rome and employed many workers of Phoenician extract, who settled there or in Ostia.[82] Coastal fishing, of course, made cities like Gadeira renowned. In Roman times, though, it was not its fish factories for which Gadeira was best known, but rather its temple of Tyrian Heracles (Melqart) with its distinctive Semitic practices.

C. *The Herakleion.* The Phoenicians of Tyre brought with them to Gadeira the worship of their famous god Melqart, identified early on with Heracles. The cult of Tyrian Melqart / Heracles enjoyed an especially powerful religious affiliation at its flourishing cult center on Gadeira, called in Greek the Herakleion (Temple of Heracles), located on the southern tip of the largest island. Little trace of the sanctuary has survived, although Greek and Roman writers give us much information about the temple's wealth and fame, its general character, and the oriental aspect of its cult—an aspect with which classical authors felt some degree of discomfort.[83] The fact that the inner sanctuary did not admit the installation of a graven image—something unthinkable in Greek or Roman religion—proved troubling to some writers, who nevertheless admired the fame of the temple's rites enough to preserve details of its cultic ritual.[84] The most important of these for our purposes is the fact that swine were strictly forbidden at the shrine. Silius Italicus tells us, among other things,

---

reminds us that "Spain is one of the four [with Sicily, Africa, and Egypt] grain-producing provinces represented in a mosaic at Ostia in the first century A.D." (*CAH* 11. 494).

[82] Albertini, *CAH* 11. 496; Tsirkin, "Phoenician Civilization," 254, 260 (cf. Strabo 3.2.5; 3.2.6), comments on the especially close ties between Gades and Italy. This has important implications for the potential spread of the Gospel to the Baetican region, as discussed below.

[83] Arrian (*Anab.* 2.16.4), for example, writing in the first part of the second century CE, makes clear the popular association of Heracles with Tyrian Melqart and recognizes the non-Greek character of the temple's rites: "Just as the Heracles honoured by the Iberians at Tartessus [sc. Gades]—a place some name the "Pillars of Heracles"—I believe to be the Tyrian Heracles, because Tartessus is a Phoenician colony, and by Phoenician custom has the Temple to Heracles been built, and by the same customs are the sacrifices also made" (καὶ τῷ Φοινίκων νόμῳ ὅ τε νεὼς πεποίηται τῷ Ἡρακλεῖ τῷ ἐκεῖ καὶ αἱ θυσίαι θύονται).

[84] Silius Italicus, who wrote in the first century CE, provides the most information about the Gadeiran cult in his *Punica* 3.14–44.

that the priests of the Herakleion forbade the entrance of women to the shrine and were careful "to keep bristly pigs away" (*curant / saetigeros arcere sues, Punica* 3.22–23). A taboo on consuming swine is a common Semitic prohibition, but its omission as a sacrificial animal would be difficult, if not impossible, for a Greek to comprehend.[85]

Silius Italicus also informs us that the doors of the Temple of Heracles displayed the Labors of Hercules,[86] a fact that not only establishes a close association between the cult of Tyrian Melqart and Greek Heracles, but one that proves the specific assimilation of the Hellenic labors and parerga of the hero to the Semitic cult. We thus have a valuable correlation between the cult of Melqart at Gadeira and stories about "Greek" Heracles.[87] In addition to this marvelous door, an independent tradition actually places the Pillars of Heracles in the Herakleion itself, in the form of two brazen columns that recorded the cost of building the sanctuary.[88] This Heraclean theme, in itself

---

[85] In classical sacrificial ritual, pigs formed a necessary part of sacrificial exigencies, particularly in offerings associated with blood purification, as in pollution caused by murder; cf. the fifth century BCE Greek *lex sacra* from Selinous in (Phoenician) Sicily; the text requires the sacrifice of a pig (χοῖρον) to Zeus in a complex purificatory rite (M. H. Jameson, D. R. Jordan, and R. D. Kotansky, *A* Lex Sacra *from Selinous* [GRBM 11; Durham: Duke University, 1993] [B5] 16, 42–43, with refs.). For similar pig-offerings and their connections with chthonian cult, especially that of Demeter, see F. Annen, *Heil für die Heiden. Zur Bedeutung und Geschichte der Tradition vom besessenen Gerasener (Mk. 5,1–20 parr.)* (FTS 20; Frankfurt am M.: Knecht, 1976) 163–64, whose observations on the Thesmophoria in particular deserve closer scrutiny.

[86] *Punica* 3.31–44, beginning: *In foribus labor Alcidae* etc.; see Tsirkin, "Labours," *RSF* 9 (1981), 21–27.

[87] Aubet argues that the myths of Heracles in Iberia arose in fourth century BCE Athens and that stories of Heracles' travels to the west and his association with Phoenician Melqart at the *Herakleion* were a relatively late attempt to bring the founding of Cádiz into closer association with the time of the Trojan War, thereby making Heracles a kind of "father of the Phoenicians" (*Phoenicians,* 169–70). But Aubet overlooks entirely the Myth of Geryon (see below), one of Heracles' famous Twelve Labors, a myth that is situated in Cádiz from the start. The whole question is linked with the delicate issue of whether the Phoenicians "expanded" to the West in the eighth century BCE, or considerably earlier in the twelfth century BCE, as archaeological finds seem to support more and more (contra Aubet).

[88] Strabo 3.5.5; Pliny *Nat. Hist.* 2.242; cf. J. G. Frazer, *Apollodorus. The Library* (2 vols.; LCL; Harvard: Harvard University Press, 1921) 1. 212, n. 1 (on Apollod. 2.5.10).

important in New Testament studies,[89] will form a significant typological trestle linking the Markan account of 5:1–20 with Tyrian Heracles, especially with regard to legends affiliated with the netherworld.[90]

D. *Lokalkolorit and Local Myth.* If certain details of the Markan narrative have confounded the placement of the "Gadarene" account within the environment of the Sea of Galilee, a setting of the story at Phoenician Gadeira seems perfectly suited. The calming of the severe ocean storm that augurs Jesus' arrival in the mystic No-Man's Land not only fits the genre of the epic voyages we have been discussing, it can also be placed rather securely at the Straits of Gibraltar hard by Gadeira; there, at the edges of the world, swirling eddies and monster-filled vortices were regularly encountered.

As for Jesus' presumed voyage to the edges of the earth, the traditional Ulysses-theme of monsters in liminal lands would surely have contributed to the popular imagination of bizarre encounters in a spectral world of the dead where fabulous events might occur. The storm that precedes his arrival in the land of the *Gadarēnoi*, if located near the Straits of Gibraltar at Gadeira, could easily be understood by readers in this western context as a reference to the dangerous tides and swirling whirlpools characteristic of the Straits of Gibraltar in general. The founding of the Gadir at the request of an oracle required three expeditions (Strabo 3.5.5) because the Straits' tempest drove the *oikists* back (Diod. S. 5.20.1–4).[91] We have also had occasion

---

[89] On the renewed interest in Heracles and the Gospels, note D. E. Aune, "Herakles," *ABD* 3 (1992) 141–43; with add. refs.

[90] See the discussion to follow. Mark 5:3–4 alone records the demoniac's inability to be tamed (δαμάσαι) or chained (δεδέσθαι), themes associated with the underworld demons of the Abyss (cf. Kotansky, "Exorcistic Amulets," 256). Even though it can be presumed that the demoniac carries the strength of the two thousand demons that are said to possess him, his rôle as a kind of uncontrollable Samson or Heracles may also be pertinent to our comparisons; however, that Jesus vanquishes this powerful nether deity and himself plays the part of the Heraclean hero who conquers evil (as monsters) will support a closer approximation between the myths of Heracles and stories of Jesus, particularly those dealing with the Underworld.

[91] Aubet, *Phoenicians*, 222.

above to discuss the Homeric Skylla and Charybdis and the tempest-like storms associated with their stories.

Mythologically, the western limits of the Mediterranean in general, and Gadeira in particular, continued in late antiquity to be emblematic of a mysterious realm beyond known reality. Centuries after Hanno's famous exploration past Gibraltar, which we shall discuss shortly, the whole western geography sustained its otherworldly mystique in popular thinking: it was an uncrossable Realm of the Dead, where even the famous "Isles of the Blessed" were believed to lie hidden.

The edges of the world are specifically associated with Gadeira in the ancient sources. Pindar, whom we have cited above, refers to the limits of human existence at the Pillars of Heracles, reminding us that one should not pass the "nether darkness" at Gadeira, lying just past the Straits.[92] Strabo, describing the founding of Gadeira, locates the Pillars of Heracles there and calls the region the "limits of the inhabited world" (τέρμονας εἶναι τῆς οἰκουμένης, 3.5.5) and notes that Gadeira was "founded at the extremities of the earth" (ἐσχάτη ἱδρυμένη τῆς γῆς, 3.1.8). Plutarch names the Straits of Gibraltar the "Gadeirean strait" (Γαδειραῖος πορθμός, *Sert.* 8.). Although there was much debate as to exactly where the Pillars of Heracles were truly located—at Gibraltar (Calpe); on either side of the narrow strait between Europe and North Africa; or on Gadeira—it is not necessary for our thesis to pinpoint the Pillars as resting precisely on Gadeira.[93]

1. Cliffs, Rocks, and Tombs.

Geologically, the whole far western realm around the Iberian Sea fits the regional anatomy of the Markan story like a glove. These coastlines of Spain bordering the Mediterranean and Atlantic are well-lined with rugged cliffs that run flush to the shore's edge, cliffs that are very difficult to account for in a context of the Sea of Galilee. One

---

[92] Pind. *Nem.* 4.69–70, Γαδείρων τὸ πρὸς ζόφον οὐ περατόν· ἀπότρεπε / αὖτις Εὐρώπαν ποτὶ χέρσον ἔντεα ναός, "Beyond Gadeira toward the gloom we must not pass, / Turn back the sails of thy ship once more to the mainland of Europe" (LCL, p. 353). Here ζόφος refers at one and the same time to the darkness of the netherworld and to the "dark quarter" of the West, signifying the farthest edges of the known world.

[93] Cf. Strabo 3.5.5, who gives a long discussion.

needs think only of the famous Rock of Gibraltar, or of the marvelous craggy citadel off the promontory near Ibiza (Balearic Islands), known to ancients as Hemeroskopeion ("Daytime Look-Out"), to envision the kind of cliffy shorelines so prevalent in mythological narratives.[94] Rocky crags and steep cliffs (κρημνοί), from which giant Cyclops, Laestrygonians, or Skyllas could rush down upon the heroes and hurl rocks, form a necessary topographical ingredient of the adventurous tales of Odysseus and Jason described above.

In particular, the Markan story tells of a herd "rushing *off* the cliff" (κατὰ τοῦ κρημνοῦ) and drowning in the sea.[95] As rightly noted by Derrett,[96] κρημνός cannot refer to a bank, but is a steep crag, the "overhanging bank" or "beetling cliff" (LSJ) of mythological dimension. To translate Mark 5:13 as "down the steep bank" (RSV, NRSV, et al.) is an attempt to accommodate the Greek phrase to a very misplaced Galilean topography. It also considerably weakens the drama of the story that plainly wishes to convey a herd plunging vertically from a mountain cliff (πρὸς τῷ ὄρει) straight into the sea,

---

[94] On Hemeroskopeion, see Strabo 3.4.6 and Rhys Carpenter, *The Greeks in Spain* (Bryn Mawr Notes and Monographs 6; Bryn Mawr, PA: Bryn Mawr College, 1925) 20–21 (with frontispiece)—a "great sheer thousand-foot tower." The cliff-like quarries pictured in Carpenter are identical to the cliff-tombs at Cádiz. In addition to Gibraltar's 1,398 ft. peak (426 meters), the whole peninsular region is surrounded by a palisade of sheer cliffs dropping straight into the sea. As Elizabeth Gebhard has communicated to me, the presence of cliffs throughout our discussion represent mythological, not historic, features; it is not necessary to locate specific cliffs in the area to corroborate the Markan narrative.

[95] "Off" or "over" is here the correct English idiom for Greek κατά + genitive, "down (into the sea)." To translate the Greek literally, rather than idiomatically, ("to rush *down* a cliff") is to misconstrue the Greek preposition. English idiom uses "off" in the sense of "off the edge" and "over" in the sense of "over (i.e., beyond) the edge," which is idiomatically peculiar vis-à-vis the Greek κατά. Modern English "down a cliff" would wrongly imply a sloping embankment. The Germanic (OE *[ʾ]ofer* etc.) is akin to the Semitic (*ʿéber*) and Greek (ὑπέρ) cognates, in the sense of "across," "beyond:" see S. Levin, *Semitic and Indo-European. The Principal Etymologies* (Amsterdam Studies in the Theory and History of Linguistic Science, Series 4: Current Issues in Linguistic Theory, 129; Amsterdam: John Benjamins, 1995) 366–76.

[96] Derrett, "Contributions," 6: "κρημνός does not mean slope; it means cliff, implying an overhang." In fact, the root is $\sqrt{\kappa\rho\epsilon\mu -}$, "to hang; suspend."

not one stampeding horizontally into the waves from a shoreline embankment.[97]

Another feature of the Gadeiran landscape that appears to fit the Markan narrative are its cliff-side tombs. Just south of the urban nucleus on the northern tip of Kotinoussa (Isla St. Petri) is a sizeable necropolis, dating from the Punic to the Roman period.[98] A Roman necropolis has also been found on the inner island of the archipelago (Isla de Léon). Particularly interesting are the cell-like catacomb-structures cut from these cliffs at the Punta de la Vaca and Los Corrales.[99] These, displaying a "cyclopean" type masonry, are open, house-like edifices formed of large square blocks hollowed out along the cliffs facing the sea. These originally Punic structures survived until Roman times and would have made a natural cliff-home for the Markan demoniac. The Punic hypogea of the Puig d'Es Molins necropolis at Ibiza are similar in representing spacious seaside underground chambers with rectangularly cut doors; they are also better excavated and afford for us the same archaeological model as the Punta de la Vaca examples do.[100]

All ancient communities buried or cremated their dead, so graves and cemeteries would have been an expected part of any extra-mural city plan. To identify graves at Gadeira or Gadara proves little, except

---

[97] The phrase ὥρμησεν . . . κατὰ τοῦ κρημνοῦ can be little different from κρημίζω, "to hurl down headlong" (with κατὰ τοῦ τείχους!) in LXX 2 Macc 6:10.

[98] The Puertas de Tierra and Punta de la Vaca necropoli, dating from the fifth century BCE to Roman times; M. E. Aubet (Semmler), "Spain," *The Phoenicians* (ed. S. Moscati, et al.; New York: Abbeville, 1988) 232; Aubet, *Phoenicians*, 224–25, 228–29 (figs.). The presence of the modern city has made the excavations of these tombs difficult. For earlier photographs, note especially Quintero, *Necrópolis* (plates); idem, *Cadiz*, 44–45 (plates). The Punta de la Vaca necropolis is famous for its anthropoid sarcophagi known since the nineteenth century (S. Moscati, "Sarcophagi," *Phoenicians*, 298–99).

[99] Plates in Quintero, *Necrópolis*; idem, *Cadiz*. For further remarks on the Gades burial practices in Roman times, note Tsirkin, "Phoenician Civilization," 265–66.

[100] Like the Cádiz tombs, which have not been studied recently (cf. Quintero, *Necrópolis*; idem, *Cadiz*; Tsirkin, "Phoenician Civilization," 253), these are large chambers with a rectangular entrance door housing stone sarcophagi. Of the 3000 to 4000 tombs in the area (used as communal graves until the Roman conquest in 123 BCE), there are three types: "hypogea dug in the rock, simple rectangular graves dug either in the rock or in the earth, and child burials inside amphorae" (Aubet, "Spain," 238–39, with beautiful color photographs).

that in the former the graves may have served a different function in the shaping of the popular folklore of the region. Since Gadeira was a kind of mythic Land of the Dead to begin with, an emphasis on tomb-dwellings in the Markan story may well be explained from the local burials at Cádiz. Mark's demoniac had his dwelling (κατοίκησις) literally "*in* the tombs" (ἐν τοῖς μνήμασιν, 5:3). Μνήματα are memorial edifices, mounds or built structures of a kind. Although "among the tombs" is a natural interpretation of the phrase in Mark, the small houselike structures of the Gadeirite cells lend themselves particularly well to the Markan structures, too, if seen as a kind of reused hypogeum or "house-tomb"-dwelling located in the western Mediterranean. Such an interpretation will also accord well with Mark's clear cliffside setting. The preposition ἐκ, unlike ἀπό ("from, away from"), signifies a coming *from out of*; when Mark 5:2 describes the demoniac coming "*out of* the tombs" (ἐκ τῶν μνημείων), it parallels Jesus' own coming "*out of* the boat" (ἐκ τοῦ πλοίου), itself a "coffin-shaped" vessel that foreshadows his resurrection out of a rock-carved tomb. Jesus had just been sleeping the "sleep of death" and comes out of the boat that has ferried him across the ocean to the Land of the Dead.

An interconnection between the archaeological structure of the rock-tombs of the Ibiza necropolis and the use of such tombs for dwellings, as suggested by Mark, surfaces in a remarkable comment by Diodorus of Sicily, about whom we shall have more to say later. The inhabitants of the Balearic Archipelago, it seems, where the Puig d'Es Molins hypogea are located, made a habit of living in hollowed-out subterranean rocks and excavated cliffs:

> And they dwell (οἰκοῦσι) underground in hollowed out rocks, and build excavated caves along the cliffs (κρημνούς), and make in general numerous subterranean places where they spend their lives.[101]

That Diodorus in the next paragraph (§ 18) goes on to describe some of the Baleareans' *burial* practices suggests that he may be confusing chambered sepulchers with chambered dwellings, but it is also possible that the island inhabitants both dwelt and buried their

---

[101] Diod. S. 5.17.3: οἰκοῦσι δ' ὑπὸ ταῖς κοιλάσι πέτραις, καὶ παρὰ τοὺς κρημνοὺς ὀρύγματα κατασκευάζοντες καὶ καθόλου πολλοὺς τόπους ὑπονόμους ποιοῦντες ἐν τούτοις βιοῦσιν, κτλ.

dead in cliff-hollows and caves. In any event, Mark's description of the demoniac making his home in the tombs among the rocky cliffs and mountains corresponds perfectly to the set of data describing the cliffs and tombs of islands off the eastern and western shores of Iberia.

2. Pigs and Herds.

Based on a real or popular etymology, the land of Gadeira will be a "land of flocks and herds."[102] The rugged terrain of ancient Spain created soil ill-suited for crops, so the raising of cattle and livestock was common. Today, hogs and beef cattle are raised more along the northern coast, with sheep elsewhere. In antiquity, "the mountaineers of the Pyrenees and the Cantabrian mountains reared pigs and exported ham which was famous."[103] At the Herakleion of Cádiz near the southern tip of Spain, pigs were held to be taboo, a fact that will have important bearing on the Markan story, so swineherding would have been prevalent in the south as well.

Despite the presence of swine in Iberia, there is some indication that Mark's herd (ἀγέλη) of pigs originally stood for a herd of cattle or oxen and that for important theological reasons the storyline has been reworked to create a group of grazing pigs, an animal considered unclean.[104] One of the reasons for this is that the Geryon myth, to which we will shortly compare the pre-Markan "Gadarene" account, deals with a herd of cattle, but there are several other causes. Pigs do

---

[102] In addition to the etymology of *gdr*, discussed above, biblical Hebrew גְּדֵרָה in Num 32:16, 36 means "pen," "sheepfold," as well as "wall" (Ps 89:42). Similarly, this and an allomorph of *gdr* with initial *ayin*, viz., *ʿdr* (Phoen., "flock;" Hoftijzer & Jongeling, *Dictionary*, 832; BH, Aram., etc. "herd;" L. Koehler & W. Baumgartner, *The Hebrew and Aramaic Lexicon of the Old Testament* 2 [Leiden: Brill, 1994] 793) links our etymology of Phoenician Gadeira closely with the Markan herd (ἀγέλη) of pigs central to his narrative. Cf. late Aramaic *ʿadərāʾ* etc. (Jastrow, *Dictionary*, 1046), an "enclosure" of animals: a "pen," "herd," or "flock." With the initial *ayin* routinely transcribed as *gamma* in Greek (cf., e.g., "Gomorrah"), this word for "herd" would become *Gadəra* (= Γαδεῖρα). The reference in Mark 5:1 to the land of "Gadirenes" would thus be a "Land of Herds" or a "Land of Pigpens."

[103] Albertini, *CAH* 11. 495. The name "Gadeira" (= enclosure; pen) in popular etymology may have referred to its large herds or pens, as much as to its having been an enclosed fort of some kind. In fact this latter etymology has little to sustain it.

[104] See below on the swine taboo associated with the temple of Heracles at Gadeira. The Geryon accounts, given below, all describe his cattle as ἀγέλη.

not occur in large herds; in fact, ἀγέλη, the term twice used in Mark (5:11,13) to describe the pigs, is always used of oxen or kine in Homer.[105] Furthermore, Derrett is right in observing, "nothing is more certain than that pigs do not move as herds . . . they do not normally move as do sheep, horses, or cows."[106] Pigs are good runners; but when Mark describes a large herd of them rushing (ὥρμησεν, 5:13) headlong over a cliff, he is characterizing a stampede of cattle, not of swine. Furthermore, the family of Suidae (pigs) are non-ruminating—they have two-chambered as opposed to three- or four-chambered stomachs—and thus they do not graze pasture like Bovidae (antelope, cattle, goats, and sheep);[107] pigs prefer forested lands. All ruminatia or "cud-chewers," on the other hand, graze wood- and vegetable-grasslands. Although *S. Scrofa,* which includes both the wild boar and the domestic pig of the genus *sus* (family: Suidae; order: Artiodactyla), do occur in groups called "sounders," in the Old World these seldom reached a size greater than twenty.[108] A sounder in the neighborhood of two thousand, such as that recorded in Mark, represents an unimaginable number of pigs from a socio-zoological point of view, and shows us once again that we are dealing with a narrative concerned with hyperbolic dimensions. We would be misled in attaching historical value to the number.

Most importantly, pigs do not drown; they are superb swimmers.[109] The preferred word for "drowning" in Greek is καταποντίζειν, found for example in Matt 18:6, or ἀποπνίγεσθαι, as used in the Lukan parallel to the "Gadarene" demoniac at Luke 8:33; the use of πνίγειν, "choke," was troubling enough for Luke to modify it and for Matthew to omit it altogether.[110] Strabo provides a fascinating sideline about the cattle of Gadeira that may shed some light on Mark's use of πνίγω. Strabo takes pains to describe the fine pasture (τὸ εὔβοτον) found

---

[105] Apart from a single mention of horses (*Il.* 19.281; LSJ, *s.v.*).

[106] Derrett, "Contributions," 5.

[107] R. M. Nowak, *Walker's Mammals of the World* (5th ed.; Baltimore and London: Johns Hopkins, 1991) 1334–35.

[108] Nowak, *Walker's Mammals,* 1338. A "sounder" of a hundred on record is apparently quite rare.

[109] Nowak, *Walker's Mammals,* 1338.

[110] For him the pigs "perish" in the waters of the Abyss (ἀπέθανον ἐν τοῖς ὕδασιν, Matt 8:32).

around Cádiz in an effort to provide an aetiology for the mythic herd of Geryon, the cattle that Heracles stole, whose myth we describe below. His remarks in particular that the milk of the cattle there carries no serum or whey (τὸ γάλα ὀρὸν οὐ ποιεῖ, 3.5.4) may explain a local custom pertinent to our story. Cheese from the Gadeirite cattle can only be made by adding large amounts of water to the viscous cream; the particularly high fat content of the milk actually causes the feeding animals to choke to death (πνίγεται τὸ ζῷον) unless the animals' veins are opened up. Oddly, this "choking" is the very fate described of the "Gadeirene" swine when they perish in the sea (ἐπνίγοντο, Mark 5:13). Strabo's reporting of such a local Gadeirite custom only makes sense as a proverbial account that has gained widespread currency, for he cites it to explain the formation of a popular local myth. The proverbial "choking" cattle of Gadeira coupled with the swine taboo of the Herakleion would have provided particularly detailed points of regional color to the Markan account, if we can locate it there; indeed, such culturally- and geographically-bound features as these will hopefully, in the end, stubbornly negotiate the thesis that ancient Cádiz lies at the very heart of the Markan story.

3. Herds, Tides, and Water Spirits.

More important perhaps is another remark by Strabo (3.2.4) concerning the cattle that live along the coastline at Gadeira. The whole of the coast from the Pillars to the Sacred Cape (Cape St. Vincent) is comprised of little hollows or bays (κοιλάδες) that tend to retain the water from the incoming tides, forming estuaries and rivulets with islands.[111] Although these estuaries prove helpful for sailing, they also pose considerable risks to ships and livestock alike: the cattle (τὰ βοσκήματα) that tend to cross over to the islets get unexpectedly swamped (ἐπεκλύσθη) by the floods and, in their attempt to swim back to land, regularly drown.[112] Drowning cattle is

---

[111] Silius Italicus *Punica* 3.45–60 also describes the vehemence of the waves crashing against the rocky land of Gadeira, an island lacking an encircling shore (*nullaque circa litora*, 3.47–48), and the eddies it thereby creates.

[112] Strabo 3.2.4: τοτὲ μὲν οὖν καὶ ἐπεκλύσθη, τοτὲ δὲ ἀπελήφθη, βιαζόμενα δ' ἐπανελθεῖν οὐκ ἴσχυεν, ἀλλὰ διεφθάρη, "Therefore, they sometimes are swept away, but other times cut off, and being forced to go back, they are not

not something remarked upon often in ancient sources, to my knowledge, and the fact that this and the choking cattle of Gadeira are described so specifically by Strabo gives us cause to reflect upon similar details of verisimilitude in Mark.

Elsewhere, Strabo goes into considerable detail regarding these peculiar tides of Gadeira and devotes several long sections to the phenomenon, citing the opinions of Polybius, Poseidonius, Athenodorus and Seleucus (3.5.7–9). It seems that there was a freshwater spring (κρήνη) in the Herakleion at Cádiz that behaved in an exactly inverse way to the rising and receding of the adjacent Ocean tides; that is, the κρήνη evacuated when the tide came in, but filled up when the tide went out.[113] This event was something of a riddle, to judge from its being repeatedly told in the context of Stoic "paradoxes" (ἐν τοῖς παραδόξοις).[114] The cause, according to Polybius, lay in the complicated working of τὸ πνεῦμα—evidently a kind of "blast"—that was cast up towards the surface from the depths of the sea (ἐκ τοῦ βάθους, 3.5.7) but blocked by the surface waves and diverted to the spring's source. That this use of πνεῦμα contains some older notion of an "entity" that Strabo is explaining along more rational lines as a "wind" or "blast" is suggested by the popular notion that the tides of the sea are to be compared to animated beings (Strabo 1.3.8; Pomponius Mela 3.1). A later author who knows the same story actually provides us with the more folkloric version. Philostratus, in his *Life of Apollonius of Tyana,* also mentions the "pneumatic" cause of the odd phenomenon of the Gadeirite tides. Philostratus (*Vit. Ap.* 5.2), who claims to have observed these tides himself, cites an epistle of Apollonius' to the effect that "the Ocean is driven by underwater blasts (or spirits) from numerous chasms" that behave in much the same way as the human body does in breathing in

---

strong enough and perish." Strabo adds the remark that the cattle have also learned to wait for the "withdrawal of the sea" (τὴν ἀναχώρησιν τῆς θαλάττης) before crossing.

[113] Cf. also Pliny *Hist. Nat.* 2.100; 2.219; Silius Italicus, *Punica* 3.45–60 (noted above); XVI.194–196; R. J. Penella, *The Letters of Apollonius of Tyana. A Critical Edition with Prolegomena, Translation and Commentary* (Mnemosyne 56; Leiden: Brill, 1979) 140 with additional refs. on such tides.

[114] Strabo 3.5.7 with H. L. Jones, *The Geography of Strabo, II* (LCL; Cambridge: Harvard Univ., 1923) 145, n. 2.

and out.[115] Philostratus then equates these ebbing and flowing πνεύματα with ocean tides that come in and remove the souls of the sick and dying: it was a popular belief that the souls of the dying will not leave their bodies so long as the tide is coming in; presumably the dying spirits are carried out with the "outgoing" marine πνεύματα:

> This theory (of underwater *pneumata*) is confirmed from those who have fallen sick around Gadeira. For during the period when the tide comes in, the souls do not leave the bodies of the dying, because this cannot occur unless a spirit also comes towards land.[116]

It is presumed that a "spirit," or even a kind of marine wind (πνεῦμα), comes in with the tide, and as the tide goes out, it claims those spirits of the dead and dying, taking them to their watery graves in the Abyss.[117] Although this belief that low tide brings death—and high tide, birth—has few direct classical echoes, Wagenvoort has deduced parallels from other folkloric traditions to establish that the concept is very primitive.[118] More importantly, he suggests that the belief described in Philostratus is linked with the notion of the kingdom of the dead as lying in the west. The out-going tide would then ferry these souls across to the other side of the ocean. In numerous ancient records, Gadeira itself was linked with the classical

---

[115] Philostr. *Vit. Ap.* 5.2: ἐν μιᾷ γὰρ τῶν πρὸς Ἰνδοὺς ἐπιστολῶν τὸν Ὠκεανόν φησιν ὑφύδροις ἐλαυνόμενον πνεύμασιν ἐκ πολλῶν χασμάτων ... χωρεῖν ἐς τὸ ἔξω καὶ ἀναχωρεῖν πάλιν, ἐπειδὰν ὥσπερ ἆσθμα ὑπονοστήσῃ τὸ πνεῦμα, "For Apollonius says in one of his letters to the Indians that the Ocean, being driven by underwater spirits/blasts from numerous chasms, . . . moves out and comes back again, just as the breath collapses in exhalation."

[116] Philostr. *Vit. Ap.* 5.2, πιστοῦται δὲ αὐτὸ κἀκ τῶν νοσούντων περὶ Γάδειρα· τὸν γὰρ χρόνον, ὃν πλημμυρεῖ τὸ ὕδωρ, οὐκ ἀπολείπουσιν αἱ ψυχαὶ τοὺς ἀποθνήσοντας, ὅπερ οὐκ ἂν ξυμβαίνειν εἰ μὴ καὶ πνεῦμα τῇ γῇ ἐπεχώρει (cf. Wagenvoort, "Journey," 116).

[117] It is immaterial whether πνεῦμα means "breath" or "wind" in this context, since the soul or spirit is believed to be carried by wind and enters the body through respiration; see Wagenvoort, "Journey," 117, n. 3, with refs. A silver amulet from Carnuntum that describes a wind demon, named Aura, coming out of the sea is discussed in relation to Mark 5:1–20 and late Christian exorcisms in R. Kotansky, *Greek Magical Amulets. The Inscribed Gold, Silver, Copper, and Bronze* Lamellae, vol. 1, *Published Texts of Known Provenance* (Abhandlungen der Nordrhein-Westfälischen Akademie der Wissenschaften, Sonderreihe Papyrologica Coloniensia 22.1; Opladen: Westdeutscher Verlag, 1994) 58–71.

[118] Wagenvoort, "Journey," 116–118, who relies on Frazer's data, with examples from—of all places—present-day Spain, Portugal, and parts of England!

Isles of the Blessed,[119] so it is clear that the out-going tide on the western coast of Spain is to be associated with the departure of the souls of the deceased. This may explain the role of the "legion" of demons in the Markan account; the demoniac's close connection with graves and the dead rightly assumes that the two thousand demons that enter the herd are the spirits of the dead among the tombs where the demoniac makes his dwelling.[120] That the legion of demons requests access to the herd and steer the pigs directly over a cliff, into the Ocean, represents the swine-spirits' longing for the tide that will carry them home to the Land of the Dead. They are kith and kin with the tidal πνεύματα of Gadeira.

Taken alone, no single one of the local "curiosities" discussed above is enough to establish a nexus between our Markan story and Phoenician Gadeira; but the assembly of stories and legends taken together, in addition to the material to be discussed below, presents a strong case for situating the Markan story of 5:1–20 in this far-western territory. Cattle were abundant in the area,[121] and the repeated remarks relating to them by Strabo and others in both regional history and myth indicate a proverbial interest in this form of livestock. This fact increases in importance in view of the etymology of *gdr* as "herd" and by virtue of the fact that the cliffs, rocks, and tombs about Iberian Gadeira seem to fit closely the topographical backdrop of Mark's story. That Mark also talks of drowning pigs in a region that held swine to be taboo and in a land where an abundance of grazing cattle were known to either choke or drown hardly seems coincidental. An association, too, of tides, spirits, and herds with Gadeira can also explain some aspects of ancient pneumatology in Mark not readily intelligible in the

---

119 Although there were other island-candidates, e.g., the Canary Islands (cf. J. F. Moffitt, "Philostratus and the Canaries," *Gerion* 8 [1993] 241–61), with respect to Cádiz, note Plut. *Sertorius* 8.1–2; Strabo 3.2.11 (Erytheia = νῆσον εὐδαίμονα); cf. Strabo 3.2.13 (Spain as the Elysian Plain); 1.1.5 ("Blessed Islands" near the Straits).

120 Gundry, *Mark*, 260, who rightly criticizes, however, the view that the dead were resistance-fighters against Rome. It is not always fully appreciated that "unclean spirits" that possess the living—including those of the New Testament—would have regularly been, in ancient pneumatological beliefs, spirits of the prematurely dead.

121 Strabo remarks on the "abundance of various cattle" (βοσκημάτων ἀφθονία παντοίων, 3.2.6) at Turdetania, the mainland region just northeast of Gadeira.

usual Galilean milieu. The story of drowning pigs does not belong to any of the Gospels' standard "demonological fare" as we know it; the account, overall, is closer to the broader Hellenistic "novella" than it is to the local Syro-Palestinian "garden variety" of exorcism. The drowning herd in Mark will point to something of greater symbolic value if we move away from the need to interpret the account as a prima facie historical event located in Galilee. Given the apparent close connection between the pre-Markan story of Legion and the topography and local color of Gadeira, it is incumbent upon us to look more closely at a particular Heraclean myth associated with the region as well.

4. The Myth of Geryon.

The local Temple of Heracles at Gadeira, with its famous prohibition of swine, seems to have been a widely respected focal point of religious activity and cult that spread far beyond the immediate region it served. Its reputation not only helped disseminate the Tyrian cult of Heracles-Melqart, it also provided a traditional depository for the telling of the famous stories of his more "Theban" counterpart. The fact that the Herakleion preserved on its temple-doors illustrations of the hero's traditional labors points to a thorough syncretism of the Tyrian Melqart with the aretalogical exploits of the Hellenic demigod.

The island Erytheia, on which ancient Gadeira was founded,[122] was also the locale of a famous myth of Geryon (or Geryoneus), the monstrous triple-bodied herdsman vanquished by Heracles to accomplish his tenth labor.[123] This regional myth, closely connected with the oriental cult of Tyrian Melqart, belongs to the last three of Hercules' canonical trials, trials that specifically deal with the theme of the conquest of Death.[124] The myth thus supports our thesis by

---

[122] See above, p. 191 and n. 79. Cf. further Strabo 3.5.4, on the authority of Pherecydes.

[123] T. Gantz, *Early Greek Myth. A Guide to Literary and Artistic Sources* (Baltimore and New York: Johns Hopkins University, 1993), 402–9; J. M. Blázquez Martínez, "Gerión y otros mitos griegos en Occidente," *Gerion* 1 (1983) 21–38; E. B. Clapp, "On Certain Fragments of Pindar," *CQ* 8 (1914) 225–29.

[124] Viz., Geryon (10), Kerberos (11), The Apples of the Hesperides (12): "All these last three are variants of one theme, the conquest of Death. The hero must go to an island in the extreme west, Erytheia, and there overcome a triple-bodied

reflecting the very theme that we have been pursuing all along in Mark.

The Geryon myth, in short, tells of the triple-bodied son of Chrysaor and Kallirhoe, daughter of Ocean, who was born in a cave on a cliff,[125] dwelt on Erytheia ("Red Island"), and owned a fabulous herd of cattle.[126] The cattle were tended by a herdsman, Eurytion, and guarded by Orthros, a two-headed dog, offspring of the monsters Echidna and Typhon. Geryon's body was joined as one at the loins and thighs but split off into three men from the waist up.[127] When Heracles was clearing Crete and Libya of wild beasts, he came to the Straits of Gibraltar to set up his celebrated Pillars. On approaching Erytheia, because of the sun's heat, an exasperated Heracles aimed his bow at Helios, but begged off at the Sun-god's behest; for his bravery, Helios nonetheless awarded Heracles his famous golden goblet (δέπας) to sail over the vastness of Ocean. This "goblet" was the very vessel which carried the night-time sun back from west to east across the Subterranean Ocean.[128]

Once Heracles actually reached Gadeira (Erytheia), so Apollodorus (2.5.10) tells us, the two-headed hound immediately recognized him (αἰσθόμενος) and rushed (ὥρμα) upon the hero. Heracles killed it right off with his club, as well as the herdsman Eurytion. Another cowherd, Menoetes, seeing the unfolding events, in turn runs off to

---

monster, Geryon, and his attendants, and take his cattle; or he must descend to the House of Hades and steal the infernal watch-dog; or, finally, he must pluck the golden apples from the dragon-guarded tree at the world's end" (H. J. Rose & C. M. Robertson, "Heracles," *OCD*², 498).

125 Stesichorus (*apud* Strabo 3.2.11).

126 According to Apollod. 2.5.10, Geryon's cattle are called "red" (εἶχε δὲ φοινικᾶς βόας).

127 Apollod. 2.5.10: τριῶν ἔχων ἀνδρῶν συμφυὲς σῶμα, συνηγμένον εἰς ἓν κατὰ τὴν γαστέρα, ἐσχισμένον δὲ εἰς τρεῖς ἀπὸ λαγόνων τε καὶ μηρῶν. Hes. *Theog.*, 287 calls Geryon "three-headed" (τρικέφαλον, *Theog.*, 287); Aesch., *Ag.* 870 and Eur. *Herc. Fur.* 423 as "triple-bodied"(τρισώματος); for additional refs., note Frazer, *Apollodorus*, 211. Gantz cites refs., including variant descriptions of Geryon's body, some including wings (*Early Greek Myth*, 402–8).

128 Refs. in Frazer, *Apollodorus*, 213, and LSJ, *s.v.* δέπας, on Stesichorus frag. 8.1–5 (see Kirk et al., *Presocratics*, 13); Pherecydes 3, frag. 18a, and other early poets (Gantz, *Early Greek Myth*, 404) record the voyage of Heracles in the goblet. The conquest of Death, of course, comes in the motif of the sea-trip as a subterranean voyage, a kind of *descensus ad infernos*.

Geryon to report what had just occurred. When the triple-bodied Geryon himself comes upon the scene, the hero, in the act of driving the cattle away, kills the giant with one of his arrows. Heracles then drives the celebrated cattle across the Ocean to the mainland at Tartessus and returns the golden goblet to Helios.

The similarities between the legends of Jesus and Heracles are noteworthy, although there are fundamental differences as well. The main dissimilarities are related to the fact that little in the myth of Heracles describes an exorcism, *per se*, as we find in Mark. For this motif we must refer the reader to the tidal spirits of Cádiz, discussed above, although Heracles' accomplishment is a form of *apopompē* that is remarkably similar to Mark's αὐτοὺς ἀποστείλῃ (5:10) and πέμψον ἡμᾶς (5:12).[129] Nor is the demoniac destroyed by the Markan hero; only the pigs are, who still behave as surrogate demons that drown in the watery Abyss. However, where a particularly "Palestinian" demonology is absent at Gadeira, it is replaced by a decidedly Near Eastern counterpart in its menagerie of theriomorphic beasts and hybrid monsters, a typically oriental manner of describing evil that had long ago penetrated deeply into the folkloric psyche of Hellenic mythography. Heracles' vanquishing of a three-headed, six-armed giant and of a two-headed offspring of Typhon and Echidna—prototypical oriental monsters, to be sure—is no less a banishing of evil than Mark's destruction of the demonic pigs.[130]

Where the Geryon myth and the *Gadarēnoi*-story best come together, I believe, is in the motif of a strong-man archetype vanquishing evil in the form of multiple entities that encounter the hero one-on-one.[131] The baneful "personalities" that Heracles and

---

[129] On the *apopompē* ("sending off," "ridding" of evil), note esp. C. A. Faraone, *Talismans and Trojan Horses: Guardian Statues in Ancient Greek Myth and Ritual* (New York and Oxford: Oxford University Press, 1992) 37, 46, 129 (with notes). This "banishment of evil" in the forms of animals deserves closer scrutiny in Mark.

[130] Note, e.g., J. Fontenrose, "Typhon among the Arimoi," *The Classical Tradition: Literary and Historical Studies in Honor of Harry Caplan* (ed. L. Wallach; Ithaca: Cornell University Press, 1966) 64–82, on the oriental origins of such monsters; and Faraone, *Talismans and Trojan Horses,* 41–53 on theriomorphic demons.

[131] There is also the singularly important motif of Heracles arriving in Cádiz on a storm-tossed ocean in the vessel of the sun. Storm-like conditions attend Heracles' arrival at the Straits of Gibraltar (Pherecydes 3 frag. 18a), just as they do that of Jesus in Mark 4:35–41, who as noted, becomes both sailor and rescuer. The rough

Jesus encounter are represented either by compound monsters or some kind of proliferation of demonic forms appointed to watch over animal herds associated with the Underworld: Geryon's cattle belong to the land of Hades,[132] and Mark's swine graze in the Land of the Dead and are returned to their watery Abyss. The giant Geryon is a monster of a peculiar three-fold form, tended by a two-headed dog; Mark's wild man is a figure in league with a whole "Legion" of demons, although they are fewer in the Matthean and Lukan versions. Both the pre-Markan catena and the Geryon myth tend to multiply the evil into a kind of intractable plurality. Is there, as well, a sort of demonic swarm or pernicious blight being hypothesized here in the presence of the attendant herds,[133] or are the droves simply souls of the dead? The Markan "reading" of the story clearly equates the swarm of the demons with the swarm of the herd, both two thousand in number. A certain cosmic harmony is thus achieved only when they are banished. Geryon's herd of cattle is less precisely equated with evil beings, though their being "driven away" (ἐλαύνειν) is particularly telling and may suggest a form of scapegoat ritual.[134] Regardless, what

seas at the Straits also seem to characterize the Phoenician founding of the city, as discussed.

132 Apollod. 2.5.10 states that "Menoetes was there tending the cattle of Hades," that is, Heracles is already in the Land of the Dead, which Erytheia (Gadeira) traditionally represented. For the Greek text, see below. Futhermore, the two-headed dog, Orthros, is a relative of Kerberos, the three-headed dog of Hades. Orthros is thus a surrogate of Kerberos.

133 As noted above, the oxen of Geryon are called "red" (viz. φοινικέα, "Phoenician"), a color associated with plague and blight; cf. Faraone (*Talismans*, 42; 51, n. 57; 64) with special reference to a red goat used in the apotropaic rite at Cyrene, a red dog used at the Roman Robigalia, and a red cow in Egyptian ritual. For the souls of the dead as bees, cf. Wagenvoort, "Journey," 121–25.

134 We cannot deal here with the notion that the Markan *apopompē* of swine contains such a ritual. The same could certainly be said of the Geryon myth, too, for the element of driving bulls away from Erytheia ("Red Island") recalls a similar removal of a ritual bull from Erythrae ("Red Lands") in Ionia (Faraone, *Talismans*, 99). In addition to sharing a common place name etymon, the Erythrae myth has a Chrysame to match Gadeira's Chrysaor, both names being associated with "gold" or "red" (Faraone, *Talismans*, 42, addresses the equation of gold with red). Also, madness is found in all three accounts: Hera drives Heracles' oxen mad; the Erythraeans go mad by eating the meat of the sacrificed oxen; and the Markan demoniac is made mad, perhaps not at having only been possessed by the "pig-demons," but having eaten the swine in the area. In any event, all these share in

is important is that both stories, in addition to the apparent geographic identity in their topography, are placed in liminal realms, precisely at the western gates of the underworld.[135]

Similarities in our parallel stories extend to the very wording of the myth found in Apollodorus. The initial encounter between the demonic hound and Heracles is expressed in terms of a recognition motif and subsequent rushing of the dog: *αἰσθόμενος* δὲ ὁ κύων ἐπ' αὐτὸν *ὥρμα* ("When the dog perceived him, he rushed upon him;" Apollod. 2.5.10); so, too, is the first meeting between Jesus and the demoniac attended by a demonic perception and ensuing charge: καὶ ἰδὼν τὸν Ἰησοῦν ἀπὸ μακρόθεν *ἔδραμεν* (5:6) . . . καὶ *ὥρμησεν* ἡ ἀγέλη κατὰ τοῦ κρημνοῦ εἰς τὴν θάλασσαν (5:13), "And seeing Jesus from afar, he ran . . . and the herd rushed off the cliff into the sea."[136] Although the specific cognate of ὁρμᾶν is reserved for the herd of swine in Mark, both accounts do, however, describe the rushing of theriomorphic demons or monsters. In Mark, it is as if the impulse of the demon rushing upon Jesus is carried through without pause into the pigs, who in turn continue the impetus by dashing off the cliff. In a sense, the invisible force of the possessing demons,

---

common the removal of animals from "one's own area of habitation" (citing Faraone, *Talismans*, 99); cf. Mark 5:10.

[135] Hesiod's description of the myth in *Theog.* 287–94; 981–983 (cf. Gantz, *Early Greek Myth*, 402–8) reminds us once again of the similarity between the settings of the two stories, especially in the πέραν-motif: *Theog.* 291–294 describes Heracles' driving the herd back to Tiryns by "crossing (διαβάς) the ford of the Ocean . . . in the dim stead out *beyond* (πέρην) glorious Ocean" (trans. H. G. Evelyn-White, *Hesiod, Homeric Hymns and Homerica* [LCL; Cambridge, MA: Harvard University Press, 1936]). Cf. Stesichorus frag. 8 [*Geryoneis, apud* Athen., *Deipn.* 11.469e], using περάσας of the crossing. The close connection, too, between the myth of Geryon and the Garden of the Hesperides (Gantz, *Early Greek Myth*, 405) underscores the netherworld context of the Geryon myth (cf. further Wagenvoort, "Journey," 115).

[136] The running at Jesus in 5:6 is immediately attended, of course, by the incongruous remark that the demon suddenly worships (καὶ προσεκύνησεν) Jesus! The worship-motif is particularly Markan and creates some tension with the fact that the demon next shouts at Jesus (Gundry, *Mark*, 259) and is untamed. There is also a kind of doublet of v. 6 in v. 1, which describes the demon "meeting" Jesus (ὑπήντησεν αὐτῷ). The structure and history of the story's text is both difficult and intriguing and cannot be addressed here. Annen gives but one useful attempt to unravel the various layers of the tradition (*Heil für die Heiden*, 70).

formerly compressed into a single body, is now visibly suffused through a whole herd of pigs.

A further similarity lies in the way in which, following the initial encounter and defeat of Orthros the hellhound, a herdsman leaves to report the events to Geryon, a kind of higher demonic power: Μενοίτης δὲ ἐκεῖ τὰς Ἅιδου βόας *βόσκων* Γηρυόνῃ *τὸ γεγονὸς ἀπήγγειλεν* ("But Menoetes, there *herding* the cattle of Hades, *reported* to Geryon *what had happened*"). So, too, once Jesus vanquishes the foe in Mark 5:1–13, herdsmen leave to report to unnamed authorities in the cities and fields what has occurred: καὶ οἱ *βόσκοντες* αὐτοὺς ἔφυγον καὶ *ἀπήγγειλαν* . . . καὶ ἦλθον ἰδεῖν τί ἐστιν *τὸ γεγονός* ("And those *herding* them [sc. the pigs < cattle] fled and *reported* in the cities and fields, and they came to see *what had happened*"). Although the higher powers are not called specifically "demonic" in Mark, the fact that they shepherd a demonic herd of swine and live in a liminal land of the dead labels them as netherworld dwellers who ultimately do not welcome Jesus but ask him to leave their frontiers (5:17). When the healed demoniac begs Jesus if he can return with him, the demoniac is refused and told rather to "go to your own (ὕπαγε . . . πρὸς τοὺς σούς) and report to them what the Lord has done for you" (5:19). The phrasing contains a poignant word-play, as τοὺς σούς, "your folk"—this form of the pronoun is found only here in all of Mark—recalls the common word for "pig," (σῦς; acc. pl. τοὺς σύας).[137] In other words, the healed "wild-man" is to return to his subterranean dwelling among his own "Pig-People."[138]

---

[137] Furthermore, since σῦς = ὗς (gen. ὑός), there may be an additional pun on the demon's addressing Jesus as Ἰη*σοῦ υἱὲ* τοῦ θεοῦ (Mark 5:7); υἱέ contains the universal, onomatopoeic "squeal" of the pig (LSJ, *svv.* ὑΐζω, ὑϊσμός), thus either making Jesus a kind of Lord of Pigs, or having the demoniac address Jesus in a "squealing" pig's voice. Another "pig" paronomasia comes in the phrases ἔξω τῆς χώρας (5:10) vs. εἰς τοὺς χοίρους (5:12)—"out of the land / into the pigs;" "χώρα" will thus, by analogy, mean "Pigland." See also the following note.

[138] On Gadeira/Gadara = "Land of Pens/Herds," see above. That the demoniac in Mark 5:20 is said to leave and preach in the Decapolis is no embarrassment to our thesis. This verse is a widely recognized editorial addition unrelated to the catena itself (cf. Guelich, *Mark*, 285–86). Not only does a Decapolitan "mission" conflict with the mandate to return to his own οἶκος (cf. κατοίκησιν in 5:3) and "family," it betrays evidence of a heavy Markan hand throughout (Guelich, *Mark*, 286, with ref.). The editor (Mark?) who had the demoniac preach in the Decapolis is the same writer who situated the story in either Gadara or Gerasa, both being

Both the Geryon myth and "Gadeirite" story show similar motifs and structures in the mythological handling of demonic forces. A particularly important parallel, too, is the fact that, just as the herd in Mark is driven into the sea, so too does Heracles drive the kine of Hades over the ocean.[139] Although these specific motifs may serve somewhat different purposes—there is no destruction of the herd in Heracles' labor—the general motif of controlling subterranean droves is consistent in both stories. The "herds of Hades/Ocean" must be related to some kind of belief in underworld forces who dwell in the watery abyss.[140]

The verbal and conceptual similarities in the Geryon and Markan accounts may do nothing more than suggest a common narrative framework in the telling of similarly structured myths; but, because of the oral nature of myth-telling in general, much of Apollodorus' account may rather be preserving oft-occurring expressions attached to the Geryon tradition; in the telling of the story over the centuries—or in one author's borrowing from another—certain key-words and phrases may have attached themselves inextricably to the

---

cities of the Decapolis. Nonetheless, the problems associated with a placement of the story in Galilee still challenge any traditional resolution of the textual conundrum.

[139] Apollodorus (2.5.10) states that Heracles drove (ἐνθέμενος) the cattle into the vessel and sailed (διαπλεύσας) to Tartessus; but Apollodorus and others continue the narrative about Heracles and tell of his eventually driving the cattle to Tiryns, either by land (across Illyricum and Italy) or across the sea (the Ionian and Adriatic). In Thrace Hera made the oxen mad, and in pursuit of them, Heracles crossed the river Strymon by making a road with huge stones (Gantz, *Early Greek Myth*, 408–9). He recovers the cattle at the Hellespont and finally takes them to Eurystheus. Other writers mention stories of the oxen in Rome (cf. Frazer, *Apollodorus*, 215–217). At Rhegium, one of the bulls, Italus, breaks away, jumps into the sea and swims to Sicily (ταῦρος . . . καὶ ταχέως εἰς τὴν θάλασσαν ἐμπεσὼν καὶ διανηξάμενος <εἰς> Σικελίαν, κτλ., Apollod. 2.5.11), giving the name "Italia" to the land. The Phoenician nexus between Gadeira and Rome is taken up in greater detail below.

[140] We remind readers that Geryon's mother was an Oceanid and that the god Ocean was said to have made trial of Heracles in his goblet on the open sea (Pherecydes *apud* Athen. 11.470C-D; Frazer, *Apollodorus*, 213, n. 2). Heracles' use of the Sun's cup to sail the subterranean Ocean also combines the motif of netherworld (Hades' realm) and watery Abyss.

story.[141] The set of correspondences presented above provides yet more grist for the comparative mill that aims to align the pre-Markan Gadara account with the western Heracles of Gadeira.

Whereas the traditional Geryon myth captures the idea of evil by describing a triple-headed anthropomorphic creature of relatively archaic pedigree, its much later pre-Markan adaptation must be viewed as considerably more "phenomonological" in approach. It deals with the demonological internalization of evil and only reverts to its archaic, more concrete 'theriomorphic' model when the demons request that they not be "sent out of the land" (5:10). The casting of the many demons *out of* the singularly possessed wild man, *into* the herd of swine, serves to concretize the phenomonology of the divine by turning the numinous host of invisible demons into a corporealized herd of animals; the theriomorphic *apopompē* of the herd belongs to older concepts of the expulsion of evil, not to the usual Palestinian exorcism of casting out unseen entities.

The development of the Geryon myth from an archaic destruction of monsters to the issue of human and demonic personalities is seen, too, in Lucian's allegorical interpretation of the Geryon myth. In his essay on friendship, *Toxaris* (§ 62), Lucian refers to the tripartite body of the monster in a more positive light than that preserved in the myth itself:

> For the union of two or three friends is like the pictures of Geryon that artists exhibit—a man with six hands and three heads. Indeed, to my mind Geryon was three persons acting together in all things, as is right if they are really friends.[142]

In Mark this concept of a multiple personality is described in contemporary military terms. The "I" of the first encounter between Jesus and the Demoniac soon yields to the grammatical "we" of the Legion of demons. The equation of the "Gadeira" demon with a

[141] Cf., for example, the consistent use of ἀγέλη, ἐλαύνειν and βοῦς to describe Heracles' driving the cattle, not only in Apollodorus, but also in Pindar, frag. 169 (151), 5–7; Paus. 3.18.13; 4.36.3 and so on.

[142] Trans. A. M. Harmon, *Lucian* (8 vols; LCL; Cambridge, MA: Harvard University Press, 1979) 5. 205. A similar sentiment is reflected in Justin (44.4.16); cf. J. M. Blázquez Martínez, "Gerión y otros mitos griegos en Occidente," *Gerion* 1 (1983) 21–38, esp. 38.

military host finds a surprising precedent in another writer's interpretation of the Geryon myth.

Diodorus of Sicily, who wrote in the generation or so before the birth of Christ, also describes the Geryon account in distinctly military terms—"demythologizing" it entirely—and thus marking a point on our mythic trajectory decidedly closer to the Markan interpretations of the Geryonic "demonic" encounter.[143]

After introducing the Geryon cattle as the subject of Heracles' tenth labor, Diodorus remarks that the cattle pastured in those regions of Iberia that inclined towards the ocean (τῆς Ἰβηρίας ἐν τοῖς πρὸς τὸν ὠκεανὸν κεκλιμένοις μέρεσιν, 4.17.1), thus providing our limen between land and sea.[144] Then Heracles, in preparation, marshalls a great army (πλῆθος στρατιωτῶν, ibid.) adequate to the challenge. But Heracles' foe, according to Diodorus, is not the triple-bodied monster, Geryon son of Chrysaor, but rather Chrysaor himself, who has three sons of great military prowess.[145] Each of these sons, in turn, possesses vast armies (μεγαλαὶ δυνάμεις) recruited from neighboring bellicose tribes.[146] In other words, Diodorus has turned the three-bodied monster into three powerful human generals with their armies. Heracles gathers his own forces at Crete—the story at least follows the traditional *geographical* line here—the place from which he chooses to launch his initial attack or "rush" (ὁρμή); surprisingly, the word ὁρμή is the same root (ὁρμᾶν) used of Mark's pigs "rushing" off the cliff (ὥρμησεν) and of Orthros' attacking (ὥρμα) Heracles in

[143] Gantz, *Early Greek Myth,* 407, refers to his "rationalizing" the story. Mark, or the author of the catena, on the other hand, would appear to be "mythologizing" a stereotypical Palestinian exorcism account in Mark 5:1–20.

[144] It becomes clear in the story that Diodorus has dispensed with Gadeira, *per se,* and has situated the story on the mainland, close by, for he consistently mentions Iberia in lieu of Gadeira, which he has previously named as a χερρονήσον (5.20.2), viz., a peninsula, or better, an island with a bridge to the mainland. Strabo 3.5.4 (on Pherecydes) makes clear that Gadeira is the true site of the conflict (Gantz, *Early Greek Myth,* 404).

[145] Diodorus 4.17.2: τρεῖς δ' ἔχει συναγωνιστὰς υἱούς, διαφέροντας ταῖς τε ῥώμαις τῶν σωμάτων καὶ ταῖς ἐν τοῖς πολεμικοῖς ἀγῶσιν ἀνδραγαθίαις, "But he (sc. Chrysaor) had three sons as fellow-fighters, who distinguished themselves both in the strength of their bodies and in the bravery of their military contests."

[146] Diodorus 4.17.2: πρὸς δὲ τούτοις ὅτι τῶν υἱῶν ἕκαστος μεγάλας ἔχει δυνάμεις συνεστώσας ἐξ ἐθνῶν μαχίμων.

Apollodorus' account. So we seem to have again the use of fixed terminology that sustains itself throughout the various tellings of the story.[147] Diodorus then informs us that Heracles cleared, along traditional lines, both Crete and Libya of wild beasts (4.17.3–5).

Diodorus continues (4.18.2–3) with Heracles' arrival at the ocean near Gadeira, his setting up of the Pillars on either side of the continents, and his crossing over to Iberia with a navy to meet the enemy. Facing the three armies of Chrysaor's sons, Heracles challenges and defeats each leader in turn. He then drives off the celebrated herd of cows[148] and "traverses the land of the Iberians" (τὴν τῶν Ἰβήρων χώραν; § 3), a phrase that again recalls our motif of the hero's displacement in a distant and foreign place.

The allegorical interpretation of Orthros, Eurytion, and finally Geryon, as three sons of Chrysaor with their vast armies, is remarkable indeed and draws even closer the connection of the Markan story with the Gadeira myth of Geryon. We have seen the development of a myth that starts with three multiple-bodied hybrid monsters into a story about a king with three sons and their powerful armies; an account of a multiply-possessed "strong-man" likened to an army (*legio*); and a metaphorical interpretation of the myth as the camaraderie of three friends.

Whether Diodorus' version of the myth with Heracles' three armies alludes to the presence of Roman armies in Spain or not is difficult to say; however, it has long been noted that the expulsion of the traditional Gadarene "legion"-demon from the land could well have been symbolic of a desired need to rid Palestine of its despised Roman presence. The same symbolism, for that matter, could apply to Spain

---

[147] The words of the Markan account belong to those that seem to carry distinctively military overtones (Derrett, "Contributions," 5) and thus seem to share something with Diodorus' version of the Geryon myth.

[148] Diodorus 4.18.2: ἀπήλασε τὰς διωνομασμένας τῶν βοῶν ἀγέλας—note again the traditional vocabulary. Diodorus adds the fact that a certain just king of the land became the recipient of some of Heracles' newly won cattle, and as a result of this largess, the king instigated annual sacrifice of the choicest of the bulls to Heracles. The practice of offering these sacred bulls to Heracles continued down to the writer's own day, we learn. The reference is clearly to the Melqart cult indigenous to the region.

as well, for Diodorus' three armies of Chrysaor will match perfectly the three legions that occupied Spain in the period ca. 44 BCE–70 CE.[149]

The Geryon myth with its otherworldly setting offers numerous linguistic, topographical, and mythological parallels with the Markan myth. In particular, the myth's netherworld livestock seem to find a consistent correlation in local folk-accounts that associate herds with the ocean: the Gadeiran cattle either drown in the nearby tidal swells or mysteriously choke en masse on their own undigested whey along the coast (ὁ αἰγιαλός). Similarly, there is a connection in the regional herds of spirits that are believed to come ashore with the rising tide and to take dying souls back to the Ocean. Mark's pigs, who perish as unclean πνεύματα in the cliffside sea, remind us of the tidal spirits that carry the souls of the deceased to their final resting place. The local myths of Gadeira, which can be directly associated with the famous Temple of Tyrian Heracles, seem to have provided much background to the unusual story we have in Mark 5:1–20. The story of Geryon will thus compete with a welter of other facts and fables pertinent to the geography of Cádiz, Tartessus, and Iberia, facts that will contribute to our interpretation of the Markan miracle catenae, in general. If the *Lokalkolorit* of the Markan "swine story" is to be found unexpectedly in faraway regions, then there may be additional regional accounts that feed into the maelstrom of traditions behind Mark 5:1–20.

5. Other Local Stories.

The Geryon myth is not alone responsible for the formation of the Markan myth of 5:1–20. Other stories of local color, as suggested in our readings of portions of Strabo and other writers, may contribute to

---

[149] That is, the Legio IV Macedonica, an Octavian legion that remained in Spain after 9 CE (Syme-Collingwood in *CAH* 10. 782); the VI Victrix, a legion of Caesar's that fought for Octavian and was later moved to the Rhineland in 69/70 CE. (Syme-Collingwood, *CAH* 10. 782, 807, 815); and thirdly, the Legio X Gemina, which transferred to Carnuntum in 63, but returned to Spain in 68 AD. Further, we know of the Legio I-II (?) Augusta, an Octavian legion that disgraced itself in Spain in 19 BC and moved to Cologne after the disaster of Varus, and the Legio V Alaudae: Caesar's legion in Narbonensis, that moved to Spain in the early principate. The Legio VII Gemina (originally the VII Galbiana for going with Galba to Rome) replaced the X Gemina in Carnuntum. It returned to Spain ca. 74 at Legio (Leon).

the general background. The portrait of the superhuman "Gadarene" demoniac, living among the tombs and crying out night and day, fits the stereotype of the wild and uncontrolled cave-dweller who dwells on the edges of the civilized world. In addition to the "Heracles Unchained" motif that corresponds to the element of superhuman strength, a whole complex of "western Mediterranean" typologies seems to feed into the Markan legend.

The *Periplus* of Hanno, that records the famous Carthaginian's voyage along the western coast of Africa, offers some valuable points of contact with our story. The brief fifth or fourth century BCE account, consisting of eighteen terse paragraphs, originally written in Punic but preserved in Greek, was said to have been dedicated in the Temple of Kronos.[150] Sailing past the Pillars, Hanno claims to have embarked with 30,000 men and women and a fleet of sixty-seven ships! In addition to describing the founding of cities and temples at some of the coastal sites of today's Morocco and Senegal, the Carthaginian enumerates some of the exotic animals and peoples he encounters: elephants (§ 4), crocodiles, hippopotami (§ 10), and other animals (§ 4); the nomadic, though friendly, "cattle-herding" Lixites (βοσκήματ' ἔνεμον, § 6); "Ethiopians" who dwelt in a "land possessed of wild beasts, cut up by great mountains" around which "dwelt men of a different shape called Cave-Dwellers" (κατοικεῖν ἀνθρώπους ἀλλοιομόρφους, Τρωγλοδύται, § 7), who could run faster than horses (§ 7); wild, stone-throwing, mountain dwellers clad in animal-skins (§ 9); jungle islands lit by night-time fires from which fearful drum-beats were heard § 14); and volcanic mountains and fiery streams (§§ 16–17).

---

150 For text and commentary on the *Periplus Hannonis*, see J. Ramin, *Le Périple d'Hannon / The Periplus of Hanno* (BAR Suppl. Ser. 23; Oxford: BAR, 1976); K. Müller, *Geographi Graeci Minores, I* (Hildesheim: Georg Olms Repr., 1855) 1–14; W. Aly, "Die Entdeckung des Westens," *Hermes* 62 (1927) 299–341, esp. 321–24. The prologue reads, "The account of Hanno, king of the Carthaginians, concerning the Libyan regions beyond the Pillars of Heracles *which he dedicated in the Temple of Kronos*" (ὃν καὶ ἀνέθηκεν ἐν τῷ τοῦ Κρόνου τεμένει). It is assumed that this temple is that of Baal-Kronos at Carthage; however, since the heading boasts of a sailing beyond the famous Pillars, which would have been at Gadeira, it seems more logical for Hanno to have made his dedication at the Kronion (Temple of Kronos) at Gadeira, not at Carthage.

Most interesting of all is the famous paragraph that ends this fabulous account. It is the mention of an island lake "full of wild people"(μεστὴ ἀνθρώπων ἀγρίων, § 18), the majority of whom were described as "women with hairy bodies" (γυναῖκες δασεῖαι τοῖς σώμασιν, § 18); these women the interpreters named "Gorillas" (Γορίλλας, § 18).[151] The males (ἄνδρες) of the species eluded capture by climbing the cliffs and defending themselves with rocks (κρημνοβάται ὄντες καὶ τοῖς πέτροις ἀμυνόμενοι, § 18), but the crew was able to capture three females who "bit and tore at" (αἳ δάκνουσαί τε καὶ σπαράττουσαι, § 18) their captors, who ended up killing and flaying the hirsute creatures.

What is intriguing about this account is that, whatever the creatures actually were, they were described as what we would call *homo sapiens*, since their sexual gender was easily distinguishable; however, nothing is said of the creatures ever speaking or requiring an interpreter, so whether Hanno's expedition described an historical encounter with real gorillas or not is difficult to say. The whole tenor of the story of a race of wild and hairy cliff-dwelling people will accord well, though, with the general picture of the demoniac of the Markan narrative. The cliff-dwelling practices (κρημνοβάται, § 18) of the inhabitants in Hanno's description matches the cliff-dwelling demoniac of Mark, whose topography requires western-like κρημνοί and whose "wild man," too, is a kind of mountain dweller (ἐν τοῖς ὄρεσιν ἦν, 5:5). Nothing is said about whether he was hairy or not, but the apparent fact that he was naked provides an excellent parallel to the concept of a primate living in the wild.[152] Certainly the inability to chain or "tame" (δαμάσαι) the creature is descriptive of a wild ape of

---

[151] See the following note. Müller, *Geographi Graeci Minores*, 1. 13 (note) gives suggested emendations of Γορίλλας to Τοραλλα (the tribe *Toorallas*) and to Γοργόνες ("Gorgons"), the latter having mythic associations with the west.

[152] Mark 5:15 implies, although the text had previously been silent on the subject, that our demoniac had been living naked in the mountains. There the demoniac (τὸν δαιμονιζόμενον!) is described as "sitting, clothed, and in his right mind" (καθήμενον ἱματισμένον καὶ σωφρονοῦνται). The whole verse comes from an independent source that was grafted onto the narrative, as indicated by differences in vocabulary (cf. Guelich *Mark*, 273, 283). For our purposes, the verse underscores the catena's need to embrace the mission to save the "Noble Savage" at the ends of the earth (cf. Eliade, *Myths*, 39–47; Romm, *Edges of the Earth*, 70–76), a concept to be explored elsewhere.

superhuman strength, and the whole would be fitting for a narrative influenced by tall tales of fabulous wild men dwelling beyond the Pillars. The wildness of the Markan demoniac, especially his cutting himself with rocks (5:5), also matches the untamed description of Hanno's "gorillas" as scratching, biting, and throwing rocks.[153]

Mark's demoniac, of course, is not a gorilla; we only argue that stories about such hairy creatures, like those saved for us in Hanno's account, would have been noised about in the region for some time to come[154] and would have contributed to the overall descriptions of the behavior of the untamed Gadeirene wild man. Such wild apes and putative stories about them were also known around and about the Straits. The Rock of Gibraltar was acclaimed, and still is today, for its famous "Barbary Ape" (*macaca sylvanus*), a species of tailless monkey that occupies the famous Spanish crag, as well as parts of North Africa.[155] One wonders whether Hanno's description in reality owes something more to observations of these European apes seen, albeit, from their habitat on the African side.

Besides the "nakedness" of the gorillas, that of the Gadeirene demoniac may owe something, too, to yet another local fact. Strabo's description of the Balearic Islands (3.5.1), near the Hemeroskopeion in the general region of Gibraltar, tells us that they were also known as the "Naked Islands" (Γυμνήσιαι νῆσοι, 3.4.7). Diodorus Siculus, whose story of Geryon we described above, explains the discrepancy as follows (5.17). The "Gymnesiae" are named from inhabitants who go naked there (γυμνοὺς τῆς ἐσθῆτος) during the summertime, but

---

[153] Pliny *Hist. Nat.* (7.2.24–25) provides an excellent parallel to some of these same concepts, though this time in the eastern "limits:" in the region of the Catarcludi in the mountains of India is a race of "fast-moving" creatures (cf. Mark 5:5: μακρόθεν ἔδραμεν) that move both on all fours and upright "in human fashion." Similarly, the forest-dwelling Choromandi there "have no power of speech, yet shriek horribly, have shaggy bodies, grey eyes, and dog-like teeth" (see Romm, *Edges of the Earth*, 105).

[154] Even the modern reference to the primate called *G. gorilla* comes directly from Hanno's description of this mysterious race of African women (Γόριλλαι, αἱ) and not from an indigenous name referring to the ape. The true reference to Hanno's "gorillas" and its etymology remain unknown.

[155] Nowak, *Walker's Mammals*, 469, 474–75. It is not known whether the species was introduced artificially onto the Rock or whether they are indigenous, but there is some indication that the Gibraltar habitat is a holdover from Pleistocene times of a *M. Sylvanus* once widespread throughout Europe.

"Balearides" comes from the fact that the folks are known to cast (βάλλειν) huge stones from slings.[156]

Strabo also informs us that, when the Phoenicians took possession of these Naked Islands, they were the first to *clothe* the inhabitants, dressing them in a type of broad-bordered tunic.[157] Given the cultural-historical context of our parallels in general, the Phoenicians as bringers of civility will correspond to Jesus who clothes and brings civility to the naked demoniac in Mark 5:15 (ἱματισμένον καὶ σωφρονοῦντα).

The coincidence of naked, rock-hurling dwellers on the Balearic Islands, in Hanno's "Libya," and at pre-Markan "Gadara" forms a remarkable coalescence of folkoric traditions, and it hardly seems impossible that some, if not all, of the accounts we have been discussing had, in one form or another, found a pathway into the formation of the Markan myth. Climbing on cliffs, throwing rocks, and even getting bruised on rough cinder-blocks go hand-in-hand with the rugged, cliffy terrain of the western Mediterranean. That cliffs, too, would have had an association with pigs hardly seems likely other than the fact that a herd of them runs off a cliff in Mark's story. But Strabo's description (3.5.1; 3.1.9) of the rocky bays around the Naked Islands as, literally, "like a hog's back" (χοιραδώδης) will provide yet one more particularly remarkable folkloric tidbit to be affiliated with the "Gadeirene" account. Χοιραδώδης (probably to be translated "rocky") is from the same root (χοῖρος) used of the cliffside herd of pigs in Mark's gospel. For some apparently visual reason, the rocky cliffs of

---

156 Livy *Epit.* 60 adds, too, that the islands may have been named from Baleus, the companion of Heracles. Strabo 14.2.10 connects Baliarides with the Phoenicians. The name of Heracles (Melqart) has many geographical associations in the west, besides those of Gadeira; see J. Schoo, "Herakles im fernen Westen der alten Welt," *Mnemosyne* 7 (1938) 1–24.

157 In the context of a discussion of the inhabitants' excellence in stone-slinging, he writes as follows:

And this art [of slinging] they have practised assiduously, so it is said, ever since the Phoenicians took possession of the islands. And the Phoenicians are also spoken of as the first to cloth the people there in tunics with a broad border (οὗτοι δὲ καὶ ἐνδῦσαι λέγονται πρῶτοι τοὺς ἀνθρώπους χιτῶνας πλατυσήμους); but the people used to go forth to their fights without a girdle on—with only a goat-skin, wrapped round the arm etc. (trans. H. L. Jones, *The Geography of Strabo* [8 vols.; LCL; London: Heinemann, 1966–70]).

the western Mediterranean were routinely described as "pig-like," owing perhaps to the jagged or rough appearance of certain hogs' backs or hides.[158] Strabo's rare adjective, apparently used only by him, is matched by the substantive χοιράδες found in descriptions of more famous rocky isles of the west, such as the "Clashing Rocks" (Symplegades), which we have had occasion to discuss above (cf. LSJ, *s.v.*, citing Theocr. 13.23). The regional use of pig-words seems to blend a tradition of associating cliff and swine not immediately clear to us, a tradition indigenous to the rocky seacoasts of the west from the Balearic Islands to Cádiz. It is entirely conceivable, too, that Mark's association of cliffs with pigs mirrors a similar bit of linguistic lore local to the region.

Naked, stone-throwing inhabitants must have been a strange sight indeed to ancient observers; it was remarkable enough to several classical writers to be written up *in extenso*. When Mark's Gospel tells us that his demoniac was not only living near cliffy shores, but also had been running about naked in the mountains, we have another possible correspondence with a far-western topography that now includes naked men, hardy cliffs, and a peculiar, "porcine" terrain. The "clothing" of naked men by Phoenician settlers on the local Balearic Islands adds a particularly interesting point of contact that may serve to associate Jesus with his Punic forebears as common bringers of civility and order. This, taken into consideration with the strong Phoenician background behind the swine-taboo of the Gadeira Herakleion, the Geryon herds of Tyrian Melqart-Heracles, and the *periplus* reports of Punic-Phoenician explorers, points strongly to an intimate connection between the sea-episodes of the Markan catena and the tales and experiences of late Phoenician traders who regularly sailed between Cádiz in the west and Tyre in the east.[159] In the context of a kind of Hellenistic *interpretatio Poenica*, the Markan story might surely have aimed at courting favor with such late Phoenician traders

---

158 That is, the wart hog (genus Phacochoerus: Nowak, *Walker's Mammals*, 1342), which, however, is indigenous to sub-Saharan Africa. English "razorbacks" similarly describes 1: "a thin-bodied long-legged hog chiefly of the southeastern U.S.," as well as, 3: "a sharp narrow back or ridge (as a range of hills)" (P. B. Gove, ed. *Webster's Third New International Dictionary of the English Language Unabridged* [Springfield, MA.: Merriam, 1981] 1888).

159 Cf. Aubet, *Phoenicians*, 133–66, esp. 144–45, 159–64.

via a retelling of their own their mythic traditions. To this topic we shall turn shortly.

VII. *Nostoi*

In the epic tradition, any valiant sea adventurer must, after all his extraordinary experiences, eventually return home to his "Ithaca." Odysseus' eagerness for home is signaled early on in the Homeric narrative, and the verb νοστέω, with πατρίς as its object (as in *Od.* 1.290), is frequently used of such homeward voyages. Νόστοι refer, as well, to generic titles of homeward voyages within the epic cycle. We have already noted the magical manner in which Odysseus is eventually wafted home from the land of the Phaeacians. When he awakens, albeit unaware at the time, Odysseus is finally found ἐν γαίῃ πατρωΐῃ, "in his own native land" (*Od.* 13.188).

A similar idea of a homeward voyage holds true for the catena's own traveler, Jesus, in the story of Mark 6:1–6. The analogy of the "τὸ Πέραν"-narratives which we have been discussing with a series of marvelous sea ventures is carried through, it would seem, even to the point of narrating the Master's own *Nostos* or "Return," although this specific word is never actually used by Mark. At the end of the last adventure in the catena-series, the story of Jairus' daughter that concludes chapter 5, Jesus is said to come back, nonetheless, to his own homeland (πατρίς): "He went away from there and came *to his own country*" (6:1).[160] Here the story's choice of words has much to tell us about the geographical mind-set of its composer: The noun is πατρίς, "homeland," the *country* of Jesus' origin, and not Ναζαρέθ, the little-known village of his upbringing, a town about which the catena has nothing to say, and Mark next to nothing.[161] It is not Nazareth that our writer intends us to understand—as, for example, in the parallel at Luke 4:16—but the entirety of Jesus' own country. It is the whole of the eastern levantine coast that we and ancient readers

---

[160] Καὶ ἐξῆλθεν ἐκεῖθεν καὶ ἔρχεται εἰς τὴν πατρίδα - the Greek of the last phrase is correctly rendered in the RSV, 2nd ed., as "his own country," not, for example, as "his home town," as in the NRSV, as if to harmonize the text with other synoptic texts that mention Nazareth.

[161] Ναζαρέθ is found only once at Mark 1:9. Elsewhere he uses the adjectival Ναζαρηνός in very limited contexts.

alike are to recognize as Jesus' *patris*! This novel reinterpretation of what must have formerly been a town-story will fit the "global" perspective of the travels of Jesus to the distant *peran*. Because our pre-Markan source is not contrasting, within the limited "historical" geography of Galilee, a land-itinerary of Jesus village-by-village, but is rather juxtaposing distant lands with distant lands on a more global and mythological scale, our Markan story assumes new meaning within the grander sphere of a trans-Mediterranean sea voyage. The "land of the Gadeirenes" in the west is being juxtaposed to "his own country" in the east. Thus the savior's voyage from one Tyrian "coast" to another, takes on decidedly more epic proportions in the telling of the Markan myth.

As Jesus sails home heroically to his own fatherland, his fame in battling the untamed elements of sea, demonic monster and death itself precedes him like an Odysseus before his return to Ithaca. But now the confines of a tiny synagogue cannot contain the power of "such *dynameis* that come from his hands" (6:2). The now empowered "son of God" rejects the performance of miracles in his own country and, eventually, sends out his own disciples two by two to perform them on his behalf (6:7–13). The Jesus of the catenae is a global seafarer to distant lands, not a mendicant healer who has merely walked from village to village.[162] His fabulous message is not for the narrow circle of his own countrymen or tribal kinsfolk (συγγενεῖς, 6:4), but belongs to the wider Gentile folk lying at the edges of the known world. But once Jesus does return from his "trans-oceanic" voyage to the Land of the Dead, he resumes again, within the Markan narrative, the more normal pattern of local synagogue healing and teaching.

VIII. Sitz im Leben and Conclusion

The "savage" demoniac of Mark 5:15, dwelling far off in the geography of unknown lands, even though properly seated, clothed, and mannered, is not allowed to voyage home with Jesus, but is to "go

[162] This interpretation may cast new light on the import of the Markan "Rejection at Nazareth," which now becomes a "Rejection in his Own Country." I hope to treat more fully this apparent "globalization" of the "Nazareth" story in Mark and its portrayal of Jesus as a shipwright (τέκτων).

to his own kind." It is widely held that the story of the swine-exorcism with the mission of the healed demoniac πρὸς τοὺς σούς indicates an early Gentile mission; it is "an exorcism in pagan territory."[163] That this pagan territory lies outside of Palestine has been suggested by the arguments of this essay. Although a voyage by Jesus across the Mediterranean to the Straits of Gibraltar borders on the fantastic, we have given no indication that he actually undertook such a journey in history. The motif of such a trek belongs to a narrative set in "mythic" time. Historically, there is nothing to lend itself to the notion that Jesus or his disciples were ever true maritime seafarers. But Paul and other early Christian missionaries were. Long before the drawing up of stories about the life and miracles of Jesus, even in pre-canonical form, an active evangelical mission had existed for at least a generation, if not longer. The rudimentary Christianity of Paul, the greatest of missionaries, knew only of "Christ and him crucified" (1 Cor. 2:2), but of little else, in terms of a kerygma of thaumaturgy. But even before Paul's conversion, the early chapters of the book of Acts imply, if not make explicit, a nascent "pagan" mission to Greeks. Of the seven Hellenists named "to serve tables" as a result of the controversy of Acts 6:1–7, only the stories of Stephen and Philip have found their way into early Christian history. Both were renowned θεῖοι ἄνδρες in their own right who had the uncanny ability to perform miracles; but neither shows any familiarity with the thaumaturgic deeds of the historic Jesus.

Philip's story is most pertinent to us. Earlier in our discussion, we remarked upon the movement of great multitudes towards the sea described in the unusual pre-Markan summary of 3:7–12, a movement that we argued brought migrations of converts towards the Mediterranean coast near Mt. Carmel or Caesarea Maritima. The size of that movement and the scope of the local ethnic groups involved might suggest to pre-Markan readers the establishment of a more permanent dominical "headquarters" along the seacoast, as opposed to a temporary stay by Jesus in houses along the shores of the Sea of Galilee.

In addition to the naming of peoples from Galilee just east of the Mediterranean shoreline and of people from Tyre and Sidon—cities

---

[163] Bligh, "Gerasene," 383.

that lie along the coast just north of Caesarea—a more general *coastal* populace seems to be included in the vast throngs of peoples that followed Jesus to the sea. The mention of Idumaea (Ἰδουμαία), named only in Mark 3:8 in all of the New Testament, would have included folks from the coastal cities of what was formerly ancient Philistia. Although not mentioned by name in the Markan summary, the individual cities of Idumaea would have included Gaza, Ascalon, Azotus (Ashdod), Joppa (Jaffa) and Jamnia had they been specified, cities far removed from the normal range of Jesus' canonical ministry, but townships suprisingly important to the early Christian mission, nonetheless.[164]

Following the famous conversion of Simon Magus in an unnamed city (Caesarea?) of Samaria (Acts 8:5), Philip the Evangelist is guided by an angel to Gaza (εἰς Γάζα, 8:26); there he converts the Ethiopian eunuch and is miraculously translated to Azotus (Φίλιππος δὲ εὑρέθη εἰς Ἄζωτον, 8:40), past Ascalon. From Azotus he preaches, passing through (διερχόμενος) each of the towns on the coast until he finally arrives in Caesarea (8:40), in the Plain of Sharon in westernmost Samaria. Thus, from south to north, the coastal cities of this early Christian missionary itinerary would have included the same cities of Idumaea implied in the naming at Mark 3:8, namely, Gaza, Azotus, Jamnia, Joppa, and Caesarea. Joppa in Acts is the scene of the famous raising of Tabitha by Peter (9:36–43)—an event parallel to the Talitha account in Mark (5:21–25; 35–43), a story that is integral to our first miracle catena. Caesarea itself becomes even more famous for the conversion of Cornelius, a centurion of the Italian Cohort, in which story the Gentiles (that is, "pagans") receive the Holy Spirit (Acts 10). Surprisingly, it is at Caesarea, too, in Peter's speech in

---

[164] In Philip's conversion of the Gentile Ethiopian minister of Candace, there is an important coastal ministry implied in the mentioning of Γάζα (Acts 8:26) and Ἄζωτος (= Ashdod) (8:40). Ἰόππη is connected with Peter's raising of Tabitha (see below), Simon the tanner's seaside home, and the Cornelius story (Acts 9:36, 38, 42–43; 10:5–6, 8, 23, 32; 11:5, 13). On the coastal cities of Idumaea, note U. Hübner, "Idumea," *ABD* 3 (1992) 382: ". . . its territory reached W into the provinces of the port cities of Gaza, Ashkelon, and Ashdod."

Cornelius' home, that one of the few references in Acts is made to the miraculous activity of Jesus (Acts 10:38).[165]

What is the import of all this? It suggests, for one, that according to the book of Acts, Caesarea Maritima must have been an early and vital center of Hellenistic missionary activity. Caesarea, too, may well have been the locus of the real or imagined headquarters of Jesus along the seacoast, according to the pre-Markan editor of Mark 3:7–12 and the catena.

Caesarea is not only the place where Philip and Peter performed numerous wonders and signs, it was there as well that early Christians began first to forge a particularly close union with the newly converted Paul, a figure who had previously been persecuting the nascent Church (Acts 8:1–3). From Caesarea, these "brethren" (οἱ ἀδελφοί) and "disciples" (οἱ μαθηταί) sent Paul to Tarsus to escape the "Hellenists" (9:29–30). At Caesarea, too, Paul disembarked following his second missionary journey (18:22); and from Caesarea Paul set sail on his long celebrated journey to Rome, having first stopped at Sidon (Acts 27:1–3).

The wonderous miracles associated with Caesarea Maritima seem to have been closely linked with the residency of traditions about Jesus as θεῖος ἀνήρ. The localization at this seaside town of healing stories both of the disciples and of Jesus (Acts 10:38) in the 30s and 40s CE points to the city as a repository of early Christian miracle stories. Miracle stories about Jesus as "benefactor and healer" (Acts 10:38) would not have existed in any written form in Philip's day. The fabulous stories of Jesus as benefactor and healer that are found in the catenae, even though pre-Markan, must have been compiled considerably later than the events surrounding Caesarea as described in Acts 8–10; nevertheless, there seems to have been a living tradition at Caesarea of god-like miracles performed by Greek-speaking Christians (and by Peter), a tradition that corresponds remarkably closely to a similar body of miracles associated with Jesus. Did the apostolic miracles in some way mimic older, "lost" traditions of Jesus'

---

[165] Acts 10:38: Ἰησοῦν τὸν ἀπὸ Ναζαρέθ, ὡς ἔχρισεν αὐτὸν ὁ θεὸς πνεύματι ἁγίῳ καὶ δυνάμει, ὃς διῆλθεν εὐεργετῶν καὶ ἰώμενος πάντας τοὺς καταδυναστευομένους ὑπὸ τοῦ διαβόλου [Σατανα E], ὅτι ὁ θεὸς ἦν μετ' αὐτοῦ.

divine activity that are never specifically mentioned in the book of Acts? Or do the apostolic miracles in Acts themselves represent the older tradition? Were Philip and Peter's rôles as "divine men" modelled after local Caesarean traditions of Jesus as divine man? Or has the exact opposite occurred? Further, could a "Hellenist" such as Philip have somehow been responsible for the actual collection of traditions about Jesus as a θεῖος ἀνήρ? If Philip himself were not the author of Mark 1–13, as suggested by Trocmé, could he possibly have been the editor of one or both of the catenae themselves?[166]

Such questions as these cannot be easily answered and perhaps need not be. It may be sufficient at this point merely to ask them and to suggest a connection between early Hellenistic missionaries at Caesarea and early missionaries commissioned by Jesus as wonder-workers, as recorded in Mark 6:7–13. These early missionaries would have found a model in the catena's own Jesus, a Divine Man who had sailed to the "beyond" and conquered death. Such a nexus could surely have occasioned the development, too, of the tradition that the Nazarene came to the important coastal city of Caesarea, and taught from its shores and stayed in its homes. After all, Mark's localization of the stories of Jesus in *specific* cities of Galilee and Judea seems relatively late when compared to the whole range of the history of New Testament literature: Acts 10:38–39, with its reference to Jesus' death by hanging on a tree, has a very primitive Christian "ring" about it; the verse knows only of "Jesus, the one from Nazareth" and mentions only broadly "the country of the Jews and Jerusalem" (ἔν τε τῇ χώρᾳ τῶν Ιουδαίων καὶ Ἰερουσαλήμ, 10:39).[167] In fact, apart from the Gospels and Acts—all relatively late documents—not a single reference is made

[166] E. Trocmé, *La Formation de l'Evangile selon Marc* (EHPR 57; Paris: Presses Universitaires de France, 1963) 202–3. The whole of Acts 8:5–40; 9:31–11:18, which contains the "Caesarean" material referred to above, appears to be an insertion into the larger body of "Antiochene" material (Acts 6:1–8:4; 9:1–30; 11:19–30; 12:25–14:23; 15:35–37), as noted by Robert Jewett, *Dating Paul's Life* (London: SCM Press, 1979 = *A Chronology of Paul's Life*, US ed.) 10, with refs. This "coastal" source—from which I would only omit 9:31 and 11:1–18 (a doublet of 10:1–48)—has numerous linguistic and theological points of contact with Mark and the catenae.

[167] Although Galilee is mentioned here in Acts 10:37 (cf. 1:11, 2:7; 5:37; 9:31; 13:31), nothing is said at all of specific cities surrounding the Sea of Galilee (see next note).

in the earliest writing of primitive Christianity to Galilee or Nazareth at all, much less to Galilean lake-side cities.[168]

The pre-Markan miracle catenae, then, which also present a relatively early portrait of Jesus as a Divine Man and are concerned largely with the θάλασσα, must have known of an ocean-side Savior, not of a teacher by the shores of the Lake of Tiberias. The first catena in particular records events that presuppose the grander scheme of coastal launchings of Jesus across the Ocean, not the smaller vision of inland lakeside "crossings." Accordingly, the sea-voyager of the catena and his crew were not concerned with mundane lakeshore activities such as mending nets and fishing, but with the stilling of seastorms, the conquering of "legions" and the raising of the dead.

We argued in detail at the outset of this study for a maritime context of the catena-stories along coastal Phoenicia or at the Acco Plain. An environment slightly more southward along the northern end of the Plain of Sharon would locate the great withdrawal of Mark 3:9 precisely at Caesarea Maritima, whose ancestry can be traced to Phoenician Sidon. The great movements of followers that are said to converge upon Jesus thus funnel together in a huge mass to the vitally important coastal focal point at Caesarea, a city that serves as a kind of centrally located geographic hub of the early Hellenistic Christian missionary movement. Within the pre-Markan catena, this monumentally important nerve-center remains unnamed precisely because of its axial position: all other regions from Tyre to Idumaea in the "geography of the mind" remain equidistant from it like spokes of an enormous wheel. As a city at the very core of the first catena's narrative, Caesarea—the homeport of Jesus' *patris*—would not require mention by virtue of the fact that it lies at the heart of its own story. Only from the more distant historical perspective of outsiders looking in would Caesarea come into the written record, as apparently happens with Acts, the only NT document to mention it. As noted, the miracle catenae are not geographically bound, to begin with, so the

---

[168] In the earliest NT documents, including the letters of Paul, of James and Peter, Hebrews etc. and the early creeds and hymns they quote, the following place names pertinent to the ministry of Jesus are entirely unknown: Galilee and Nazareth; Bethany, Bethlehem, Bethsaida, Bethphage, Cana, Capernaum, Chorazim, Gadara, Gennesaret, Gergesa, Golgotha, Dalmanoutha, Decapolis, Emmaus, Idumaea, Jericho, Magdala, Nain, Samaria, Sidon, and Tyre.

naming of cities in them is rare, and when cities are found their identifications are nebulous, being the apparent result of later textual maneuverings. Pre-Markan Christianity seems to know almost nothing of Galilean villages and towns.

Given the first miracle catena's apparent focus on the actual sea-crossing itself, rather than on its geographical destiny, we have interpreted the *Peran* as a kind of boundary between two very different worlds. On the one hand, we encounter the Jewish life of Judaea and Galilee: its villages, houses, and synagogues; its scribes and Pharisees. On the other hand, the Gentile world of the Other Side betrays no historical referencing of this kind. Gone are Capernaum, Nazareth, and Bethsaïda—not even Galilee is mentioned—only a kind of hazy region of cliffs and monsters lying "beyond the sea." Its tales, instead, relate the sort of mythic, allegorical, and symbolic themes particularly appealing to its "pagan" audience.

We have had occasion to identify the land at which Jesus arrives in Mark 5:1 as Phoenician "Gadeira" (Cádiz), rather than Galilean "Gadara." The catena's interest in describing such a mythic voyage to a terminal boundary at the edges of the world, with its dramatic affiliations of death, magic, and mystery, must have made a deep impression on those who read or heard its stories. Its prodigy of untamed chaos, sea-storms, cliffs, and drowning pigs would have sounded a familiar ring to any audience steeped in the popular myths and legends of divine heroes like Jason, Odysseus, or Heracles. The celebrated temple of Tyrian Heracles located at Cádiz, with its famous taboo on swine and the association of its cult with the Heracles-Geryon myth, appears to have left an indelible mark in the shaping of the pre-canonical story in Mark 4:35–5:20. The impact of its cult, along with details of its day-to-day economy, animal husbandry, and burial practices, all seem to point to the profound contribution that Phoenician Cádiz must have made to the makeup of the unusual pre-Markan story that we have examined. The Tyrian Heracles, Melqart—the principal "dying and rising" deity of Gadeira[169]—must

---

[169] On the annual *egersis* of Melqart, see Joseph. *Ant.* 8.5.3; *Ap.* 1.119 (see above, note 35); cf. Paus. 9.4.6; Aubet, *Phoenicians*, 128–30; A. I. Baumgarten, *The* Phoenician History *of Philo of Byblos: A Commentary* (EPRO 69; Leiden: Brill, 1981) 210–11, with additional evidence.

also have found his Christian counterpart in a far greater "dying and rising" son of god, Jesus, who could not only raise up the blade of grain from the earth (cf. Mark 4:26–29), but could also quell the tempest, defeat evil, and raise the dead.

All the data about Cádiz and its cult that we have presented will point to an interest in accommodating a public familiar with its own religious and mythological culture. A western mission whose main target must have been the conversion of Punic-Phoenician traders who lived at sea would appear to be a good candidate for the specific *Sitz im Leben* of so important a composition as the first miracle catena; the broad implications of a "Cádiz reading" of Mark 5:1–20 will point in the grander scheme to an early pre-Markan mission to the west, a mission specifically aimed at spreading the Gospel to the Iberian peninsula.[170] In order to evangelize the west, it would have been imperative to win over the powerful Tyrian merchants who controlled trade between Phoenician Tyre and Cádiz. Ancient Cádiz's primary commercial market was Rome, with a great many of Rome's own population relocating to this busiest of Spanish ports, and with Ostia's hotels and taverns continually saturated with the prattle and barter of Gadirite hawkers and merchants. Could not our miracle catena—or even Mark's gospel in general—have had as an eventual missionary goal the vastly important cosmopolitan citizenry of Cádiz, a folk that would have been especially susceptible to the propagation of new and unexplored cults and religious beliefs, especially if those beliefs were discreetly articulated within the cultural framework, mythological setting, and social features with which these "late Phoenicians" would have felt the greatest fraternity? That there are other interests in things Phoenician in Mark's gospel at large is a matter that has, so far, apparently escaped scholarly attention. It is an issue yet to be explored, but one that I leave for another time.

---

[170] Independent sources name Spain as an evangelical target of Paul's mission (cf. *1 Clem.* 5.6–7). Note, further, R. Jewett, "Paul, Phoebe, and the Spanish Mission," *The Social World of Formative Judaism and Christianity: Essays in Tribute to Howard Clark Kee* (ed. J. Neusner; Philadelphia: Fortress, 1988) 142–61, with much indispensable material. Paul would not have been the only one to sail west from Caesarea; others, like Titus or Philip, could hardly have ignored the vast ocean vista lying at their doorsteps.

Jesus and the Romans in Galilee: Jews and Gentiles in the Decapolis

David E. Aune

I. Introduction

Roy Kotansky proposes a reading of the stories of the Stilling of the Storm and the Exorcism of the Gerasene Demoniac in Mark 4:35–5:43 that is strikingly different from those reflected in previous Markan scholarship. This imaginative new reading centers on a recontextualization of the geographical references in sections of Mark which he considers pre-Markan. After deconstructing the more conventional understanding of the admittedly confused geography in Mark 4:35–5:43 (and its larger context), the author advances detailed arguments in support of a mythological reading of Mark 4:35–5:43 in its pre-Markan context as nothing less than mythic sea voyage of Jesus to the Land of the Dead, a kind of nautical *descensus ad inferos* of Jesus the hero to the island of Gadeira or Cádiz beyond the Pillars of Heracles, associated in ancient popular imagination with the Underworld. As bizarre as this interpretation may appear at first, Kotansky bases his proposal on a close reading of the text of Mark particularly in terms of its possible utilization of pre-Markan sources with an original meaning which differed considerably from the way in which they were used by the Second Evangelist.

I. Exploring the Geography of Mark

Each of the canonical gospels has a geographical framework which organizes the story of Jesus as a travel narrative centering on movement within Galilee, in part focused on the Sea of Galilee, and movement between Galilee and Jerusalem.[1] The geographical and

[1] This is essentially in line with the claim of C. W. Hedrick that Mark's "geographical references and spatial locations . . . constitute the only immediately recognizable over-all narrative structure to an otherwise highly episodic narrative" ("What is a Gospel? Geography, Time and Narrative Structure," *Perspectives in Religious Studies* 10 [1983] 255–68).

topographical references which meet the reader at every turn encourage the formulation of a "mental map" which provides a spatial context for understanding the unfolding story of Jesus.[2] The geography and topography of the Gospel of Mark (as of the other Gospels), arguably constitutes a structural system which has its own *internal* coherence, regardless of the extent to which it corresponds or fails to correspond to *external* historical geographies.[3] Ancient as well as modern readers necessarily approach Mark (and the other Gospels) with their own imaginary map which is modified as they journey with Jesus and his disciples through the text. This imaginary map is primarily informed by the geographical references mediated by the text itself, but can also be informed by a direct or indirect acquaintance with Palestinian geography and topography, or even by consulting maps which reconstruct the historical geography of first century Palestine (a luxury unavailable to ancient readers). The imaginary map that a reader might draw based on the data presented by the text itself would very likely be strikingly different from maps reconstructed by historical geographers. In the Gospel of Mark, for example, it would not be absolutely necessary for a reader to distinguish between the Sea of Galilee and the Mediterranean coast, particularly since the word θάλασσα, as Kotansky reminds us, can either be used as a synonym for λίμνη, "lake" or with the more usual Greek meaning "sea."[4]

At first sight, the notion of a cognitive geography which encourages the creative imagination of the reader seems inimical to traditional historical criticism, for critics like Dalman have meticulously attempted to correlate the geographical and topographical references in the

---

[2] P. Gould and R. White, *Mental Maps* (2d. ed; Boston: Allen & Unwin, 1986); P. S. Alexander, "Early Jewish Geography," *ABD* 2. 977–88.

[3] The "narrative space" of Mark has been treated in detail as a system amenable to structuralist analysis by E. Struthers Malbon (*Narrative Space and Mythic Meaning in Mark* [San Francisco: Harper & Row, 1986]), but of course the coherence of the internal geographical-topographical "system" is dependent on the extent to which sources have been integrated into the final composition of Mark.

[4] See the imaginary map drawn by S. van Tilborg, based on the geographical data presented in the Gospel of John, in which "the sea" is located on the west side of the map and much larger than "the lake of Galilee," Jerusalem is in the lower center, while Galilee, Samaria and Judea are located in the top, middle and lower range of the east side of the map (*Reading John in Ephesus* [NovTSup 83; Leiden: Brill, 1996] 62).

Gospels (particularly Mark and Luke) with the reconstructed historical geography of first century Palestine, exposing all the real or imagined missteps of the evangelists.[5] The game of correcting Mark's geography and topography, of course, is a very old one, which began with Matthew and Luke and was continued by copyists trying to make sense of the exemplars with which they were working. The generally recognized geographical confusion in Mark and Luke has often led to the conclusion that the evangelists were unfamiliar with most or all of Palestine and that Luke in particular was not a very good historian.[6] For many, however, there is a middle way. The earlier redaction critics focused on many of the geographical peculiarities of Mark and Luke, which they attempted to integrate into the theological agenda of each evangelist.[7] Since Jesus makes several trips from Galilee to Jerusalem according to the Fourth Gospel, and several passages in the Synoptics presuppose more than a single visit to Jerusalem,[8] it became evident that the portrait of Jesus' activity in Galilee (Mark 1–9), followed by a single fateful journey of Jesus from Galilee to Jerusalem (Mark 10–16), replicated in Matthew and Luke, was a theologically motivated creation of the Second Evangelist.[9] The term "Galilee" is largely, if not exclusively, redactional,[10] representing the place of Jesus' ministry, his eschatological activity and the point of departure for the gentile mission, precisely because Galilee has special significance for the Christian community of Mark's day, while "Jerusalem" is the place of

---

[5] G. Dalman, *Sacred Sites and Ways: Studies in the Topography of the Gospels* (New York: Macmillan, 1935).

[6] See the brief review of the problem in M. Hengel, "Luke the Historian and the Geography of Palestine in the Acts of the Apostles," idem, *Between Jesus and Paul* (Philadelphia: Fortress, 1983) 97–100. R. Pesch observes: "Mark has . . . no personal knowledge of Galilean geography around the Sea of Galilee" (*Das Markusevangelium* [HTKNT; Freiburg: Herder, 1976] 1. 10).

[7] H. Conzelmann, *The Thelogy of St. Luke* (New York: Harper & Row, 1960) 18–94; W. Marxsen, *Der Evangelist Markus: Studien zur Redaktionsgeschichte des Evangeliums* (Göttingen: Vandenhoeck & Ruprecht, 1959) 33–77.

[8] K. L. Schmidt, *Der Rahmen der Geschichte Jesu* (1919; reprinted Darmstadt: Wissenschaftliche Buchgesellschaft, 1964) 271–73; Marxsen, *Der Evangelist Markus*, 34.

[9] Marxsen, *Der Evangelist Markus*, 34.

[10] Schmidt, *Der Rahmen*, 43; Marxsen, *Der Evangelist Markus*, 36–37, 40; J.-M. van Cangh, "La Galilée dans l'évangile de Marc: un lieu théologique?" *RB* 79 (1972) 59–75.

the death of Jesus.[11] Mark also occasionally refers to various unidentified "mountains" as the venues for Jesus' quest for solitude (3:13; 6:46; 9:2).[12]

II. The Focal Text: Mark 4:35–5:43

Kotansky's primary focus is on the pre-Markan source or sources used by the Second Evangelist. The four miracle stories found in Mark 4:35–5:43 are widely thought to have constituted a pre-Markan collection or cycle.[13] Keck and Pesch, followed with qualifications by Guelich, have argued for a larger pre-Markan collection of six miracle stories introduced with the pre-Markan summary in 3:7–12 at the beginning and concluding with the two miracle stories of the feeding of the 5,000 and Jesus walking on the water in 6:32–52.[14] Kuhn, unware of Keck and Achtemeier, examines the possibility of a pre-Markan collection of six miracle stories in Mark 4:35–6:52, but is not certain that all six stories belonged to a single collection.[15] Achtemeier argued for an even larger pre-Markan collection of two miracle catenae consisting of ten miracle stories which formed two parallel series of five stories which begin with sea miracles and end with

---

[11] W. G. Kümmel, *Introduction to the New Testament* (rev. ed.; Nashville: Abingdon, 1975) 88–89.

[12] Normally one would regard a "mountain" (ὄρος) as a significantly higher elevation than a "hill" (βουνός, ὀρεινή, θίς), though the canonical gospels use only ὄρος of elevations, never βουνός or other synonyms for "hill." The Hebrew word הר similarly includes higher and lower elevations distinguished in English by the terms "mountain" and "hill."

[13] J. Weiss, *Das älteste Evangelium* (Göttingen: Vandenhoeck & Ruprecht, 1903) 179–80; K. L. Schmidt, *Der Rahmen,* 150–52; F. C. Grant, *The Gospels: Their Origin and Growth* (New York: Harper & Row, 1957) 92; V. Taylor, *The Formation of the Gospel Tradition* (London: Macmillan, 1953) 39, 169; idem, *The Gospel According to Mark,* (2d ed.; Grand Rapids, MI: Baker Book House, 1966) 94–95; H.-W. Kuhn, *Ältere Sammlungen im Markusevangelium* (SUNT 8; Göttingen: Vandenhoeck & Ruprecht, 1971) 27–28; C. Bryan, *A Preface to Mark: Notes on the Gospel in Its Literary and Cultural Settings* (New York: Oxford University, 1993) 49.

[14] L. Keck, "Mark 3:7–12 and Mark's Christology," *JBL* 84 (1965) 341–58; Pesch, *Das Markusevangelium,* 1. 198, 277–81; R. Guelich, *Mark 1–8:26* (WBC 34A; Dallas: Word, 1989) 142–44, 261–63.

[15] H.-W. Kuhn, *Ältere Sammlungen im Markusevangelium,* 191–213; Keck, "Mark 3:7–12 and Mark's Christology;" P. Achtemeier, "Toward the Isolation of Pre-Markan Miracle Catenae," *JBL* 89 (1970) 265–91.

feeding miracles, framing three healing miracles (* = Matthean parallel; + = Lukan parallel; # = Johannine parallel):[16]

Catena I	*Catena II*
*+Stilling of the storm (4:35–41)	*#Jesus walks on the sea (6:45–51)
*+Gerasene demoniac (5:1–20)	Blind man of Bethsaida (8:22–26)
*+Woman/hemorrhage (5:24b–34)	*Syrophoenician woman (7:24b–30)
*+Jairus' daughter (5:21–23, 35–43)	Deaf-Mute (7:32–37)
*+#Feeding of the 5,000 (6:34–44, 53)	*Feeding of the 4,000 (8:1–10)

Achtemeier's proposal has been accepted by a few American scholars,[17] but it has had little discernible impact on others.[18] His identification of two pre-Markan miracle collections is supported by the fact that they are analogous to the pre-Johannine Signs Source utilized by the Fourth Evangelist. Surprisingly, Achtemeier does not capitalize on the fact that the miracle of the feeding of the 5,000 and the story of Jesus walking on the water are juxtaposed in John 6:1–21, just as in Mark 6:30–52, for there appears to be an obvious affinity between aspects of the Johannine "Signs Source" and the pre-Markan miracle collection. However, the fact that the feeding of the 5,000 ends his Catena I, while the story of Jesus walking on the water begins Catena II, does not provide support for a theory of *two* collections.[19]

---

[16] Achtemeier also argues that two large blocks of material involving the teaching and disputing activity of Jesus were inserted into the catenae (6:1–33 into the first; 7:1–23 into the second), and that the following material in the catenae is possibly or probably editorial: Catena I: 4:35; 5:21c, 24, 43a; 6:34bc, 35b; Catena II: 6:45c, 50c, 51b; 7:36; 8:1a ("Toward the Isolation of Pre-Markan Miracle Catenae," 291). He also considers 7:31 to be part of the Markan geographical framework (ibid., 287).

[17] H. C. Kee, *Community of the New Age: Studies in Mark's Gospel* (Philadelphia: Westminster, 1977) 32–34; B. L. Mack, *A Myth of Innocence* (Philadelphia: Fortress, 1988) 216–19, 230–33; J. H. Elliott, Review of H.-W. Kuhn, *Ältere Sammlungen im Markusevangelium*, *CBQ* 34 (1972) 370; W. Kelber, Review of H.-W. Kuhn, *Ältere Sammlungen im Markusevangelium*, *JBL* 93 (1974) 307.

[18] The Belgian scholar J.-M. van Cangh discusses Achtemeier's proposal in some detail, but is skeptical of his methodology ("Les sources de l'Evangile: les collections pré-marciennes de miracles," *RTL* 3 [1972] 76–85).

[19] R. T. Fortna reconstructs the pre-Johannine source behind John 6:1–25 in which the miracle of the feeding of the 5,000 and Jesus walking on the water are linked, but similarly finds no reason to mention the parallel structure in Mark 6:30–52 (*The Fourth Gospel and Its Predecessor* [Philadelphia: Fortress, 1988] 79–93). The parallels between Mark 6:30–52 and John 6:1–25 are examined and judged to be derived from a common earlier tradition by C. H. Dodd (*Historical Tradition in the Fourth Gospel* [Cambridge: Cambridge University, 1965] 211) and M. Smith

Following Achtemeier, Kotansky considers Mark 4:35–5:43 to be part of the first of two pre-Markan miracle catenae, the first catena consisting of Mark 4:35–5:43, 6:34–44, 53 [?], and the second consisting of Mark 6:45–52; 7:24b–30; 7:32–8:10 (though Kotansky is concerned only with Catena I).[20] The distinctive feature of the ten miracle stories in Mark 4:35–8:26 is that they ignore the conflicts between Jesus and Jewish religious leaders and emphasize rather the supernatural power of Jesus. Achtemeier finds parallels to aspects of his two collections, that is, the two sea miracles and the two feeding miracles, in Hellenistic Jewish traditions of Moses as a miracle-working divine man, including elements from the Elijah-Elisha traditions.[21] More speculatively, Achtemeier suggested that the function of such miracle stories was epiphanic and that they revealed Jesus as a *deus praesens.* He also suggested that such a recital may have served as an interpretive liturgy accompanying a eucharistic meal, which consisted primarily of bread.[22] Therefore the community within which the two miracle catenae arose probably espoused a "divine man" christology, though it is clear that Mark did not share this christology and therefore Mark tried to correct what he considered a one-sided emphasis on Jesus the miracle worker.[23] This, of course, reflects the dated view that the notion of the divine man is a key to understanding the triumphant title "Son of God" in Mark, which was corrected by the evangelist's emphasis on the suffering "Son of Man" christology, a thesis eloquently argued by Weeden and which was popular in the 1970s, but has more recently been treated more cautiously or even with benign neglect.[24]

(*Clement of Alexandria and a Secret Gospel of Mark* [Cambridge: Harvard University Press, 1973] 158–63).

[20] Though Achtemeier includes the healing of the blind man of Bethsaida (Mark 8:22–26) in the second position in Catena II, Kotansky omits it entirely without comment.

[21] P. Achtemeier, "The Origin and Function of the Pre-Markan Miracle Catenae," 202–5.

[22] Ibid., 205–9.

[23] Ibid., 209–212, 218–19.

[24] T. J. Weeden, *Mark: Traditions in Conflict* (Philadelphia: Fortress, 1971); J. D. Kingsbury, *The Christology of Mark's Gospel* (Philadelphia: Fortress, 1983) 25–45; B. L. Mack, *A Myth of Innocence,* 75–76.

While Kotansky basically accepts the two miracle collections identified by Achtemeier (though he is primarily interested in Catena I), he substitutes his own speculations for the speculative suggestions of Achtemeier concerning the patterns and function of these collections. Kotansky proposes that the two miracle catenae are set on the Mediterranean coast rather than the Sea of Galilee, and that the target cities of both catenae (5:1, the country of the Gerasenes; 8:10, the regions of Dalmanoutha), with their confusing textual history, accord better with an extra-Palestinian destination. The two catenae constitute a kind of mini-epic (in Kotansky's terms a kind of novella, *Märchen,* or Argonaut-like *mythos*) narrating the western voyage of Jesus and his followers across the Mediterranean sea to the mythic Land of the Dead supposedly associated with the island of Gadeira just west of the Strait of Gibraltar. His procedure is to atomize the first hypothetical pre-Markan miracle collection (his primary focus) into constituent motifs which he claims allude to Greek and Near Eastern myths. Kotansky speculates that Caesarea Maritima was the place to which Jesus withdrew in Mark 3:7, for it was an important early Christian urban center with a strong miracle tradition. He further suggests that Philip the Evangelist may have edited one or both of the pre-Markan miracle catenae.[25] If we should ask why Caesarea Maritima is unnamed in the pre-Markan miracle catenae or the Synoptic tradition generally, Kotansky has an answer: "Within the pre-Markan catena-narrative, this monumentally important nerve-center [that is, Caesarea Maritima] remains unnamed precisely because of its axial position: all other regions from Tyre to Idumaea in the 'geography of the mind' remain equidistant from it like spokes of an enormous wheel."

III. Sea of Galilee or Mediterranean Sea?

Lake Kinneret, the ancient name for the Sea of Galilee, is a prominent natural feature of northern Palestine which serves as a main theater of activity for Jesus and his disciples according to all the canonical Gospels. The most ancient designation for this body of water was "Lake Kinneret" (ים כנרת; Num 34:11; cf. *Tg. Onq.* Num 34:11, or

---

[25] Following E. Trocmé, *The Formation of the Gospel according to Mark* (London: SPCK; Philadelphia: Westminster, 1975) 257–59.

ים כנרות (the plural form); Josh 12:3; 13:27). A later name of the lake was Lake Gennesar (an etymological development of Kinneret), known to Pliny the Elder, who reports that some call it "Lake Taricheae" (*Hist. Nat.* 5.71), the Greek name for Magdala, north of Tiberias on the west side of Lake Kinneret, referred to frequently by Josephus.[26] Similarly, *Tg. Jon.* Josh 12:3 and 13:27 use the phrase *yam ginnesar* or *yam ginessar* (Aramaic: *ymʾ dgnysr*). The Markan term for this natural feature is "the Sea of Galilee" (ἡ θάλασσα τῆς Γαλιλαίας), a phrase which occurs just twice (1:16; 7:31),[27] while the remaining seventeen occurrences of θάλασσα are generally assumed to refer to that same Sea of Galilee.[28] The peculiar feature of this usage is that the term θάλασσα was normally reserved for much larger bodies of water such as the Mediterranean Sea.[29] Lake Kinneret, a moderately sized inland body of water, is only called a θάλασσα in the canonical gospels (with the exception of Luke), and a few passages in the Septuagint (Num 34:11; Josh 12:3; 13:27). The Septuagint similarly refers to the Dead Sea as a θάλασσα (Gen 14:3; Num 34:3, 12; Deut 3:17; Josh 3:16; 12:3; 4 Kgdms 14:25; Joel 2:20).[30] This usage is usually explained by the fact that the Hebrew or Aramaic term ים can mean either "sea" or "lake" depending on the context, so that θάλασσα in the Gospels can be considered a Septuagintism (in modern Israel,

---

[26] Josephus *Vit.* 155–57; *Bell.* 2.252, 573, 634–35; 3.445, 457, 462–65. There is a discrepancy between Pliny (*Hist. Nat.* 5.71), who locates Taricheae at the southwest part of Lake Kinneret, near the Jordan outlet, and Josephus, who was more familiar with the topography and locates Taricheae 30 stades (3 1/2 miles) from Tiberias.

[27] Both references to "of Galilee" were probably added by the Evangelist (Schmidt, *Der Rahmen*, 43; Willi Marxsen, *Der Evangelist Markus*, 36, 44).

[28] The phrase "Sea of Galilee" occurs twice in Matthew (4:18; 15:29), both references derived from Mark (1:16; 7:31), while in the Gospel of John the lake is referred to once as the "Sea of Tiberias" (21:1; Josephus also uses the expression "Lake Tiberias" in *Bell.* 3.57; 4.456), and once with the conflated expression the "Sea of Galilee of Tiberias" (6:1). The designation "Tiberias" presupposes the local perspective of that lakeside city, founded by Herod Antipas in AD 20, and named in honor of the reigning emperor.

[29] Theissen cites Porphyry, quoted by Macarius Magnes *Apokritikos*, to the effect that there is in fact no "sea" (θάλασσα) in Palestine, but rather a "lake" (λίμνη) (*The Gospels in Context: Social and Political History in the Synoptic Tradition* [Minneapolis: Fortress, 1991] 105–6).

[30] Josephus refers to the Dead Sea as "Lake Asphaltitis."

Lake Kinneret is called Yam Kinneret). Beyond this Theissen has suggested that the local perspective of the inhabitants might have considered Lake Kinneret as the θάλασσα for people who had never seen the Mediterranean.[31] Luke was careful about this, and never uses θάλασσα of Lake Kinneret, but prefers the designation λίμνη.[32] Luke uses the phrase ἡ λίμνη Γεννησαρέτ, "lake Gennesaret," once (5:1), substitutes λίμνη one time where Mark and Matthew have θάλασσα (Luke 8:33 = Mark 5:13 = Matthew 13:32), and twice substitutes ὕδωρ for θάλασσα in Mark (Luke 8:24–25 = Mark 4:39–40).[33] However, it is not a matter only of Luke's lexicographical purity, for he also omits Mark's references to the sea, to Jesus going to the sea and to Jesus teaching on or by the sea (Mark 2:13; 3:7, 9; 4:1; 5:21; 7:31). Josephus, like Luke, uses the term λίμνη of Lake Kinneret, never θάλασσα (*Bell.* 2.573; 3.57, 463, 506, 522; *Ant.* 18.28, 36; *Vit.* 96, 153, 304, 327, 349).

Kotansky suggests that there is some ambiguity in the use of the term θάλασσα ("sea, lake") in Mark 4:35–5:43 and that sometimes θάλασσα points to the coast of the Mediterranean. He in fact argues that *all* sea-crossings in the catenae involve the Mediterranean[34] and furthermore that Galilee forms no part of the catenae geographies; the exception is the difficult passage Mark 7:31, which Kotansky considers a gloss but which most scholars regard as part of the Markan redaction. The story of the Syro-Phoenician woman (7:24–30) is set in the coastal regions about Tyre, according to Kotansky, but since the villages controlled by the Greek cities of Tyre and Sidon stretched inland for many miles, it is possible, but certainly not necessary, that Mark here depicts Jesus and his entourage as visiting the

---

[31] Theissen, "Meer und See in den Evangelien: Ein Beitrag zur Lokalkoloritforschung," *Studien zum Neuen Testament und seiner Umwelt* 10 (1976) 5–25; *The Gospels in Context*, 107.

[32] H. J. Cadbury, *The Style and Literary Method of Luke* (Cambridge: Harvard University Press, 1920) 186.

[33] Lake Kinneret is called τὸ ὕδωρ τοῦ Γεννησαρ, "Lake Gennesar," in 1 Macc 11:67 and Josephus *Ant.* 13.158.

[34] There are *four* sea-crossings in the sections Achtemeier has identified as miracle collections ("Toward the Isolation of Pre-Markan Miracle Catenae"): (1) 4:35 ("let us go across to the other side") and 5:1 ("the other side of the sea"); (2) 5:25 ("the other side"); (3) 6:45 ("to the other side, to Bethsaida"); (4) 8:10 (to Dalmanoutha).

Mediterranean coast between Tyre and Sidon.[35] More telling perhaps is the fact that no terms for "sea" or "coastal regions" are mentioned in the pericope. Furthermore, there is not even a hint in the Synoptic tradition that Jesus was ever active on the Mediterranean coast.[36] There is, in fact, no good contextual reason for construing θάλασσα to mean anything but the Sea of Galilee. The first two mentions of θάλασσα in Mark occur in the phrase "the Sea of Galilee" (Mark 1:16 [twice]), as does the last non-metaphorical mention of the term (7:31). Kotansky observes that neither Galilee (apart from the editorial remark of 7:31), Capernaum or Nazareth are part of the geography of the catenae, and that "If Galilee forms no part of the catenae geographies, references to a generic 'sea' in them will not describe the Sea of Galilee, but the greater littoral of the adjoining seacoast." In the second catena, of course, Bethsaida is mentioned as the intended destination of the disciples when they saw Jesus walking on the water (6:45–52), though they actually end up landing at Gennesaret (6:53);[37] in the Johannine parallel in John 6:17, the destination is Capernaum, where they are also said to land (John 6:21).

The intention of crossing the sea is first mentioned in Catena I in 4:35 in the phrase "let us go over to the other side." To decide what "sea" is implied, Kotansky argues that one must refer back to 3:7 where Jesus and his disciples are said to "withdraw to the sea" (ἀνεχώρησεν

[35] Tyre and Sidon had extensive territories. The territory of Tyre reached to Cadasa in the mountains overlooking the Huleh valley, while that of Sidon shared a common border with Damascus, far inland.

[36] Luke alone uses the term παράλιος, "coastal area," a single time to specify more closely the origin of those from Tyre and Sidon who came to see, hear and be healed by Jesus (6:17). The Mediterranean is referred to frequently in the LXX simply as ἡ θάλασσα, and more specifically as as the "Great Sea" (e.g., Josh 9:1; 13:8; Ezek 47:20). Alternate designations for Lake Kinneret in early Judaism include "Sea of Joppa" (θάλασσα Ιόππης) in 2 Chron 2:15; Ezra 3:7, and "Sea of Jamnia" (θάλασσα Ἰαμνίας) in *T. Naph.* 6:1.

[37] Bethsaida is probably Bethsaida Julias which was situated on the shores of the Sea of Galilee just east of the Jordan in lower Gaulanitis or Trachonitis (Pliny *Hist. Nat.* 5.71; Josephus *Bell.* 2.168; 3.515), and though perhaps not technically in Galilee, it was so near Galilee that it is informally referred to as "Bethsaida of Galilee" in John 12:21 and by Ptolemaeus *Geographia* 5.15.3 (ed. C. F. A. Nobbe, *Geographia* [3 vols.; Leipzig: O. Holtze, 1843–45]). Bethsaida was reportedly the home of three of Jesus' disciples: Philip, Andrew and Peter (John 1:44; 12:21), and according to Luke 9:10 was the site of the feeding of the 5,000.

πρὸς τὴν θάλασσαν). The meaning of θάλασσα in 3:7 should not be determined by the immediate context, he cautions, for 3:7–12 is probably pre-Markan,[38] though most critics judge the passage to be the product of Markan redactional activity.[39] Note, however, that he wants to have it both ways, for he wants to use the "sea" in 3:7, which he thinks refers to the Mediterranean coast, as the context for understanding the "sea" implied in the crossing mentioned in 4:35.[40] "Withdrawing to the sea" cannot mean the Sea of Galilee, he argues, for the term ἀναχωρεῖν implies a considerable distance, and it would be absurd to suggest that Jesus should "withdraw" to an area where he is already located, at Capernaum in the synagogue (3:1–6). The difficulty with this argument, however, is that ἀναχωρεῖν has at least two distinct meanings in the New Testament: (1) "to move away from a location, implying a considerable distance," appropriately glossed as "to withdraw, retire, go away," and (2) "to move back to a point or area from which one has previously departed, but with more explicit

[38] In footnote 15, Kotansky claims to follow R. Guelich, *Mark 1–8:26,* 142–44 (who emphasizes five significant *hapax legomena* in 3:7, 9–10), who in turn follows Pesch, *Das Markusevangelium,* 1. 198. However, Pesch is virtually alone among recent critics in regarding 3:7–12 as pre-Markan, for Guelich (*Mark 1–8:26,* 143) in fact follows L. Keck ("Mark 3:7–12 and Mark's Christology," 346–47) in regarding 3:7, 9–10 as pre-Markan (though he dissents from Keck's view in some details, including the view that "from Galilee" in v. 7 belongs to the Markan redaction).

[39] Schmidt, *Der Rahmen,* 105–7; R. Bultmann, *Die Geschichte der synoptischen Tradition* (8th ed.; Göttingen: Vandenhoeck & Ruprecht, 1967) 366; Grant, *The Gospels,* 90; Marxsen, *Der Evangelist Markus,* 39; D. E. Nineham, *Saint Mark* (Philadelphia: Westminster, 1963) 112; E. Schweizer, *The Good News According to Mark* (Atlanta: John Knox, 1970) 78–79; Trocmé, *The Formation of the Gospel according to Mark,* 195; J. Gnilka, *Das Evangelium Nach Markus (Mk 1–8, 26)* (Zürich: Benziger; Neukirchen-Vluyn: Neukirchener, 1978) 1. 133. However, note the reconstruction by Keck in which it is precisely the *geographical* references in 3:7–8 which are attributed to Mark, though the remainder of 3:7–12 is judged pre-Markan ("Mark 3:7–12 and Mark's Christology," 346–48). Keck proposes a reconstruction of the Urtext of Mark 3:7–12 (English translation of his Greek text): "And Jesus with his disciples withdrew to the sea and a large multitude followed. And he told his disciples to prepare a boat for him because of the crowd, that they might not crush him, for he had healed many so that all those who had diseases pressed about him in order to touch him" ("Mark 3:7–12 and Mark's Christology," 347).

[40] This would be possible if he considered 3:7–12 as part of the first catena, as does Keck ("Mark 3:7–12 and Mark's Christology").

emphasis upon the return," glossed as "to move back, return."[41] Since ἀναχωρεῖν occurs just once in Mark (3:7), it is imprudent to insist on the first meaning when the second meaning fits equally well: "Then Jesus, his disciples, *returned* to the sea." Of course, it cannot be assumed that the reader would know that Capernaum is located on the northwest shore of the Sea of Galilee, although Capernaum and the Sea of Galilee are placed in close proximity by Mark.[42] There is a clear polarity in Mark between Jesus seeking human association and turning away from it in retreats to the seaside, the hills or "the mountain" (Mark 1:35; 6:30–31, 46). John 6:15, a passage which links the story of the feeding of the 5,000 in John 6:1–14 and the story of Jesus walking on the lake in John 6:16–21, says that Jesus "withdrew" (ἀνεχώρησεν) to a mountain, whence he came to the disciples in the boat as they struggled in a storm, apparently supposing that Jesus could see the disciples in trouble from his mountain.

Further, Kotansky claims that, after Jesus *withdrew* to the sea (3:7), a great crowd of people followed him (in geographical sequence) from Galilee, Judea, Jerusalem, and then from Idumea, the other side of the Jordan, and the area about Tyre and Sidon. The sea in question, however, cannot be the Sea of Galilee, Kotansky contends, for how can Galileans whose principal towns and villages are on the shores of the Sea of Galilee be said to *withdraw* there?[43] This is a misrepresentation of the text, however, for according to Mark 3:7 there were *two* great multitudes, distinguished by two verbal clauses, one from Galilee

---

[41] J. P. Louw and E. A. Nida, *Greek-English Lexicon of the New Testament Based on Semantic Domains* (2 vols.; New York: United Bible Societies, 1988) vol. 1, § 15.53, § 15.89.

[42] Capernaum is mentioned just three times in Mark (1:21; 2:1; 9:33). The pericope on the calling of the first disciples by the Sea of Galilee (1:16–20) is followed by the pericope on Jesus' preaching in the synagogue of Capernaum (1:21–28). The transition between the two in 1:21 says only that "they entered into Capernaum," implying only that it must be in the vicinity of the Sea of Galilee. The pericope on the healing of the paralytic in Capernaum (2:1–12) is immediately followed by the call of Levi by the sea (2:13–14), again indicating their close proximity. In the canonical gospels, only John (6:17, 24) speaks of going to Capernaum by boat, clearly assuming that it is a lakeside village.

[43] Though Capernaum was a lakeside village, it would be perfectly appropriate to imagine a "withdrawal" to a remote part of the lake.

which *followed*[44] Jesus and another from Judaea, Jerusalem, Idumea and beyond the Jordan, and from the region of Tyre and Sidon which *came* (ἦλθον) to Jesus. It seems clear that the great multitude from Galilee occupies a special position in the view of the evangelist, and the great multitude from outside Galilee is described from a Galilean perspective.[45] Kotansky's claim that Mark's Galilee contains *only* lakeside inhabitants is contradicted by Mark 1:9, 39; 6:7. Although these references to Jesus' activity in Galilee are admittedly redactional, they nevertheless reveal the evangelist's interest in the broader population of Galilee. At least one early reader of Mark understood the great multitude from Galilee of Mark 3:7 as "a great crowd of his disciples" and maintained a Galilean venue for the great crowd who came to hear Jesus *from* all Judea and Jerusalem and *from* the seacoast of Tyre and Sidon (Luke 6:17).[46] The mention of a crowd coming to Jesus from *Idumaea* has great significance for Kotansky, for he claims that the unmentioned individual cities of Idumaea would have included Gaza, Ascalon, Azotus,[47] Joppa and Jamnia,[48] important centers of early Christianity mentioned in the Acts of the Apostles. However, none of these former Philistine coastal cities were ever considered part of Idumaea,[49] whose principal cities, according to literary sources, included Hebron, Marisa, Adora and Betabris.[50] Nevertheless, Kotansky is probably on the right track in detecting a

---

44 The term used is ἠκολούθησεν, which Mark tends to reserve for serious followers of Jesus.

45 E. Lohmeyer, *Das Evangelium des Markus* (Göttingen: Vandenhoeck & Ruprecht, 1959) 72.

46 The parallels in Matthew and Luke differ from Mark 3:7–8. Matt 4:25 reads "Great crowds followed him from Galilee and the Decapolis and Jerusalem and Judea and from beyond the Jordan" (omitting Mark's mention of Idumea and Tyre and Sidon, but including the Decapolis). Luke 6:17 omits mentions of crowds from Galilee, Idumea, and beyond the Jordan.

47 Azotus, the Greek name of the Phoenician city Ashdod, had an inland city center called *Azotus Mesogaios* or Ashdod and a coastal center known as *Azotus Paralius* or Ashdod-Yam.

48 The inland city of Jamnia or Yavneh (Jabneel) also had a coastal center at Yavneh-Yam.

49 Gaza, Azotus and Jamnia are excluded from Idumea in 1 Macc 4:15 (= Josephus *Ant.* 12.308 and Josephus *Ant.* 13.395), while the Judaeans, Idumaeans, Gazaeans and Azotians are distinguished in Strabo 16.2.2.

50 Josephus *Ant.* 12.353; 13.207, 257; *Bell.* 1.63.

Christian motivation for inserting the list of regions and cities in Mark 3:7, which probably has less to do with the origins of the followers of the historical Jesus,[51] than it does with the Jewish areas in which sizable Christian groups existed when the Gospel of Mark was compiled.[52]

With Jesus situated near the Mediterranean coast in Mark 3:7 and 4:1, according to Kotansky, when he says to his disciples "let us go to the other side" (Mark 4:35), "the reader is prepared for a large sea-crossing—or a series of them—not a mere jaunt across a lake."[53] However, at least one early reader of Mark understood the phrase "let us go to the other side" to mean "let us go across to the other side *of the lake*" (Luke 8:22; here λίμνη can only refer to Lake Kinneret). Similarly, when it is said that "they came to the other side of the sea, to the country of the Gerasenes" (Mark 5:1), Luke again understands the venue to be the trans-Jordan, for he adds "which is opposite Galilee" (8:26). Luke 9:10 places the feeding of the 5,000 in Bethsaida, a place-name which Luke probably derived from Mark 6:45,[54] the first verse of Luke's so-called Big Omission of Mark 6:45–8:26, though Bethsaida in Mark 6:45 is where the disciples head *after* the feeding of the 5,000 (even though, according to Mark 6:53, they arrive at Gennesaret). As noted above, Capernaum is their destination in the Johannine parallel (John 6:17).[55] At the conclusion of the story of the exorcism of the Gerasene demoniac (Mark 5:1–20), it is said that the exorcised man "began to proclaim in the *Decapolis* how much Jesus had done for him (Mark 5:20).[56] This mention of the Decapolis (notably absent from Matthew and Luke) clearly indicates that Mark has situated the story of the Gerasene demoniac east of Galilee. However, just because Matthew and Luke, as well as Mark himself, placed the two pre-Markan miracle

---

[51] The view of Schmidt (*Der Rahmen*, 106).

[52] Lohmeyer, *Das Evangelium des Markus*, 72; Marxsen, *Der Evangelist Markus*, 39.

[53] However, by referring to "the *reader*," Kotansky has again apparently moved from pre-Markan tradition to the context of the final redaction of Mark.

[54] J. A. Fitzmyer, *The Gospel According to Luke (I-IX)* (AB 28; Garden City, NY: Doubleday, 1981) 765.

[55] This suggests that the version of Mark used by Luke read "Bethsaida" in Mark 6:45.

[56] Both Gerasa and Gadara were generally counted among the Greek cities of the Decapolis (see Pliny *Hist. Nat.* 5.74, where "Galasa" is usually emended to "Gerasa" [modern Jerash]).

collections (or whichever parts of the collections Matthew and Luke reproduced) in the geographical context of Lake Kinneret does not necessarily mean that the same must be said for the pre-Markan collections. However, the case for placing the pre-Markan catenae in a Lake Kinneret setting is strengthened by the Johannine Signs Source, in which two of the miracle stories of the pre-Markan miracle catenae, the feeding of the 5,000 (John 6:1–14; parallel to Mark 6:34–44) followed by the story of Jesus walking on the water (6:16–21; parallel to Mark 6:45–51), exhibit no signs of literary dependence on Mark (or the other Synoptic Gospels) even though the sequence is identical.[57] Moreover, the Fourth Evangelist situates the two connected miracle stories on "the other side of the Sea of Galilee, which is the Sea of Tiberias" (John 6:1).

IV. Crossing the Sea: Gadeira or Bust

Gadeira, the Greek name for the Phoenician city Gadir (founded in the eighth century), called Gades by the Romans (modern Cádiz), is located on a promontory (originally an island; cf. Pliny *Hist. Nat.* 4.119–20) on the west coast of the Iberian peninsula just northwest of the Strait of Gibraltar. Kotansky argues that "Gadeira" is the toponym that originally stood in Mark 5:1 as the destination of Jesus and his disciples and that the toponyms now found in the variants, whether "Gerasenes" (the reading preferred by all modern critical editions of the Greek New Testament)[58] or the more weakly attested "Gadarenes"

---

[57] Dodd, *Historical Tradition in the Fourth Gospel,* 211; Smith, *Clement of Alexandria and a Secret Gospel of Mark,* 158–63. The two stories are linked in very similar ways in Mark and John. In Mark, the feeding of the 5,000 is linked to the story of Jesus walking on the water by Mark 6:45–46, which narrates the intended return of the disciples by boat to Bethsaida (which Kotansky suggests is a gloss; they actually land at Gennesaret according to Mark 6:53), while Jesus himself dismissed the crowd and went to a mountain to pray. In John, the same two stories are linked by 6:15 in which Jesus, aware that the crowd intended to make him king, withdrew alone to a mountain.

[58] The parallel to Mark 5:1, Matthew 8:28, reads "Gadarenes" for Mark's "Gerasenes," which is generally regarded as an attempt to correct Mark, since Gerasa was located thirty-seven miles south southeast of Lake Kinneret. Gadara, the toponym substituted by Matthew, is five miles southeast of Lake Kinneret on the ruins of the Umm Qeis (E. M. Meyers, ed., *The Oxford Encyclopedia of Archaeology in the Near East* [5 vols.; New York: Oxford University Press, 1997] 5. 281–82). Its territory formed the eastern boundary of Galilee (Josephus *Bell.* 3.37) and

or "Gergesenes" etc., are all later attempts to historicize an embarrassing mythical geography. Since most scholars agree that Matthew used Mark, Kotansky insists that Matthew must have read "Gadarenes" in Mark 5:1,[59] which was itself a very early historicizing correction of his preferred but unattested original reading "Gadeirenes." Of course, one cannot be sure that the version of Mark used by Matthew was identical with canonical Mark (although in my view "Gerasenes" was probably the original reading in Mark 5:1, since it is reproduced in Luke 8:26). "Gadarenes" in Matt 8:28 is generally considered to be a correction of Mark by the First Evangelist, who knew that Gerasa could not have been the scene of the story of the Gerasene Demoniac. The Semitic stem גדר (with the basic meaning "build a wall," hence "fortress") was used as the name for many ancient Semitic towns,[60] and there is often a great deal of confusion in the identification of these towns.[61]

---

probably extended to Lake Kinneret, a conclusion suggested by Matt 8:28 and the existence of coins from Gadara depicting a ship; E. Schürer, *The History of the Jewish People in the Age of Jesus Christ* (rev. and ed. G. Vermes, F. Millar and M. Black; 3 vols.; Edinburgh: T. & T. Clark, 1973–87) 2. 132–33). Both Gadara and Gerasa were included in lists of cities making up the Decapolis (Pliny *Hist. Nat.* 5.74; with the non-existent "Gelasa" emended to "Gerasa"). The Lukan parallel to Mark 5:1 takes over the Markan toponym "Gerasencs," and further specifies it as "opposite Galilee" (Luke 8:26).

[59] This is, of course, an extremely rigid approach to the complex problem of how Matthew and Luke used Mark and why they omitted, changed and transposed material found in Mark.

[60] These include Geder, one of thirty-one cities of the Canaanites conquered by the Israelites (Josh 12:13); Gederah, a town in the lowland of Judah (Josh 15:36; 1 Chron 4:23); Gederoth, a town in the lowland of Judah (Josh 15:41; 2 Chr 28:18); Gederthaim, a town in the lowland of Judah (Josh 15:36); and Gedor = Khir bet Jedur (Josh 15:58), a town in the hill country of Judah.

[61] For example, in *Ant.* 14.91, Josephus includes "Gadara" on a list of five administrative districts, although this is almost certainly an error for "Gazara." Gaza, the southernmost of five principal Phoenician cities widely known by that name in antiquity (Diodorus 19.59.2; Strabo 19.59.2; 19.80.5; Arian *Anabasis* 2.26–27; Strabo 16.2.21; Josephus *Ant.* 13.215 [*var. lect.*]), was also known as Gazara (1 Macc 13:43, 53; 14:34; Josephus *Ant.* 13.215). Gazara was occasionally called Gadara (Strabo 16.2.29 [*Gadaris* is located on the coast before Azotus and Ascalon]; 16.2.45; Josephus *Ant.* 12.308 [*var. lect.*]), probably in error. This is complicated by the fact that the ancient city of Gezer (Josh 21:21; 1 Kgs 9:15, 17) was also called Gazara (1 Macc 4:15; 9:52; Josephus *Ant.* 13.261; *Bell.* 1.50) and occasionally also Gadara (Josephus *Ant.* 14.91), unless this too is an error, while

Kotansky tries to substantiate his proposal by observing that the destinations of Jesus and his disciples, when traveling by boat, do not accord with the known geography of the region surrounding the Sea of Galilee: (1) Does Jesus land at Gerasa, Gadara, Gergesa or somewhere else in 5:1 (Mark 5:1 reads "Gerasenes," while Matt 8:28 reads "Gadarenes," and Luke 8:26 reads, with Mark, Gerasenes)? (2) Where does Jesus make landfall when he comes again to the other side in 5:21 (the text simply reads "And when Jesus had crossed again to the other side")? (3) Do the disciples sail "to the other side, to Bethsaida" as Mark 6:45 has it (εἰς τὸ πέραν πρὸς βηθσαϊδάν) or to "the Beyond" (εἰς τὸ πέραν) as the parallel in Matt 14:22 reads?[62] (4) Where is the Dalmanoutha mentioned in Mark 8:10 (called Magadan in Matt 15:39)? These are some, though not all, of the indications of geographical confusion in Mark, who appears to have retained toponyms which he found in the traditions he used, even though he was apparently not personally familiar with the geography of Galilee.[63] Kotansky then concludes that there was an attempt by later editors, perhaps Mark himself, to harmonize the fabulous lands of the collection of miracle stories with the known topography of Palestine.

When examined closely, Kotansky argues, the various features of the stories in Mark 4:35–5:43, which make little sense in a Galilean geographical context, suddenly make sense when read as references to the geography and associated mythology of Iberian Gadeira. Kotansky claims that Gadeira, as well as the western limits of the Mediterranean, continued into late antiquity to represent a mysterious realm beyond known reality,[64] a kind of mythic Land of the Dead. The Pillars of Heracles, or Strait of Gibraltar, he reminds us, marked the threshhold of the known world in post-Homeric Greek literature. Attempts to go farther than the Strait are motivated by excessive pride in mortals, for only heroes and divine figures could sail to the ends of the earth and return safely again. In the expedition narrated in Catena I, he

---

Gadara was also the name of a city in the Decapolis (Josephus *Bell.* 1.86, 155, 170) and a city in Perea, earlier Gilead (Josephus *Bell.* 4.413; Schürer, *The History of the Jewish People*, 1. 268, n. 5; 2. 134–36).

[62] The translation of εἰς τὸ πέραν as "to the Beyond" is only a remote possibility.

[63] Pesch, *Das Markusevangelium*, 1. 10.

[64] For this he cites Pind. *Nem.* 4.69–70 and Strabo 3.1.8; 3.5.5.

maintains, Jesus sails west to the limits of the known world and crosses mystically into the underworld (suggested by the toponym "Gadeira"), just as Odysseus crossed over the stream Ocean to the underworld. In fact, he maintains, the pre-Markan catenae narratives were modeled after a voyage like that of Odysseus or the Argonauts. Themes of death dominate the narrative in 4:35–5:43, including the beginning of the voyage at nightfall, Jesus sleeping in the boat, the sea symbolizing the waters of death, the demoniac who comes from the tombs, to name a few. He construes the miracle of the Stilling of the Storm (Mark 4:35–40) as the motif of the mystic calm which is a prelude to the arrival in mythical places where normal geographies do not obtain (here Kotansky depends heavily on sequences of motifs from the Odyssey). The story of the exorcism of the demoniac (Mark 5:1–20), like some of Odysseus' adventures, he believes, can be more appropriately set on the island of Gadeira near the Strait of Gibraltar. While there are no cliffs on the eastern shore of Lake Kinneret,[65] on the Iberian island of Gadeira itself, there were steep cliffs running to the edge of the shore, the presence of flocks and herds (including pigs), cliff-side house-tombs (on the island of Cotinussa) and other features, all of which combine to suggest that Iberian Gadeira fits the topography of Mark 5:1–20 better than does the geography on the east shore of Lake Kinneret. The pigs in Mark 5:1–20 have replaced cattle in the earlier version of the mythic narrative, for pigs are not raised in large herds, certainly not herds of 2,000, and do not easily drown—all pertinent observations which nearly all commentators have missed. Further, the presence of the temple of the Tyrian deity Melqart-

[65] Contrary to what Kotansky maintains, there is a wide, relatively steep cliff at one place on the eastern shore, near modern El Koursi, identified by some as "Gergesa," a variant of "Gerasenes" in Mark 5:1 which appears to have been suggested first by Origen (B. M. Metzger, *A Textual Commentary on the Greek New Testament* [2d. ed.; Stuttgart: Deutsche Bibelgesellschaft, 1994] 72), who claims to have visited Gergesa and to have seen a steep area which drops down to the lake (*Comm. in. Ioh.* 6.24), though this resolution of Mark's geographical error is hardly satisfactory. Kotansky claims that the only cliff-like formations are on the western shore of Lake Kinneret to the north and south of Tiberias, and cites the aerial photographs in R. Cleave, "Satellite Revelations: New Views of the Holy Land," *National Geographic* 187.6 (1995) 89 (overleaf), as proof. However, the satellite photo referred to was taken some miles east of Lake Kinneret and shows only the topography of the west shoreline, not the east shoreline.

Heracles at Gadeira (actually on the island of Cotinussa where the cemetery is located), with its swine taboo and close association with the labors of Heracles, provides a wealth of local mythological associations for victorious struggles with monsters and symbolic conquests of death and the underworld. Kotansky claims that the prohibition against eating and sacrificing swine were Semitic customs and that the latter would be particularly difficult (if not impossible) for a Greek to understand.[66] Kotansky focuses on the relevance of the tenth labor, the struggle with Geryon, an archtypal strong-man with a triple body, who owned a fabulous herd of cattle, tended by a herdsman and Orthros, a two-headed dog. Heracles kills him and drives off his cattle. For Kotansky, Jesus himself is a Herculean hero who defeats a man too strong to be confined by chains. Further, stories of wild, naked, stone-throwing people dwelling on cliffs are reported in accounts of voyages along the coast of Africa from the fourth century BCE, encouraging comparison with the Gerasene Demoniac.[67]

There is, of course, an entirely different way of assessing the "evidence" which Kotansky has presented for this final phase of his Gadeiran hypothesis. First, despite the author's claim that "Gadeira was a kind of mythic Land of the Dead," he cites no ancient text which substantiates that judgment. The earliest text he cites is Pind. *Nem.* 4.69 from the early fifth century: "No man may pass what lies to the sunset beyond Gadeira." This text is apparently a mythic fragment used to underline the point that the achievements of the house of Peleus are beyond detailed consideration.[68] In this mythic fragment,

[66] There were, however, wide variations in Greek sacrificial protocol, and there is some evidence to indicate that the sacrifice of pigs was generally taboo in cults of Aphrodite, who apparently preferred goats. Texts include the explicit prohibition of sacrificing pigs to Aphrodite in the Corinthian περίβολος, mentioned by Pausanias 2.10.5 and referred to generally in Aristoph. *Ach.* 793: "A pig is no sacrifice to Aphrodite!"). However, Athenaeus quotes the testimony of Callimachus or Zenodotus to the effect that the people of Argos sacrificed pigs to Aphrodite at a festival called Ὑστήρια (*Deipn.* 3.96), though this may be based on a pun involving the word μυστήρια.

[67] The recent article by G. Mobley is a reminder that the motif of the "wild man," which is certainly present in Mark 5:1–20, is as common in the eastern Mediterranean world as it is in the west ("The Wild Man in the Bible and the Ancient Near East," *JBL* 116 [1997] 217–33).

[68] Translation by C. M. Bowra, *Pindar* (Oxford: Clarendon, 1964).

Gadeira *itself* is not the Land of the Dead, but rather represents the limits of the known world, a view also preserved in Kotansky's references to Strabo (born ca. 64 BCE), who speaks of Gadeira as "situated at the extremeties of the earth" (3.1.8) and as the "limits of the inhabited world" (3.5.5), since west of there is the boundless ocean. In Strabo's discussion of the geography of Spain (Book 3), he provides detailed discussions of Gadeira and environs several times, but provides no indication whatsoever that Gadeira was "emblematic of a mysterious realm beyond known reality," a view which continued into late antiquity, according to Kotansky. The author, in fact, does not provides us with a scintilla of literary evidence to support his assertion that Gadeira was "a kind of mythic Land of the Dead." As for the presence of flocks and herds and steep cliffs on Gadeira, and tombs on nearby Continussa, how rare are these phenomena in the Mediterranean world? And, as far as the cult of Melqart-Herakles is concerned, the region of Tyre is the place of its origin.[69] Furthermore, the many journeys of individuals and groups to the realm of the dead in Mediterranean mythologies unfailingly make it perfectly obvious to the hearers and readers that a perilous visit to the dreaded underworld is in view, yet the stories in Mark 4:35–5:43 require allegorical manipulation to elicit such an underworld journey.

The positive arguments for understanding Mark 4:35–5:43, even in its hypothetical pre-Markan form, as set in a Lake Kinneret context still seem to me to be compelling. First, to suggest that references to the "Decapolis" (Mark 5:20), "Bethsaida" (Mark 6:45) and "the Sea of Galilee and the Decapolis" (Mark 7:31) are later glosses, while not impossible, is a bit too convenient. Further, the association of the stories in Mark 6:30–52 in the pre-Markan catenae with Lake Kinneret finds support in the similar setting of the parallel pre-Johannine stories in John 6:1–21. While Kotansky is correct in exposing the many Markan geographical blunders, socio-cultural contradictions and possible symbolic features in the narrative in Mark 4:35–5:43, it is simply misguided to press for geographical and historical accuracy by changing the venue to Iberian Gadeira. Rather, the simplest

---

[69] C. Bonnet, *Melqart: cultes et mythes de l'Héraclès tyrien en Méditerranée* (Studia Phoenicia 8; Leuven: Peeters, 1988); D. E. Aune, "Heracles," *Dictionary of Demons in the Bible* (ed. K. van der Toorn et al.; Leiden: Brill, 1995) 765–72.

explanation for Mark's location of that story in the region of Gerasa is that, in the tradition available to him, the exorcism of the demoniac was associated with Gerasa (which Mark correctly associated with the Decapolis, according to 5:20), though Mark wanted to link it with the fantastic story of the destruction of the herd of pigs in the sea (5:11–13), apparently to connect this miracle with the cycle of stories centering on Lake Kinneret.[70] Further, the political features of the story of the demoniac in Mark 5:1–20 are difficult to ignore.[71] The tensions between the Gentile inhabitants of the Decapolis and the Jews provide a possible vantage point from which to interpret the story. The demon who reveals that his name is "legion," that is, representing an entire Roman army, wants to stay in the land it occupies (5:10). This "legion" of demons is driven into the sea (perhaps symbolic for the underworld), reflecting the Jewish desire to drive the Romans out of the land. The Roman tenth legion Fretensis, stationed in Syria from 6 BCE on, and in Judaea following the first Jewish revolt, had the image of a boar on its standards and seals. These are just a few of the considerations which suggest the appropriate setting of Mark 4:35–5:43 within the vicinity of Lake Kinneret.

V. Conclusion

While Kotansky has presented us with a boldly innovative and creative reading of Mark 4:35–5:43 and supported it with great erudition, the details of his proposal simply do not hold up to critical scrutiny. The author has, however, rightly exposed a number of features of the Markan narrative, many of which appear rooted in pre-Markan miracle collections, which do not cohere well with the known geography and socio-cultural features of the eastern shore of Lake Kinneret during the first century CE. The geographical confusion in Mark is of course well known. But some of the phenomena pointed out by Kotansky, such as the impossibility of a herd of 2,000 pigs drowning in the sea, suggest an obvious symbolic meaning and need to be dealt with by future Markan commentators. Also salutary are the author's emphasis on the symbolism of death which pervades much of

---

[70] J. F. Craghan, "The Gerasene Demoniac," *CBQ* 30 (1968) 522–30; Guelich, *Mark 1–8:26*, 272–75.

[71] Following Theissen, *The Gospels in Context*, 109–112.

the narrative in Mark 4:35–5:43. While all of these supposed motifs are not equally compelling, their presence and significance must be seriously evaluated in future analyses of Mark, even though many of us might not want to travel all the way to Gadeira to find a solution to the problem.

A Case Study of Scripture and Culture: Apocalypticism as Cultural Identity in Past and Present

Ithamar Gruenwald

Preface

The pendulum that swings between the Bible and culture, the two terms used in the title of this conference, touches upon two disciplines: Religious Studies and Cultural Studies. This essay examines the possibility of engaging both disciplines in a complementary way to assess apocalypticism.

This essay also attempts to follow up on Professor Betz's article "Zum Problem des religionsgeschichtlichen Verständnisses der Apokalyptik."[1] It should be noted that he is always aware of the need to establish the *religionsgeschichtliche* context of his research and study. Professor Betz also makes his readers aware of the relevance of the study of the ancient world to the understanding and assessment of the cultural situation of our own time. This essay attempts to do the same.

The methods employed in this esay are, as noted above, those of Religious Studies and Cultural Studies.[2] It is assumed that, when

---

[1] Originally published in *ZTK* 63 (1966) 391–409; reprinted in H. D. Betz, *Hellenismus und Urchristentum: Gesammelte Aufsätze I* (Tübingen: Mohr [Siebeck], 1990) 52–71.

[2] The term "Cultural Studies" as an academic discipline has not yet received widespread recognition. What the term is intended to convey in the present context will become clear in the course of the ensuing discussion. The term "culture," however, is differently defined by various scholars. Two examples will show how complicated the issue is. Ruth Benedict in her land-mark study, *Patterns of Culture* (Boston: Houghton Mifflin, 1961), views "culture" in its diverse anthropological forms and in a framework of what is often referred to as primitive societies and religions. In other words, in comparison to the approach adopted in this essay, "culture" in Benedict's usage implies *less* than what it does here. Clifford Geertz, in his equally important *The Interpretation of Cultures* (New York: Basic, 1973), argues that religion belongs to a cultural system. In this respect, there is a basic affinity between the approach maintained here and that of Geertz: "culture" has wider terms of reference than "religion." However, unlike the approach here, in which "culture" is used of more sophisticated forms of human behaviour and

viewed from these two vantage points, the same phenomenon—apocalypticism—may be assessed in correspondingly different ways. Religious Studies examines ideas, notions, beliefs, doctrines and practices that constitute the religious life of individuals and groups, mostly in the past. Cultural Studies, however, has a different spectrum of considerations. It aims at highlighting the anthropological, social and psychological aspects of the subject matter. In many respects, cultural perspectives imply secular modes of consideration. Engaging Cultural Studies for the study of a religious phenomenon means that aspects of religious life and practice are highlighted and viewed in a different light than that of Religious Studies.

Applying, as I propose to do, these two approaches to the study of a single phenomenon—apocalypticism—is likely to result in a deeper understanding of the general implications of that phenomenon. The ontology, or epistemology, of my research is a composite one. Its point of departure is the notion that it is vital for a comprehensive assessment of religious phenomena to go beyond the basic facts and proceed to their cultural assessment, even evaluation. In other words, the critical assessment of the religious phenomenon studied here aims at drawing attention to significant aspects that do not constitute a functional part of the original phenomenon.

Let me be more specific about this issue. As will be shown, the subject of apocalypticism is likely to appear in a different light when viewed in the context of the history of religions alone, than it does when complementarily viewed in the context of Cultural Studies. That which, in the context of the study of religions, looks like a positive, driving force may have a completely different configuration, at times even negative aspects, when studied from the point of view of Cultural Studies. In the pages that follow it will be shown how this dual approach works in the study of apocalypticism.

I have chosen the subject of apocalypticism to honour my dear friend, Hans Dieter Betz. We both share a deep concern for culture and its overall sanity and sociological hygiene. It seems that there is nothing that can exemplify this concern better than the subject of apocalypticism. On the one hand, apocalypticism is the quintessence

---

expression, Geertz sees "culture" as mainly expressive of the complex of attitudes, mostly symbolic, of "primitive" societies, so called.

of hope, promise and expectation. Among other things, it intensifies and rejuvenates many utterances in scriptural prophecy about the future. It also attempts at specifying the manner in which the realization of those utterances can be contextualized historically. In doing so, apocalypticism is often described as redeeming prophecy from what may be referred to as its own failure of nerve.[3]

On the other hand, cumulative impressions gained from years of studying the relevant apocalyptic texts reveal undercurrents in which disturbing features can be discerned. Among them, one can name dualistic estrangement of the "other," the animalization of the enemy, and the radicalization of social and political issues. In themselves these features are common ways of fighting enemies. However, the apocalyptic world picture is deterministic, total and universal: it leaves no room for those who "do not belong," even when they are not actively engaged in fighting the apocalyptic groups.

Apocalypticism creates a certain type of identity. Its basic features derive from a pervasive sense of dissatisfaction with current events. In fact, it is nourished by a denial of the social and political structure of the culture-creating establishment, and may, thus, be viewed as breeding revolutionary drives. Furthermore, apocalypticism fosters feelings of frustration as well as personal and social agony. People finding nourishment in such perverse feelings abide by a nervous time table and impatiently wait for the historical enactment of these drives. This means that reasonable solutions to the prevailing situation are totally ruled out. Hence, one discovers in apocalypticism an indulgence in historical solutions that reflect a policy of intolerance. These solutions are believed to be divinely inspired and desired. Thus, effectiveness is believed to be dependent on the degree of radicalism that is reached. Other aspects of this identity that require more detailed consideration will be discussed below.

Modern forms of apocalyptic behaviour strengthen these impressions.[4] This can be explained by the fact that politics becomes the

---

[3] The subject of the crisis of unfulfilled prophecies has often been discussed in scholarly writings in its relationship to apocalypticism. Still relevant, in this respect, is P. von der Osten-Sacken, *Die Apokalyptik in ihrem Verhältnis zur Prophetie und Weisheit* (München: Kaiser, 1969).

[4] A good illustration of what I have in mind, though written from a different point of view, is Walter Burkert's comment to the effect that ". . . the religious

chief form of expression of a radical ideology that embodies the apocalyptic features mentioned above. Understandably, apocalypticism should signal a warning light to those who care. Trying to put into action an overdose of expectations in matters that require calculated reasoning and consideration is likely to result in historical hyper-activity. Apocalypticism can easily be shown to foster extreme forms of political strategy. Experience, however, shows that optimal results are seldom attained by the application of violence alone. Such results are more likely to be achieved by the application of political realism and pragmatic sophistication. However, apocalyptic drives are more likely to be linked with a paucity of these qualities than an abundance of them.

In fact, apocalypticism reveals the persistence of an ethos of violence. No wonder, then, that it is likely to create a feeling of uneasiness in critics with concern for cultural issues, such as social justice and democratic structures. On a more pragmatic level, however, apocalypticism makes the cultural critic explore in depth and detail what is likely to happen, when hope becomes a misguiding principle. In being misused, hope is likely to wind up in despair and destruction.

I

Assessing a religious phenomenon from a cultural point of view requires that the scholarly practice of focusing on the phenomenon itself be expanded so as to include a wider spectrum of considerations. Among other things, this means that one becomes intellectually more involved with the subject matter. A dominant requirement in Religious Studies is maintaining strict personal detachment. In fact, detachment is considered a *conditio sine qua non* in Religious Studies. Allegedly, it

---

forces remain unexpectedly tenacious and impetuous, nay dangerous and sometimes disastrous. We are puzzled by the drawing power of new cults and sects, we are horrified by the passions of the strife in many contemporary conflicts, we are apprehensive of the growing tide of fundamentalism in different encampments." See idem, *The Creation of the Sacred: Tracks of Biology in Early Religions* (Cambridge, MA and London: Harvard University Press, 1996) ix-x. It must be observed, though, that in light of the "biological" context as suggested by Burkert, his comments sound all the more deterministic and threatening. I am not sure that I can follow Burkert all the way, in this respect.

prevents interference of the scholar's personal convictions and beliefs with his academic interests and studies.[5] In other words, it is praised as scholarly objectivity. In a number of cases, this detachment is operative in avoiding the need to come to grips with the realities studied. The vantage point of Cultural Studies is less loaded from a confessional point of view. It, therefore, allows a less rigid attitude to establish itself in regard to the scholar's maintaining such detachment. As a result, one is unimpeded in showing a sincere intellectual concern for the cultural implications of the subject matter.

In my view of the matter, then, the scholarly assessment of apocalypticism will gain significantly from discussing it as a potentially omnipresent cultural factor.[6] The key notion here is the "omnipresence of the apocalyptic factor." It conveys a certain perception, to the effect that apocalypticism should no longer be confined to a shaded corner in the distant past, lighted only for a few curious scholars. Being confined to such a corner, apocalypticism loses much of its intellectual and, for that matter also, historical significance. Furthermore, such a corner inadvertently sanctions the kind of scholarly handling of the subject matter, according to which apocalypticism is confined to a socially isolated, that is, primarily sectarian settings.[7] Finally, such a position strengthens the view,

---

[5] The problem of the attitudes maintained by scholars in the area of Religious Studies has been discussed recently in I. Gruenwald, "The Study of Religion and the Religion of Study," *Religious Propaganda and Missionary Competition in the New Testament World: Essays Honoring Dieter Georgi* (ed. L. Bormann et al.; Leiden: Brill, 1994) 3–21.

[6] Only rarely does the study of Apocalypticism in the framework of Religious Studies receive a more widely ranging framework than the historical and philological ones. See, however, C. Rowland, *Radical Christianity* (Maryknoll, NY: Orbis, 1988), which is a rare exception to this rule. Deplorably, Rowland's book does not always receive the kind of attention it deserves in this respect.

[7] In the present discussion of sectarianism, I follow S. J. D. Cohen, *From the Maccabees to the Mishnah* (Philadelphia: Westminster, 1989) 124–173. Although I accept in principle Cohen's definition of "sect," I cannot follow his sweeping usage of the term. Cohen writes: "A sect is a small, organized group that separates itself from a larger religious body and asserts that it alone embodies the ideals of the larger group because it alone understands God's will" (ibid., 125). As will be argued below, such a definition assumes that there was a "larger group" from which a sect could differentiate itself. However, a normative kind of Judaism in the period discussed here is still an assumption and no proven fact.

frequently maintained in scholarly circles, to the effect that apocalypticism was mainly a literary phenomenon, the historical enactment of which was rare. As will be shown, apocalypticism did not only have a strong presence in the past, but its spirit is also present in contemporary events.[8] Furthermore, its sectarian confinement is likely to downgrade its overall presence and impact.

In short, the common approach to the study of apocalypticism—chiefly stressing qualities of literary genre, utopian or inert ideas, and a sectarian setting—all too often sidetracks cultural issues that are vital for its comprehensive assessment as a phenomenon with a real historical presence. To me, then, the intellectual challenge of studying apocalypticism now lies in realizing its various manifestations in their pervasive omnipresence and as dynamic cultural factors in the past as well as in the present. The implications that this approach has for the assessment of the apocalyptic phenomenon in general seems to be of a decisive nature.[9]

In the eyes of its own advocates, however, apocalypticism singularly signals the great historical chance of social change and progress. It stimulates people to engage in something that is tantamount to the total annihilation of the powers of evil, often detected in the oppositional "other" and the corrupted worldly regime. However, the student of culture who reflects on the nature of apocalypticism is likely to see in it something different from what is usually presented in modern studies. This student is likely to notice different aspects and shaded corners, the existence of which is neither readily admitted by the advocates of apocalypticism, nor quickly recognized as such by scholars of Religious Studies. In short, he may see in apocalypticism anomalies of historical behaviour that are seldom discussed in scholarly writings.

There are several features that justify the manner in which the student of culture is likely to see apocalypticism. For this student, apocalypticism figures as the ideological platform that calls for waging

---

[8] A recent and notable exception to that rule is J. Marcus, "Modern and Ancient Jewish Apocalypticism," *JR* 76 (1996) 1–27. See also I. Gruenwald, "Apocalypticism, Mysticism, Messianism and Political Assassination," *Criterion* 35 (1996) 11–17.

[9] See also the interesting comments of C. Rowland, *Radical Christianity*, 66–88.

a holy war. Holy wars, against whomever they are fought, crystallize in non-negotiable settings. Usually, no compromises are conceivable in such settings. People are convinced that God is behind their cause and that His name can invest their banners with special powers. The Qumran "War of the Sons of Light against the Sons of Darkness" is apocalyptically modelled and may serve as an apocalyptic text-book for every interested student.[10] In spite of their aims as holy wars they can easily change their course and become an uncontrolled outburst of chaotic impulses. Consequently, disorientation and the loss of the pre-set tracks of redemptive functions are likely to replace every single bit of hope that apocalypticism is likely to imbue in its advocates.

The student of culture is likely to be struck by the fact that such wars, that so often lead to self-destruction, are formally and theologically sanctioned as divinely inspired. The ideology of divine vengeance upsets the notion that wars should be fought only to guarantee physical and territorial existence. The setting of a holy war may be viewed by the outsider as vainly glorifying the commitment to seek extreme forms of behaviour, such as martyrological self-destruction. In any event, the notion of the eschatological holy war has become emblematic of the whole apocalyptic setup. Naturally, the cultural critic hits the nail on the head when raising the question of the price versus the rather speculative gains of such wars.[11]

We live at the turn of the twentieth century. We have seen many wars and revolutions that started as historical necessity. They often began in loud declarations, advocating the good that lies in store for those who are willing to sacrifice all and everything. However, the subsequent developments and the final outcome tell a totally different story. In this story, the destruction that was conceived as an inevitable tool, or tactics, in the annihilation of evil often becomes an end in itself in which the acquisition of power rather than the annihilation of evil is the main driving force. Destruction never has pre-set boundaries that can effectively prevent the destroyers from turning against

---

[10] Aspects of holy war are discussed by G. von Rad, *Holy War in Ancient Israel* (Grand Rapids: Eerdmans, 1991 [with an updated bibliography by J. E. Sanderson]).

[11] See A. Yarbro Collins, *Crisis and Catharsis: The Power of the Apocalypse* (Philadephia: Westminster, 1984), esp. 84–140.

themselves. It can be stopped only after self-destruction has set in. In this respect, the twentieth century was one of the most apocalyptic centuries in human history.

Looking back, one can hardly avoid noticing that the apocalyptic events in our century demanded an atrociously high price. In fact, their constructive potentials were quickly shown to be self-deception. They were totally submerged in their own destructive impulses. In other words, since the forces set free in the apocalyptic outbursts of violence can hardly be contained in their alleged potentials as corrective and redeeming factors, cultural criticism has to set in and pronounce its verdict in prophetic words of condemnation.

II

Leaving cultural criticism aside for a moment, some of the major questions that bear on the study of apocalypticism as a religious factor are:

(1) What are the source materials and the historical circumstances that contributed to the shaping of apocalypticism? This question will not be addressed here.

(2) What did apocalypticism accomplish for its advocates that either was not or could not be accomplished in the framework of the then established forms of religious notions and practiced ritual? In other words,

(3) What did apocalypticism add to the so-called mother religion, in our case scriptural Judaism?

Connected to these questions is:

(4) In what ways did apocalypticism contribute to the shaping of subsequent, not specifically apocalyptic, attitudes of Judaic religiousness?

To me, these questions constitute the central issues in the study of apocalypticism as a religious factor. In other words, these are major issues in the study of apocalypticism from the point of view of Religious Studies.

Related to the above is the question,

(5) What forms did ancient apocalypticism take on in the course of history? I shall address this question in connection with a few modern manifestations of apocalypticism.

Since, as will be shown, apocalypticism participates in the shaping of the religion in which it grows, it also plays an important role in shaping the cultural layout of the people concerned. The question in this connection is:

(6) Aside from its religious configuration, what kind of cultural identity did apocalypticism create?

Culture, as has been shown, means aspects of life and behaviour that are not necessarily related to, and shaped so as to achieve, religious goals. Culture is here viewed in wider terms of reference than religion. In general terms, culture is a multi-structured system of socially-centred components that, functionally speaking, are cross-referential in shaping the existence and the forms of self-identification of individuals and groups. Religion is part of culture and adds unique ideological and ritual (or cultic) elements to it. It creates a transformative context the main components of which are oriented towards achieving modes of existence that allegedly are either directed by or relating to God.

Since the social layout connected with apocalypticism is a key issue in the latter's formation, the questions to be asked are:

(7) Socially speaking, can one identify certain types of people that are more inclined than others either to create or adapt apocalyptic views and forms of expression?

(8) Does apocalypticism represent a mainstream or a sectarian type of religiousness?

The last questions will receive intensive attention in the present essay.

There are a few more questions that scholars dealing with apocalypticism from the point of view of Religious Studies have to consider. Since the space at my disposal is not unlimited, questions, for instance, of historical affiliation and development, as also of cultural contextualization, will be avoided in the present essay. These questions will receive proper attention in a separate study.

Speaking of apocalypticism, attention has evidently to be given to the life of the people concerned. In other words, philological and text-historical questions will not be the major concern here, but issues that shed light on people's life and culture. Since apocalypticism played an important role in the shaping of subsequent forms of Judaism (and Christianity), I shall avoid viewing it, as is often the case in scholarly writings, in a primarily sectarian setting. The sectarian aspects of apocalypticism are often viewed as its most striking feature.[12] The extent to which this assumption is correct cannot be discussed at length in the present context. However, there are good reasons to believe that apocalypticism was not primarily sectarian.

Briefly, our knowledge of the labeled social and ideological stratification of the Judaic world in pre-Christian times is largely dependent on Philo, Flavius Josephus and the New Testament. When the Dead Sea Scrolls had become known, they were immediately interpreted as confirming that particular way of understanding. The information contained there was immediately compared to that found in the Apocrypha and Pseudepigrapha to the effect that similarities could easily be pointed out. Doubtlessly, there are writings like those found in the Qumran library that are basically inspired by a sectarian spirit.[13] Several apocalyptic writings, too, convey notions of exclusive election of at least a certain fraction of the people. The sectarian implications of these materials cannot be overlooked. In addition, the famous calendric differences, so emphatically maintained in the groups in question, evidently contributed to notions of sectarian separatism.

However, the absolute confidence maintained in scholarly writings in regard to the sectarian nature of apocalypticism cannot go undisputed. One has, for instance, to admit that essential parts of the Qumran library, as also a few apocalyptic writings (for example, *Jubilees*), are clearly non-sectarian. Similarly, the implications of the alleged prevalence of the lunar calendar over against the allegedly sectarian solar-lunar calendar are to an essential extent dependent on the assumption that the lunar calendar of rabbinic Judaism as advocated in the Mishnah and Talmud was always the normatively prevailing one. Dialectically speaking, however, one may argue that it was the lunar calendar that was adopted for polemical reasons, rather

---

[12] See, for instance, D. Dimant, "Qumran Sectarian Literature," *Jewish Writings of the Second Temple Period* (ed. Michael E. Stone; Assen: Van Gorcum, 1984) 483–549. For a recent discussion of the sociological background of apocalyptic groups, see S. L. Cook, *Prophecy and Apocalypticism: The Post Exilic Social Setting* (Minneapolis: Fortress, 1995). In several respects Cook's book comes close to our line of argumentation, though in the final resort he sticks to the group [basically, sectarian] theory.

[13] The sect's *Rule* is a notable example to that effect.

than the other way around. The solar calendar was widely maintained in the Ancient Near East. Thus, one may argue that the lunar calendar was introduced by certain groups in ancient Israel as a polemical substitute in the cultural war waged against Ancient Near Eastern "idolatry."[14]

As noted above, special attention is given in the present essay to the chaotic and uncontrolled aspects of apocalypticism. In this respect, it seems safe to say that these aspects were mainly found where sectarian concerns prevailed. In other words, notions of sociological marginality enhance drastic, hence apocalyptic, solutions. However, since apocalypticism played a substantially constructive role in the shaping of the Judaic world view in the Second Temple period and thereafter, it is inconceivable that sectarianism was its only sociological setting. The opposite must be true. Essential components of Rabbinic Judaism in the Mishnah period were indebted to their "forerunners" as developed in the framework of Apocalypticism. To repeat, it is quite inconceivable that these components, to which more attention will be given below, are by and large attributable to a sectarian dynamic.

III

Scholars have studied extensively the various features that constitute apocalypticism as a general factor in Judaic religiosity. Viewed from a religious angle, apocalypticism suggests a purposeful structure conducive to the fulfillment of the yearning towards experiencing the divine and building a social structure that precipitates the coming of the eschatological era. As a cultural phenomenon, though, more complex issues come into play.

One aspect of apocalypticism has so far received insufficient attention in scholarly writings. It concerns the dynamics of substitution. It should be noted, though, that substitutional factors had occupied the centre of the religious scene in Judaism long before apocalypticism as

---

[14] One cannot altogether rule out the possibility that two different types of calendar simultaneously prevailed in ancient Israel, though for different purposes. In other words, reading Philo and other authors as if truthfully reflecting a pervasive type of social and ideological stratification, is not overwhelmingly corroborated by the evidence at our disposal. Since the issue is not central to our line of argumentation here, we shall leave it at this point.

a movement or special ideology came into being.[15] They also persisted long after apocalypticism had ceased to be the dominant form of expression that it used to be.[16]

Henceforth, we shall focus on the element of substitution. It will receive full attention in the framework of two major forms of discourse, the "discourse of interpretation" and the "discourse of visions." One famous example of the "discourse of interpretation" is Torah-study and its institutionalization after the destruction of the Second Temple and the cessation of its sacrificial rites. However, as Professor Michael Fishbane has convincingly shown,[17] several parts of Scripture (for example, Deuteronomy and Chronicles) evolved in the context of scriptural interpretation. In many of these cases, inner-scriptural interpretation attempted to create alternative versions of scriptural passages. It substituted one literary unit with another. Arguably, then, interpretation became part of the process of creating the scriptural canon! It seems safe to say that full justice cannot be done to interpretation, and particularly to its radical nature, unless its substitutional qualities are properly highlighted. In the final analysis, though, every interpretation—including, for that matter, the simple exegetical work—has a certain tendency to substitute its interpretation for the text.[18]

Substitutional factors are not necessarily geared towards negative ends. This is certainly the case, when exegetical work is done with no manipulative aims in mind.[19] As mentioned above, it is often argued

---

[15] The various aspects of substitution in scriptural Judaism—in a sacrificial context—are discussed in J. D. Levenson, *The Death and Resurrection of the Beloved Son: The Transformation of Child Sacrifice in Judaism and Christianity* (New Haven and London: Yale University Press, 1993) 43–52.

[16] See the discussion of M. Fishbane, *The Kiss of God: Spiritual and Mystical Death in Judaism* (Seattle and London: University of Washington Press, 1994) 87–124.

[17] See M. Fishbane, *Biblical Interpretation in Ancient Israel* (Oxford: Clarendon, 1985).

[18] See I. Gruenwald, "Midrash and 'The Midrashic Condition:' Preliminary Considerations," *The Midrashic Imagination: Jewish Exegesis, Thought and History* (ed. M. Fishbane; Albany, NY: State University of New York Press, 1993) 6–22.

[19] One may, of course, argue that delimiting manipulative aims is tantamount to subjective criticism. It is indeed difficult to tell when exegesis is breaking the rules of the game, since those rules are arbitrarily set by an interested audience. It may be argued that *bona fide* intentions, tact, and disinterest in polemical stances are the major components of a non-manipulative type of exegesis.

that when the Second Temple had been destroyed, Torah-study—like its counterpart, prayer—became a substitutional institution in the religious life of the people. To begin with, there is plenty of evidence for the conclusion that Torah-study was a well established institution with substitutional dimensions long before the destruction of the Jerusalem Temple. This was the case in the Diaspora or else in circles that opposed the Jerusalem priesthood and Temple. These circles were not necessarily sectarian. Opposition to the Temple should not automatically be identified as a sectarian activity. Admittedly, people opposing the Temple may easily find themselves marginalized by the cult-oriented establishment. Understandably, this is likely to prepare the way for sectarian clustering, but does not necessarily do so. If, as suggested above, apocalypticism, too, is not by definition sectarian, then the whole process of institutionalizing the substitutional functions of Torah-study in an apocalyptic, as later on in a rabbinic, milieu is not necessarily embedded in sectarian thinking.

One further question to be considered at this point is: if the substitutional dimensions of Torah-study—so articulately professed by the Qumran people—had really been sectarian, as some would argue, would the rabbis really have adopted them without risking an intellectual blunder? I incline to think that the substitutional tendencies are much more widespread than in their alleged sectarian settings. Hence, no negative aims were attached to them originally. Consequently, the rabbis could adopt them in an unhampered manner. If this is the case, then one may argue that the alleged split between the rabbis of Mishnaic times and earlier groups that were not "temple-based," was not as emphatically marked as is sometimes assumed. In fact, it may have reflected the (latent?) opposition of the Rabbis to the priests associated with the Temple, rather than to groups that were not temple oriented! Thoughts of this kind have been brought up in recent scholarship in various ways.

If the process of interpretative substitution indeed had its beginning in Scripture, the part played, in this respect, by apocalypticism may be described as its radicalization. Radicalization here means that nothing in the history of the people is optional or the result of free will and choice, not even the introduction of the substitutional process. This process reflects conditions in which the interpretative substitution was the only option given in reading

Scripture and maintaining its relevancy in a context configured by eschatological considerations. As the Qumranites put it, the very process and its various timings are pre-determined by divine will according to a secret plan, referred to as a mystery (רז) and revealed only to a select group of people.

Another aspect of this radicalization is the belief that the Torah actually belongs to a select group of "Israelites." Not every Israelite is entitled to share it. This will guarantee the fact that only those who really deserve to receive the blessings of the Torah will do so. Evidently, this notion prefigures the Pauline one regarding the "Israel according to the Spirit" that is substituted for the "Israel according to the flesh." Since the world is divided between predetermined and irreconcilable groups, ethical dilemmas involving good and evil make no sense. Every conceivable solution to the situation is envisioned as a total—and therefore merciless—annihilation of the "other." Personal and moral identity is fixed in such a manner that the notion of *teshuvah*, repentance, ceases to make sense.

On another, somewhat paradoxical, level of thinking, the interpretative dimension of apocalypticism, whether shaped as a pesher or as a narrative (*Jubilees*, *1 Enoch*), played a pivotal role in suggesting the inner dynamic of the scriptural constant. The process of reshaping, substituting, and replacing major parts of Scripture makes no sense if there is no constant that requires that process. In many cases, the results of this process were writings that received the label "pseudepigrapha." However, the term "pseudepigraphy" makes full sense only when the names of the respective "writers" in Scripture are really authentic. The question to be asked in this respect is: is the "Moses" of Scripture more real than the Moses of the pseudepigraphic writings attributed to him?[20] Hence, it is safe to conclude that "pseudepigraphy" entails no value judgement in regard to literary authenticity. At best, what it does is express the extra-canonical

[20] An interesting overview of "Moses the Pseudepigrapher at Qumran" is given by J. Strugnell in idem, "4QApocryphon of Moses[b?]," in *Qumran Cave 4: XIV, Parabiblical Texts, Part 2* (DJD 19; Oxford: Clarendon, 1995) 131–136. See also, G. W. E. Nickelsburg, ed., *Studies in the Testament of Moses* (Cambridge, MA: Society of Biblical Literature, 1973).

provenance of a certain book.[21] Still, one has to bear in mind that Pseudepigraphy is not an extra-scriptural invention. Some books in Scripture (such as Deuteronomy) are pseudepigraphs in the full sense of the term.[22] Their inclusion in the scriptural corpus saved them from the fate of pseudepigraphy![23]

In any event, the latitude created between the scriptural constant and the various modes of interpretation as formed, for instance, in apocalypticism is the space in which religious renewal and cultural change happen as an ongoing prolongation of the scriptural constant. That prolongation, organically growing out of the scriptural constant, is generally conceived as tradition. However, as has been noted above, there is always the danger of misusing interpretation for group-oriented purposes. Such misuse sows the seeds out of which the chaotic nightmares of apocalypticism grow. The nightmarish tones subdue the voices of peace that could have been heard had another type of interpretation been allowed to prevail.

This is another lesson that history teaches: the manner in which (a religious) culture develops is often dependent on the type of (scriptural) interpretation that is allowed to prevail. People tend to seek shelter for their troubled self in ways of life that are assumed to be culturally justifiable. As indicated, cultural justification—and hence identity—often amounts to adopting a specific type of interpretation or an alternate narrative that creates for the people in question their desired ideology. For instance, as a consequence of the belief in the approach of the "end of times" people are drawn towards kinds of

---

[21] See further M. Smith, "Pseudepigraphy in the Israelite Literary Tradition," *Pseudepigrapha I: Pseudopythagorica, Lettres de Platon, Litterature pseudepigraphe juive* (ed. K. von Fritz; Entretiens sur l'antiquité classique 18; Geneva: Fondation Hardt, 1972) 191–227; M. Hengel, "Anonymität, Pseudepigraphie und literarische Fälschung in der jüdisch-hellenistischen Literatur," *Judaica et Hellenistica: Kleine Schriften 1* (Tübingen: Mohr [Siebeck], 1996) 231–251.

[22] See I. Gruenwald, "Prophecy, Jewish Apocalyptic and the Problem of Uncanonical Books" in idem, *From Apocalypticism to Gnosticism* (Frankfurt am Main: Peter Lang, 1988) 13–52.

[23] The question of the canonical, or quasi-canonical, status of certain apocryphal writings has recently been brought up in scholarly writings. See, most recently, G. W. E. Nickelsburg, "Scripture in *1 Enoch* and *1 Enoch* as Scripture," *Texts and Contexts: Biblical Texts in Their Textual and Situational Contexts: Essays in Honor of Lars Hartman* (ed. T. Fornberg and D. Hellholm; Oslo: Scandinavian University Press, 1995) 333–354.

radical ideology that would sanction "apocalyptic" solutions. The cultural critic would diagnose here cases of hyper-interpretation.

However, the crust that builds around the social context in which such interpretations become possible effectively prevents the intrusion of voices that would warn against the reckless adaptation of forms of interpretation that outlaw the "other" without giving him any chance of survival. The prevailing strategy in such cases is that the "End" justifies any and every means. The urge to find in almost every word of Scripture a call for the application of aggression and destructive forces builds on radical deconstruction and verges on total anarchy. It can certainly be explained on psychological grounds. However, what matters is that psychological drives here seek and even find theological justification. When this happens, they quickly become the horror stories of humankind. The price that has to be paid in such cases is always high. It is indeed likely to affect the culture that makes such interpretations possible. The manner in which this happens will be discussed on another occasion.

In a humanistic world view, culture ideally assumes the role of the control centre in which the application of the destructive forces in human nature are put under close surveillance or else sublimated. However, uncontrolled modes of interpretation that crystallize in an "apocalyptic culture" easily transform culture and cause it to change its very essence. Such a culture quickly turns into an anti-culture. In this kind of anti-culture, nothing but self-destruction and chaos can stop the anarchic snowballing from crashing into the culture of the "other." There are indeed cases in which the student of culture cannot but perceive the revitalization of primordial chaos in the process of re-writing Scripture as accomplished in apocalypticism. Here, the story of the Flood, as told in Genesis, has prototypal functions.

IV

Another major component that shapes the unique nature of apocalypticism is the "discourse of visions." It has two principal forms of expression: visions of the heavenly court room and visions of the cosmological order. Visions of the heavenly realms were one of the basic religious experiences in apocalypticism and subsequently in

Merkavah Mysticism.[24] It has been pointed out in various ways that initially visions of the heavenly courtroom replaced the visions of God in His earthly Temple.[25] Whether this is true or not need not be discussed here. However, visions of the cosmological order have a different kind of agenda. Rather than drawing an astronomical map, they set cosmological structures for eschatological events.[26] They fix past and future events in an astronomical setting. Doing so, they determine for the apocalyptic group(s) the boundaries of their special, rather than spatial, "cosmos" of historical experience. In many cases, the context of these visions is that of the final judgment and of the eschatological, often messianic, redemption. In short, the time beat of eschatological time can be discovered in astronomy.[27]

Apocalypticism radically transforms the historical orientation and perspective of the people concerned. To use familiar terms, the "Urzeit" becomes the "Endzeit." Apocalypticism sets a time table that transforms the notion of "religious" time as maintained in Scripture. In the common religious view, time is principally structured, even consecrated, in ritual cycles. It creates the notion of "memory" and endows it with ritual qualities, or perspectives.[28] Memory principally recalls past events. In enacting memory as ritual, people are transplanted in their consciousness from their existence in the present to the past. Thus, they create a mental predisposition in which they are

---

24 The extent to which heavenly visions were also part of the scriptural milieu need not be discussed here. Elsewhere, I have pointed out that one of the distinctive characteristics of apocalypticism over against Scripture was that in Scripture visionaries are never described as ascending to heavenly realms, while in apocalypticism visionaries often experienced heavenly ascents.

25 See J. D. Levenson, "The Jerusalem Temple in Devotional and Visionary Experience," *Jewish Spirituality: From the Bible Through the Middle Ages* (ed. A. Green; London: Routledge & Kegan Paul, 1986) 32–61.

26 The most detailed scholarly discussion of this subject can be found in E. Rau, "Kosmologie, Eschatologie und die Lehrautorität Henochs," (Ph.D. diss., Hamburg, 1974).

27 The connection between astronomy, eschatology and mysticism is discussed in M. E. Stone, "Lists of Revealed Things in the Apocalyptic Literature," *Selected Studies in Pseudepigrapha and Apocrypha* (Leiden: Brill, 1991) 379–418.

28 See J. H. Yerushalmi, *Zakhor: Jewish History and Jewish Memory* (Seattle: University of Washington Press, 1982). Yerushalmi basically takes the vantage point of the historiographer. Ritual aspects receive little attention.

able to participate, naturally on a ritual level, in the events of the past.[29]

However, apocalypticism transforms notions of the past into visions of the future. Most of its interpretative work has that aim in mind. Apocalyptic visions of the future, and in this respect of the heavenly realms, too, may be described as a ritual enactment of the future performed in the present. Consequently, the apocalyptic anticipation of the *future* is endowed with a ritual dimension or function. It should be remarked, though, that this anticipation also has an element of historical evasion. Dialectically speaking, in postponing the realization of the expected changes to an indefinite future, the people involved may rid themselves of the responsibility of taking measures to change their own conditions, here and now.

The visionary experience and interpretative anticipation of the future often entail the use of figurative or allegorical language. Frequently, that language is explained as a literary device aimed at camouflaging the events and the people referred to in the visionary discourse. However, it seems to me that this process has a deeper motivation. It is embedded in yet another process of interpretative substitution. When, for instance, one year (even one day) becomes a millennium, and a week is turned into a septennium, time loses its explicit historical immediacy. When beasts stand for monarchs, a demonization of the worldly political order and the enemy sets in.[30] In both cases, a cultural atmosphere is created in which history is dehumanized.[31] In a sense, history loses touch with any specific reality. Those who think that historical events do not play into their hands

---

[29] This notion is particularly stressed in *m. Pesaḥ* 10:5: "In every generation a person is duty-bound to regard himself as if he personally has gone forth from Egypt . . . ." (English translation by J. Neusner, *The Mishnah: A New Translation* [New Haven: Yale University Press, 1988]).

[30] See, for instance, E. Pagels, "The Social History of Satan, the 'Intimate Enemy:' A Preliminary Sketch," *HTR* 84 (1991) 105–128.

[31] Attention should be drawn to the term "dehumanization." See O. y Gasset, *The Dehumanization of Art and Other Writings on Art and Culture* (Garden City, NY: Doubleday, 1956). For Ortega y Gasset "dehumanization" mainly signifies a notion characterizing aspects of artistic creation. The [modern] artist creates "unlived," and for that matter dehumanized, situations. In the present context the term has a more psychological significance. It implies a tendency towards creating a situation in which a humane, or humanistic, attitude toward man is abrogated.

lose interest in history, past and present, and invest that interest in the redemptive future. The solutions expected of the future have to match a world picture in which the enemy is depicted as a satanic demon, or is symbolically represented by an animal. In other words, the brutal aspects of some of the apocalyptic solutions match the bestial forms of behaviour of the adversaries.

What really deserves our attention is the fact that in a great number of cases apocalyptic time flows mainly in one direction: from the present to the future. In this respect, the expectation of the future is largely substituted for the memory of the past. It has been pointed out that apocalypticism entails notions of radical change. However, the past cannot be changed except by rewriting it. Changing the narrative of the past, though, does not change the present reality. Thus, the future becomes the main subject in the apocalyptic ideology of change. Visionary speculations about the prospective changes, their timing and the means of attaining them fill the pages of apocalyptic writings.

Reflecting upon, or rewriting, the past, amounts to actually inventing it.[32] Doing so, the visionaries retrospectively justify their visions of the radical changes of the future.[33] Thus, the rewriting of Scripture is functional not only in accomplishing hermeneutical stances but also in creating the historical basis for any changes in the future.[34] The history of the people of Israel is rewritten so as to

---

[32] See the interesting discussion in E. Hobsbawm and T. Ranger, *The Invention of Tradition* (Cambridge: Cambridge University Press, 1983).

[33] There are many interesting examples to that effect. In this respect, the manner in which the oral tradition of rabbinic Judaism is conceptualized is an interesting and sophisticated example. Practically speaking, it becomes an indispensable tool in reshaping, or reconstructing, the past. This is accomplished when, in rabbinic writings, the notion of the past is predominantly conceived in ritual terms. The relevancy of past events is preserved only inasmuch as it is considered as contributing to the shaping of newly shaped concepts of ritual practice and performance. In this respect, even the patriarchs—Abraham, Isaac and Jacob—are depicted as observing, if not altogether responsible for creating, the precepts of the Law, written and oral alike. Another example is the belief adopted by the early Christians in regard to the pre-existence of the Messiah: his "works" are explained as reflecting his creative essence as shaped in primordial times. Being identical to the divine Logos, he is described as participating in the creation of the world.

converge with a certain notion of the historical future.[35] In other words, it is common for people whose hopes and actions are motivated by a certain ideology to reconceptualize their perception of reality, including for that matter their own past and tradition. In short, one kind of past is made to substitute for another.

In other words, the attitude towards the past and the manner in which it is shaped in the minds of different groups represents the manner in which they conceive of their own identity. In this respect, the notion of the election of Israel is intensified in apocalypticism so as to create an identity that is shaped by dualistic dichotomization, or polarization. Conceivably, such processes are characteristic of marginalized groups, but not necessarily so.[36] Even in groups that claim to occupy the sociological centre, the so-called establishment, changes of direction, political as well as ideological, are likely to bring about changes in their respective perception of the past, and consequently of their own identity. This happens, when those changes concern the very existence of the group. In any event, those who by the merit of their own power consider themselves to be the "centre" can more easily accept the past without interfering with its official documentation. Such documentation is often treated as having scriptural status.

We have referred to the visions of the cosmological order. When viewed on a large cosmic scale, human history is somewhat deprived of its immediate social relevance. The meta-human cosmic framework contributes to depersonalizing, even dehumanizing as we said, history.[37] Consequently, aspects of the history of the past and the

---

[34] The subject of rewriting Scripture has received attention in recent scholarly writings. See, for instance, I. Gruenwald, *Apocalyptic and Merkavah Mysticism* (Leiden and Köln: Brill, 1980) 3–28; G. W. E. Nickelsburg, "The Bible Rewritten and Expanded," *Jewish Writings of the Second Temple Period*, 89–156.

[35] Obviously, the details of this assumption have to be discussed at length. However, limits of space dictate a delay of this discussion.

[36] Marginality can be either objective or subjective. In fact, many people and groups foster, so to speak, notions of marginality. The reasons for that can be various. In many cases, though, it reflects a damaged defence system or the desire to maintain it in adverse conditions.

[37] See D. Flusser, "The Fourth Empire—An Indian Rhinoceros," *Judaism and the Origins of Christianity* (Jerusalem: Magnes, 1988) 345–354; see also, ibid., 317–344. See further, D. Dimant, "The 'Pesher on the Four Periods' (4Q180) and 4Q181,"

present are likely to lose some of their authority as models. At best, history can become an anti-model. When the history of the people is viewed in the context of astronomical measurements and other cosmic powers, notions of free will and moral choice lose their personal immediacy.[38] In this connection, one should be reminded of the fact that in antiquity astronomy was not differentiated, as it is in modern science, from astrology and, for that matter, also from mythic forms of expression. This brings us back to the notion that apocalypticism is embedded in a deterministic world view. In that deterministic environment narrow margins are allowed,[39] if any, for the expression of free will and personal initiative. Even divine interference with events becomes possible only because it has been pre-programmed into the world order. This is where the notion of pre-programmed, or prefigured, "ends," most specifically maintained in several of the Qumran writings, receives special meaning. The consequences such concepts have for the possibility of maintaining a free humanistic world-view are rather disturbing, from a cultural point of view.

The deterministic world view that evolves in the framework of Apocalypticism is in many respects a novelty in Judaic thought. In the Deuteronomic world picture, the human being faces moral choices between clearly specified modes of good and evil, life and death.[40] It is made clear what God expects the human being to choose. However, in an apocalyptic setting (that is, the Qumran writings) dualism is viewed in more mythic terms. Satan and the Angel of Darkness, with all their hordes of rebellious creatures, become the order-upsetting rivals of God. They create a mythic split in the world, in which personal choices

---

Israel Oriental Studies 9 (1979) 77–102. Recently these subjects have received extensive attention in J. J. Collins, *Daniel* (Hermeneia; Minneapolis: Fortress, 1993) passim.

[38] This is certainly the case in the "Two Ways" doctrine as developed among the Qumran people. A major feature of that doctrine is its predestination. It maintains a permanent separation between the Sons of Light and the Sons of Darkness.

[39] The feeling of being constrained by time [and space] is a formative issue in the shaping of the apocalyptic *Weltanschauung*. See the interesting discussion of H. Blumenberg, *Lebenzeit und Weltzeit* (Frankfurt am Main: Suhrkamp, 1986) 71–79. I owe this reference to Professor H. D. Betz.

[40] See Deut 30:15–20. Attention should be paid to the fact that, in this passage, life and death are viewed in connection with the presence of the people of Israel in their Promised Land.

lose all their moral significance. Fighting against these mythic figures means waging a cosmic war. As indicated above, in such a setting, solutions are sought that are commensurate to the situation. Forms of extreme political activism are one aspect of this kind of cosmic war, dramatically viewed as a world conflagration.[41] Often it is enacted as a suicidal type of rebellion. The great rebellion of 66 C.E. and the Bar Kokhva war may in this respect be viewed as events motivated by an apocalyptic spirit.[42] To all familiar with the history of these events, the consequences of these wars cannot but be seen as signaling an apocalyptic catastrophe, the redeeming parts of which are almost indefinitely postponed.

In other words, there is little in the apocalyptic culture that can be viewed as historical processes of a controlled and civilized nature. Rather, it is the arena in which violence is all too readily enacted and its ethos willingly adopted. Furthermore, the separation of history from culture removes the carpet of moral responsibilities from underneath human behaviour, and carries chaotic potentials for that culture. What is meant is this. As we saw, apocalypticism preserves the relevance of the past by significantly rewriting it. Culturally speaking, then, the apocalyptic reshaping of the past can be assessed in two different ways. On the one hand, it may basically be a creative stance in the framework of which the past is constantly revived so as to maintain its live relevance to ongoing changes in historical circumstances. In particular, this is done so as to provide the needed justification for newly created forms of identity. On the other hand, one may view in the retelling of the past—actually, its invention—symptoms of (pathological) instability in maintaining cultural identity. In this respect, changing the past is indicative of a crisis that is overcome only by "forging" one's own layers of existence and identity.

Psychologically speaking, there cannot be anything as potentially threatening to culture as the voluntary rewriting of its past. Changing

---

[41] See P. van der Horst, "The Idea of Cosmic Conflagration in Hellenism, Ancient Judaism, and Early Christianity," *Hellenism—Judaism—Christianity: Essays on Their Interaction* (Kampen: Kok Pharos, 1994) 227–251.

[42] It is more common, though, to see the Bar Kokhva uprising in messianic terms. There is an often quoted saying attributed to Rabbi Akiva to the effect that Bar Kokhva was the Messiah. Other rabbinic authorities were more skeptical, or realistic, in this matter.

the past is tantamount to a process of negation and denial. Nevertheless, when this happens, the newly shaped past becomes the groundwork of a fictitiously founded cultural identity. Cultures that are fictitiously shaped—that is, cultures that are artificially severed from their real history—can easily take on any desired and selfishly chosen direction.[43] Nobody feels obliged to account, or take responsibility, for the idiosyncratic turn that history takes in the process of being arbitrarily rewritten. What matters in the eyes of those engaged in the process is the platform that is thereby created for envisioning historical programming that can be characterized by caprice and theological arbitrariness.

V

In many respects, the foregoing characterization of apocalypticism—and particularly its cultural assessment—owes many of its insights to a close examination of current events, mostly happening in today's Israel. In my view of the matter, some aspects of these events are shaped apocalyptically. This at least is the feeling many people had after the assassination of Yitzhak Rabin. In a state like Israel, stricken by conflict, the political situation easily attaches itself to extreme positions. A messianic consciousness prevails in certain groups of the population and is responsible for the ethos of violence that is their major behavioral characteristic. Violence here takes on many forms: from the vocabulary used in certain speech forms, through abrupt and arbitrary forms of thinking used in scriptural interpretation to violence enacted in street demonstrations. All these create in people a sense of nervous urgency that cannot be controlled easily by the complementary sense of historical responsibility.

In a wider spectrum, mystical—that is, Qabbalistic—notions are brought into play, too. They aggravate the situation by engaging interiorized—or spiritual—modes of religious experience on the historical—that is, external—scene. All these become the platform of political circles that maintain right wing views in regard to the political questions that the state faces in its relations with the Arabs. What is

---

[43] For processes similar to the ones discussed here, see G. W. Bowersock, *Fiction as History* (Berkeley: University of California Press, 1994).

significant here is the fact that political views are linked to a religious agenda as discussed above.

The major actors in the play are certain students of Rav Avraham Yitzhaq Halevi Kook.[44] Rav Kook was Chief Rabbi of British Palestine until his death in 1935. He was an interesting figure who wrote extensively on the processes of the redemptive, or messianic, setting of modern Jewish history. Most of his writings interpret the situation in terms taken from the Judaic mystical tradition and in their own interesting way give expression to a moderate view in regard to the messianic enactment of historical events. However, after the Six Days War in 1967, the writings of Rav Kook became a source of messianic inspiration for people whose arguments were mainly shaped as messianic norms.

It is often argued that Rav Kook represents a rather moderate type of messianic zeal. However, there are passages in his writings that render a different picture. One of them is worth quoting here. Writing on "The War," Rav Kook says:

> When there is a great war in the world, the power of the messiah awakens . . . the wicked ones are driven out of the world and the world is "filled with perfume" . . . . The few ones that are killed without judgment in the course of the catastrophe that marks the torrent of the war, display the principle that the death of the righteous ones is atoning [for the rest of the world]. They rise up [to heaven] to [lit., in] the root of life, and the essence of their life becomes valuable to the good and the blessing of the building of the world [after the war] . . . . Then, after the war is over, the world is renewed with a new spirit, and the traces of the footsteps of the messiah are more clearly manifested. In accordance with the "greatness" of the war, quantitatively and qualitatively speaking, the expectation of the traces of the footsteps of the messiah intensifies . . . .[45]

---

44 See A. Ravitzky, *Messianism, Zionism, and Jewish Religious Radicalism* (Chicago and London: University of Chicago Press, 1996). The apocalyptic implications of that book are discussed by J. Marcus, "Modern and Ancient Jewish Apocalypticism," 1–27. See also I. Gruenwald, "Apocalypticism, Mysticism, Messianism and Political Assassination," 11–17. See also I. Gruenwald, "Mysticism and Politics in the State of Israel," *Religion and the Political Order: Politics in Classical and Modern Christianity, Islam and Judaism* (ed. J. Neusner; Atlanta: Scholars Press, 1996) 95–108.

45 Rav Avraham Yitzhaq Ha Cohen Kook, *Orot* ("Lights"), Jerusalem, 1984, p. 13. A. Ravitzky quotes from this passage (*Messianism, Zionism, and Jewish Religious Radicalism*, 109). However, he skips the lines that speak of the dialectic of war and messianism!

The implications of these words cannot be mistaken. In the last hundred years, similar words were often voiced, reflecting anything from dialectic materialism to the Shi'ite denial of life for the sake of heavenly bliss. The principle is clear. It reflects a type of Qabbalistic-messianic dialectic: the worse the situation becomes the better the chances are for the coming of the messianic redemption. Everybody acquainted with the apocalyptic spirit of antiquity knows the kind of historical determinism that is implied in these notions. A terrible war, whether "Armagedon" or "Gog and Magog," must precede the birth of the messianic age. Birth is anticipated by the inevitable "pains."

The Six Day War was taken to be such a pre-messianic event. One result of that war was the retrieval of considerable parts of the Holy Land by the Jewish people. This was considered to be a divine act. Conceivably, therefore, no part of the newly conquered territories should be handed back into Arab hands, nor even traded for peace. In their zeal, the followers of Rav Kook's writings elaborated upon his theology, justifying a hard line in current political decisions.

In their messianic zeal, the new students of Rav Kook's writings found an interesting ally. They were inadvertently assisted by the non-Zionist Lubavitchers, who—inspired by their Qabbalisitic messianism—ardently helped along the process of delegitimizing any governmental decision that advocated a peace-policy involving the giving back of land. No havoc was ruled out as inconceivable by the people who saw themselves as the Forces of God (*Tziv ot Ha-Shem*) or by those who considered it their duty to usher in the messianic era.

In short, the Lubavitchers and the students of Rav Kook's writings were the two sources from which the modern messianism of *Gush Emunim*, the groups of "Settlers" and some other political extremists, fetched their ideological waters. Qabbalah provided the rhetoric and the ideological foundations not only for the politically oriented declarations made by the Lubavitcher Hasidim, but also for the violent street demonstrations in which they and others engaged. Qabbalah, in this respect, was used to justify patterns of thinking and action that are typical of the ethos of violence so prevalent in apocalypticism.

It was this ethos of violence, so characteristic of apocalypticism, that was the driving force behind the political snowballing that brought about about the murder of Yitzhak Rabin. In being predisposed to apocalyptic ways of thinking and expression, many of the neutral onlookers did not care to heed the ominous insinuations contained in the messages which had been spread long before that event. The fascination with the threatening tones of the *Dies Irae* was easily transformed into political zeal. And if an American comparison is needed, the case of David Koresh in Waco, Texas, can easily, with small modifications, serve that purpose.

To use the language of the Book of Daniel—in itself one of the most interesting specimens of the apocalyptic tradition—the writing on the wall was clearly seen. However, only few understood its meaning and foresaw its implications. Those who should have noticed the writing and the music that accompanied the messianic orgies totally failed in drawing the necessary conclusions. The results are known and sad.

If this presentation makes sense, then the events leading to the assassination of Yitzhak Rabin had all the ingredients of an apocalyptic drama. Prior to the assassination, the Labour-led government had often been designated by its opponents as the "Kingdom of Wickedness" (*Malkhut Ha-Zadon*).[46] The term is also well known from its apocalyptic usage. Violence for the sake of divine redemption was very much in the air, if not virtually enacted in the streets. In short, a type of culture evolved in which the apocalyptic ethos of violence was allowed to prevail.

In line with what has been said above, it is once again interesting to note that this modern type of apocalypticism was not sectarian. It was widely preached and openly enacted. In fact, those who did not succumb to that outbreak of apocalyptic zeal were ruthlessly marginalized. Thus, apocalypticism swayed high and undisturbed. Its opponents, however, were the ones who were considered the sect of unbelievers, a very large sect in this respect. In any event, this outbreak of apocalyptic zeal rendered one thing clear: it aimed at shaping the identity of Zionism along the lines of apocalyptic and messianic ideas.

---

[46] In the Jewish Prayer Book, such terminology is reserved for "Rome," used literally and metaphorically [for example, signifying Christianity]. See also Jer 50:31–32, referring to the People of Babylonia or its king.

Epilogue

The notions of "apocalyptic culture" or the "culture of apocalypticism" have repeatedly been referred to in the present essay. In addition, we have seen that apocalypticism is likely to create a cultural identity. Thus, it can best be viewed in contrast to other forms of religious identity. In many respects, the ultimate goal of the Judaic way of life as viewed in the context of the scriptural world is the "holiness" and "righteousness" of the individual and the community. Cultic, socio-political, and communal factors are variously stressed in the different parts of Scripture. The framework, though, is predominantly a priestly one.

Apocalypticism, however, stresses the prevalence of heavenly and meta-historical factors. Angelic beings and the heavenly court are mostly substituted for the priests and the temple cult.[47] At times, the messianic figures and regime replace the earthly monarch and kingdom.[48] These and some other features constitute what is here referred to as the "apocalyptic culture." It was basically characterized by the factor of substitution. The new apocalyptic identity is shaped mainly by people's absolute confidence in the redeeming structure and function of the historical future and the cultic reorientation that looks upward to heavenly realms. This confidence and reorientation are the operative factors in the reconfiguration of the past that, psychologically speaking, is another major characteristic of the apocalyptic transformation of identity.

In speaking about the apocalyptic ideology of change, messianism had to be mentioned as one of its peaks. Evidently, it fits into the substitutional process mentioned above. The future Messiah is entrusted with all the tasks connected with the redemption of the

---

[47] In this respect, the "Angelic Liturgy" from Qumran is highly significant. The angels are referred to in these texts as priests. See C. Newsom, *Songs of the Sabbath Sacrifice: A Critical Edition* (Atlanta: Scholars Press, 1985). However, the picture is not devoid of dialectic tones. See I. Gruenwald, *From Apocalypticism to Gnosticism* (Frankfurt am Main: Peter Lang, 1988) 125–173. See also the next footnote.

[48] See also I. Gruenwald, "From Priesthood to Messianism: The Anti-Priestly Polemic and the Messianic Factor," *Messiah and Christos: Studies in the Jewish Origins of Christianity Presented to David Flusser* (ed. I. Gruenwald et al.; Tübingen: Mohr [Siebeck], 1992) 75–93.

people.[49] These tasks had previously been viewed as being in the hands of God to accomplish. The promise of the future redemption as voiced in Deut 30:1–10, in Jeremiah and in several of the other prophets of ancient Israel, reflects the *magnalia dei* in the history of the people of God. In later times, however, everything connected to the future redemption of the people was entrusted to the Messiah. Evidently, this signals another aspect in the above-mentioned layout of substitution: The Messiah substitutes for God! He is more than simply an emissary or intermediary figure, substituting for the earthly king. As in the concept of divine kingship in the Ancient Near East, the king—and later on the Messiah—substituted for God.[50]

We have seen that, essentially speaking, apocalypticism enhanced the establishing of norms of change and innovation in search of a new identity. Interpretation, visions, the rewriting of Scripture, substitution, and replacement became the major tools in the apocalyptic culture. The question always is, what are the limits of these changes and innovations crystallizing in interpretation? It seems that in apocalypticism the limits are set without regarding the catastrophic implications. It is often said that many of the characteristic features of apocalypticism are the result of nervousness and impatience felt by people who placed all their hopes in one basket, that of radical change. Anxiety is the emotional space in which radical changes are usually conceived as the only operable option. In many cases, it is likely to breed monstrous manifestations of violence.[51]

---

[49] See S. Mowinckel, *He That Cometh* (Oxford: Basil Blackwell, 1959). See also the next footnote.

[50] See H. Frankfort, *Kingship and the Gods* (Chicago and London: University of Chicago Press, 1978).

[51] Naturally, anxiety has to be discussed as a psychological phenomenon. However, a classic discussion of anxiety in terms of its religious and cultural manifestations is E. R. Dodds, *Pagan and Christian in an Age of Anxiety* (Cambridge: Cambridge University Press, 1965). See, however, Peter Brown, *The Making of Late Antiquity* (Cambridge, MA: Harvard University Press, 1978) 5, who comments that "anxiety" does not adequately describe the spiritual climate of the third century. Brown stresses the element of change so pervasive in that period. I believe that, from a historian's point of view, the centuries under discussion (second to sixth C. E.) could well be described as manifesting the echo-waves of the Judaic/early-Christian apocalyptic spirit! Speculations are a scholarly luxury; however, I would like to know what kind of review A. D. Nock would have written of Dodds' book!

Under such circumstances, a different, less critical, kind of assessment of apocalypticism loses much of its relevance. If some cultural sanity is to prevail in the pursuit of a future in which our children and grandchildren will find a peaceful corner, then the ominous tones of apocalypticism should be heeded and its echoes stopped from spreading.

Cross-Cultural Reflections on Apocalypticism

Jonathan Z. Smith

Professor Gruenwald's contribution is not only specifically appropriate to this celebration, recalling, as it does, Dieter Betz's important 1966 methodological contribution to the study of late antique apocalypticism, which insisted that the latter constitutes an integral phenomenon (albeit within the context of "syncretism") which cannot be reduced to a motley list of "traits."[1] Ironically, given our topic, the textual examples Betz treats in detail have to do, in part, with a horror, by the apocalypticists, at the "evil . . . of shedding blood." It is also appropriate to the work of Betz's colleagues on this faculty, ranging from the Collins's work on defining the genre, "apocalypse," an effort which has attained wide consensus, to McGinn's ongoing project of exhibiting and interpreting later Christian apocalypticisms—both labors reaching a sort of culmination in the projected millenarian dictionary.[2]

Gruenwald's discussion of the "history of religions" understanding of apocalypticism has advanced the question, most particularly, his insistence on "mainstreaming" apocalypticism and his focus on "substitution" and "interpretation." In the remarks which follow, I will, therefore, focus on his cultural assessment.

Gruenwald's chosen term, "apocalypticism," is a fairly recent generic and comparative coinage of the mid-nineteenth century—the period, between the 1830s and 1860s that produced the bulk of the "isms" which continue to plague the study of religion—although its roots go back to early Christian Greek; the majority of the references to "apocalyptic" prior to "apocalypticism's" coinage have reference to the last book of the Christian canon. The phenomenon so named has appeared earlier under a variety of titles, each influenced, at first application, by elements in intra-Christian discourse, and often reflect

---

[1] Hans Dieter Betz, "Zum Problem des religionsgeschichtlichen Verständnisses der Apokalyptik," *ZTK* 63 (1966) 391–409.

[2] John J. Collins, Bernard McGinn and Stephen Stein, eds., *The Encyclopedia of Apocalypticism* (3 vols.; New York: Continuum, 1998).

a perceived link with violence. Beyond the generic "heresy," and the early usage, "millenarian" or "millenialism," the first self-conscious history of Christian movements later denoted "apocalyptic" was, most probably, Heinrich Corrodi's, *Critical History of Chiliasm*, published in three volumes in four parts in Frankfort-Leipzig, 1781–83.[3] In the eighteenth century, "fanaticism" moved from a general term for "inspiration" to a specific French term indicating millenarian violence in polemics against the Protestant Camisards. In the eighteenth century as well, "enthusiasm" underwent a similar history (culminating, perhaps, in R. A. Knox's spleenful *Enthusiasm: A Chapter in the History of Religion*[4]), although it has been more successful in retaining its original connotations. The extension of "apocalyptic" beyond Christianity, first to Jewish, Islamic and Iranian traditions, then to its current status as a ubiquitous religious phenomenon (an extension that began with James Mooney's 1896 study of the Native American Ghost Dance[5]), has given rise to a bewildering assortment of terminology which, by and large, refuses specifically Christian connotation: "crisis cult," "cargo cult," "nativistic movements," "revitalization movements"—to name but a few, a project which has as its emblems comparative works such as Lanternari's *The Religions of the Oppressed*[6] and Bryan R. Wilson's *Magic and the Millennium*.[7] Working through the titles of the enormous scholarly literature listed in Ted Daniels's *Millenialism: An International Bibliography* will provide you with the complete nomenclature.[8] The most recent coinage, "militant fundamentalism," marks an unfortunate return to the earlier practice of Christian exemplification.

---

[3] Heinrich Corrodi, *Kritische Geschichte des Chiliasmus* (3 vols.; Frankfort-Leipzig: 1781–83).

[4] R. A. Knox, *Enthusiasm: A Chapter in the History of Religion* (Oxford: Clarendon, 1950).

[5] James Mooney, *The Ghost-Dance Religion and the Sioux Outbreak of 1890* (Washington: Government Printing Office, 1896).

[6] Vittorio Lanternari, *Movimenti religiosi di libertà e di salvezza dei popoli oppressi* (Milano: Feltrinelli, 1960).

[7] Bryan R. Wilson, *Magic and the Millennium* (New York: Harper & Row, 1973).

[8] Ted Daniels, *Millenialism: An International Bibliography* (New York: Garland, 1992).

Gruenwald's proposal, to view apocalypticism as an "omnipresent . . . cultural factor, past and present," takes its place within a tradition of study that arose, first, in relation to World War II and the Cold War, and emphasizes the political implications of "apocalypticism," particularly more ancient forms in relation to modern totalitarianisms of both the left and the right. While the privileged term changes, one thinks of Jakob Taubes's *Occidental Eschatology* (1947);[9] Norman Cohn's *The Pursuit of the Millennium* in its successive editions from 1957;[10] J. L. Talmon's two studies, *The Origins of Totalitarian Democracy* (1960)[11] and *Political Messianism: The Romantic Phase* (1960),[12] as well as Eric Voegelin's varied studies which employ the term "gnostic" to a similar end.[13]

More recently, a set of extreme cases, in the United States and elsewhere, has raised in an acute form the question on which Gruenwald focuses—the relationship of contemporary apocalyptic movements to violence. Its leading scholars are associated with the social sciences—most prominently, Michael Barkun and David C. Rapoport—generating a large literature, as well as specialized journals and series (for example, *Terrorism and Political Violence*,[14] *Syzygy*, and the CASS Series on Political Violence, the latter devoting its second volume to *Millenialism and Violence*[15]). Because of the criminal aspects of such movements, a complex anthropologically influenced legal literature is in the process of formation, carefully reported in journals such as the *Review of Law and Social Change* and *Behavioral Sciences and the Law*.

---

[9] Jakob Taubes, *Abendländische Eschatologie* (Bern: A. Francke, 1947).

[10] Norman Cohn, *The Pursuit of the Millennium* (Fairlawn, NJ: Essential Books; London: Secker and Warburg, 1957).

[11] J. L. Talmon, *The Origins of Totalitarian Democracy* (New York: Praeger, 1960).

[12] J. L. Talmon, *Political Messianism: The Romantic Phase* (New York: Praeger, 1960).

[13] Eric Voegelin, *Science, Politics and Gnosticism: Two Essays* (A Gateway Edition 6118; Chicago: H. Regnery Co., 1968).

[14] *Terrorism and Political Violence* is a quarterly journal published in London by F. Cass since 1989.

[15] *Syzygy* is a journal published in Exton, PA, by Closed Quantum Publishing since 1996. Michael Barkun, ed., *Millenialism and Violence* (CASS Series on Political Violence 2; Portland, OR and London: CASS, 1996).

All of this is to say that Professor Gruenwald has directed our attention to a worthy and difficult subject. But it is by no means clear that Gruenwald's "horror story" has any sort of inevitability to it. Indeed, the older critique of "apocalypticism" took the opposite point of view, that its "determinism" and "ethical disassociation" led to passivity rather than aggression. One cannot but agree with the Canadian scholar, Thomas Flanagan:

> A worthwhile project for comparative research would be a systematic study of the conditions under which religious millenarianism becomes politically activist. Eclectic reading of the literature suggests that a deliberate, calculated resort to arms is exceptional; more common is a dialectic of threat and counter-threat between millenarian believers and the state, which at some point breaks out into violence, perhaps by miscalculation.[16]

This would seem as true of the American example of Waco as it is of the Israeli example of the assassination of Rabin.

As I should not have to argue in the presence of Walter Burkert and Robert Jewett, apocalypticism seems no more inherently violent than other religious modes—or, for that matter, other spheres of human culture. Culture and violence are not oppositional categories. The interesting question is what prompts one group, at a particular place and time, to turn to violence in contradistinction to another moment in their own history, or to another group with similar ideology and structure.

Perhaps the most important suggestion Gruenwald puts forth with respect to this question concerns the issue of "reinterpretation." Some scholars, among them Michael Barkun, Rodney Stark and William S. Bainbridge, have been pointing to this as one possible catalytic element for violence. They distinguish (in varying vocabularies, at times unfortunately wedded to distinctions of "sect" and "cult") between those groups which emerge within an established tradition which they idiosyncratically reinterpret, usually in a coherent and consistent manner which can be, with effort, decoded—see, most recently, Stephen D. O'Leary's important, *Arguing the Apocalypse: A Theory of Millennial Rhetoric*[17]—and those groups which exhibit an

---

16 Thomas Flanagan, "The Politics of the Millennium," in M. Barkun, ed., *Millenialism and Violence*, 164–75.

17 Stephen D. O'Leary, *Arguing the Apocalypse: A Theory of Millennial Rhetoric* (New York: Oxford University Press, 1994).

extreme eclecticism, constructing a novel patchwork system from a diversity of partially assimilated sources. These latter are inaccessible to outsiders, not only, thereby, increasing the distance between the group and its surroundings, but making it difficult for public institutions (for example, governments and the press) to generalize from one group to another, rendering policy impossible, except through the imposition of inadequate categories such as "cult," "brainwashing," or the like (or, for that matter, the scholarly category "syncretism")—a double failure at communication which makes violence all the more probable.

Among other implications, this state of affairs suggests the hope that future students of religion will undertake efforts of translation between the apocalyptic groups and the public, with respect both to the internal language of the group and the provision of adequate public categories. As reported in James Tabor and Eugene Gallagher's *Why Waco?*,[18] the example of Phillip Arnold's and Tabor's ability to reason with David Koresh within the terms of his system, gaining his assent to an alternative (and pacific) reinterpretation of his previously violent interpretation of the Apocalypse's "fifth seal" over and against the authorities' inability to concede any religious context at Waco, provides both a possibility and a warning for future confrontations. The fact that this instance, as difficult as it may appear, was with respect to a tradition-based movement and not the far more intractable eclectic sort, only furthers a sense of urgency.

---

[18] James Tabor and Eugene Gallagher, *Why Waco?: Cults and the Battle for Religious Freedom in America* (Berkeley: University of California Press, 1995).

Beatitudes and Their Illocutionary Functions*

David Hellholm

1. Methodological Approaches and Consequences

Exegetical work is always dependent on the text's situational context on the one hand and its literary co-text on the other. The two, however, are to a certain degree interdependent. Furthermore, the literary co-text can and must be divided into what is normally called *intra-textuality*, that is, references to texts within one and the same literary unit and *inter-textuality,* that is, references to texts outside of the literary entity to be interpreted.[1] In the case of ancient literature the situational context in most cases has to be established by means of interpretations of texts belonging to the two types of literary co-texts just mentioned. Consequently, there is an interrelationship between the level of literary co-texts and that of the situational contexts.

In the case of the Sermon on the Mount (SM) and the Sermon on the Plain (SP), this distinction is crucial. Especially with regard to *intra-textuality,* the problems have become greater and the solutions increasingly more difficult. To this state of affairs our jubilarian has contributed greatly, and he has done so to such a degree that a paper like the present one eventually became not only a possibility but actually also a necessity.

If interpreters of the redaction-critical school until recently could rely on the Gospel of Matthew as the immediate intra-textual co-text when interpreting the SM and the Gospel of Luke when interpreting the SP, this is no longer possible to the same extent or with the same self-evident truth after Hans Dieter Betz's essays[2] and his monumental

* Leif Vaage and Adela Yarbro Collins checked and improved my English, for which I am most grateful.

[1] See, e.g., H. F. Plett, ed., *Intertextuality* (Research in Text Theory 15; Berlin and New York: de Gruyter, 1991).

[2] H. D. Betz, *Essays on the Sermon on the Mount* (Philadelphia, PA: Fortress 1985); *Studien zur Bergpredigt* (Tübingen: Mohr [Siebeck], 1985); *Synoptische Studien. Gesammelte Aufsätze II* (Tübingen: Mohr [Siebeck], 1992).

commentary.[3] This is true, of course, when for methodological reasons one limits oneself to the interpretation of these sermons as individual entities on their own and not as part of the extant Gospels. At that level, the intra-textual co-text of the sermons has simply been lost and that of the Beatitudes—to which I will turn below—drastically reduced.

The situation has become even more precarious than that. If literary-critics, as well as form-critics, could still view the SM and the SP as texts formed by the group behind Q, this is no longer possible either, if we follow Prof. Betz. When he argues that the sermons constitute separate *epitomes*,[4] which were taken over by and integrated into separate versions of Q (Q^{Matt} and Q^{Luke}) at a rather late stage,[5] these epitomes stand on their own as literary units and as theological summaries more or less independent of the Q-redactions. Not only the Matthean or Lucan, but also the Q co-texts are viewed as secondary with the result that no *intra*-textual connections exist at the epitome-level, and we are entirely dependent on *inter*-textual relations for these early sermons.

With regard to *inter-textuality* the situation has also changed. On the inter-textual level of Matthew and Luke the loss is the same as at the level of intra-textuality, since these Gospels are late. At the inter-textual level of the SM and the SP vis-à-vis Q, the situation has definitively improved, since the different Q-versions as well as the not yet gnosticized *Gospel of Thomas* are now (after reconstruction) available as approximately contemporaneous comparative materials from the earliest stages of Christianity.[6] As far as the inter-textual material from Jewish and Greco-Roman sources is concerned, the situation in principle has not changed to any considerable degree,

---

[3] Idem, *The Sermon on the Mount. A Commentary on the Sermon on the Mount, including the Sermon on the Plain (Matthew 5:3–7:27 and Luke 6:20–49)* (Hermeneia; Minneapolis: Fortress, 1995).

[4] Idem, "The Sermon on the Mount (Matt. 5:3–7:27): Its Literary Genre and Function," *Essays,* 1–16; and *Synoptische Studien,* 77–91; especially idem, *Sermon on the Mount,* 70–80. Cf. also I. Opelt, "Epitome," *RAC* 5. 944–73; W. Schmid, "Epikur," *RAC* 5. 682–819; A. Malherbe, *Moral Exhortations* (Library of Early Christianity; Philadelphia, PA: Westminster, 1986) 85.

[5] Betz, "The Sermon on the Mount and Q," *Synoptische Studien,* 249–69, here 249, 266–69; idem, *Sermon on the Mount,* 43–44.

[6] See H. Koester, *Ancient Christian Gospels. Their History and Development* (London: SCM; Philadelphia: Trinity, 1990) 75–128, especially 95.

except for the fact that new comparative material of the same *genre* (for example, Epicurus, *Kyriai doxai*[7]) has been utilized and that we now are more aware of the different levels on which we pose our questions.

In view of the *situational context*, we are almost in the same situation as with regard to the level of inter-textuality. There is loss with regard to the *situation* of Matthew and Luke, gain, however, with regard to the earlier periods in view of the *settings* of the Q-versions, the *Gospel of Thomas*, and the Greco-Roman and Hellenistic-Jewish materials including the epitomaic writings.

As far as the intra-textual context is concerned, let me illustrate the complexity of this state of affairs by using the introductory and closing frames in Matthew and Luke as examples. When the sermons are classified as epitomes, not only their character as "breviers" or "summaries" of "already existing sources, written, oral, or both"[8] has been established, but also the question of recipients has been determined. Epitomes are not composed for strangers or beginners but, as Epicurus phrases it, for

> those who have made some advance in the survey of the entire system . . . (καὶ τοὺς προβεβηκότας δὲ ἱκανῶς ἐν τῇ τῶν ὅλων ἐπιβλέψει . . .) (Diog. Laer. 10.35).[9]

To whom are now the SM and the SP respectively addressed? In Matthew as well as in Luke we encounter a discrepancy concerning the addressees. In Matt 5:1–2 we read:

> When he saw the crowds, he went up the hill. There he took his seat, and when his disciples had gathered round him he began to address them.

Here Matthew is referring to the crowd mentioned in 4:25; and in Luke 6:17 we read:

---

[7] This text was referred to in connection with the question of the genre of Q already by P. Vielhauer in his *Geschichte der urchristlichen Literatur* (de Gruyter Lehrbuch; Berlin and New York: de Gruyter 1975) 316–19. In connection with the epitome-genre it was utilized by Betz, see above note 2.

[8] Betz, *Sermon on the Mount*, 76.

[9] Text and trans. R. D. Hicks, *Diogenes Laertius: Lives of Eminent Philosophers,* (2 vols.; LCL; London: Heinemann; Cambridge, MA: Harvard University Press, 1970).

He came down the hill with them (sc. his disciples) and took his stand on the plain. There was a large concourse of his disciples and great numbers of people . . . .

Thereafter Jesus' speech is introduced with a special reference to his disciples (v. 20):

Then turning to his disciples he began to speak.

In both instances the evangelists are of the opinion that the Sermons were directed to the crowds, which is substantiated in the closing formulas, which in their present form are supplied by the respective evangelists.[10] They are—textgrammatically speaking—"substitutions on abstraction-level," that is, they constitute a type of resumption in which the *substituens* has a larger range of meaning than the *substituendum*.[11] In Matt 7:28 we read:

When Jesus had finished this discourse, the people were astounded at his teaching . . . ; cf. 8:1: After he had come down from the hill, he was followed by a great crowd.

In Luke we encounter the corresponding statement in 7:1:

When he had finished addressing the people, he went to Capernaum.

The discrepancy was noticed already by Bultmann, who, however, thought that "*already in Q* there must have been a *small introductory sentence* in which the μαθηταί were named as listeners."[12] If the sermons, however, are epitomes incorporated into different versions of Q as Betz maintains, is it not then as reasonable to try to differentiate between the epitomes and the versions of Q, into which these sermons were incorporated, as to differentiate between Q and the Evangelists? The introductory sentence referring to the disciples was, in my opinion, probably already part of the SM and the SP and not only of Q.

Can such a claim be substantiated? I think so, indeed! It is after all remarkable that *at the end* of both sermons, we encounter situational

---

[10] See D. Hellholm, "Substitutionelle Gliederungsmerkmale und die Komposition des Matthäusevangeliums," *Texts and Contexts. Biblical Texts in Their Textual and Situational Contexts. Essays in Honor of Lars Hartman* (ed. T. Fornberg and D. Hellholm; Oslo: Scandinavian University Press, 1995) 11–76, here 33–39.

[11] Cf. Hellholm, "Gliederungsmerkmale," 31.

[12] R. Bultmann, *Geschichte der synoptischen Tradition* (6th ed.; FRLANT 29; Göttingen: Vandenhoeck & Ruprecht, 1964) 358 (italics mine).

descriptions, both of which are to be characterized as "substitutions on abstraction-level." They record unanimously that the addressees were in fact the crowds (ὄχλοι/λαός) and not just the disciples. The formulations, as we now have them, are, of course, each typical of their Evangelists, but the simple fact that such substitutions occur in the accounts of both Gospels, strongly suggests that *some sort of closing formula* was added to the sermons, when they were incorporated into Q^{Matt} and Q^{Luke} respectively.[13] If the Q-tradition thus depicts the addressees as being the crowds, then the introductory description of the disciples as the addressees must belong to another level, most likely to that of the epitome. If so, then we have to reckon with the following, yet incomplete, development:

(1) In the *epitomes* the disciples were addressed for "educational purposes related to the training of early Christian disciples."[14]

(2) In Q^{Matt} and Q^{Luke} the disciples and the crowds were addressed; the emphasis in both Q-traditions is decisively on the crowds as the closing formulas clearly show.

(3) In Matthew and Luke respectively the Q-settings are partly retained and partly further developed.

In addition, we have to discern whether the disciples as addressees reflect the setting in the life of the historical Jesus as well. This question will be addressed at the end of this essay (paragraph 6).

2. *The Compositional Structure of Macarisms in Matthew and Luke*

The SM and the SP begin with τὰ κυριώτατα serving as *exordia*[15] for each sermon.[16] The compositional structure of the macarisms in the SM/SP indicate, as Prof. Betz has rightly emphasized,[17] two *series* of

---

[13] See also Bultmann, *Geschichte,* 359, n. 1: "Evidently Matthew found this formula in Q serving as a transition from the Sermon on the Mount to the story of the centurion; for Matt 7:28 corresponds to Luke 7:1." Bultmann refers to B. H. Streeter, *The Four Gospels* (London: Macmillan 1924) 262 and E. von Dobschütz, "Matthäus als Rabbi und Katechet," *ZNW* 27 (1928) 341.

[14] Betz, *Sermon on the Mount,* 44.

[15] Betz, *Sermon on the Mount,* 50, 59, 66, 571.

[16] Cf. W. Schmid, "Epikur," 659: "An der Spitze der Sammlung [sc. *Kyriai doxai*] stehen 4 Sprüche, deren Gehalt als das 'Wichtigste' (τὰ κυριώτατα) galt . . . ."

[17] Betz, "Die Makarismen der Bergpredigt (Matthäus 5,3–12). Beobachtungen zur literarischen Form und theologischen Bedeutung," *ZTK* 75 (1978) 3–19, here

beatitudes and not just isolated macarisms.[18] Methodologically this is an important observation, since as E. Coseriu has pointed out "there are text-units (*Texteinheiten*) which do not coincide with sentences but can be expressed through sentences. A text consists just as little of sentences as sentences of words. 'Sentence' and 'text' rather comprise in each case specific functional units."[19] In this connection the apt question of W. Raible, "whether one shouldn't consider the speech-acts in Searle's sense as textfunctions," can only be fully endorsed[20] and will be the supposition for my own deliberations in this essay.

In the SM Betz reckons with a series of ten, while in my opinion the last one constitutes an expanded and thus comprehensive Beatitude.[21] Even if we only glance briefly at the first part (vv. 3–10) we immediately observe that it is an original unit vis à vis the second part

8; reprinted in *Studien*, 17–33, here 22; and in *Synoptische Studien*, 92–110, here 97. English version: "The Beatitudes of the Sermon on the Mount (Matt. 5:3–12): Observations of Their Literary Form and Theological Significance," in *Essays*, 17–36, here 23. See now the series of macarisms from 4Q525 2 ii 1–13 (= 4QBéat) and hereto with text and trans. J. A. Fitzmyer, "A Palestinian Collection of Beatitudes," *The Four Gospels 1992. FS Frans Neirynck* (ed. F. Van Segbroeck et al.; BETL 100-A; Leuven: Peeters 1992) 509–15; and B. T. Viviano, "Eight Beatitudes in Qumran and in Matthew. A New Publication from Cave 4," *SEÅ* 58 (1993) 71–84.

[18] Series of macarisms are found in Jewish wisdom and apocalyptic literature, e.g. Ps 119:1–3; Sir 14:1–2, 20–27; 25:7–10; Tob 13:14–16; *2 Enoch* 42:6–14; 52:1–14; *Sib. Or.* 4.24–34; 4Q525 [4QBéat] 2. ii. See also K. Berger, *Formgeschichte des Neuen Testaments* (Heidelberg: Quelle & Meyer, 1984) 190. Noteworthy is the lack of series of macarisms in Greco-Roman literature. In Egypt there seems to have been no series of macarisms either, see J. Assmann, "Weisheit, Loyalismus und Frömmigkeit," *Studien zu altägyptischen Lebenslehren* (ed. E. Hornung and O. Keel; OBO 28; Freiburg: Universitätsverlag; Göttingen: Vandenhoeck & Ruprecht, 1979) 11–72, here 36.

[19] E. Coseriu, in his contribution to the discussion in *Textsorten. Differenzierungskriterien aus linguistischer Sicht* (2d ed.; ed. E. Gülich and W. Raible; Wiesbaden: Athenaion, 1975) 138.

[20] W. Raible in his contribution to the discussion in *Textsorten*, 140.

[21] Hellholm, "'Rejoice and Be Glad, for Your Reward is Great in Heaven'. An Attempt at Solving the Structural Problem of Matt 5:11–12," *Festschrift Günter Wagner* (ed. Faculty of Baptist Theological Seminary, Rüschlikon, Switzerland; International Theological Studies: Contributions of Baptist Scholars 1; Bern: Peter Lang, 1994) 47–86.

(vv. 11–12).[22] The apodosis of the first and the eighth macarism is identical: "for theirs is the Kingdom of Heaven" (ὅτι αὐτῶν ἐστιν ἡ βασιλεία τῶν οὐρανῶν). Thus they establish a rhetorical *inclusio*, which "suggests that everything from 5:3 through 5:10 is to be read as a single unit."[23] According to Prof. Betz "the inclusio is clear: the sequence of virtues in vv. 3a–9a, combined with the eschatological promises in vv. 3b–9b, is held together by the theme of the Kingdom of Heaven, in which righteousness reigns and will ultimately prevail."[24] The eight macarisms are further made up of two stanzas each:[25] (a) According to M. A. Powell the first encompasses the first four Beatitudes (5:3–6) with its promise of "eschatological *reversal* to those who are unfortunate,"[26] or more precisely, according to Betz, in the first three macarisms the "situation of deprivation" is described as "motivating the 'hunger and thirst for righteousness'" in the fourth (3+1).[27] Thus, "the first set of four Beatitudes emphasizes themes of *pursuing* righteousness."[28] Only the first stanza exhibits the internal p-alliteration and only it has parallels in the SP (Luke 6:20b–21). (b) As far as Powell is concerned, the second stanza encompasses the last four Beatitudes (5:7–10) with its promise of "eschatological *reward* to people who exhibit virtuous behavior,"[29] or more precisely, according to Betz, in the first three macarisms of the second stanza "human activities" and "virtues" are described "that meet with persecution for

---

22 See further Hellholm, "Rejoice," 58, n. 58 with references; cf. also Viviano, "Beatitudes," 77.

23 M. A. Powell, "Matthew's Beatitudes: Reversals and Rewards of the Kingdom," *CBQ* 58 (1996) 460–79, here 475; so also Betz, *Sermon on the Mount*, 105, 142, 146; W. Schenk, *Die Sprache des Matthäus. Die Text-Konstituenten in ihren makro- und mikrostrukturellen Relationen* (Göttingen: Vandenhoeck & Ruprecht, 1987) 352.

24 Betz, *Sermon on the Mount*, 146.

25 Cf. U. Luz, *Das Matthäusevangelium. 1. Teilband Mt 1–7* (EKKNT 1/1; Zürich: Benziger; Neukirchen: Neukirchener Verlag, 1985) 199–200.

26 Powell, "Beatitudes," 463, 469 (italics mine); similarly already J. Weiss, *Die Predigt Jesu vom Reiche Gottes* (2d ed.; Göttingen: Vandenhoeck & Ruprecht, 1900 [repr. 1964, with supplement from the 1st ed. 1882]) 127, 186–87; Strecker, "μακαρισμός, *EWNT* 2. 928; cf. Betz, *Sermon on the Mount*, 121.

27 Betz, ibid., 142; "If one follows the thought of the SM, this hunger is the fruit of insight into the human condition" (ibid., 129).

28 Betz, ibid., 142 (italics mine).

29 Powell, "Beatitudes," 470 (italics mine); similarly Weiss, ibid., 186–87; Strecker, ibid.

the sake of righteousness" in the fourth and last Macarism (3+1).[30] Thus, "the second set of four speaks of *endurance* for the sake of righteousness."[31] In addition to the different kinds of descriptions of those addressed in the two stanzas, the protases of the last macarism in each stanza by means of the qualifying adverbial expressions, τὴν δικαιοσύνην and ἕνεκεν δικαιοσύνης respectively, underline the delimitation of the series of beatitudes into two stanzas. In this way the two stanzas—in spite of their differences—are connected and thus kept together, with the result that "all of the virtues of vv. 3–10 are testimonies of human strength, rather than weakness. All of this is said to a community that at present lives under distress."[32]

If theoretically the textfunction of the series is one and the same, consistency in its interpretation is required. Powell's solution is unsatisfactory insofar as he considers the first stanza to be declarative/performative promising *reversals* to the unfortunate, while the second is said to be directive/prescriptive promising *reward* to the virtuous. Betz evidently understands the function of the whole series as directive/prescriptive, when he talks about "the sequence of *virtues* in vv. 3a–9a," but seems to me to be inconsistent when he constantly advocates a prescriptive-ethical understanding of the beatitudes in the SM and at the same time claims that the situation of the first three beatitudes is one of "*deprivation*," and that they promise "*reversal*."[33] It seems to me that Betz has not fully reconciled an illocutionary function, at a stage prior to the composition of the SM, of at least the first three macarisms with the one controlling the whole series. An attempt at solving the problem will be given in paragraph 5.2.2. of this essay.

In the SP we encounter a series of four *macarisms* (vv. 20b–23) corresponding to a series of four *Woes* (vss 24–26). As in the case of the series in the SM, the series of macarisms here is also divided into two parts: the first part is made up of three beatitudes in the form of *distiches* (vv. 20b–21) followed by a comprehensive Beatitude (v. 22), "in which the description of the situation is given in the form of a

---

30 Betz, *Sermon on the Mount,* 142; cf. further ibid., 126, 136, 139, 146.

31 Betz, ibid., 142 (italics mine).

32 Betz, ibid., 146.

33 Betz, ibid., 142 and 121 respectively; see, however, my interpretation below.

subordinate circumstantial sentence introduced by the temporal conjunction ὅταν."[34] The series of woes immediately following the beatitudes is similarly structured,[35] with the exception that in the last one the "rejoinder"-clause is missing, since the *protasis*-line is short and simple.[36] The parallelism between the series of macarisms and that of the woes is indeed important for the correct interpretation of the beatitudes in the SP.[37]

In my further deliberations, I must on this occasion limit myself mainly to the first and the last macarisms in the SM and the first in the SP.

3. Beatitudes and Their Illocutionary Functions

In the "oldest preserved treatise on language,"[38] namely, Plato's dialogue *Kratylos*, language is characterized as a means of action: "Isn't speaking also a way of acting?" (ἆρ' οὖν οὐ καὶ τὸ λέγειν μία τις τῶν πράξεών ἐστιν . . . [387b]). In this dialogue Plato developed a tool kit model (ὄργανον—*Werkzeugmodell*) in regard to the function of language.[39] This understanding was taken up by the German psychologist Karl Bühler in his theory of language, when in 1933 he described human speech as "a form, a mode of action."[40] After the

---

[34] Hellholm, "Rejoice," 70–71 (quotation from p. 71).

[35] Contra Betz, *Sermon on the Mount*, 571.

[36] See Hellholm, "Rejoice," 74.

[37] See below, paragraph 5.2.

[38] F. von Kutschera, *Sprachphilosophie* (2d ed; UTB 80; München: Fink, 1975) 32; cf. E. Gülich and W. Raible, *Linguistische Textmodelle. Grundlagen und Möglichkeiten* (UTB 130; München: Fink, 1977) 24–25.

[39] See E. Heitsch, "Platons Sprachphilosophie im 'Kratylos.' Überlegungen zu 383a4-b2 und 387d10–390a8," *Hermes* 113 (1985) 44–62, especially 56–58; cf. also the examples given in Aristot. *Poet.* 19.7 (1456b): "command (ἐντολή), prayer (εὐχή), narrative (διήγησις), threat (ἀπειλή), question (ἐρώτησις), reply (ἀπόκρισις), and all the like (καὶ εἴ τι ἄλλο τοιοῦτον)" (text and trans. in S. Halliwell, *Aristotle: Poetics* [LCL; Cambridge, MA and London: Harvard University Press, 1995] *ad loc.*); this text is quoted in connection with speech acts in J. G. Cook, *The Structure and Persuasive Power of Mark. A Linguistic Approach* (Semeia Studies; Atlanta, GA: Scholars Press, 1995) 106, n. 31.

[40] K. Bühler, *Axiomatik der Sprachwissenschaften*, Einleitung und Kommentar von E. Stöcker (2d ed.; Frankfurt am Main: Klostermann, 1976) 59; cf. also 43 and 48 [first published in *Kant-Studien* 38 (1933) 19–90, here 48; cf. also 37 and 40]; see further Bühler, *Sprachtheorie. Die Darstellungsfunktion der Sprache* (Ullstein Buch

intimation by L. Wittgenstein, the speech-act theory by J. L. Austin, further developed by J. R. Searle, also emphasized the importance of illocutions, that is to say, "how to do things with words."[41]

As will be obvious from our deliberations on the understanding of the beatitudes in the SM and the SP, it is of utmost importance to realize that there is an interrelationship between the *semantic meaning* of words, syntagmata, sentences, textparts, and texts, on the one hand, and the *illocutionary function*[42] of the same, on the other. In most cases it is not possible to determine the illocutionary function (*Sinn*) without knowing the meaning (*Bedeutung*) of an utterance. This makes the establishment of illocutionary functions so difficult.

3392; Frankfurt am Main: Ullstein, 1965) 24–26, 48–69 [reprint of the 2d ed. from 1965 = 1st ed. 1934].

[41] J. L. Austin, *How To Do Things with Words*. The William James Lectures delivered at Harvard University in 1955. (2d ed.; ed. J. O. Urmson and Marina Sbisà; Cambridge, MA: Harvard University Press, 1975); J. R. Searle, *Speech Acts* (Cambridge: Cambridge University Press, 1969); idem, *Expression and Meaning. Studies in the Theory of Speech Acts* (Cambridge: Cambridge University Press, 1979/85); idem, *Intentionality. An Essay in the Philosophy of Mind* (Cambridge: Cambridge University Press, 1983/85); J. R. Searle and D. Vanderveken, *Foundations of Illocutionary Logic* (Cambridge: Cambridge University Press, 1985). Cf. also J. R. Searle, ed., *The Philosophy of Language* (Oxford Readings in Philosophy; Oxford: Oxford University Press, 1971/74) (with contributions by i.a. Austin, Searle, Grice and Strawson); K. Bach and R. M. Harnish, *Linguistic Communication and Speech Acts,* (Cambridge, MA; London: MIT, 1982); and K. Brinker, "Textfunktionen: Ansätze zu ihrer Beschreibung," *ZGL* 11 (1983) 127–48. Speech act theories have been discussed from an exegetical point of view by D. Hellholm, *Das Visionenbuch des Hermas als Apokalypse. Formgeschichtliche und texttheoretische Studien zu einer literarischen Gattung,* vol. 1, *Methodologische Vorüberlegungen und makrostrukturelle Textanalyse* (CB.NT 13/1; Lund: Gleerup, 1980) 52–61, and applied by Cook, *Structure,* 106–16 and L. Hartman, "Doing Things with the Words of Colossians," *Text-Centered New Testament Studies. Text-Theoretical Essays on Early Jewish and Early Christian Literature* (WUNT 102; Tübingen: Mohr [Siebeck] 1997) 195–209.

[42] Cf. J. Lyons' condensed definition of Austin's locutionary, illocutionary and perlocutionary acts: "(i) A locutionary act is an *act of saying*: the production of a meaningful utterance. . . (ii) An illocutionary act is an act performed *in saying* something: making a statement of promise, issuing a command or request, asking a question, christening a ship, etc. (iii) A perlocutionary act is an act performed *by means of saying* something: getting someone to believe that something is so, persuading someone to do something, moving someone to anger, consoling someone in his distress etc." (*Semantics* [Cambridge: Cambridge University Press 1977] 2. 730 [italics mine]).

Without using technical terminology the illocutionary function of the beatitudes has long been discussed as the history of research shows.[43] Two types of functions have been proposed: (1) the *declarative/performative* function, according to which the beatitudes have been interpreted as declarations of consolation with the promise of reversal; the emphasis here is on the consolation by the sender and the *perlocutionary* acceptance on the part of the addressees of this declaration; (2) The *directive/prescriptive* function, according to which the beatitudes have been understood primarily as ethical exhortations, but occasionally as doctrinal or cultic admonitions with the promise of reward; the emphasis here is on the exhortation to fulfill the requirement for the blessing or to maintain it. The *perlocutionary* effect[44] is, of course, also different: The reaction will be to fulfill or not to fulfill the requirement.

(a) *Grammatically*, macarisms are vague, since their *protasis*-lines in most instances consist of nominal-clauses, substantivized adjectives and participial constructions that lack the possibility of expressing *modi*.[45] When interpreted, these expressions have to be supplemented not only with a copula but also with a subordinate clause introduced by a fitting conjunction. Syntactically, the conjunctions can be co-ordinate or subordinate in character and semantically, they indicate the type of relationship,[46] be it *conditional* (if; ἐάν, εἰ), *causal* (since; ὅτι, διότι,

---

[43] Cf., e.g., G. Strecker, *Die Bergpredigt. Ein exegetischer Kommentar* (2d ed.; Göttingen: Vandenhoeck & Ruprecht, 1985) 30; Luz, *Matthäusevangelium I*, 202–4; W. D. Davies and D. C. Allison, *The Gospel according to Saint Matthew*, vol. 1 (ICC; Edinburgh: T. & T. Clark, 1988) 439–40; H. Weder, *Die "Rede der Reden." Eine Auslegung der Bergpredigt heute* (Zürich: Theologischer Verlag, 1985) 44–45; Powell, "Beatitudes." It is confusing when R. A. Guelich calls the question of "virtues" vs "ultimate blessings" a question of "content," since this is a semantic and not an illocutionary and pragmatic concept or lexeme respectively ("The Matthean Beatitudes: 'Entrance Requirements' or Eschatological Blessings?" *JBL* 95 [1976] 415–34, here 415–16).

[44] Cf. M. Ulkan, *Zur Klassifikation von Sprechakten. Eine grundlagentheoretische Fallstudie* (Linguistische Arbeiten 174; Tübingen: Niemeyer, 1992) 12, 36–38.

[45] Cf. J. Blomqvist and P. O. Jastrup, *Grekisk/græsk Grammatik* (Copenhagen: Akademisk Forlag, 1991) 232 [§ 275, 2] (all trans. of quotations from the Swedish are mine).

[46] Cf. E. Hentschel and H. Weydt, *Handbuch der deutschen Grammatik* (Berlin and New York: de Gruyter, 1990) 257 (all trans. of quotations from the German are mine).

ὡς, ἐπεί, ἐπειδή), *descriptive-circumstantial* (when, by being; ὅτε, ὁπότε, ἐπεί) or *concessive* (although; εἰ καί, κἄν, καίπερ, καίτοι).

The difference between the *descriptive-circumstantial* and the *causal* clauses lies in their relation to a presupposed condition: in the case of a descriptive-circumstantial utterance the condition is *actual* and *sufficient*, while in the case of a causal utterance the condition is *necessary*.[47] The descriptive-circumstantial clauses only indicate an asserted sort of circumstances (*Begleitumstände*) to an action,[48] not a causal connection.[49] As distinguished from the *temporal* clauses, the descriptive-circumstantial clauses "do not answer to specific questions regarding the action's placement in time . . . but give more general information regarding the background of the action."[50] The *concessive* clauses express either a condition, a ground, or an actual circumstance; thereby they express concessions of the "ineffectual counterargument."[51]

As an example we might look at the possible variants of the first macarism in the SM. Since this is more easily done in the second person, I will here—and throughout the entire essay—change the third person into a second person beatitude:

(1) Blessed are you, since/when/although you are poor in the spirit for yours is the Kingdom of Heaven.

(2) Blessed are you, if you become/if you remain poor in the spirit for yours is the Kingdom of Heaven.

Depending upon the decomposition of the nominal-clause, one will end up with a consoling or an admonishing declaration, that is, a declarative/performative or a directive/prescriptive function for the beatitude.

---

[47] For this distinction, see Hellholm, "Enthymemic Argumentation in Paul: The Case of Romans 6," *Paul in His Hellenistic Context* (ed. T. Engberg-Pedersen; Edinburgh: T. & T. Clark, 1994; Minneapolis: Fortress, 1995) 119–79, here 147–48. This distinction was brought up in the discussion following my presentation in Chicago by Prof. Edgar Krentz.

[48] Cf. Hentschel and Weydt, *Handbuch*, 273.

[49] Regarding causal connections, see Blomqvist and Jastrup, *Grammatik*, 252 [§ 292].

[50] Blomqvist and Jastrup, *Grammatik*, 255 [§ 294].

[51] Hentschel and Weydt, *Handbuch*, 272; see further Blomqvist and Jastrup, *Grammatik*, 251 [§ 291].

Important here is the distinction between performatives and prescriptives with regard to the agent and recipient of a speech-act: "a promise leads to a commitment on the part of the speaker, an exhortation to a commitment on the part of the addressee."[52] In macarisms, however, there is always a commitment on the part of the *agent*; that is true regardless of the illocutionary type: (α) in a *performative* utterance the commitment is entirely and unconditionally on the part of the speaker; (β) in a *prescriptive* utterance the commitment is also on the part of the speaker, who here, however, conditionally promises the blessing. The commitment on the part of the *recipient* differs according to the illocutionary function: (α) in a *performative* utterance the addressee simply has to accept (or reject) the promise, (β) while in a *prescriptive* utterance the addressee must commit him/herself to fulfilling the requirements demanded by the speaker.[53]

(b) *Form-critically*, almost all of the macarisms in the SM/SP are *distiches*, with a statement of the reason.[54] All except the last one in the SM are formulated in the third person plural, while the first one in the SP exhibits a somewhat uncommon form insofar as the protasis is given in the third person plural[55] while the apodosis is formulated in

[52] D. Wunderlich, "Über die Konsequenzen von Sprechhandlungen," *Sprachpragmatik und Philosophie* (ed. K.-O. Apel; Theorie-Diskussion; Frankfurt am Main: Suhrkamp, 1976) 441–62, here 454. See also E. U. Große, *Text und Kommunikation* (Stuttgart: Kohlhammer, 1976) 58–59, and Ulkan, *Klassifikation*, 19: "Informationshandlungen" vs "Aufforderungshandlungen."

[53] Cf. Betz, *Sermon on the Mount*, 97: "Thus, the benefit of this revelation [sc. the encouragement by the speaker through the predicate attribute μακάριοι] goes hand in hand with the *demand of a response*" (italics mine). How Betz, nevertheless, a few lines later can state that the beatitudes are pronounced "*without* condition" is beyond my comprehension, especially in view of his statement on p. 574: "Contrary to today's assumptions, the promise of salvation is thus *not* given *without* condition" (italics mine).

[54] This is also the case with most beatitudes from the Egyptian material; see Assmann, "Weisheit," 21: the "macarism form" over against the "mutuality form."

[55] Cf. Luz, *Matthäusevangelium I*, 201, n. 14; Luz argues that, since "die spärlichen aramäischen und hebräischen Makarismen in der 2. Pers Plur immer mit Suffix formuliert (z.B. Jes 32,20 [אשריכם]) (sind)," the word-by-word translation ought to be μακάριοι ὑμεῖς, as is the formulation in *Herm. Vis.* 2.2.7 and *Sim.* 9.29.3. In the LXX, however, Isa 32:20 is translated μακάριοι οἱ σπείροντες [as I noticed afterwards, this has been observed also by H. Schürmann, *Das Lukasevangelium. Erster Teil* (HTKNT 3; Freiburg: Herder, 1969)

the second person plural, as is also the case with logion 54 in the *Gospel of Thomas*.

Unfortunately, form-criticism is of no help with regard to determining the illocutionary function of individual macarisms, since none of the functions can be tied exclusively to one or the other form: (α) macarisms in the third person plural can exhibit *performative* (Ps 1:1–3; *Pss. Sol.* 4:23), as well as *prescriptive* (*1 Enoch* 81:4; *2 Enoch* 42:6–8), functions and macarisms in the second person plural correspondingly exhibit both *performative* (*1 Enoch* 58:2) and *prescriptive* (Eccl 10:17) functions; (β) the difference between macarisms with relative clauses and those with participial constructions or substantivized adjectives following the attributive μακάριος/μακάριοι does not establish a form-critical criterion for the determination of function either, since both constructions are semantically equivalent and allow for one or the other illocutionary aspect: Ps 1:1–3; *Homeric Hymn to Demeter* 480 (with relative clauses) and *Pss. Sol.* 4:23 (with participial construction) are *performative*, while, for example, Prov 3:13; *1 Enoch* 81:4; *2 Enoch* 42:6–8 (with relative clauses) and Aristoph. *Ra.* 1482 (with participial construction) are *prescriptive.*

This means that there are no rules, at the level of *langue*, that constitute criteria for determining the illocutionary function. Determinative are the *parole*-conditioned co-texts and contexts, in which each individual Macarism or each series of Macarisms is embedded.[56]

(c) The *philosophers of language* have been instrumental in working out the different aspects of how language functions. With the help of their models, it is at least possible to understand how the beatitudes could and still can be interpreted so differently. In the theory of

---

330, note 29]. The second person singular (אשריך) is indeed found in Deut 33:29 (LXX: μακάριος σύ Ισραηλ), Ps 128:2 (LXX 127:2: μακάριος εἶ) and Eccl 10:17 (LXX: μακαρία σύ, γῆ). Consequently, the formulation in Luke 6:20a is not as awkward as Luz maintains, in spite of the formulation of the woes in Luke 6:20–23: οὐαὶ ὑμῖν.

[56] For the terms *langue* and *parole*, see F. de Saussure, *Course in General Linguistics* (New York, NY: McGraw-Hill, 1966) 9 and 13–14 and further the discussion in Hellholm, "Methodological Reflections on the Problem of Definition of Generic Texts," *Mysteries and Revelations. Apocalyptic Studies since the Uppsala Colloquium* (ed. J. J. Collins and J. H. Charlesworth; JSPSup 9; Sheffield: Sheffield Academic Press, 1991) 135–63, here 136–38.

language, one distinguishes first of all between *theoretical* sentences with truth-value and *atheoretical* sentences without truth-value.[57]

(I) Theoretical sentences	(II) Atheoretical sentences
(a) assertive function	(a) commissive function
(α) descriptive function	(b) directive/prescriptive function
(β) informative function	(c) declarative/performative function
	(d) expressive function

J. R. Searle and D. Vanderveken are convinced that there is "a rather limited number of things one can do with language."[58] In fact they maintain that there are only five illocutionary points or types:[59]

---

[57] See already Aristot. *De Interpretatione* 17a 2–4: "Every sentence (λόγος) is significant (σημαντικός)—not as a tool (ὄργανον) but, as we said, by convention (συνθήκη)—but not every sentence is a statement-making sentence (ἀποφαντικός), but only those in which there is truth or falsity (ἐν ᾧ τὸ ἀληθεύειν ἢ ψεύδεσθαι ὑπάρχει). There is not truth or falsity in all sentences: a prayer [or better: petition/wish (εὐχή)—DH] is a sentence but is neither true nor false" (trans. J. L. Ackrill, *Aristotle's Categories and De Interpretatione* [Clarendon Aristotle Series; Oxford: Clarendon, 1963] *ad loc.*). Cf. H. Weidemann, *Aristoteles: Peri Hermeneias* (Aristoteles Werke in deutscher Übersetzung, 1/2; Darmstadt: Wissenschaftliche Buchgesellschaft, 1994) 191–92; further E. Coseriu, "Die Ebenen des sprachlichen Wissens. Der Ort des 'Korrekten' in der Bewertungsskala des Gesprochenen," *Energeia und Ergon. Sprachliche Variation—Sprachgeschichte—Sprachtypologie*, vol. 1, *Schriften von Eugenio Coseriu (1965–1987)* (ed. J. Albrecht; Tübingen: Narr, 1988) 327–64, here 352, notes 50–51. The distinction between sentences that are subject to truth or falsity and those that are not is mentioned also in (Pseudo-[?]) Apuleius, *Peri Hermeneias* 1.146.4–14: ". . . the one of these (sc. various kinds of speech) which is the most important for my topic is that which is called statement (*pronuntiabilis*). It expresses a complete meaning and is the only one of all of them that is subject to truth or falsity . . ." (. . . *est una inter has ad propositum potissima, quae pronuntiabilis appellatur, absolutam sententiam comprehendens, sola ex omnibus veritati aut falsitati obnoxia* . . ."); text and trans. D. Londay and C. Johanson, *The Logic of Apuleius, Including a Complete Latin Text and English Translation of the Peri Hermeneias of Apuleius of Madaura* (PhAnt 47; Leiden: Brill, 1987) 82 and 83; see the reference in Cook, *Structure*, 106, n. 31.

[58] Searle and Vanderveken, *Foundations*, 51; see the review article by E. Rolf, "Eine handlungsanalytische Kritik der Sprechakttheorie," *Linguistische Berichte* 106 (1986) 470–83. Cf. W. Raible in his contribution to the discussion in Gülich and Raible, eds., *Textsorten*, 140: "Die Zahl der möglichen Sprechakte ist so ungeheuer groß, daß man versuchen muß, sie zu reduzieren. Dies kan man tun, indem man nicht Sprechakt und Text, sondern Sprechakt und Textfunktion gleichsetzt. Ein Text bestünde dann aus mehreren Sprechakten, die nicht durch Einzelsätze ausgedrückt werden müssen." Concerning a hierarchy of speech-acts, see especially I. Rosengren, "Hierarchisierung und Sequenzierung von Illokutionen: zwei interdependente Strukturierungsprinzipien bei der Textproduktion,"

(1) "The *assertive* point is to say how things are," that is, to tell others what the case is. The assertives include, among others, the following verbs:[60] *assert* (as the primitive illocutionary force), assure, claim, deny, argue, inform, predict, remind, et cetera. Any proposition can be the content of an assertion. The preparatory condition of all assertive illocutionary forces is the *speaker's* evidence or ground for his assertion (truth-value).

(2) "The *commissive* point is to commit the *speaker* to doing something," that is, to binding oneself to fulfill certain tasks.[61] The commissives include, among others, the following verbs: *commit* (as the primitive illocutionary force), promise, pledge, accept, guarantee, threaten, et cetera. The proposition must represent some future course of action by the *speaker* vis à vis the hearer. The preparatory condition of commissives is the speaker's ability to perform the act to which he has committed himself.

(3) "The *directive* [or *prescriptive*] point is to try to get *other people* to do things," that is, to try to make them carry out certain things. The directives include, among others, the following verbs: *direct* or *prescribe* (as the primitive illocutionary force), order, request, warn, command, recommend, invite, et cetera. The propositional content represents a future course of action of the *hearer*. The preparatory condition is that the hearer is capable of doing what he is directed to do.

(4) "The *declarative* [or *performative*] point is to change the world by saying so," that is, to cause changes by means of utterances. The declaratives are among other performative verbs: *declare* (as the

---

Zeitschrift für Phonetik, Sprachwissenschaft und Kommunikationsforschung 40 (1987) 28–44.

[59] For the following, see Searle and Vanderveken, *Foundations*, 37–40; 54–59. Cf. Brinker, "Textfunktionen," 139–40; Ulkan, *Klassifikation*, 51 et passim; S. Kanngießer, "Sprachliche Universalien und diachrone Prozesse," *Theorie-Diskussion. Sprachpragmatik und Philosophie* (ed. K.-O. Apel; Frankfurt am Main: Suhrkamp, 1976) 273–393, here 342–43. A somewhat longer list of illocutionary types is to be found in D. Wunderlich, *Studien zur Sprechakttheorie* (suhrkamp taschenbuch wissenschaft 172; Frankfurt am Main: Suhrkamp, 1976) 77; a shorter list is found in Bach and Harnish, *Communication*, 39–55: constatives, directives. commissives, acknowledgments.

[60] A "Semantical Analysis of English Illocutionary Verbs" is to be found in Searle and Vanderveken, *Foundations*, Chapter 9, 179–216.

[61] Cf. Ulkan, *Klassifikation*, 184–86, 193.

primitive illocutionary force), approve, endorse, name, christen, bless, curse, excommunicate et cetera." Searle/Vanderveken state that "by definition, a declarative illocution is successful only if the *speaker* brings about the state of affairs represented by its propositional content in the world of the utterance" and they continue by stating that "all successful declarations have a true propositional content and in this respect declarations are peculiar among speech acts in that they are the only speech acts whose successful performance is by itself sufficient to bring about a word-world fit. In such cases, 'saying makes it so,'" and further they claim that "all declarative illocutionary forces have the mode of achievement that the *speaker* invokes his power or authority to perform the declaration and the general preparatory condition that the speaker has the power or authority to change the world by the performance of the appropriate utterance act."[62]

As was pointed out most convincingly by M. Wörner,[63] Austin's first theory was that of the "performative," in which the success of an utterance was bound to the *institutional* backing of the speaker;[64] Austin's second theory was his "speech-act theory," with a set of illocutions and perlocutions, that was not bound to an institution but could be performed by anyone.[65] In his analysis of illocutionary points and forces, Searle[66] has incorporated Austin's performatives in his declaratives as can be seen from the verbs listed in Searle/Vanderveken and referred to above: to christen and excommunicate are bound to church institutions; to nominate and appoint are mainly bound to political or judicial institutions. As Searle/Vanderveken write: "Thus, when one adjourns a meeting, pronounces a couple man and wife, . . . or appoints a chairman, an *extralinguistic institution* empowers an appropriately situated speaker to bring about a word-world match solely in virtue of his speech act."[67] They recognize, however, that there are exceptions to this general requirement of an

---

[62] Searle and Vanderveken, *Foundations,* 57.

[63] M. H. Wörner, *Performative und sprachliches Handeln. Ein Beitrag zu J.L. Austins Theorie der Sprechakte* (IKP-Forschungsberichte Reihe 1.64; Hamburg: Buske, 1978); cf. also D. Hellholm, *Visionenbuch,* 52–58.

[64] Wörner, *Performative,* 15–21.

[65] Wörner, ibid., 244.

[66] Searle, *Expression,* 16–20.

[67] Searle and Vanderveken, *Foundations,* 56–57.

extralinguistic institution. As an example of such a successful performance of declaration they point to "supernatural declarations" like God's utterance, "Let there be light." Here there is no need for an extralinguistic institution, because of the "supernatural powers" involved.[68]

(5) "The *expressive* point is to express feelings and attitudes," that is, to bring out emotions and views. In addition to exclamations the expressives are among other performative verbs: apologize, congratulate, condole, deplore et cetera. There seems to be no general propositional content, although particular expressives can have quite precise propositional contents. There is, of course, usually also a difference of degree of strength among expressives. The preparatory condition is that the propositional content must be true.

From Austin's and Searle's speech-act-theory,[69] we know that the grammatical structure of a sentence is independent of its illocutionary function,[70] and we have seen examples of this already. This is furthermore extremely important in cases of *primary* or *implicit* utterances in contrast to *explicit* ones[71] with metapropositional bases,[72] which provide instructions to the addressees how to interpret the illocution.[73]

The type of function which sees the beatitudes as *declarative/performative* interprets them as consoling declarations. The beatitudes do not merely inform or describe (as theoretical sentences) what is actually true regarding the addressees, but in fact through this

---

68 Searle and Vanderveken, ibid., 57.14

69 See above, note 41.

70 Cf., e.g., von Kutschera, *Sprachphilosophie,* 143: "Der Satz 'es regnet' kann sowohl als Mitteilung verwendet werden wie als Warnung ('Geh nicht ohne Regenschirm hinaus') und als Aufforderung ('Schließ die Fenster, damit es nicht hereinregnet'). Welche Rolle sie jeweils spielt, steht nicht im Satz selbst, sondern ergibt sich erst aus dem pragmatischen Kontext der Äußerung;" see further 168–69; cf. also Coseriu's contribution to the discussion in Gülich and Raible, eds., *Textsorten,* 138: "Es existiert eine Textfunktion 'Aufforderung,' die sehr oft nicht mit der Satzfunktion 'Imperativsatz' zusammenfällt." See also the discussion above related to notes 19 and 20.

71 Cf. Austin, *How to Do Things,* 32, 56–65.

72 See Große, *Text,* 15–16.

73 See further the discussion in Hellholm, *Visionenbuch,* 57.

statement pronounce an assurance. And this assurance is proclaimed unconditionally.

The other type, which understands these beatitudes as *directive/prescriptive,* interprets them as exhortations, especially ethical exhortations. As prescriptive the beatitudes do not merely inform or describe (as theoretical sentences) what is actually true regarding the addressees, nor do they proclaim an unconditional promise, but do in fact primarily admonish the addressees either to become what they are not or to remain as they are. Thus, the promise they deliver is conditional.

These different speech-act-functions, however, are dependent first of all upon the situational context and then, of course, upon the literary co-texts, that is, the intra- as well as the inter-textual co-texts. This is why it becomes precarious when co-textual connections and contextual settings are lost or diminished.

Before I turn to the SM/SP, I will illustrate the problem of different illocutionary functions using materials from Jewish and Greco-Roman literature.

4. Types of Beatitudes in Jewish and Greco-Roman Literature

It is the merit of Professor Burkhard Gladigow to have tried to establish a first, although selective, typology of macarisms from ancient Greek and Roman materials.[74] To my knowledge, Professor Betz was the first New Testament scholar to utilize this typology for the classification of the beatitudes in the SM/SP.[75]

In what follows I will rely on their insight and pursue it still further by systematically addressing first the *time aspect* (eschatological or present) and secondly the *illocutionary function* (directive/prescriptive or declarative/performative) in the Jewish and Greco-Roman material.[76] Here I can only give a few examples of each type:

---

[74] B. Gladigow, "Zum Makarismos des Weisen," *Hermes* 95 (1967) 404–33.

[75] Betz, "Makarismen," [reprinted in *Studien* and *Synoptische Studien*]. English version: "Beatitudes," in *Essays.*

[76] As Assmann, "Weisheit," passim, has shown, all macarisms in the rich Egyptian material are of the basic distichal structure A—B: "'Wer (Gott gegenüber) A ist/tut, dem wird (von Gott) B zuteil' bzw. 'Wohl dem, der A ist/tut, denn ihm wird B zuteil' . . . Selig, wer ihn schaut: dessen Sonne ist aufgegangen [Urk IV 1722]" (p. 21). This means they are all conditional macarisms (Assmann,

(1) The Conventional Macarisms

These are concerned with wealth, fortune, beauty, and the like. Persons who have obtained these attributes or qualities are declared happy or blessed. In the Greek tradition since Homer this type is common. An example is to be found in Anaximenes, *Rhetorica ad Alexandrum* (35.1440b):[77]

> τοὺς γὰρ ἰσχυροὺς καὶ τοὺς καλοὺς καὶ τοὺς εὐγενεῖς καὶ τοὺς πλουσίους οὐκ ἐπαινεῖν ἀλλὰ μακαρίζειν προσήκει.
>
> Since it is appropriate for the strong and handsome and well-born and rich to receive not praise but congratulation on their good fortune.

Another example is Menander, *Fragment* 114:[78]

> Μακάριος ὅστις οὐσίαν καὶ νοῦν ἔχει·
> χρῆται γὰρ οὗτος ἃ δεῖ ταύτῃ καλῶς.
>
> Blessed is the man who has both mind and money,
> for he employs the latter well for what he should.

In the Jewish and Christian tradition this type is rare. 4 Macc 18:9 is an example:[79]

> Μακάριος μὲν ἐκεῖνος,
> τὸν γὰρ τῆς εὐτεκνίας βίον ἐπιζήσας.
>
> Happy was he,
> for the life he lived was blessed with children.

In Sir 31:8 a conventional macarism is on its way to becoming a beatitude of another type, namely, the macarism of the wise, as indicated by the two relative clauses:[80]

> Μακάριος πλούσιος, ὃς εὑρέθη ἄμωμος
> καὶ ὃς ὀπίσω χρυσίου οὐκ ἐπορεύθη.

---

ibid., 29 and 31), that is to say, their function is directive/prescriptive, although not in an ethical sense; see below, note 98.

[77] Text and trans. H. Rackham, *Aristotle XVI: Rhetorica ad Alexandrum* (LCL; Cambridge, MA: Harvard University Press; London: Heinemann 1983) 257–449. This text is referred to in E. Klostermann, *Das Matthäusevangelium* (HNT 5; 3rd ed. 1927 [= 4th ed.]; Tübingen: Mohr [Siebeck] 197) 34.

[78] Text and trans. F. G. Allinson, *Menander. The Principal Fragments* (LCL; Cambridge, MA: Harvard University Press; London: Heinemann 1964) 342–43.

[79] Trans. H. Anderson, "4 Maccabees," *OTP,* 2. 531–64.

[80] Trans. NEB.

Happy the rich man, who has remained free of its taint
and has not made gold its aim.

This type is almost exclusively *present-oriented* in nature, since the blessedness it promises is happiness in this life and not in that to come. Functionally it is also *performative.* A prescriptive impulse is only indirectly present.[81]

(2) The Macarism of the Wise or the Inverted Conventional Macarism

This type is concerned with wisdom and virtues and turns the conventional macarism upside down.[82] Its origin is in critical reflection on the conventional macarism. An instructive example is Sir 25:8, where the conventional blessing of the man who has found a beautiful and rich wife (for example, Aristoph. *Av.* 1725–27) is replaced by another evaluation:[83]

Μακάριος ὁ συνοικῶν γυναικὶ συνετῇ.

Happy the husband of a sensible wife.

The illocutionary function of this macarism is not easy to ascertain, since the intra-textual co-text is mainly made up of sentences and gnomae. Yet, it seems likely that it is primarily *performative* and only secondarily *prescriptive,* but certainly not in an ethical sense. The happiness is proclaimed for the *present* and not for the future.

An example from Greek literature is found in Aristoph. *Ra.* 1482:[84]

Μακάριός γ' ἀνὴρ ἔχων ξύνεσιν ἠκριβωμένην.

Happy the man who possesses a keen intelligent mind.

This beatitude, stripped of its co-text, is certainly *performative.* As part of its intra-textual co-text it attains *in addition a prescriptive* function,

---

[81] Cf. K. von Fritz, *Philosophie und sprachlicher Ausdruck bei Demokrit, Plato und Aristoteles* (New York, Leipzig and London: Stechert,1938) 33: "Pracht und Glanz, Macht und Reichtum, Gesundheit und Schönheit macht den ὄλβος aus. Der ὄλβος ist das Glück in seiner äußeren Erscheinung gesehen, als gegenwärtiger Zustand;" further Gladigow, "Makarismos," 405.

[82] Gladigow, "Makarismos," passim; Betz, "Makarismen," *Studien,* 28 [= *Synoptische Studien,* 104]; Engl. version: "Beatitudes," *Essays,* 30–31.

[83] Trans.: NEB.

[84] Text and trans.: B. B. Rogers, *Aristophanes, Frogs* (LCL; Cambridge, MA: Harvard University Press; London: Heinemann, 1924).

although not ethical, but rather exhortative in respect to patriotism: "The Chorus sings an ode in praise of the man of true intelligence, who, they claim, will avoid socratic subtleties and bring practical benefit to his kinsmen and to the citizens in general."[85] The *present-oriented* aspect is in this case obvious.

(3) The Religious Macarism.

This type can be divided into two kinds:

(3.1) The Religious Macarism of the Wise.

This type is common among the Psalms of the Old Testament and in Wisdom literature. The most evident example is Ps 1:1–2.[86]

Μακάριος ἀνήρ, ὃς οὐκ ἐπορεύθη ἐν βουλῇ ἀσεβῶν
καὶ ἐν ὁδῷ ἁμαρτωλῶν οὐκ ἔστη
καὶ ἐπὶ καθέδραν λοιμῶν οὐκ ἐκάθισεν,
ἀλλ' ἢ ἐν τῷ νόμῳ κυρίου τὸ θέλημα αὐτοῦ,
καὶ ἐν τῷ νόμῳ αὐτοῦ μελετήσει ἡμέρας καὶ νυκτός.

Happy is the man
who does not take the wicked for his guide
nor walk the road that sinners tread
nor take his seat among the scornful;
the law of the Lord is his delight . . . .

Another example is *Pss. Sol.* 4:23:[87]

Μακάριοι οἱ φοβούμενοι τὸν κύριον ἐν ἀκακίᾳ αὐτῶν·
ὁ κύριος ῥύσεται αὐτοὺς ἀπὸ ἀνθρώπων δολίων καὶ ἁμαρτωλῶν.

Blessed are those who fear God in their innocence;
the Lord shall save them from deceitful and sinful people.

Here the religious wise person is declared happy already *here and now* without any reference to the other-world. The co-texts of both macarisms show that we have to do with *performative* beatitudes, which are declarations of grace to those who fear God in contrast to the accusations and woes over the ungodly and unjust.

---

85 W. B. Stanford, *Aristophanes, The Frogs* (2d ed.; Basingstoke and London: Macmillan, 1963) 197–98.

86 Trans. NEB

87 Trans. R. B. Wright, "Psalms of Solomon," *OTP,* 2. 656.

This type of macarism is, as far as Greek religion is concerned, to be found in the cult of Dionysos as the well-known example from Euripides, *Bacchae* 72–74 shows:[88]

Ὦ μάκαρ, ὅστις εὐδαίμων	O blessed he, who in happiness
τελετὰς θεῶν εἰδὼς	knowing the rituals of the Gods
βιοτὰν ἁγιστεύει καὶ	makes holy his way of life and
θιασεύεται ψυχάν.	mingles his spirit with sacred band.

B. Gladigow has pointed out that here Euripides has transferred to the disciples of Dionysos a religious macarism that originally applied to the Eleusinian mysteries.[89] Here we can observe a change from a religious eschatological macarism to a religious macarism of the wise, as has been noticed by E. R. Dodds in his commentary on this text: "The present passage, like these (sc. *The Homeric Hymn to Demeter* and Pind. *Fragment* 137), bases the promise of happiness on a religious experience, but its promise, unlike theirs, is for this world, not for the next—the happiness which Dion[ysos] gives is here and now."[90] Thus, this macarism is *present-oriented* and not eschatological and furthermore, it is *performative* and not prescriptive.

(3.2) The Religious Eschatological Macarism

This type is common in the intertestamental apocalyptic literature and in the Hellenistic mystery religions.

I will give two examples from the *Ethiopic Book of Enoch (= 1 Enoch)*; first from 58:2:[91]

> Blessed are you, the righteous and chosen,
> for your lot will be glorious!

Also from the immediate co-text it is clear that the apodosis-line is *eschatologically* qualified:

---

[88] Text: D. Ebener, *Euripides Tragödien. Sechster Teil* (SQAW 30,6; Berlin: Akademie-Verlag, 1980) 122–23; trans.: G. S. Kirk, *The Bacchae of Euripides* (Englewood Cliffs, NJ: Prentice-Hall,1970) 33–35.

[89] Gladigow, "Makarismen," 404.

[90] E. R. Dodds, *Euripides. Bacchae: Edited with Introduction and Commentary* (Oxford: Clarendon 1986 [= 2nd ed. 1960]) 75. There are, however, indications that the macarisms of the Eleusinian mysteries were not exclusively eschatological but also this-worldly, see below *ad* notes 94, 95 and 99.

[91] Trans.: M. A. Knibb, "1 Enoch," *The Apocryphal Old Testament* (ed. H. F. D. Sparks; Oxford: Clarendon, 1984) 169–319, here 236–37.

And the righteous will be in the light of the sun,
and the chosen in the light of eternal life;
and there will be no end to the days of their life,
and the days of the holy will be without number.

From the co-text it is further evident that we are here dealing with a *performative-consoling* and not with a *prescriptive-ethical* macarism.

The other example is taken from 81:4:[92]

Blessed is the man,
who dies righteous and good,
concerning whom no book of iniquity has been written,
and against whom no guilt has been found [on the day of judgement].

In contrast to the previous one this *eschatological* beatitude can only be interpreted as *prescriptive-ethical* as is evident from the co-text in 81:3 and 81:6–8.

The eschatological perspective, which is characteristic of these Jewish macarisms, is also to be found in Greek texts from the mystery religions. In *The Homeric Hymn to Demeter* 480–82 we read:[93]

ὄλβιος ὃς ταδ' ὄπωπεν ἐπιχθονίων ἀνθρώπων·
ὃς δ' ἀτελὴς ἱερῶν, ὃς τ' ἄμμορος, οὔ ποθ' ὁμοίων
αἶσαν ἔχει φθίμενός περ ὑπὸ ζόφῳ εὐρώεντι.

Blessed is the mortal on earth who has seen the rites,
but the uninitiate who has no share in them
never has the same lot once dead in the dreary darkness.

In his commentary N. J. Richarson writes: "The Poet proclaims the blessed state of those who have seen the mysteries, and the unhappy fate after death of the uninitiated . . . . It is natural to assume that this refers both to the present life and also to the life after death . . . . The emphasis here, however, is more on the second . . . .;"[94] and W. Burkert says it even more strongly: "There is no attack on the joys of living, but the accent is indeed on the other side."[95]

---

[92] Trans.: Knibb, ibid., 270 with note 11.

[93] Text: N. J. Richardson, *The Homeric Hymn to Demeter* (Oxford: Clarendon, 1974) 134; text and trans. H. P. Foley, *The Homeric Hymn to Demeter. Translation, Commentary and Interpretative Essays* (ed. H. P. Foley; Princeton, NJ: Princeton University Press, 1994) 26–27.

[94] Richardson, *Hymn to Demeter,* 310–11.

[95] W. Burkert, *Ancient Mystery Cults* (Cambridge, MA and London: Harvard University Press, 1987) 21.

In the macarism found in 486–89, the stress, however, lies on happiness *now* and the "prosperity in this life, rather than happiness after death:"[96]

> μέγ' ὄλβιος ὅν τιν' ἐκεῖναι
> προφρομέως φίλωνται ἐπιχθονίων ἀνθρώπων·
> αἶψα δέ οἱ πέμπουσιν ἐφέστιον ἐς μέγα δῶμα
> Πλοῦτον, ὃς ἀνθρώποις ἄφενος θνητοῖσι δίδωσιν.

> Highly blessed is the mortal on earth
> whom they graciously favor with love.
> For soon they will send to the hearth of his great house
> Ploutos, the god giving abundance to mortals.

Concerning the question of consolation or exhortation in these macarisms it is clear that "there is no hint at an ethical viewpoint here, no suggestion that initiation requires good conduct, or that evil deeds will be punished."[97] The question of function, however, is not decided by the denial of an ethical viewpoint, since the prescriptive function need not be ethical but "theological," or perhaps better: cultic, in the sense that the exhortation here is in fact an urgent invitation to be initiated into the mysteries.[98] I believe that both functions, the *performative* as well as the *prescriptive*, apply in this case. Concerning the *time aspect*, it is evident that the blessings are for this world as well as for the next.[99]

A characteristically eschatological macarism is the one in Pind. *Fragment* 137 (Snell/Maehler; Bowra, *Fragment* 121), where the text reads:[100]

---

[96] Richardson, ibid., 316–17; text: Richardson, ibid., 134–35; text and trans.: Foley, *Homeric Hymn,* 26–27.

[97] Richardson, ibid., 311.

[98] Macarisms with directive/prescriptive function of a non-ethical character are also found in Egypt; see Assmann, "Weisheit," 42: ". . . (selig) er, der eingeführt ist in (deine Lehre), der unterwiesen ist (. . .) er wird immer deine Stimme hören . . .;" see further ibid., 39 and 43: "Appellfunktion."

[99] See Foley, *Hymn to Demeter,* 63: "It [sc. happiness] can include worldly success (. . .) as well as a different relation to the afterlife;" J. Rudhardt, "Concerning the Homeric Hymn to Demeter," *Hymn to Demeter,* 198–211, esp. 208: "The *Hymn* teaches us that the Mysteries procure for their initiates advantages both in this world and in the Other World (480–82)." So also in the Amarna-macarisms; see Assmann, "Weisheit," 33.

[100] Text: B. Snell and H. Maehler, *Pindarus. Pars II: Fragmenta. Indices* (Bibl. Teub.; 4th ed.; Leipzig: Teubner, 1975) 112; C. M. Bowra, *Pindar* (Oxford:

ὄλβιος ὅστις ἰδὼν κεῖν' εἶσ' ὑπὸ χθόν'·
οἶδε μὲν βίου τελευτάν,
οἶδεν δὲ διόσδοτον ἀρχάν.

Happy is he who, having seen those things, passes under the earth;
He knows the end of life,
And knows the god-given beginning.

The *eschatological* perspective in this Eleusinian beatitude is underlined by E. R. Dodds, Fritz Graf and C. M. Bowra.[101] In the Orphic-Pythagorean appropriation of the Eleusinian macarisms, however, we can—as Graf has pointed out—observe an ethicizing shift, as is indicated in Aristophanes, *Frogs* 448–55.[102] An ethical admonition is not included in this macarism, even if a *prescriptive* component with the exhortation to experience the *orgia* is not to be excluded. Graf emphasizes the *performative* function when he says: "The 'secret society' of the mystery cult is concerned with the depiction to its members of their splendid lot ...."[103]

From the Orphic tablets we now know that the Orphic and Eleusinian worlds are closely related and that the *eschatological* promises, and sometimes threats, are given in the form of macarisms.[104]

The result of the functional analysis shows that there is no automatic connection between eschatological promise and ethical or cultic exhortation. This is true of the Jewish, as well as of the Greco-Roman, eschatological macarisms.

These two types of religious beatitudes, the macarism of the wise and the eschatological macarism, diverge mainly in regard to how the time aspect is related to their illocutionary functions: the macarisms of the wise are almost exclusively *performative*, while the apocalyptic-

Clarendon, 1964) 90; trans. Bowra. See now also text and trans. in W. H. Race, *Pindar II* (LCL; Cambridge, MA and London: Harvard University Press, 1997) 370–71.

101 Dodds, *Bacchae*, 75; F. Graf, *Eleusis und die orphische Dichtung: Athens in vorhellenistischer Zeit* (RVV 33; Berlin and New York: de Gruyter, 1974) 79–80; Bowra, *Pindar*, 90.

102 See Graf, *Eleusis*, 81–94, esp. 81–82, 86–87, 89, and 93.

103 Graf, *Eleusis*, 80.

104 F. Graf, "Dionysian and Orphic Eschatology: New Texts and Old Questions," *Masks of Dionysus* (ed. T. H. Carpenter and C. A. Faraone; Myth and Poetics; Ithaca, NY and London: Cornell, 1993) 239–58, esp. 241–42 et passim; W. Burkert, "Bacchic Teletai in the Hellenistic Age," *Masks of Dionysus*, 259–75.

eschatological macarisms, depending on the context, can either be *declarative/performative* or *directive/prescriptive* or sometimes even *both.*

5. Interpretation of the Macarisms in the Sermon on the Mount and in the Sermon on the Plain

When I now turn to the SM/SP I will restrict myself to a few macarisms, namely, the first in the SM and the SP, and the eighth in the SM, which has no parallel in the SP; both, however, have parallels in the *Gospel of Thomas.* Thereby I will concentrate on the functional aspect in conjunction with the semantic understanding of these beatitudes.

The macarisms I will discuss here are all "distiches made up of a *protasis*-line consisting of the adjective μακάριοι, functioning as a predicate attribute, followed by a substantivized adjective or participial construction, functioning as the subject of the protasis but lacking the copula as predicate, thus being an elliptic construction;[105] this part of the protases functions at the same time as a description of the *preconditioned situation* of those who are called 'blessed.'"[106] In this way they are statements about the addressees.

The *apodosis*-line is made up of a causal clause introduced by the conjunction ὅτι; thereby the first and the eighth are identical. It is also "pertinent to observe that the causal connection . . . is not with the subject part of the protasis but throughout with the predicate attribute μακάριοι. Thus the apodoses render the reason for the affirmation of felicity, which in turn is the result of the preconditioned situation referred to in the subject part of the protases."[107]

---

105 Cf. F. Blaß, A. Debrunner and F. Rehkopf, *Grammatik des neutestamentlichen Griechisch* (14th ed.; Göttingen: Vandenhoeck & Ruprecht, 1976) 105–6 [§ 128.1].

106 Hellholm, "Rejoice," 54–55; similarly now Viviano, "Beatitudes," 73; cf. also Betz, "Beatitudes," *Essays,* 30: ". . . the characteristic feature of the first line of the macarism in Matt. 5:3 is the designation of those addressed;" "Makarismen," *Studien,* 28; [= *Synoptische Studien,* 104].

107 Hellholm, "Rejoice," 55; cf. Viviano, ibid., 73; Betz, *Sermon on the Mount,* 118 and also 93. The beatitudes in 4Q525 2 II 1–13 are sapiential rather than eschatological (Fitzmyer, "Collection," 513–14), and they are not *distiches* with a protasis containing the affirmation and the description of the addressees followed by an apodosis that brings the reason for the affirmation; rather "the second clause in each pair is . . . in antithetical parallelism with the first clause" (Viviano, ibid., 76).

5.1. The Sermon on the Mount

5.1.1. The First Macarism in the SM (Matt 5:3)

The first macarism in the series is also the "leading" one of which the others are variants, according to Professor Betz.[108] This beatitude is complicated in so far as the *syntagma* οἱ πτωχοὶ τῷ πνεύματι is unique in the NT, early Christian literature and Greek literature at large. How should it be understood semantically? As pure economic poverty? The importance of a functional analysis is made evident by Betz in his discussion of the possible interpretation of οἱ πτωχοὶ τῷ πνεύματι as referring to economic poverty or rather economically poor people. The functional possibilities formulated in the second person plural would then be:

(1) Declarative/performative function:
Blessed are you,

causal:	*since* you are economically poor
circumstantial:	*when* you are economically poor
concessive:	*although* you are economically poor

for yours is the Kingdom of Heaven.

(2) Directive/prescriptive function:
Blessed are you,

conditional—	
ingressive:	*if* you *become/*
durative	*if* you *remain* economically poor

for yours is the Kingdom of Heaven.

As far as the declarative function is concerned, Betz rules out the causal interpretations, when he states that "it is important to realize that the SM does *not* regard the condition of poverty as a blessing."[109] The circumstantial and concessive interpretations, however, are acceptable, since "even though the condition of poverty is not blessed, persons living in such conditions can be blessed."[110] With these statements he has in fact also ruled out the possibility of the directive/prescriptive function and spells this out implicitly when emphasizing that "praising the condition of poverty as such would hardly be conceivable in antiquity, unless it were done as an act of folly

---

108 Betz, "Beatitudes," *Essays*, 24; *Sermon on the Mount*, 130, 136.

109 Betz, *Sermon on the Mount*, 114.

110 Betz, ibid.

or cynicism. Also, praising the poor simply because they are poor economically would be equally cynical because experience indicates that poor people may be good or bad like everyone else."[111] Thus, material deprivation as such cannot be the reason for the blessing in the SM.

The syntagma οἱ πτωχοὶ τῷ πνεύματι, however, can hardly mean just economically poor,[112] since then the adverbial qualifier would be redundant. Can it be interpreted as purely metaphorical, be it in the *positive* sense of "humble, pious or even meek,"[113] or in the *negative* sense of "fainthearted, desperate or despondent"?[114]

When trying to arrive at a cohesive interpretation of the polysemic syntagma "the poor in (the) spirit," we are limited first of all with respect to the intra-textual co-text to the series of macarisms and then to the SM itself; with respect to the inter-textual co-texts, this applies first of all to the SP and the *Gospel of Thomas* and only secondarily to other materials of a compatible nature, Christian, Jewish, and Greco-Roman or Egyptian.[115] The *semantic* as well as *illocutionary* alternatives can, in my opinion, best be evaluated by means of the following juxtaposition formulated in the second person plural:

(1) Declarative/performative function:
Blessed are you,

positive-causal:	*since* you are humble/pious/meek
positive-circumstantial:	*when* you are humble/pious/meek
negative-concessive:	*although* you are fainthearted/ desperate/despondent

---

[111] Betz, ibid.; see, however, my critique of this generalization by Betz, below in note 178. H. Merklein, "πτωχός κτλ.," *EWNT* 3. 469.

[112] Πτωχός means poor in the sense of beggar, but it can also be used in a more general sense; see *LSJ*, 1550, *s.v.* πτωχός: AP 9.258 (Antiphan.): [πηγή] πτωχὴ νυμφῶν; Gal 4:9: ἀσθενῆ καὶ πτωχὰ στοιχεῖα; 1 Cor 15:10 v.l.: πτωχὴ οὐκ ἐγενήθη; cf. W. Bauer, F. W. Gingrich and F. Danker, *A Greek-English Lexicon of the New Testament and Other Early Christian Literature* (2d ed.; Chicago and London: The University of Chicago Press, 1979) *s.v.* πτωχός 2.

[113] Cf., e.g., E. Schweizer, "πνεῦμα κτλ.," *TWNT* 6. 398–99; Strecker, *Bergpredigt*, 33–34.

[114] Cf., e.g., E. Best, "Matthew V.3," *NTS* 7 (1960–61) 255–58; Powell, "Beatitudes," 463.

[115] The inter-textual co-texts of Jewish, Greco-Roman and Egyptian provenance play—as expected—an important role in Professor Betz's interpretation of the Beatitudes in the SM and the SP.

for yours is the Kingdom of Heaven.

(2) Directive/prescriptive function:

Blessed are you,

positive-conditional—

ingressive:	*if* you *become/*
durative:	*if* you *remain* humble/pious/meek

negative-conditional—

ingressive:	*if* you *become/*
durative:	*if* you *remain* fainthearted/desperate despondent

for yours is the Kingdom of Heaven.

It will now become even more evident how important the determination of the functional aspect in fact is for the interpretation of the syntagma "poor in (the) spirit." In the case of a *declarative/performative* designation, on the one hand, both the supposed positive and the negative interpretations are possible, since it is reasonable to affirm felicity causally or circumstantially to "humble, pious or meek" disciples/crowds as well as concessively to "fainthearted, desperate or despondent" disciples/crowds.[116]

In the case of a *directive/prescriptive* designation, on the other hand, the negative is excluded and only the positive interpretation possible, since it is unreasonable to assume that in the SM an exhortation to become or to remain "fainthearted, desperate or despondent" should be given; but it is indeed plausible to admonish people to become or remain "humble, pious and meek."

Before we try to make a decision between the two functions, we should take a look at the proposal by Prof. Betz regarding the *semantic* meaning of "poor in (the) spirit." In his commentary Betz suggests that the expression is not really metaphorical but refers to "the *intellectual insight* into the human conditions,"[117] conditions which he

---

[116] A positive concessive understanding is ruled out by definition; see above in relation to note 51.

[117] Betz, *Sermon on the Mount*, 115. Similarly already T. Zahn, *Das Evangelium des Matthäus* (KNT 1; Leipzig: Deichert, 1903) 178: "Es drückt nicht den Mangel an irgend etwas, sondern die Haltung des Bedürftigen aus." This interpretation comes close to the philosophers' reinterpretation of the macarisms of the mysteries as asserted by Richardson, *Hymn to Demeter*, 313: "Later the μακαρισμός of the mysteries is taken over by the philosophers, who proclaim the blessed happiness of those who have gained *enlightenment* by contemplation, and who

designates as poverty, desertion and misery; this intellectual insight is then characterized as "humility" over against "hubris."[118] This interpretation relies on a familiar *topos* in antiquity, in Judaism[119] as well as in Greek philosophy;[120] this is its strength. Its weakness lies in the lack of philological parallels and—as far as I can see—Professor Betz has given no explanation for the odd syntagma οἱ πτωχοὶ τῷ πνεύματι.[121] To be sure, he refers, as others before him,[122] to עניי רוח in 1QM 14:7 and to the difficult passage 1QH 14:3,[123] but insists at the same time that "the original language of the SM was Greek, not Aramaic"[124] and much less Hebrew. As W. D. Davies/D. C. Allison rightly have pointed out, "the Hebrew, like Mt 5.3, (unfortunately) can bear several senses:" humble, fainthearted or voluntarily poor;[125] thus, the Hebrew syntagma עניי רוח is of little

---

understand the nature of the world in the same way that the initiate has *insight or knowledge of the nature of his existence*" (italics mine). In Egyptian macarisms the emphasis is on God's action, as pointed out by Assmann, "Weisheit," 49: " . . . Gottes Wirken im Horizont des menschlichen Daseins und der Bezogenheit, des Umgriffenseins der conditio humana vom Göttlichen . . . ."

118 Betz, ibid., 116, 146; cf. Zahn, *Matthäus*, 182.

119 Especially in connection with the ענוים piety; see R. Martin-Achard, "ענה II elend sein," in: *THAT* II (München: Kaiser; Zürich: Theologischer Verlag, 1976) 341–350; E. Gerstenberger ענה, in: *TWAT* 6. 247–270; Betz, *Sermon on the Mount*, 116.

120 Betz refers to the Socratic and Cynic schools as advocates of a "positive evaluation of poverty, *understood as self-understanding*," ibid., 116 (italics mine); see also the material referred to ibid., 114–15.

121 Since the syntagma οἱ πτωχοὶ τῷ πνεύματι is syntactically unique in Greek literature—as Betz has rightly pointed out—its metaphorical meaning is unknown; see *LSJ*, 1550, *s.v.*, πτωχός, where the only evidence for the metaphorical meaning is said to be Matt 5:3.

122 E.g., H.-T. Wrege, *Die Überlieferungsgeschichte der Bergpredigt* (WUNT 9; Tübingen: Mohr [Siebeck] 1968) 6: "Die Qumrantexte haben für diesen Zusatz die Präformation erbracht: 1QM 14,7 begegnet בעניי רוח als Selbstbezeichnung der Sektenglieder und zwar im synonymen Parallelismus zu den 'Vollkommenen des Wandels;'" H. Braun, *Qumran und das Neue Testament. Band I* (Tübingen: Mohr [Siebeck], 1966) 13.

123 Betz, ibid., 116 with references to literature in note 178, where the reference should be to 1QH 14:3 and *not* to *1QM* 14:3(!). It is noteworthy that in connection with the designation עניי רוח no macarisms occur, and in the series of macarisms in 4Q525 (Béat) this designation is missing.

124 Betz, ibid., 125.

help in monosemizing the Greek syntagma οἱ πτωχοὶ τῷ πνεύματι, regardless of whether the reference is to individuals or to a particular group of pious people (designating themselves as ענוים). At the end of this essay, I will try to provide an explanation for the odd Greek syntagma. In view of the question of function, Professor Betz's *semantic* proposal will come out as follows:

(1) Declarative/performative function:
Blessed are you,

causal:	*since* you are aware of the human conditions of poverty, desertion and misery.
circumstantial:	*when* you are aware of the human conditions of poverty desertion and misery.
concessive:	*although* you are aware of the human conditions of poverty, desertion and misery.

for yours is the Kingdom of Heaven.

(2) Directive/prescriptive function:
Blessed are you,

conditional-ingressive:	*if* you *become* aware of the human conditions of poverty, desertion and misery.
conditional-durative:	*if* you *remain* aware of the human conditions of poverty, desertion and misery.

for yours is the Kingdom of Heaven.

This *semantic* interpretation in itself allows a declarative/performative as well as a directive/prescriptive illocution; in the *performative* case the causal and circumstantial interpretations are possible, while the concessive by definition is excluded;[126] in the *prescriptive* case, both the ingressive and the durative options are reasonable as admonitions to obtain or maintain these insights.

Before we continue our functional analysis of the semantic proposal by Prof. Betz, we have to ask which functional aspect could be

[125] Davies and Allison, *Matthew I,* 444; see also Luz, *Matthäusevangelium I,* 206; the meaning "voluntarily poor" is again recently advocated by Schenk, *Sprache des Matthäus,* 424.

[126] See above, in relation to note 51.

intended in the epitome as far as the *usual* semantic interpretation is concerned? In both cases we are dependent on the intra-textual co-text of the SM. From its "self-understanding" (Matt 7:24–27),[127] its "hermeneutical principles" (5:17–20),[128] the "antitheses" (5:21–48),[129] and its inherent "soteriological basis" (6:25–34),[130] it is clear that the introductory series of macarisms has to be understood in the first place as *prescriptive-ethical* sayings.[131] If this is the case, then the common negative *metaphorical* interpretation as "fainthearted" or "despondent" is excluded and we are left with the positive *metaphorical* sense "humble, pious" or even "meek." But then we get into difficulties with the third macarism and the blessing of the πραεῖς there,[132] which has caused some commentators to regard this macarism as a later insertion.[133] J. Wellhausen, by reversing the order of the second and third macarisms and at the same time presupposing the use of ענו and עני respectively, proposed that the first and the third once constituted a *parallelismus membrorum*,[134] and Betz, without following Wellhausen's reversal, still insists that "meek" is a variation of the "poor in spirit."[135] The understanding of πραΰς as a variation of οἱ πτωχοὶ τῷ πνεύματι is certainly intelligible in the series of macarisms, but it is not yet, in my opinion, distinctive enough, especially if the first

---

[127] Betz, "Eschatology in the Sermon on the Mount and the Sermon on the Plain," *Synoptische Studien,* 219–29.

[128] Betz, "The Hermeneutical Principles of the Sermon on the Mount (Matt. 5:17–20)," *Essays,* 37–53; German in *Studien,* 34–48 [= *Synoptische Studien,* 111–126].

[129] P. Hoffmann, "Die Begründung einer neuen Ethik in den Antithesen der Bergpredigt," *Studien zur Frühgeschichte der Jesus-Bewegung* (Stuttgarter Biblische Aufsätze 17; Stuttgart: Katholisches Bibelwerk, 1994) 73–94.

[130] Betz, "Cosmogony and Ethics in the Sermon on the Mount," *Essays,* 89–123; German in *Studien,* 78–110 [= idem, *Synoptische Studien,* 155–87].

[131] See, e.g., Strecker, *Bergpredigt,* 34; Luz, *Matthäusevangelium I,* 205, 207; Davies and Allison, *Matthew I,* 440; Betz, *Sermon on the Mount,* 97 et passim.

[132] Cf. F. Hauck and S. Schulz, πραΰς, *TWNT* 6. 645–51.

[133] See, e.g., J. Wellhausen, *Das Evangelium Matthäei* (2d ed.; Berlin: Reimer, 1914) 15; Klostermann, *Matthäusevangelium,* 37; Bultmann, *Geschichte,* 115; T. W. Manson, *The Sayings of Jesus* (London: SCM, 1949) 152; Bammel, πτωχός κτλ., *TWNT* 6. 903–4; S. T. Lachs, *A Rabbinic Commentary on the New Testament. The Gospels of Matthew, Mark, and Luke* (Hoboken, NJ: KTAV, 1987) 74.

[134] Wellhausen, ibid.; Lachs, ibid.; Davies and Allison, *Matthew I,* 449; cf. also D. A. Hagner, *Matthew 1–13* (WBC 33A; Dallas, TX: Word Books, 1993) 93.

[135] Betz, *Sermon on the Mount,* 125.

macarism functions as the "leading," "basic," and overarching one, of which "all others are climactic developments of some sort."[136] The specific and distinctive semantic meaning of the other macarisms must be established before one can determine the inter-relationship between the two stanzas and between the singular macarisms within each stanza. This task, however, must be left for another occasion.

If we return to the semantic proposal by Prof. Betz, the indicated difficulty could be removed and the *directive/prescriptive* function of the first macarism would be as follows: becoming aware of the deprived human condition "is essential for one's understanding of life; it is also the starting point of an ethic."[137] This means ethical encouragement or exhortation of the disciples to become what they are not or to remain as they are, namely, aware of the human conditions of poverty, desertion and misery.

The *apodosis*-line (ὅτι αὐτῶν ἐστιν ἡ βασιλεία τῶν οὐρανῶν) is in a different way important for the functional aspect,[138] but it is especially important for the *time aspect.* As it now stands in the SM, it renders the reason for the affirmation of felicity and refers to the eschatological end-time when God is to judge.[139] Thus the "Kingdom of Heaven" is an "altogether eschatological concept," an anticipation of an *eschatological* verdict in the afterworld.[140] This is even more obvious in the co-text on the *Matthean level* as the judgement scene in Matt 25:31–46 shows.[141] What should be noted already here, however, is the striking difference between the apodoses-lines in the first and the eighth macarisms, that are formulated in the present tense, and

---

[136] Betz, ibid., 109.

[137] So Betz, ibid., 115.

[138] See my discussion below in paragraph 6 on its significance for the historical Jesus in contrast to its meaning in the SM/SP and Matthew/Luke.

[139] Cf. Strecker, *Bergpredigt,* 32; Luz, *Matthäusevangelium I,* 208; Davies and Allison, *Matthew I,* 445.

[140] Betz, "Beatitudes," *Essays,* 34; "Makarismen," *Studien,* 18; [= *Synoptische Studien,* 108]; *Sermon on the Mount,* 118.

[141] Cf. Betz, "Beatitudes," *Essays,* 26; "Makarismen," *Studien,* 10–11; [= *Synoptische Studien,* 100]; note, however, that Betz is using here the intra-textual co-text of the Gospel of Matthew without reflecting on the fact that he has declared the co-text in Matthew as not directly relevant for the interpretation of the epitome. Only as an inter-textual co-text of a much later document can Matthew 25 here be operational.

those in between, that are all formulated in the future tense, whether in the active or passive voice.[142]

If, as Professor Betz claims, the macarisms in the SM are to be interpreted as *inverted* beatitudes,[143] that is, as "eschatological macarisms of the wise man," it is pertinent to examine of what concepts they are inversions.[144] With regard to the usual understanding, it is in most cases rather easy to establish the antonyms as, for example, to "the poor" (οἱ πτωχοί), "those who mourn" (οἱ πενθοῦντες), "the meek" (οἱ πραεῖς), namely, "the rich" (οἱ πλούσιοι, οἱ εὔποροι),[145] "those who laugh" (οἱ γελῶντες),[146] "the brutal" (οἱ ἀγριότητες)/"the angry" (οἱ ὀργιλότητες)[147]/"the cruel" (οἱ χαλιπότητες).[148] With regard to the syntagma οἱ πτωχοὶ τῷ πνεύματι, the antonyms that come closest are those listed as antonyms to οἱ πραεῖς. What those blessed in fact are deprived of are the characteristics that constitute the antonyms to the description of the addressees' situation in the protases.[149]

With regard the interpretation of the recipients as those with "insight into the *condicio humana*," the deprivation that Betz also envisages[150] cannot in the *first* place consist of the antithetical concepts that are made up of the antonyms to "misery," "grief," "meekness" etc. listed above, which will have to be done in a *second* round, but rather of an antithetical concept to "the insight, the enlightenment" into

[142] See further below, pp. 333–34.

[143] Betz, "Beatitudes," *Essays*, 33; "Makarismen," *Studien*, 30 [= *Synoptische Studien*, 107]; *Sermon on the Mount*, 97 et passim; so also A. Kodjak, *A Structural Analysis of the Sermon on the Mount* (Berlin: Mouton de Gruyter, 1986) 42.

[144] Cf. H. Geckeler, *Strukturelle Semantik und Wordfeldtheorie* (München: Fink, 1971) 103: "Die Geltung eines Wortes wird erst erkannt, wenn man sie gegen die Geltung benachbarten und opponierenden abgrenzt. Nur als Teil des Ganzen hat es Sinn; denn nur im Feld gibt es Bedeuten;" citation from J. Trier, *Der deutsche Wortschatz im Sinnbezirk des Verstandes, Band I* (Heidelberg: Winter, 1931 [= 2nd ed. 1973]), 6.

[145] See Luke 6:24; cf. F. Hauck, "πτωχός im Griechischen," *TWNT* 6. 886–87; Betz, *Sermon on the Mount*, 112.

[146] See Luke 6:25.

[147] For the last two, see Betz, *Sermon on the Mount*, 126.

[148] F. Hauck and S. Schulz, "πραΰς κτλ.," *TWNT* 6. 645.

[149] Cf. Assmann, "Weisheit," 39 and 47.

[150] Betz, *Sermon on the Mount*, 142.

these human conditions. Consequently, the antonym for the first three macarisms will be one and the same, namely, "the ignorance" of these conditions, which in itself is not yet but could easily develop into "hubris."[151]

In the series of macarisms in the SM, this abstract semantic intimation has its real advantage insofar as it allows for all beatitudes in the first stanza to obtain the same prescriptive function.[152] Then both stanzas would be directive/prescriptive, promising a conditional reward, and the whole series of eight can "be read as a single unit" also from an illocutionary point of view.[153]

The interpretation presented here is furthermore compatible with the observation that the first stanza is made up of 3+1 macarisms,[154] where the last one forms the consequence of the preceding three. If in the first three beatitudes, the moira of which the blessed were deprived was not spelled out, but had to be established in the form of the antonym "ignorance," here in the fourth one, that of which they are deprived is explicitly stated as the "pursuit of righteousness."

5.1.2. The Eighth Macarism in the SM (Matt 5:10)

This beatitude concludes the series of macarisms formulated in the third person plural, and its apodosis-line is identical with that of the first macarism. It is only found in the SM and in the *Gospel of Thomas*. It reads:

Matthew 5:10	*Gospel of Thomas* 69a[155]
Μακάριοι οἱ δεδιωγμένοι ἕνεκεν δικαιοσύνης, ὅτι αὐτῶν ἐστιν ἡ βασιλεία τῶν οὐρανῶν.	Μακάριοι οἱ δεδιωγμένοι ἐν τῇ καρδίᾳ αὐτῶν, ἐκεῖνοι εἰσιν οἱ γνόντες τὸν πατέρα ἐπ᾽ ἀληθείας.

If, as some scholars including our jubilarian assert, the structure of the SM is 3+1 in the first set regarding "pursuing righteousness" and 3+1 in the second set speaking of "endurance for the sake of

---

151 See note 118 above.

152 A coherent directive illocution would otherwise be difficult to establish because of the second macarism that blesses those who mourn.

153 Contra Powell; see note 23.

154 See above, note 27.

155 The Greek trans. from the Coptic is from H. Greeven, *Synopsis of the First Three Gospels* (Tübingen: Mohr [Siebeck], 1981) 30.

righteousness,"[156] there still is a difference between the concluding macarisms in each section. The accusative object τὴν δικαιοσύνην in v. 6 brings about a metaphorization, as does to a certain extent τῷ πνεύματι in v. 3 and perhaps the phrase "the belly of him who desires" in logion 69b in the *Gospel of Thomas.* In the eighth macarism of the SM, however, the adverbial prepositional phrase ἕνεκεν δικαιοσύνης does not lead to a metaphorization, but simply states the reason for persecution, a persecution which is real.[157] The corresponding beatitude in logion 69a of the *Gospel of Thomas,* on the other hand, has been given a metaphorical meaning through the adverbial addition ἐν τῇ καρδίᾳ αὐτῶν, "in their heart" or "within themselves."[158]

Before discussing the illocutionary function, we have to determine the meaning of ἕνεκεν δικαιοσύνης. Is it referring to a "human way of acting" or to "God's gift"? Since the reception of δικαιοσύνη from God can hardly be a reason for persecution, while striving for righteousness as a human way of acting could well be, it is more reasonable to assume that the phrase refers to human conduct rather than to God's gift.[159]

If the eighth macarism expresses blessedness for those actually being persecuted because of their striving for righteousness, how should we understand the illocutionary function of this beatitude? Formulated in the second person plural, the alternatives are as follows:

(1) Declarative/performative function:
Blessed are you,

---

[156] Betz, *Sermon on the Mount,* 142.

[157] Persecution "for the sake of righteousness" does not make it any less real than persecution for any other reason.

[158] See M. Meyer, *The Gospel of Thomas. The Hidden Sayings of Jesus* (San Francisco, CA: Harper, 1992) 96: "Saying 69 specifies that the place of persecution is within. In *Who is the Rich Man* 25, Clement of Alexandria asserts that the 'most difficult persecution is from within,' from pleasures and desires and passions: 'The one being persecuted cannot escape it, for he carries the enemy around within himself everywhere.'"

[159] So also Luz, *Matthäusevangelium I,* 214; Strecker, *Bergpredigt,* 45: "Die *conditio sine qua non* dieser Seligpreisung is also eine ethische Haltung der Menschen;" Davies and Allison, *Matthew I,* 459–60; Betz, *Sermon on the Mount,* 146; see also idem, "Principles," *Essays,* 52, n. 62; "Prinzipien," *Studien,* 47 with n. 61 [= *Synoptische Studien,* 124 with n. 61]. Otherwise Powell, "Beatitudes," 467–68.

causal: *since* you are persecuted for the sake of righteousness,
circumstantial: *when* you are persecuted for the sake of righteousness
concessive: *although* you are persecuted for the sake of righteousness

for yours is the Kingdom of God.

(2) Directive/prescriptive function:
Blessed are you,
conditional-durative:[160] *if* you *are persecuted* for the sake of righteousness

for yours is the Kingdom of God.

Before a decision can be made regarding the illocutionary function, it is necessary to pursue the interpretation of the declarative/performative alternatives further. The *causal* understanding connects *macarios* primarily with the reason for persecution, that is, righteousness and secondarily with the act of persecution itself. Then martyrdom would be a necessary condition for the blessing and, consequently, the persecution would in a way become the proof of righteousness.

The *circumstantial* reading supposes the beatitude to be an address to people in situations of actual persecution due to their striving for righteousness. Escape is acceptable, perhaps even desirable; it is certainly not regarded as a prerequisite for the blessing.

The *concessive* understanding seems at first farfetched, but is it really? In this case the *macarios* is primarily connected with persecution as a fact and only secondarily with its cause. The persecution then is something to be avoided even for the righteous ones, since it is unjust. Once persecution is a fact, however, the macarism functions as a consolation.

The *conditional* understanding seems possible only under one condition, namely, that persecution or even martyrdom is an ideal. This is the interpretation of Professor Betz when, with regard to the *inclusio* made up by the first and the eighth macarism in the SM, he writes: "If humility is the most elementary of the *virtues*, persecution

[160] Because of the perfect participle δεδιωγμένοι only the durative alternative is relevant.

[but only in the passive sense of being persecuted or in the active sense of seeking martyrdom—DH] is the highest."[161]

All four options are possible, but from the structure of the SM as a unit the *directive/prescriptive* function is the most likely after all, as is also emphasized by Betz in his commentary when he writes: "Since striving for righteousness is the highest goal for the SM (see especially 6:33; also 5:6, 20; 6:1; 7:21–23), persecution for the sake of that goal must also be the highest test and virtue." The reward is, as in the first beatitude, the *eschatological* promise of the Kingdom of Heaven.

As far as the SM is concerned, we can now state that in the series the beatitudes are primarily *eschatological* in character and *directive/prescriptive* in function. They are, according to Betz, "conditions of an ethical sort" and "laid down for admission into paradise."[162] In his commentary from 1995, he has modified his view with regard to the time aspect insofar as he now maintains that they "have eschatological as well as this-worldly implications."[163] As far as the illocutionary function goes, he still holds to the opinion that they have "a close relationship to morality and ethics. By revealing a new way of life, the beatitude effects moral behavior and demands an ethical awareness."[164]

5.2. The Sermon on the Plain

5.2.1. The First Macarism in the Sermon on the Plain (Luke 6:20b)

The first macarism in the SM has its parallels in Luke 6:20b (= SP) and in *Gospel of Thomas*, logion 54. I presuppose here that a not yet gnosticized *Gospel of Thomas* may have contained logia that are as old as or older than corresponding sayings in the synoptic Gospels.[165] There are three striking differences between these three texts: (a) in the SP

---

161 Betz, *Sermon on the Mount*, 146 (italics mine).

162 Betz, "Beatitudes," *Essays*, 34; "Makarismen," *Studien*, 32 [= *Synoptische Studien*, 108]; so already H. Windisch, *Der Sinn der Bergpredigt. Ein Beitrag zum Problem der richtigen Exegese* (UNT 16; Leipzig: Hinrichs, 1929) 10 [2nd ed. 1937, 63, n. 1], and also Strecker, *Bergpredigt*, 34; Schenk, *Sprache des Matthäus*, 352.

163 Betz, *Sermon on the Mount*, 96; cf., however, already idem, "Cosmogony," *Essays*, 94; "Kosmogonie," *Studien*, 83 [= *Synoptische Studien*, 160].

164 Cf. Betz, *Sermon on the Mount*, 97.

165 Cf. Koester, *Gospels*, 84–113; C. W. Hedrick, *Parables as Poetic Fiction. The Creative Voice of Jesus* (Peabody, MA: Hendrickson, 1994) 236–51.

and the *Gospel of Thomas* the adverbial qualifier "in the spirit" is missing;" οἱ πτωχοί is thus by all likelihood more original;[166] (b) in the apodosis-line the second person plural is again common for SP and *Gospel of Thomas* over against SM and in my view probably more original; (c) the SM and *Gospel of Thomas* both have βασιλεία τῶν οὐρανῶν over against SP, which has βασιλεία τοῦ θεοῦ. This shows that the expression "Kingdom of Heaven" need not be a Matthean redaction; rather the other way around: Matthew has by all likelihood taken over this formulation form the SM or Q^{Matt}. The *Gospel of Thomas* seems to have had access to traditions that go back to the SP, as well as to the SM or possibly Q^{Matt} and Q^{Luke}.

Before a decision can be made regarding the illocutionary function, we must determine the *semantic* meaning of οἱ πτωχοί in the series. As we have seen already, οἱ πτωχοί can designate "economically poor people," but also more generally "people who are lacking something."[167] In order to determine the meaning within the series, we must look for the meaning of the remaining beatitudes as well as of the corresponding characterizations of those addressed in the concomitant "woes" in vv. 24–26.[168] Consequently, the meaning, not only of the designations of those addressed in the macarisms, but also of their antonyms in the "woes," must be localizable on the same level of concretion or abstraction respectively: either they are all used in a literal sense or all in a metaphorical sense of one kind or another.

Interpreted in a *literal* sense, the juxtapositions would be "poor" (πτωχοί) vs "rich" (πλούσιοι), "hungry" (πεινῶντες) vs "well-fed"

---

166 Cf. Wrege, *Überlieferungsgeschichte*, 7: the Qumran texts show "daß τῷ πνεύματι weder literarischer Zusatz des Mt noch ursprünglicher Bestandteil des Makarismus sein kann;" Luz, *Matthäusevangelium I*, 200.

167 See above, note 112.

168 Series of "woes" can be found, e.g., in Isa 5:8–23; *1 Enoch* 94:6–9; 95:4–7; 96:4–8; 97:7–8; 98:9–15; 99:1–2; 99:11–16; 100:7–9; *2 Enoch* 52:1–14. Macarisms and woes beside each other are only rarely found, e.g., in Eccl 10:16–17; Tob 13:12–14; *2 Enoch* 52; *2 Apoc. Bar.* 10:6–7; *Did.* 1:5. See further E. Schweizer, "Formgeschichtliches zu den Seligpreisungen Jesu," *NTS* 19 (1973) 121–26, here 121–22. An example from Egypt is quoted by Assmann, "Weisheit," 41: "Selig (*rš-wj*), wer auf dich vertraut! Wehe dem, der dich angreift!" (Turin Stele 1454bis), who continues by stating: "Ich möchte so weit gehen zu sagen, dass jede Seligpreisung einen derartigen Weheruf impliziert, wenn sie in ihrer vollen Bedeutung als Aufruf zur Entscheidung verstanden werden will."

(ἐμπεπλησμένοι), "weeping" (κλαίοντες) vs "laughing" (γελῶντες). If the first macarism in the SP—as in the SM—constitutes the overarching principle,[169] then the following beatitudes are in fact not only subsumptions but also specifications of that principle without the first one losing its literal meaning.[170] The same applies, of course, to the "woes" in the *exordium*.[171]

In his commentary Professor Betz primarily—although not exclusively—advocates a more *abstract and general* interpretation of the first beatitude that comes close to a metaphorical meaning of poverty as "a broader concept referring to an entire attitude toward life rather than merely to economic conditions."[172] In his analysis Betz comes to the conclusion that there is no stark contrast between "the poor in the spirit" in SM and "the poor" in the SP, "rather the SM simply spells out what the SP suggests."[173] Even with this general or figurative understanding of poverty as an "attitude toward life," it can serve as an overarching concept for a figurative meaning of the following two beatitudes:[174] hunger (and thirst) were often used metaphorically in antiquity,[175] as was weeping, that could refer to all kinds of grief, including "weeping over the conditions of this world and the suffering resulting from them."[176] Thus the antonym to the overarching concept

---

169 For the SM as well as for the SP; see above, in relation to note 136; cf. already Weiss, *Predigt*, 183.

170 Cf. Betz, *Sermon on the Mount*, 576: "The connection between poverty . . . and hunger is traditional;" ibid., 577: "weeping is part of poverty."

171 Cf. Betz, *Sermon on the Mount*, 585: " . . . the filled stomach, fun and laughter, and of course flattery, of which the rich can never get enough."

172 Betz, *Sermon on the Mount*, 576.

173 Betz, ibid.

174 In addition to notes 136 and 169 above, see also E. Boring, "The Historical-Critical Method's 'Criteria of Authenticity:' The Beatitudes in Q and Thomas as a Test Case," *The Historical Jesus and the Rejected Gospels (Semeia 44)* (ed. C. W. Hedrick; Atlanta, GA: Scholars Press, 1988) 9–43, here 28: " . . . blessing on the poor/hungry/crying, are not concerned with three different groups, but with three aspects of one group . . .;" C. M. Tuckett, *Q and the History of Early Christianity* (Edinburgh: T. & T. Clark; Peabody, MA: Hendrickson, 1996) 226.

175 See Bauer, Gingrich and Danker, *Greek-English Lexicon*, 640, *s.v.* πεινάω 2; L. Goppelt, "πεινάω κτλ.," *TWNT* 6. 18–22; Betz, *Sermon on the Mount*, 129, n. 289, and 576.

176 Betz, *Sermon on the Mount*, 577; cf. further Bauer, Gingrich and Danker, *Greek-English Lexicon*, 432, *s.v.* κλαίω 1; Bultmann, "πένθος, πενθέω," *TWNT* 6. 43.

of "awareness of the conditions of life" would be the corresponding "unawareness" or "non-enlightenment" as in the SM.

Although Betz maintains that there is no major difference between the SM and the SP and that the former only spells out what is entailed in the latter, he still recognizes a significant difference between them as far as their views of human society is concerned: the SM separates people "into groups of righteous and unrighteous," while the SP "divides human society into poor and rich."[177] Thus, the difference between οἱ πτωχοὶ τῷ πνεύματι in the SM and οἱ πτωχοί in the SP is, in my opinion, not negligible. The *explicit* metaphorization in the first, as well as in the fourth, macarism in the SM stands after all in sharp contrast to the merely *implicit* figurative use in all of the beatitudes in the SP.

The question of the *illocutionary function* must now be posed anew, since the designation here of those addressed is different from the SM and so not only in its formulation:

(1) Declarative/performative

Blessed are you,

causal:	*since* you are poor
circumstantial:	*when* you are poor
concessive:	*although* you are poor

for yours is the Kingdom of God.

(2) Directive/prescriptive

Blessed are you,

conditional-ingressive:	*if* you *become* poor
conditional-durative:	*if* you *remain* poor.

for yours is the Kingdom of God.

Interpreted in a *literal* sense semantically, all five alternatives are possible in principle, that is, under certain conditions or presuppositions: the performative-causal as part of a strict poverty ideal,[178] the performative-circumstantial and -concessive as part of a

[177] Betz, *Sermon on the Mount*, 572.

[178] Cf. F. Bovon, *Das Evangelium nach Lukas I (Lk 1,1–9,50)* (EKKNT 3/1; Zürich: Benziger; Neukirchen-Vluyn: Neukirchener, 1989) 300; Betz, *Sermon on the Mount*, 572 and 575: "Just as calling the poor blessed is a traditional topos, so also is threatening the rich;" cf., however, Betz's statement, ibid., 114, quoted above in relation to note 111; each of these statements is clearly too general, which seemingly leads to a contradiction!

sympathy ideal,[179] the prescriptive-ingressive and -durative as a poverty ideal, according to which the directives must be achieved or maintained.

Taken in a more *general* or *figurative* sense, the illocutionary function of all three macarisms can be declarative/performative as well as directive/prescriptive:

(1) Declarative/performative

Blessed are you,

causal:	*since* you are aware of the conditions of poverty, hunger, and grief
circumstantial:	*when* you are aware of the conditions of poverty, hunger, and grief
concessive:	*although* you are aware of the conditions of poverty, hunger, and grief

for yours is the Kingdom of God.

(2) Directive/prescriptive

Blessed are you,

conditional-ingressive:	*if* you *become* aware of the conditions of poverty, hunger, and grief
conditional-durative:	*if* you *remain* aware of the conditions of poverty, hunger, and grief.

for yours is the Kingdom of God.

In the declarative/performative case, the causal and circumstantial interpretations are possible, while the concessive by definition is excluded; in the directive/prescriptive case, the ingressive as well as the durative options are reasonable as admonitions to obtain or maintain these insights just as in the SM.

Since the macarisms and the "woes" make up a unit in the *exordium* of the SP, the question of the *illocutionary function* must be posed to both categories. As we have seen, beatitudes can either have declarative/performative function as words of *comfort* and *consolation*, or directive/prescriptive function as words of *admonition* and *exhortation*. Similar—although not identical—illocutionary points are true of the "woes:" as declaratives/performatives they are *curses*,[180] as

179 Cf. Bovon, ibid.

180 Cf. Betz, *Sermon on the Mount*, 586, and above, pp. 300–301.

directives/prescriptives they are *warnings*,[181] and as commissives they are *threats*.[182]

Within the framework of the SP, however, as Professor Betz has shown, the *directive/prescriptive* function is predominant;[183] this is true especially in view of the paraenetical wording of the body section of the SP (Luke 6:27–45) with its "rules for the conduct of disciples" vis à vis the outside as well as the inside world.[184]

The *apodosis*-line is also in the SP of significance, in particular with regard to the time aspect: it is also here mainly *eschatological* in an afterworldly sense.[185] Within the framework of the SP, it renders the reason for the affirmation of felicity, and it does so with reference to the eschatological end-time when God is to judge. The eschatological perspective, in addition to the future tense in the second and third apodoses, is further accentuated by the addition of the temporal adverb νῦν, in the protases, which, however, occurs only in those macarisms and "woes" where the verbs stand in the future tense (vv. 21 and 25). In the two series it serves a contrasting purpose by separating the "now" from the "then."[186]

5.2.2. "Poor" (SP) and "Poor in the Spirit" (SM)

I shall now return to an observation I made when discussing the first beatitude in the SM, namely, the lack of a linguistic Greek parallel to the expression οἱ πτωχοὶ τῷ πνεύματι ("poor in [the] spirit"). Can a reasonable explanation be given for this curious expression? If the SM and SP are independent of each other,[187] Professor Betz's statement quoted above that "the SM simply spells out what the SP suggests"[188] is not to be taken as an indication that he is advocating a

[181] Cf. Betz, ibid., 585, 587, and above, pp. 300–301.

[182] Cf. Betz, ibid., 585, 586, and above, pp. 300–301.

[183] Betz, ibid., 572, 574–75, 586.

[184] Betz, ibid., 66–68, 574–75, 599–601.

[185] Betz, ibid., 572, 574; Hoffmann, "QR und der Menschensohn. Eine vorläufige Skizze," *The Four Gospels 1992. FS Frans Neirynck* (ed. F. Van Segbroeck et al.; BETL 100A; Leuven: Peeters, 1992) 421–56, here 447.

[186] See also Hoffmann, "Die Basileia-Verkündigung Jesu und die Option für die Armen," in idem, *Studien*, 43 and Bovon, *Lukas I*, 300, note 46.

[187] Betz, *Sermon on the Mount*, 43–45.

[188] Betz, ibid., 576.

literary dependence of the SM on the SP. If this is true, however, the most likely explanation is that in a formulation prior and common to the SM/SP, which possibly originated somehow with Jesus,[189] the characterization of the addressees was οἱ πτωχοί and that the people behind the SM minimized the alteration they felt necessary in order to avoid misunderstanding by keeping the original wording and just adding the adverbial phrase τῷ πνεύματι, parallel to and possibly under influence of the Hebrew עניי רוח (1QM 14:7 and 1QH 14:3?).[190] This is a rather conservative way of reformulating tradition in order to give it a new meaning, or perhaps better, in order to retain the metaphorical meaning already established in an earlier appropriation. Since the expression עניי רוח and similar expressions (cf. 1QH 5:22; 1QM 11:9; 4QpPs 37 II 8) in the Dead Sea Scrolls were used as self-designations,[191] it is rather likely that the corresponding expression οἱ πτωχοὶ τῷ πνεύματι in the SM,[192] as well as the simple expression οἱ πτωχοί in the SP,[193] were used as self-designations by the early Christians.

6. *Jesus and the Beatitudes*

When I now briefly turn to Jesus in the hope of finding more original meanings and functions of the beatitudes than those in the SM/SP, this must by necessity be tentative. My questions will be the same as before: what is the *sigmatic reference*, the *semantic meaning*, the *time aspect* and the *illocutionary function* in the beatitudes of the historical Jesus? If the intra-textual co-texts were radically curtailed in

---

189 See the next paragraph.

190 Gerstenberger, ענה, *TWAT* 6. 270.

191 See the quotation from Wrege, *Überlieferungsgeschichte*, 6 above in note 122, and further Bammel, "πτωχός C.III. Qumran," *TWNT* 6. 896–99; J. Maier, *Die Texte vom Toten Meer. Band II* (München: Reinhardt, 1960) 83–87; J. Dupont, "Les πτωχοὶ τῷ πνεύματι de Matthieu 5,3 et les עניי רוח de Qumran," *Neutestamentliche Aufsätze. FS J. Schmid* (ed. J. Blinzler et al.; Regensburg: Pustet, 1963) 53–64; W. Grundmann, *Das Evangelium nach Matthäus* (THKNT 1; Berlin: Evangelische Verlagsanstalt, 1968) 120–21; J. Gnilka, *Das Matthäusevangelium I. Teil* (HTKNT I/1; Freiburg: Herder, 1988) 121; Gerstenberger, ענה, *TWAT* 6. 253.

192 So Wrege, *Überlieferungsgeschichte*, 7.

193 So Robinson, "The Sayings Gospel Q," 366–68, referring to Gal 2:10, Rom 15:26 and Epiph. *Haer.* 30. This is denied, however, by Schürmann, *Lukasevangelium I*, 327.

reference to the SM/SP, things are far more complicated as far as the historical Jesus is concerned. Through the analysis of the narrative frames of the SM and the SP, we tried to differentiate between the recipients of the SM/SP, on the one hand, the disciples, and those of Q, on the other, the crowds.[194] In this connection a further question should be raised, whether there are indications in the epitomes themselves that would allow us to differentiate between the recipients of the SM/SP and those of the proclamation of Jesus. If so, it would enable us to get one step closer to the teaching of the historical Jesus. In the epitomes (SM/SP), the recipients of Jesus' teaching are the disciples, as shown above. This causes no problem as long as we confine ourselves to the beatitudes, but once we turn to the woes in the SP (Luke 6:24–26), the question of the addressees becomes complicated, since it is rather unlikely that these woes originally were addressed to Jesus' disciples, who in all likelihood were neither "rich," nor "well-fed," nor "laughing."[195] Three options seem possible: either these woes were directed to well-to-do people in the Church and thus comprise secondary sayings,[196] or they were directed to rich individuals or groups in Jesus' encounter with them and thus constitute more or less original sayings of Jesus, or a combination of both, in which the

---

[194] See above pp. 287–89.

[195] Although disregarding the co-text of the SP, the problem is discussed in R. Kieffer, "Weisheit und Segen als Grundmotive der Seligpreisungen bei Matthäus und Lukas," *Theologie aus dem Norden* (ed. A. Fuchs; *SNTU* A.2.; Linz: Fuchs, 1977) 29–43, here 36. The statement that in *the text of the SP*, a sudden change of addressees from disciples in the macarisms to potential enemies in the woes is unwarranted in view of the compositional structure of the SP: neither needs "πλήν to signal a change of addressees" (so Bovon, *Lukas I*, 301), since the conjunction is best interpreted as presaging "the turning point between promise of salvation and warning against disaster" (Betz, *Sermon on the Mount*, 585); nor need the introductory formula ἀλλὰ ὑμῖν λέγω τοῖς ἀκούουσιν (Luke 6:27) indicate a return to the addressees of the macarisms (so Schürmann, *Lukasevangelium I*, 337), since it is best explained as marking "the beginning of a new section," as well as designating the following text as "authoritative teaching material" (Betz, ibid., 592). The *series* of woes should not be understood as "a kind of parenthesis" (so Kieffer, ibid.), but rather as a warning to wealthy disciples in the community of the SP. A methodological awareness of the distinction between the literary level of the SP and the (reconstructed) historical level of Jesus is an absolute requirement in our exegetical discipline.

[196] Cf. I. Broer, *Die Seligpreisungen der Bergpredigt. Studien zu ihrer Überlieferung und Interpretation* (BBB 61; Bonn: Hanstein, 1986) 33–34.

first alternative constitutes an appropriation of the second. If the last two options are viable, then we would have here an indication that at least parts of the tradition preserved in the SM/SP were directed to people Jesus met on his wanderings in and around Galilee. In Jesus' setting these woes in the form of declarative/performative illocutions functioned as *curses*[197] and in form of commissives as *threats*[198] to rich people Jesus addressed. In the form of directive/prescriptive illocutions within the "Sitz im Leben" of the SP, they functioned as *warnings*[199] to well-to-do people in the early Church. It is not appropriate, however, to take the present co-texts (SM/SP) as indications of the original meaning and function of these beatitudes and woes in their proclamation by the historical Jesus.

The *series* of macarisms are literary phenomena, as are the *sermons* of which they are *exordia,* and as such they do not apply to the historical Jesus. These *logia* are, consequently, to be interpreted as *single, isolated* beatitudes directed to individuals or groups of individuals.[200] Syntactically, these were probably formulated in the second person plural (SP + *Gospel of Thomas*) or singular, respectively.[201] Scholars who have declared the third person as original[202] have not taken seriously the fact that the comparative material they have drawn on for the most part is literary and thus inadequate as parallels to orally formulated macarisms in Jesus' actual encounter with individuals or groups of individuals. The formulations in the second person were used in specific cases "in which a single person (or persons—DH) in a given exceptional situation was

---

197 See above, note 180.

198 See above, note 182.

199 See above, note 181.

200 See note 224, below.

201 See above, paragraph 5.2.1. In view of the LXX transl. of Isa 32:20 quoted in note 55 above and the parallels from early patristic literature registered in Broer, *Seligpreisungen,* 34–35, note 73a, the second person seems to be well attested; cf. also *1 Enoch* 58:2 quoted above, paragraph 4 (3.2.); see further M. Dibelius, *Die Formgeschichte des Evangeliums* (6th ed.; Tübingen: Mohr [Siebeck], 1971) 248; J. Becker, *Jesus von Nazareth* (Berlin and New York: de Gruyter, 1996) 197.

202 So, e.g., Weiss, *Predigt,* 182; Bultmann, *Geschichte,* 114; S. Schulz, *Q. Die Spruchquelle der Evangelisten* (Zürich: Theologischer Verlag, 1972) 77; Kieffer, "Weisheit," 35; Bovon, *Lukas I,* 297.

addressed."[203] As far as the *usage of lexemes* is concerned, it is almost common agreement among scholars that in the first macarism, the simple οἱ πτωχοί (SP + *Gospel of Thomas*) is more original than the syntagma οἱ πτωχοὶ τῷ πνεύματι (SM);[204] neither is the lexeme πλούσιοι in the first woe in the SP provided with an adverbial qualifier;[205] the concrete expression οἱ κλαίοντες (SP) is also regarded as original vis à vis the more general οἱ πενθοῦντες (SM);[206] the same is true of the simple οἱ πεινῶντες (SP + *Gospel of Thomas*), which is less developed than the complex syntagma οἱ πεινῶντες καὶ διψῶντες τὴν δικαιοσύνην (SM).[207] In both cases where the protases of the *Gospel of Thomas* possess equivalents to the synoptic beatitudes, its text is closer to the SP than to the SM in that no adverbial additions bringing about metaphorical interpretations are present. As far as authenticity is concerned here the rule of multiple attestation can be applied.[208]

M. A. Powell has pointed to the fact that the description of those addressed in the macarisms in the first stanza in the *Sermon on the Mount* can be interpreted as privations:

(1) Lack of hope = fainthearted/despondent (οἱ πτωχοί τῷ πνεύματι);[209]
(2) Lack of happiness = miserable (οἱ πενθοῦντες);[210]
(3) Lack of power = humiliated/oppressed (οἱ πραεῖς).[211]

---

[203] Schweizer, "Seligpreisungen," 123.

[204] In addition to references given in note 166, see, e.g., J. Jeremias, *Neutestamentliche Theologie. Erster Teil* (Gütersloh: Mohn, 1971) 114; Schulz, *Q. Die Spruchquelle,* ibid.; Luz, *Matthäusevangelium I,* 205; J. M. Robinson, "The Sayings Gospel Q," *The Four Gospels 1992. FS Frans Neirynck,* 361–88, here 369.

[205] Jeremias, ibid.

[206] See, e.g., Luz, ibid., 208; Robinson, ibid.

[207] See, e.g., Robinson, ibid.

[208] Cf. G. Theißen and A. Merz, *Der historische Jesus* (Göttingen: Vandenhoeck & Ruprecht, 1996) 116–19; James Breech, *The Silence of Jesus: The Authentic Voice of the Historical Man* (Philadelphia: Fortress, 1983) 127, and Boring, "Historical-Critical Method," 25.

[209] Powell, "Beatitudes," 463–64; Best, "Matthew V.3," 255–58; Davies and Allison, *Matthew 1,* 444.

[210] Powell, ibid., 465–66.

[211] Powell, ibid., 466–67; K. Wengst, *Humility: Solidarity of the Humiliated* (Philadelphia, PA: Fortress 1988) 16; Davies and Allison, *Matthew* I, 449; Hagner, *Matthew 1–13,* 92–93.

In the macarisms of the *Sermon on the Plain* we encounter the following privations:

(1) Lack of economical means = poor (οἱ πτωχοί);
(2) Lack of food = hungry (οἱ πεινῶντες);
(3) Lack of joy = weeping (οἱ κλαίοντες).

If these *negative* connotations can be applied to the first three Beatitudes of the SM and the SP, it not only has a bearing on the identification of the groups of people addressed by Jesus but also on the illocutionary function exerted by him in proclaiming these addressees μακάριοι. The very fact that—when disregarding the co-text in both sermons on all levels—the utterances about the addressees can be interpreted in a non-metaphorical sense—not only in the SP but indeed also in the SM—strongly indicates that the concrete meanings of the characterization actually apply to the referents, that is, the individuals or groups of individuals whom Jesus proclaimed blissful. Consequently, these macarisms of Jesus are of the *inverted* religious type; but are they also eschatological macarisms—and if so, in what sense?

Regarding the *time aspect*, we have already observed that the two apodosis-lines in the SM containing the expression "Kingdom of Heaven" and strategically framing the central six beatitudes with apodoses-lines formulated in the future tense are both formulated in the *present tense* (ἐστίν),[212] which I take to be a preservation of the original wording, that could not be altered even in the SM. It is further noteworthy that the apodosis of logion 69a in *Gospel of Thomas*—although it does not mention the Kingdom of God and clearly is gnosticized—gives the reason for felicity in present-oriented terms: "they are the ones who have truly come to know the Father."[213] In the SP we encounter a similar pattern: the apodosis of the first beatitude, as well as that of the first woe, are formulated in the present tense (ἐστίν/ἀπέχετε) while the concomitant macarisms and woes are formulated in the future tense. As we saw earlier, the temporal

[212] Kodjak, *Analysis*, 45–46. Cf. Betz, "Cosmogony," *Essays*, 94; "Kosmogonie," *Studien*, 83 [*Synoptische Studien*, 160]; F. Hauck and S. Schulz, "πραΰς κτλ.," *TWNT* 6. 650; S. Schulz, *Q. Spruchquelle*, 81; Davies and Allison, *Matthew I*, 446.

[213] Trans. Meyer, *Gospel of Thomas*, 53; Greek trans. by H. Greeven; see above, note 155.

adverb νῦν functions as a contrasting agent for promotion of an eschatological-future interpretation of the macarisms in the series.[214] There is, however, nothing in the formulation of these beatitudes in itself that requires a temporal reference to an eschatological end-time. From a logical point of view, the tense in these apodosis-lines can only be future, which means that the three beatitudes, as well as the woes, as preserved in the SP actually can be conceived of as eschatological and present-oriented in character.[215] This cognizance speaks in favor of νῦν having been added by the time those macarisms were included into the SP. Our observation with regard to the future tense is substantiated by the formulation of the apodosis-line in the parallel beatitude in logion 69b in the *Gospel of Thomas*, where the Greek translation by H. Greeven reads:[216] μακάριοι οἱ πεινῶντες, ὅτι χορτασθήσεται (ἵνα—ασθῇ) ἡ κοιλία τοῦ θέλοντος. The Coptic has šina, which can be used causally also in the Greek.[217]

The observation made by Powell, that the four beatitudes in the first stanza in the SM per se rather suggests promises of "eschatological *reversal* to those who are unfortunate" than "eschatological *reward* to people who exhibit virtuous behavior,"[218] is an indication that the function of at least some of the single macarisms in fact once was declarative/performative. The verification must be conducted by means of a countercheck vis à vis the illocutionary function of the beatitudes within the series.[219] From what we know, among other things, from the *core material* examined, for example, by James E. Breech,[220] it is unreasonable to believe that Jesus admonished individ-

---

214 See above, in relation to note 186.

215 Cf. Hoffmann, "Basileia-Verkündigung," 48; Becker, *Jesus*, 197; contra Theißen and Merz, *Jesus*, 232.

216 Greeven, *Synopsis*, 30.

217 See Hellholm, "Rejoice," 69, nn. 108 and 109 with references.

218 See above, notes 26 and 29.

219 Cf. Becker, *Jesus*, 19, who, however, only considers the question of semantics, not that of function.

220 Breech, *The Silence of Jesus*, especially the synopsis 227–28 and further, in connection with photodramatic parables (Matt 13:44–46// *Gos. Thom.* 109 and cf. 76; Matt 13:31–32//Mark 4:30–32//Luke 13:18–19// *Gos. Thom.* 20; Matt 13:33//Luke 13:20–21//*Gos. Thom.* 96; Matt 18:12–14//Luke 15:4–6// *Gos. Thom.* 107; Luke 15:8–10; Mark 4:3–8// *Gos. Thom.* 9), 231 and phonodramatic parables (Luke 10: 25–35; 15:11–32; 16:1–8; Matt 20:1–16; Matt 22:1–14//Luke

uals to become or remain "poor," "hungry," "weeping," "despondent," "miserable" and "oppressed;" thus the directive/prescriptive illocution is excluded, while the circumstantial or possibly the concessive interpretation is possible, that is to say, the macarisms proclaimed by Jesus were declaratives/performatives and thus functioned as consolations to people in need.[221]

Space does not permit even a cursory investigation regarding the teaching of Jesus, but I propose that the illocutionary function of the sayings of Jesus were not directive/prescriptive, either ethical or cultic, but on the contrary *declarative/performative* and so, in a circumstantial sense, they were unconditioned consolations in miserable situations,[222] and what he promised was that they were to be congratulated, not directly because he liberated them "from their miserable conditions,"[223] but because the Kingdom of God was at hand.[224] As we have noted already, the four apodosis-lines that contain the expression "Kingdom of Heaven/God" are formulated in the *present tense.* As has

---

14:16–29//*Gos. Thom.* 64), 235–40. See also Bultmann, *Jesus* (Siebenstern-Taschenbücher 17; Hamburg: Siebenstern, 1964) 138–40.

[221] I cannot see any reason for taking these macarisms as *causal* utterances, making the preconditioned situation a necessity. The blessedness is not dependent upon the recipients' misery! Correctly, K. Wengst, *Pax Romana. Anspruch und Wirklichkeit* (München: Kaiser, 1986) 84: "Sie werden nicht selig gepriesen, *weil* sie arm, hungrig und voller Trauer sind, sondern weil ihnen als solchen eine Verheißung gegeben ist, die jeweils ein Begründungssatz nach der Zusage ausdrücklich nennt, die Verheißung nämlich, daß ihr niedriger Zustand in sein genaues Gegenteil umgekehrt werden soll. Das ist evident bei der zweiten und dritten Seligpreisung: Die Hungernden sollen satt werden, und die Weinenden sollen lachen;" cf. also Schürmann, *Lukasevangelium I,* 328–29; Bovon, *Lukas I,* 300.

[222] Cf. Weder, *Rede der Reden,* 48: "Aber genau diese Unbedingtheit ist ein Charakteristikum Jesu: genau so unbedingt vergibt er Sünden, ruft er in die Nachfolge, stellt er den Menschen ins Zentrum auch am Sabbat . . ., dann kann die Seligpreisung der Armen niemals eine Aufforderung sein . . . ."

[223] Betz, *Sermon on the Mount,* 113.

[224] Cf. already Weiss, *Predigt,* 127–28: As words of the historical Jesus, the macarisms of Matt 5:3–6, 10 were "himmlische Trost- und Segenssprüche . . . Einladungen und Heilsrufe an solche, die bisher nicht daran gedacht haben, dass ihnen von den Segnungen der messianischen Zeit etwas zu teil werden könnte," and what these people were promised was "Ausfüllung und Ersatz ihres bisherigen Mangels" (186); nowadays: Weder, *Rede der Reden,* 47: "Jesus wandte sich offenbar an vor ihm stehende Arme und spricht ihnen die Seligkeit zu ... mit einer sprachlichen Handlung, mit einem Sprechakt."

been argued recently by Hartmut Stegemann[225] and Werner Zager,[226] the unique expression "Kingdom of God" or "Kingdom of Heaven" is neither present-oriented nor futuristic, but eschatological in the sense of an immediately commencing realization of the Kingdom of God (cf. Matt 12:28//Luke 11:20; Luke 10:18; Mark 2:19–20; 3:27; Matt 13:16–17//Luke 10:23–24; Matt 11:12–13//Luke 16:16; Matt 11:5–6//Luke 7:22–23; Luke 10:18 and John 12:31).[227] Thus, Jesus is here promising individuals or groups of individuals[228] in need their immediate share in the Kingdom, which he is envisaging or even experiencing in his teaching and his actions.[229] "The people who benefit when God rules, Jesus declares, are those who otherwise have no reason for hope or cause for joy, who have been denied their share of God's blessings in this world and deprived of justice . . . . For such people, the coming of God's Kingdom is a blessing, because when God rules, all this will change and things will be set right."[230]

---

[225] H. Stegemann, "Der lehrende Jesus. Der sogenannte biblische Christus und die geschichtliche Botschaft Jesu von der Gottesherrschaft," *NZSTh* 24 (1982) 3–20; idem, *Die Essener, Qumran, Johannes der Täufer und Jesus. Ein Sachbuch* (Herder Spektrum 412; 4th ed.; Freiburg: Herder, 1994) 316–30.

[226] W. Zager, *Gottesherrschaft und Endgericht in der Verkündigung Jesu. Eine Untersuchung zur markinischen Jesusüberlieferung einschließlich der Q-Parallelen* (BZNW 82; Berlin and New York: de Gruyter, 1996) esp. 311–13.

[227] Cf. Hoffmann, "Basileia-Verkündigung," 48–52; Breech, *Silence,* 37; H. Weder, *Gegenwart und Gottesherrschaft. Überlegungen zum Zeitverständnis bei Jesus und im frühen Christentum* (BThSt 20; Neukirchen: Neukirchener, 1993) 26–28; H. Hübner, *Biblische Theologie des Neuen Testaments. Band 3* (Göttingen: Vandenhoeck & Ruprecht, 1995) 260–62; G. Theißen, "Jünger als Gewalttäter (Mt 11,12f.; Lk 16,16)," *Mighty Minorities? Minorities in Early Christianity: Positions and Strategies. Essays in Honor of Jacob Jervell on his 70th Birthday, 21 May 1995, ST* 49 (1995) 183–200; Theißen and Merz, *Jesus,* 232–53; H. Schürmann, *Das Lukasevangelium, Zweiter Teil. Erste Folge* (HTKNT III 2/1; Freiburg: Herder, 1994) *ad loc.*; Weiss, *Predigt,* 92–93; Hedrick, *Parables,* 75–76; Stegemann, "Der lehrende Jesus," 15; Becker, *Jesus,* 124–54.

[228] Cf. Gerstenberger, ענה, *TWAT* 6. 262, with reference to Isa 3:15 and 61:1: "Parallel zur Kollektivierung läßt sich aber auch eine Individualisierung des Begriffs feststellen. So meinen manche Plurale deutlich eine aus Einzelpersonen zusammengesetzte Gruppe;" cf. also ibid., 264.

[229] Stegemann, *Essener,* 323–330; Hoffmann, "Basileia-Verkündigung," 48; Becker, *Jesus,* 176–233; Theißen and Merz, *Jesus,* 460 et passim.

[230] Powell, "Beatitudes," 470, although Powell wrongly presents this interpretation as Matthew's understanding of the macarisms instead of Jesus' own message to those whom he encountered when wandering around in Galilee (see

As we have seen already, all declarative/performative illocutionary forces "have the mode of achievement that the *speaker* invokes his power or authority to perform the declaration and the general preparatory condition that the speaker has the power or authority to change the world by the performance of the appropriate utterance act."[231] With what kind of power or authority could Jesus declare people he encountered "blessed" or "happy"? In order for the beatitudes to function as declarative/performative utterances, an *extralinguistic institution* was supposed to empower Jesus to proclaim "blissfulness" to his listeners. Typical of the narratives about Jesus in the Gospels, however, is the explicit denial of such institutionalized authorization, as can be deduced from the redactional material in all three Gospels: "And they were astonished at his teaching, for he taught them as one who had authority, and not as the scribes" (Mark 1:22; cf. Matt 7:28–29);[232] "By what authority are you doing these things, or who gave you this authority to do them?" (Mark 11:28//Matt 21:23//Luke 20:2).[233]

Powell's own reservation with regard to his interpretation of the first stanza of beatitudes in the SM; 476). This performative/present-oriented type of beatitude is still to be found—although different in content—in the Coptic *Apoc. Peter* (70:21–25) (trans. by A. Werner, *New Testament Apocrypha*, vol. 2, [ed. W. Schneemelcher and R. McL. Wilson; Cambridge: Clarke & Co., and Louisville, KY: Westminster-Knox, 1992] 705):

> Blessed are those who belong to the Father,
> <who> is above the Heaven,
> who has revealed life through me to those who come from life,
> since I have reminded (them of it).

[231] See above, note 62.

[232] Cf. Stegemann, "Der lehrende Jesus," 14–17, especially 17: this authority is also true of Jesus' interpretation of the Torah. Further D. Lührmann, *Das Markusevangelium* (HNT 3; Tübingen: Mohr [Siebeck] 1987) 50: "Diese ἐξουσία ist die Nähe des Reiches Gottes, die den Schriftgelehrten eben fehlt (vgl. 12,34);" Theißen and Merz, *Jesus*, 208–9.

[233] Theißen and Merz, *Jesus*, 214: "Er tritt der Tempelaristokratie in einer Haltung gegenüber, die diese um so mehr herausfordern mußte, als hier ein einfacher Galiläer eine 'Vollmacht' in Anspruch nahm, die angesichts seiner niedrigen Herkunft nur als Anmaßung erlebt werden konnte. Mit Recht fragte die Tempelaristokratie Jesus nach der Tempelreiningung: 'In welcher Vollmacht tust du das?' (Mk 11,28)."

If such an extralinguistic institutional backing is missing or even explicitly denied,[234] an explanation for Jesus' authoritative claim[235] must be sought in the same direction as Searle/Vanderveken suggested in view of the creation narrative:[236] it is based on "supernatural powers," since the obvious response to the authorities' question about Jesus' authority would have had to be the same as the equally obvious response by the authorities to Jesus' counterquestion whence John the Baptist got his authority, namely from Heaven = from God (Mark 11:27–33 parr).[237] Jesus' performance of such speech-acts could not have been perceived as anything less than "supernatural declarations" to individuals or groups of individuals in distress and misery.[238] Here there is no need for an extralinguistic institutional backing because of the "supernatural powers" involved: the Kingdom of God/Heaven is at hand—therefore μακάριοι ἔστε! The reports in the Gospels that the authorities did not accept Jesus' actions and his teaching as signs of God's power[239] only confirms his implicit and explicit claims.

In my brief interpretation of the original macarisms proclaimed by Jesus I have been keen on discarding the co-text on all literary levels,[240]

---

[234] Cf. Hoffmann, "Basileia-Verkündigung," 63.

[235] Cf. Stegemann, "Der lehrende Jesus," 9, note 33: "Untersuchungen zur Frage eines 'Messiasbewußtseins' Jesu oder zu seiner soteriologisch motivierten 'Todesbereitschaft' behandeln nur Teilaspekte und bleiben recht spekulativ. Was fehlt, ist eine gründliche Untersuchung zu der Art seines 'Autoritätsanspruches;'" see also Becker, *Jesus*, 337–87. The present treatment of the beatitudes as pronouncements by the historical Jesus is partly meant to be a small contribution to that question. I hope to return to this issue in another context.

[236] See above, note 68.

[237] See Lührmann, *Markusevangelium*, 198.

[238] This result of my speech-act analysis leads to a specification of the illocutionary function of the elements in Jesus' teaching and action mentioned in N. A. Dahl, "The Crucified Messiah," in idem, *Jesus the Christ. The Historical Origins of Christological Doctrine* (Minneapolis, MN: Fortress, 1991) 27–47, here 42: "Jesus' sovereign attitude to the prescriptions of the law, his relation to the poor and to many suspect individuals, and especially his public appearance in the temple — all this, in conjunction with his eschatological preaching, could appear to be a revolt against the established religio-political order."

[239] Cf. Theißen and Merz, *Jesus*, 208–16.

[240] See, e.g., Breech, *Silence*, 160–61, 185 et passim.

since they are likely to be products of the various literary editors and thus reflect their social contexts.

A discussion of the different *perlocutionary* reactions on the side of the various addressees ought to follow here, but considerations of space do not allow for it.

7. The Question of "Sitze im Leben"

It is, in my opinion, likely that macarisms were pronounced in connection with Jesus' encounter with poor, disillusioned or even persecuted people and not as part of didactic and liturgical systems. The latter must be regarded as a later, literary development. Formulated in the words of James M. Robinson: "The historical origin of the beatitudes may have been Jesus' affirmation of the victims of fate that he encountered on all sides, which came to expression variously as the poor, the hungry, the mourning, etc. But this stamp of approval pronounced on the miserable of the village was *progressively appropriated* by the Jesus movement for the disciples themselves."[241] This progressive appropriation took place on the lexical and text-syntactic as well as on the semantic, sigmatic and pragmatic-illocutionary levels, as I have tried to show throughout this essay. Such a diachronic investigation on all semiotic levels requires a much more thorough inquiry than I have been able to undertake here;[242] that will have to wait for another occasion.[243]

---

241 Robinson, "Sayings Gospel Q," 368–69 (italics mine); cf. also H. Koester, "The Sayings Gospel Q and the Quest of the Historical Jesus: A Response to John S. Kloppenborg," *HTR* 89 (1996) 345–49, here especially 348–49.

242 Cf. Kanngießer, "Sprachliche Universalien," 287: "Die Perspektive . . . wird durch die Bezugnahme auf *diachrone* Aspekte (immer wenn von Kontingenz, von Veränderung und Veränderungsfähigkeit die Rede ist, stehen diachrone Aspekte zur Debatte) offenkundig noch erheblich kompliziert."

243 In the history of religions such appropriations are well known; see above, in relation to note 104 and note 118 with regard to the ethical or religious reinterpretation of the macarisms of the mysteries by the philosophers; the ethical reinterpretation of the Eleusinian macarisms by the Orphic-Pythagorean philosophers is a remarkable parallel to the ethicizing of Jesus' consolation in the SM/SP and later traditions (Q and Matt/Luke); with regard to the usage of macarisms on Orphic gold leaves, see below, note 246.

If in Q^{Matt} and Q^{Luke}, those addressed are the crowds outside and within the community,[244] then the illocutionary function most likely is prescriptive, even more precisely, *conditional-ingressive* for those outside and *conditional-durative* for those within; in both instances with an eschatological end-time perspective.

If in the SM, as well as in the SP, those addressed are the disciples and the illocutionary function is prescriptive with an eschatological end-time perspective also, what kind of prescription do we encounter in these epitomes: a conditional-ingressive or a -durative? From the frequent statements in Betz's commentary that the *macarisms* as well as the *woes* are "reminders" given *didactically to the disciples*,[245] it is clear that their functions can be defined more precisely as prescriptive-*durative*: blessed are those who keep their insight into the misery of human conditions as "unrighteous" (SM) or "poor" (SP) respectively. At an earlier stage, possibly *cultic* (baptism?) in nature,[246] the illocution to the *neophytes* in all likelihood was prescriptive-*ingressive* with an eschatological future consolation: blessed are those, who are now receiving the insight into what it means to be a part of the community of the Poor (in spirit).[247]

---

244 See above, note 184.

245 Betz, *Sermon on the Mount*, 59, 95, 572, 573. Betz's characterization of the beatitudes as "reminders," however, is ambiguous: is it a reminder of the semantic content or the illocutionary function? This is dependent on the reconstruction of the pre-SM/SP level: if the illocution there is *prescriptive*, then the beatitudes in the SM/SP can be characterized as "reminders;" if the illocution on the pre-SM/SP level is *performative*, then the beatitudes in SM/SP cannot be "reminders" of the pragmatic function; they can still be "reminders" of the semantic content, but now with a change in function: from performative to prescriptive, i.e. from "consolation" to "exhortation."

246 So Betz, ibid., 59, 95, who refers to a parallel macarism on Orphic gold leaves (G. Zuntz, *Persephone: Three Essays on Religion and Thought in Magna Graecia* [Oxford: Clarendon, 1971] 322–23: text A.1. line 8]), presumably revealed to initiates in connection with an initiation ceremony; in this connection one should also refer to Jewish beatitudes connected to the mystery cults, especially *Jos. Asen.* 16:7–8 (Betz, ibid., 100 with text and trans.). From the perspective of performatives, see Wörner, *Performative*, 26 and 96; further Wunderlich, *Sprechakttheorie*, 312–13.

247 This development can be viewed in terms of a possible development from עני = poor to ענוה = humble, pious. This is of special importance, since עני is used for the individual person(s) (57 times in the singular and 19 times in the plural), while ענוה is used almost exclusively collectively (once in the singular and

The social setting in which Jesus performed his teaching and actions was his encounter with individuals or groups of individuals, occasions on which he assured victims of fate of blissfulness with reference to the immediately commencing realization of the Kingdom of God. This is the origin for the later appropriation just demonstrated.

The progression is also clearly recognizable in the change from the usage of the second person in Jesus' direct proclamation to people he met to the third person plural in the series of the SM: the second person plural or singular is more congenial with the congratulatory meaning of the declarative/performative illocution, while the more general third person plural is more consonant with the exhortative meaning of the directive/prescriptive illocutionary function.[248]

In my outline of the development of the various usages of beatitudes, I have taken seriously the insight formulated by J. S. Kloppenborg that "... the act of literary composition presupposes a social context that is simply not identical with that of the various oral performances of Jesus."[249]

---

nineteen times in the plural); see Gerstenberger, ענה, *TWAT* 6. 259: "Möglicherweise ist aber eine bewußte Entwicklung auf *ᶜanijjim* = Arme; *ᶜanawim* = Demütige, Fromme hin festzustellen . . . ." More cautious is Martin-Achard, "ענה II elend sein," *THAT* 2. 343; cf. also Grundmann, "ταπεινός κτλ.," *TWNT* 8. 1–27, here 6–7.

[248] See N. Walter, "Die Bearbeitung der Seligpreisungen durch Matthäus," *Studia Evangelica IV. Papers presented to the Third International Congress* (ed. F. L. Cross; TU 102; Berlin: Akademie-Verlag, 1968) 246–58, here 253: "allgemeingültige Aussage" vs "Zuspruch;" Schweizer, *Das Evangelium nach Matthäus* (NTD 2; Göttingen: Vandenhoeck & Ruprecht, 1973) 45; Powell, "Beatitudes," 477: "it establishes the blessed as a field of persons which is not limited to the disciples of Jesus" and " . . . creates an initial distance that allows Jesus' audience to hear his words impartially before realizing the direct application to themselves;" and 478, where he recognizes that the second person plural in the ninth beatitude in the series in the SM has a totally different meaning than the second person singular or plural in Jesus' setting, namely, that "the sudden shift to the second person in 5:11 assaults Matthew's [or better: the SM's—DH] readers in the world outside the story as surely as it does the disciples within the story." Cf. also Betz, *Sermon on the Mount*, 93–94, who, however, is of the opinion that the second person plural "appears to reflect more directly the primary function in the ritual . . ." rather than the encounter of Jesus with unfortunate people.

[249] J. S. Kloppenborg, "The Sayings Gospel Q and the Quest of the Historical Jesus," *HTR* 89 (1996) 307–44, here 322.

8. Conclusion

In conclusion let me present *setting, function, time* and *addressees* in relation to each other at various stages in the development of the tradition:

Setting	Function	Time	Addressees
Jesus' direct encounter	performative	present-oriented/eschatological	individuals/groups
Pre-SM/SP: cultic-liturgical	performative? prescriptive: conditional-ingressive	present-oriented/eschatological? eschatological	neophytes neophytes
SM/SP: didactic	prescriptive: conditional-durative	future-eschatological	disciples
Q^Matt^/Q^Luke^	prescriptive: conditional-ingressive conditional-durative	future-eschatological	crowds from the outside and from the inside

The most striking result is the sigmatic differentiation among the recipients on all levels, which in turn is due to the different settings; these different settings are also pre-conditions for the various functions; finally, in connection with the change in the time-aspect of the "Kingdom of God/Heaven" from an immediately commencing realization to a futuristic concept, a change in illocution occurred: from a performative to a prescriptive function.

At the beginning of this essay, I lamented the curtailment or even loss of the intra-textual co-texts when interpreting the SM/SP as epitomes. Now at the end, I would like to turn the tables and point to what, in my view, has been gained by Professor Betz's accomplishments. In addition to the abundance of new materials and insights, the methodological benefit is, as far as I can see, at least six-fold: (1) erroneous intra-textually conditioned interpretations can be avoided, for instance, supposedly substantial Matthean or Lucan redactional influences; (2) new inter-textual connections at earlier stages in the tradition can in this way be uncovered, for example, the relationship to a not yet gnosticized *Gospel of Thomas*; (3) this in turn can help to establish new and different situational contexts for the two sermons, for example, the differences between the SM and the SP in their views of human society: the separation of people into groups of "righteous and unrighteous" in the SM and "poor and rich" in the SP;[250] (4) another benefit is the discovery of very early collections of sayings material in the early Church, and the significance of theological divergences at such an early stage; (5) the opening of new ways to unearth the teaching of Jesus—even if only by means of very tentative results or suggestions; (6) insight into the literary and theological rearrangement of the narrative and sayings material through various stages up until its preservation in our extant Gospels. All this and much more is the result of the intense and creative work over the years by Hans Dieter Betz, my distinguished teacher, colleague and friend.

---

[250] Betz, *Sermon on the Mount*, 572.

Beatitudes and Mysteries

Detlev Dormeyer

0. Introduction

The "Jubilarian" Hans Dieter Betz has collected all of the important historical material into his exhaustive commentary on "The Sermon on the Mount" of 1995. In dealing with some text-theoretical considerations, I simply clarify details and set new accents in response to Professor Hellholm. Because the validity of a case must be attested by two or more witnesses, I gladly join the phalanx of those who appropriate the rhetorical and literary analysis of Professor Betz and confirm it with great profit.

1. Text-theoretical Definition of the "Beatitude"

According to Professor Betz the term "macarism" or "beatitude" "designates a literary genre."[1] Professor Hellholm confirmed this definition. The roots go back to the Old Testament and to Egypt. Therefore, "the beatitudes in the SM and the SP are not drawn from ancient Greek mystery cults, but they have developed out of a Jewish matrix."[2] We will consider whether this opposition is strictly exclusive or merely a matter of emphasis. Professor Hellholm listed the different types of beatitudes, but neglected the mystery-cult genre. I want to explore this genre.

The main conclusions about the beatitudes, according to Professor Betz, are the following:

1. Their original function (*Sitz im Leben*) is in ritual;
2. Their nature is that of declarative statements;
3. Their future orientation is eschatological as well as this-wordly;
4. They are connected with ethics and morality.[3]

---

[1] H. D. Betz, *The Sermon on the Mount: A Commentary on the Sermon on the Mount, including the Sermon on the Plain (Matthew 5:3–7:27 and Luke 6:20–49)* (Hermeneia; Minneapolis: Fortress, 1995) 92–93.

[2] Ibid., 93.

[3] Ibid.

These definitions are short and precise. But there is a tension between points 1 and 4. According to the history of tradition, the beatitudes lost their original ritual function and acquired a didactic and doctrinal function within the redactional environment of the sermons.[4] But according to point 4, the beatitudes were originally connected with ethics and morality. Professor Hellholm demonstrated the ethical function for the distinct stages of the tradition. We will see later that the redaction has also combined the ritual function with the ethical function; it has not abolished the usual ritual function, but given it a new sense. Some remarks are also possible on point 2, on the nature of "declarative statements." Professor Hellholm discussed this point extensively. And the third, well-known point of eschatological tension, "already now—not yet," is closely connected with points 1 and 4 and can also be clarified in the discussion with Professor Hellholm.

With regard to point 2: according to Professor Betz, the genre of the beatitude belongs to "gnomological literature" and constitutes "a subgenre of the *sententia*."[5] I agree:[6] but what is a Greek *gnome* and a Latin *sententia*? Are they possible but inapt genres for describing the logia of Jesus, as Bultmann argued and therefore avoided these terms,[7] or are they the main genre of the indicative and interrogative sayings of Jesus, as I conclude?[8]

Bultmann's definition and the Greek genre γνώμη are not really incompatible. Bultmann took over from Jer 18:18 the differentiation of wisdom-saying (עצה), prophetic saying (דבר) and priestly rule (תורה).[9] The genre γνώμη can be classed with the wisdom-saying. Now new problems arise. What about the "priestly rules"? Are they included in the "legal sayings and community rules (Gesetzesworte und Gemeinderegeln)" as Bultmann maintains?[10] How many subgenres does the *gnome* or *sententia* have?

---

[4] Ibid., 93–95.

[5] Ibid., 96.

[6] D. Dormeyer, *Das Neue Testament im Rahmen der antiken Literaturgeschichte: Eine Einführung* (Darmstadt: Wissenschaftliche Buchgesellschaft, 1993) 80–83.

[7] Rudolf Bultmann, *Die Geschichte der synoptischen Tradition* (Göttingen: Vandenhoeck & Ruprecht, 1957) 73.

[8] Dormeyer, *Das Neue Testament*, 70–74.

[9] Bultmann, *Geschichte*, 73.

[10] Ibid.

Before Bultmann created a series of subgenres, he argued in a fundamentally rhetorical way. He differentiated between "constitutive" and "ornamental" motifs:

> Zu den letzteren gehören Formen wie Vergleich, Metapher, Paradoxie, Hyperbel, Parallelismus der Glieder, Antithese und dergl. Motive, die einzeln wie verbunden bei verschiedenen Grundformen angewandt werden, aber auch fehlen können (To the latter belong forms like comparison, metaphor, paradox, hyperbole, parallelism of the parts of a sentence, antithesis and similar motifs, which are used individually and together in various basic forms, but may also be lacking).[11]

This definition of "ornamental" refers to the *lexis* or style, the third level of a speech. The constitutive motifs belong to the *dispositio* or outline, the second level within the hierarchy of speech-elements. These motifs constitute the genre: "Konstitutive Motive nenne ich solche, die die Form eines Spruches konstituieren (I call those motifs constitutive which constitute the form of a saying)."[12] They are given "by the logical form of a sentence."[13] The logical syntactic forms of sentences are three: "1. Principles = *Grundsätze* (the declarative form = *Form der Aussage*); 2. Admonitions = *Mahnworte* (the imperative form = *Form des Imperativs*); 3. Questions = *Fragen*."[14]

These excellent considerations are supported by contemporary speech-act theory. Austin differentiates all speech-acts into illocutionary and constative sentences. "Principles" and "admonitions" describe correctly the deep-structure of the sentences, as we heard from Professor Hellholm. Only the wisdom-question does not have a separate deep-structure and can be classified normally as a constative speech-act, as a "principle." The wisdom-questions of Jesus are rhetorical constative calls, not real questions.[15] The listener has to agree with the proposition implied by the question.

It is another matter with the similarity between priestly rules and "legal sayings and community rules." Without argument Bultmann merely asserts this coincidence. But he mixes the modern genres "legal sayings, community rules" with the ancient genre "priestly rules." The

---

[11] Ibid.

[12] Ibid.

[13] Ibid., 74.

[14] Ibid., 73–74.

[15] H. Lausberg, *Elemente der literarischen Rhetorik* (München: Hüber, 1963) § 445.

priestly class and the sacrificial cult did not exist within the Christian communities. Therefore, there is no continuity from the priestly rules of the Old Testament to the pre-easter and post-easter sayings of Jesus. A linguistic analysis shows that the "legal sayings" and "community rules" belong to the constative and illocutionary wisdom-sayings, that is, to the constative *sententia* and to the prescriptive illocutionary *sententia*.[16]

On the other hand, the sub-distinctions of the wisdom-sayings contain the subgenre "beatitude."[17] This classification is right, but without significance. For Bultmann did not give any description of the structure of the beatitude. The thesis of Professor Betz is much more productive. The beatitude belongs to both forms of the *gnome* or *sententia* and is connected with ritual, especially with Hellenistic and Jewish-Hellenistic mystery-rituals.[18] The modern genres "legal sayings, community rules" (*Gesetzesworte, Gemeinderegeln*) do not give immediate insights into the life of the early Christian communities, as reconstructions of the history of these traditions normally claim. For these sayings are well-known, universal *sententiae* for the popular Hellenistic philosophical life. But the beatitudes are a distinct genre expressing a special type of communal life and opening windows to the ritual dimension of their social setting. Professor Hellholm showed rightly that "grammatically the beatitudes are vague." They can be "declarations of consolation" as well as "ethical exhortations" in a constative way. This double structure gives the beatitudes their special power. The difference between grammatical structure (declaration) and speech-act-function (constative and prescriptive function) allows the reconstruction of possible stages of the tradition. Professor Hellholm formed a useful tool for linking specific meanings of the beatitude with specific situations of communication: historical Jesus, SM, SP, Q, Q^{Matt} and Q^{Luke}. I observe here more intensively the stage of the redaction, especially the pragmatic dimension of the *genre*, which as cultural co-text gives specific sense to the beatitude.

---

[16] K. Berger, "Hellenistische Gattungen im Neuen Testament," *ANRW* 2.25.2 (1984) 1085–86; Dormeyer, *Das Neue Testament*, 71–72.

[17] Bultmann, *Geschichte*, 75.

[18] Betz, *Sermon on the Mount*, 97–105.

2. *Intertextuality of the beatitudes of Matt 5:3–12*

I do not want to bring owls to Chicago, the new Athens. Professor Betz has listed the uses of the terms μακάριος/ὄλβιος/εὐδαίμων, and Professor Hellholm has deepened this matter.[19] The pre-texts from the Old Testament are clearly shown to belong mostly to the wisdom literature (Psalms; Proverbs; Ecclesiastes; Wisdom; Sirach), especially to the apocalyptic type of wisdom (Tob 13:15–16; Sir 48:11). Jewish literature brings the genre beatitudes "into association with the mystery cult"[20] and into association with apocalypticism.[21] The beatitudes have the position of a prologue in the Sermon on the Mount, as well as in the wisdom-psalm Ps 1:1–2 and in the Jewish wisdom-book Ps-Phocylides.[22] Thus, the dependence of the beatitudes-prologue Matt 5:3–12 on the Old Testament and Jewish literature seems to be indisputable.

But the Hellenistic mystery texts, which Professor Betz quotes or cites extensively, should get more attention. Professor Hellholm also mentions the mystery-cult beatitudes. But he merely added them to the complex "apocalyptic-eschatological macarism" and neglected their ritual function. Why did Matthew pick up the three beatitudes from Q (Q 6:20–21a-b), expand them to a poem with eight beatitudes and an appendix of two[23] or one beatitude[24] and set them in the position of a prologue? Matthew is interested in extending the Jewish holy scriptures into the time of Jesus and the church. So Matthew tries to write in the style of the Old Testament. But his structure of election, selection and transformation is determined by Hellenistic culture. Does the mystery-function of the Hellenistic beatitude make sense for the Gospel of Matthew as whole?

---

[19] Ibid., 92–110.

[20] Ibid., 100: *Joseph and Aseneth* 16:7–8.

[21] Betz, *Sermon on the Mount,* 101–2: *2 Enoch* 42:6–14; 4Q525 3.

[22] Betz, *Sermon on the Mount,* 104.

[23] Ibid., 105–7.

[24] D. Hellholm, "Rejoice and Be Glad, For Your Reward is Great in Heaven:" An Attempt at Solving the Structural Problem of Matt 5:11–12," *Festschrift Günter Wagner* (ed. Faculty of Baptist Theological Seminary Rüschlikon, Switzerland; Bern: Peter Lang, 1994) 47–79.

3. The Gospel of Matthew as a member of the genre βίος */"biography" and the beatitudes*

The Gospel of Matthew is a subgenre of the hellenistic genre βίος/"biography."[25] What have mystery beatitudes to do with the biography βίβλος γενέσεως Ἰησοῦ Χριστοῦ υἱοῦ Δαυὶδ υἱοῦ Ἀβραάμ ("the book of the origin of Jesus Christ, son of David, son of Abraham," Matt 1:1). The first epithet Χριστός (Christ) indicates a story about a king; the second epithet υἱὸς Δαυίδ strengthens this title of majesty. Jesus continues and fulfills the kingdom of his ancestor David. The third epithet opens this title for all nations; Abraham is the father of the Jews and the believing gentiles.[26]

But what does the life of the earthly Jesus have to do with mystery cults? Matthew took over the singular word μυστήριον from Mark (Mark 4:11) and changed it from singular to plural. Jesus introduces the explanation of the parable of the sower with the following sentence ὅτι ὑμῖν δέδοται γνῶναι τὰ μυστήρια τῆς βασιλείας τῶν οὐρανῶν, ἐκείνοις δὲ οὐ δέδοται ("because it is given to you to know the mysteries of the Kingdom of the heavens, but to them it is not given," 13:11). The parables-speech in chapter 13 stands near the center of Matthew, that is, the confession of Jesus' messiaship by Peter (16:13–20). The μυστήρια (mysteries) of the Kingdom of the heavens were given before the parables-speech and should be given after this speech. The way of Jesus Christ seems to be the same as the way of the mystery cults. Jesus as "hierophant," that is, as revealer of the mysteries of God's kingdom, invites all God-seekers to go the way of the mysteries with him and to experience their gradual revelation. But Jesus is more than a revealer of Eleusis; the Kingdom of God has begun in Jesus himself; he is the bringer of God's kingdom *and* the main actor in the mystery play.

---

[25] D. Dormeyer, *Evangelium als literarische und theologische Gattung* (ErFor; Darmstadt: Wissenschaftliche Buchgesellschaft, 1989); R. A. Burridge, *What are the Gospels?: A Comparison with Graeco-Roman Biography* (Cambridge: Cambridge University Press, 1992); Dormeyer, *Das Neue Testament,* 199–228.

[26] D. Dormeyer, "Mt 1,1 als Überschrift zur Gattung und Christologie des Matthäusevangeliums," *The Four Gospels, 1992: FS F. Neirynck* (ed. F. van Segbroeck, et al.; BETL 100; Leuven: Leuven University Press, 1992) 1361–83; H. Frankemölle, *Matthäus: Kommentar 1* (Düsseldorf: Patmos, 1994) 133–35.

The assembling of the crowd and of the four disciples, who have been just called, belongs to the beginning of the publication of God's Kingdom (4:12–5:2) and the procession to the death-mystery in Jerusalem. The Galilean mountain is the place of the beginning. The beatitudes are the beginning of the welcoming speech. The revelation of the mysteries ends with the appearence of the risen Christ on the Galilean mountain again. The difference between crowd and disciples is the difference between initiates and non-initiates. After the Sermon on the Mount, the crowd reacts positively and many from the crowd follow him (7:28–8:1). At the beginning of the mission-speech in chapter 10, the number of the twelve disciples is also completed from the crowd.

Eleusis and Samothrake, the most famous mystery-sites in the ancient world, have exactly this ritual pattern. Every year a procession went from Athens to Eleusis to return the statue of Demeter, which had previously been taken to Athens. Initiates and aspirants walked together. At the great gate of Eleusis, the Προπύλαια, the priest-hierophant welcomed the people. The liturgical speech has not been handed down, but can be reconstructed from the Homeric hymn to Demeter,[27] from the *The Frogs*, a comedy of Aristophanes, and other testimonies. The hierophant greets the crowd.[28] After this reception the procession walked on the holy street to some stations, like the cave of Pluton, and to the Τελεστήριον, that is the meeting hall. A ceremony follows here, symbolizing the whole myth of Demeter.[29] At what point the aspirants became initiated cannot be determined exactly. The position of the beatitude, according to the end of the *Hymn to Demeter* (476–482), should be after the first step of initiation. An ancient relief shows the initiation into the Eleusinian mystery-cult.[30] The μύστης, the aspirant, is sitting with covered head on a stool; to the left a priest is pouring out a drink-offering; on the right a priestess is standing with two lowered torches. Marion Giebel argues

---

[27] W. Burkert, *Antiken Mysterien: Funktionen und Gehalt* (München: Beck, 1990) 78–80.

[28] M. Giebel, *Das Geheimnis der Mysterien: Antike Kulte in Griechenland, Rom und Ägypten* (München: Deutscher Taschenbuch, 1993) 38–40.

[29] Burkert, *Antiken Mysterien,* 78–79.

[30] Ibid., 58–59.

that this initiation-scene was celebrated at the great gate.[31] After the removal of the cloth, the μύστης can watch the mystery plays of the myth of Demeter in the cave of Pluton and in the Telesterion.[32] This reconstruction is supported by *The Frogs* of Aristophanes. Before arriving at the great gate, the choir of the procession is singing the hymn of Iakchos on the meadow outside of Eleusis. The choir names itself: χοροποιόν, μάκαρ, ἥβαν ("lovely, youthful chorus," V 352). The beatitude begins at the great gate of Eleusis.

Similarly, before the SM the disciples and the crowd lost a little bit of their blindness by hearing Jesus' preaching that the Kingdom of the heavens has arrived (Matt 4:17). The opening of their eyes continues with the SM, with the revelation to the little ones (Matt 11:25), with the revelation by means of parables (Matt 13:11–17) and with the confession of Jesus' messiaship by Peter (Matt 16:13–20). The last two speeches also have beatitudes (Matt 13:16; 16:17). "But blessed are your eyes, for they *see* and your ears, for they hear" (13:16). "Blessed are you, Simon Bar-Jona, for flesh and blood has not *revealed* this to you, but my father who is in heaven" (16:17). The beatitude at the end of the *Hymn to Demeter* shows a picture similar to that of these verses (Matt 5:3–12; 16:13–20 and especially 13:11–17). Compare "Happy is he among humans on earth who has *seen* these mysteries; but he who is uninitiate and who has no part in them, never has lot of like good things once he is dead, down in the darkness and gloom" with "To you it has been given to know the secrets of the kingdom of the heaven, but to them it has not been given" (Matt 13:11).

It is tempting to equate Matthew's Gospel with a pagan mystery cult. The beatitude 11:6 praises John's acceptance of Jesus; the last beatitude in 24:46 praises the faithful servant as a future possessor of God's Kingdom. The Matthean beatitudes (5:3–12; 11:6; 13:16; 16:17; 24:46) mark the way of Jesus as a way of gradual revelation of the mysteries of God's Kingdom. But Galilee is not Eleusis and the βίβλος about Jesus is not the ritual book of an annual mystery feast. But mystery language is also used in a metaphorical sense in philosophy and literature. Professor Betz named Euripides (*Ba.* 72–77) and Apuleius (*Met.* 11.16) for literature, Hesiod (*Theog.* 954–55) and

[31] Giebel, *Das Geheimnis der Mysterien*, 38–40.

[32] Ibid., 32–33.

Epicurus (Diog. Laer. 10.139) for philosophy. Plato (*Resp.* 1.354a; *Phaedr.* 250b) can be added.

Like a philosophical teacher, Matthew's Jesus creates a school by expressing his theology in the language of the mysteries. Thus the use of the verb διδάσκω starts after the call of the first four disciples (4:23) and is repeated in the introduction to the Sermon on the Mount. Forming an inclusio, this verb and the related noun end the speech (7:29).

But Jesus is more than a teacher of theological mysteries. According to the title in Matt 1:1, he is the Christ and the son of David. So a third line must be constructed, that is, the emperor-cult. Augustus was very cautious with regard to the emperor-cult. He invented the new goddess *Roma* and allowed the Greek-speaking half of the empire to worship the *Dea Roma* and to honor her most important servant, the living emperor. After his death Augustus was deified. Tiberius did not force the imperial cult, Caligula overacted crazily, Claudius retarded the development again, but Nero tried a new way. Seneca was to help him to become both an emperor as well as a philosopher and poet. This Platonic and peripatetic ideal influenced Seneca as well as Plutarch. After Nero's nasty death, a new dimension of the imperial cult was manifested in relation to Vespasian. Miracle-working was attributed to him in accordance with the pattern of the *theios anēr*.[33] The adopted emperors fulfilled the plan of Seneca and Nero. Hadrian and Marcus Aurelius became emperors *and* philosophers. They neglected the miracle-working, but they exaggerated the cult-function. Hadrian allowed the cultic worship of his person and founded new cults for his friends, for example, for his favorite, Antinoos.

There was a broad palette of exceptional qualifications for the emperor-cult. The weakest point was the foundation of a new imperial-mystery-cult.[34] The deification of Antinoos was quite ridiculous and funny (compare Wis 14:15). The emperors remained real human

---

[33] B. Kollmann, *Jesus und die Christen als Wundertäter: Studien zu Magie, Medizin und Schamanismus in Antike und Christentum* (FRLANT 170; Göttingen: Vandenhoeck & Ruprecht, 1996) 106–9.

[34] H.-J. Klauck, *Die religiöse Umwelt des Urchristentums II: Herrscher- und Kaiserkult, Philosophie, Gnosis* (Stuttgart: Kohlhammer, 1996) 63–64.

beings, but they were believed to be able to mediate between human beings and gods.[35]

Matthew's portrait of Jesus combined the separate functions "teaching, miracle-working, school-forming, revealing mysteries" and emphasized the last function "revealing mysteries." Jesus became a counterpart of the emperor, who held the worldly functions "tax-collecting, administration, law and war" (Matt 22:15–22; 27:1–66). These were the classical functions of the *princeps* (*Res gestae* 1–10.18) as well as for the messiah from the house of David.

The mystery cults and the philosophical schools were compatible with official society.[36] If Matthew portrayed Jesus as a founder of a philosophical school with an appeal like that of the mysteries, the "knowledge of the mysteries of the Kingdom of the heavens" (13:11) becomes also compatible with the Roman empire. The portrait of Jesus Christ has both sides. For Jewish hearers Jesus fulfills the Old Testament promises of the Davidic messiah and collects an eschatological Israel into the circle of the twelve; for Hellenistic hearers he creates a new mystery community, which is rooted in the archaic Jewish religion.

The beatitudes perform what they say in mystery language. They declare the hearers as the possessors of present blessedness and promise the fulfillment of all blessedness for the future. Therefore I do not agree totally with Professor Betz and Professor Hellholm, who emphasized the *prescriptive* function of the redactional meaning of the beatitudes. In that case the beatitudes have only a didactic and dogmatic function, but not a ritual function. Let us return to the beginning. According to Betz, the "first recipients of the Sermons may remember baptism as their initiation ceremony, but neither the SM nor the SP mentions baptism."[37] Do the first recipients really remember their baptism? Are the beatitudes necessarily connected with baptism, and is this connection demonstrated by early baptismal formulas? The Gospel of Matthew as a whole does not know baptism of the disciples of Jesus or of the crowd around Jesus. Also the mystery

---

[35] Tacitus *Annals* 4.37.3: the speech of Tiberius; Klauck, *Die religiöse Umwelt des Urchristentums II*, 72.

[36] Burkert, *Antiken Mysterien*, 35–56.

[37] Betz, *Sermon on the Mount*, 95.

cults are not limited to the ritual of washing and initiation, but deepen the mystery-beatitudes by their repetition in the yearly rituals till the hopeful death of the initiates.

In Eleusis and Samothrake the cultic function is therefore strongly woven together with ethical and didactic functions.[38] The eschatological tension is also present in the promises of the mystery cults, which are limited to individual salvation. Therefore, the ritual function of the beatitudes includes the whole process of hearing and following Jesus like the life according to philosophy and the mystery cult. Seneca mocks the Isis mystery cult in his work *Apokolokyntosis*: after his death and deification, the emperor Claudius was condemned to Hades and expelled from heaven. At the door of the underworld "Narcissus" cries: "Claudius is coming." The dead murdered by Claudius run out and sing an allusion to the Isis-cult, to the finding and reviving of Osiris: εὑρήκαμεν, συγχαίρομεν ("we have found him, we rejoice;" Seneca, *Apokolocyntosis* 13–14; compare Matt 5:12).[39] The murdered dead allude to the enjoyment of putting Claudius on trial and accusing him. Initiation into the mystery cult does not save villains from the underworld trial.[40] This portion of the parody makes use of the ritual procession from the Isis-cult and the Eleusinian mysteries, which have similarities with the beginning of the SM in a metaphorical sense. Like Claudius and Narcissus, the crowd and the four disciples are walking to Jesus. He offers the beatitudes and joins them, reviving the seekers of God's Kingdom. Nero produced Seneca's parody after his victories at the Olympic games. He staged his arrival in Rome (68) as a triumph combined with a mystery ritual which seems to imitate the ritual of Eleusis. Dio Cassius writes:

> When he entered Rome, a portion of the wall was torn down and a section of the gates broken in, because some asserted that each of these ceremonies was customary upon the return of crowned victors from the games. First entered men bearing the crowns which he had won, and after them others with wooden panels borne aloft on spears, upon which were inscribed the name of the games, the kind of contest, and a statement that Nero Caesar first of all the

---

38 Giebel, *Das Geheimnis der Mysterien*, 109–10.

39 W. Schöne, *Apokolokyntosis: die Verkürbissung des Kaisers Claudius* (Munich: E. Heimeran, 1957) 68.

40 Aristoph. *Ra.* 455–57: the catalogue of evils; Giebel, *Das Geheimnis der Mysterien*, 109–10.

> Romans from the beginning of the world had won it. Next came the victor himself on a triumphal car, the one in which Augustus had once celebrated his many victories; he was clad in a vestment of purple covered with spangles of gold, was crowned with a garland of wild olive, and held in his hand the Pythian laurel. By his side in the vehicle rode Diodorus the lyre-player. After passing in this manner through the Circus and through the Forum in company with the soldiers and the knights and the senate he ascended the Capitol and proceeded thence to the palace. The city was all decked with garlands, was ablaze with lights and reeking with incense, and the whole population, the senators themselves most of all, kept shouting in chorus: "Hail, Olympian Victor! Hail, Pythian Victor! Augustus! Augustus! Hail to Nero, our Hercules! Hail to Nero, our Apollo! The only Victor of the Grand Tour, the only one from the beginning of time! Augustus! Augustus! O, Divine Voice! Blessed are they that hear thee" (Dio C. 63.20.1–5).[41]

As Heracles and Apollo incarnate, Nero mediates at this moment divine power and immortality. The structure of the beatitudes is the same as the structure of the beatitudes in Matthew 5. Does the allusion to Nero redivivus in Revelation (Rev 13:3) include the memory of this mystery-triumph? But Dio Cassius did not accept this pretension. He continues:

> I might, to be sure, have used circumlocutions, but why not declare their very words? The expressions that they used do not disgrace my history; rather, the fact that I have not concealed any of them lends it distinction (63.20.6).[42]

The mystery ritual becomes a hidden contextual structure of the gospel-book (Matthew) as whole. The Christians who are in the process of receiving and deepening the mysteries of God need to hear and follow the book (βίβλος) of Jesus Christ within their communities. The book also plays an important role for the mystery cult of Isis (Apul. *Met.* 11.17).[43] But especially for the philosophical schools, the books of and about the founder became the basis for the whole of life. Plato compares the contemplation of beauty with the mystery cult procession:

> Now in the earthly copies of justice and temperance and the other ideas which are precious to souls there is no light, but only a few, approaching the images through the darkling organs of sense, behold in them the nature of that which

---

[41] Text and trans. E. Cary, *Dio Cassius: Roman History* (9 vols.; LCL; Cambridge, MA: Harvard University Press, 1961).

[42] Cary, ibid.

[43] R. Merkelbach, *Roman und Mysterium in der Antike* (München: Beck, 1962) 113.

> they imitate, and these few do this with difficulty. But at that former time they saw beauty shining in brightness, when, with a blessed company—we following in the train of Zeus, and others in that of some other god—they saw the blessed sight and vision and were initiated into that which is rightly called the most blessed of mysteries, which we celebrated in a state of perfection, when we were without experience of the evils which awaited us in the time to come, being permitted as initiates to the sight of perfect and simple and calm and happy apparitions, which we saw in the pure light, being ourselves pure and not entombed in this which we carry about with us and call the body, in which we are imprisoned like an oyster in its shell (Plat. *Phaedr.* 250b-c).

The word δικαιοσύνη ("righteousness") opens this paragraph. The adjective εὐδαίμων describes the choir, μακάριος and θεός qualify the view, going μετὰ Διός ("with Zeus") is parallel to "Immanuel" (Matt 1:23). The idea of "God with us" is realized when Jesus sits and teaches on the mount (Matthew 5). Plato's words, ἐτελοῦντο τῶν τελετῶν ("and were initiated"), correspond to "to know the mysteries of God's Kingdom" (Matt 13:11). This metaphorical mystery-speech is transformed in the biographies of philosophical men to a specific way of life associated with the mystery procession. The biography of the founder included the qualifications of the ideal emperor; see, for example, the *Life of Pythagoras.* Further, the archaic city-founders and reformers were pictured by Plutarch according to the ideal of the philosopher-King, for example, Romulus, Numa, Theseus, Lykurgus and Solon. Therefore, Jesus Christ is pictured by Matthew as an archaic philosophical founder-teacher and eschatological Christ. Baptism is only a preparatory rite, like the washings before the ritual processions in Eleusis and elsewhere, which are followed by the first initiation. For this reason Matthew can put the command regarding baptism of future Christians at the end and emphasize the ethical, wonder-working, theological and mystery-language of Jesus Christ. The last mandate of the risen Christ combines baptism with the complex teaching (28:19–20) which had ritual, ethical and didactic functions.

The Sermon on the Mount and its prologue of beatitudes begin the formation of a new community, with a new mystery-knowledge, behavior and way of life, which continues till the end of the world.

Conversion and Culture: A Comparative Study of the Conversions of Paul and Two Twentieth-Century African Christians[1]

Kathleen O'Brien Wicker

I. Introduction

Many Christians develop their ideas about religious conversion from dramatic conversion stories about Paul, Augustine, and other heroes and heroines of the Christian tradition. These narratives describe conversions as sudden, total and permanent transformative religious experiences in which individuals recognize that they have been chosen by a God who demands their exclusive loyalty and commitment.[2]

---

[1] I am pleased to thank the following colleagues and friends for helpful comments on various versions of this paper and for obtaining relevant materials for me: Esther Acolatse, M. L. Daneel, Sue E. Houchins, Simeon Ilesanmi, Elizabeth Leitch, Birgit Meyer, Jacob K. Olupona, Kofi Asare Opoku, Emmanuel Kweku Osam and Vincent Wimbush.

[2] One influential example of this approach to conversion is the classic study of conversion by A. D. Nock, *Conversion: The Old and the New in Religion from Alexander the Great to Augustine of Hippo* (Oxford: Oxford University Press, 1933). Any definition or description of conversion is, of course, predicated upon a particular definition of religion. Nock defines religion as a system which requires an "all or nothing" commitment and a particular "view of the world and of the soul" (p. 160). He describes forms of religious activity that tolerate inclusiveness as cults. He argues that the term conversion should be applied only to change of religion, and not to adhesion to cults. There are many critics of Nock's narrow definition of conversion. Hubert Cancik, in his essay in this volume, "Lucian on Conversion: Some Remarks on Lucian's Dialogue *Nigrinos*," states that Nock treats the conversion literature in Greco-Roman antiquity either incompletely or not at all. The historian Ramsay MacMullen presents a different account of the history of conversions to Christianity in antiquity from that of Nock, including a recognition of the phenomenon of group conversion (*Christianizing the Roman Empire: A.D. 100–400* [New Haven: Yale University Press, 1984]). Eugene V. Gallagher offers a thoughtful critique of various modern views of conversion, including that of Nock, from a religious studies perspective (*Expectation and Experience: Explaining Religious Conversion* [Atlanta: Scholars Press, 1990] 110–33).

This commonly accepted view of conversion oversimplifies the process of conversion, which is rarely sudden or total, and is inevitably dynamic rather than static. It also ignores the historical and cultural contexts of the conversion experience. The traditional view fails to recognize how those contexts prepare potential converts to be receptive to new religious experiences, and the ways in which other people aid them to interpret the significance of their experiences and provide a supportive environment in which they can mature in their new faiths.[3]

The transformation of Paul from a zealous Pharisee to a missionary of the risen Jesus to the Gentiles has been understood throughout Christian history as a conversion experience. Such events occur, according to Hans Dieter Betz and others, when a space for change opens up between other bounded options. Paul found such a space in the interstices between Judaism and Hellenism, which allowed his personal transformation, as well as the development of a new religious movement.[4] But Betz says that the term conversion should be used to describe Paul's experiences only in a qualified way. He points out that, while Paul changed his party allegiance within Judaism, he did not change his religious tradition.[5]

The assumption that conversion means change of religion rather than change or renewal within a tradition is not universally accepted, however. In the Hebrew prophetic tradition, conversion was under-

---

[3] A number of modern studies of conversion stress the importance of balancing individual factors and cultural and social influences in the assessment of conversion experiences. See, for example, Robert W. Hefner, ed., *Conversion to Christianity: Historical and Anthropological Perspectives on a Great Transformation* (Berkeley: University of California Press, 1993); Eugene V. Gallagher, *Expectation and Experience: Explaining Religious Conversion*; Lewis R. Rambo, *Understanding Religious Conversion* (New Haven: Yale University Press, 1993).

[4] Hans Dieter Betz, "The Apostle Paul between Judaism and Hellenism: Creating a Space for Christianity" (forthcoming).

[5] Hans Dieter Betz, *Galatians: A Commentary on Paul's Letter to the Churches in Galatia* (Philadelphia: Fortress Press, 1979) 62–75. I agree that Paul did not call himself a convert, that he would not have been understood as a convert from a strict Jewish perspective, and that he could not, historically, have been a convert to Christianity.

stood as a return to full commitment through repentance and a change of heart.[6]

First century Judaism probably considered as converts only those changing from paganism to Judaism. But Hubert Cancik provides examples from the philosophical literature of antiquity which indicate that a change from one philosophical school to another was described as conversion.[7] Since the various "schools" in first century Judaism and in early Christianity[8] often used the language of philosophy and compared themselves to philosophical schools, describing Paul's change from one "school" within Judaism to another as a conversion also seems historically valid. Paul's conversion experience cannot be reduced simply to a prophetic call to a mission to the Gentiles.[9]

An examination of religious conversion from a modern perspective also legitimates calling Paul a convert.[10] Utilizing insights from the modern conversion literature, I will suggest a conceptual framework of

---

[6] In later Jewish tradition, however, conversion was understood primarily as a change of mind which required renewed observance of the Law. Conversion was thus a process which happened often in the life of the individual. See Johannes Behm and Ernst Würthwein, "νοέω κτλ.," *TDNT* 4. 980–99; Georg Bertram, "στρέφω κτλ.," *TDNT* 7. 719–20; 723–26. In these cases there was no question about change of religion *per se*. Modern examples of changes from one form of a religious tradition to another that are understood as conversions can also be adduced. Two such examples will be discussed in this essay.

[7] Cancik, "Lucian," 36.

[8] Hans Dieter Betz, "Christianity as Religion: Paul's Attempt at Definition in Romans," *Paulinische Studien. Gesammelte Aufsätze III* (Tübingen: J.C.B. Mohr [Paul Siebeck], 1994) 207, n. 4.

[9] Betz has correctly observed that "Paul's 'conversion' to the Christian faith disappears behind his vocation to the apostolate" in his letters (*Galatians*, 69). But this does not mean that Paul did not have a conversion experience. Beverly Anne Roberts Gaventa discusses the history of the view that Paul received a call but was not converted ("Paul's Conversion: A Critical Sifting of the Epistolary Evidence" [Duke University: Ph.D. Dissertation, 1978] 71–74). See also Krister Stendahl, "Call Rather Than Conversion," *Paul Among Jews and Gentiles and Other Essays* (Philadelphia: Fortress Press, 1976) 7–23. The description of Paul's experience as a prophetic call has its own problems. There are limits to how far this analogy can be extended without distorting Paul's theology. See Betz, *Galatians*, 70, n. 139. In addition, Hebrew prophets were not ordinarily given a mission to go outside of Israel to convert people. Jonah is an exception.

[10] Alan F Segal argues for the application of the terms convert and conversion to Paul from a modern Jewish perspective (*Paul the Convert: The Apostolate and Apostasy of Saul the Pharisee* [New Haven: Yale University Press, 1990] 6).

conversion which emphasizes the historical and cultural[11] dimensions of this type of religious experience. I will then use this framework to show that the manner in which Paul describes his life, his visions of Jesus, and his subsequent mission are characteristic of contemporary understandings of religious conversion experiences.

I will also compare Paul's conversion experience with those of two twentieth-century African Christians, Johane Marange[12] of Zimbabwe and John Sam Amedzro[13] of Ghana. The conversion experiences of each of these men inspired them to found new types of Christian churches in their communities. Comparisons of the two African converts and Paul are appropriate for several reasons. All were members of cultural and religious communities characterized by diverse forms of interpretation and praxis; all had their conversion experiences within the context of imperial or colonial regimes and, perhaps as a result, developed an eschatological orientation in their theologies; all regarded their experiences as new revelations about the religious traditions of which they were already a part; and all acted as catalysts for the transformation and diversification of these traditions.

My broader goals in examining the topic of conversion in this comparative context are twofold: I want to acquaint readers with aspects of the history of Christianity in Africa and to show the

---

[11] Ithamar Gruenwald, in his contribution to this volume, defines culture as follows: "In general terms, culture is a multi-structured system of socially-centred components that, functionally speaking, are cross-referential in shaping the existence and the forms of self-identification of individuals and groups" (idem, "A Case Study of Scripture and Culture: Apocalypticism as Cultural Identity in Past and Present," 260). This definition is consistent with my use of the term culture in this essay.

[12] Johane Marange founded the African Apostolic Church of Johane Marange as an Independent Christian Church in then Southern Rhodesia in 1932. Congregations of this church now extend from South Africa to Zaire. He died in 1963. Family members provided leadership for the Church after Marange's death. For a parallel to succession within the family, consider James and the cousins of Jesus. See Ernst Bammel, *Jesu Nachfolger: Nachfolgeüberlieferungen in der Zeit des frühen Christentums* (Heidelberg: L. Schneider, 1988).

[13] Samuel Yao Amedzro, or John Sam Amedzro, his conversion name, founded an Independent Christian Church known as *Abelengor* in Ghana in 1961. By 1985, however, he transformed the church into a healing church known as The Lord's Pentecostal Church, its present designation. After his death, he was succeeded by his son, Rev. Stanley Amedzro.

similarities and parallels in the religious phenomena experienced by prominent and well-known Christian figures, such as Paul, with Marange and Amedzro, who are largely unknown outside their immediate communities.

II. Conversion and the Conversion Literature

References to conversion are found frequently in religious communities, art, literature and the media. Despite these cultural representations, and recent studies and conferences devoted to the topic of conversion,[14] however, there is still a lack of consensus on the nature and definition of religious conversion.

One obvious reason for this situation is the multivalency of the term conversion. The terms most commonly used in the literatures of Greco-Roman and Judeo-Christian antiquity to describe the process of religious conversion are, in Greek, μετανοεῖν, ἐπιστέφειν, ἀποστρέφειν and their cognates and related forms, and in Latin, *convertere* and its cognates.[15] These terms suggest a turning or a change that can be applied to many different spheres of human activity.[16] But even when this terminology of conversion is used to describe religious transformation, it may refer to change of mind (an intellectual act), change of heart (an attitudinal stance), change of behavior, or to a combination of two or more of these elements.

The multidimensionality of conversion experiences is another reason for the lack of consensus about the nature of conversion. A distinction is usefully made between the precipitating conversion event and the other contributing factors involved in the process of conversion. Conversion experiences also need to be distinguished from

---

[14] An important conference on conversion, "Conversion to World Religions: Historical and Ethnographic Interpretations," was held at Boston University, April 14–15, 1988. The papers from this conference are published in Robert W. Hefner, ed., *Conversion to Christianity*, cited above.

[15] Johannes Behm, "νοέω κτλ.," *TDNT* 4. 999–1008; Bertram, "στρέφω κτλ.," *TDNT* 7. 721–22; 726–29.

[16] Thus, Cancik distinguishes between philosophical and religious conversion in antiquity ("Lucian," 28, 30). His thoughtful analyses of types of conversion in three dialogues of Lucian, and in writings of Seneca and Apuleius, suggest to me, however, that philosophical and religious categories of conversion cannot be totally distinguished from one another phenomenologically.

conversion narratives which are expressions of retrospective self-understanding, like Augustine's *Confessions*, or are the views of a community influenced by a convert's transformation, such as Luke's accounts about Paul in Acts. These narratives, constituted as a new story of identity and meaning, are best regarded as "biographical reconstructions," and not as objective interpretations of the conversion process.[17] Such narratives may, however, be accurate representations of the self-understanding of an individual or a community at a particular historical moment. Individuals and communities may also change their conversion narratives over time to reflect further experiences and insights, as has been observed in Augustine's writings.[18]

Modern historical studies of conversions and investigations of conversion experiences utilizing psychological, sociological and anthropological methods of research both complicate and refine understandings of conversion which are based solely on literary narratives about these experiences. They also render inadequate A. D. Nock's classic definition of conversion as:

> . . . the reorientation of the soul of an individual, his deliberate turning from indifference or from an earlier form of piety to another, a turning which implies a consciousness that a great change is involved, that the old was wrong and the new is right."[19]

Robert W. Hefner offers different descriptions of conversion based on studies of conversion in a variety of cultural traditions:

> The most necessary feature of religious conversion . . . is not a deeply systematic reorganization of personal meanings but an adjustment in self-identification through the at least nominal acceptance of religious actions or beliefs deemed more fitting, useful, or true . . . . conversion implies the

[17] Cancik emphasizes the narrative character of conversion stories in Graeco-Roman antiquity ("Lucian," 31, 38). He observes that they "have a long, rich, pre-Christian tradition." David Snow and Richard Machalek describe the process as biographical reconstruction ("The Convert as a Social Type," *Sociological Theory*, [ed. R. Collins; San Francisco: Jossey-Bass, 1983] 259–89). See also Mary M. Gergen and Kenneth J. Gergen, "The Social Construction of Narrative Accounts," *Historical Social Psychology* (ed. K. J. Gergen and M. M. Gergen; Hillsdale, NJ: Erlbaum, 1984) 173–89.

[18] Paula Fredriksen, "Paul and Augustine: Conversion Narratives, Orthodox Traditions, and the Retrospective Self," *JTS* 37 (1986) 3–44.

[19] Nock, *Conversion*, 7.

> acceptance of a new locus of self-definition, a new, though not necessarily exclusive, reference point for one's identity .... conversion need not reformulate one's understanding of the ultimate conditions of existence, but it always involves commitment to a new kind of moral authority and a new or reconceptualized social identity.[20]

Modern studies of conversion in Africa suggest that religious conversion is mediated within the particular social and political circumstances of people's lives. They stress the importance of both utilitarian and spiritual aspects of religion. Frequently, they focus on the conversion of groups of people, rather than individuals, and on "religious creativity."[21]

A number of studies have explored whether the adoption of the monotheistic traditions of Islam and Christianity in Africa represents a radical shift in world view from that of traditional religions.[22] Robin Horton argues that African traditional religions, in addition to their microcosmic perspective, also have a macrocosmic dimension, that is, a universal sense of the divine, which gains prominence when these religions come in contact with other macrocosmic traditions, such as Islam and Christianity. Therefore, the radical change of world view essential for conversion does not take place.[23]

J. D. Y. Peel observes that conversions usually occur when there is a correspondence between the needs of converts and the features of the

---

[20] Hefner, *Conversion to Christianity*, 17.

[21] Mario I. Aguilar uses this term to refer to situations "where more than two traditions are actively interacting in an African region, or in the life of an African community" ("Rethinking African Conversion: Assessing Syncretism through Diversification," Paper presented at the African Studies Association meeting, November, 1996).

[22] For background on the religious traditions of Africa and their interpretation, see Jan G. Platvoet, "The Religions of Sub-Saharan Africa in their Historical Order," and "From Object to Subject: A History of the Study of the Religions of Africa," *The Study of Religions in Africa: Past, Present and Prospects* (ed. Jan G. Platvoet, James L. Cox, and Jacob K. Olupona; Cambridge: Roots & Branches; Harare: University of Zimbabwe Press, 1996).

[23] Horton's views, referred to as an "intellectualist" approach to the study of African religions, are found in three programmatic essays: Robin Horton, "African Conversion," *Africa* 41.2 (1971) 85–108; "On the Rationality of Conversion, Part I," *Africa* 45.3 (1975) 219–325; "On the Rationality of Conversion, Part II," *Africa* 45.4 (1975) 373–99.

new religion.[24] Religious adherence itself often becomes the mark of political identity in African communities, at both the local and the global levels.[25] David D. Laitin argues that Islam and Christianity are often perceived to address the problems of modernization better than traditional religions do.[26] But Terence Ranger has demonstrated that Christianity and Islam can also operate microcosmically and traditional religions macrocosmically in African cultures. He concludes that the tension between the local and the global is observable in all of these religious traditions.[27]

Humphrey J. Fisher has argued against Horton that the radical changes involved in conversion do occur in Africa, but that not all affiliations with new religions can be labeled conversions.[28] Scholars have also shown that conversion in Africa has not proved to be a unidirectional process of evolution from so-called lower to higher forms of religion. Converts sometimes reaffiliate with their former traditions,[29] or they continue to practice traditional religion after they convert to Islam or Christianity. The two systems address quite different, and not oppositional, aspects of devotees' lives, according to Jon Kirby.[30] Or, as Terence Ranger has suggested, this fluidity of

---

[24] J. D. Y. Peel, "Conversion and Tradition in Two African Societies: Ijebu and Buganda," *Past and Present* 76 (1977) 108–41. Jean and John Comaroff analyze how certain southern Africans tried historically to appropriate Christianity to make it serve their interests (*Of Revelation and Revolution: Christianity, Colonialism and Consciousness in South Africa*, vol. 1 [Chicago: The University of Chicago Press, 1991]).

[25] Peel, "Conversion and Tradition," 139.

[26] David D. Laitin, *Hegemony and Culture: Politics and Religious Change among the Yoruba* (Chicago: The University of Chicago Press, 1986) 37.

[27] Terence Ranger, "The Local and the Global in Southern African Religious History," *Conversion to Christianity*, 65–98.

[28] Humphrey J. Fisher, "Conversion Reconsidered: Some Historical Aspects of Religious Conversion in Black Africa," *Africa* 43.1 (1973) 27–40. He describes three phases of religious change in Africa, two of which are modeled on Nock's categories of "adhesion" and "conversion" (pp. 33–35).

[29] Mario I. Aguilar, "African Conversion from a World Religion: Religious Diversification by the Waso Boorana in Kenya," *Africa* 65.4 (1995) 525–44.

[30] Jon P. Kirby, "Cultural Change & Religious Conversion in West Africa," *Religion in Africa: Experience & Expression* (ed. Thomas D. Blakely et al.; Portsmouth, NH: Heinemann, 1994) 56–71.

religious identity is an expression of "creative and resilient religious pluralism."[31]

Studies indicate that people change only as much of their world views and behaviors as is demanded by new experiences. They do not completely replace their old world views with new ones. The usual pattern is to integrate new perspectives into old cosmologies and behavior patterns. This may require a change in the interpretations given to the old ideas and behaviors, but not the elimination of traditional patterns except if they are in direct conflict with the new beliefs. Jacob K. Olupona reflects this view of the conversion process:

> . . . elements from the world views that "make sense" are added while those which have proven inadequate are deleted. The process occurs in all cultures, for world views themselves are dynamic organisms. Conversion, then represents both a continuity and discontinuity with the old traditions.[32]

In the modern literature on the phenomenology of conversion, Lewis R. Rambo has developed an inclusive model of religious conversion drawn from the experiences of people of diverse religious and cultural traditions. He also incorporates methodological studies of the religious, cultural, social and psychological factors that affect conversion. He divides the process of conversion into seven stages: context, crisis, quest, encounter, interaction, commitment, and consequences. He recognizes that individuals are often impelled toward conversion by specific events of personal life, for which they seek resolution, or by a desire for a more satisfying explanation of the meaning of life. In the process, the potential convert comes into contact with persons of other persuasions, who offer new alternatives. Potential converts must engage the new tradition and its members before making the commitment to reconstruct their self-understandings in the new context, which will affect world view, perceived moral authority, social identity and behavior.[33]

Rambo makes a number of important contributions to the discussion of conversion. He observes that the transformation in the

---

[31] Ranger, "The Local and the Global," 73.

[32] Jacob K. Olupona, *Kingship, Religion, and Rituals in a Nigerian Community: A Phenomenological Study of Ondo Yoruba Festivals* (Stockholm: Almqvist & Wiksell International, 1991) 172.

[33] Rambo, *Understanding Religious Conversion*, passim.

potential convert's world view and behavior is a process which takes place over time. Recognizing that the events which precipitate conversion are often ambiguous and require interpretation, he highlights the importance of interaction between the individual and the religious community in the conversion process. In addition, he gives breadth to the understanding of the conversion experience by including examples from a variety of religious traditions and by utilizing the results of studies based on differing methodologies.

Enlarging upon Rambo's discussion of conversion, I distinguish among related but separable aspects of the individual's conversion *experience*: the *antecedents* to conversion, including cultural, historical, economic and personal factors; the conversion *event/s* and their interpretation; the *transformation* in the self-understanding, world view and behavior of the convert, including the *call* or *mission* received as part of the conversion *experience*; and a description and interpretation of the conversion experience in a conversion *narrative.*

I regard religious conversion as a process in which an individual or a group experiences a renewal within their own religious tradition, or shifts beliefs from one tradition to another. Usually conversion is catalyzed by such spiritual experiences as dreams, visions, intellectual or life quests, or revelations about the meaning of problematic life events. The process occurs through a dynamic interaction at two levels: socially, between the converts and the adepts in the religion, and personally, between the converts' old perspectives and those of the new religion. The integration achieved by a convert or group can range from simple affiliation with a new group to a major transformation in self-definition, world view and behavior. The conversion experiences of Paul, Johane Marange, and John Sam Amedzro, which are the subject of the next two sections of this essay, were characterized by profound revelatory experiences. These men interpreted their experiences from the perspective of particular religious traditions or "schools," but their interpretations were also affected by broader social, political and historical contexts. The impact of their conversion experiences also extended to other people through the mission activity they carried out as a response to their conversion calls.

III. Paul's Conversion Experience

A clearer understanding of Paul's conversion can be gained by applying to his life and experiences the conceptual framework of conversion sketched above. The antecedents to conversion in Paul's life, the religious experiences which constituted his conversion event, and the context of its interpretation will be examined first. Then, the post-conversion transformation in Paul's self-understanding, world view and behavior will be interpreted as continuities or discontinuities with these antecedent factors. Finally, the possibility that Paul constructed a retrospective conversion narrative will be examined.

Antecedents to Conversion

Individuals learn within specific cultural communities how to interpret the meaning of life, to understand the way the world works, and to behave in a manner suited to their place in the community. The particular political, social, religious and personal realities of their lives may also create the interstitial spaces in which radical change may occur.

The political and social contexts of the Roman empire and the religious context of first century Judaism were important antecedent factors in Paul's conversion experience. These factors were so closely intertwined in his life that it is impossible to consider them separately. Undoubtedly, personal factors also played their part, but almost none of them are known to us.

The first century Roman Empire was a colonizing power which often exploited its citizens and political dependencies and deprived them of freedom, while claiming to assure a reign of *pax et securitas.* The political order was maintained through careful control of potentially volatile areas, such as Judea. The patronage system, which anchored the privileged social structure of the colonial regime, promised personal success and advantage to those willing to contribute to the aggrandizement of their patrons and of the regime which supported them.[34]

---

[34] For an historical perspective, see Neil Elliott, *Liberating Paul: The Justice of God and the Politics of the Apostle* (Maryknoll: Orbis Books, 1994) 184–89.

Individuals and communities responded to the realities of this situation in the ways that colonized peoples have always done: through assimilation, passive resistance or active subversion.[35] Philosophers reflected upon the "possibilities of human freedom" in such a political context and found it only in the self-sufficiency of the philosopher and in the control of the individual over when to end life.[36]

Jewish responses to Roman colonization were varied. For some, Roman domination was God's will, since history demonstrated that God had in the past used foreign rulers to punish Israel for its infidelities.[37] The group which Josephus (*Ant.* 18.9) designated the "Fourth Philosophy" advocated non-violent resistance to Rome, because they rejected the thesis that God would rule Israel through foreign powers.[38] Later in the first century, however, the rejection of foreign domination by the Jewish community in Judea became more actively subversive.[39]

Endurance and submission were characteristic responses of the Pharisees, who believed that the divine plan permitted the Roman domination of Israel for a limited time.[40] Some apocalypticists even claimed they had visions which assured them that God was still enthroned on high and his plan still operative in the world.[41]

---

[35] For a discussion of colonial theory, see Benedict Anderson, *Imagined Communities: Reflections on the Origin and Spread of Nationalism.* (rev. ed.; London: Verso, 1983).

[36] Hans Dieter Betz, "Paul's Concept of Freedom in the Context of Hellenistic Discussions about Possibilities of Human Freedom," *Paulinische Studien. Gesammelte Aufsätze III* (Tübingen: J.C.B. Mohr [Paul Siebeck], 1994) 110–25.

[37] Elliott, *Liberating Paul*, 160.

[38] Elliott, *Liberating Paul*, 151–54.

[39] For a more extensive examination of the zealot movement, see Martin Hengel, *The Zealots: Investigations into the Jewish Freedom Movement in the Period from Herod I until 70 A.D.*, (Edinburgh: T. & T. Clark, 1989); Martin Goodman, *The Ruling Classes of Judaea: The Origins of the Jewish Revolt against Rome A.D. 66–70* (Cambridge: Cambridge University Press, 1987); Richard A. Horsley, *Jesus and the Spiral of Violence: Popular Jewish Resistance in Roman Palestine* (San Francisco: Harper & Row, 1987).

[40] Elliott, *Liberating Paul*, 159–67.

[41] On Jewish apocalypticism, see Gershom Scholem, *Jewish Gnosticism, Merkabah Mysticism, and Talmudic Tradition* (New York: The Jewish Theological Seminary of America, 1960); Ithamar Gruenwald, *Apocalyptic and Merkavah Mysticism* (Leiden: E. J. Brill, 1980); Christopher Rowland, *The Open Heaven: A Study of Apocalyptic in*

Followers of the crucified Jesus of Nazareth interpreted his death as part of God's plan to mark the beginning of the end of the evil age. This interpretation was confirmed, they claimed, by appearances and visions of the resurrected Jesus.[42]

The Pre-Conversion Paul

Paul was born into this complex political and social context. He was a free male and probably a citizen of the empire,[43] as well as a diaspora Jew who may also have had connections with the Jewish community in Judea.[44] A devout Pharisee, he was also well educated by Hellenistic or Judean schools in textual exegesis, rhetorical arts, and philosophical and theological discourse.[45] Had Paul wished to deemphasize his Jewishness, he could have sought a Roman education, acculturated by adopting prevailing cultural norms, and perhaps gained success as the client of a prominent patron. But since he chose to affirm his Jewish traditions, his possibilities for advancement within the prestige systems of the empire were limited.[46]

Paul chose a Jewish identity and commitment. As a member of the Pharisaic "school," he tells us that he was zealous in his fidelity to the traditions of the fathers (Gal 1:14). He was critically aware of the Roman system of political domination, but he appears to have adopted the stance of endurance and submission which characterized the

---

Judaism and Early Christianity (New York: Crossroad, 1982); David Hellholm, ed., *Apocalypticism in the Mediterranean World and the Near East: Proceedings of the International Colloquium on Apocalypticism, Uppsala, August 12–17, 1979* (Tübingen: J.C.B. Mohr [Paul Siebeck], 1983); Elliot R. Wolfson, *Through a Speculum That Shines: Vision and Imagination in Medieval Jewish Mysticism* (Princeton: Princeton University Press, 1994).

[42] See Paula Fredriksen, *From Jesus to Christ: The Origins of the New Testament Images of Jesus* (New Haven: Yale University Press, 1988).

[43] M. Hengel, *The Pre-Christian Paul* (In collaboration with Roland Deines; London: SCM, 1991) 1–17.

[44] Ibid., 18–53. Hengel argues forcefully for Paul's connection with Judea, but this is a debated issue.

[45] Paul's knowledge of the philosophical traditions was most likely mediated through his Jewish education.

[46] See Segal, *Paul the Convert,* 87 for the options available to Jews in this period.

Pharisees.[47] Paul became affiliated with a group which had the mystical and eschatological orientation cultivated within apocalyptic Judaism and in the communities out of which *merkavah* mysticism developed.[48] Like other mystics in this tradition, he may well have received revelations assuring him that God was still on his throne or that the period of Roman domination was limited.

Paul's mystical experiences may account for his negative response to another Jewish group which claimed that the death and resurrection of Jesus indicated that God was about to introduce the messianic age. Paul perhaps recognized within this apocalyptic movement an impulse toward radical political action.[49] Paul undertook a campaign of active suppression of this group's message, perhaps recognizing the potential for retaliation on the whole Jewish community if such an intent were suspected by Roman officials.[50]

The Conversion Event and Its Interpretation

Acts provides a triple account of Paul's conversion event, which is not replicated in Paul's letters.[51] In all likelihood, however, a mystical experience, perhaps involving both vision and audition, was the catalyzing event for Paul's conversion.[52] In 1 Cor 9:1 and 15:8, Paul

---

[47] This view differs from Betz's interpretation that Paul is sympathetic with Roman political views. See Betz, "Paul's Concept of Freedom," *Paulinische Studien III*, 117.

[48] Segal, *Paul the Convert*, 34–71.

[49] Ithamar Gruenwald carefully analyzes this impulse toward radical action in apocalypticism as an effort to transform historical events into cosmological processes ("A Case Study of Scripture and Culture," 268, 271–72, 277). In such efforts, cultural ethical values are lost, and destruction and chaos prevail.

[50] Elliott, *Liberating Paul*, 143–49; Hengel suggests that the opposition between Paul and followers of Jesus originally took place in Jerusalem (*Pre-Christian Paul*, 71–86). Rudolf Bultmann ("Paul," *Existence and Faith: Shorter Writings of Rudolf Bultmann* [ed. Schubert Ogden; New York: Meridian Books, Inc., 1960] 113) and Günther Bornkamm (*Paul*, [New York and Evanston: Harper & Row, 1971] 12) speculate that Paul might have been a missionary of Judaism to the diaspora Gentiles.

[51] The general scholarly consensus is that these accounts are narratives informed by Luke's agenda rather than strictly historical accounts of Paul's experiences.

[52] For a discussion of Paul's visions as Jewish apocalyptic experiences, see Gruenwald, *Apocalyptic*, 90–92; Rowland, *Open Heaven*, 374–86; John J. Collins, *The*

claimed that he had seen an appearance of the risen Jesus. In Gal 1:12, he stated that he received his gospel by a revelation from Jesus Christ, and in 1:16 that he had been called by God who had revealed his son in him. 2 Cor 12:1–4 reports the visions and revelations of a man, probably himself, who had been caught up to the third heaven.[53] These accounts may be different versions of a single revelatory event or a report of several separate mystical experiences. One or more of them may have constituted the precipitating conversion event for Paul. Paul asserted that his conversion was the work of God alone, but this would not preclude his having consulted one or more religious communities to interpret his revelations.

Paul says (Gal 1:17) that immediately after the conversion event he went to Arabia and then returned to Damascus. Martin Hengel has suggested that the Jewish Hellenists who left Jerusalem after the Stephen incident may have gone to Damascus, where Paul could have engaged in discussions with them after his revelatory experience.[54] Hellenistic Jewish Jesus communities which included Gentile God-fearers appear to be the most likely social contexts in which Paul arrived at his interpretation of the significance of his experiences. Paul's short visit to Peter, leader of the Hebrew Jesus movement, three years later may also have been part of this process of interpreting and affirming his conversion experience (Gal 1:18–20). After this visit, Paul proceeded to Syria and Cilicia on his missionary activities (Gal 1:21).

The Transformation of the Convert

As was noted earlier, the transformation of a convert produces discontinuities and continuities with the person's pre-conversion world view and behavior. Discontinuities for Paul include his new understanding that the risen Jesus is the δόξα ("glory") of God whose death and resurrection mark the beginning of the messianic age; his reevaluation of the role of the Gentiles in the divine plan of salvation;

Apocalyptic Imagination: An Introduction to the Jewish Matrix of Christianity (New York: Crossroad, 1984), 207–9.

53 Betz takes a different view (*Der Apostel Paulus und die sokratische Tradition: Eine exegetische Untersuchung zu seiner "Apologie" 2 Korinther 10–13* [BTH 45; Tübingen: Mohr {Siebeck}, 1972] 83–92).

54 Hengel, *Pre-Christian Paul,* 63–86.

and his recognition of his own call to play a unique role in the salvation of the Gentiles.

Paul's revelation that Jesus is the δόξα of God, probably through an enthronement vision,[55] radically contradicted his preconversion perceptions of Jesus and of the movement which developed after his death. The theological implications of the revelation that Jesus is the δόξα of God absorbed Paul for the rest of his apostleship. He came to view the Jewish tradition itself as radically transformed by this new revelation of the significance of Jesus.

Paul's conversion experience also required him to relinquish his expectation of salvation through the ethnic distinctiveness of Judaism in favor of a more universal conception of salvation. Judaism, of course, did allow Gentiles to become part of the Jewish ἔθνος through conversion or affiliation. But it now became clear to Paul that God had given the Gentiles an opportunity to become a more integral part of salvation history through faith in Jesus, without the requirements of conversion to Judaism.[56]

The community of Hellenistic Jews and Gentiles within which Paul interpreted his conversion experience and revelation had apparently developed a theological perspective on the equality of Jews and Gentiles in the Jesus movement. This perspective is reflected in their baptismal formula, which Paul quotes in Gal 3:26–29:

> You are all sons of God through [the] faith in Christ Jesus. For as many of you as were baptized into Christ have put on Christ. There is neither Jew nor Greek; there is neither slave nor freeman; there is no male and female. For you are all one in Christ Jesus. If, however, you belong to Christ, then you are Abraham's offspring, heirs according to [the] promise.[57]

This formula asserts not that differences no longer exist but that power relations are equalized. The spaces between these categories have been eliminated by the insertion of the σῶμα τοῦ Χριστοῦ.[58] In adopting this position, Paul radically departed from views on the

---

[55] Segal, *Paul the Convert*, 58–71.

[56] See the discussion of this issue in Paula Fredriksen, "Judaism, the Circumcision of Gentiles, and Apocalyptic Hope: Another Look at Galatians 1 and 2," *JTS* 42.2 (1991) 532–64.

[57] Translation by Betz, *Galatians*, 181.

[58] Betz, "Between Judaism and Hellenism."

nature of social relationships commonly accepted both by Jews and by others in the Roman empire.[59]

Paul's conversion also involved a call to a special apostolic role among the Gentiles. Whether this call came simultaneously with his revelation of Jesus as the δόξα of God is not certain. Possibly Paul received further revelations during the three years before he undertook his missionary activities in Syria and Cilicia (Gal 1:21). The full implications of his revelation and his mission may have been recognized by Paul only after a period of reflection and observation of the work of Jewish and Gentile missionaries in the Gentile world.

The radical demand of Paul's call to a mission to the Gentiles should not be underestimated. He chose not to observe *halakhah*, which he had previously observed faithfully. Instead he dealt directly with people whom Pharisaic Judaism would have considered impure. He became the best known spokesperson for the movement which enabled him to interpret his conversion experience.

But there were also continuities between the pre-conversion and the post-conversion Paul. Paul maintained a continual dialogue in his letters, and undoubtedly in his preaching as well, between his gospel about Jesus and Jewish scriptural traditions. He retained an apocalyptic eschatological orientation, as is reflected in his continued use of dualistic and mythohistoric language to explain his theology of righteousness through faith in Jesus. He used his considerable exegetical skills, learned earlier in Jewish schools, to make these arguments. He also drew upon themes explored by Hellenistic philosophy to distinguish between these perspectives and those afforded by his understanding of the revelation of the risen Jesus.

Paul's revelations did not cause him to change his political stance of endurance and submission to Roman power, though his message of salvation through faith in a crucified and risen Messiah had definite

---

[59] Betz has documented that ideals of egalitarianism were also expressed in the philosophical discussions of antiquity with which Paul may have been acquainted (*Galatians*, 190). However, he accords a special significance to this position in the Christian context, stating: "There can be no doubt that Paul's statements [in Gal. 3:26-28] have social and political implications of even a revolutionary dimension. The claim is made that very old and decisive ideals and hopes of the ancient world have come true in the Christian community . . . . Christians have renounced the social, religious, and cultural distinctions characteristic of the old world order."

political implications. Further, his teaching on ethical behavior and his call for Gentile observance of the Noachic laws challenged many of the social practices within the larger culture, thus both narrowing and widening the gap between Jewish and Gentile values and behaviors.

Paul's views on morality and ethics appear to have remained consistent with his pre-conversion perspectives, despite his adoption of the Hellenistic baptismal formula in Gal 3:26–29. Sheila Briggs points to Paul's inconsistency in using this formula and then following it in the next chapter of Galatians with the Hagar and Sara analogy, the cogency of which is based on assumptions about the nature of slavery.[60] Antoinette Wire also argues that an inevitable tendency toward recuperation is reflected in Paul's reassertion in 1 Corinthians of the legitimacy of some power relationships in the Christian community based on status, ethnicity or gender.[61] And Bernadette Brooten demonstrates that Paul's views on homoeroticism in Romans reflect traditional Jewish views and are not reflective of a new understanding of human relationships.[62]

But Paul's connection to his Jewish tradition is perhaps nowhere more vividly expressed than in his efforts to retain unity between the Gentile and Hebrew Jesus movements. He respected the choice of Jews within the Hebrew Jesus movement to interpret the significance of Jesus within traditional Jewish paradigms. But he also persuaded James, Peter and John to accept the legitimacy of his mission, which they did by extending the right hand of fellowship to him and Barnabas. This averted for a time a crisis within the Jewish Jesus movement, which would have reduced it to two competing traditions.

Ultimately, however, the accommodation that Paul had reached with "the pillars" in Jerusalem failed. Tradition tells us that the collection, which was intended to symbolize the unity of the diverse communities of the Jesus movement, was not accepted. Its delivery endangered Paul. By the end of Paul's life, or shortly thereafter, and in some measure due to his efforts to define Christianity as a religious

---

[60] Sheila Briggs, "Galatians," *Searching the Scriptures: A Feminist Commentary* (ed. Elisabeth Schüssler Fiorenza; New York: Crossroad, 1994) 218–36.

[61] Antoinette Clark Wire, *The Corinthian Women Prophets: A Reconstruction through Paul's Rhetoric* (Minneapolis: Fortress Press, 1990).

[62] Bernadette J. Brooten, *Love Between Women: Early Christian Responses to Female Homoeroticism* (Chicago: The University of Chicago Press, 1996).

tradition,[63] the unity among the groups within the Jesus movement dissolved. Judaism could not tolerate the loss of its own ethnic religious identity which it understood that Paul's theology demanded. Shortly after Paul's death, Christianity became a religion separate from Judaism.

Paul's Conversion Narrative

Hans Dieter Betz and other scholars hypothesize that Paul probably created a conversion narrative which he used in his preaching.[64] Galatians 1–2 may be an *epitome* of this conversion narrative. If so, then Paul's conversion story probably began with an allusion to some special circumstances of Paul's birth which signaled his subsequent election.[65] It continued by describing Paul's religious practice as a devout Jew, referred briefly to the special revelation of Christ to Paul and reported his movements after the conversion event. Finally, it detailed some of his encounters with the leadership of the Hebraic Jesus movement and legitimates his understanding of his mission.

IV. The Conversions of Marange and Amedzro

History of Christianity in Africa

After Paul's death, Christianity developed as a religion separate from Judaism, even while claiming that it was the authentic heir of God's covenant with Israel. It spread rapidly throughout the Roman empire, including Africa.[66] The Coptic Christian community in Egypt claimed apostolic origins, and the North African churches played an

---

[63] See Betz, "Christianity as Religion," *Paulinische Studien, III,* 206–39; idem, "The Birth of Christianity as a Hellenistic Religion: Three Theories of Origin," *JR* 74 (1994) 1–25.

[64] Betz, *Galatians,* 64; Hengel, *Pre-Conversion,* 66; Gerd Luedemann, *The Resurrection of Jesus: History, Experience, Theology* (Minneapolis: Fortress Press, 1994) 65.

[65] It is not uncommon in conversion narratives for hitherto insignificant details of the person's life to take on new meaning in light of the conversion experience. In Gal 1:15, Paul claims that God set him aside from his mother's womb. However, he does not elaborate further on this statement.

[66] For the history of Christianity in Africa, see Elizabeth Isichei, *A History of Christianity in Africa* (Grand Rapids: Eerdmans Publishing Company, 1993) and Lamin Sanneh, *West African Christianity: The Religious Impact* (Maryknoll, NY: Orbis Books, 1989).

important role in early Christian history. But Christianity was almost eliminated by Islam in Africa, except in Egypt and Ethiopia, before the end of the first millennium. However, it reasserted itself from the sixteenth century on in the wake of European colonial expansion.

The missionaries took advantage of the interstices created largely by colonialism to evangelize Africa.[67] In the late eighteenth century, the North Atlantic evangelical revival movement, with its apocalyptic orientation, stressed the necessity of the conversion of all nations as a prerequisite to the second coming of Christ.[68] Africa became one of the important destinations for the mission societies, influenced apparently by the abolitionist literature which had created vivid images of a raped and despoiled African Eden and of its exiled sons and daughters.[69]

Africans perceived missionaries as part of the colonial project, whether or not they actively colluded with the colonial administrations, because colonial power made their evangelization programs possible.[70] The spiritual and social messages of Christianity had an appeal for some Africans.[71] But Africans also recognized that conversion had its practical advantages. Education and medical treatment, for example, were available to converts at the mission station. Whatever their reasons for conversion, Africans' acceptance of the Christian gospel also inevitably entailed the adoption of European modernity.

---

[67] Jean and John Comaroff document the history of the European missionary movement among the Southern Tswana and its relationship to the colonial system (*Revelation*, 252–308).

[68] Isichei, *History*, 81–97; Andrew F. Walls, *The Missionary Movement in Christian History: Studies in the Transmission of Faith.* (Maryknoll, NY: Orbis Books, 1996).

[69] Comaroff, *Revelation*, 109–17.

[70] For a contemporary African perspective on Africans' assessment of the missionary project, see Kofi Asare Opoku, "The West Through African Eyes," *The International Journal of Africana Studies* 4:1–2 (1996) 82–97.

[71] The great diversity among African peoples and cultures has produced a variety of responses to Christianity in all the different ways they have encountered it. What people of one culture have found appealing in the Christian message, for example, its interpretation of the meaning of death, may be insignificant to another community with well-articulated and affirming beliefs in a lineage which includes the ancestors, the living, and the not-yet-born.

The missionary program of translating the Bible into local languages, though problematic in several ways,[72] allowed the message of Christianity to be more widely disseminated.[73] This program allowed Africans to play a primary role in the evangelization of other Africans,[74] and it also had two further consequences: the preservation and valorization of African cultural traditions and the development of indigenous African biblical exegesis.[75]

Despite Africans' success in evangelizing Africa, however, European Christians, with few notable exceptions,[76] generally were reluctant to promote African leadership in the mission churches, especially when it meant that Africans would have authority over white Christians. The tragic debacle which followed the appointment of Samuel Ajayi Crowther of Sierra Leone as the first African Anglican bishop for the Niger Mission in 1864[77] was a catalyst for the foundation by African

---

[72] The Comaroffs point to the inadequacy of many of the local interpreters and the missionaries' assumptions "about the ('indexical') properties of language and the possibility of knowledge that transcended human differences" (*Revelation*, 216).

[73] See Lamin Sanneh, "Theology and the Challenge of Ethnicity: The Ethnic Issues in Bible Translation with Reference to Africa" (Yale-Edinburgh Conference Paper, 1996).

[74] Isichei critiques those histories of Christianity in Africa in which "the foreign Christian is the heroic actor, and African communities merely the backdrop for her or his good deeds" (*History*, 75). For an example of scholarship which recognizes the significance of African evangelists, see Gerdien Verstraelen-Gilhuis, *From Dutch Mission Church to Reformed Church in Zambia: The Scope for African leadership and initiative in the history of a Zambian mission church* (Netherlands: T. Wever, Franeker, 1982) and "Rewriting the History of Christianity in Africa," *A New Look at Christianity in Africa* (Gweru: Mambo Press, 1992) 75–98. More recently, see Paul Stuart Landau, *The Realm of the Word: Language, Gender, and Christianity in a Southern African Kingdom.* (London: James Currey, 1995) 131–59.

[75] Lamin Sanneh describes the role of missionaries in preserving traditional cultures, thus preserving resources for future indigenous nationalism (*Translating the Message: The Missionary Impact on Culture* [Maryknoll, NY: Orbis Books, 1989] 106–8). He also regards biblical translation as a conscious effort to recontextualize Christianity, thus allowing more ethnic visions to shape the Christian tradition.

[76] Church Mission Society Honorary Secretary Henry Venn (1841–72), for example, envisioned the "euthanasia" of missions brought about by African leadership, but his perspective no longer prevailed in the late nineteenth century. See Isichei, *History*, 164.

[77] For the history of the life and mission of Bishop Crowther and the debacle at the end of Crowther's life, see Kwame Bediako, *Christianity in Africa: The Renewal of*

Christians of the so-called Ethiopian or African churches and the Independent churches at the end of the nineteenth century.

The Ethiopian churches, while retaining the ritual practices of the Protestant mission churches and their traditions of biblical interpretation, advocated African leadership and the inclusion of African cultural practices in Christian churches. The story of the converted Ethiopian official in Acts 8 was often used to justify their claims to apostolic succession and their responsibility for the conversion of Africans.[78] The Independent Church movement, which was more critical of both traditional practices and the mainline churches, provided an alternative approach to the appropriation of Christianity in Africa.[79]

Antecedents to the Marange and Amedzro Conversions

Applying the model of the conversion experience elaborated earlier, it is clear that family, personal and traditional Shona and Ewe cultural world views and experiences, in which religion is life,[80] as well as the political, social and religious dimensions of colonization, were important antecedent factors to conversion in the lives of Johane Marange and Samuel Yao Amedzro. The religious systems of the Shona[81] and the Ewe[82] include belief in a supreme God, other divinities or spirits, ancestors, and lesser beneficent or avenging spirits. All are understood to affect, positively or negatively, the lives of members of the community. Each community recognizes spirit

---

a Non-Western Religion (Edinburgh: Edinburgh University Press, 1995) 198–200 and Lamin Sanneh, *West African Christianity*, 169–73 and passim.

78 See Isichei, *History*, 125–27 and passim.

79 Ibid., 179–82 and passim. Birgit Meyer, "Beyond syncretism: Translation and diabolization in the appropriation of Protestantism in Africa," *Syncretism/Anti-Syncretism: The Politics of Religious Synthesis*, (ed. Charles Stewart and Rosalind Shaw; London and New York: Routledge,1994) 45–68.

80 Kofi Asare Opoku, *West African Traditional Religion* (Accra: FEP International Private Limited, 1978) 1.

81 For the Shona world view, see M. L. Daneel, *Old and New in Southern Shona Independent Churches*, vol. 1: *Background and Rise of the Major Movements* (The Hague: Mouton, 1971) 79–184; Michael Bourdillon, *The Shona Peoples* (3rd ed; Gweru: Mambo Press, 1987).

82 Opoku, *West African Traditional Religion*, passim. See also Sandra E. Greene, "Religion, History and the Supreme Gods of Africa: A Contribution to the Debate," *Journal of Religion in Africa* 26.2 (1996) 122–38.

mediums, who communicate between the divinities and ancestors and the community, and diviner-healers, who diagnose problems and provide remedies for personal and social disruptions and imbalances, which are often attributed to evil spirits or to witches and wizards.

The social structures of the Shona[83] and the Ewe[84] are based on complex systems of hierarchical social relationships which establish unambiguously the relative position of each person in relation to every other member of the family and the community. Family units are further organized into villages under a headman, villages are organized into wards, and wards in turn form a chiefdom with a chief at the apex of the political structure. The primary economic bases of these communities in the precolonial period were livestock, agricultural production, and fishing.

British colonial administrators destablized traditional Shona and Ewe communities by rejecting and denigrating the world views which legitimated their social practices, and altered the people's productive activity and relationship to the land. They promoted instead a social structure based on the individual and the single family unit and a new political organization in which the colonial authorities had ultimate power, while traditional social and political organizations were altered, if not replaced, and subordinated to the patterns of colonial administration.[85]

The Shona in what is now called Zimbabwe resented the appropriation of their ancestral lands, which forced many, like the young Johane Marange, to seek employment outside their traditional areas. The Ewe were required to enrich the British colonial economy,[86] first through the production of cotton and then cocoa. When cocoa became an unaffordable luxury for export during World War II, the

---

[83] M. L. Daneel, *Old and New*, 1. 17–78.

[84] D. E. K. Amenumey, *The Ewe in Pre-Colonial Times* (Accra: Sedco Publishing Limited, 1986); Sandra Greene, *Gender, Ethnicity, and Social Change on the Upper Slave Coast: A History of the Anlo-Ewe* (London: James Currey, 1996) 1–135.

[85] Neil Parsons, *A New History of Southern Africa* (New York: Holmes & Meier Publishers, Inc., 1983) 107–320; Greene, *Gender*, 136–80.

[86] For the role of the missionaries in encouraging consumerism among the Ewe, see Birgit Meyer, "Commodities and the Power of Prayer. Pentecostalist Attitudes Towards Consumption in Contemporary Ghana" (Unpublished Paper presented at the "Globalization and the Construction of Communal Identities" Conference, Amsterdam, 29 February—3 March, 1996) 3–10.

Ewe economy entered a decline from which it has not yet recovered. These circumstances produced many indigent people, like Samuel Yao Amedzro, who had been deprived of traditional social structures and lacked other means to support themselves.

The Shona were missionized by several Christian churches and missionary societies.[87] The diverse theologies and practices of the Dutch Reformed and Catholic missionaries in Marange's area created confusion among the Shona about Christian beliefs and practices. This ultimately allowed for the development of or receptivity to new forms of Christianity by the Shona, such as the Independent African Apostolic Church which Johane Marange was later to found.[88]

In the mid-nineteenth century, the German Pietist missionaries of the *Norddeutsche Missionsgesellschaft* (NMG) began the evangelization of the Peki Ewe in what is now Ghana and Togo.[89] They were succeeded by pastors from the Evangelical Presbyterian Church (EPC). These churches had an apocalyptic theology with a dualistic world view based on the polarization of God and Satan. They identified traditional Ewe spirits as agents of Satan or the devil and linked them with witchcraft. They also taught that the Christian God was more powerful than the traditional Ewe spirits. The Ewe responded to the claims of the Christian God's power by converting in large numbers and developing a theology "from the bottom up," stressing the competing powers of Jesus and the demons, thus producing a hybridization of traditional culture and mission teaching.[90]

The life of Johane Marange and the development of the Apostle Church which he founded has been documented and analyzed by

---

[87] M. L. Daneel, *Old and New,* 1. 185–281.

[88] For a discussion of the Independent Church movement in Southern Africa, see Inus [M. L.] Daneel, *Quest for Belonging: Introduction to a Study of African Independent Churches* (Gweru: Mambo Press, 1987).

[89] Birgit Meyer, "'Komm herüber und hilf uns' of hoe zendelingen de Ewe met andere ogen gingen bekijken," *Etnofoor* 2 (1989) 91–111.

[90] Birgit Meyer, "'If You are a Devil, You are a Witch, If You are a Witch, You are a Devil.' The Integration of 'Pagan' Ideas into the conceptual Universe of Ewe Christians in Southeastern Ghana," *Journal of Religion in Africa* 22.2 (1992) 98–132. A popular writing in West Africa which reflects this theology and, according to Meyer (Personal correspondence, June 21, 1996), "forms a model for the conceptualization of conversion" is Emmanuel Eni, *Delivered from the Powers of Darkness* (Ibaden: Scripture Union [Nigeria] Press and Books Ltd., 1987).

Zimbabwean missiologist M. L. Daneel.[91] Marange was born into a traditional family.[92] His mother was an important spirit medium and his ancestral family held chiefly rank. From age six, he exhibited special spiritual powers, which he later reported in a book called *The New Witness of the Apostles*.[93] In it, he described his first vision of the Spirit:

> I saw a white cloud which thundered and the whole world was full of the noise. The Holy Spirit filled me and I started to sing a New Song saying Halelua, Halelua. I was given a Bible in my hand, I stood on top of an anthill and started to preach. My father and brothers came there. They knelt in front of me and started worshiping God.[94]

His visions were noted at the American Methodist Mission where he attended catechism classes and was baptized. After Standard 2 he left school to become a wage worker in an urban area.

Amedzro's life and the history and theology of the churches he founded, *Abelengor* and The Lord's Pentecostal Church, have been studied by Amsterdam anthropologist Birgit Meyer, who has done extensive fieldwork among the Peki Ewe in Southeastern Ghana.[95] In contrast with Johane Marange, Amedzro displayed no spiritual propensities in his youth, though he was baptized in the Evangelical Presbyterian Church. He was influenced by traditional culture through his father and by Christianity through his mother, a member of an Independent Church. Later, as he described himself, "he took to reckless living, indulging in all kinds of social vices."[96]

---

[91] My reliance on Daneel's work will be documented in the footnotes. For a study of the Apostles in Zaire, see Bennetta Jules-Rosette, *African Apostles: Ritual and Conversion in the Church of John Maranke* (Ithaca: Cornell University Press, 1975).

[92] M. L. Daneel, *Old and New*, 1. 315–39.

[93] John Marange, *The New Witness of the Apostles* (Marange: Bocha, c. 1953). This book is considered a canonical addition to the Bible in the Apostle Church. I thank Dr. E. K. Osam of The University of Zimbabwe for obtaining a copy of this text for me.

[94] John Marange, *New Witness*, 1.

[95] References to Meyer's work will be cited in the footnotes.

[96] John Sam Amedzro, *A Brief History of the Lord's Pentecostal Church* (n.d.) 2. Cited in Birgit Meyer, "Translating the Devil. An African Appropriation of Pietist Protestantism. The Case of the Peki Ewe, 1847–1992" (Ph. D. Diss., University of Amsterdam, 1995) 184.

Conversion and Call Events

Johane Marange had his first vision of Jesus Christ in 1926 at about age fourteen while he was herding cattle. Following this experience, he had a vision in which "[he] went to many countries and a multitude of people followed [him] while [he] was flying and leading them with a rod in [his] hand."[97] His visions and spiritual experiences continued after he went to work in Mutare (Umtali). In one vision, he was told by "a tall man who wore snow white garments"[98] that he would return to baptize Marange at the end of June, 1932, after which he was to found the Apostle Church. The figure "dressed [him] in a long garment and he gave [him] a rod and a big book."[99] Maranke was twenty years of age at the time. Johane's decisive commissioning came on July 17, 1932:

> [He] was walking home when a flash of light surrounded him. A voice came out of heaven saying "Thou art John the Baptist and Apostle." Go into all the countries, teach and convert people, telling them not to commit adultery, not to steal, not to covet, not to be easily angered.[100]

He returned home in a trance state and began to speak in tongues.

The story of Samuel Yao Amedzro's conversion began when he became ill in 1958. Since neither traditional healing nor western medicine was able to cure him, he threw his "medicine" (magical substances) into the toilet and went with his mother to a village where an EPC prayer group had a Healing Centre. In his fifth month at the Centre, he had a vision of an angel writing "John" on his forehead. This was followed in the eighth month by a second vision which he interpreted as a call to a special mission. After these experiences he was healed.[101]

---

97 Marange, *New Witness,* 2.

98 Ibid.

99 Marange, *New Witness,* 6.

100 Marange, *New Witness,* 7.

101 Amedzro, *Brief History,* 2. Cited in Meyer, "Translating the Devil," 184.

Interpretation of the Conversion Event

Consistent with Shona practice, Johane's revelations were interpreted by his family, close relatives and friends.[102] Having determined that he was possessed neither by a traditional spirit or by the Spirit of a local Independent Church prophet, they agreed that his spirit was the Christian Spirit. In addition, his family and other Christians may have assisted Johane in interpreting the biblical allusions to Joseph, Moses, John the Baptist and Paul in his visions and his call to a new mission.

Amedzro's interpretive community was the EPC Healing Centre, where the devil causing his illness was identified and exorcised. Pastors at the Centre regarded his illness as a work of the devil, and his visions, about which they counseled him, and his cure as demonstrations of God's power in his life. They encouraged him to accept the commission that God had given him.

Conversion Transformations

After his conversion, Johane Marange received further revelatory directives about the African Apostolic Church, or *vaPastori*, that he had been commissioned to found. The first converts were from his immediate family, but the church grew rapidly. Marange devoted the remainder of his life to preaching and baptizing. By the time of his death in 1963, the Apostle church, characterized by "a presupposed Christology, a prominent pneumatology and a realized-futuristic eschatology,"[103] extended from South Africa to Zaire.

Marange was critical of both mission Christianity and traditional religion. Reinterpreting the Ham story in Genesis 9, the *vaPastori* taught that:

> for whites the time of grace is past because they killed Jesus and suppressed the biblical message of the Holy Spirit. Now the time has come for Africa to be blessed. The house of Ham, long trampled underfoot, is now summoned to carry on the task of Jesus Christ. The banner which the descendants of Shem

---

102 Daneel, *Old and New*, 1. 319–21. Among his informants was Johane's brother, Anrod.

103 M. L. Daneel, *Old and New in Southern Shona Independent Churches* (Gweru: Mambo Press, 1988) 3. 123.

and Japheth have trampled has been picked up by Johane who marches triumphantly at the head of the once oppressed race, the House of Ham.[104]

The importance of the Bible in Marange's visions and ministry is significant. It provided him with a symbol of authority and a source of legitimation for his practice of a Christian ministry. Instead of imitating European missionaries, Maranke's ministry was conducted in imitation of that of Jesus and the apostles. He reported: "I went to many villages preaching, casting out demons, and healing. Many people walked in fire."[105]

Marange also rejected traditional views of the spirits and the ancestors, the role of the traditional healers, and certain objects associated with witchcraft. His brother Anrod described Johane's stance toward traditional religion as "an immense relief from the old binding practices which were often exploited by the *nganga* to serve their own ends."[106] He did, however, preserve traditional singing and dancing, healing and the discernment of spirits.

John Sam Amedzro's mission began after he returned from the Healing Centre with his new commission. He rejoined his local EPC congregation in 1960, where he set up a healing prayer group. Facing opposition in the church, however, he next established an Independent Church known as *Abelengor* ("there is life ahead") in 1961. Traditional cultural practices were introduced, but in 1985, when the EPC church decided to "Africanize" church practice, he did away with all indigenous elements in *Abelengor* and transformed it into The Lord's Pentecostal Church.[107]

The Pentecostal Church movement was introduced into Ghana from the United States in the 1980s.[108] These churches differ from the

---

104 Ibid., 114–15. For further references to the Ham legend in African and diasporic contexts, see Robert E. Hood, *Begrimed and Black: Christian Traditions on Blacks and Blackness.* (Minneapolis: Fortress Press, 1994); Sue Houchins and Kathleen O'Brien Wicker, "The Blessing of Ham: Re-Sacralizing and Re-Contextualizing the Narrative of Nation" (forthcoming in *Research in African Literatures*).

105 Marange, *New Witness,* 10.

106 Daneel, *Old and New,* 1. 325.

107 These developments are chronicled in Amedzro, *Brief History.*

108 Paul Gifford, "Ghana's Charismatic Churches," *Journal of Religion in Africa* 3 (1994) 241–65.

Independent Churches in their global, rather than local, perspective and in their negative attitude toward all aspects of traditional religion. They emphasize deliverance from the power of Satan, a strong eschatology, healing, reliance on the Bible alone and renunciation of idols. They also reflect the theological synthesis created by Africans in the mission churches about the relationship between demonic forces and the power of Jesus.[109]

The ministries of John Sam Amedzro and Stanley Amedzro, his son and successor, in The Lord's Pentecostal Church are based on pentecostal theological perspectives. Their prayer meetings are healing sessions in which possessing demons are identified and exorcised. They adopt the problem-solving function of traditional religion in attempting to deal with pressing daily needs, but they also stress the importance of exorcising people from the demons of materialism and modernism which distract them from God and spiritual values.[110]

Conversion Narratives

The conversion experiences of Johane Marange and John Sam Amedzro are described in the narrative histories of their churches, *The*

---

[109] Birgit Meyer has documented the historical and theological development of Pentecostal churches among the Peki Ewe of Ghana. See Meyer, "African Pentecostal Churches, Satan and the Dissociation from Tradition" (Paper presented at the American Anthropological Association, November, 1995); "Beyond Syncretism: Translation and diabolization in the appropriation of Protestantism in Africa," *Syncretism/Anti-syncretism: The politics of religious synthesis* (ed. C. Stewart and R. Shaw; London and New York: Routledge, 1994) 45–68; "'If You are a Devil, You are a Witch and if You are a Witch, You are a Devil': The Integration of 'Pagan' Ideas into the Conceptual Universe of Ewe Christians in Southeastern Ghana," *Journal of Religion in Africa* 22.2 (1992) 98–132; "Magic, Mermaids and Modernity: The Attraction of Pentecostalism in Africa," *Etnofoor* 8.2 (1995) 47–67. Ruth Marshall offers an insightful analysis of the Pentecostal churches in Nigeria and how they understand themselves as "changing society and making history" ("Power in the Name of Jesus," *Review of African Political Economy* 52 [1991] 21–37; here p. 37). She cautions against placing too much emphasis on the foreign origins of Pentecostal churches.

[110] See Birgit Meyer, "Commodities and the Power of Prayer: Pentecostal Attitudes Towards Consumption in Contemporary Ghana" (Paper presented at the "Globalization and the Construction of Communal Identities" Conference, Amsterdam, 1996); "'Delivered from the Powers of Darkness:' Confessions of Satanic Riches in Christian Ghana," *Africa* 62.2 (1995) 236–55.

New Witness of the Apostles and the *Brief History of the Lord's Pentecostal Church.* The Marange narrative is primarily a collection of his visions, filled with biblical allusions, which legitimate him as a successor to Old Testament figures, Jesus and the apostles. It also provides a brief description of his mission activities and deals with issues of succession in the church. The *Brief History*, after a short report of Amedzro's evil life prior to conversion and his subsequent transformation,[111] describes how the church separated itself from the mainline EPC church, established a Healing Centre and organized itself in branches on the model of the mission church.[112]

The model for both of these texts appears to be Acts, where Paul's conversion is also told as part of the larger account of the development of the early church. And, like the Lucan account, some of the events described in Marange's *New Revelation* may have been redactionally edited and reinterpreted in light of later developments in the church.[113]

Acts also provides several representations of Paul's conversion which serve as models for those of Maranke and Amedzro. Paul's transformation from an evildoer to a servant of God is explicitly

---

[111] Birgit Meyer observes: "Conversion here, indeed, is modeled on that of St. Paul. I am not sure that in the early beginnings the founders were so very conscious of this, as this model of conversion has been popularized into Protestant missionary tradition ever since missions started to operate on the 'dark continent.' And even missionaries themselves tended to describe their own conversion in these terms. Of course, St. Paul's model of conversion has been taken up by one of the most important works of popular literature: John Bunyan's *Pilgrim's Progress*, a book which has been translated into more than 300 languages, one of them Ewe. The Ewe translation was achieved by a native evangelist and published even before the whole Ewe bible was translated. Virtually everybody in Peki knows the *Pilgrim's Progress* and I think that this is a very important meditation on St. Paul's conversion experience" (Personal communication, Feb. 28, 1997).

[112] Birgit Meyer, Personal correspondence, Feb. 28, 1997.

[113] Daneel observes: "The visions recorded in the *Umboo utsva* [New Witness] may not have been generally known before Johane's inspiration by the Holy Spirit in July 1932. These may therefore have been partly construed and elaborated on at a later stage for the purpose of clarifying moral directives and to impress upon the followers the uniqueness of his calling. The calling may in fact have been much less vivid and clear than this 'Apostolic Bible' portrays. It nevertheless reveals the African's need for a clear charter for the new Church and the importance attached to a direct calling from God, in much the same way as the Biblical prophets of old" (*Old and New*, 1. 318).

applied to Amedzro and also, though somewhat less prominently, to Marange.[114] Light is a manifestation of the divine in the account of Marange's conversion. Revelatory visions in the conversion process are prominent in all three accounts. Interestingly, though, it is not Paul, but rather John the Baptist with his message of repentance and deliverance, whose name each man received in the conversion process.

Marange and Amedzro share with the Paul of the letters an apocalyptic and eschatological theology. Like Paul, Amedzro envisions the struggle between death and life, and Christ and Satan, as the ultimate human and spiritual reality. Marange, as Paul before him, believed he had been chosen from birth for his mission,[115] and had mystical experiences, in which he was transported to the divine realm, which informed his mission and his teaching. Finally, the teachings of all three reflect the view discussed earlier, that the conversion process always reflects "both a continuity and discontinuity with the old traditions."[116]

Conclusion

From Paul's time to the days of Johane Marange and John Sam Amedzro in the twentieth century, the Spirit has utilized the spaces between the divine and the human realms to communicate with human beings. In conversion experiences, It manifests itself variously as light—Acts 9:3 tells us that "a light from heaven flashed around" Paul on his way to Damascus, and Marange reports that a "rock flashed and engulfed" him prior to the manifestation of a man whose "eyes were like a flame of fire;"[117] as voice—which spoke to Johane Marange, saying: "Tomorrow you invite people and tell them that Jesus Christ

---

[114] A transcription of a sermon given by The Rev. Rameck Zvanaka, a Zionist Apostolic Church Bishop, in Zimbabwe in 1984 expresses the same sentiment about Paul: "We see such a change in the life of Paul. Paul himself said, 'What I intended is not what I did; what I did is not what I was thinking of.' For when Paul grew up he was a bad man, a destroyer of those who followed Christ. He did this for quite sometime, until one day he was filled with the Spirit of Jesus Christ. Christ brought this about because he knew that Paul was planning to persecute some more of his followers." Quoted in M. L. Daneel, *Fambidzano: Ecumenical Movement of Zimbabwean Independent Churches* (Gweru: Mambo Press, 1989) 608.

[115] Paul, Gal 1:15; Marange, *New Revelation*, 5.

[116] Olupona, *Kingship*, 172.

[117] Marange, *New Witness*, 2.

sent [you]. Come and I shall teach you the Gospel of the Lord;"[118] as vision—"an angel writing 'John' on [Amedzro's] forehead."[119]

The Spirit also allows its chosen ones to "be caught up to Paradise" and to hear "things that man is not permitted to tell," as with Paul's "man in Christ" in 2 Corinthians 12, and to see visions such as Johane Marange saw when he

> sat in the air looking up into the sky and there came a cloud. [He] went on watching and an Angel descended past [him]. A third Angel also went past [him] down to earth. On their way up, they took [him] with them. They put [him] in the middle and led [him] to Heaven where [he] saw a very big temple.[120]

Or, as with John Sam Amedzro, the Spirit manifests itself in the war between Jesus and the demons which he saw being fought in the bodies and souls of the people he treated. Nigerian Pentecostal convert Emmanuel Eni described a healing session similar to those which Amedzro conducted to drive out demons:

> . . . a few [Christians] came out to pray for me. As they started with "In Jesus' name" I heard a big bang inside me and fell on the floor. Immediately the flying demon in me went into action. I started running . . . because of the stronger power in the room. Two opposing forces went into action and the atmosphere changed. I suddenly stood up and became very violent etc. A demon went out of me and possessed a boy in their midst . . . This continued till 7:00 a.m. I was physically exhausted and became quiet so the brethren gathered around me again and started shouting "name them," "who are they" etc. I kept quiet. After waiting a long time and I said nothing they were deceived to believe that I was delivered. They prayed and we dismissed.[121]

Later, however, Jesus appeared to Eni directly and showed him his fate if he continued under the power of the devil. Eni renounced his former ways and put himself under the protection of Jesus.

When the Spirit manifests itself, It utilizes the interstices in the realm of human history and culture to communicate with human beings. For Saul, the interstices were among the various forms of first century Judaism and between the cultures of Hellenistic Judaism and the Roman empire. And, as Hans Dieter Betz has already shown, the converted Paul then played a very important role in "creating a space

---

118 Ibid., 9.

119 Amedzro, *Brief History*, 2.

120 *New Witness*, 3.

121 Eni, *Delivered*, 35.

for Christianity" between Judaism and Hellenism.[122] Several centuries later, Hellenism was transformed into a Christian Roman culture and Christianity regarded Judaism as its spiritual origins.

The interstices in Johane Marange's pre-conversion experience were between traditional religion and culture and colonial culture, including missionary Christianity. Conversion to a new Christian mission meant for him carving out a bounded space between missionary Christianity and traditional religion. The *vaPastori*, the Independent Church he founded, continues to live in that space, separate from both traditional culture and from other Christian groups as well, because they believe that they alone are "the truly saved people of God."[123]

Prior to his conversion, Samuel Yao Amedzro fell into the void created by the disjunction between colonialism and traditional culture. The illness which this produced in him drew him back into contact with mission Christianity. Once he was named John, however, and called to a healing ministry, mission Christianity no longer seemed an appropriate spiritual home. He then founded Abelengor, an Independent Church created in the interstices between traditional religion and mission Christianity. But even this option did not satisfy him. So he located another of the spaces among the Christian options and established The Lord's Pentecostal Church, which reflected a global rather than a local Christian option. However, even that option, rooted in an eschatology "from the bottom up," may be more grounded in a *metisságe* of traditional and mission culture than he realized.

Conversion, inspired by the spirit, always occurs in specific cultural contexts. Rather than opposing religion and culture, then, this discussion suggests that the two must always be understood in relation to each other. Paul remained a Jew, historically and culturally, and yet

---

[122] Betz, "Between Judaism and Hellenism."

[123] M L. Daneel states: "The vaPastori have pretty rigid and exclusive teachings about salvation, loyalty to Johane, the true Apostle of Africa, and purity of life, the Apostolic way. They consider themselves the truly saved people of God, the real Apostles in accordance with biblical norms. Consequently their motivation for ecumenicity and interaction with the 'lesser' Christians—particularly the Zionists, whose perception of the Holy Spirit they consider inadequate—is rather limited" (Personal communication, November 1, 1996).

radically transformed his understanding of that reality and no longer observed Jewish Torah.[124] Johane Marange and John Sam Amedzro remained Africans, while they experienced their spirit-inspired conversions in the interstices between worlds. But, like Paul, they carried out their missions in the two worlds simultaneously, transforming each in the process.

---

[124] Paul, Gal 2:11–14; 2 Cor 9:19–23.

Conversion as a Native Category

Arthur J. Droge

I am very pleased indeed to respond to Professor Wicker's paper, first, because it has forced me to reflect on the meaning and explanatory utility of the term "conversion," and, second, because it affords me the opportunity to acknowledge, publicly, my gratitude to Hans Dieter Betz, whom I have known now for almost twenty years, and who, I am honored to say, is my teacher, colleague, and friend.

In my response this afternoon, I want to address both the "What?" and the "So What?" of Professor Wicker's fine paper on the subject of conversion. But it seems necessary first to reflect for a moment on the inherently problematic nature of the category itself (something that became apparent, I think, in the lively discussion that followed Professor Cancik's paper on Tuesday). It is generally assumed that the term "conversion" refers to a distinct kind of religious experience. However extraordinary a particular conversion experience may be, the category itself is an ordinary component of the way Western culture, in general, and the Western academy, in particular, understand religion. Indeed, what William Scott Green has said about "religion" seems to me to apply with equal validity to "conversion." Put simply, for the West, "conversion" is a *native* category. In general we accept the idea that it is natural or legitimate for people to have a religious experience called "conversion." And, because conversion is a native category, we use it both abstractly and concretely. As an abstraction—much like the category "culture" or even the term "religion" itself—conversion is a concept, a theoretical entity, that allows us to identify, label, and make sense of the discrete particulars of our own or other religions. Yet, like all native categories, conversion also claims to be concrete, self-evident, and inherently significant. Consequently, it is evocative but inarticulate. We take conversion for granted as a meaningful and conventional trait of being religious, but we grasp and employ conversion intuitively more than we discern and deploy it discursively.

We apprehend conversion better than we comprehend it; we think better *with* conversion than we do *about* it.[1]

Take Paul, for example, a religious virtuoso if there ever was one. Like many students of early Christianity, Professor Wicker chooses to describe Paul's experience—whether on the road to Damascus or in the third heaven—as a "conversion," though to her credit she recognizes that Paul did not describe his own experience(s) as such. Nevertheless, she maintains that "the rhetoric of transformation that is the central message of Paul's gospel is the language of conversion." And she goes on to say that "Paul undoubtedly formulated *a* conversion narrative detailing events of his transformation which he shared with his communities." Now permit me to ask a few simple questions. How do we know this? What is the language of conversion, such that we know it when we see it? How do we know that conversion (understood here as transformation) is a better description of Paul's religious experience than, say, "call," especially since Paul's *language* in Galatians 1 is reminiscent of Jeremiah's self-presentation? Does it make a difference? I suspect not, and that says something about the adequacy of the categories we employ in a desire to make sense of apparent change. Since Paul claimed to be set apart by God before he was born, I can imagine the beloved apostle saying, "I am not a convert, that is not what I am at all." How are the competing (and often conflicting) interests inherent in the convert's and the external observer's explanations of apparent change to be negotiated? Further, will Professor Wicker's understanding of conversion as transformation have the same explanatory utility in contexts other than Paul's? Again to her credit, Professor Wicker wants to use the term conversion comparatively, not just with respect to Paul but as an adequate description of the religious experiences of two twentieth-century African Christians. I shall want to question the adequacy of this specific comparative move, but for now let me ask: Does the understanding of the category conversion change as a result of its deployment in a comparative context? And if so, how?

In the spirit of Dieter Betz, Professor Wicker wants to stress the importance of historical context in understanding Christianity. One of

---

[1] Forward to Eugene V. Gallagher, *Expectation and Experience: Explaining Religious Conversion* (Atlanta, GA: Scholars Press, 1990) vii.

the two arguments she seeks to advance in her paper is that "conversion experiences cannot be adequately understood apart from the cultural contexts of the converts." As she put it in an earlier version of her paper, "We cannot afford to *minimize* the influence of cultural contexts in the development of Christian history and theology." More particularly, in her comparative analysis of the conversions of Paul, Marange, and Amedzro, she admitted to being struck by "just how pervasive a factor culture was in their lives, before, during, and after their conversions." Now several things occurred to me as I read these statements of her thesis. Why can't we afford to minimize cultural context in the development of Christian history and theology? What, exactly, is lost by so doing? Next, I wondered who Professor Wicker's intellectual adversaries were in this statement. It is not immediately apparent to me who does advocate *minimizing* cultural context, or who contends that conversion experiences *can* be adequately understood apart from the cultural contexts of the converts. For analytical purposes and in the interests of stimulating discussion, let me try to re-state her thesis more sharply. To frame it roughly in her terms, Can we afford to *maximize* the influence of cultural context in the development of Christian history and theology? Put differently: What are the consequences of *maximizing* the influence of cultural context, both for the study of religion generally and of conversion in particular?

For one thing, such an approach would require, I think, questioning the notion that there is an "essence" of Christianity which is timeless and unchanging and which only manifests itself in particular historical contexts, what George Lindbeck has called the "experiential-expressivist" model of religion; that is, that different religions are diverse expressions or objectifications of a common core experience, and that it is this experience which identifies them as religions. By contrast, maximizing the influence of cultural context would seem to require adopting (what Lindbeck calls) the "cultural-linguistic" model of religion, which views religion as a kind of cultural and/or linguistic framework or medium that shapes the entirety of life and thought, indeed, makes possible the description of realities, the formulation of beliefs, and the experiencing of inner attitudes, feelings, and sentiments. Consider the matter this way: Do religions shape individual subjectivities or do religions manifest them?

Now I should like to hear Professor Wicker's reflections on this theoretical question, because, as I read her paper, I detect a certain ambiguity. On the one hand, she wants to insist on the importance of cultural context for understanding conversion experiences, but on the other hand, she can refer, both at the beginning and conclusion of her paper, to conversion experiences as "spiritual phenomena" and assert that such experiences are "inspired by the spirit." The tension between these two dispositions with respect to understanding conversion remains unresolved and a little disconcerting. Is the historian of religions in the business of de-mystifying or re-mystifying? Is the goal explanation or preserving the mystery intact? This far and no farther.

Professor Wicker has argued "that there are parallels between the spiritual conversion experience of Paul . . . and those of Marange and Amedzro." In the earlier version of her paper, she put it this way: "the conversion narratives of Paul, Marange, and Amedzro reflect broad similarities phenomenologically among their conversion experiences." If I have understood her correctly, I take her to mean that the interpreter does not have access to the conversion experience itself, only the retrospective account or narrative of that experience. But insofar as Professor Wicker classifies conversion experiences as "spiritual phenomena" and attributes them to the "inspiration of the spirit," the implication is that, however pervasive a role cultural and historical circumstances play in conversion, conversion accounts themselves reflect, however ambiguously and imperfectly, the raw reality of experience, and the raw reality of experience influences or structures the accounts of conversion.

I would choose to construe the matter differently, following Gene Gallagher's recent analysis of conversion. So-called "conversion experiences," rather than being "spiritual phenomena" or "inspired by the spirit," and thus appearing as something fixed and determinative, are something more fluid and malleable; conversion accounts, rather than reflections of raw reality, become constructions of it. If such is the case, then conversion accounts should be viewed as first order explanations of conversion. Like any explanation, they are shaped in crucial ways by the concrete situation of the person doing the explaining, and, as that situation changes, so also will the explanation, and, I submit, *the experience.* To illustrate my point, let me touch very briefly on one of the exchanges following Professor Cancik's paper. In response to the questioner who asked, "How can one distinguish between 'real' and 'fictive' conversion accounts?," Professor Krentz put it this way, "You can't have a *real* conversion narrative without a conversion experience." In my view, it is just the other way round: "You can't have a *real* conversion experience without a conversion narrative."

Let me be clear: I am in general agreement with Professor Wicker's emphasis on the importance of historical context in the shaping of conversion, but this would require, I think, a thicker description of the historical contexts of the three converts she seeks to analyze, interpret, and explain. The "parallels" or "broad phenomenological similarities" she sees reflected in the three conversion narratives are not particularly striking, at least not in the sense she takes them to be, inasmuch as Marange and Amedzro were converts to what is loosely called African Christianity, where the Lukan account of Paul's conversion was frequently read and, no doubt, served a paradigmatic function; that is to say, played a role in *shaping* the conversion accounts of Marange and Amedzro, in much the same way, I suspect, that the language of Jeremiah shaped Paul's conversion narrative.

Since any account of conversion is retrospective, the representation of experience (and, I would add, the experience itself) can change as the situation of the convert changes. With respect to Paul, for example, I do not think the representation of his "conversion experience" in the first chapter of his letter to the Galatians can be taken at face value. More attention needs to be paid to the highly charged and polemical situation of the letter—in short, to the "rhetoric of conversion," which necessarily influences or shapes the representation of the conversion experience. It is one of the strengths of Professor Wicker's paper to emphasize that conversions are *not* "once and for all," appearances to the contrary notwithstanding. Conversion is an on-going process; that is to say, people continue to convert themselves, as they continually adjust their accounts of conversion to reflect their current situations, commitments, and beliefs. As Gallagher puts it, converts are continually "converting their conversions" to bring them into closer harmony with their current circumstances, all the while maintaining the fiction of their conversion experience as something fixed and determinative.

What are the implications of this? In contrast to Professor Wicker's hypothetical, I do not think that Paul "formulated *a* conversion narrative detailing events of his transformation which he shared with his communities." If we are going to hypothesize, I think it more likely that Paul was continually reinterpreting his conversion and therefore continually formulating conversion narrative*s* according to the circumstances in which he found himself. And this is why we have had such a difficult time reconstructing Paul's conversion narrative. It is not just that the Lukan fiction of the Damascus road has distorted our vision (as well as Paul's) in this regard. The reason that passages like Galatians 1, Philippians 3, 1 Corinthians 15 and 2 Corinthians 12 do not fit together neatly is that they do not stem from a *single* narrative. Rather, they reflect a Paul in process of "converting his conversion." And it would make for an interesting comparison, I submit, to see whether this is also true of the conversion accounts of Marange and Amedzro.

Finally, as important as historical context is for understanding conversion, I do not think it is the crucial determinant, nor even is it the nature of the experience itself, had we access to it. What is crucial are the explanatory interests and assumptions of the observer—in short, the theory, which commits one in advance to a particular understanding of religion, and determines in advance what will be accepted as evidence. Simply put, explanations of conversion express the fundamental interests of the person doing the explaining, and this is as true of Paul as it is of Wicker and Droge.

BIBLIOGRAPHY

Achtemeier, P. "The Origin and Function of the Pre-Markan Miracle Catenae." *JBL* 91 (1972) 198–221.

Achtemeier, P. "Toward the Isolation of Pre-Markan Miracle Catenae." *JBL* 89 (1970) 265–91.

Ackrill, J. L. *Aristotle's Categories and* De Interpretatione. Clarendon Aristotle Series. Oxford: Clarendon, 1963.

Aguilar, M. I. "African Conversion from a World Religion: Religious Diversification by the Waso Boorana in Kenya." *Africa* 65.4 (1995) 525–544.

Aguilar, M. I. "Rethinking African Conversion: Assessing Syncretism through Diversification." Paper presented at the African Studies Meeting. November, 1996.

Aharoni, Y. *The Land of the Bible: An Historical Geography. Revised and Enlarged Edition.* 2d. ed. Philadelphia: Westminster, 1979.

Albertini, E. "The Latin West: Africa, Spain and Gaul." *CAH* 11, ed. S. A. Cook *et al.* Cambridge: At the University Press, 1954, 479–510.

Albertz, R. *A History of Israelite Religion in the Old Testament Period.* 2 vols.; London: SCM, 1994.

Alexander, P. S. "Early Jewish Geography." *ABD* 2, ed. D. N. Freedman. New York: Doubleday, 1992, 977–88.

Allison, D. C., Jr. "The Structure of the Sermon on the Mount." *JBL* 106 (1987) 423–45.

Alpers-Gölz, R. *Der Begriff 'Skopos' in der Stoa und seine Vorgeschichte.* Hildesheim and New York: Olms, 1976.

Aly, W. "Die Entdeckung des Westens." *Hermes* 62 (1927) 299–341.

Amedzro, J. S. *A Brief History of the Lord's Pentecostal Church.* n. d.

Amenumey, D. E. K. *The Ewe in Pre-Colonial Times.* Accra: Sedco Publishing Limited, 1986.

Amir, Y. "Die jüdische Eingottglaube als Stein des Anstoßes der hellenistisch-römischen Welt." *JBTh* 2 (1987) 58–75.

Anderson, B. *Imagined Communities: Reflections on the Origin and Spread of Nationalism.* Rev. ed. London: Verso, 1983.

Anderson, G. "Lucian's *Nigrinos*, the Problem of Form." *GRBS* 19 (1978) 367–74.

Annen, F. *Heil für die Heiden: Zur Bedeutung und Geschichte der Tradition vom besessenen Gerasener (Mk 5, 1–20 par.).* FTS 20. Frankfurt am Main: Knecht, 1976.

Arnim, H. F. A. von. *Stoicorum Veterum Fragmenta.* 4 vols. Leipzig: Teubner, 1968.

Assmann, J. "Weisheit, Loyalismus und Frömmigkeit." *Studien zu altägyptischen Lebenslehren.* Ed. E. Hornung and O. Keel. OBO 28. Freiburg: Universitätsverlag; Göttingen: Vandenhoeck & Ruprecht, 1979, 11–72.

Assmann, J. "Zur Geschichte der Herzens im Alten Ägypten." *Die Erfindung des inneren Menschen.* Ed. J. Assmann. Gütersloh: Gütersloher, 1993, 81–113.

Assmann, J., ed. *Die Erfindung des inneren Menschen.* Gütersloh: Gütersloher, 1993.

Aubet, M. E. *The Phoenicians and the West: Politics, Colonies and Trade.* Cambridge: Cambridge University Press, 1993.

Aune, D. E. "Heracles." *Dictionary of Deities and Demons in the Bible.* Ed. K. van der Toorn, B. Becking, and P. W. van der Horst. Leiden: Brill, 1995, 765–72.

Aune, D. E. "Herakles." *ABD* 3 (1992) 141–43.

Aune, D. "Romans as a Logos Protreptikos in the Context of Ancient Religious and Philosophical Propaganda." *Paulus und das antike Judentum.* Ed. M. Hengel and U. Heckel. Tübingen: Mohr (Siebeck), 1992, 91–124.

Austin, J. L. *How To Do Things with Words.* The William James Lectures delivered at Harvard University in 1955. 2d ed. Ed. J. O. Urmson and M. Sbisà. Cambridge, MA: Harvard University Press, 1975.

Babbit, F. C., ed. *Plutarch's Moralia. Volume 1.* LCL. Cambridge, MA and London: Heinemann, 1969.

Bach, K. and Harnish, R. M. *Linguistic Communication and Speech Acts.* Cambridge, MA and London: MIT, 1982.

Baker, D. W. "Girgashite." *ABD* 2, ed. D. N. Freedman. Garden City, NY: Doubleday, 1992, 1028.

Bammel, E. "πτωχός κτλ." *TWNT* 6, ed. G. Kittel and G. Friedrich. Stuttgart: Kohlhammer, 1959, 885–915.

Barclay, J. *Jews in the Mediterranean Diaspora, from Alexander to Trajan (323 BCE–117 CE).* Edinburgh: T. & T. Clark, 1996.

Barkun, M. ed. *Millenialism and Violence.* CASS Series on Political Violence 2. Portland, OR and London: Cass, 1996.

Barnard, L. W. *Justin Martyr: His Life and Thought.* Cambridge: Cambridge University Press, 1971.

Barr, J. *Old and New in Interpretation: A Study of the Two Testaments.* London: SCM, 1966; 2nd ed. 1982.

Barton, J. "The Significance of a Fixed Canon in the Hebrew Bible." *Hebrew Bible/Old Testament: The History of its Interpretation.* Vol. 1,

From the Beginnings to the Middle Ages. Ed. M. Sæbø. Göttingen: Vandenhoeck & Ruprecht, 1996, 67–83.

Baumgarten, A. I. *The* Phoenician History *of Philo of Byblos: A Commentary*. EPRO 69. Leiden: Brill, 1981.

Becker, J. *Jesus von Nazareth*. Berlin and New York: de Gruyter, 1996.

Bediako, K. *Christianity in Africa: The Renewal of a Non-Western Religion*. Edinburgh: Edinburgh University Press, 1995.

Behm, J. and Wurthwein, E. "νοέω κτλ." *TDNT* 4, ed. G. Kittel and G. Friedrich. Grand Rapids: Eerdmans, 1967, 948–1022.

Bellido, A. García y. "Hércules Gaditanus." *Archivo Español de Arqueologia* 36 (1963) 70–152.

Benedict, R. *Patterns of Culture*. Boston: Houghton Mifflin, 1961.

Berger, K. *Formgeschichte des Neuen Testaments*. Heidelberg: Quelle & Meyer, 1984.

Berger, K. "Hellenistische Gattungen im Neuen Testament." *ANRW* 2.25.2, ed. H. Temporini and W. Haase. Berlin and New York: de Gruyter, 1984, 1031–1432.

Berger, K. "Innen und Außen in der Welt des Neuen Testaments." *Die Erfindung des inneren Menschen*. Ed. J. Assmann. Gütersloh: Gütersloher, 1993, 161–67.

Bergren, A. L. T. *The Etymology and Usage of* ΠΕΙΡΑΡ *in Early Greek Poetry*. American Classical Studies 2. New York: APA, 1975.

Bertram, G. "στρέφω κτλ." *TDNT* 7, ed. G. Kittel and G. Friedrich. Grand Rapids: Eerdmans, 1971, 714–29.

Best, E. "Matthew V.3." *NTS* 7 (1960–61) 255–58.

Betz, H. D. *2 Corinthians 8 and 9: A Commentary on Two Administrative Letters of the Apostle Paul*. Hermeneia. Philadelphia: Fortress, 1985.

Betz, H. D. *Der Apostel Paulus und die sokratische Tradition. Eine exegetische Untersuchung zu seiner "Apologie" 2 Korinther 10–15*. BTH 45. Tübingen: Mohr (Siebeck), 1972.

Betz, H. D. "Eine jüdenchristliche Kult-Didache in Matthäus 6,1–18." *Jesus Christus in Historie und Theologie: Neutestamentliche Festschrift für Hans Conzelmann zum 60. Geburtstag*. Ed. G. Strecker. Tübingen: Mohr (Siebeck), 1975, 445–57.

Betz, H. D. *Essays on the Sermon on the Mount*. Philadelphia: Fortress, 1985.

Betz, H. D. *Galatians: A Commentary on Paul's Letter to the Churches in Galatia*. Hermeneia. Philadelphia: Fortress, 1979.

Betz, H. D. "Gottmensch II (Griechisch-römische Antike und Christentum)." *RAC* 12, ed. T. Klauser *et al.* Stuttgart: Hiersemann, 1983, 234–311.

Betz, H. D. *Hellenismus und Urchristentum. Gesammelte Aufsätze I.* Tübingen: Mohr (Siebeck), 1990.

Betz, H. D. "Jesus and the Cynics: Survey and Analysis of an Hypothesis." *JR* 74 (1994) 453–75.

Betz, H. D. *Lukian von Samosata und das Neue Testament. Religionsgeschichtliche und paränetische Parallelen. Ein Beitrag zum Corpus Hellenisticum Novi Testamenti.* TU 76. Berlin: Akademie-Verlag, 1961.

Betz, H. D. *Paulinische Studien. Gesammelte Aufsätze III.* Tübingen: Mohr (Siebeck), 1994.

Betz, H. D. *Synoptische Studien. Gesammelte Aufsätze II.* Tübingen: Mohr (Siebeck), 1992.

Betz, H. D. "The Apostle Paul Between Judaism and Hellenism: Creating a Space for Christianity." Forthcoming.

Betz, H. D. "The Birth of Christianity as a Hellenistic Religion: Three Theories of Origin." *JR* 74 (1994) 1–25.

Betz, H. D. "The Sermon on the Mount in Matthew's Interpretation." *The Future of Early Christianity: Essays in Honor of Helmut Koester.* Ed. B. A. Pearson. Minneapolis: Fortress, 1991, 258–75.

Betz, H. D. *The Sermon on the Mount: A Commentary on the Sermon on the Mount, Including the Sermon on the Plain (Matthew 5:3–7:27 and Luke 6:20–49).* Hermeneia. Minneapolis: Fortress, 1995.

Betz, H. D. "Zum Problem des religionsgeschichtlichen Verständnisses der Apokalyptik." *ZTK* 63 (1966) 391–409. Reprinted in *idem, Hellenismus und Urchristentum: Gessamelte Aufsätze I.* Tübingen: Mohr (Siebeck), 1990.

Betz, H. D., ed. *Plutarch's Ethical Writings and Early Christian Literature.* SCHNT 4. Leiden: Brill, 1978.

Blänsdorf, J. *Das Paradoxon der Zeit.* Heidelberger Texte 13. Freiburg and Würzburg: Ploetz, 1983.

Blázquez Martínez, J. M. "Gerión y otros mitos griegos en Occidente." *Gerion* 1 (1983) 21–38.

Bligh, J. "The Gerasene Demoniac and the Resurrection of Christ." *CBQ* 31 (1969) 383–90.

Blomqvist, J. and Jastrup, P. O. *Grekisk/græsk Grammatik.* Copenhagen: Akademisk Forlag, 1991.

Blumenberg, H. *Lebenzeit und Weltzeit.* Frankfurt am Main: Suhrkamp, 1986.

Bompaire, J. *Lucien ècrivain.* Paris: de Boccard, 1958.

Bonhoeffer, A. "Ein heidnisches Pendant zum Neutestamentlichen Gleichnis von Sämann." *ARW* 11 (1908) 571–72.

Bonhöffer, A. *Die Ethik des Stoikers Epiktet.* Stuttgart: Enke, 1894.

Bonnet, C. *Melqart: cultes et mythes de l'Héraclès tyrien en Méditerranée.* Studia Phoenicia VIII. Leuven: Peeters, 1988.

Bonnet, H. *Reallexikon der ägyptischen Religionsgeschichte.* Berlin: de Gruyter, 1952.

Boring, E. "The Historical-Critical Method's 'Criteria of Authenticity': The Beatitudes in Q and Thomas as a Test Case." *The Historical Jesus and the Rejected Gospels. Semeia* 44, ed. C. W. Hedrick. Atlanta: Scholars Press, 1988, 9–43.

Bornkamm, G. "Der Aufbau der Bergpredigt." *NTS* 24 (1978) 419–32.

Bornkamm, G. *Paul.* New York and Evanston: Harper & Row, 1971.

Bourdillon, M. *The Shona Peoples.* 3d ed. Gweru: Mambo, 1987.

Bovon, F. *Das Evangelium nach Lukas I (Lk 1,1–9,50).* EKKNT 3/1. Zürich: Benziger; Neukirchen-Vluyn: Neukirchener, 1989.

Bowersock, G. W. *Fiction as History.* Berkeley: University of California Press, 1994.

Bowra, C. M. *Pindar.* Oxford: Clarendon Press, 1964.

Brashear, W. "Nachtrag zum Zauberformular P. Berol. 11734." *APF* 38 (1992) 27–32.

Brashear, W. "Zauberformular." *APF* 36 (1990) 61–74.

Braun, H. *Qumran und das Neue Testament. Band I.* Tübingen: Mohr (Siebeck), 1968.

Breech, J. E. *The Silence of Jesus.* Philadelphia: Fortress, 1983.

Bremmer, J. *The Early Greek Concept of the Soul.* Princeton, NJ: Princeton University Press, 1983.

Briggs, S. "Galatians." *Searching the Scriptures: A Feminist Commentary.* Ed. E. Schüssler Fiorenza. New York: Crossroad, 1994, 218–236.

Broer, I. *Die Seligpreisungen der Bergpredigt. Studien zu ihrer Überlieferung und Interpretation.* BBB 61. Bonn: Hanstein, 1986.

Brooten, B. J. *Love Between Women: Early Christian Responses to Female Homoeroticism.* Chicago: University of Chicago Press, 1996.

Brown, P. *The Making of Late Antiquity.* Cambridge, MA: Harvard University Press, 1978.

Brunner, E. *The Divine-Human Encounter.* London: SCM, 1944. German original, *Wahrheit als Begegnung.* Berlin: Furche-Verlag, 1938.

Brunner, E. "The Significance of the Old Testament for our Faith." *The Old Testament and Christian Faith.* Ed. B. W. Anderson. New York: Harper and Row, 1963, 243–64. German original, "Die Bedeutung des Alten Testaments für unsern Glauben." *Zwischen den Zeiten* 8 (1930) 30–48.

Bryan, C. *A Preface to Mark: Notes on the Gospel in Its Literary and Cultural Settings.* New York and Oxford: Oxford University, 1993.

Bühler, K. *Axiomatik der Sprachwissenschaften. Einleitung und Kommentar von E. Stöcker.* 2d. ed. Frankfurt am Main: Klostermann, 1976.

Bühler, K. *Sprachtheorie. Die Darstellungsfunktion der Sprache.* Ullstein Buch 3392. Frankfurt am Main: Ullstein, 1965.

Bultmann, R. *Die Geschichte der synoptischen Tradition.* 8th ed. Göttingen: Vandenhoeck & Ruprecht, 1967.

Bultmann, R. *Jesus.* Siebenstern-Taschenbücher 17. Hamburg: Siebenstern, 1964.

Bultmann, R. "Paul." *Existence and Faith: Shorter Writings of Rudolph Bultmann.* Ed. S. Ogden. New York: Meridian Books, 1960, 111–46.

Bultmann, R. "πένθος, πενθέω." *TWNT* 6, ed. G. Kittel and G. Friedrich. Stuttgart: Kohlhammer, 1959, 40–43.

Burchard, C. "Hippos." *KP* 2 (1979) 1177–78.

Burkert, W. *Ancient Mystery Cults.* Cambridge, MA and London: Harvard University Press, 1987.

Burkert, W. *Antiken Mysterien. Funktionen und Gehalt.* 2d. ed. München: Beck, 1991.

Burkert, W. "Der geheime Reiz des Verborgenen: Antike Mysterienkulte." *Secrecy and Concealment: Studies in the History of the Mediterranean and Near Eastern Religions.* Ed. H. G. Kippenberg and G. S. Stroumsa. Leiden: Brill, 1995, 79–100.

Burkert, W. *Homo Necans: The Anthropology of Ancient Greek Sacrificial Ritual and Myth.* Berkeley: University of California Press, 1983.

Burkert, W. *Lore and Science in Ancient Pythagoreanism.* Cambridge, MA: Harvard University Press, 1972.

Burkert, W. *The Creation of the Sacred: Tracks of Biology in Early Religions.* Cambridge, MA: Harvard University Press, 1996.

Burkert, W. *The Orientalizing Revolution: Near Eastern Influence on Greek Culture in the Early Archaic Age.* Cambridge, MA: Harvard University Press, 1992.

Burridge, R. A. *What are the Gospels? A Comparison with Graeco-Roman Biography.* Cambridge: Cambridge University Press, 1992.

Cadbury, H. J. *The Style and Literary Method of Luke.* Cambridge: Harvard University, 1920.

Cancik, H. "Bios und Logos. Formengeschichtliche Untersuchungen zu Lukians 'Demonax'." *Markus-Philologie.* Ed. H. Cancik. Tübingen: Mohr (Siebeck), 1984, 115–30.

Cancik, H. "Gnostiker in Rom. Zur Religionsgeschichte der Stadt Rom in 2. Jh. n. Chr." *Gnosis und Politik.* Ed. J. Taubes. Paderborn: Fink, 1984, 163–84.

Cancik, H. and Cancik-Lindemaier, H. "*patria – peregrina – universa.* Versuch eine Typologie der universalistischen Tendenzen in der

Geschichte der römischen Religion." *Tradition und Translation. Zum Problem der Übersetzbarkeit religiöser Phänomene. Festschrift für Carsten Colpe zum 65. Geburtstag.* Ed. C. Elsas *et al.* Berlin and New York: de Gruyter, 1994, 64–74.

Cancik, H. and Cancik-Lindemaier, H. "Senecas Konstruktion des Weisen. Zur Sakralisierung der Rolle des Weisen im 1. Jh. n. Chr." *Weisheit. Archäologie der literarischen Kommunikation.* Ed. A. Assmann. München: Fink, 1991, 205–22.

Cancik-Lindemaier, H. "Der Diskurs Religion im Senatsbeschluß über die Bacchanalia von 186 v. Chr. und bei Livius (B. XXXIX)." *Geschichte – Tradition – Reflexion. Festschrit für Martin Hengel zum 70. Geburtstag.* Vol. 2, *Griechische und römische Religion.* Ed. H. Cancik *et al.* Tübingen: Mohr (Siebeck), 1996, 77–96.

Cancik(-Lindemaier), H. *Untersuchungen zu Senecas* Epistulae morales. Spudasmata 18. Hildesheim: Olms, 1967.

Cangh, J.-M. van. "La Galilée dans l'évangile de Marc: un lieu théologique?" *RB* 79 (1972) 59–75.

Cangh, J.-M. van. "Les sources de l'Évangile: les collections pré-marciennes de miracles." *RTL* 3 (1972) 76–85.

Carlston, C. E. "Betz on the Sermon on the Mount: A Critique." *CBQ* 50 (1988) 47–57.

Carpenter, R. *The Greeks in Spain.* Bryn Mawr Notes and Monographs 6. Bryn Mawr, PA: Bryn Mawr College, 1925.

Carson, D. A. and Williamson, H. G. M., eds. *It Is Written: Scripture Citing Scripture. Essays in Honor of Barnabas Lindars.* New York: Cambridge University Press, 1988.

Catchpole, D. R. *The Quest for Q.* Edinburgh: T & T Clark, 1993.

Cerro, M. Martinez de. *Un Paseo por Cadiz. Ensayo historia intinerario artistico.* Cadiz: Editorial Escelicer, S. A. del Cerro, 1966.

Chapman, D. W. "Locating the Gospel of Mark: A Model of Agrarian Biography." *BTB* 25 (1995) 24–25, 28–36.

Childs, B. S. *Biblical Theology in Crisis.* Philadelphia: Westminster, 1970.

Childs, B. S. *Biblical Theology of the Old and New Testaments: Theological Reflection on the Christian Bible.* Minneapolis: Fortress, 1983.

Clapp, E. B. "On Certain Fragments of Pindar." *CQ* 8 (1914) 225–29.

Clay, D. "Lucian of Samosata: Four Philosophical Lives. " *ANRW* 2.36.5, ed. W. Haase and H. Temporini. Berlin and New York: de Gruyter, 1992, 3406–3450.

Cleave, R. "Satellite Revelations. New Views of the Holy Land." *National Geographic* 187/6 (1995) 88–105.

Cohen, S. J. D. *From the Maccabees to the Mishnah.* Philadelphia: Westminster, 1989.

Cohn, N. *The Pursuit of the Millennium.* Fairlawn, NJ: Essential Books; London: Secker and Warburg, 1957.

Colli, G. and Montinari, M., eds. *Friedrich Nietzsche. Sämtliche Briefe. Kritische Studienausgabe.* 15 vols. 2nd ed. München: Deutscher Taschenbuch Verlag, 1988.

Collins, A. Yarbro. *Crisis and Catharsis: The Power of the Apocalypse.* Philadelphia: Westminster, 1984.

Collins, A. Yarbro. "Rulers, Divine Men, and Walking on the Water (Mark 6:45–52)." *Religious Propaganda and Missionary Competition in the New Testament World. Essays Honoring Dieter Georgi.* Ed. L. Bormann *et al.* Leiden: Brill, 1994, 207–27.

Collins, J. J. *The Apocalyptic Imagination: An Introduction to the Jewish Matrix of Christianity.* New York: Crossroad, 1984.

Collins, J. J. *Daniel.* Hermeneia. Minneapolis: Fortress, 1993.

Collins, J. J. *Jewish Wisdom in the Hellenistic Age.* Old Testament Library; Louisville: Westminster JohnKnox, 1997.

Collins, J. J. "Natural Theology and Biblical Tradition: The Case of Hellenistic Judaism." *CBQ* 60 (1998) 1–15.

Comaroff, Jean and Comaroff, John. *Of Revelation and Revolution: Christianity, Colonialism, and Consciousness in South Africa.* Vol. 1. Chicago and London: University of Chicago Press, 1991.

Conzelmann, H. *The Theology of Saint Luke.* New York: Harper and Brothers, 1960. German original, *Die Mitte der Zeit.* Tübingen: Mohr (Siebeck), 1954.

Cook, E. "Ferrymen of Elysium and the Homeric Phaeacians." *JIES* 20 (1992) 239–67.

Cook, J. G. *The Structure and Persuasive Power of Mark: A Linguistic Approach.* SBLSS. Atlanta: Scholars Press, 1995.

Cook, S. L. *Prophecy and Apocalypticism: The Post Exilic Social Setting.* Minneapolis: Fortress, 1995.

Corrodi, H. *Kritische Geschichte des Chiliasmus.* 3 vols. Frankfort-Leipzig: 1781–83.

Cosieru, E. "Die Ebenen des sprachlichen Wissens. Der Ort des 'Korrekten' in der Bewertungsskala des Gesprochenen." *Energeia und Ergon. Sprachliche Variation – Sprachgeschichte – Sprachtypologie.* Vol. 1, *Schriften von Eugenio Coseriu (1965–87).* Ed. J. Albrecht. Tübingen: Narr, 1988.

Craghan, J. F. "The Gerasene Demoniac." *CBQ* 30 (1968) 522–36.

Cranfield, C. E. B. *The Gospel According to Saint Mark.* Cambridge: Cambridge University Press, 1966.

Dahl, N. A. *Jesus the Christ: The Historical Origins of Christological Doctrine.* Minneapolis: Fortress, 1991.

Dalman, G. *Sacred Sites and Ways: Studies in the Topography of the Gospels.* London: SPCK; New York: Macmillan, 1935.

Daneel, I. [M. L.] *Quest for Belonging: Introduction to a Study of African Independent Churches.* Gweru: Mambo, 1987.

Daneel, M. L. *Fambidzano. Ecumenical Movement of Zimbabwean Independent Churches.* Gweru: Mambo, 1989.

Daneel, M. L. *Old and New in Southern Shona Independent Churches.* Vol. 1., *Background and Rise of the Major Movements.* The Hague: Mouton, 1971; Vol. 2., *Church Growth: Causative Factors and Recruitment Techniques.* The Hague: Mouton, 1974. Vol. 3., *Leadership and Fission Dynamics.* Gweru: Mambo, 1988.

Daniels, T. *Millenialism: An International Bibliography.* New York: Garland, 1992.

Davies, W. D. and Allison, D. C. *The Gospel according to Saint Matthew, Volume 1.* ICC. Edinburgh: T & T Clark, 1988.

Derrett, J. D. M. "Contributions to the Study of the Gerasene Demoniac." *JSNT* 3 (1979) 2–17.

Derrett, J. D. M. *The Making of Mark: The Scriptural Basis of the Earliest Gospel.* Warwickshire: Drinkwater, 1985.

Dibelius, M. *Die Formgeschichte des Evangeliums.* 6th ed. Tübingen: Mohr (Siebeck), 1971.

Dibelius, Martin. "The Isis Initiation in Apuleius and Related Initiatory Rites." *Conflict at Colossae.* Rev ed. Ed. F. O. Francis and W. A. Meeks. SBLSBS 4. Missoula: Scholars Press, 1975, 61–121. German Original, "Die Isisweihe bei Apuleius und verwandte Inititations-Riten." *Botschaft und Geschichte.* Ed. G. Bornkamm. 2 vols. Tübingen: Mohr (Siebeck), 1956, 2.30–79.

Diels, H., and Kranz, W. *Die Fragmente der Vorsokratiker, griechisch und deutsch.* 18th ed. 3 vols. Zurich: Weidmann, 1942.

Dihle, A. *The Theory of Will in Classical Antiquity.* Berkeley: University of California Press, 1982.

Dillon, J. *The Middle Platonists: A Study of Platonism, 80 B.C. to A.D. 220.* London: Duckworth, 1979.

Dimant, D. "Qumran Sectarian Literature." *Jewish Writings of the Second Temple Period.* Ed. M. E. Stone. CRINT 2/2. Assen: Van Gorcum, 1984, 483–549.

Dimant, D. "The 'Pesher on the Four Periods' (4Q180) and 4Q181." *IOS* 9 (1979) 77–102.

Dobschütz, E. von. "Matthäus als Rabbi und Katechet." *ZNW* 27 (1928) 338–48.

Dodd, C. H. *Historical Tradition in the Fourth Gospel.* Cambridge: Cambridge University, 1965.

Dodds, E. R. *Euripides Bacchae. Edited with Introduction and Commentary.* Oxford: Clarendon, 1986.

Dodds, E. R. *Pagan and Christian in an Age of Anxiety.* Cambridge: Cambridge University Press, 1965.

Dodds, E. R. *Plato. Gorgias.* Oxford: Clarendon, 1957.

Donaldson, T. L. *Paul and the Gentiles: Remapping the Apostle's Convictional World.* Minneapolis: Fortress, 1997.

Dormeyer, D. *Das Neuen Testament im Rahmen der antiken Literaturgeschichte. Ein Einführung.* Darmstadt: Wissenschaftliche Buchgesellschaft, 1993.

Dormeyer, D. *Evangelium als literarische und theologische Gattung.* ErFor 263. Darmstadt: Wissenschaftliche Buchgesellschaft, 1989.

Dormeyer, D. "Mt 1,1 als Überschrift zur Gattung und Christologie des Matthäusevangeliums." *The Four Gospels, 1992: FS F. Neirynck.* Ed. F. van Segbroeck *et al.* BETL 100. Leuven: University Press, 1992, 1361–83.

Dornseiff, F. *Echtheitsfragen antik-griechischer Literatur.* Berlin: de Gruyter, 1931.

Dupont, J. "Les πτωχοὶ τῷ πνεύματι de Matthieu 5,3 et les ענוי רוח de Qumran." *Neutestamentliche Aufsätze. FS J. Schmid.* Ed. J. Blinzler *et al.* Regensburg: Pustet, 1963, 53–64.

Düring, I. *Chion of Heraclea.* Göteberg: Wettergren & Kerbers, 1951.

Ebeling, G. "The Meaning of 'Biblical Theology'." *JTS* 6 (1955) 210–25. Reprinted in *idem, Word and Faith.* London: SCM, 1963, 79–97.

Ehrlich, C. S. "Geder." *ABD* 2, ed. D. N. Freedman. Garden City, NY: Doubleday, 1992, 924–25.

Ehrlich, C. S. "Gederah." *ABD* 2, ed. D. N. Freedman. Garden City, NY: Doubleday, 1992, 925.

Eliade, M. *Myths, Dreams and Mysteries: The Encounter between Contemporary Faiths and Archaic Realities.* Repr. ed. San Francisco: Harper & Row, 1975.

Elliott, J. H. Review of H.-W. Kuhn, *Ältere Sammlungen im Markusevangelium. CBQ* 34 (1972) 368–71.

Elliott, N. *Liberating Paul: The Justice of God and the Politics of the Apostle.* Maryknoll: Orbis, 1994.

Eni, E. *Delivered from the Powers of Darkness.* Ibadan: Scripture Union (Nigeria) Press and Books Ltd., 1987.

Evelyn-White, H. G. *Hesiod, Homeric Hymns and Homerica.* LCL. Cambridge, MA: Harvard University Press, 1936.

Faraone, C. A. *Talismans and Trojan Horses: Guardian Statues in Ancient Greek Myth and Ritual.* New York and Oxford: Oxford University Press, 1992.

Fishbane, M. *Biblical Interpretation in Ancient Israel.* Oxford: Clarendon, 1985.

Fishbane, M. *The Kiss of God: Spiritual and Mystical Death in Judaism.* Seattle: University of Washington Press, 1994.

Fisher, H. J. "Conversion Reconsidered: Some Historical Aspects of Religious Conversion in Black Africa." *Africa* 43 (1973) 27–40.

Fitzmyer, J. A. "A Palestinian Collection of Beatitudes." *The Four Gospels 1992. FS Frans Neirynck.* Ed. F. Van Segbroeck *et al.* BETL 100-A. Leuven: Peeters, 1992, 509–15.

Fitzmyer, J. A. *The Gospel According to Luke (I-IX).* AB 28. Garden City, NY: Doubleday, 1981.

Flanagan, T. "The Politics of the Millennium." *Millenialism and Violence.* Ed. M. Barkun. CASS Series on Political Violence 2. Portland OR and London: CASS, 1996, 164–75.

Flusser, D. *Judaism and the Origins of Christianity.* Jerusalem: Magnes, 1988.

Foley, H. P., ed. *The Homeric Hymn to Demeter. Translation, Commentary and Interpretative Essays.* Princeton: Princeton University Press, 1994.

Fontenrose, J. "Typhon among the Arimoi." *The Classical Tradition: Literary and Historical Studies in Honor of Harry Caplan.* Ed. L. Wallach. Ithaca: Cornell University, 1996, 64–82.

Forschner, M. "Das Gute und die Güter. Zur Aktualität der stoischen Ethik." *Aspects de la philosophie hellénistique.* Ed. H. Flashar. Entretiens sur l'antiquité classique 32. Vandoeuvres-Genève: Fondation Hardt, 1985, 325–50.

Forschner, M. *Die stoische Ethik. Über den Zusammenhang von Natur-, Sprach- und Moralphilosophie im altstoischen System.* 2d. ed. Darmstadt: Wissenschaftliche Buchgesellschaft, 1995.

Forschner, M. *"Über das Glück des Menschen." Aristoteles, Epikur, Stoa, Thomas von Aquin, Kant.* Darmstadt: Wissenschaftliche Buchgesellschaft, 1993.

Fortna, R. T. *The Fourth Gospel and Its Predecessor.* Philadelphia: Fortress, 1988.

Fraenkel, E. *Aeschylus. Agamemnon.* 3 vols. Oxford: Clarendon, 1950.

Frankemölle, H. *Matthäus: Kommentar 1.* Düsseldorf: Patmos, 1994.

Frankfort, H. *Kingship and the Gods.* Chicago: University of Chicago Press, 1978.

Fredriksen, P. *From Jesus to Christ: The Origins of New Testament Images of Jesus.* New Haven: Yale University Press, 1988.

Fredriksen, P. "Judaism, the Circumcision of Gentiles, and Apocalyptic Hope: Another Look at Galatians 1–2." *JTS* 42 (1991) 532–564.

Fredriksen, P. "Paul and Augustine: Conversion Narratives, Orthodox Traditions, and the Retrospective Self." *JTS* 37 (1986) 3–44.

Fritz, K. von. "ΕΣΤΡΙΣ ΕΚΑΤΕΡΩΘΙ in Pindar's second Olympian and Pythagoras' Theory of Metempsychosis." *Phronesis* 2 (1957) 85–89.

Fritz, K. von. *Philosophie und sprachlicher Ausdruck bei Demokrit, Plato und Aristoteles.* New York, Leipzig and London: Stechert, 1938.

Fumarola, V. "Conversione e satira antiromana nel Nigrino di Luciano." *Parola del Passato* 6 (1951) 182–207.

Gaiser, K. "Das Gold der Weisheit. Zum Gebet des Philosophen am Schluß des *Phaidros.*" *RhM* 132 (1989) 105–40.

Gaiser, K. "Ein Lob Athens in der Komödie (Menander, Fragmentum Didotianum b)." *Gymnasium* 75 (1968) 193–219.

Gallagher, E. V. *Expectation and Experience: Explaining Religious Conversion.* Atlanta: Scholars Press, 1990.

Gamble, H. Y. *Books and Readers in the Early Church.* New Haven: Yale University Press, 1995.

Gamble, H. Y. "The Pauline Corpus and the Early Christian Book." *Paul and the Legacies of Paul.* Ed. W. S. Babcock. Dallas: Southern Methodist University Press, 1990, 265–80.

Gantz, T. *Early Greek Myth: A Guide to Literary and Artistic Sources.* Baltimore and New York: Johns Hopkins University, 1993.

Gasset, O. y. *The Dehumanization of Art and Other Writings on Art and Culture.* Garden City, NY: Doubleday, 1956.

Gaventa, B. Roberts. *Paul's Conversion: A Critical Sifting of the Epistolary Evidence.* Ph.D. Dissertation, Duke University, 1978.

Gaventa, B. Roberts. *From Darkness to Light: Aspects of Conversion in the New Testament.* Philadelphia: Fortress, 1986.

Geckeler, H. *Strukturelle Semantik and Wordfeldtheorie.* München: Fink, 1971.

Geertz, C. *The Interpretation of Cultures.* New York: Basic, 1973.

Gergen, M. M. and Gergen, K. J. *Historical Social Psychology.* Hillsdale, NJ: Erlbaum, 1984.

Gerstenberger, E. "ענה." *TWAT* 6, ed. G. J. Botterweck and H. Ringgren. Stuttgart: Kohlhammer, 1989, 247–70.

Giannantoni, G. *Socratis et Socraticorum Reliquiae.* 4 vols. Naples: Bibliopolis, 1990.

Giebel, M. *Das Geheimnis der Mysterien. Antike Kulte in Griechenland, Rom und Ägypten.* München: Deutscher Taschenbuch, 1993.

Gifford, P. "Ghana's Pentecostal Churches." *Journal of Religion in Africa* 3 (1994) 241–265.

Gigon, O. "Antike Erzählungen über die Berufung zur Philosophie." *Museum Helveticum* 3 (1946) 1–21.

Glad, C. E. *Paul and Philodemus: Adaptability in Epicurean and Early Christian Psychagogy*. NovTSup 81. Leiden: Brill, 1995.

Gladigow, B. "Zum Makarismos des Weisen." *Hermes* 95 (1967) 404–33.

Gnilka, J. *Das Evangelium Nach Markus (Mk 1–8,26)*. Zürich, etc.: Benziger; Neukirchen-Vluyn: Neukirchener, 1978.

Gnilka, J. *Das Matthäusevangelium I. Teil*. HTKNT 1.1. Freiburg: Herder, 1988.

Goodman, M. *Mission and Conversion: Proselytizing in the Religious History of the Roman Empire*. Oxford: Clarendon, 1994.

Goodman, M. *The Ruling Classes of Judaea: The Origins of the Jewish Revolt against Rome A.D. 66–70*. Cambridge: Cambridge University Press, 1987.

Goppelt, L. "πεινάω κτλ." *TWNT* 6, ed. G. Kittel and G. Friedrich. Stuttgart: Kohlhammer, 1959, 12–22.

Gould, E. P. *A Critical and Exegetical Commentary on the Gospel According to Saint Mark*. ICC. Edinburgh: T & T Clark, 1896.

Gould, P. and White, R. *Mental Maps*. 2d ed. Boston: Allen & Unwin, 1986.

Graf, F. "Dionysian and Orphic Eschatology: New Texts and Old Questions." *Masks of Dionysius*. Ed. T. H. Carpenter and C. A. Faraone. Myth and Poetics. Ithaca, NY and London: Cornell, 1993, 259–75.

Graf, F. *Eleusis und die orphische Dichtung Athens in vorhellenistischer Zeit*. RVV 33. Berlin and New York: de Gruyter, 1974.

Grant, F. C. *The Gospels: Their Origin and Growth*. New York: Harper & Row, 1957.

Grant, R. M. *Greek Apologists of the Second Century*. Philadelphia: Westminster, 1988.

Greene, S. *Gender, Ethnicity, and Social Change on the Upper Slave Coast: A History of the Anlo-Ewe*. London: James Currey, 1996.

Greene, S. "Religion, History and the Supreme Gods of Africa." *Journal of Religion in Africa* 26 (1996) 122–138.

Grese, W. C. "De profectibus in virtute (Moralia 75A–86A)." *Plutarch's Ethical Writings and Early Christian Literature*. Ed. H. D. Betz. SCHNT 4. Leiden: Brill, 1978, 11–31.

Gresseth, G. K. "The Homeric Sirens." *TAPA* 101 (1970) 203–218.

Griffin, M. T. *Seneca. A Philosopher in Politics*. Oxford: Clarendon, 1986.

Griffiths, J. G. *Apuleius of Madauros. The Isis-Book (Metamorphoses, Book XI). Edited with an Introduction, Translation and Commentary*. Leiden: Brill, 1975.

Grimal, P. *Sénèque: ou la conscience de l'Empire.* Paris: Belles Lettres, 1978.

Grimm, J., and Grimm, W. *Deutsche Mythologie.* Repr. ed. 3 vols. Graz: Akademische Druck, 1953.

Grimm, J., and Grimm, W. *Deutsche Sagen.* Repr. ed. Darmstadt: Wissenschaftliche Buchgesellschaft, 1977.

Große, E. U. *Text und Kommunikation.* Stuttgart: Kohlhammer, 1976.

Gruenwald, I. *Apocalyptic and Merkavah Mysticism.* Leiden: Brill, 1980.

Gruenwald, I. "Apocalypticism, Mysticism, Messianism and Political Assassination." *Criterion* 35 (1996) 11–17.

Gruenwald, I. *From Apocalypticism to Gnosticism.* Frankfurt am Main: Peter Lang, 1988.

Gruenwald, I. "From Priesthood to Messianism: The Anti-Priestly Polemic and the Messianic Factor." *Messiah and Christos: Studies in the Jewish Origins of Christianity Presented to David Flusser.* Ed. I. Gruenwald *et al.* Tübingen: Mohr (Siebeck), 1992, 75–93.

Gruenwald, I. "Midrash and 'The Midrashic Condition': Preliminary Considerations." *The Midrashic Imagination: Jewish Exegesis, Thought and History.* Ed. M. Fishbane. Albany: SUNY, 1993, 6–22.

Gruenwald, I. "Mysticism and Politics in the State of Israel." *Religion and the Political Order: Politics in Classical and Modern Christianity, Islam and Judaism.* Ed. J. Neusner. Atlanta: Scholars Press, 1996, 95–108.

Gruenwald, I. "The Study of Religion and the Religion of Study." *Religious Propaganda and Missionary Competition in the New Testament World: Essays Honoring Dieter Georgi.* Ed. L. Bormann *et al.* Leiden: Brill, 1994.

Grundmann, W. *Das Evangelium nach Matthäus.* THKNT 1. Berlin: Evangelische Verlagsanstalt, 1968.

Guelich, R. A. "The Matthean Beatitudes: 'Entrance Requirements' or Eschatological Blessings?" *JBL* 95 (1976) 415–34.

Guelich, R. *Mark 1–8:26.* WBC 34A. Dallas: Word, 1989.

Gülich, E. and Raible, W. *Linguistische Textmodelle. Grundlagen und Möglichkeiten.* UTB 130. München: Fink, 1977.

Gülich, E. and Raible, W., eds. *Textsorten. Differenzierungskriterien aus linguistischer Sicht.* 2d. ed. Wiesbaden: Athenaion, 1975.

Gummere, R. M., ed. *Seneca: Ad Lucilium epistulae morales.* 3 vols. LCL. Cambridge, MA and London: Harvard University Press, 1953.

Gundry, R. H. *Mark: A Commentary on His Apology for the Cross.* Grand Rapids: Eerdmans, 1993.

Guthrie, W. K. C. *A History of Greek Philosophy.* Vol. 3, *The Fifth-Century Enlightenment.* Cambridge: Cambridge University Press, 1969.

Hachmann, E. *Die Führung des Lesers in Senecas Epistulae morales.* Orbis Antiquus 34. Münster: Aschendorff, 1995.

Hagner, D. A. *Matthew 1–13.* WBC 33A. Dallas: Word Books, 1993.

Halliwell, S. *Aristotle: Poetics.* LCL. Cambridge, MA and London: Harvard University Press, 1995.

Hansen, P. A. *Carmina Epigraphica Graeca Saeculi IV A. Chr. N.* Texte und Kommentar 15. Berlin: de Gruyter, 1989.

Harmon, A. M. *Lucian.* 8 vols. LCL. Cambridge, MA: Harvard University Press, 1979.

Hartman, L. "Doing Things with the Words of Colossians." *Text-Centered New Testament Studies: Text-Theoretical Essays on Early Jewish and Early Christian Literature.* Ed. L. Hartman. WUNT 102. Tübingen: Mohr Siebeck 1997, 195–209.

Hauck, F. and Schulz, S. "πραΰς πραΰτης." *TWNT* 6, ed. G. Kittel and G. Friedrich. Stuttgart: Kohlhammer, 1959, 645–51.

Hauck, F. "πτωχός im Griechischen." *TWNT* 6, ed. G. Kittel and G. Friedrich. Stuttgart: Kohlhammer, 1959, 886–88.

Heckel, T. K. *Der Innere Mensch. Die paulinische Verarbeitung eines platonisches Motivs.* Tübingen: Mohr (Siebeck), 1993.

Hedrick, C. W. *Parables as Poetic Fiction: The Creative Voice of Jesus.* Peabody, MA: Hendrickson, 1994.

Hedrick, C. W. "What is a Gospel? Geography, Time and Narrative Structure." *Perspectives in Religious Studies* 10 (1982) 255–68.

Hefner, R. W., ed. *Conversion to Christianity: Historical and Anthropological Perspectives on a Great Transformation.* Berkeley: University of California Press, 1993.

Heinisch, P. *Die griechische Philosophie im Buche der Weisheit.* Münster: Aschendorff, 1908.

Heitsch, E. "Platons Sprachphilosophie im 'Kratylos'. Überlegungen zu 383a4–b2 und 387d10–390a8." *Hermes* 113 (1985) 44–62.

Hellholm, D. "'Rejoice and Be Glad, for Your Reward is Great in Heaven'. An Attempt at Solving the Structural Problem of Matt 5:11–12." *Festschrift Günter Wagner.* Ed. Faculty of Baptist Theological Seminary, Rüschlikon and Switzerland. International Theological Studies: Contributions of Baptist Scholars 1. Bern: Peter Lang, 1994, 47–86.

Hellholm, D. *Das Visionenbuch des Hermas als Apokalypse. Formgeschichtliche und texttheoretische Studien zu einer literarischen Gattung.* Vol. 1, *Methodologische Vorberlegungen und makrostrukturelle Textanalyse.* CB.NT 13/1. Lund: Gleerup, 1980.

Hellholm, D. "Enthymemic Argumentation in Paul: The Case of Romans 6." *Paul in His Hellenistic Context.* Ed. T. Engberg-Pedersen. Edinburgh: T & T Clark, 1994; Minneapolis: Fortress, 1995, 119–79.

Hellholm, D. "Methodological Reflections on the Problem of Definition of Generic Texts." *Mysteries and Revelations. Apocalyptic Studies since the Uppsala Colloquium.* Ed. J. J. Collins and J. H. Charlesworth. JSPSup 9. Sheffield: Sheffield Academic Press, 1991, 135–63.

Hellholm, D. "Substitutionelle Gliederungsmerkmale und die Komposition des Matthäusevangeliums." *Texts and Contexts: Biblical Texts in Their Textual and Situational Contexts. Essays in Honor of Lars Hartman.* Ed. T. Fornberg and D. Hellholm. Oslo: Scandinavian University Press, 1995, 11–76.

Hellholm, D., ed. *Apocalypticism in the Mediterranean World and the Near East: Proceedings of the International Colloquium on Apocalypticism, Uppsala, August 12–17, 1979.* Tübingen: Mohr (Siebeck), 1983.

Helm, R. "Lukian und die Philosophenschulen." *Neue Jahrbücher für das klassische Altertum* 9 (1902) 188–213; 263–78; 351–69.

Helm, R. *Lukian und Menipp.* Leipzig and Berlin: Teubner, 1906.

Hengel, M. *Between Jesus and Paul.* Philadelphia: Fortress, 1983.

Hengel, M. *Judaica et Hellenistica: Kleine Schriften 1.* Tübingen: Mohr (Siebeck), 1996.

Hengel, M. *The Zealots: Investigations into the Jewish Freedom Movement in the Period from Herod I until 70 A.D.* Edinburgh: T. & T. Clark, 1989.

Hengel, M., in collaboration with Deines, R. *The Pre-Christian Paul.* London: SCM, 1991.

Henrichs, A. "Zwei Fragmente über die Erziehung." *ZPE* 1 (1967) 45–53.

Hentschel, E. and Weydt, W. *Handbuch der deutschen Grammatik.* Berlin and New York: de Gruyter, 1990.

Hesse, B. "Pig Lovers and Pig Haters: Patterns of Palestinian Pork Production." *Journal of Ethnobiology* 10 (1990) 195–225.

Hesse, H. *Weg nach Innen.* West Germany: Deutsche Buch-Gemeinschaft, 1973.

Heubeck, A. and Hoekstra, A. *A Commentary on Homer's Odyssey, 2: Books IX-XIII.* Oxford: Clarendon, 1990.

Heubeck, A., West, S., and Hainsworth, J. B. *A Commentary on Homer's Odyssey, I: Introduction and Books I-VIII.* Oxford: Clarendon, 1990.

Hobsbawm, E. and Ranger, T. *The Invention of Tradition.* Cambridge: Cambridge University Press, 1983.

Hoffmann, P. "QR und der Menschensohn. Eine vorläufige Skizze." *The Four Gospels 1992. FS Frans Neirynck.* Ed. F. Van Segbroeck *et al.* BETL 100-A. Leuven: Peeters, 1992, 421–56.

Hoffmann, P. *Studien zur Frühgeschichte der Jesus-Bewegung.* Stuttgarter Biblische Aufsätze 17. Stuttgart: Katholisches Bibelwerk, 1994.

Hood, R. E. *Begrimed and Black: Christian Traditions on Blacks and Blackness.* Minneapolis: Fortress, 1994.

Horsley, R. A. *Jesus and the Spiral of Violence: Popular Jewish Resistance in Roman Palestine.* San Francisco: Harper & Row, 1987.

Horst, P. van der. *Hellenism – Judaism – Christianity: Essays on Their Interaction.* Kampen: Kok Pharos, 1994.

Horton, R. "African Conversion." *Africa* 41 (1971) 85–108.

Horton, R. "On the Rationality of Conversion." 2 parts. *Africa* 45 (1975) 219–35, 373–399.

Houchins, S. and Wicker, K. O'Brien. "The Blessing of Ham: Re-Sacralizing and Re-Contextualizing the Narrative of Nation." *Research in African Literatures.* Forthcoming.

Hübner, H. *Biblische Theologie des Neuen Testaments.* 3 vols. Göttingen: Vandenhoeck & Ruprecht, 1990–95.

Hübner, H. "Idumea." *ABD* 3, ed. D. N. Freedman. Garden City, NY: Doubleday, 1992, 382–83.

Irmscher, J. *Götterzorn bei Homer.* Leipzig: O. Harrassowitz, 1950.

Isichei, E. *A History of Christianity in Africa.* Grand Rapids: Eerdmans, 1995.

Jaeger, W. *The Theology of the Early Greek Philosophers.* Oxford: Clarendon, 1947.

Jameson, M. H., Jordan, D. R. and Kotansky, R. D. *A* Lex Sacra *from Selinous.* GRBM 11. Durham: Duke University, 1993.

Jeremias, J. *Neutestamentliche Theologie. Erster Teil.* Gütersloh: Mohn, 1971.

Jewett, R. *Dating Paul's Life.* London: SCM, 1979.

Jewett, R. "Paul, Phoebe, and the Spanish Mission." *The Social World of Formative Judaism and Christianity: Essays in Tribute to Howard Clark Kee.* Ed. J. Neusner *et al.* Philadelphia: Fortress, 1988, 142–61.

Johnson, L. T. *The Real Jesus.* San Francisco: Harper San Francisco, 1996.

Jones, C. P. *Culture and Society in Lucian.* Cambridge and London: Harvard University Press, 1986.

Jones, C. P. *Plutarch and Rome.* Oxford: Clarendon, 1971.

Jones, H. L. *The Geography of Strabo.* 8 vols. LCL. London: Heinemann, 1966–70.

Jules-Rosette, B. *African Apostles: Ritual and Conversion in the Church of John Maranke.* Ithaca: Cornell University Press, 1975.

K. Brinker, "Textfunktionen: Ansätze zu ihrer Beschreibung," *ZGL* 11 (1983) 127–48.

Kanngießer, S. "Sprachliche Universalien und diachrone Prozesse." *Theorie-Diskussion. Sprachpragmatik und Philosophie.* Ed. K.-O. Apel.

Theorie-Diskussion. Frankfurt am Main: Suhrkamp, 1976, 273–93.

Kassel, R. and Austin, C., eds. *Poetae Comici Graeci.* Berlin and New York: de Gruyter, 1995.

Keck, L. "Mk 3,7–12 and Mark's Christology." *JBL* 84 (1965) 341–58.

Kee, H. C. *Community of the New Age: Studies in Mark's Gospel.* Philadelphia: Westminster, 1977.

Kelber, W. H. Review of H.-W. Kuhn, *Ältere Sammlungen im Markusevangelium. JBL* 93 (1974) 306–8.

Kelly, J. N. D. *The Pastoral Epistles.* HNTC. San Francisco: Harper & Row, 1960.

Kieffer, R. "Weisheit und Segen als Grundmotive der Seligpreisungen bei Matthäus und Lukas." *Theologie aus dem Norden.* Ed. A. Fuchs. SNTU A.2. Linz: Fuchs, 1977, 29–43.

Kingsbury, J. D. *The Christology of Mark's Gospel.* Philadelphia: Fortress, 1983.

Kingsley, P. *Ancient Philosophy, Mystery and Magic. Empedocles and Pythagorean Tradition.* Oxford: Clarendon, 1995.

Kirby, J. "Cultural Change & Religious Conversion in West Africa." *Religion in Africa: Experience & Expression.* Ed. T. D. Blakely, W. E. A. van Beek and D. L. Thomson. London: James Currey, 1994, 56–71.

Kirk, G. S. *The Bacchae of Euripides.* Englewood Cliffs, NJ: Prentice-Hall, 1970.

Kirk, G. S., Raven, J. E. and Schofield, M. *The Presocratic Philosophers.* 2d ed. Cambridge: Cambridge University Press, 1983.

Klauck, H. J. *Die religiöse Umwelt des Urchristentums II. Herrscher- und Kaiserkult, Philosophie, Gnosis.* Stuttgart: Kohlhammer, 1996.

Kloppenborg, John S. "The Sayings Gospel Q and the Quest of the Historical Jesus." *HTR* 89 (1996) 307–44.

Klostermann, E. *Das Matthäusevangelium.* 4th ed. HNT 5. Tübingen: Mohr (Siebeck), 1971.

Knox, R. A. *Enthusiasm: A Chapter in the History of Religion.* Oxford: Clarendon, 1950.

Kodjak, A. *A Structural Analysis of the Sermon on the Mount.* Berlin: de Gruyter, 1986.

Koester, H. *Ancient Christian Gospels: Their History and Development.* Philadelphia: Trinity, 1990.

Koester, H. "The Sayings Gospel Q and the Quest of the Historical Jesus: A Response to John S. Kloppenborg." *HTR* 89 (1996) 345–49.

Kollmann, B. *Jesus und die Christen als Wundertäter. Studien zu Magie, Medizin und Schamanismus in Antike und Christentum.* FRLANT 170. Göttingen: Vandenhoeck & Ruprecht, 1996.

Kotansky, R. "Greek Exorcistic Amulets." *Ancient Magic & Ritual Power.* Ed. M. Meyer and P. Mirecki. RGRW 129. Leiden: Brill, 1995.

Kotansky, R. *Greek Magical Amulets. The Inscribed Gold, Silver, Copper, and Bronze Lamellae, I: Published Texts of Known Provenance.* Abhandlungen der Nordrhein-Westfälischen Akademie der Wissenschaften. Sonderreihe Papyrologica Coloniensia 22/1. Opladen: Westdeutscher, 1994.

Kraemer, H. J. *Platonismus und die hellenistische Philosophie.* Berlin and New York: de Gruyter, 1971.

Kuhn, H.-W. *Ältere Sammlungen im Markusevangelium.* SUNT 8. Göttingen: Vandenhoeck & Ruprecht, 1971.

Kümmel, W. G. *Introduction to the New Testament.* Rev. and ed. P. Feine and J. Behm. Nashville: Abingdon, 1973.

Kutschera, F. von. *Sprachphilosophie.* 2d ed. UTB 80. München: Fink, 1975.

Kvalbein, H. "Die Wunder der Endzeit: Beobachtungen zu 4Q521." Paper presented at the Society for New Testament Studies Annual Meeting. Strasbourg, 1996.

Kyriakou, P. "ΚΑΤΑΒΑΣΙΣ and the Underworld in the *Argonautica* of Apollonius Rhodius." *Philologus* 139 (1995) 256–64.

Lachs, S. T. *A Rabbinic Commentary on the New Testament. The Gospels of Matthew, Mark, and Luke.* Hoboken: KTAV, 1987.

Laitin, D. *Hegemony and Culture: Politics and Religious Change among the Yoruba.* Chicago and London: The University of Chicago Press, 1986.

Landau, P. S. *The Realm of the Word: Language, Gender, and Christianity in a Southern African Kingdom.* London: James Currey, 1995.

Lang, F. G. "'Über Sidon mitten ins Gebiet der Dekapolis'. Geographie und Theologie in Markus 7,31." *ZDPV* 94 (1978) 145–60.

Lanig, K. *Der handelnde Mensch in der Ilias.* Ph. D. Dissertation, Erlangen, 1953.

Lanternari, V. *Movimenti religiosi di libertà e di salvezza dei popoli oppressi.* Milano: Feltrinelli, 1960.

Larcher, C. *Études sur le Livre de la Sagesse.* Paris: Gabalda, 1969.

Lausberg, H. *Elemente der literarischen Rhetorik.* München: Hüber, 1963.

Ledergerber, J. *Lukian und die altattische Komödie.* Einsiedeln: Benziger, 1905.

Lesky, A. *Göttliche und menschliche Motivation im homerischen Epos.* SHAW 4. Heidelberg: Carl Winter Universitätsverlag, 1961.

Levenson, J. D. *The Death and Resurrection of the Beloved Son: The Transformation of Child Sacrifice in Judaism and Christianity*. New Haven: Yale University Press, 1993.

Levenson, J. D. "The Jerusalem Temple in Devotional and Visionary Experience." *Jewish Spirituality: From the Bible Through the Middle Ages*. Ed. A. Green. London: Routledge & Kegan Paul, 1986, 32–61.

Levin, S. *Semitic and Indo-European. The Principal Etymologies*. Amsterdam Studies in the Theory and History of Linguistic Science IV/129. Amsterdam: Benjamins, 1995.

Lewis, E. "The Stoics on Identity and Individuation." *Phronesis* 40 (1995) 89–108.

Lipsius, R. A. and Bonnet, M., eds. *Acta Apostolorum Apocrypha*. Repr. ed. Darmstadt: Wissenschaftliche Buchgesellschaft, 1959.

Lloyd-Jones, H. *The Justice of Zeus*. Berkeley: University of California Press, 1971.

Lohmeyer, E. *Das Evangelium des Markus*. Göttingen: Vandenhoeck & Ruprecht, 1957.

Londey, D. and Johanson, C. *The Logic of Apuleius, Including a Complete Latin Text and English Translation of the* Peri Hermeneias *of Apuleius of Madaura*. PhAnt 47. Leiden, etc.: Brill, 1987.

Long, H. S. "A Study of the Doctrine of Metempsychosis in Greece from Pythagoras to Plato." Thesis, Princeton University, 1948.

Long, H. S., ed. *Diogenes Laertius. Vitae philosophorum*. 2 vols. Oxford: Clarendon, 1964.

Louw, J. P. and Nida, E. A. *Greek-English Lexicon of the New Testament Based on Semantic Domains*. 2 vols. New York: United Bible Societies, 1988.

Ludwig, W. "Plato's Love Epigrams." *GRBS* 4 (1963) 59–82.

Luedemann, G. *The Resurrection of Jesus: History, Experience, Theology*. Minneapolis: Fortress, 1994.

Lührmann, D. *Das Markusevangelium*. HNT 3. Tübingen: Mohr (Siebeck), 1987.

Lührmann, D. *Die Redaktion der Logienquelle*. WMANT 33. Neukirchen-Vluyn: Neukirchener, 1969.

Luschnat, O. "Das Problem des ethischen Fortschritts in der alten Stoa." *Philologus* 102 (1958) 178–214.

Luz, U. *Das Matthäusevangelium. 1. Teilband Mt 1–7*. EKKNT 1/1. Zürich: Benziger and Neukirchen: Neukirchener, 1985.

Luz, U. *Die Jesusgeschichte des Matthäus*. Neukirchen-Vluyn: Neukirchener, 1993.

Luz, U. "Die Wundergeschichten von Mt 8–9." *Tradition and Interpretation in the New Testament: Essays in Honor of E. Earle Ellis for his 60th Birthday*. Ed. G. F. Hawthorne and O. Betz. Grand Rapids: Eerdmans, 1987, 149–65.

Luz, U. "Fiktivität und Traditionstreue im Matthäusevangelium im Lichte griechischer Literatur." *ZNW* 84 (1993) 153–77.

Luz, U. *Matthew 1–7: A Commentary*. Minneapolis: Augsburg, 1989.

Lyons, J. *Semantics, volume 1*. Cambridge: Cambridge University Press, 1977.

MacDonald, D. R. *The Acts of Andrew and the Acts of Andrew and Matthias in the City of the Cannibals*. Society of Biblical Literature Texts and Translations 33; Christian Apocrypha 1. Atlanta: Scholars Press, 1990.

Mack, Burton L. *A Myth of Innocence: Mark and Christian Origins*. Philadelphia: Fortress, 1988.

MacMullen, R. *Christianizing the Roman Empire: A.D. 100–400*. New Haven: Yale University Press, 1984.

Maier, J. *Die Texte vom Toten Meer*. München: Reinhardt, 1960.

Malbon, E. Struthers. "Galilee and Jerusalem: History and Literature in Marcan Interpretation." *CBQ* 44 (1982) 242–55.

Malbon, E. Struthers. *Narrative Space and Mythic Meaning in Mark*. San Francisco: Harper & Row, 1986.

Malherbe, A. "'Gentle as a Nurse': The Cynic Background to 1 Thessalonians 2." *NovT* 12 (1970) 203–17. Reprinted in *idem*, *Paul and the Popular Philosophers*. Minneapolis: Fortress, 1989, 35–48.

Malherbe, A. *Moral Exhortations*. Library of Early Christianity. Philadelphia: Westminster, 1986.

Malherbe, A. *Paul and the Thessalonians: The Philosophic Tradition of Pastoral Care*. Philadelphia: Fortress, 1987.

Manson, T. W. *The Sayings of Jesus*. London: SCM, 1949.

Marange, J. *The New Witness of the Apostles*. Marange: Bocha, c. 1953.

Marcus, J. "Modern and Ancient Jewish Apocalypticism." *JR* 76 (1996) 1–27.

Markschies, C. "Die platonische Metapher vom 'inneren Menschen'. Eine Brücke zwischen antiker Philosophie und altchristlicher Theologie." *ZKG* 105 (1994) 1–17.

Markschies, C. "Innerer Mensch," *RAC* 18, ed. E. Dassmann. Stuttgart: Hiersemann, 1997, 266–312.

Marshall, R. "Power in the Name of Jesus." *Review of African Political Economy* 52 (1991) 21–37.

Martin-Achard, R. "ענה II elend sein." *THAT* 2, ed. E. Jenni and C. Westermann. München: Kaiser; Zürich: Theologischer Verlag, 1976, 341–50.

Marxsen, W. *Der Evangelist Markus: Studien zur Redaktionsgeschichte des Evangeliums.* Göttingen: Vandenhoeck & Ruprecht, 1959.

Maurach, G. *Der Bau von Senecas* Epistulae morales. Heidelberg: Winter, 1970.

McCown, C. C. "Gospel Geography, Fiction, Fact and Central Section." *JBL* 57 (1938) 51–66.

McRay, J. "Gerasenes." *ABD* 2, ed. D. N. Freedman. Garden City, NY: Doubleday, 1992, 991.

Merkelbach, R. *Roman und Mysterium in der Antike.* München: Beck, 1962.

Merkelbach, R., and West, M. L. *Fragmenta Hesiodea.* Oxford: Clarendon, 1967.

Merklein, H. "πτωχός κτλ." *EWNT* 3, H. Balz and G. Schneider. Stuttgart: Kohlhammer, 1983, 193–95.

Mesk, J. "Lukians *Nigrinus* und Iuvenal." *Wiener Studien* 34 (1912) 373–82; 35 (1913) 1–33.

Metzger, B. M. *A Textual Commentary on the Greek New Testament.* 2nd ed. Stuttgart: Deutsche Bibelgesellschaft, 1994.

Metzger, B. M. *The Text of the New Testament. Its Transmission, Corruption and Restoration.* 3d ed. New York: Oxford, 1992.

Meuli, K. *Gesammelte Schriften.* Basel: Schwabe, 1975.

Meyer, B. "'Delivered from the Powers of Darkness': Confessions of Satanic Riches in Christian Ghana." *Africa* 62 (1995) 236–255.

Meyer, B. "'If You are a Devil, You are a Witch and if You are a Witch, You are a Devil.': The Integration of 'Pagan' Ideas into the Conceptual Universe of Ewe Christians in Southeastern Ghana." *Journal of Religion in Africa* 22 (1992) 98–132.

Meyer, B. "'Komm herüber und hilf uns' of hoe zendelingen de Ewe met andere ogen gingen bekijken." *Etnofoor* 2 (1989) 91–111.

Meyer, B. "African Pentecostal Churches, Satan and the Dissociation from Tradition." Paper presented at the American Anthropological Association. November, 1995.

Meyer, B. "Beyond Syncretism: Translation and Diabolization in the Appropriation of Protestantism in Africa." *Syncretism/Anti-syncretism: The Politics of Religious Synthesis.* Ed. C. Stewart and R. Shaw. London and New York: Routledge, 1994, 45–68.

Meyer, B. "Commodities and the Power of Prayer: Pentecostalist Attitudes Towards Consumption in Contemporary Ghana." Paper presented at the "Globalization and the Construction of Communal Identities" Conference. Amsterdam, 1996.

Meyer, B. "Magic, Mermaids and Modernity: The Attraction of Pentecostalism in Africa." *Etnofoor* 8 (1995) 47–67.

Meyer, B. "Translating the Devil. An African Appropriation of Pietist Protestantism. The Case of the Peki Ewe, 1847–1992." Ph.D. Dissertation, The University of Amsterdam, 1995.

Meyer, M. *The Gospel of Thomas: The Hidden Sayings of Jesus.* San Francisco, CA: Harper, 1992.

Meyers, E. M., ed. *The Oxford Encyclopedia of Archaeology in the Near East.* 5 vols. New York and Oxford: Oxford University, 1997.

Mitchell, M. M. "Rhetorical Shorthand in Pauline Argumentation: The Functions of 'The Gospel' in the Corinthian Correspondence." *Gospel in Paul.* Ed. A. Jervis and P. Richardson. JSNTSup 108. Sheffield: Sheffield Academic Press, 1994.

Mobley, G. "The Wild Man in the Bible and the Ancient Near East." *JBL* 116 (1997) 217–33.

Moffitt, J. F. "Philostratus and the Canaries." *Gerion* 8 (1993) 241–61.

Mooney, J. *The Ghost-Dance Religion and the Sioux Outbreak of 1890.* Washington: Government Printing Office, 1896.

Moscati, S., *et al.*, eds. *The Phoenicians.* New York: Abbeville, 1988.

Mowinckel, S. *He That Cometh.* Oxford: Basil Blackwell, 1959.

Mühll, P. von der. *Epicuri Epistulae tres et ratae sententiae.* Stuttgart: Teubner, 1975.

Müller, K. *Geographi Graeci Minores, I.* Hildesheim: Georg Olms Repr., 1855.

Müller, W. G. "Der Brief als Spiegel der Seele. Zur Geschichte eines Topos der Epistolartheorie von der Antike bis zu Samuel Richardson." *Antike und Abendland* 26 (1980) 138–57.

Murray, A. T. *The Odyssey: Homer.* 2 vols. LCL. Cambridge, MA: Harvard University Press, 1960–75.

Neirynck, F. "Q: From Source to Gospel." *ETL* 71 (1995) 421–30.

Neirynck, F. "The First Synoptic Pericope: The Appearance of John the Baptist in Q?" *ETL* 72 (1996) 41–74.

Newsom, C. *Songs of the Sabbath Sacrifice: A Critical Edition.* Atlanta: Scholars Press, 1985.

Nickelsburg, G. W. E. "Scripture in *1 Enoch* and *1 Enoch* as Scripture." *Texts and Contexts: Biblical Texts in Their Textual and Situational Contexts. Essays in Honor of Lars Hartman.* Ed. T. Fornberg and D. Hellholm. Oslo: Scandinavian University Press, 1995, 333–54.

Nickelsburg, G. W. E. "The Bible Rewritten and Expanded." *Jewish Writings of the Second Temple Period.* Ed. M. E. Stone. CRINT 2/2. Assen: Van Gorcum, 1984, 89–156.

Nickelsburg, G.W.E., ed. *Studies in the Testament of Moses.* Cambridge, MA: Society of Biblical Literature, 1973.

Nineham, D. E. *Saint Mark.* Philadelphia: Westminster, 1963.

Nobbe, C. F. A., ed. *Geographia*. 3 vols. Leipzig: O. Holtze, 1843–45.

Nock, A. D. *Conversion. The Old and the New in Religion from Alexander the Great to Augustine of Hippo*. London, Oxford and New York: Oxford University Press, 1972.

O'Leary, S. D. *Arguing the Apocalypse: A Theory of Millennial Rhetoric*. New York: Oxford University Press, 1994.

Oberbreyer, M., ed. *Lucian's ausgewählte Schriften*. Trans. C. M. Weiland. Leipzig: P. Reclam, 1877.

Olupona, J. K. *Kingship, Religion, and Rituals in a Nigerian Community: A Phenomenological Study of Ondo Yoruba Festivals*. Stockholm Studies in Comparative Religion 28. Stockholm: Almqvist & Wiksell International, 1991.

Opelt, I. "Epitome." *RAC* 5, ed. T. Klauser. Stuttgart: Hiersemann, 1962, 944–73.

Opoku, K. A. "The West Through African Eyes." *The International Journal of Africana Studies*. 4.1–2 (1996) 82–97.

Opoku, K. A. *West African Traditional Religion*. Accra: FEP International Private Limited, 1978.

Osten-Sacken, P. von der. *Die Apokalyptik in ihrem Verhältnis zur Prophetie und Weisheit*. München: Kaiser, 1969.

Padel, R. *In and out of the Mind. Greek Images of the Tragic Self*. Princeton, NJ: Princeton University Press, 1992.

Pagels, E. "The Social History of Satan, the 'Intimate Enemy': A Preliminary Sketch." *HTR* 84 (1991) 105–128.

Park, E. C. *The Mission Discourse in Matthew's Interpretation*. WUNT 2/81. Tübingen: Mohr (Siebeck), 1995.

Parsons, N. *A New History of Southern Africa*. New York: Holmes & Meier, 1983.

Peel, J. D. Y. "Conversion and Tradition in Two African Societies: Ijebu and Buganda." *Past and Present* 76 (1977) 109–141.

Pelikan, J. *Christianity and Classical Culture. The Metamorphosis of Natural Theology in the Christian Encounter with Hellenism*. New Haven: Yale University Press, 1993.

Pelliccia, H. *Mind, Body, and Speech in Homer and Pindar*. Göttingen: Vandenhoeck & Ruprecht, 1995.

Penella, R. J. *The Letters of Apollonius of Tyana. A Critical Edition with Prolegomena, Translation and Commentary*. Mnemosyne 56. Leiden: Brill, 1979.

Perry, B. E., ed. *Aesopica*. Vol. 1, *Greek and Latin Texts*. Urbana, IL: University of Illinois Press, 1952.

Pesch, R. *Das Markusevangelium*. 3d. ed. HTKNT 2/1–2. Freiburg: Herder, 1980.

Pfohl, G. ed., *Das Epigramm: Zur Geschichte einer inschriftlichen und literarischen Gattung.* Darmstadt: Wissenschaftliche Buchgesellschaft 1969.

Platvoet, J. G., *et al.*, eds. *The Study of Religions in Africa: Past, Present and Prospects.* Cambridge: Roots & Branches; Harare: University of Zimbabwe Press, 1996.

Plett, H. F., ed. *Intertextuality.* Research in Text Theory 15. Berlin and New York: de Gruyter, 1991.

Powell, M. A. "Matthew's Beatitudes: Reversals and Rewards of the Kingdom." *CBQ* 58 (1996) 460–79.

Quintero, P. *Cádiz. Primeros Pobladores: Hallazgos Arqueológicos.* Cádiz: Manuel Alvarez, 1917.

Quintero, P. *Necrópolis Ante-Romana de Cádiz. Descripción de las excavaciones efectuadas, acompañada de un estudio de D. Antonio Vives sobre las monedas antiquas Gades.* Madrid: Hauser y Menet, 1915.

Rad, G. von. *Holy War in Ancient Israel.* Grand Rapids: Eerdmans, 1991.

Rambo, L. R. "Conversion." *The Encyclopedia of Religion* 4, ed. M. Eliade. New York: MacMillan; London: Collier Macmillan, 1987, 73–78.

Rambo, L. R. *Understanding Religious Conversion.* New Haven and London: Yale University Press, 1993.

Ramin, J. *Le Périple d' Hannon / The Periplus of Hanno.* British Archaeological Reports Supplementary Series 23. Oxford: British Archaeological Reports, 1976.

Ranger, T. "The Local and the Global in Southern African Religious History." *Conversion to Christianity: Historical and Anthropological Perspectives on a Great Transformation.* Ed. R. W. Hefner. Berkeley: University of California Press, 1993, 65–98.

Rappe, G. *Archaische Leiberfahrung. Der Leib in der frühgriechischen Philosophie und in außereuropäischen Kulturen.* Berlin: Akademie Verlag, 1995.

Rau, E. *Kosmologie, Eschatologie und die Lehrautorität Henochs.* Ph.D. Dissertation, Hamburg, 1974.

Rausch, D. A. *Messianic Judaism: Its History, Theology, and Polity.* Texts and Studies in Religion, 14. New York: Mellon, 1982.

Ravitzky, A. *Messianism, Zionism, and Jewish Religious Radicalism.* Chicago: University of Chicago Press, 1996.

Reider, J. *The Book of Wisdom.* New York: Harper, 1957.

Rein, T. W. *Sprichwörter und sprichwörtliche Redensarten bei Lucian.* Tübingen: Mohr (Siebeck), 1894.

Reinhard, K. *Aischylos als Regisseur und Theologe.* Bern: A. Francke, 1949.

Reynolds, L. D., ed. *L. Annaei Senecae ad Lucilium epistula morales.* 2 vols. Oxford: Clarendon, 1965.

Rist, J. M. *Augustine. Ancient Thought Baptized.* Cambridge: Cambridge University Press, 1994.

Rist, J. M. *Epicurus: An Introduction.* Cambridge: Cambridge University Press, 1972.

Rist, J. M. "Seneca and Stoic Orthodoxy," *ANRW* 2.36.3, ed. W. Haase and H. Temporini. Berlin and New York: de Gruyter, 1989, 1993–2012.

Rist, J. M. *Stoic Philosophy.* Repr. ed. Cambridge: Cambridge University Press, 1980.

Ritschl, D. *The Logic of Theology.* London: SCM, 1986.

Ritschl, D. "'Wahre,' 'reine' oder 'neue' biblische Theologie? Einige Anfragen zur neueren Diskussion um 'biblische Theologie.'" *JBTh* 1 (1986) 135–50.

Robinson, C. *Lucian and His Influence in Europe.* Chapel Hill: University of North Carolina Press, 1979.

Robinson, J. M. "The *Incipit* of the Sayings Gospel Q." *Hommage à Étienne Trocmé. RHPR* 75 (1995) 9–33.

Robinson, J. M. "The Sayings Gospel Q." *The Four Gospels 1992. FS Frans Neirynck.* Ed. F. Van Segbroeck *et al.* BETL 100-A. Leuven: Peeters, 1992, 361–88.

Robinson, J. M. "The Sequence of Q: The Lament over Jerusalem." *Von Jesus zum Christus: Christologische Studien für Paul Hoffmann.* Ed. U. Busse and R. Hoppe. New York: de Gruyter, 1998.

Robinson, J. M., ed. *The Nag Hammadi Library in English.* Rev. ed. Leiden: Brill, 1988.

Rolf, E. "Eine handlungsanalytische Kritik der Sprechakttheorie." *Linguistische Berichte* 106 (1986) 470–83.

Rolke, K.-H. *Die bildhaften Vergleiche in den Fragmenten der Stoiker von Zenon bis Panaitios.* Hildesheim and New York: Olms, 1975.

Romm, J. S. *The Edges of the Earth in Ancient Thought: Geography, Exploration, and Fiction.* Princeton: Princeton University Press, 1992.

Rose, H. J. and Robertson, C. M. "Heracles" *OCD* 2d ed. Ed. H. H. Scullard. Oxford: Clarendon, 1970, 498–99.

Rose, V., ed., *Aristotelis. Fragmenta.* 3d. ed. Leipzig: Teubner, 1886.

Rosengren, I. "Hierarchisierung und Sequenzierung von Illokutionen: zwei interdependente Strukturierungsprinzipien bei der Textproduktion." *Zeitschrift für Phonetik, Sprachwissenschaft und Kommunikationsforschung* 40 (1987) 28–44.

Ross, W. D., ed. *Aristotelis. Fragmenta Selecta.* Oxford: Clarendon, 1955.

Rowland, C. *Radical Christianity.* Maryknoll: Orbis, 1988.

Rowland, C. *The Open Heaven: A Study of Apocalyptic in Judaism and Early Christianity.* New York: Crossroads, 1982.

Russo, J., Fernandez-Galiano, M., and Heubeck, A. *A Commentary on Homer's Odyssey, Volume III: Books XVII-XXIV*. Oxford: Clarendon, 1992.

Sandbach, F. H. *The Stoics*. Bristol: Bristol Press, 1989.

Sandys, J. E. *The Odes of Pindar. Including the Prinicíple Fragments*. Rev. ed. LCL. Cambridge, MA: Harvard University Press, 1961.

Sanneh, L. "Theology and the Challenge of Ethnicity: The Ethnic Issues in Bible Translation with Reference to Africa." Paper presented at the Yale-Edinburgh Conference. 1996.

Sanneh, L. *Translating the Message. The Missionary Impact on Culture*. ASMS 13. Maryknoll, NY: Orbis, 1989.

Sanneh, L. *West African Christianity: The Religious Impact*. Maryknoll, NY: Orbis, 1983.

Saussure, F. de. *Course in General Linguistics*. New York: McGraw-Hill, 1966.

Schenk, W. *Die Sprache des Matthäus. Die Text-Konstituenten in ihren makro- und mikrostrukturellen Relationen*. Göttingen: Vandenhoeck & Ruprecht, 1987.

Schmid, W. "Epikur." *RAC* 5, ed. T. Klauser. Stuttgart: Hiersemann, 1962, 682–819.

Schmidt, K. L. *Der Rahmen der Geschichte Jesu*. Repr. ed. Darmstadt: Wissenschaftliche Buchgesellschaft, 1964.

Schmidt, O. *Metapher und Gleichnis in den Schriften Lucians*. Winterhus: Geschwister Ziegler, 1897.

Schmitt, A. *Selbständigkeit und Abhängigkeit menschlichen Handelns bei Homer*. AAWM 5. Mainz: Akademie der Wissenschaften und der Literatur, 1990.

Schneck, R. *Isaiah in the Gospel of Mark, I-VIII*. BIBAL Dissertation Series 1. Vallejo: BIBAL, 1994.

Scholem, G. *Jewish Gnosticism, Merkabah Mysticism, and Talmudic Tradition*. New York: The Jewish Theological Seminary of America, 1960.

Schoo, J. "Herakles im fernen Westen der alten Welt." *Mnemosyne* 7 (1938) 1–24.

Schulz, S. *Die Spruchquelle der Evangelisten*. Zürich: Theologischer Verlag, 1972.

Schumate, N. *Crisis and Conversion in Apuleius' Metamorphoses*. Ann Arbor: University of Michigan Press, 1996.

Schürer, E. *The History of the Jewish People in the Age of Jesus Christ*. 3 vols. Rev. and ed. G. Vermes, F. Millar and M. Black. Edinburgh: T. & T. Clark, 1973–87.

Schürmann, H. *Das Lukasevangelium. Erster Teil*. HTKNT 3. Freiburg: Herder, 1969.

Schürmann, H. *Das Lukasevangelium. Zweiter Teil. Erste Folge.* HTKNT 3.2/1. Freiburg: Herder, 1994.

Schweizer, E. "πνεῦμα κτλ." *TWNT* 6, ed. G. Kittel and G. Friedrich. Stuttgart: Kohlhammer, 1959, 330–453.

Schweizer, E. *The Good News according to Matthew.* Atlanta: John Knox Press, 1975.

Schweizer, E. *Das Evangelium nach Matthäus.* NTD 2. Göttingen: Vandenhoeck & Ruprecht, 1973.

Schweizer, E. "Formgeschichtliches zu den Seligpreisungen Jesu." *NTS* 19 (1973) 121–26.

Schweizer, E. *The Good News According to Mark.* Atlanta: John Knox, 1970.

Searle, J. R. and Vanderveken, D. *Foundations of Illocutionary Logic.* Cambridge: Cambridge University Press, 1985.

Searle, J. R. *Expression and Meaning: Studies in the Theory of Speech Acts.* Cambridge: Cambridge University Press, 1985.

Searle, J. R. *Intentionality. An Essay in the Philosophy of Mind.* Cambridge: Cambridge University Press, 1985.

Searle, J. R. *Speech Acts.* Cambridge: Cambridge University Press, 1969.

Searle, J. R., ed. *The Philosophy of Language.* Oxford Readings in Philosophy. Oxford: Oxford University Press, 1974.

Seaton, R. C. *Apollonius Rhodius. The Argonautica.* LCL. Cambridge, MA: Harvard University Press, 1961.

Segal, A. F. *Paul the Convert: The Apostolate and Apostasy of Saul the Pharisee.* New Haven: Yale University Press, 1990.

Segal, C. *Singers, Heroes, and Gods in the Odyssey.* Ithaca and London: Cornell University, 1994.

Silberling, K. J. "Orality and Intertextuality in Matthew: A Case for Literary Stratigraphy in the Gospel of Matthew." Ph.D. Dissertation, Claremont Graduate School, 1997.

Smend, R. "Theologie im AT." *Die Mitte des Alten Testaments.* Ed. R. Smend. Munich: Kaiser, 1986, 104–17. Reprinted in *Verifikationen: Festschrift für Gerhard Ebeling zum 70. Geburtstag.* Ed. E. Jüngel *et al.* Tübingen: Mohr, 1982, 11–26.

Smith, E. J. "Note. On Lucian's *Nigrinos.*" *AJP* 18 (1897) 339–41.

Smith, M. *Clement of Alexandria and a Secret Gospel of Mark.* Cambridge: Harvard University Press, 1973.

Smith, M. "Pseudepigraphy in the Israelite Literary Tradition." *Pseudepigrapha I: Pseudopythagorica, lettres de Platon, literature pseudepigraphe juive.* Ed. K. von Fritz. Entretiens sur l'antiquité classique 18. Geneva: Fondation Hardt, 1972, 191–227.

Snell, B. *The Discovery of the Mind.* Oxford: Blackwell, 1953. German original, *Die Entdeckung des Geistes.* Hamburg: Claaszen & Goverts, 1946; 4th ed. repr., Göttingen: Vandenhoeck & Ruprecht, 1975.

Snell, B., ed. *Lexikon des frühgriechischen Epos.* Göttingen: Vandenhoeck und Ruprecht, 1955-.

Snow, D. and Machalek, R. "The Convert as a Social Type." *Sociological Theory.* Ed. R. Collins. San Francisco: Jossey-Bass, 1983.

Sourvinou-Inwood, C. *'Reading' Greek Death: To the End of the Classical Period.* Oxford: Clarendon, 1995.

Stanford, W. B. *Aristophanes, The Frogs.* 2d. ed. Basinstoke and London: Macmillan, 1963.

Stanton, G. N. Review of H. D. Betz, *Essays on the Sermon on the Mount. JTS* 37 (1986) 521–23.

Stegemann, H. "Der lehrende Jesus. Der sogennante biblische Christus und die geschichtliche Botschaft Jesu von der Gottesherrschaft." *NZSTh* 24 (1982) 3–20.

Stegemann, H. *Die Essener, Qumran, Johannes der Täufer und Jesus. Ein Sachbuch.* 4th ed. Herder Spektrum 4128. Freiburg: Herder, 1994.

Steinmetz, P. "Die Stoa." *Grundriss der Geschichte der Philosophie. Begründet von F. Ueberweg. Völlig neu bearbeitete Ausgabe. Die Philosophie der Antike.* Vol. 4/2. Ed. H. Flashar. Basel: Schwabe, 1994, 495–716.

Stendahl, K. "Matthew." *Peake's Commentary on the Bible.* Ed. M. Black and H. H. Rowley. Middlesex: Nelson, 1962.

Stendahl, K. *Paul Among Jews and Gentiles and Other Essays.* Philadelphia: Fortress, 1976.

Stone, M. E. *Selected Studies in Pseudepigrapha and Apocrypha.* Leiden: Brill, 1991.

Strecker, G. *Die Bergpredigt. Ein exegetischer Kommentar.* 2d ed. Göttingen: Vandenhoeck & Ruprecht, 1985.

Strecker, G. "μακαρισμός." *EWNT* 2, ed. H. Balz and G. Schneider. Stuttgart: Kohlhammer, 1981, 926–32.

Streeter, B. H. *The Four Gospels.* London: Macmillan, 1924.

Strugnell, J. "Moses the Pseudepigrapher at Qumran." In idem, "4QApocryphon of Moses[b?]," in *Qumran Cave 4: XIV, Parabiblical Texts, Part 2.* DJD 19. Oxford: Clarendon, 1995, 131–36.

Stückelberger, A. "Seneca: Der Brief als Mittel der persönlichen Auseinandersetzung mit der Philosophie." *Didactica Classica Gandensia* 20 (1980) 133–48.

Syme, R. and Collingwood. R. G. "The Northern Frontiers From Tiberius to Nero." *CAH* 10, ed. S. A. Cook *et al.* Cambridge: Cambridge University Press, 1952, 781–805.

Szlezák, T. A. "Unsterblichkeit und Trichotomie der Seele im zehnten Buch der Politeia." *Phronesis* 21 (1976) 31–58.

Tabor, J. and Gallagher, E. *Why Waco? Cults and the Battle for Religious Freedom in America.* Berkeley: University of California Press, 1995.

Talmon, J. L. *Political Messianism: The Romantic Phase.* New York: Praeger, 1960.

Talmon, J. L. *The Origins of Totalitarian Democracy.* New York: Praeger, 1960.

Taubes, J. *Abendländische Eschatologie.* Bern: A. Francke, 1947.

Taylor, V. *The Formation of the Gospel Tradition.* London: Macmillan, 1953.

Taylor, V. "The Original Order of Q." *New Testament Essays: Studies in Memory of T. W. Manson, 1893–1958.* Ed. A. J. B. Higgins. Manchester: Manchester University Press, 1959, 246–69. Repinted in *idem, New Testmaent Essays,* 95–118.

Theißen, G. "Meer und See in den Evangelien: Ein Beitrag zur Lokalkoloritforschung." *SNTU* 10 (1976) 5–25.

Theißen, G. *The Gospels in Context: Social and Political History in the Synoptic Tradition.* Minneapolis: Fortress, 1991.

Theißen, G. and Merz, A. *Der historische Jesus.* Göttingen: Vandenhoeck & Ruprecht, 1996.

Theißen, G. "Jünger als Gewalttäter (Mt 11,12f.; Lk 16,16)." *Mighty Minorities? Minorities in Early Christianity: Positions and Strategies. Essays in Honor of Jacob Jervell on his 70th Birthday, 21 May 1995. ST* 49, ed. D. Hellholm *et al.* Oslo, etc.: Scandinavian University Press, 1995, 183–200.

Thesleff, H., ed. *The Pythagorean Texts of the Hellenistic Period.* Abo: Akademie, 1965.

Thraede, Klaus. *Grundzüge griechisch-römischer Brieftopik.* Zetemata 48. München: Beck, 1970.

Tilborg, S. van. *Reading John in Ephesus.* NovTSup 83. Leiden: E. J. Brill, 1996.

Trapp, M. B., ed. *Maximus of Tyre*: The Philosophical Orations. *Translated with an Introduction and Notes.* Oxford: Clarendon, 1997.

Trier, J. *Der deutsche Wortschatz im Sinnbezirk des Verstandes, Band I.* Heidelberg: C. Winter, 1931.

Trobisch, D. *Die Entstehung der Paulusbriefsammlung: Studien zu den Anfängen christlicher Publizistik.* NTOA 10. Göttingen: Vandenhoeck & Ruprecht, 1989.

Trocmé, E. *La Formation de l'Évangile selon Marc.* EHPR 57. Paris: Presses Universitaires de France, 1963.

Tsafrir Y. and Di Segni, L. *Survey of Israel: Iudaea Palestina. Eretz Israel during the Hellenistic, Roman and Byzantine Periods.* Jerusalem: Israel Academy of Sciences and Humanities, 1993.

Tsekourakis, D. *Studies in the Terminology of Early Stoic Ethics.* Hermes Einzelschriften 32. Wiesbaden: Steiner, 1974.

Tsirkin, J. B. "The Labours, Death and Resurrection of Melqart as Depicted on the Gates of the Gades Herakleion." *RSF* 9 (1981) 21–27.

Tsirkin, J. B. "The Phoenician Civilization in Roman Spain." *Gerion* 3 (1985) 246–70.

Tuckett, C. M. *Q and the History of Early Christianity.* Edinburgh: T & T Clark; Peabody, MA: Hendrickson, 1996.

Ulkan, M. *Zur Klassifikation von Sprechakten. Eine grundlagentheoretische Fallstudie.* Linguistische Arbeiten 174. Tübingen: Niemeyer, 1992.

Verstraelen-Gilhuis, G. *From Dutch Mission Church to Reformed Church in Zambia: The Scope for African Leadership and Initiative in the History of a Zambian Mission Church.* Netherlands: T. Wever, Franeker, 1982.

Verstraelen-Gilhuis, G. "Rewriting the History of Christianity in Africa." *A New Look at Christianity in Africa.* Ed. G. Verstraelen-Gilhuis. Gweru: Mambo, 1992.

Vielhauer, P. *Geschichte der urchristlichen Literatur.* de Gruyter Lehrbuch. Berlin and New York: de Gruyter, 1975.

Viviano, B. T. "Eight Beatitudes in Qumran and in Matthew. A New Publication from Cave 4." *SEÅ* 58 (1993) 71–84.

Voegelin, E. *Science, Politics and Gnosticism: Two Essays.* A Gateway Edition 6118. Chicago: H. Regnery Co., 1968.

Voelke, A. J. *L'idée de volonté dans le stoicisme.* Paris: Presses Universitaires de France, 1973.

Voigt, C. *Überlegung und Entscheidung. Studien zur Selbstauffassung des Menschen bei Homer.* Repr. ed. Meisenheim: A. Hain, 1972.

Voigt, E., ed. *Sappho et Alcaeus.* Amsterdam: Athenaeum, 1971.

Wagenvoort, H. "The Journey of the Souls of the Dead to the Isles of the Blessed." *Mnemosyne* 24 (1971) 113–61.

Walls, A. F. *The Missionary Movement in Christian History: Studies in the Transmission of Faith.* Maryknoll, NY: Orbis, 1996.

Walter, N. "Die Bearbeitung der Seligpreisungen durch Matthäus." *Studia Evangelica IV. Papers presented to the Third International Congress.* Ed. F. L. Cross. TU 102. Berlin: Akademie-Verlag, 1968, 246–58.

Weder, H. *Die "Rede der Reden." Eine Auslegung der Bergpredigt heute.* Zürich: Theologischer Verlag, 1985.

Weder, H. *Gegenwart und Gottesherrschaft. Überlegungen zum Zeitverständnis bei Jesus und im frühen Christentum.* BThSt 20. Neukirchen: Neukirchener, 1993.

Weidemann, H. *Aristoteles*: Peri Hermeneias. Aristoteles Werke in deutscher Übersetzung 1/2. Darmstadt: Wissenschaftliche Buchgesellschaft, 1994.

Weinreich, O. "Alexander der Lügenprophet und seine Stellung in der Religiosität des 2. Jahrhunderts n. Chr." *Neue Jahrbücher für das klassische Altertum* 24 (1921) 129–51.

Weiss, J. *Das älteste Evangelium.* Göttingen: Vandenhoeck & Ruprecht, 1903.

Weiss, J. *Die Predigt Jesu vom Reiche Gottes.* 3d ed. Göttingen: Vandenhoeck & Ruprecht, 1964.

Wellhausen, J. *Das Evangelium Matthäei.* 2d ed. Berlin: Reimer, 1914.

Wengst, K. *Humility: Solidarity of the Humiliated.* Philadelphia: Fortress, 1988.

Wengst, K. *Pax Romana: Anspruch und Wirklichkeit.* München: Kaiser, 1986.

West, M. L., ed. *Iambi et Elegi Graeci ante Alexandrium Cantati.* 2d. ed. 2 vols. Oxford: Oxford University Press, 1989.

Wilson, B. R. *Magic and the Millennium.* New York: Harper & Row, 1973.

Windisch, H. *Der Sinn der Bergpredigt. Ein Beitrag zum Problem der richtigen Exegese.* UNT 16. Leipzig: Hinrichs, 1929. 2d. ed., 1937.

Winston, D. *The Wisdom of Solomon.* Anchor Bible 43; New York: Doubleday, 1979.

Wire, A. C. *The Corinthian Women Prophets: A Reconstruction through Paul's Rhetoric.* Minneapolis: Fortress, 1990.

Wolfson, E. R. *Through a Speculum That Shines: Vision and Imagination in Medieval Jewish Mysticism.* Princeton: Princeton University Press, 1994.

Wörner, M. H. *Performative und sprachliches Handeln. Ein Beitrag zu J. L. Austins Theorie der Sprechakte.* Forschungsberichte des Instituts für Kommunikationsforschung und Phonetik der Universität Bonn 1/64. Hamburg: Buske, 1978.

Wrege, H.-T. *Die Überlieferungsgeschichte der Bergpredigt.* WUNT 9. Tübingen: Mohr (Siebeck), 1968.

Wright, G. E. *God Who Acts.* London: SCM, 1952.

Wunderlich, D. *Studien zur Sprechakttheorie.* Suhrkamp Taschenbuch Wissenschaft 172. Frankfurt am Main: Suhrkamp, 1976.

Wunderlich, D. "Über die Konsequenzen von Sprechhandlungen." *Sprachpragmatik und Philosophie.* Ed. K.-O. Apel. Theorie-Diskussion. Frankfurt am Main: Suhrkamp, 1976, 441–62.

Yerushalmi, J. H. *Zakhor, Jewish History and Jewish Memory*. Samuel and Althea Stroum Lectures in Jewish Studies. Seattle: University of Washington Press, 1982.

Zager, W. *Gottesherrschaft und Endgericht in der Verkündigung Jesu. Eine Untersuchung zur markinischen Jesusüberlieferung einschließlich der Q-Parallelen*. BZNW 82. Berlin and New York: de Gruyter, 1996.

Zahn, T. *Das Evangelium des Matthäus*. KNT 1. Leipzig: Deichert, 1903.

Ziegler, K. “Mariandynoi.” *KP* 3 (1979) 1024–25.

Zuntz, G. *Persephone: Three Essays on Religion and Thought in Magna Graecia*. Oxford: Clarendon, 1971.

INDEX TO ANCIENT WRITINGS

C. NEW TESTAMENT

Matthew

INDEX TO MODERN AUTHORS